THE ZUNI CAFE COOKBOOK

THE ZUNI CAFE

COOKBOOK ✤ JUDY RODGERS

WINE NOTES & SELECTIONS ✤ GERALD ASHER

PHOTOGRAPHY ✤ ✤ ✤ GENTL & HYERS / EDGE

W. W. NORTON & COMPANY

NEW YORK ✤ LONDON

For information about permission to reproduce selections from this book, write to
Permissions, W. W. Norton & Company, Inc., 500 Fifth Avenue, New York, NY 10110

The text of this book is composed in Foundry Old Style with the display set in Garamond 3
Composition by Tom Ernst
Manufacturing by R. R. Donnelley & Sons.
Book design by Jean Orlebeke
Production manager: Andrew Marasia

Library of Congress Cataloging-in-Publication Data

Rodgers, Judy.
The Zuni Cafe cookbook / Judy Rodgers ; wine notes, selections, Gerald Asher ;
photography, Gentl & Hyers/Edge.
p.   cm.
Includes bibliographical references and index.
ISBN 0-393-02043-6
1. Cookery. I. Zuni Cafe (Restaurant) II. Title.

TX714 .R614 2002

641.5'09794'61—dc21   2002026477

W. W. Norton & Company, Inc., 500 Fifth Avenue, New York, N.Y. 10110
www.wwnorton.com

W. W. Norton & Company Ltd., Castle House, 75/76 Wells Street, London W1T 3QT

1 2 3 4 5 6 7 8 9 0

Méfie-toi du cinéma dans la cuisine

~Jean-Baptiste Troisgros

CONTENTS

✦ ✦
✦

ACKNOWLEDGMENTS

✦ ✦
✦

Among the many pleasures I enjoyed over the course of writing this book was the unconditional generosity of many colleagues and friends. First among them is Vince Calcagno, my partner at Zuni Café, who for several years shouldered a disproportionate burden of duties there with grace and agility. There would be neither cookbook nor Zuni without him. Likewise Carol Bever, Quang Nguyen, Cynthia Shea, and Rymee Trobaugh, who never said no to any request for help~more often they simply figured out what I needed and stepped in before I asked. Indeed, the same can be said of all of the cooks at Zuni. Their kindness and patience made the writing possible, and much of what I share in the pages that follow is distilled from their questions, and their solutions.

My gratitude to Bill Fujimoto, Trino Cruz, and the staff of Monterey Market in Berkeley, for their generosity and assistance, and for teaching me something about produce nearly every time I shopped there for over 20 years.

I am grateful to the many people who, usually with scant notice, agreed to critique some part of the text, answer a nagging question, or research a conundrum I had become obsessed with: Kate Arding, Sue Conley, and Peggy Smith of Cowgirl Creamery; Meredith Benke; Rolando Berramendi, Carolyn Buck, Brooke Thornton, Ed Valenzuela, and David Albee of Manicaretti; Will Borgeson of Bodega Marine Lab; Bob Bruno of De Choix Foods; Maria Colonna; Jim Ferguson; John Finger and Mike Watchorn of Hog Island Oyster Company; Michelle Fuerst; Jim Galle of Grimaud Farms; Cesare Gallo; Steve Giambalvo and Mike Cisneros of Cheeseworks West; Ihsan Gurdal of Formaggio Kitchen; Alison Hooper of Vermont Butter and Cheese; Paul Johnson and Tom Worthington of Monterey Fish Company; David Karp; Billy Marinelli of Marinelli Shellfish; Harold McGee; Edward Mills, Ph.D., Associate Professor of Dairy and Animal Science, Penn State University; Mark Palladini of Niman Ranch; Gianluigi Peduzzi of *Rustichella d'Abruzzo;* Gilbert Pilgram; Tim Ports of The Fresh Fish Company; Molly Stevens; Michael Thomey of Abco Laboratories; Michel Troisgros; Gary Vullis; Glenn Witte; Bob Wolke, Professor Emeritus of Chemistry, University of Pittsburgh; and Adrienne and Martin Zausner.

For recipe testing, I am indebted to Bob Chambers and his culinary staff, Donna Bianco, John Peelen, and Bernadette Pochet. Thanks to Martha Buser, Markus Dobler, and Cameron Finoki as well. Particular thanks to Deirdre Davis for tackling the roughest of the recipes, restructuring their unwieldy formats along the way.

Very special thanks to Jean Orlebeke, Andrea Gentl, Marty Hyers, Michael Pederson, and Steven Rothfeld for making this book lovely. Gerald Asher added heart with each wine choice. Judith Sutton carefully read every word of the original manuscript and gently fixed the many that were errant.

Warm thanks to Doe Coover, whom I nearly forget is my agent, since she cared for me and this book more like a mother. Thanks also to everyone at W. W. Norton, for their daring to embrace this book and then lavishing it with extraordinary attention; in particular I am indebted to Louise Brockett, Sue Carlson, Erik Johnson, Star Lawrence, Georgia Leibman, Jeannie Luciano, Andrew Marasia, Drake McFeely, Debra Morton Hoyt, Nancy Palmquist, Don Rifkin, Bill Rusin, and Susan Sanfrey. I will be forever grateful to my editor, Maria Guarnaschelli, who challenged and nurtured at all the right times, making the book better at every pass. She imagined, and championed, an ambitious book I'd never have had the vision to compose on my own. And to Kirk Russell I owe more than to anyone, for constantly reminding me to share what is true.

Heartfelt thanks to Kate and Olivia for their forbearance~taming my anxiety with patience, laughter, and love.

INTRODUCTION

Zuni cafe occupies an unlikely triangular space in a 1913 building at the corner of Rose Alley and Market Street in San Francisco, a few blocks to the wrong side of Civic Center. The front door opens into a gaping bar with two-story window walls framed by a handful of brick and iron columns. Liquor and wine bottles are improbably arrayed against the Market Street glass. During the day the natural light is stunning, and after dusk the space glows like a jeweled box from two blocks away. The restaurant feels barely contained. It's not fancy, there are no expensive finishes, just handsome spaces. When there are just a few customers, the space is airy and relaxing, a haven for reading or chatting over drinks and a simple plate of anchovies or a comforting bowl of polenta. When it's crowded, the room warms to the bustle and excitement, and the same austere plate of anchovies or shaky tower of shoestring potatoes becomes part of the glamour. A mezzanine dining room overlooks this bar and leads to a warren of smaller dining rooms, mostly more intimate, although one offers a bird's-eye view of the kitchen below. Sixteen tables skirt the wide-open kitchen, face a glowing hearth, and back up to a dozen more slender, twelve-foot windows on Market Street.

I was smitten on sight when I walked into Zuni in 1987. I'd been offered the chef's job, and suspected it could be a good place to serve the mostly regional French and Italian food I adored. The crowd was eclectic ~ young, old, middle-aged, dressed up, dressed down, in noisy groups or quiet deuces, some there for the place, some for the drinks, some for the food, some for each other. I took in the space and imagined you could eat as simply or as grandly as you wanted in this setting, and that the food would only be a part of the seduction. Zuni was a wonderful gathering place, it had a sense of romance and felt as if it had been there forever.

FIFTEEN YEARS LATER, I USUALLY ENTER THROUGH THE BACK DOOR, WHERE MOST OF the romance is tamed by the realities of running a busy restaurant. Deliveries are late, the dishwasher breaks down, we're short a thousand napkins on a Saturday, one hundred fifty chickens come in four ounces too small. The glowing hearth and brick oven require constant maintenance, the graceful window walls get broken, and, in earthquake country, beautiful old brick pillars require costly seismic braces. And yet, in that engaging setting, many thousands of clients, and well more than a hundred cooks over the years, have sustained our mostly traditional repertory. Love of those culinary traditions, both familiar and obscure, and the cultures and remarkable individuals that have nurtured them, drives our cooking. {Even where our techniques are unconventional ~ for example, we salt most proteins in advance, and we don't skim the fat off stock while it is cooking ~ it usually turns out they are seeded in traditional cooking habits.} And the privilege of working with a generous variety of organic products year-round has been a defining force. Receiving these treasures has been a constant delight, and the task of showing them at their best is one of my favorite responsibilities. Seeking just the right preparation to magnify the charms of a knobby potato, skinny stalk of asparagus, or the first freshly shelled walnuts of the year is always a happy challenge, especially when the ingredients are so good they need little done to them. In this context, I rediscover daily that the best dishes are the result of honoring the ingredients, continually tasting, and heeding not just the season, but also the weather outside, which has an immeasurable effect on how well a dish works. Like much of what is thought of as culinary wisdom, this sense of what to cook, and when, is distilled through experience and is a pleasure to acquire. The other bits of culinary knowledge that guide me daily are mostly the casual gifts of many teachers and fellow cooks, and such shared wisdom, coupled with simple observation and an interest in food chemistry, is at the heart of all my methods.

The recipes here represent our entire repertory: a battery of appetizers; a group of mostly leafy salads; the hot dishes that make a hearty middle course or a comforting one-course meal; a collection of vegetable dishes, preserved things, and sauces; the fish, poultry, and meat-centered preparations they interchangeably complement; suggestions for after-dinner cheese; and, finally, desserts. You will find a number of labor-of-love-intensive dishes; having made them hundreds of times, we've learned which extra steps guarantee depth of flavor, making the extra minutes more than worthwhile. But most often these dishes take their time, not the cook's time. Many other recipes call for little active work and require only the skill and will to select excellent ingredients, perhaps the most useful culinary skill of all. These simple dishes, celebrating the particular affinity of two or three ingredients, can either stand alone or quietly frame more elaborate dishes in a meal. I have included recipes that, while obscure sounding, are representative of our cooking, have consistently proven satisfying, and show not just what, but how we cook, and how to change a dish to suit your ingredients and palate. A number of the recipes may sound inconvenient ~ for example, most of you won't rush to start deep-frying, or stuffing sausage first thing after skimming these pages ~ but with just a little experience, both become fun. Like the restaurant, this book asks you to consider trying something unfamiliar, along with that friendly, popular roast chicken ~ if not right away, then as you become more intrepid.

The best meals are more than a succession of great dishes resulting from a number of great recipes. They are fashioned with wisdom and experience and are shaded, always, with spontaneity. So don't chart every turn before going to the market, and don't feel you must follow a recipe slavishly. As you use this book, choose a few recipes, or suggestions, that appeal to you ~ then shop with those in mind, but be prepared to change plans if the market doesn't deliver or the weather changes abruptly. As you cook, taste constantly, watch closely, smell and touch the ingredients as they change, and then adjust ~ for your palate, for the weather, for the ingredients, for your equipment. Make dishes more than once, and pay attention to the slight or substantial differences in each variable and how each affects the results, for the better or the worse. This effort, more important than any recipe, rewards even the most experienced cook with insights and surprises. Recognizing the little differences in ingredients, and learning how to optimize them rather than dilute or ignore them, is a mantra in the kitchen at Zuni. Along with sharing our repertory, I hope to show that this approach to cooking is not only accessible to everyone, but is also fun, and essential to producing consistently delicious food.

❖ ❖ ❖

MY EDUCATION IN COOKING BEGAN UNASSUMINGLY IN 1973 WITH A DELICIOUS HAM sandwich on chewy, day-old *pain de compagne,* a spoonful of very spicy mustard, tarragon-laced cornichons, and a few sweet, tender crayfish as an hors d'œuvre. Jean Troisgros chose the menu for us and prepared our little meal with enthusiasm, surprising to me at four in the morning after a flight from New York and a high-speed seven-hour drive from Paris to Roanne. It was actually our second ham sandwich of the night; our first was a nondescript effort on stale baguette that we left half-eaten in an all-night autoroute *resto-stop*. But I am sure the redundancy was no coincidence; Jean had it in mind to demonstrate how good such a sandwich could be, and his dark brown eyes twinkled when I finished and then reached for another slice of ham. We ate standing in his kitchen, which was dark and quiet and gave no hint of its legendary status, except for the rich aroma of a veal stock slowly reducing to demi-glace. This was my first meal in the best restaurant in France. I had the singular good fortune to spend the year that followed under Jean's wing, and in the embrace of his brother, Pierre, and their extended family and staff at their restaurant, Les Frères Troisgros.

Chefs weren't stars in 1973; *nouvelle cuisine* had not been pronounced, and "California Cuisine" had just been seeded. As a sixteen-year-old from Saint Louis, I had never taken an interest in cooking, and nearly everything I ate in Roanne was as unfamiliar as it was delicious. Happily, I was prodded by the neighbor at home who had arranged for my stay with his French friends, the Troisgros, to document everything I ate there. As a result, and with the brothers' blessing, I recorded recipes for every dish on the menu, and then some. Their focus on raw ingredients was relentless, and the attention they lavished on each detail of every preparation was as routine for them as it was revelatory for me. Hearing about the traditions surrounding each dish made each one more memorable. What had begun as a high school exchange student sojourn veered swiftly away from academics and toward *la cuisine*. Although I had not landed at a restaurant, much less Les Frères Troisgros, by any design, observing this routine became all-consuming. As soon as I got home from school, I headed for the kitchen to watch, listen, and take notes. Jean relished calling me Mata Hari, and he punctuated the accusation with a thrust of his meat fork, which was his favorite all-purpose kitchen tool. Having made the joke, Jean would return to the *piano* {the edge of the stove}, pause, and then dispense a bit of culinary wisdom as he checked the doneness of a *côte de bœuf*.

"Do you see how this pan is *à taille* {the right size}? This is the first and most important thing to know. Always choose a pan that is the right size. Too small, and you crowd the meat and steam it; too large, and you burn the fat you are cooking in, and it's not so good for the pan either. This is why we have the *batterie de cuisine*."

He turned to the array of copper casseroles, six to eighteen inches wide, hanging behind him. Jean could always explain cooking techniques in a practical and logical way.

Following this unplanned curriculum, I learned many of the lessons I still apply daily, although I never really cooked at Les Frères Troisgros. Timidity and respect for their *métier* held me back. I occasionally summoned the confidence to help sort through spinach leaves with a *commis* {beginning cook}, or gingerly pluck a thrush before dropping it whole into a Robot-Coupe for their famous *mousse de grives,* but mostly I watched, and wrote.* But if my hesitation cost me hands-on experience, Jean, Pierre, and their cooks compensated; they made sure I tasted as many dishes, as frequently, and in as many stages of preparation, as possible.

"It tastes different today, the cream, *n'est-ce pas?* You see? It's more acidic and thicker. We'll use less lemon in the sauce."

Or, "Taste this. Do you like it? It's a truffle. First of the year. But they'll get better."

Jean had just popped a whole truffle steamed over Sauternes in my mouth.

I watched Pierre measure portions of aged Charollais beef by eye, carve them with nonchalant precision, and then taste a sliver of the raw meat that clung to his knife. Always checking. A lesson I have never forgotten.

A parade of Troisgros devotees from a dozen countries passed through the kitchen that year and most confided to me that this was not the usual three-star restaurant. It was not just the best food, it was also the simplest and purest, and the restaurant the most convivial. The seasonality and regional character of the food, coupled with lack of pretension, brought clients back over and over. The most frequent diners were business people, purveyors, neighbors, fellow restaurateurs, and the local taxman, all of whom stopped in the kitchen for a visit before Jean or Pierre prepared a simple lunch for them "off-menu." *Les amis* dined on a plain dish ~ an omelette, half a roast chicken left from the *repas du personnel* {staff meal}, or the signature Troisgros escalope of salmon, but without their legendary sorrel sauce ~ just perfect local salmon, barely cooked, strewn with freshly chopped herbs, and moistened with olive oil and lemon juice. These clients ate very, very well.

And I learned from *le Patron,* Jean-Baptiste Troisgros, Jean and Pierre's father. I shared some of my most memorable meals with him. A proud Burgundian, Jean-Baptiste was the patriarch of the house, who held court at table and struck a mix of fear and adoration in all who attended to him. The *Patron,* feisty at eighty-six, wore wire-rimmed glasses with dark gray lenses that enhanced his mystique tremendously. Although he could have anything he wanted, on or off

---

* I did once prepare an American carrot cake from scratch and proudly announced that it was better than most American cakes, which came from a box and were full of *préservatifs.* This provoked gales of laughter, since that is the French word for condom. The cake was not very good, and I cheerfully returned to learning about French food for the duration of my stay.

the menu, Jean-Baptiste favored simple food and became utterly euphoric when presented with a carefully fried egg deglazed with sherry vinegar, flanked by *pain grillé* {toast}, and followed by a salad of *pissenlits au lard* {dandelion greens and bacon}. Likewise, he was never more irritated than when he thought a dish was even slightly overwrought, not honest or "*généreux.*" *Le Patron* admonished me never to be taken in by "*cinéma dans la cuisine*" ~ akin to saying "food for show." His culinary edicts were always passionate, and I wrote all of them down.

The Troisgros *sœur,* Madeleine Troisgros Serraille, also did her part. At least twice a week she'd fetch me from her brothers' restaurant and calmly produce a perfect family meal in her own modest kitchen ~ a *blanquette de veau, pot-au-feu,* or *gratin de nouilles* {macaroni and cheese, sort of}. I loved her *miroton,* a homey beef and onion casserole, based on the leftover *pot-au-feu* she had deliberately made too much of. Madeleine was a champion of the salad course and was rigorous about its seasonality ~ she was visibly thrilled to dress the first mâche or tender dandelion of the season. She loved every leafy thing you could eat *en salade* ~ escarole, frisée, watercress, endive, *roquette* {arugula}, Batavia or butter lettuce ~ and had a knack for choosing one or two nonleafy things ~ nuts, or croûtons, or hard-cooked egg ~ that made the salad more satisfying. Every leaf was in impeccable condition, and the ritual of dressing it at table was an important moment in every meal. There was never a leaf left over. Then, before clearing the salad plates, Madeleine served the cheese. This course, never omitted, consisted of a few perfect cheeses, always in season, and just right for the dishes that had preceded ~ whether a local goat cheese, the regional Fourme d'Ambert, or a chunk of Beaufort she had brought back from the Alps. She never offered too many choices, lest they compete or clash or overwhelm. She tended to sample only one herself, knowing which was the best that day. Madeleine fashioned perfect meals; beyond being generous in flavor and tradition, there was a balance and focus to the menu: everything complemented everything else in an uncanny way. And there was always a simple dish with the *goût du revenez-y* ~ "the taste you return to" for another nibble that prolongs the meal. Her cooking never demanded your attention, it simply kindled conviviality.

Within a very few months, I had succumbed to the philosophy that guides Zuni cooking today. While growing international attention swirled around the more glamorous three-star restaurants, and parades of gastronomic pilgrims clamored after the fanciest, cleverest, and most exclusive truffle, lobster, and foie gras dishes incorporating exotic fruits and Japanese garnishes, I was taking thorough notes on how Michel made *hachis parmentier* {shepherd's pie *à la française*} for the staff meal. Or I was heading for the slightly drab but friendly café up the street with Jean on his night off for a hanger steak and perfect *pommes frites.* My mentor always congratulated the café owner on the delicious *bifteck* and insisted this was as good a meal as any, lest one think classical or *nouvelle cuisine* could challenge the virtues of simplicity. There was surely a place for creative new restaurant cooking, and even for classical cuisine, but it wasn't for every day. And Jean constantly reminded me that the food we eat every day ought to be taken just as seriously. It deserved to be just as well prepared, and just as celebrated.

WHEN I RETURNED TO AMERICA IN 1974, I HAD NO PLANS TO BECOME A COOK, much less a chef or restaurateur; it was obviously too late. A *commis* at Troisgros enrolled by age fourteen, and I was already seventeen. I headed to California to college. But late in 1977, a friend told me about an unusual restaurant in Berkeley where the menu was based on the best seasonal ingredients, and changed daily. She was already working at Chez Panisse and described a community of passionate cooks and kindred spirits. I booked a table a few weeks later and walked into Chez Panisse with a stack of Troisgros recipes, my meticulous food logs, and the tantalizing hope that the enchantments of that year in France could be conjured in America. I was not disappointed. Alice Waters pushed the *Patron*'s notion of *cuisine généreuse* into new territory ~ no effort was spared to offer the most delicious, beguiling, satisfying meals. Every detail of preparation and presentation was favored with care, from the handwritten menus to the extraordinary flowers that graced the dining room. When Alice shocked me with the proposal that I help out at Saturday lunch, I discarded a stack of graduate school applications and asked her what cookbooks to buy. It was too good to be true, but I was scared to death. I graduated a few months later to cooking lunch every day by myself, although the convenient title "lunch chef" was not really apt, since I was "chief" to no one. But being in charge of myself was plenty, given that I had never actually cooked many of the things I had so carefully recorded. I rapidly learned that a simple pan of crispy, golden sautéed potatoes, no problem for the tenderest *commis* chez Troisgros, was beyond my reach. My potatoes often stuck viciously to the pan ~ when they didn't jump to the floor. And when they didn't stick, I had no idea why. I did begin each day with an exceptional advantage: the delicious leftovers from the night before ~ I just had to avoid wrecking them. However, considering my limited skills, even this was fraught with risks and resulted in plenty of nervous scrambles. But Alice made a point of coming through the kitchen in the late morning, when she carefully tasted and corrected my troubled efforts ~ she seemed to sense where a dish should go and could always make it better {or gently suggest that we did not have to serve it, which was a revelation to me}. I wasn't sure how she arrived at these miraculous fixes, but her example ingrained in me the habit of reconsidering every option at every stage of preparation. Alice and her colleague, pastry chef Lindsey Shere, along with chefs Jean-Pierre Moullé and Mark Miller, were generous, inspiring, adventurous, and patient. I managed, thanks to them, and to the very best leftovers in America, to look competent. I am convinced there was no better place in America to learn to cook.

While at Chez Panisse, I set out to learn the repertory of french cuisine, classical and traditional, reading cookbooks every night after work. I pored over Richard Olney's *Simple French Food* ~ the thorough, practical lessons reminded me of Jean. I cooked through Elizabeth David's volumes on French food, partially in the kitchen and partially in my head, and, almost incidentally, made tentative forays into her brilliant compendium of Italian food. This too sounded like the generous, honest cooking Jean-Baptiste craved and demanded. And I fell for Waverly Root when I saw he subdivided France based on cooking fats.

TWO YEARS LATER, I RETURNED TO FRANCE, THIS TIME TO TRAVEL. At the urging of a friend in Paris, I headed to the Southwest into Les Landes, an idyllic region of pine forests, two-lane roads, and small farms. My friend arranged a ride for me and mentioned I'd be dropped off at a friend's restaurant. {She had also told her friend I'd like to stay and cook there. I hadn't heard that part.} Thus I happened into an apprenticeship with Pepette Arbulo at l'Estanquet, her tiny café-bar-restaurant-inn-*tabac*-post office in a village of twenty people and hundreds of ducks. In her care, Pepette made sure I learned how to use every part of that bird, and did her best to convince me there was no place for butter in the kitchen except on toast in the morning. *La graisse* {duck fat} was the choice for every preparation. I admired her gentle dogmatism, and more, I loved her ultratraditional food, especially the offbeat things like preserved goose gizzards, *carcasses grillées* {roasted bones}, *graisserons* {a scrappy sort of gelée-bound terrine made from the leavings at the bottom of the confit pot}, and *merveilles* {pastry fried in duck fat}. Pepette had a foolproof method for preserving fresh anchovies, and simple ones for putting up porcini mushrooms {in duck fat, of course} and for stockpiling stone fruits in a stunning amount of Armagnac. In Pepette's kitchen, foie gras was not an aristocratic exclusivity to embellish and transform for special occasions, it was simply a treasured regional staple whose delicacy you did your best not to violate. Her favorite recipe for foie gras calls for foie gras, sea salt, and experience. Pepette's was not really restaurant food; it was farmhouse cooking at a restaurant.

I stayed in France until I ran out of money, and after returning to California, I turned to Alice for advice. She suggested that I meet with her friend Marion Cunningham, who needed a chef for an American restaurant project she was working on. And so I stumbled into good luck again, and had the chance to work with Marion at the Union Hotel in Benicia. Her commitment to unpretentious American cooking was irresistible. It felt odd to set aside *French Country Cooking,* but the assignment ~ to prepare a set menu of simple, traditional American dishes ~ could not have been more timely. Marion's work on *The Fannie Farmer Cookbook* had breathed new life into American food. She was persuading America that delicious food did not have to be French, and that home cooking belonged in restaurants too. The menu featured pickled beets and eggs, scrapple, spoon bread, and oyster loaf. And Marion put Caesar salad on the menu, which at the time was considered a bit retro ~ hard to imagine now. The panfried chicken, cured in rock salt, then soaked in milk, was unusually succulent, and became too popular ~ with only six burners, we couldn't fry enough fast enough.

I first heard the phrase "New American Cooking" about three months later. And I recognized that this homey, American fare had a lot in common with traditional French cuisine. Jean-Baptiste would have loved scrapple. And we could make a boiled dinner as lovingly as Madeleine made her *pot-au-feu.* Thinking of Pepette, I preserved and pickled every fruit and vegetable in season. When we ground our hamburger in-house daily, I remembered the *Patron* declaring a great *steak haché* could be worth an *entrecôte à la moelle,* if made with the same care. Inspired by these memories, I was determined to explore the entire repertory of regional American cooking and New World ingredients. To do this, the set menu had to go.

But romance, variety, and discovery were not the most important rewards for that change. Chez Panisse had taught me to heed the ingredients first of all, and to change course if it meant the result would be better. A set menu often stymied that agenda. It left little room to alter a dish to improve it, and some pressure to accept less-than-brilliant, overpriced product to meet the demands of a printed page. No ingredient was spectacular all the time, and no dish was appealing every day. A short, changing daily menu eliminated these problems and was, in truth, the only way I knew how to cook. This seemed the best of both worlds, but still, with time, the Old World beckoned. Many American dishes had roots in Europe, and I started looking more closely, and longingly, at those sources when they were Italian.

In 1983, I left the hotel and booked a farmhouse outside Florence. From day one, I wrote down everything I ate, a time-consuming old habit, and then started making lists of everything I saw in every market. I tasted and cooked everything I could. I didn't understand why they gave me green tomatoes when I said they were for salad, or why salt was sold with stamps and tobacco at the bar down the street, and I was shocked by how "fresh" some of the salami was {it looked raw}, but took a chance, found it tasty, and lived. The prosciutto with fur {wild boar ham} got my attention, as did the columns of little birds in the market {smaller even than the precious ortolan I'd had in France}. I caught the brief season of *minutina* {a salad green shaped like a blade of grass} and sampled the collection of edible weeds for sale at the Mercato Centrale. I liked the ritual of peeling raw favas to nibble with fresh pecorino, and enjoyed daily salads of slivered raw artichokes and pine nuts, remembering that Madeleine had made a similar salad, explaining that it was a Provençal specialty. I ate dozens of *porchetta* sandwiches {to make sure they were really supposed to be so salty}, and tried to figure out how to make rice ice cream. I pursued every rumor of "stale bread" dishes ~ *pappa, panzanella, acquacotta, ribollita* ~ and recorded the variations. Researching outside the markets, it was easy to find traditional food in restaurants in Italy, much easier than in France, where *haute* and *nouvelle cuisine* competed so vigorously. Stopping in Roanne on the way home, sharing travel stories with the Troisgros, I could not help but focus on how delicious the food was in Italy. I should not have been surprised that they also shared that view. So much for Gallic chauvinism. No one seemed the least bit bothered by this apparent "defection" ~ if anything, it was evidence I had inherited their affection for authentic, generous food to celebrate every day.

I had found a culinary home in the Tuscan idiom, and on subsequent trips, fell for the charms of Umbria, Sicily, the Abruzzo, Campania, and so on. But by the time I headed back to California that first year I had a goal. I would look for the restaurant where I could settle down to cook both French and Italian traditional food and evoke the spirit of dinner at Madeleine's.

BILLY WEST OPENED ZUNI CAFE IN 1979, WITH A HUGE HEART AND EXACTLY TEN thousand dollars. In the early years, the restaurant consisted of a narrow storefront with a creaky mezzanine, roughly one-quarter of its current size. To capitalize on the neighboring and highly visible corner cactus shop, {where Billy had been a partner until it became clear cactus sales wouldn't support three partners}, he hand-plastered the walls and banquettes of his new space to give it a Southwestern adobe look. He chose the name Zuni, after the Native American tribe, and decided to feature a few simple and authentic Mexican dishes, drawing inspiration from Diana Kennedy's cookbooks. A Weber grill was an important early investment, and was rolled onto the back sidewalk for each day's service. This unpretentious arrangement attracted writer Elizabeth David's attention when, wandering through the neighborhood antique shops, she smelled something delicious and followed her nose to find Billy grilling chicken in the alley behind the restaurant. She came back for dinner twice that week and made a point of returning whenever she came to San Francisco. After the grill came an espresso machine, which doubled as a stove, since you could scramble eggs with the milk steamer. The waiters made this dish to order. Barely two years later, Billy hired Vince Calcagno to help run his struggling café, when helping to run the café meant not just managing the books and the entire front-of-house operations but also stripping floors and laying Mexican pavers, and making biweekly trips to the wholesale flower market and regular dawn produce runs to South San Francisco. And worrying about the kitchen as well: Vince occasionally called friends to help cook when Billy was understaffed in the kitchen. {I received one of those calls and recall a frantic but happy evening of making countless Caesar salads, harvesting sizzling croûtons from an overworked toaster oven that was tethered to the single kitchen outlet with a daisy chain of extension cords.} But, ever-resourceful and passionate, Billy and Vince made a success of the improbable restaurant. By 1986, Zuni had absorbed the adjacent storefront and spilled into the former cactus shop. That transformation created the romantic space everyone falls for today.

When Billy and Vince, now partners in the business, asked me to be chef in 1987, the restaurant was busy and well respected. The food was delicious; milk-steamer eggs had gone away and there was an indoor grill and exhaust system. The menu still had a vaguely Mexican bent and the most popular dish was the made-to-order Caesar salad. The second most successful item was an excellent made-to-order guacamole, served in the *molcajete,* with fried-to-order chips {until the Health Department declared the coarsely pitted mortar a threat to public health, forcing it off the menu}. The *à la minute* approach was cumbersome, but taste had always undermined efficiency at Zuni. I accepted the job. I was confident that the owners' affection for France and Italy, and for traditional food, would sanction lots of experimentation and change. Vince, who has Sicilian and Apulian roots, seemed particularly enthusiastic as the Italian focus promised to drift farther and farther south. I told Billy and Vince that we really needed a brick oven, and within a few months there was a twelve-by-eight-foot hole in the middle of the main dining room, decorated with plenty of bright yellow caution tape.

That brick oven ushered in a litany of dishes ~ smoky, creamy potato gratins with sorrel or wild mushrooms; tomato and onion *panade;* Madeleine's *miroton;* salmon braised with fresh shelling beans, red wine, and bacon; sea bass *à la boulangère* {with leeks, potatoes, white wine, thyme, and chicken stock}; monkfish with homemade sauerkraut and Riesling; crostini with house-cured salt cod and charred tomatoes; savory onion tartlets and roasted apple charlottes; roasted porcini mushrooms with hazelnut *aïllade;* and quail roasted with cherries and squab roasted with figs. The brick oven made everything taste better ~ and sell better.

And, one fateful afternoon when I was feeling overworked, under the weather, and debating what to cook in the brick oven that night, I floated an idea with Billy and Vince.

"Why not just roast a chicken? A whole chicken, to order. People could share it. It would be delicious out of that oven and *simple.* I bet people would go for it."

I rushed off to salt the chicken in advance, thinking it would make it succulent, like the Union Hotel fried chicken.

People did go for it. We never stop apologizing for the wait, but we just can't roast enough chickens fast enough. Juggling up to nineteen birds, and their bread salads, on about twelve not-very-accessible square feet of oven deck is a feat.

Other dishes took a little more selling: we featured bony cuts of meat in long-simmered, rather monochrome braises {oxtails caught on, baby goat did not} and proposed Pepette's *choux farci* {stuffed cabbage} to the well-heeled, Saturday night pre-opera crowd. We offered potato omelettes for dinner, as at Madeleine's house, and I was very happy to sell three or four a night, to the thankful few who craved exactly that. We served lamb's tongues *à la Sainte-Menehould* {with mustard and bread crumbs}, preserved mackerel in white wine, sealed rabbit in crocks with prunes, and offered *potée landaise, pot-au-feu,* or *bollito misto* once a week. People puzzled over unfamiliar words on the menu~dishes like *garbure* and *salsiccia all'uva* didn't "sell themselves," but, so long as we didn't overbuy, the restaurant didn't lose money on them. A dish was considered a success when those who ordered it found it delicious; no one required it to sell well from day one, or even within a month. This odd formula became a permanent part of our menu strategy.

My old friend Marsha McBride, a colleague from the Union Hotel, was kitchen manager, charged with, among too many other things, finding all the odd or undervalued ingredients not on anyone's product list. She attacked these problems with cheerful tenacity, procuring fresh duck blood for Pepette's *sanguette* {fried blood} and writhing eels for *matelote.* Our fish broker enjoined local fishermen not to throw back the skate, because Zuni needed it {to serve with "black butter" and pickled glasswort}. When Marsha explained we could really use a regular supply of live anchovies, our broker bought into a bait boat. With this triumph, we filled the shelves of the walk-in refrigerator with the salted fish, along with house-made pickles, brandied fruit, homemade jam, curing olives, terrines of foie gras, and five types of confit. Experimental duck hams and house salami dangled from hooks under the compressor. Billy and Vince installed a second walk-in.

The Zuni Caesar Salad survived the transition, and remained impractical. With a dozen on order and seventy more on the horizon, squeezing fresh lemon for every one and whisking the egg to order was as time-consuming as ever. After a few dozen salads, the challenge of tasting each little batch of dressing for garlic, lemon, anchovy, and salt and keying it to that day's romaine can lose its mystique. One very busy evening, someone accidentally called it a "Seizure Salad," and of course it stuck.

To compete with the venerable Caesar, we offered *frisée aux lardons,* then frisée with duck fat croûtons and preserved gizzards, then with a poached, truffle-scented egg, and later with a crown of fried onions and scattering of roasted Zante grapes. Arugula showed up in combination with different crostini, or cheeses, or fennel, or beets, or figs, or nuts~depending on what else was on the menu that evening. My food logs from dinner at Madeleine's reminded me to serve lamb's lettuce, endive, watercress, and every member of the tangled chicory family, each with something to set off its flavor and texture. A local farmer agreed to grow the diminutive *minutina* I'd seen growing outside the farmhouse in Tuscany, and to clip it at infancy. But I am still looking for the exact type of wild dandelion you need for the *Patron*'s favorite salad.

As winter became spring, the Italian repertory started to dominate. We stuffed and braised artichokes with mint, fried pencil-thin asparagus and thin lemon slices, and stewed fresh favas with sage. Diligent prep cooks figured out how to extract the ink sacs from tiny local squid for black risotto with peas. Buying frozen cuttlefish ink would have been too easy. *Pearà* {warm bread crumb–marrow sauce} sounded a little scary to many of our customers, but it was delicious and became a standard with grilled beef. That summer, servers struggled to explain that *pappa al pomodoro* {literally, "tomato pap"} was not exactly a soup, but kind of like one. Foreign words and odd dishes created romance and confusion in about equal doses, and both were effective in getting people to try stale bread soup or stuffed duck necks. For friends ~ especially other chefs who came in on their night off ~ we put *onglet* {hanger steak} on the menu, and I wished Jean could come to dinner. And when we served peaches in red wine, generously littered with wild strawberries, I knew Jean-Baptiste would like that.

I was intent on offering cheese, but a *grand plateau de fromage* didn't seem right for our casual restaurant, nor could we in those days get enough great cheeses to populate one. A more sensible and satisfying way to eat cheese seemed to be Madeleine-style, one cheese at a time and at its prime. Worried that our clientele would find this austere, I decided to pair each choice with a condiment, not an all-purpose garnish, but instead a specific variety of apple, or pear, or cherry, or fig, or a type of nut, or ribbons of fennel, seeking tastes and textures to flatter each individual cheese, the way those favas made that Tuscan pecorino taste better. This cheese program became my most personal and idiosyncratic contribution to the menu and may be the only aspect of our repertory that is even vaguely original.

Everything else, I am very proud to say, is derivative. I cannot make a dish without trying to conjure where it came from, and where I first had it, or read about it, or who made it, or taught me to make it. And who grew the vegetables, raised the chickens, or made the cheese, and where. In this way, the simplest dish can recall a community of ideas and people. I hope that some of my ~ and your ~ efforts in the kitchen sustain that community or provoke you to explore and sustain different ones on your own. Jean Troisgros always insisted that cooking is not an art, but is *artisanal.* His distinction acknowledges the necessity of cooking, and honors the collaborative genius of community in coming up with good cooking. I have written this book for those who wish to linger at times over details in that continuum of ideas, and who consider cooking a labor of love. Indeed, food itself is only part of the seduction of cooking.

AND SO, THE ZUNI REPERTORY IS AN EVOLVING HYBRID OF THE CUISINES THAT I love, made possible by the generosity of many teachers and colleagues. I hope I can in this volume honor and convey some of their collective wisdom and passion. If our food is delicious, it is due to that passion, and to the extraordinary quality of the products we obtain, and to the talent and devotion of every cook who has embraced it with heart.

✢
✢ ✢

✢ ✢
✢

WHAT TO THINK ABOUT BEFORE YOU START, *&* WHILE YOU ARE COOKING

✢ ✢
✢ ✢

DECIDING WHAT TO COOK

A TRULY GOOD MEAL DEPENDS ON A CAVALCADE OF SOUND JUDGMENTS, MANY OF which occur well before you lift a knife. When you decide what to cook, you are deciding whether a meal can be really good or not. If you choose to do a dish you can't get good ingredients for, one you are completely unfamiliar with, or one you don't have the time or proper equipment to prepare, you may be setting the stage for a mediocre meal that will be no fun to produce. Even if you have made a dish before, or at least eaten a delicious version of it, and you have the right equipment, the best recipe can only "doll up" mediocre product. The process of deciding what to cook should always begin with deciding where to shop and what to buy {or, if you are lucky, what to harvest}. Only then should you settle on the preparation, which should suit the qualities of those ingredients, as well as your experience, time frame, and equipment. I add a premium for choosing a dish that suits the weather. To assess and balance these things well is no mean accomplishment, and a good sense of what to buy and how to use it is not developed overnight. Such skills are, however, a pleasure to acquire.

DECIDING WHERE TO BUY YOUR FOOD

COOKBOOKS WILL GIVE YOU IDEAS, BUT THE MARKET WILL GIVE YOU DINNER ~ STUDY your market at least as avidly as your library. Look for a market that takes pride in featuring local, seasonal produce, however modest it may be in variety, and pay attention to that produce most of all. Clamor for organic and sustainably farmed foods. If there is a farmers' market in your area, shop there. Talk and listen to the growers. You can learn from the people who raise the food; they probably have more insight into the corn or lettuce that you are about to buy than any cookbook. Fewer handlers and handlings mean that the grower can dare to pick ripe, and that more flavorful but fragile fruit and vegetable varieties become a viable option. By contrast, large-scale-for-long-distance packing practices demand hardy varieties and uniformity. They favor shelf life and looks, not flavor and fragrance. I'd rather pay the premium for a low-yield but delicious variety of melon or berry in peak season than swallow the cost of waxing apples or gassing strawberries just so they conform to an ideal market standard at any time of year, and any distance from the garden. Raw ingredients trump recipes every time; farmers and ranchers who coax the best from the earth can make any of us appear to be a great cook.

Choosing Ingredients

I err when I take casual chances on unfamiliar ingredients, combinations, or methods, or, foolishly, all three at once. When I cook with what I know, I make the best food, which leads to the underlying requirement: as you decide what to buy and then how to cook it, take stock of what you know and build on that. Don't shop for lots of things you've never bought or tasted, much less cooked. In general, it makes most sense to build meals around ingredients or dishes you know and know you love; then enjoy learning about unfamiliar ingredients and techniques at the fringes of the menu, or in the optional areas. I often buy a little of an "unknown" to experiment with, taste, and learn from~ but I don't base a whole meal on it. {Although a thoughtful little experiment can be the star of a meal.} If you don't feel you know very much, then start with what you really like. If you really like apples or lamb or olive oil or rice, then buy that product regularly, trying different varieties, cuts, or vintages, until you are confident you know what you like best and, eventually, how to choose it. For example, make simple dishes using every variety of rice you can find~ or start with every brand of Carnaroli you can find, then expand to include other risotto rices, then other Italian rices, and then branch into the plump Spanish rices you might have heard about by now, since you are paying attention to Mediterranean rice. Notice what the grains look like~ their size, shape, and color~ and what they feel like~ smooth or rough, dusty or shiny, heavy or light. Compare the "same" product from different countries or local regions, and from the current versus a prior year's harvest. {The pantry "staples" olive oil and rice are at issue here; both degenerate with time. I appreciate it when the label provides the harvest date.} With fresh produce, the process is similar: pay attention to the differences in taste, texture, smell, appearance, availability, and price between two apple varieties that you like, first raw, and then in different preparations. Look as closely at the specimens that don't taste great as you do the ones you favor. Track one variety of apple over the course of its season. *Learn what its season is.* Then expand that kind of attention to other things you like to eat. Constant variety is seductive, but the truth is you will only develop an eye or nose for a given product if you use it frequently. {The same may be said for recipes. Making even a simple dish three times in two weeks can teach you more about cooking than trying three different dishes in the same period of time. Pay attention to the process of making it, and to the small and large differences in the results. Then take what you have learned about those ingredients and techniques and apply it to other dishes.}

If you nurture this shopping sense, you will find yourself drawn to what is in season and of good quality. It is sensible and fun to go to the market with a few recipes in mind, but if the tomatoes in your market are lousy, forget about tomato salad. Wander instead toward the lettuces or arugula or tender frisée. A handful of leaves may not seem as "substantial" as that hoped-for tomato affair, but you can cosset them with shavings of cheese or ripe pears or good nuts, or all three, when all three are perfect. Or trust that excellent oil and vinegar can make a simple salad of stand-alone greens genial. When I arrive at the market {or at the restaurant to find the day's deliveries}, I have hopes, expectations, and a few ideas in mind, but I don't decide exactly what to cook until I can see, smell, feel, or taste the raw ingredients. I also consider what condiments, pickles, and cured things we have in stock. And I look for tasty "leftovers," which we nearly always try to generate; often they become the heart of the next dish. You will find many recipes in this book where I exhort you to "make extra" and to capitalize on by-products. For example, cooking and marinating a few extra sardines when you are making Pasta with Sardines and Tomato Sauce will provide a few hors d'œuvre options later in the week, when you may not have the time or spirit to start from scratch. Deliberately making too much *farrotto* provides for an easy second meal of farro soup {page 200}; extra *fideus* can become a great frittata {page 181}; "leftover" panfried *panade* {page 230} can be better than the parent dish. The most versatile leftover, and my favorite, is bread: heels, crusts, crumbs, wads of crusted bread ~ all these scraps profit from being appreciated {along with oil, salt, aromatics, and drippings} and appear throughout this book. Aside from being fun and efficient, this habit of "making extra" spares you the worry of calculating exact yields for uncertain appetites, and it pleasantly forces you to revisit and reconsider the ingredients and original recipe as you use the extra. Seeing how much things have changed, or not, and whether you like them more, or less, cannot help but make you a more capable cook.

Having taken inventory of what is available, it is fun to decide how to use it. If we have plenty of gorgeous, flavorful, tender tomatoes, I may show them off in generous slices with little else on the plate. If they are a little less gorgeous, but still flavorful and tender and deserve to be used raw and at their peak, I may slide them into an heirloom tomato–BLT, or stack them in our tomato summer pudding {page 258}. If they are tasty but a little overripe, I'll look elsewhere for the hors d'œuvre or salad course, and turn them into tomato sauce. If we ordered ripe heirloom tomatoes, but had to send back a stack of underripe or disappointing varieties, I'll happily make *pappa al pomodoro* with the rich, ripe Roma or gnarly but delicious Pink Paste tomatoes we bought instead.

And then there is the weather. {A dodgy condition to consider in San Francisco, where we can visit four seasons in a day.} There is great pleasure in tailoring a menu to the elements, and often the adjustments are simple to make. On the simplest level, food with butter, cream, or high butterfat cheeses seems to taste best when it is cold out, and in warm weather I turn to olive oil–based dishes almost exclusively. Braised dishes with reduced juices, or rich risotto or polenta dishes, which comfort when it's cool and overcast, can pall when it's hot. Texture matters too: on a typical fog-dreary summer morning, we may plan a puréed potato soup with butter or bacon to flavor it, but if the day starts to clear and turn warm, we'll put away the blender and the bacon and cook the same chunks of potatoes into a brothy potato soup with sweet corn and cilantro. And if the weather warms just before we are ready to place a hearty beef braise in the oven, we'll adapt it by adding more tomato to the pan, and choose a different side dish ~ an arugula or watercress salad, or wilted spinach with orange zest, instead of mashed potatoes. Nevertheless, when you are expecting a heat wave, don't plan to serve pot roast in the middle of it. Simply grilled or sautéed meat, garnished with fresh salsa, will be more welcome. Most of these decisions do not require sophisticated expertise ~ they are sort of analogous to thinking about the weather before choosing what to wear. Substituting olive oil for butter, choosing a lightly cooked, brothy dish over a rich, long-simmered one, or choosing a cold dish rather than a hot or room-temperature one are just a few examples of characteristics you might contemplate as you decide what to cook.

THE HABIT *of* TASTING, *&* FINDING FLAVOR BALANCE

RECIPES DO NOT MAKE FOOD TASTE GOOD; PEOPLE DO. Once you to start to prepare the excellent ingredients you have chosen, you have constant opportunity to optimize them. But in order to do this, you need to taste as you cook.

I remember the first time that Jean Troisgros, my first teacher, told me he needed to add acidity to a cream sauce; he said so before he had tasted it ~ he could tell from the look of the crème fraîche that it was mild. But almost before I had registered his declaration, he dipped his finger in the cream and tasted it as well. He needed to be sure, and tasting does become an irrepressible habit. Experience is a good predictor of how you'll need to season and adjust food, but it is no substitute for vigilant tasting.

Tasting, looking, smelling, and feeling as you cook is not difficult. Adjusting for what you taste, or don't taste, need not be intimidating. You just have to get in the habit. And you will learn the most if you taste dishes early, and often. I am fairly intrepid about tasting everything raw or partially cooked, from squash and potatoes to quince and eggplant. {I have also learned you don't have to swallow to taste.} Tracking how flavors and textures change and then discovering or mastermiding the best balance of flavor is fun. And striking that balance is not a skill reserved for an elect group with extraordinary palates. You need most of all to trust and pay attention to your own palate. Even if it isn't yet your habit to taste as you cook, training yourself to recognize where you need more salt, sweetness, fat, or acidity, or where a dish needs more cooking to concentrate or soften flavors, or improve the texture, is eminently doable. And if you can easily learn to recognize defects, a little thought and cautious adjusting will teach you to know if an already good-tasting dish can be made even better.

I have found that the best, and safest, way to approach correcting a dish is to tinker with a small amount of it. First spoon or trim off a few sips or nibbles into a separate dish and then taste it. Now add a little of anything you suspect is lacking {it's okay to guess}, taste again, and ask yourself if you like it better. If you do, add more and more to that little sample until it is excessive in that thing. Now you have taught yourself what that dish tastes like both under- and over-*something*. The most obvious place to start is with salt, but you might also adjust a dish with something sweet {sugar, honey, sweet wine, well-cooked onions, or more of another relatively sweet element that is already in the dish, like tomato paste}, something acidic {vinegar, citrus, wine, or tomato}, something bland {water or light stock, or, in some cases, egg or stale bread}, something rich and succulent {butter, cream, olive oil, cheese, or other fat}, and so on. Similarly, it is sometimes revealing to reduce a spoonful of what you are cooking to see what concentration or longer cooking will do to flavor and texture. When combining raw ingredients, whenever possible, taste the individual elements, then taste them combined. It is often worth pinching or spooning off a little and cooking a sample or two, especially where tasting raw is not possible, as in sausage making~but always cook the sample in a way that approximates what you will be doing to the whole batch. For example, don't panfry a sample of something that will be served poached, unless you factor in the effect of evaporation and surface browning. And consider the temperature of your sample~it will be most revealing if it is the same temperature as the finished dish will be, although you can teach yourself to correct for a discrepancy. The recipes in this book offer lots of suggestions in these matters.

Having checked and corrected the flavor on a small scale, you can confidently adjust a whole dish, still tasting as you go. This technique prevents big mistakes when you have little experience, but I still use it regularly when I cook. Although I am fairly confident in my ability to judge salt, I often tinker with small amounts of soup, vinaigrette, purée, or stew, adding tiny doses of seasonings when I am anything shy of thrilled with the dish as it is. A dish need not be desperate for "correction" to benefit from "adjustment." A splash of cream can round out a pretty good soup, a trickle of vinegar can improve the flavor of a fairly tasty sorbet mixture, a pinch of salt can heighten the flavor of tart fillings. Straining and reducing the liquid from a delicious braised dish may make it even more delicious. Adding a splash of strategically chosen liqueur to a vinaigrette can marry it to the elements in a salad~for example, Frangelico with hazelnuts and tender lettuces, or Chartreuse with grapefruit and endive~though it may turn out to be a piece of fine tuning particular to a day and a salad that you may never exactly duplicate.

The more you taste as you cook, the better you will understand how each addition you make to a preparation affects the flavor and texture of the dish, immediately and eventually. Thoughtful tasting equips you to make tomorrow's dish better for what you cooked today, even if the two dishes are very different. Finally, this sort of attention forms the basis of being able to imagine what foods will go together well and how they should be prepared and combined for the best effect. This knowledge permits you to "experiment" wisely, and so prepare successful dishes of your own invention.

THE PRACTICE *of* SALTING EARLY

IT WAS MIDNIGHT, AND WE WERE CLEANING THE KITCHEN OF RESTAURANT LOUS Landès in Paris after a busy service. A *cuisinier* {line cook} had just told owner Georgette Descat, the chef and formidable eighty-ish matriarch of *cuisine landaise* in Paris, that there were a few pounds of sea bass left.

«*Mets-y du sel. Ça bougera pas.*» {"Salt it. It won't budge," meaning, "It will keep perfectly."}

I was tired and uncomfortable from a day of working in duck fat, but that didn't sound right.

And then, with finality, as she walked away: *«C'sera meilleur même.»* {"It'll be even better."}

This was a galvanizing statement to a California cook schooled in the dictum "always salt at the last minute so you don't dry things out." I'd never have challenged Georgette, but I might have ignored it if her food weren't so deeply flavorful and succulent. And her food was not salty, just tasty all the way through. Her daughter, Pepette Arbulo, my mentor and friend, had gotten my attention a few months before when she sprinkled salt in her chicken stock ~ I sensed a pattern here.

And there was. Umpteenth-generation *landaises,* {les Landes, in Southwestern France, being the land of confit ~ salted duck, goose, or pork, cooked and stored in its own fat} Georgette and Pepette knew salt first as the thing that keeps you from starving; one used it to preserve food through lean times ~ in their case, through the world wars. This practice is nearly ubiquitous in traditional cuisines, but it is notable that traditional *landaise* food is not typically salty; even their hams and sausages are not, in my experience, as salty as many other French or Italian counterparts. Confits are salted just enough to keep, and this quiet "keeping" concept hummed through every culinary operation I observed. But beyond that, what Georgette's *afterthought* suggested was that a little salt early made for better results than the same amount, or more, later. The food didn't just keep, often it got better, for reasons I couldn't understand. But Georgette and Pepette did not talk science, they talked tradition and flavor.

And so, over the years, I have tracked the taste and texture of every type of meat, bird, and fish I have cooked to see which ones benefit from an early sprinkle of salt, or a bath of brine. Many do, especially tough cuts of meat, and some meaty fish. Likewise some vegetables in certain situations. How early I salt foods is a function of their size, amount of surface area, and density or expected toughness. I tend to salt large, dense cuts, such as chuck roasts, and sinewy cuts, like oxtails, farther in advance than skinny, loosely textured cuts, like skirt steak, or small birds, like quail. This book urges you to add your salt "early" in many situations, echoing a technique we have used at Zuni for more than a decade. The Zuni Roast Chicken and Zuni Hamburger both depend on salting in advance ~ and are compelling cases for the method.

Aside from simply allowing time to diffuse the seasoning throughout the food, which is reason enough to try the technique, early salting also promotes juiciness and improves texture. This is the felicitous result of a few reliable processes. First, salt helps dissolve some of the proteins within and around muscle fibers that would otherwise resist chewing. A second process is more complex. Initially, salt does draw moisture from cells ~ whence the widely accepted belief that it dries food out. However, the quiet trauma of osmosis is temporary. With time, the cells reabsorb moisture in reverse osmosis. When they do, that moisture is seasoned with salt. {And, I've found, sugar or other aromatics you might have used. A little salt in a marinade seems to assist in the movement of other flavors into food. When we add aromatics to a Pork Brine [page 400], or black pepper and thyme to our Rabbit Cure [page 413], we are capitalizing on this effect.} What is more, that intruder salt changes the proteins~they "open up," enabling them to entrap more moisture than before. When you heat these transformed proteins, they don't coagulate and squeeze out moisture quite the same way unaltered proteins do; some of the recovered moisture survives the ravages of heat. All of this results in seasoned, moisture-laden cells, less tenaciously attached to one another than their unseasoned counterparts. I love this tender succulence and aim to use just enough salt, and allow enough time, to achieve it.

In a less complex process, selected vegetables, in selected situations, can also benefit from salting in advance. In these instances, the dose of salt may be minimal and the lead time may be only five to fifteen minutes, just long enough for osmosis to deflate and soften the cells. This permits them to cook to uniform tenderness in less time, or with less heat, and they end up with more bright vegetable flavor intact. This technique produces excellent grilled onion slices, and we also use it for grilled broccoli rabe, peppers, thickly sliced summer squash, and so on. I distinguish this habit from traditional "salt purging," which is sometimes done to prepare vegetables for pickling.

Where meats and poultry are concerned, I sometimes use the word "cure" to describe the early salting process, whether it is a dry-salting or wet-brining operation, although I caution that these lightly treated foods are not preserved for the long term. The goal of traditional cures, which use much more salt, *was* to preserve for the long term, and interesting taste and texture changes were nice by-products. The goal of our "preseasoning" is to manage and improve flavor, succulence, and texture; any resulting "keeping" ability is the nice by-product. In practice, where most meat and poultry is concerned, we plan ahead and buy early~one to five days in advance~so we have time to lightly cure them. {Fish is a different case; freshness remains imperative. When I preseason fish, it is for a few hours at most.} Such planning is not complicated, and the salting operation usually takes no more than a few minutes. I usually unwrap and season whatever is at issue as soon as I get it home from the store, and place it in the refrigerator, then don't think about it again until I begin to cook the dish. Happily, barring fish, these several-hour to multiday cures do have the advantage of being "extendable." They will forgive you for changing your mind and making a dish a day or two later than originally planned. And if you need to abbreviate these cures, you can do that too. The effect will be more superficial~the salt may not have time to reach the very center of the piece of meat or poultry, but the parts it does reach will benefit, making it worth the effort. Given that the salt may not completely diffuse, in such cases, err on the side of less salt than usual.

Concerning timing, bear in mind that temperature affects how quickly salt moves through the piece of meat. Cold slows down the process {though it will not stop it until you reach freezing, which triggers a different set of changes}. If the chicken you are salting is quite cold, it will cure more slowly than one that is warmer. Wet brines should be cool when you add meats to them, but not ice-cold, or they may not "cure" the meat at all. Once salted or brined, these meats should be refrigerated.

Since seasoning early means seasoning "raw," it requires a leap of faith. You can't effectively "salt to taste" unless you know what your taste in salt "looks like" on the surface of a given piece of raw meat. {But this is a little tricky, since that "look" varies with the size of the piece of meat~freshly salted large cuts will look awfully "salty" compared to small cuts, since large objects tend to have less surface area to volume.} For consistent results, the best solution is to quantify the amount of salt you find you like per pound of meat, then measure the appropriate amount for the weight of what you're preparing. To help you to that end, you'll see that in certain recipes I provide, as a starting point, the ratios or amounts of salt that I like and find effective per pound. Those ratios are pretty consistent, but be assured that you can adjust them to your taste. If you want more or less salt than I suggest, you can easily figure out the amount per pound that suits you after trying only one such recipe, say the roast chicken. {And then, if you find you like the effect, and get in the habit of seasoning in advance, you can fairly rapidly train your hand and eye to consistent freehand salting to your taste. This will be more fun and gratifying than weighing and measuring.} The distinctive thing in these preparations is not how much, but when you add the amount of salt you like. You may find that by seasoning judiciously in advance, you use less salt overall, as you eliminate the habit of repeated doses, and accidental overdoses, of "surface salt" at table.

CHOOSING AMONG SALTS

AT ZUNI AND AT HOME, I GENERALLY USE PLAIN SEA SALT. The type I use has the texture of coarse cornmeal. Unfortunately, most widely distributed commercial sea salts are processed to be either "coarse" like gravel or "fine" like superfine sugar. The medium grade I like is often sold in bulk bins, and it may be labeled simply "sea salt" or, confusingly, "fine sea salt." Its slightly coarse texture makes it easier to sprinkle evenly than brand-name "fine" sea salt, and, for regular use, it is more practical than the gravelly crystals that you must crush or grind. I have lately encountered iodized sea salt, as well as sea salt adulterated with free-flow/anticaking agents, but I use neither. Iodized salt can taste vaguely medicinal or metallic on some foods~and I don't mind if my salt gets clumpy. Likewise, I don't use iodized "table salt," which sometimes hides a dose of dextrose, and avoid "plain table salt" when it is laced with free-flow agents. Nevertheless, issues of flavor and purity aside, such products will behave like plain sea salt, with respect to the desirable changes triggered by preseasoning.

My second choice for general use is plain kosher salt, which has a clean, some say "light," flavor. I think this latter impression owes at least partially to its shape, which ordains that with equal volumes of kosher and other salts, you get less of the flaky kosher stuff than you get with other crystals, because they aren't packed as densely. {Kosher salts vary in flakiness, but testing just a few brands, I found a cup of our sea salt to weigh anything from one and a quarter times to nearly twice as much as a cup of kosher salt.} A teaspoon of salt *does* salt less when it's kosher, because it *is* less salt. This can matter in curing and sausage recipes where salt is measured in volume, usually teaspoons or tablespoons. If you use kosher salt you will get a milder cure, unless you increase the dose a little. In recipes where you are seasoning to taste, this crystal-shape issue is not relevant.

Fleur du sel is a coarse, irregular, slightly humid salt efflorescence harvested from salt marshes. Unrefined, its flavor varies with its source, but I have liked every one I have used. I use it primarily for last-minute seasoning at table, where its texture and flavors will bloom to order. It often sells at impressive prices, and seems most worth the money when you do not dilute its character and squander its crunch through cooking. If you do elect to cure with it, you should pack it, like brown sugar, when measuring by volume. And still, as with kosher salt, you may get less salt than with other salt crystals. When seasoning to taste, this is not an issue.

Mined salts, confusingly called "rock salts" {"rock" refers to their provenance here~dry land versus the sea~not their form}, may have extra mineral components and can taste very nice. I have also tasted bland ones, as well as one that tasted too minerally, a bit like wet concrete smells.

So long as you respect the caveats regarding crystal shape and how it affects measurement, all of these salts will work in these recipes.

On Weighing *&* Measuring

Most of us who cook professionally {read "constantly, and in quantity"} have at least once scoffed that we never measure, and don't use recipes. This is usually what we believe, and we don't mean it in a cavalier way, but it can be off-putting to home cooks, and frankly, it is not entirely true. We may not take out a tool to measure ingredients, or look at a piece of paper, but we measure with our eyes and weigh with our hands and scroll through memories of prior cooking experiences for the unwritten script for the current one. And if we don't put a premium on knowing in advance how many onions or tomatoes will be needed, it is because we have the luxury of sacks and cases at hand to shop from. But beyond this, most of us shun exact weights, measurements, and temperatures because we have learned that many unmeasured and unmeasurable variables can render fixed numbers devilishly misleading. We routinely sacrifice set measures at the altar of variables ~ differences in product quality, tools, appetite, and changes in our own palate from one day, or year, to the next. We learn to adjust. Our unwritten recipes become fluid, producing a variety of different, but related, results, all of which may be delicious.

But if absolutely reliable weights and measures are not possible, that is not to say that weighing and measuring are not worth doing. Composing this book, I have bedeviled and amused every cook in the restaurant and every member of my family, wielding scales, cups, spoons, and tape measures, not to trap the truth of good cooking in numbers, but to state parameters, attaching a number, where it might be helpful, to a condition. In general, weight is a more dependable measure than volume, especially when it comes to solids ~ coarse or fluffy ones in particular {like whole nutmeats or grated cheese}, where the notion of "level" can be hard to apply and "lightly packed" leaves lots of room for interpretation. In such cases, and for virtually all baking, weight is the better measure ~ but I generally provide both weight and volume in these recipes. And be aware that measuring tools are not always reliable: we had a few sets of measuring spoons at Zuni for years that we only lately discovered proposed very different standards. One tablespoon held a quarter more than another did. Our "reliance" on them was always tempered by the habit of tasting, so no one noticed. Likewise, many of our ladles and measuring cups that are marked in ounces and quarter-cups but were manufactured in metric-system countries have been wildly inaccurate.

In these recipes, then, consider numbers as guidelines. They are almost always subordinate to certain described conditions, such as "to coat," "until golden," "until just firm," or "to taste," but they can certainly help you shop and plan your time. I might have prefaced nearly every quantity with "about," because most could be adjusted in either direction without catastrophic results, but instead I have generally provided fixed numbers, not as guarantees but as points of reference. They offer, at a minimum, a notion of scale and a sense of the relative scale of different ingredients, temperatures, and amounts of time. Relative to each other, and to the other variables I pay attention to, these numbers can be very revealing. Tracking proportions of ingredients ~ of liquid to solid, or of vinegar to oil ~ you will begin to notice patterns in groups of dishes, like vinaigrettes or pastry doughs. Easy to remember, ratios are like portable foundations, providing solid insights for attacking a class of dishes. In the case of vinaigrette, they make it possible to confidently assemble dishes by eye and taste alone. With pastry dough, you can learn to tell by looking at basic ratios of fat to starch whether a recipe will be really rich or lean, and how much you may want to adjust it.

Having a few concrete numbers is surely most helpful the first time you make a recipe ~ even if you don't adhere to them exactly. By the second and third time you make a dish, you will probably not depend on them in the same way at all. It is likely you will adjust some of the amounts, tailoring them, with growing confidence, to your circumstances and personal taste. Indeed, a great pleasure lies in transforming a recipe, adjusting it somewhat for the best result each time you make it. If you think yourself unable to make adjustments by eye and taste, ask yourself whether you measure the exact amount of sugar or milk you add to your coffee or tea. Familiarity, and knowing what you like, breeds the necessary confidence.

But if you aren't already very familiar with a dish, paying attention to temperatures, quantities, and proportions and observing how they affect results can help you abbreviate the romantic but lengthy learning process one might characterize as "guess, feel, botch, puzzle, try again, and try to remember what you did." Having a foundation in carefully measured quantities, you may unconsciously begin to trust your eye and hand, knowing what a quarter cup of liquid looks like in your favorite bowl, what two ounces feel like in the palm of your hand, or how many of your pinches fit in a quarter teaspoon.

And still, appreciating the numbers is not more critical than the attention you pay to selecting ingredients, planning menus, and the methods you use, although instructions in those areas are scarcely foolproof either. Ironically, most of us who have scoffed that measurements can be misleading are quick to insist on "perfectly ripe fruit," or "very tender this-or-that" ~ important specifications but, like numbers, not perfectly reliable ones, especially if the listener is not sure he has ever encountered exactly that thing before. These suggestive guidelines can be as flawed as measurements, but both are helpful, and I rely on both types constantly.

Together, they can help you picture the dish I have in mind, even though neither pretends to guarantee a perfect reproduction of it. Happily, since many delicious versions of a dish are possible, there is no reason that your "imperfect" rendition would not be as delicious as, or more delicious than, my prototype.

CONSIDER YOUR TOOLS

I ONCE IMAGINED THAT I COULD GUARANTEE A PERFECT MEAL IN SOMEONE ELSE'S kitchen 2000 miles away by simply bringing all the ingredients with me. This ambitious naïveté ignores the fact that using poor tools, or the wrong tools, can compromise a cook ~ or at least require you to modify your technique or your recipe to your circumstances. An inadequate pan can doom a dish; a dull knife can make cooking a chore and can spoil the results.

The following is a discussion of the principal pieces of equipment that I use frequently and that are critical to the success of the recipes in this book. The list is not exhaustive; you will use other basic, everyday tools that I don't go into here, such as spatulas, tongs, cutting boards, and wooden spoons. A few tools specific to particular dishes are discussed in their respective recipes ~ for example, omelette pans, *spätzle* makers, tart pans, meat grinding equipment. I am certain there are sensible tools and gadgets I don't call for, either because I don't know about them or because I am conservatively attached to some of the rituals of working by hand or with traditional equipment.

SHARP THINGS

Knives
I favor softer stainless steel knives over the hardest stainless. After years of wielding thick, heavy knives, I now reach for a number of relatively inexpensive knives, whose slender blades and gently beveled edges glide through food. Although they can lose their edge more easily, that edge is also very easy to reconstitute to razor sharpness. The hardest abruptly beveled stainless knife may hold that initial edge a little better, but it is much harder work to repair once it is compromised. Old-fashioned carbon steel is easy to make very sharp, although the constant threats of

corrosion and its reacting with acidic foods are disadvantages. Softer stainless steel knives offer a happy, inexpensive compromise solution.

Keeping your knives razor sharp enables you to work much more quickly and keeps your hands and arms from tiring out, even after hours of preparation. Furthermore, a sharp knife glides through food with little pressure; so long as you watch what you are doing, you aren't more likely to cut yourself than with a dull knife. Indeed, a dull knife forces you to exert pressure; it doesn't get purchase on what you are cutting and is apt to slip from the mark. This means you are more prone to cut "off course," and the force you apply to compensate for dullness will worsen the possible wound to yourself. Finally, a dull knife tends to smash rather than slice its way through ingredients, damaging them more than necessary, and leaving them ripe for texture and flavor degeneration.

To maintain your knife's edge, use a sharpening steel to correct the edge before and after every use, and during use, if you feel your knife is losing its bite. When slicing lots of tomatoes or peppers, or trimming artichokes, all of which challenge the edge, I reach for the steel every five minutes or so. Hand wash and dry your knives thoroughly, and be especially prompt when you have been handling high-acid items. Wash your sharpening steel as well when it gets food on it. Don't wash knives or steels in the dishwasher; high heat, chemicals, and slow drying compromise the blade and are unfriendly to lots of grips. Always store knives in a rack where they won't crash into each other, or other tools. And the first time you notice that a few strokes of the steel fail to bring back razor sharpness, or if you notice a tiny nick or burr, it is time to reconstitute the edge with a whetstone or oil stone. Be aware that each time you sharpen your knife on a stone you are actually removing metal, but if you act before the edge becomes truly dull you can usually correct the edge with little loss. Both types of stones are generally sold with guidelines on their use; learning to use one is as gratifying as it is easy. Sending your knives to a stranger to grind on a wheel is costly and inconvenient, and you risk getting back a lot less blade than you sent off.

You can make the recipes in this book with only four different knives, although I would not discourage you from building a larger, specialized collection.

 ⁑ **Paring knife:** I favor a lightweight, 2-1/2-inch parer with a slightly flexible blade and curved edge. I find that expensive, thick, stiff-bladed paring knives can be awkward for most of the small jobs they confront, and I find my hands tire more quickly with a stocky knife. I use paring knives constantly to core onions before halving and peeling them, to turn and fillet citrus, trim artichokes, peel garlic, dice shallots, trim vegetables, and so on.

+ **10-inch chef's knife:** The other workhorse knife. I like mine to have a wide blade with a gently curved cutting edge. The long edge can cover lots of territory, which makes chopping go more quickly, and the curved shape of the edge allows you to rock the knife back and forth ~ momentum replaces muscle power to get the chopping done. The blade is long enough to safely split a whole head of cabbage and sturdy enough to cleave poultry, rabbit, and fish bones. I also find this knife excellent for carving boneless roasts; being heavier than most slender French carves or ham slicers, it allows better control of the angle of carving and the thickness of the slice. So long as it is sharp, it will almost fall through a tender roast with no sawing action.

+ **Boning knife:** Mine has a 5-inch long, 1/2-inch wide blade, which is slightly flexible. It is the obvious choice for boning, but I also reach for it when I slice foie gras or pâté ~ the slender blade doesn't stick and drag. In a pinch, I can fillet fish with it.

+ **Bread knife:** Choose a fairly heavy, stiff-bladed, serrated, and beveled knife, and remember that the bevels are on one side of the serration ~ so the knife will tend to steer to the beveled side, usually to the right. This protects your fingertips ~ if you are right handed. But always keep your fingers away from the blade. A bread knife can stay sharp for years so long as you use it just for tender things and keep it clean and dry. Many people use serrated bread knives to slice tomatoes; if you do, wash and dry it afterward. Replace dull bread knives; they invite forceful sawing gestures that easily go awry. Most types cannot be effectively sharpened ~ standard steel or whetstone techniques just wear down the tips of the serrations.

Other sharp tools

+ **Citrus zester:** Perhaps the most worthwhile of single-use tools. My zester produces five delicate filaments per stroke. If you wash and dry it promptly after every use it ought to stay sharp for quite a while. If you have to press very hard to get pretty zest, either your citrus is dehydrated and rubbery, or the zester is dull. There is no fix for this and it is not worth the struggle. Replace it. I don't use common strippers whose single, scalloped edge digs a deep channel into the tasteless, or bitter, pith of the citrus.

+ **Vegetable peeler:** The double-bladed knife that most of us take for granted and don't take care of. I prefer the type with facing blades that swivel as you set them against the vegetable. The cutting edges are prone to corrosion, so wash and dry by hand immediately after using and replace it once you notice that you, not the blade, are doing the work. Aside from their obvious utility in peeling vegetables, peelers are useful for cutting shallow, wide citrus zest to flavor stews, compôtes, and ice creams.

+ **Mandoline:** An adjustable slicing tool that replaces your paring or chef's knife when you want lots of consistent, pretty slices of a vegetable, fruit, or hard cheese in a hurry. The results will be more regular than can be achieved by even the most practiced hand. Most will cut little strings {julienne} as well. I use a Japanese mandoline {made by Benriner} for slicing items directly onto the serving plate. Not handling the fragile slivers means they look more elegant and taste brighter. A footed French mandoline is a little more cumbersome to use, but it is also a friendly tool for slicing pounds of potatoes at a time and comes with built-in blades for alternatives cuts, like french fries. Wash and dry by hand.

⁺ **Dough cutter or pastry scraper:** A stiff, rectangular metal plate with one not-too-sharp edge and a wide grip on the opposing one. Though I never use mine to portion dough {I use a knife for that}, it is very helpful when assembling any sort of pastry or yeast dough by hand and is essential for making our rough puff pastry. You will need one or two of them for chopping granita. This tool is also convenient for coarsely chopping juicy canned tomatoes without spreading the juice all over the counter or floor {I corral them in a shallow roasting pan, then chop with the scraper}. I use mine constantly to scrape my work surface clean, no matter what I am cooking.

Assisted chopping

⁺ **Food processor:** I use a processor for making bread crumbs and a few other operations, such as grinding nuts and puréeing fruit. In a few recipes I stipulate it as an alternative to hand chopping or in place of a meat grinder. To keep the work-horse serrated chopping blade sharp, wash it promptly and by hand. Store it where it won't get nicked.

⁺ **Blender:** A jar- or canister-type blender homogenizes, emulsifies, and aerates as it purées, which can be desirable for absolutely smooth soups. If you don't have a canister blender, you can sometimes achieve this consistency with a processor if you drain off and reserve most of the cooking liquid and then process the solids for a few minutes. Add back the reserved liquid and process again. Do likewise if you are using a handheld immersion blender. This type of blender is quite convenient to use, but, like a food processor, usually fails to completely homogenize purées as well as a canister blender does.

DULL THINGS

⁺ **Pestle and mortar:** I use a 2-cup stone pestle and mortar almost daily for cracking or pulverizing spices, crushing garlic cloves, pummeling salt cod, or pounding nuts. I love the perfume and flavor of freshly crushed spices and am not bothered by a little irregularity in texture.

⁕ **Pepper grinder:** Although I often crack pepper in a mortar, a grinder is more convenient, especially at table. Choose one that allows you to adjust the grind from fine to very coarse~I usually call for coarsely ground or cracked pepper.

⁕ **Meat pounder:** A flat-faced metal "palate," preferably with an offset handle. Most efficient if it weighs a few pounds; it will flatten things with its own momentum, not your force. Essential for pounding carpaccio, but very efficient for pitting olives and shelling nuts. Just place either in a scattered colony between clean towels and pound gently to split the skins or crack the shells. Also useful for crushing crab or lobster shells for shellfish fumet or bisque.

⁕ **The flat face and back side of a wide-bladed chef's knife:** Although not a separate piece of equipment, it's worth including these overlooked parts of the knife with other crushing and smashing tools. You can use the flat face to split the skins of garlic cloves so they are easier to peel. Use the back side to pound and "bruise" sprigs of fresh sage or rosemary before you add them whole to infuse oil, braises, or stews.

HEAT SOURCES: WHAT YOU COOK *On*, OR *In*

⁕ **Burners:** Both gas and electric burners have their advantages, and these recipes require only that you are, or that you become, familiar with the range of heat possible on your stove top and the time it takes to achieve the temperature adjustments. Temperature changes are slower to achieve and stabilize on electric burners, so slide the pan from the heat to mitigate this problem, or use a Flame Tamer to muffle strong heat. And remember, medium-heat on a high BTU professional gas stove in one home kitchen is not the same as medium heat on an old residential gas stove. Be aware that terms like "low" and "medium-low" heat are not absolute, even if they are printed on your control knob. I use them in these recipes as guidelines only. Remember also that the type of pan you are using~how efficient it is~plays a major role in how much heat you need to apply. In any case, descriptions of what the food should look, sound, and smell like at any given point are the most useful indicators that the temperature is correct.

⁕ **Grills:** At home, I usually grill outside over hardwood or mesquite charcoal, on heavy iron grills whose bars are spaced 1/2 to 3/4 inch apart. But I have grilled successfully on hibachis, on commercial barbecues with not-very-heavy wire grills, and on oven racks balanced on firedogs in the fireplace of my family home in Saint Louis. Most important is that the grills are clean and very hot when you place the food on them and that the distance between the grill and the coals is managed. For quickly cooked items, the grill may be only 2 or 3 inches from the heat; for thick pieces of meat, it may need to be 4 to 6 inches above it. Being able to adjust this distance at will is an equipment advantage. The size of the bed of coals and whether they are flaming, glowing red hot, grizzled orange, or waning dusty gray, matters as much as the above consideration.

Grilling over gas jets or flame-heated rocks won't deliver the flavor of live fire, but it does at least treat the surface of the food to blistering direct heat, which is a major reason for grilling. This flavor-neutral option is preferable to grilling over commercial briquettes whose composition is uncertain.

◦ **Ovens:** I have always used a gas oven and broiler at home. Gas ovens pre-heat more rapidly than electric ovens, and recover more rapidly after you open the door. Given the fact that gas ovens always have flues, the heat is more turbulent than in an electric oven. Since movement magnifies the effect of a given tempera-ture~think of windchill~this distinction explains why a gas oven usually browns food more rapidly, or effectively, than an electric one set to the same temperature. Electric ovens do, however, have an advantage over gas. They maintain steadier temperature, which is very desirable for baking. Electric ovens are typically engi-neered to vary no more than 15° before the thermostat triggers a correction~gas ovens may vary 20° or more.

Many of these recipes were tested in a gas oven~if you use electricity and you find dishes aren't browning as rapidly as I suggest, you may need to nudge the heat up 25°. Either type of oven will brown more effectively, and cook more rapidly if you are using a convection function. A convection fan blows the heat evenly around the chamber and compensates for the relatively stagnant heat of an electric oven chamber. Many cookbooks suggest you use lower heat, and for less time, when cook-ing with convection~and for much baking this is wise; for some dishes, however, such as our roast chicken, you may get the best results at full temperature and with convection. The browning effect of convection can be evident in as little as five min-utes, so it's easy to experiment and decide what works best in your oven.

Whatever type of oven you use, it is important to know its idiosyncrasies. Use an oven thermometer to make sure it is accurately calibrated, and, if you have convection, whether it was calibrated with the convection on or off. {Check the owner's manual or call the manufacturer.} Know also if it has hot spots or cool spots. You can use an oven thermometer to find out, but if you study how evenly your oven browns a sheet pan of croûtons, bread crumbs, or cookies you'll have a good idea. As far as how well your oven retains heat during the cooking process, keep in mind that a deep oven with a small door will retain heat better than a wide, shallow chamber with a big door.

We have a wood-fired brick oven at Zuni, the launching pad for countless roast chickens, pizzas, and braises. It has two chambers ~ a lower one serving as a firebox, and whose live coals we cook on, and an upper one as the roasting shelf. The low arched ceiling and placement of the flue create enormous turbulence and precipitate a marvelous smoky scent on anything we place in there. Notwithstanding, for this book I reworked many of our brick-oven dishes to suit the relatively calm, smokeless heat of my home oven. If you do have a wood-fired oven, I encourage you to use it for the roasted bird dishes {pages 342, 355, 359, and 363} and the fish dishes on pages 322 through 328, although you will no doubt need to modify the execution to suit the design of your oven.

COOKING VESSELS

A COMPLETE, HEAVY-GAUGE *BATTERIE DE CUISINE* ~ A FULL RANGE OF POT SIZES and shapes ~ will allow you maximum culinary flexibility, but to make most of these recipes, which are for 4 servings, you can get by with a few pots and matching lids. I use heavy, stainless-clad aluminum pots that conduct and diffuse heat quickly and evenly across the bottom and up the sides of the vessel. Stainless-clad copper is an even more faithful heat conductor, and you will tend to use lower heat if you cook in copper. If you cook with tin-lined copper, you know it conducts heat well; however, it should not be used for acidic preparations and is high-maintenance.

A good set of pans can last a lifetime so long as you don't abuse them by leaving them empty on the heat for very long. If the pan doesn't have a passenger to deliver the heat to, it will warp, if not on the first occasion of abuse, then eventually, as you repeatedly strain the metal's tolerance. Likewise, let a very hot pan cool somewhat on its own before you plunge it in water; rapid temperature changes strain and weaken the metal. If you choose saucepans, skillets, and sauté pans with all-metal handles, you will discover they can double as braising and roasting vessels as well. I frequently transfer a stovetop operation directly to the oven.

The multipurpose pans I use nearly every day
  + 12-inch and 10-inch curved-sided skillets with matching lids: You will use these constantly for sautéing; the flared sides encourage rapid evaporation and, hence, good coloration.

+ **3-quart {10-1/2-inch} sauté pan with lid:** The wide, straight-sided pan that the French call a *sauteuse.* I use it for wilting greens, poaching gnocchi, stovetop braising and stewing, and some shallow frying. I rarely actually sauté in this pan, finding that the straight sides thwart the "jumping" action and somewhat restrict evaporation. I sauté in skillets instead.

+ **4-quart {8-inch} saucepan with lid:** Beyond sauces, small stews, shelling bean cookery, risotto, and custard making, this pot is big enough to boil green vegetables or 2 servings of pasta, and for small batches of stock, fumet, or confit.

+ **2-quart saucepan with lid:** Use for cooking small amounts in general, and particularly for operations where you need to crowd a little bit of solid food in a little bit of liquid, such as poaching a few pears, or making a small batch of stock. Use this pot for dishes where you need a small surface area in contact with the burner to allow long, slow cooking, such as onion marmalade.

+ **8- to 10-quart {2- to 2-1/2-gallon} stockpot or deep casserole with lid:** Essential for boiling lots of pasta or crab and for stock making. For stock making in particular, your stockpot should be taller than it is wide, so that it will hold the solid ingredients snugly, and therefore will take a minimum of liquid to submerge them. I explain the importance of this crowding concept in Stocks and the Sauces They Make Possible {page 54}.

Other pans I'm glad I have

+ **Nonstick pans:** Nonstick skillets make easy work {and clean up} of egg dishes, and a small, nonstick saucepan can be handy for reheating small amounts of dense things, such as crostini toppings, without them scorching or drying out. I store nonstick pans individually in paper bags so the surrounding *batterie* doesn't scratch them.

+ **A cast-iron pan, 8, 10, or 12 inches wide {depending on how many you are cooking for}:** A good choice for shallow-frying, stove-top hamburgers, polenta hash, and similar dishes where you want a crunchy crust.

+ **Double boiler:** I have a 1-quart porcelain-nested-in-copper beauty that I almost always forget to use. It always seems easier to construct an *ad hoc* assembly, poising whatever bowl or pan I am already using strategically over another pan of water. If this is your option, the top pan or bowl shouldn't touch the floor of the bottom pan or its contents won't be fully insulated from the burner heat. However you choose to "insulate," bear in mind that the term "double boiler" should not imply that the water in the lower vessel is necessarily boiling; it can be warm, hot, or boiling. To moderate the burner heat uniformly, the bottom of the top pan should be just above the surface of the simmering water ~ in the steady heat of steam. But for projects where very gentle heat is called for, say for melting chocolate, I actually submerge the bottom of the pan in the water, making sure the water is hot but not boiling.

Double boilers are known as *bain-maries* in French, although that name also embraces the type of water bath you place custards and pâtés in when you place them in the oven. Deep roasting pans are good vessels for this sort of *bain-marie.*

MEASURING

⁜ **Scale:** While cups and spoons are adequate to measure some ingredients, a scale is easy to use and generally does a much better job, since results aren't dependent on product size or shape, or subjective considerations like "packed-ness." I generally use a spring-type scale that measures up to 5 pounds in 1/2-ounce increments. Not a high-performance machine, it is important to keep this sort of scale dry, and always lift it by the base, not by the plate. Store it upright and never store anything on it. Check to make sure it is reading true and that the needle returns unerringly to zero before every use. {If it sticks or misses, the spring is failing and you ought to replace the scale.} Also, make sure you read weights from the same angle as you check for trueness. If you move the scale, or stand in a different position, you will get a different view of where the needle rests, and you can come up with an inaccurate weight, depending on how fat the needle is and how widely spaced the markings are.

Electronic scales can be expensive, but are worth it for fast, clear readings. For really small increments they are more useful than a spring scale where markings can be crowded and hard to read. My electronic scale displays 1/8-ounce incre-ments~believe it or not, such small increments matter quite a lot when it comes to light, fluffy things like flour, which is dodgy when it comes to volume measure-ment. Nevertheless, remember that digital readings aren't gradual; they jump from one increment to the next. To make sure you aren't actually over the displayed weight, always lift a little measured product from the scale, until the reading drops to the next lower weight. Then gradually re-add what you removed, stop-ping just when the reading blinks back to the desired weight. All of this said, such precise measurement ought to be a temporary tool, useful only so long as you are not yet confident to rely on your hands, eyes, and palate, which, ultimately, are more important tools~invaluable for detecting and measuring the nuances that make food delicious. {See On Weighing and Measuring, page 40.}

⁜ **Meat thermometer:** Instant-read digital thermometers give you quick, clear temperature readings, both advantages over conventional, dial-type thermometers. I recommend you use a model whose sensor is in the very tip of the probe. Many thermometers, digital or otherwise, house the sensor partially up the shaft, which complicates the task of getting a reading at the center of anything, since you have to factor in the extra bit of shaft when you shoot for the center of a roast. Furthermore, if the sensor is too far up the shaft you may not be able to get it all the way to the center of really large roasts. Most manufacturers mark the sensor location with a dimple in the shaft. If you can't find one, and the packaging offers no help, consider contacting the manufacturer, or the store where you bought the thermometer. Thermometers whose probes are attached to a cable allow you to leave the probe in place as you cook, which has great advantages: it eliminates the need to open the door ~ and lose heat ~ and greatly simplifies the process of monitoring your roasts {see Successful Roasting, page 391}. I recommend that you check the accuracy of your thermometer, both when brand new and from time to time thereafter. You can test it by submerging the sensor in boiling water. More than once I have returned brand-new thermometers that registered only 200°.

✦ **Oven thermometer:** Handy for checking the accuracy of your oven and identifying the inevitable temperature variations within the chamber. Mercury-type thermometers can be left in the oven and will remain more accurate over the long term than will the bimetal spring-type {common dial-type thermometers}. The latter lose accuracy if left in the oven, or with frequent use. To check your oven, place the thermometer in the center of the oven and allow the oven to preheat fully. For electric ovens this may take two heating cycles. Move the thermometer around to check for variation. Bear in mind that even a well-calibrated oven will necessarily vary within a range of temperatures, and door opening can affect temperature dramatically {see Ovens, page 47}.

✦
✦ ✦

CHOOSING THE WINES

by GERALD ASHER

JUDY RODGERS'S COOKING IS ROOTED IN THE TRADITIONS OF REAL PEOPLE IN real places. The wines I've chosen for it are also real: they, too, express people and places. Each one of them complements a dish and strengthens the web of memories it brings to the table. Mostly the associations are universal and obvious, but sometimes they're personal. For example, I shall always associate blood sausage with the wines of the Côte de Brouilly. Sometimes on a brisk autumn day at Château Thivin, my old friend Yvonne Geoffray would grill a few slices of her homemade sausage over the embers of vine cuttings in the dining-room grate, and we'd wash them down with a pitcher of new wine drawn from one of the huge wooden casks in the cellar below the house. And I cannot think of *stracciatelle* without remembering the bright red wine of Bonarda, a simple variety common in the Po Valley of Northern Italy. I first tasted both the wine and the soup at the kitchen table of a grower near Pavia whose wife had asked me, out of the blue, to stay for supper. I watched as she beat the eggs and flour and stirred them into a pot simmering on the stove. In these pages, I have suggested some of the great classic wines where appropriate. But mostly I have tried to draw attention to neglected or unfamiliar wines that can add an unexpected dimension, an element of surprise, to the simplest occasion. They are good wines, delicious wines, wines with a real history, and all of them made by serious growers. That's why they are in this book.

❖
❖ ❖

✢ ✢
✢

STOCKS & THE SAUCES THEY
MAKE POSSIBLE

✢
✢ ✢

ONE OF THE INDELIBLE LESSONS OF MY COOKING CAREER OCCURRED THE DAY Pepette Arbulo scolded me for approaching the stockpot to skim her *bouillon de volaille* {her chicken stock}. Looking at me as though I were a traitor, she asked what I was doing and to please stop. "You must leave the fat on top. What are you worried about? Skim it off, and the *bouillon* will have no flavor." I obeyed and discovered that the resulting broth was sunny yellow, brightly flavored, and clear. After years of hearing and reading admonitions to scrupulously and constantly skim every shadow of fat from the surface of a stock, this discovery was a delight.

The next morning, I noticed she dumped a demitasseful of *sel de mer* into that day's broth just as she lit the flame. She responded to my quizzical look with, "You have to salt it, *non?*"

«*D'accord,*» I said, although I would not have agreed the week before I arrived in her kitchen. I arranged to stay for the rest of the summer.

I have never strayed from Pepette's method, though I retest the premise from time to time. And whenever I see a tub of not-brilliant or not-bright-tasting stock at the restaurant, I investigate and discover someone forgot the salt altogether, added it at the last minute ~ too late to do its job ~ or skimmed all of the fat at the beginning, thinking they were doing a good thing. Another point I stress in making stock is the maintenance of steady heat ~ I like a gentle simmer and am adamant about keeping fluctuation to a minimum. Too high, and you will churn the fat under and "oxidize" the delicate broth. Too low, and a dirty, bony taste can intrude. Even a brief period of either situation can flaw the stock ~ especially when it's chicken. For the same reason, I insist that stocks be strained as soon as they are ready; once the flame is off, we scramble to get the liquid off the bones, lest unwanted flavors leach out of the bones and spoil the delicacy of the broth. We don't stir stocks, although if at any time a limb, root, or stalk is poking prominently above the surface, we give it a shove to make sure it contributes its flavor to the brew.

I encourage cooks to taste every half hour or so after the stock begins to simmer {or every few minutes for fish fumet}. This allows us to track the development of the flavor ~ it improves steadily until, at some point, the stock doesn't taste better than before. It may taste stronger, but not better or brighter. The goal is to catch the stock just before this happens, before the meat and vegetable flavors are overcooked. And, since we add only enough liquid to cover the meaty bones and vegetables, plus a few inches at most, the flavor is fairly concentrated at the point it peaks. If you use too much water at the outset, the flavor will still be dilute when it peaks. Reducing such dilute stock is not a great fix. Reducing delicate chicken stock or fish fumet {whether strained or "on the bones"} dulls the flavors even as you concentrate them; you can't evaporate the water without changing the character of the flavor components themselves.

Each of our formulas call for a heavy load of the cartilage, sinews, and connective stuff that give stock lovely body. Your stock will be most reliably delicious if you use all fresh parts, although that may not always be practical. Using a portion of carefully wrapped and frozen scraps or bones, the by-products of an earlier project, won't usually compromise the stock and is a sensible concession to economy of time, money, and product. But a stock made exclusively from long- or sloppily frozen bones and scraps may taste tired.

COMPOUND STOCKS

COMPOUND STOCKS ARE MEAT AND POULTRY STOCKS WE MAKE WITH MEATY BONES, scraps, and carcasses, browned and then moistened with our chicken stock or chicken stock plus water. Since it is flavorful and slightly gelatinous already, chicken stock gives these second-generation stocks a kick-start. They achieve lovely body in fewer hours, without overcooking the new flavors ~ beef, pork, lamb, rabbit, duck, squab, or other meats you might make into stock. This method "compounds" flavor and produces a rich, albeit costly, stock. We think it is worth the extra expense and time. {And the exhausted chunks of meat can be delicious if you eat them right after straining the stock.} All of these stocks are brewed with a combination of muscle, bone, and connective tissue, although the respective proportions vary. You can use less meat ~ at some loss of flavor ~ but I can't suggest that without recalling an extraordinary and generous cook, Catherine Brandel, who looked at me Pepette-like when she saw nothing but bits of trim in the bone pile we were about to roast for some unenlightened stock years ago. "You're adding some meat, no? This will taste like boiled bones." Zuni switched to Catherine's method that day. Use only impeccable product ~ even an ounce of off-smelling scrap will ruin a whole stock.

These recipes begin by roasting the meat and bones, and it is here that subtle damage can be done to a stock. Always arrange the parts in a shallow pan that crowds them in a single, even layer. This way they will brown evenly, and the pan will not scorch. Roast in a fairly hot oven; long, slow roasting would dry them out and could damage the proteins that give the stock body. But do watch that none of the tallest protruding bits burns. Even a small amount of burned product will taint the flavor of the stock. {If any parts do burn, trim them off before you assemble the stock.} Use tongs to rearrange endangered bits of meat or bone, or rotate the roasting pan if necessary. Roast to a caramel color, to give the stock a nice roasty flavor and golden hue. Remove the pan from the oven while the parts still look, and smell, delicious. The meat should still have bounce when you press it or bend a joint. In most ovens, meaty bones take no more than 45 minutes to color superficially while remaining moist inside.

For the best flavor, assemble the stock promptly, with still-warm parts. Place in a stockpot, one narrow enough that the bones form a pile at least as deep as it is wide. Pour off any fat from the roasting pan, then moisten the pan with a little cold water and simmer to loosen or dissolve any stubborn but still-golden bits. Taste to make sure these "deglazed" drippings are tasty; if they are, add them to the stockpot. Then moisten the bones with cold chicken stock. Most of these recipes call for you to finish with a measure of cold water. If you are short on chicken stock, don't hesitate to alter the balance, but, obviously, using more water will produce a stock with less body and less complex flavor. If you must choose, however, even all water produces a better stock than one made with any amount of poor-tasting chicken stock. If using all water, add a few pinches of salt.

The larger the beast or bones, the more slowly they will yield their proteins and flavor. And you can't rush this extraction by flooding the parts with liquid, raising the heat, and boiling the stock. That technique tends to grab the color, and some of the flavor from the meat and bones, but it usually fails to properly tease out the proteins, or, worse, churns them, along with impurities and fat, into an unappetizing murk.

The vegetables and aromatics recommended for each stock are chosen, dosed, and sized for the meat in question. For example, pork tends to be rich and sweet, so there's no carrot in the pork stock. Or, since rabbit can make a stock that is thin in flavor, and peaks quickly, we boost it with a generous measure of vegetables and cut them small so they express all of their flavor just as quickly. For clarity of flavor, we add the vegetables raw to most of these stocks. To sauté or roast them with the bones is to squander their distinct, fresh flavors in favor of caramelization. This can make the finished stock too sweet. I make an exception for tomato, which I sometimes like to roast with the bones.

Each of these stocks will keep for about a week refrigerated.

REDUCTION: TURNING STOCK *into* SAUCE

IT IS EASY TO TURN THESE COMPOUND STOCKS INTO SATINY, RICHLY FLAVORED sauces that are nearly fat-free. As long as the initial chicken stock was not oversalted, the resulting *glace,* or reduction, will not be too salty. Impeccable raw ingredients, which you take care not to overbrown, and which you simmer only until their flavor peaks, will tolerate reduction by up to 80 percent and still taste bright. On the other hand, even a bit of burned bone, hard boiling, or tardy straining can introduce off flavors that will bloom and dominate all others when you reduce the stock. {Such flawed reductions can sometimes be mellowed with a lump of unsalted butter, whisked in at the last minute over high heat. You can also, for that matter, whisk butter into an unflawed reduction, but I don't crave the dairy taste and prefer the clean, unenriched version. Although I did spend years proudly *monter*-ing *au beurre*~beating in butter.} You can also partially reduce any of these stocks and use that *demi*{half}-*glace* to moisten braises or stews.

To reduce a strained compound stock, first cool it completely and remove the cap of fat from the surface. Scrape off any opaque sludge that may sit on top of the semisolid stock. Pour into a saucepan, or sauté pan, scraping the jellied stock from the sides of the storage vessel but taking care to avoid any sludgey stock that may be at the bottom. Simmer steadily and gently, uncovered, skimming impurities as they veil the surface of the reducing stock. The most efficient way to remove these evanescent "skins" is to rest the underside side of a wide, flat serving spoon on them~the veil will cling to the spoon. Lift and gently pivot the spoon, so that the skin doesn't slide back into the reduction, then rinse the spoon clean. Repeat as needed. This way you discard only impurities, not precious reduction. You can adjust the flavor of the reducing stock by adding a little bit of sliced carrot, celery, and/or onion, or a bay leaf or peppercorns, or by introducing new aromatics like thyme, garlic, rosemary, or shallot, where they suit the dish the reduction is meant to sauce. Reduce to the desired consistency, which you can test by dribbling a little of the sauce-in-progress onto a room-temperature or cold plate. How long the reducing will take will depend on the amount of stock, pot size and shape, and heat level. A few cups of already jellied stock may take only ten minutes to reach a velvety consistency in a wide sauté pan, but twice as long in a narrower saucepan. How much reduction you will obtain from any of these recipes is a tricky question as well. It depends on how rich your initial chicken stock was, exactly what mix of bones and meat you used, how much body you teased from them, and how thick you want your sauce. Still, I include approximate reduction yields with each recipe.

These reductions keep well for weeks and are nice to have on hand to sauce grilled, sautéed, or roasted meats. One to 2 tablespoons reduction per person will be enough.

ZUNI CHICKEN STOCK

THIS IS THE STOCK WE USE FOR MOST OF OUR SOUPS, FOR MEAT AND POULTRY braises, for moistening certain fish dishes, and for making compound meat stocks. It calls for lots of meaty chicken, but is worth the investment; it delivers plenty of balanced, bright flavor. A brew made from the economical "backs, necks, and wing tips" triumvirate does not compare. Chicken stock brewed from mostly bones, especially stockpiled, tired ones, tastes dull to me and isn't worth the trouble, or even the small expense. I have tasted, and tested with, a dozen different canned chicken stocks, and a few in wax boxes ~ mostly salted, some salt-free, a few all-natural and organic candidates, most 99 percent fat-free ~ and found none that has the clear flavor I seek. Odd additives {potato starch, turmeric, dextrose, corn syrup, onion powder, MSG} could explain the muddy flavor. "Artisanal" chicken stocks, available at specialty food markets, usually frozen, offer hope ~ they can be excellent, as good as the ingredients, recipe, and cook responsible for them {see Sources and Resources, page 000}. But even if they offer convenience, they are not as economical as homemade stock ~ even this one using whole chicken.

Whole birds ~ with their head {or at least the jointy neck} and feet ~ are my first choice for stock making. They provide a convenient combination of the meat, bone, connective fibers, and fat that produce great flavor and body. Asian markets are a good place to look for "head-and-feet-on" chickens, and other poultry. And since about 15 percent of the weight is head and feet, they are typically less expensive per pound than "dressed" chicken. Still, you can substitute a small whole chicken and make up the balance with fresh chicken wings, which deliver bright flavor and viscosity. Don't supplement with backs.

If you make double or triple batches of this stock, you probably won't need to quite double or triple the amount of water; this will depend on your pot's dimensions. Pay attention to coverage, not quarts. You might also need to increase the cooking time by as much as a few hours to account for a smaller surface-area-to-volume ratio, which restricts evaporation. The amount of salt you use is subject to taste and intended purpose. I use the full measure indicated in the recipe when I am certain to use the chicken stock for a clear soup or risotto. I use the smaller amount when the stock will end up as a reduced sauce, especially one where the compound stock has little added water, as for duck, quail, squab, guinea hen or rabbit.

FOR 8 TO 10 CUPS:

One 5-1/2-pound chicken, preferably with head and feet, or a smaller dressed chicken plus extra wings to equal 5-1/2 pounds

About 4 quarts cold water {to cover}

1 large carrot {about 4 ounces}, peeled and cut into 2-inch chunks

1 stalk celery {about 1 ounce}, leaves trimmed off and cut into 2-inch chunks

1 large yellow onion {about 12 ounces}, root end trimmed flat, peeled, and quartered

1 to 1-1/2 teaspoons salt {a little more if using kosher salt}

Remove the giblets from the chicken, if included. Don't remove the lump of fat you find inside the cavity; it will add flavor. Rinse the chicken. Remove the breast meat {usually 10 to 12 ounces' worth} for another use: To remove the breasts, poke the tip of your boning knife flat against the sternum {breastbone}, then slide the blade smoothly along its length. Repeat on the other side of the sternum. Feel for the collarbone {which is the wishbone}, and cut along its inside contour on both sides of the sternum. Use your fingers to pry the breast muscle away from the carcass on one side of the breast. Then, cutting flat against the bone, use the tip of your knife to gradually free the meat as you tug the breast with the other hand. The breast meat sometimes slips free of its skin as you do this. If so, leave the skin attached to the carcass; it will add flavor to the stock. Repeat with the other breast. Next, slash the thigh and leg muscles to encourage the greatest release of flavor during cooking. Cut off the feet, if the bird has them. {This is only so they won't poke above the surface of the water.} Place the feet and chicken in a deep 8- to 10-quart stockpot that holds the chicken snugly. Add the cold water. If 4 quarts of water doesn't cover the chicken, it is likely your pot is a little too wide~ *don't add more water.* Instead, remove the chicken, cut off the legs at the hip joint, and then replace all the parts in the pot, arranging them so they sit low enough to be submerged. If a stubborn wing still refuses to stay submerged, cut it off as well and then drop it back in the water. {But don't, in this effort to consolidate, resort to cutting through the backbone or breast-bone.} Bring to a simmer over high heat and skim the foam. Stir the chicken under once~just to allow the last of the foam to rise~reduce the heat, and skim

\ *continued*

the foam carefully, taking care to leave behind any bright yellow fat that may be starting to appear on the surface. Add the vegetables and salt and stir them under. Bring back to a gentle simmer and adjust the heat to maintain it. If you taste the water now, you will barely be able to detect the salt. Don't cover the pot. Maintain that gentle simmer and taste the broth regularly. Don't add more water, don't stir, and don't skim the fat, which will gradually form a "cap" on the broth. Once the stock has a rich, bright, chickeny flavor, usually in about 4 hours, turn off the heat. Leave a minute, to allow the simmer to stop, then pour through a wide strainer. Tipping the hot, heavy pot can be awkward ~ start by ladling some of the stock through the strainer, enough to make tipping manageable. Or you may choose to fish out the carcass and vegetables as they are gradually exposed. I usually strain the stock first through a medium strainer to filter out the obvious solids, then pour the stock through a fine mesh strainer. When we are serving our chicken stock as clear soup or with *Stracciatelle* {page 158} or pastina in it, we ladle the strained stock through a clean cotton napkin moistened with water. This broth-soup rarely needs any doctoring.

Don't discard the cooked bird. Every cook I know loves to nibble on the warm meat from the spent stock chickens ~ it isn't succulent, having given all it has to the stock, but if you catch it while it is still warm, it is comforting and tasty, especially when you have made the stock with salt. I like it with tarragon vinaigrette or Four-Minute Egg Gribiche {page 291}.

Cool the stock to room temperature, then cover tightly and place in the refrigerator. Remove the cap of solidified fat only just before you use the stock ~ it will keep out some air until then. Because it is lightly salted, this stock will keep for about a week refrigerated, but it is practical to divide it into several smaller containers and freeze right away what you won't need within that time. For freezing, use odorless plastic containers with tight-fitting lids that allow room for expansion as ice crystals form. Remove all the fat from the stock first, and make sure the stock is cold when you fill the containers. Thaw frozen stock slowly in the refrigerator, or slide from the storage vessel into a pot and melt over low heat. For the best flavor, don't freeze chicken stock for more than a few weeks.

✢
✢ ✢

Rich Pork Stock

We make one or two 20-gallon batches of this delicious stock per week. We use it to moisten braised pork dishes, to enrich the juices from our Mock Porchetta {page 408}, and to deglaze the pan when we make Standing Rib Roast of Pork {page 403}. But most often, we reduce it to make a pristine sauce for House-Cured Pork Chops {page 400}.

Making such large batches, we find it convenient and economical to use a whole pig's head,* to add succulence and body. At home, making a small batch of stock, it is more practical to use a piece of pig's foot, which contains a comparable combination of skin, cartilage, meat, and bone. {Many supermarkets carry them, or can get them with a day's notice, and they are usually available at Latin and Asian markets. Have them cut in chunks, or split, and freeze what you don't need right away.} The main flavor component of the stock, however, is the "meaty" bones; we use a combination of inexpensive fresh pork shank and more costly bone-in, lean shoulder butt, sometimes called Boston butt. Shank gives the stock body and depth of flavor; shoulder gives it brightness. You can use other bony cuts, such as ribs, as long as they aren't too fatty and are fairly meaty. Otherwise, add a pound of meat to 1-1/2 pounds clean bones; without meat, the stock will have body but lack flavor. Make sure the bones and scraps smell very fresh and are not tacky to the touch.

\ *continued*

---

* The pig's head is a dramatic thing. Passing through the kitchen their first or second week at Zuni, more than a few servers {and cooks} have recoiled at the sight of a caramel-colored, 15-pound pig's head peering from the stockpot. And there is the nearly unbelievable tale of pig head–snatching: Our "low-boy" stockpot burners are positioned near the receiving entrance and are in full view of the back window. Anyone walking past the back of the restaurant can look in the kitchen window and see *frittos* frying, gnocchi bobbing, or a pig peering from a pot. One morning at about 2 A.M., as the closing manager was checking windows and the clean-up crew was ferrying in supplies, a curiously motivated stranger slipped in the back door, nabbed the steaming head barehanded from the pot, sped out, and scrambled up the alley behind the restaurant. The manager was caught between concern and hilarity, but he composed a careful note explaining events to the kitchen manager, who would now have a deficient pork stock. The thief, in the meantime, dropped his scalding prize within 30 yards. The police apprehended the uncomfortable culprit and suggested restitution of the cost of the pig's head {$7.50 at the time}. We let it go.

FOR 4 TO 5 CUPS {*ABOUT 1 TO 2 CUPS REDUCTION*}:

2-1/2 pounds lean bone-in pork shoulder or shank {fresh, not smoked}, cut into 3-inch chunks

1/2 small pig's foot {about 1 pound}, split

4 cups cold Chicken Stock {page 58} {enough to barely cover the meat and bones}

About 4 cups cold water {enough to cover the meat and bones by about 1 inch}, plus a little to deglaze the pan and stockpot

1 large yellow onion {12 ounces}, halved

2 stalks celery {2 ounces}, leaves trimmed off

1 bay leaf

A few whole black peppercorns

Preheat the oven to 450°.

Crowd, but without piling them up, the pork and pig's foot in a shallow roasting pan or in a 10- or 12-inch ovenproof skillet. {If you briefly preheat the pan over a low flame before you add the pork, it will sear on contact and be less likely to stick later on.} You should barely see the bottom of the pan; otherwise, the drippings will tend to burn in the exposed spots. Roast until golden, 30 to 40 minutes. Check the progress after about 25 minutes, and rearrange the pork, or turn it over, as needed, to promote even coloring. You may need to rotate the pan.

Transfer the pork and foot, still warm, to a deep 8- to 10-quart stockpot. Pour off all of the fat from the pan, then add about 1/4 cup cold water to it, set over low heat, and scrape and stir to melt any gold or chestnut-colored drippings; don't work on any black ones. Taste. If they are nice and porky, pour these reconstituted drippings into the stockpot; if the liquid tastes at all scorched ~ like over-browned bacon ~ discard it. Add the cold chicken stock, then add water to cover by about an inch. {If using unsalted chicken stock, add a few pinches of salt.} Bring to a simmer and skim the foam. Poke under any exposed chunks of meat, then skim any new foam that rises to the surface. Add the onion, celery, bay leaf, and peppercorns and stir them under. Simmer uncovered, without skimming or further stirring but tasting regularly, for 4 to 5 hours, until the stock is richly flavored and the color of maple syrup, and has some body; check for this last by chilling a few drops of stock on a plate. You may need to adjust the heat to control the simmer, and you may need to poke the bones or add a few ounces of water to keep the meat and bones submerged during the long extraction.

Strain the stock promptly; leave the meat and vegetable chunks in the strainer to continue dripping. Immediately pour about 1/4 cup of water into the stockpot and swirl it briefly, to liquefy and capture the syrupy stock that is clinging to the pan. Pour this over the meat and vegetables, to rinse some of the rich syrup from their surfaces into the strained stock below. Leave the stock to cool completely. If not using right away, cover and refrigerate with the layer of fat intact ~ it will help preserve the stock until needed.

Return to the strainer: you will see that the meat chunks are absolutely tender and spent ~ they will collapse upon touch. Salvage and enjoy them, still warm, smashed between slices of focaccia, crowned with a smear of fresh ricotta and lots of cracked black pepper, or moistened with a spoonful of Chimichurri {page 298} or Salsa Verde {page 292}.

⁘
⁘

BEEF STOCK

We SERVE THIS BEEF STOCK AS A BROTH SOUP, GARNISHED WITH A POACHED EGG {see Beef Broth with Marrow Croûtons and a Truffled Egg, page 160}, Martha's Spätzle {page 220}, or pastina. It flavors our rich Porcini *Pearà* Sauce {page 311} and makes braised beef dishes rich and delicious, particularly if you reduce it somewhat to make demi-glace before you add it to the braise. Reduced to a glaze, we use it to sauce *onglet* {hanger steak}, skirt steak, or roasted beef fillet. We include the optional tomato when the final dish welcomes that flavor.

Our standard formula calls for beef shank exclusively, which may seem a costly requirement, but the shank is a convenient and ideal package of bone, muscle, and connective matter and guarantees the consistent, rich yields that we depend on for so many preparations. Ask your butcher to slice the whole shank and give you the bony, cartilaginous joint ends as well as the meaty center ~ this ought to drop the per-pound price. Alternatively, you can produce a delicious stock using half the amount of shank complemented with equal parts lean chuck and other beef bones. That combination makes a bright-tasting, slightly less viscous stock.

\ *continued*

FOR 6 TO 8 CUPS *{1 TO 2 CUPS REDUCTION}:*

About 3 pounds beef shank, cut osso
  buco–style into 1/2- to 1-inch-thick
  slices, or a combination of 1-1/2
  pounds shank plus 1-1/2 pounds
  beef bones and lean chuck in equal
  proportions {see Note}
1 small ripe tomato {optional}
6 cups cold Chicken Stock {page 58}
  {enough to barely cover the meat
  and bones}

About 6 cups cold water {enough to
  cover the meat and bones by about
  2 inches}, plus a little to deglaze
  the pan and stockpot
1 large carrot {4 ounces}, peeled
1 large yellow onion {12 ounces},
  halved
2 stalks celery {2 ounces}, leaves
  trimmed off
1 bay leaf
A few whole black peppercorns

Note: If using shanks, poke out the plug of marrow from each slice, place in a
few cups of water, and store refrigerated for up to a week, changing the water as it
turns from pink to ruddy. Use for Melting Marrow Gremolata {page 296}, or to
flavor the aforementioned Marrow Croûtons, or *Pearà.* Or, if you don't have plans
to use it soon, soak it for a day only, then drain, dry, wrap in several layers of
plastic, and freeze.

Preheat the oven to 450°.

Crowd, but without piling it up, the meat, or meat and bones, in a shallow
roasting pan or ovenproof 12-inch skillet. {If you preheat the pan over low heat
before you add the beef, it will sear on contact and be less likely to stick later on.}
You should only barely see the bottom of the pan; otherwise, the drippings will
tend to burn in the exposed spots. If using the tomato, nest it between two
accommodating chunks of meat, not directly on the pan bottom, so it will roast
without burning.

Roast until evenly browned and delicious smelling, 30 to 45 minutes. Since
shank slices tend to sit flat, you may need to turn them over to brown both sides.
You also may need to rotate the pan to promote even coloring.

Transfer the beef, still warm, to a deep 8- to 10-quart stockpot. Drain all the fat
from the roasting pan. If there are any promising caramelized drippings, add about
1/4 cup cold water, set over low heat, and scrape and stir to reconstitute them.
Taste. If the deglazed liquid is bright and beefy tasting, pour it into the stockpot; if
it tastes at all burned or acrid, discard it. Add the cold chicken stock, then top with
cold water to cover by about 2 inches. {If using unsalted chicken stock, add a few

pinches of salt.} Bring to a simmer and skim the foam. Poke any exposed meat under the surface, then skim any new foam that appears. Add the carrot, onion, celery, bay leaf, and peppercorns and stir them under. Simmer uncovered, without stirring or skimming but tasting regularly, for 4 to 5 hours, until the stock is full flavored and the color of strong black tea, and has a little body; to check for this last, trickle a little stock onto a plate and chill ~ it should set like very soft Jell-O. You will need to adjust the heat to control the simmer, and you may need to add water to keep the meat and bones submerged during the long extraction.

Strain the stock promptly; leave the meat and vegetables in the strainer. Add about 1/4 cup water to the stockpot, swirl, and then pour this liquid over the strained meat and vegetables into the stock. {This technique captures the syrupy stock that is clinging to the stockpot and solids.} Leave to drip for 5 to 10 minutes, then leave the stock to cool completely.

For a primitive meal, salvage the warm tender meat and serve with Salsa Verde {page 292} or mustard vinaigrette.

✦ ✦
✦ ✦

LAMB STOCK

WE MAKE LAMB STOCK PRIMARILY TO TURN IT INTO A REDUCED SAUCE FOR Roasted Leg of Lamb {page 394} or grilled lamb chops. We usually make the stock with the bones and lean trim from a leg of lamb, about 2 pounds total, supplemented with 1/2 pound of inexpensive meaty neck bones. Foreshank and breastbones are fine choices as well. Ask the butcher to cut the bones so they will fit into your intended pot. All of the usual advisories apply to lamb stock, with two additional caveats: Trim every bit of lamb fat from the parts before you roast them. Otherwise, its persuasive flavor will dominate the stock, no matter how gently it is simmered. And don't roast lamb bones as aggressively as beef or pork bones; very high heat and thorough browning tend to produce a scorched-tasting lamb stock.

\ *continued*

FOR ABOUT 4 CUPS {*ABOUT 1 CUP REDUCTION*}:

About 2-1/2 pounds lamb bones and
    meaty scraps from the leg, neck,
    shank, and/or breast
4 cups cold Chicken Stock {page 58}
    {enough to barely cover the meat
    and bones}
About 4 cups cold water {enough to
    cover the meat and bones by about
    1 inch}, plus a little to deglaze the
    pan and stockpot

1 carrot {3 ounces}, peeled
1 large yellow onion {12 ounces},
    quartered
1 stalk celery {1 ounce}, leaves
    trimmed off
1 bay leaf
A few whole black peppercorns
A few unpeeled garlic cloves, lightly
    crushed {optional}

Preheat the oven to 425°.

Crowd the bones and meat in a shallow roasting pan or in an ovenproof
12-inch skillet. {If you preheat the pan, the bones will be less likely to stick.}

Roast until lightly browned, about 30 minutes. Rotate the pan or rearrange
the bones and meat if they threaten to burn at any point.

Transfer to a deep 8- to 10-quart stockpot, or a 4-quart saucepan if the chunks of
bone are small enough, taking care to leave every drop of rendered fat in the roasting pan. Pour off the fat from the pan. If there are any golden drippings in the
roasting pan, moisten with about 1/4 cup cold water, set over low heat, and stir and
scrape to melt them. Taste the result. If it is pleasant, pour it over the bones.

Moisten the bones with the chicken stock, then add cold water to cover by 1
inch. {If using unsalted chicken stock, add a pinch of salt.} Bring to a simmer and
skim the foam. Jiggle and poke the bones gently, then skim any new foam that
floats to the surface. Add the carrot, onion, celery, bay leaf, peppercorns, and garlic, if using, stir them under, and adjust the heat to maintain a gentle, steady simmer. Simmer uncovered, without stirring but skimming and tasting regularly,
until the stock is bright in flavor and golden brown, 3 to 4 hours.

Strain promptly; leave the bones and meat in the strainer. Swirl a few spoonfuls of water in the warm stockpot, and pour this through the strainer as well.

+
+ +

Duck, Quail, Squab, Guinea Hen, or Rabbit Stock

Stocks made from these creatures are wonderful for saucing their respective meats or for moistening such braises. A stingy tablespoon of squab reduction can make a simple Roast Squab {page 363} an elegant event, and guinea hen stock will make a brilliant "Saltimbocca" {page 357} or sauce for Roasted Guinea Hen with Bay Leaves, Madeira and Dates {page 355}. Rabbit stock gives extra character to Rabbit with Marsala and Prune-Plums {page 414} and, reduced to a glaze, is delicious with Rabbit Sausage {page 426}. You also can use this formula to make goose, pheasant, or other game bird stocks.

I group these stocks because they share characteristics that determine how we get the best results from them. They all present skinny bones that need to be browned very quickly but that will suffer the most if roasted to brittleness. In most cases, you will be making a small amount of tasty stock from a small pile of wing tips, feet, or necks from the animal you are cutting up to braise or roast. If using whole carcasses, break them up after roasting them; otherwise, just a few pounds of the gangly skeletons will require too large a pot and too much stock to submerge. A supplement of raw chicken parts contributes body. All these stocks have the best flavor and body after just a few hours of simmering.

FOR ABOUT 3 CUPS {ABOUT 1 CUP REDUCTION}:

1 pound bones {carcasses, wing tips, necks, feet, and/or heads} and meat scraps from the chosen bird or rabbit

8 ounces chicken wings and/or necks

About 4 cups cold Chicken Stock {page 58} {enough to barely cover the meat and bones}

About 2 cups cold water {enough to cover the meat and bones by 1/2 inch}, plus a little to deglaze the pan and stock pot if need be

1 medium carrot {2 ounces}, peeled and sliced about 1/2 inch thick

1 medium yellow onion {8 ounces}, thickly sliced

1 bay leaf

A few whole black peppercorns

A few garlic cloves, unpeeled, lightly crushed {optional}

A small sprig of fresh thyme {optional}

Preheat the oven to 475°.

\ continued

If using duck, trim off the fat and slabs of skin. Set aside to render for another use {see page 432}.

Crowd all the bones and meat scraps except the chicken parts in a small, shallow roasting pan or small, ovenproof skillet. Roast until golden but not brittle, 20 to 30 minutes; rotate the pan or rearrange the bones and meat if necessary.

Crowd the roasted parts and raw chicken in a 2-quart saucepan, breaking any carcasses into pieces as needed so they will fit snugly. If there are any appetizing golden drippings in the roasting pan, first pour off any fat, then moisten with a few tablespoons cold water, set over low heat, and stir and scrape to melt them. If the result is tasty, pour it over the bones.

Add the cold chicken stock, then water to cover by 1/2 inch. {If using unsalted chicken stock, add a pinch of salt.} Bring to a simmer and skim the foam. Poke the bones under and skim any new foam that rises to the surface. {Don't skim the fat.} Add the carrot, onion, bay leaf, peppercorns, and garlic and/or thyme, if using. Stir them under and adjust the heat as needed to bring back to a steady, slow simmer.

Simmer uncovered, without stirring but tasting regularly, until the stock is golden and rich in flavor, usually about 2 hours. If the specific flavor of any of these birds or rabbit is unfamiliar to you at the outset, fear not: stock making, and progressive tasting, is the ideal way to "learn" that flavor as it develops in the broth.

Strain promptly. If the stock feels fairly rich and sticky ~ some birds will make such a stock ~ add a few tablespoons cold water to the empty pot, swirl it around, and then pour this over the strained meat and bones into the finished stock.

❖
❖ ❖

FISH FUMET

Fish stock is usually called "fumet," a pretty word that suggests that the brew is little more than a scent of fish. Indeed, it should be delicate in character and smell. A well-made fish fumet will enhance any fish stew or braise.

Quickly made, fumet is an easy alternative to water, or the brash commercial candidate, clam juice.

When making fumet, use only impeccably fresh bones that smell as good as the fish you are serving. For clarity of flavor, we make each fumet to match the fish we are serving~hence, monkfish fumet, or bass fumet, or rockfish fumet. {Likewise, we don't use fish fumet in shellfish dishes; we make shellfish fumet or shellfish essence; see page 172.} If you aren't filleting your own fish, and thus yielding your own bones, specify what kind of bones you want at the fishmonger. Also, unless a variety of fishes appear together in a dish, we don't make composite fish stocks, anymore than we would combine beef, lamb, and pork in the same stock. We do, on the other hand, sometimes use up to 20 percent brightly flavored chicken stock, as opposed to all water, to moisten the fumet, finding that it can flatter and frame the perfume of many types of fish, and it contributes body as well.

Fish fumet happens rapidly~the slippery bones usually yield their protein in less than half an hour, by which time the broth will taste just-cooked and delicate. The vegetables need to be thinly sliced so they release a maximum of flavor in the short time it takes the fish bones to release theirs. It only takes a small amount of fresh herb or lemon zest to perfume fumet; where it suits the final dish, we sometimes add those. As with all stocks, maintain a steady, gentle simmer and strain promptly once the flavor is at its peak.

I never reduce fish stock, finding that it makes the flavor dingy.

FOR 3 TO 4 CUPS:

About 1 pound fresh fish bones, fins, head and/or trimmings from the type of fish you are serving

1 cup dry white wine

About 1/3 cup {1-1/2 ounces} thinly sliced carrot

About 1/3 cup {1-1/2 ounces} sliced celery, leaves trimmed off

About 1/3 cup {1-1/2 ounces} thinly sliced yellow onions

A few whole black peppercorns

A wide strip of lemon zest, removed with a vegetable peeler {optional}

A sprig of fresh thyme and/or parsley {optional, depending on the destination of the fumet}

About 4 cups cold water {to not quite cover the bones and vegetables} or 3 cups cold water plus 1 cup cold Chicken Stock {page 58}

Up to 1/2 teaspoon salt {a little more if using kosher salt}

\ *continued*

Quickly rinse the bones and trimmings, checking for viscera and clotted blood. If using a fish head, remove the gills.

Pour the wine into a 4-quart saucepan or 3-quart sauté pan and bring to a boil. Reduce the heat and simmer for about 30 seconds. Turn off the heat.

Add the bones and trimmings and scatter with the carrot, celery, onion, peppercorns, zest, and thyme and/or parsley, if using. Add cold water, or water and stock, to not quite cover. Bring to a simmer, skim the foam, and taste. Season with salt, keeping in mind that you will not be reducing this broth, so it should taste nearly fully seasoned. Adjust the heat to maintain a gentle simmer; don't stir. Taste every 5 minutes, and notice how the taste of raw fish evolves into a pleasant, complex, round flavor. Prepared in a small quantity like this, most fumet will be at its best with only 15 to 25 minutes of gentle simmering. After 15 minutes, I begin tasting every couple of minutes to pick out the peak of flavor, which announces itself with a sudden note of sweetness. This may last only a few minutes. It may take slightly overcooking a fumet or two, before you will learn to choose this point. {There is no bay leaf in this recipe, to simplify detecting that fleeting sweetness~you can, of course, add bay leaf when you use the fumet in a recipe.}

Pour the fumet immediately through a fine strainer. The fumet may be slightly hazy, but as it cools and the solids settle, it will tend to clear. Carefully pour into a storage vessel, tilting slowly, as if you were decanting a bottle of old red wine. Alternatively, pour it through a coffee filter first moistened with water. Cool completely. Freeze any fumet you don't plan to use the same day.

✦
✦ ✦

DISHES TO START A MEAL

THE APPETIZERS IN THIS BOOK FALL INTO SEVERAL CATEGORIES, BUT ALL AIM TO pique the appetite, rather than stun it with complexity or quantity. Small portioning is an obvious strategy for first courses, but I like the little nibble to be big enough to allow you to appreciate the ingredients. The tiniest of *amuse-gueles* {"gullet entertainments" ~ the most unfortunate of French culinary metaphors, I think} sometimes fail me in this respect. If only out of reverence for the ingredients, I'd rather have a second, or even a third, bite, and less variety.

The traditional distinction between hors d'œuvres, or antipasti ~ both of which are meant to be deployed "outside" the meal ~ and "first courses," which then begin the real thing, is hard to sustain. All of the dishes that follow can be served outside or within the "main menu" and in smaller or larger portions than specified, to suit how you use them in a meal, and how many of them you serve. Some might become the main course of a simple meal.

A few of these dishes consist of little more than an excellent product, such as raw oysters or cured meat, with little or no cooking. Others, the crostini in particular, may initially appear more complicated, but will be logical choices for your menu when you have one of the base ingredients in the "larder," or left over from a prior meal ~ a few spoonfuls of meaty pasta sauce, or onion marmalade, or preserved tuna. Indeed, that is how many of these dishes were born. I do, of course, suggest you set the stage for this sort of pseudo-improvisation by making extra of these condiments when they make their principal appearance elsewhere in the book.

The beginning of a meal is a good place to be adventurous when menu planning, and when learning to cook. While you may not be brave enough to invest all your hope in raw beef carpaccio or season with salted tuna roe when it concerns the main event, you might consider taking risks with appetizers, where you generally encounter hearty appetites and, if the nibbles are entertaining and delicious, open minds.

⁺
⁺ ⁺

ZUNI SALT-CURED ANCHOVIES

THIS METHOD FOR CURING ANCHOVIES IS ANCIENT. I learned it in the southwest of France from Pepette Arbulo when her fisherman husband released an incidental catch of five pounds of live anchovies onto the work table in her small kitchen. Pepette was very enthusiastic about the delivery ~ this was an hors d'œuvre that would supplant her perfect foie gras for special friends all summer long. She calmly pushed aside that day's fortune in raw duck liver to pack the fish in salt.

Choose only bright, shiny, fresh anchovies up to 4 inches long. Expect about 20 fish per pound and allow about 2 pounds rock salt per pound of fish. Gut them by hand, pinching and twisting off the heads, which should tug the viscera from the belly at the same time. Then use your index finger to pry open the tender belly, sliding it along the vertebrae to wipe the cavity clean. Rinse each fish briefly under a gentle stream of cold water. Don't attempt to clean them perfectly; you don't want to waterlog them or wash away all their oil. Loosely layer the fish in a colander, scattering with about one-quarter of the rock salt as you go. Place the colander over a bowl and leave the anchovies to drain overnight in the refrigerator. The next day, carefully repack the fish, layering with the remaining rock salt in wide jars or earthenware crocks. Cover tightly and refrigerate. Thus preserved, the anchovies will keep well for nine months, which allows a year-round supply if you are diligent and prepare enough during fresh anchovy season {late April to mid-September in California}. They are especially delicious, however, after only a few days of curing. We serve them as soon as 18 hours after the second packing.

To serve, first rinse the fish, then soak in cool water until pliable, about 5 minutes. Next, starting at the natural seam at the base of the dorsal fin, use your fingers to ease the fillets free of the central bone. Rinse each fillet, rubbing gently to remove the scales, collarbone, and remaining fins. Taste and keep rinsing, or resoak in cool water until the fish is only mildly salty and quite tender. Arrange the fillets in a single layer on an absorbent towel. Cover with another towel and press to draw out the water~the fillets should now have a nutty, tender texture. Place them in extra-virgin olive oil to just cover. Serve immediately, or cover and refrigerate for up to a few weeks.

Our signature hors d'œuvre at the restaurant consists of 6 or 7 neatly displayed fillets of these glistening anchovies, flanked by slivers and shards of Parmigiano-Reggiano and cold, crisp, sliced celery, topped with a grind of black pepper, a few Niçoise olives, and a squeeze of lemon.

If you are lucky enough to find very small fresh sardines, try the same method. They are stronger and meatier and are nice with Picholine olives and fleshy roasted red and yellow bell peppers.

Wine: Muscadet de Sèvre-et-Maine, Cuvée 1, Louis Métereau, 2000

✧
✧ ✧

Choosing, Storing, & Serving Oysters

My first oyster was unforgettable. It was not quite cold, and looked to me like a large, milky gray raw egg spilled into the pearly shell. I dangled the whole thing from the little fork and glanced around before committing. It did not taste good, but given the august setting I found myself in, a tufted Parisian three-star, I didn't consider I had an option. Tears welled in my eyes as I swallowed it whole. I looked away just as the *garçon* returned with the platter and a gracious *"Encore une?"*

I ate my second oyster thirteen years later, and twenty-three more that same evening at Zuni. Perched like diamonds in the rough on plenty of ice, casually entangled in seaweed fronds, the tiny, ruffled Pacific oysters were so beautiful I suddenly had an appetite for them. I did work my way as well through the ritual fan of thinly sliced dense rye, flanked by a generous slab of unsalted butter and a ramekin of shallot vinegar, adjusting to this new taste, but it was hardly torture. A flute of Champagne helped, as it usually does.

One of the finest hors d'œuvres we are lucky to be able to offer is oysters, and I never forget that romance makes oysters better. Knowing you can have more is delightful; that they are pristine, bracingly cold, and presented grandly makes this primitive food seem a great indulgence. We sell at least four thousand per week, all on the half-shell. Allowing for more modest sales in the early years, this adds up to over four million oysters.

On a given day we may offer as many as fifteen different oysters. Beyond the local Tomales Bay product, our broker receives thrice-weekly deliveries of a lavish selection from the Pacific Northwest, North Atlantic Coast, and, during our summer, the Southern Hemisphere. We purchase only the ones we think are at their best. Stored in a moist environment, at 36° to 45° ~ the lower end of that range is preferable to the higher end ~ oysters will live for as long as two weeks, although we sell through our stock in two days or less. Flavorwise, more recently harvested oysters have an advantage in that the seawater in their shells is fresher. Once harvested, oysters live in, and on, the water in their shells, which necessarily changes flavor. For that reason, some people choose to pour this "liquor" off when an oyster is not straight from the sea. But healthwise, it is perhaps less important how long oysters have been stored than how well. Even a brief period of higher temperatures favors the reproduction of bacteria, which is unhealthy for diners, and can kill the oyster.

We list oysters first by species, and then by market name, which is usually the location of harvest, or of the oyster farm that cultivates them. I compare this to a wine list that is divided into varietals, and then wineries. Furthering the analogy, I like to explain that two oysters of the same species, say *virginica,* which is the native East Coast oyster, will taste very different if grown in different locations. Hence a Blue Point* from off Long Island is distinct from a *virginica* harvested off the coast of Wellfleet, Massachusetts, or one from Cape Breton, Malpeque, or our own Tomales Bay {where Hog Island Oyster Company harvests a precious, delicious few every year}. Like four different crops of Cabernet Sauvignon, *virginica* may grow successfully in many places, but they will always taste distinctly of their aquatic "*terroir.*" Indeed, being filter feeders, oysters usually taste *exactly* of their *terroir.*

To simplify the matter of species identification, I list the species we offer as follows:

In the genus *Crassostrea:*

Virginica ~ the Atlantic oyster, by which I mean that one native to, and hence most familiar on, the East Coast and around the Gulf of Mexico. The oysters can be had quite large, the shells are thick and heavy, and the meats tend to fill the shallow shells. On the whole, oysters of this species are milder than other species. Some taste like raw egg white to me.

Gigas ~ a Japanese native, the most widely cultivated species in the Pacific Northwest, Europe, and elsewhere; what the French sometimes call *portugaise.*† It is the fastest-growing of the species, attaining 2 inches in twelve to eighteen months, and sometimes reaching three times that size. The deeply ruffled shells are often striated with showy bands of gray, white, gold, black, green, or purple ~ or all those colors ~ and hold the meat in deep cups. Flavor, firmness, creaminess, and size of meat vary tremendously from farm to farm, and from harvest to harvest at the same farm, but most have fresh, cucumbery or melony notes I adore.

---

* Blue Point, on Long Island Sound, no longer supplies oysters commercially. The Blue Point Oyster Company, in business since the 1800s, was sold to a developer in 1997. There are, however, still oysters out there.

† This because a load of the strain of *gigas,* called *angulata,* migrated to Portuguese waters from its native Taiwan, courtesy of the great explorers. In the late 1800s, a load of these tasty transplants ~ en route to English markets ~ was dumped for dead into the waters off Bordeaux. Some lived, to be harvested and enjoyed by the French, who christened this new type of oyster *portugaise.* By the mid-1970s, an oil spill and an Atlantic Ocean virus had destroyed this Asian native. The oyster beds were replanted with seed from a similar but virus-resistant Japanese cousin, also a *gigas.* It assumed the familiar moniker.

Sikamea~ another Japanese native, which was revived in the Pacific Northwest in the 1940s as a summer oyster. This commercial motive was thought to have preserved the species, though, happily, native stock has recently been identified in Japan. Known as the Kumamoto, the Japanese prefecture it came from, it is very successful gastronomically. It outsells every other oyster at Zuni 5 to 1. "Kumis" are small, with very deeply cupped, ruffled shells; the meats usually fill the shell and are often creamy. Flavor varies from sweet to mild to alkaline and depends, as with all oysters, on food supply, water temperature, and time of year.

In the genus *Ostrea:*

Conchaphila {formerly known as *lurida*}~ the tiny flat oyster native to and once gloriously abundant all along our Pacific Coast. San Francisco Bay once had a fabulous population, well before the arrival of Europeans. It was already declining rapidly when Gold Rush pollution fouled the Bay and all but finished the job. These have rebounded somewhat as the Bay has gotten cleaner, although for now they are commercially limited to the Olympic Peninsula, in Washington, where the oyster was christened the Olympia. They are very slow to grow; I do not know of "Olys" having been farmed with commercial success anywhere else. They have flat, slightly ruffled shells with ample meat for their size. They usually have a creamy texture and a pleasant, metallic flavor note, sometimes with a lovely, subtle mushroomy taste.

Edulis~ the flat oyster native to the coastal waters of most of Europe. The increasingly rare French Belon and Marennes oysters are *edulis*. Shells are always rather round and flat with a modestly ruffled edge. When they are cultivated in New World waters, the meats tend to be small and very briny, with otherwise mild flavor notes. More often lean than creamy, they are often dry~ their shallow design doesn't hold much brine, and they require care in handling so what there is doesn't drain out. Apparently they can be "trained" to stay closed, and the French shuttle them into intertidal zones to do that. Some growers ship "flats" with rubber bands around them.

I offer few specifics here on flavor, because it is perilous to generalize about a species or even a farm. In my notes, I find "watermelon" next to certain *gigas* oysters, "algal," "metallic," "briny," "iodine," "Milk of Magnesia" {!} next to others, but the more I taste, the less I generalize. I know I like "leaner" oysters~ literally, not full of food, stored as creamy glycogen, which is chemically equivalent to cornstarch. Leaner oysters have clearer, smaller meat and bright flavor notes, and they don't coat your mouth. In the extreme, however, say, after heavy storms, when oysters find their supply of microorganisms totally disrupted, they go from pleasantly lean to starving; the meats are miniature and tasteless. These we avoid. Likewise oysters that have just finished spawning. This cycle varies with genus and species; for example, *gigas* are excited by warming waters, but *virginicas* may spawn, or not, at any time of year. During spawning, oysters change radically in flavor and texture. If you look closely, you can see translucent "channels" in the swollen white meat. Spawning oysters tend to be runny, and I find their flavor to run from insipid to rank tasting. But they are not harmful to eat.

I have been taught that the colder the water, the saltier the oyster, but only because the water itself may be saltier. This could be useful if you know how cold the water in a given inlet, or oyster bed, is; latitude and season are not entirely reliable guidelines. More significant is the amount of freshwater intrusion, whether from local rivers or recent rain, which will dilute the salinity of any temperature of water. This factor renders the temperature-saltiness guideline largely academic. A more critical concern with warming, or always-warm, waters is the proliferation of naturally occurring bacteria, which collect in the filter feeder and can be passed on to the diner in these higher concentrations. This is the reason we are advised to avoid raw oysters outside the "r" months, although the calendar is not a perfect predictor of water temperature. Some locales harvest safely nearly year-round. But all raw oysters contain bacteria; individuals with compromised immune systems should not eat them.

To serve oysters on the half-shell requires little culinary skill. Purchase oysters from a vendor you trust and who knows exactly what he is selling and when the oysters came in. He ought to know or be able to find out when they were harvested. The oysters ought to be stored in a cold, moist spot {but never submerged in water}, between 36° and 45°. They should be bedded in ice if they are not in a refrigerator. Choose oysters that are tightly closed and with shells intact, not cracked or crushed. They should be neither too heavy for their size {or they may be filled with silt!}, nor feel hollow. But don't worry if they are a little muddy on the outside~it is better that they be washed just before opening anyway. If you don't serve the oysters the day you buy them, store them cup side down in the coldest part of your refrigerator, draped with a damp towel, with an ice cube or two on top to keep the towel damp.

To open oysters, simply rinse them in cold water to rid them of the surface mud you don't want to transfer inside. Set the oyster cup side down {this is usually obvious in all but the flattest of flat oysters}, and look for the spot where the shells are joined. This is also usually obvious, but if not, look closely at the whorl pattern of growth rings on the shell: the lines in the whorl are most compressed near the joint. Hold the oyster securely in place with a gloved hand or a towel and probe at the joint with an oyster knife, or, yes, a sterilized sharp screwdriver, and gently work the flat blade into this tiny slit. Usually you can ease the shells apart with a patient rocking, probing motion. Sometimes they pop easily. If you run into a recalcitrant one, work at it, then set it aside. Often it will be easier in five minutes. Once you have popped the top shell free, slide in your knife {if you are using a screwdriver, switch to a paring knife for this step}, flat against the top shell. Feel for and cut through the connective muscle, which resembles a small, tough scallop, then lift off the top shell. Smell the oyster. Discard it if it smells off. Now slide your knife under the oyster meat, close against the cupped side of the shell, and free that side of the muscle. Contrary to custom, we don't turn the oysters over in their shells; I think the topside of the meat is gorgeous with its ruffles, folds, and shades of gray, silver, black, cream, and beige. The underside is plain by comparison. Inspect the oyster for bits of shell, mud, or, yes, the rare tiny pearl. Arrange the opened oysters as you go on a bed of ice, first dusted with salt to stabilize it and make it shed cold, on a wide, shallow platter. Take care to place the oysters level, so they don't spill their juice. Open oysters at the last possible moment; if this is not possible, keep shucked oysters level and well chilled until serving. Properly stored, oysters on the half-shell do not spoil immediately, but they can take up lots of space and are vulnerable to mishap and contamination. "Managing" opened oysters and transferring them from one tray to another is no less labor than shucking at the last minute. Holding them on ice can be fine as long as your tray has a drain; otherwise, the oysters will shortly be inundated in their melting bed. We insist on opening every oyster to order, which can result in backlogs at our beleaguered oyster bar, but the alternative can pose health risks and is always a challenge to quality.

We serve oysters on the half-shell with the simplest garnishes and condiments, hoping to let the complex flavors of each oyster bloom in the diner's mouth. The strongest condiment we offer is lemon. For preserving and flattering an oyster's flavor, I favor a traditional *sauce mignonette.* Make it about half an hour before needed, and keep it cold; heat will dull the flavor.

Wine: Chablis Premier Cru Vaillons, Christian Moreau et Fils, 1999

SAUCE MIGNONETTE

ENOUGH FOR A FEW DOZEN OYSTERS:

1/4 cup dry white sparkling wine or
    Champagne
2 tablespoons Champagne vinegar or
    white wine vinegar

1 medium shallot {about 1/2 ounce}
Freshly cracked black pepper

Combine the wine and vinegar. Finely mince the shallot using a razor-sharp knife; a dull knife will smash the shallot and release acrid flavors. You should get about 2 teaspoons. Add the shallot to the wine-vinegar, along with plenty of pepper, and stir. Serve in ramekins for dipping the oysters, or in a bottle, with a split cork for a spout, to sprinkle on the half-shells.

I use leftover mignonette plus unsalted butter, bay leaf, lots of lemon zest, and a sprig of thyme for steaming mussels or clams.

❖
❖ ❖

CURED MEAT

CURED MEAT, PAIRED WITH A CONDIMENT OR TWO OR THREE, MAKES SIMPLE WORK of the appetizer course in a meal. Buy cured meat where they sell a lot of it, and where they slice it perfectly and are careful to lay down each slice neatly overlapping the preceding one. Cured meat will taste and look best if you buy it within a few hours of serving it, but if you need to purchase it further in advance, then refrigerate it promptly and keep the package flat. For the best flavors and easiest handling, bring it out about half an hour before serving.

The dishes that follow are particularly good before a meatless main course of eggs, pasta, or gnocchi, or before grilled fish or poultry. Well-presented, cured meat can add luxury and finesse to a meal, with minimal scrambling in the kitchen.

SOME THOUGHTS *on* THE CURED MEATS SUGGESTED *in* THESE RECIPES

AVAILABILITY OF THESE CURED MEATS VARIES REGIONALLY BUT OUGHT TO IMPROVE as they are better appreciated. You may not find smoked prosciutto as easily as prosciutto, but a store that cares enough to stock excellent-quality Parma prosciutto may be interested in carrying it, along with fine air-dried beef or coppa, if they learn their clients will buy it.

We use Parma prosciutto at Zuni, choosing brands that are deep, fleshy pink, and firm but not hard. I avoid prosciutto that has an unnatural, "glowing" pink hue, evidence of excessive curing salt. While not as readily available, prosciutto di San Daniele can be an excellent choice as well. I have not tasted a domestic prosciutto that approaches the highest Italian standard. Fine, sweet-salty, satiny prosciutto tolerates nothing but elegance on its plate~in particular, succulent, low-acid fruit. The combinations I describe toy with the softness, the subtle nutty-sweet animal flavor, and the sensuality of the best prosciutto.

Firmer and saltier than plain prosciutto, smoked prosciutto stands up to bigger flavors and coarser textures. Pressed and aged for about six months, it yields gorgeous petals of burnished maroon meat edged with ivory fat. Do not confuse cold-smoked prosciutto with hot-smoked cooked hams, such as Westphalian. Some smoked prosciutto is called *speck*. Speck is a product of the Alto Adige/Südtirol in Northern Italy, where it has been made for nearly five hundred years and is justifiably treasured. {But since speck can be made with loin, belly, shoulder, neck, or leg, not all speck is actually smoked prosciutto.} We use both imported smoked prosciutto and speck.

Spanish serrano ham, lately available in the United States, is a delicious alternative to smoked prosciutto in these recipes. It is not a smoked ham, but is similarly firm, dense, intensely flavored, and full of character. Salty-sweet raw Smithfield ham, which can be delectable served thinly sliced, is another good choice.

All three of these hams can be excellent with cheese, olives, or pickled fruit and anchor an antipasto that has more than one big flavor.

I favor very coarsely ground all-pork salami. We use a four-inch wide "flattened-log" type, marketed as soppressata. Currently no Italian salami is permitted for import in the United States; the one we use is made in California and sold under the label Ticino. Traditionally, fat logs of soppressata were pressed, to force out air and improve the chances of successful drying, which accounts for its name, but I have seen proud round ones in American markets; modern methods often render old words more charming than meaningful. Their shape and size notwithstanding, I choose firm salami, and only those that are distinctly freckled ruddy red and pearly white. Rustic in all ways, salami shows best in informal arrangements with simple, accessible flavors.

The coppa we use is a log of cured rolled pork shoulder. It presents a bold swath of pearly fat in each slice. {In Italy, the name coppa can apply to both shoulder and loin products, and, confusingly, in Southern Italy similar confections are sometimes called capocollo.} Coppa tends to be salty, and spicy coppa is rubbed with cayenne pepper before it is rolled, cased, and dry-aged for up to 3 months. There is nothing subtle about coppa; it will overwhelm delicate, fruity, or faint-heated condiments. We pair it with big, earthy flavors.

Currently, Italian coppa and capocollo cannot be imported into the United States; however, there are tasty domestic coppas to choose from. We use coppa and spicy coppa made by Molinari in San Francisco, which is widely distributed. {Do not confuse this type of traditional dry-cured coppa with cooked coppa or other cooked domestic products called capocollo.}

"Bresaola," an awkward but lovely word, refers to a flavorful air-dried beef from the Valtellina in Northern Italy. Originally known as *salaa come brisa,* it is made from one of five lean hind leg muscles {from the top, bottom, or eye of the round}. It is first soaked in a proprietary saltwater brine containing perhaps pepper, juniper, and coriander seeds, then cased, dried, and aged for at least 2 months. It is log shaped. Bündnerfleisch, made in the Grisons region of Switzerland, is another fine air-dried beef that I recommend. It is not cased and tends to be firmer than bresaola. It is brick shaped, producing pretty rectangular slices. The edges may be flecked or well frosted with harmless ~ indeed it is protective ~ white mold. This is easy to scrape or trim off. Beefy, salty, and lean, and with a wonderful leathery texture, both types of air-dried beef are up to many flavor challenges, so long as one of them is a generous splash of oil to compensate for its lack of fat.

+ + + + +

WINE & CURED MEATS

THOUGH MOST OF THE WINE SELECTIONS HERE ARE INTERCHANGEABLE, each has been chosen for a particular affinity with the garnish and for any regional association it might have. If the dish is served as a first course {rather than as a main course for a light lunch or supper}, the wine chosen should lead gracefully to whatever wine or food is planned to follow.

+ + + + +

PROSCIUTTO & MELON *in* SAMBUCA

A<small>N INTOXICATING VARIATION ON A FAMILIAR PAIRING</small>. Use ripe cantaloupe or other firm orange-fleshed melon. This combination is also nice with thinly sliced soppressata.

A note on choosing melon: Melon should be heavy for its size, and if it has netting, the rind under the netting no longer raw green. Sometimes a tender stem end is a good sign. Scent can be a good guideline, but I have had some great melons that didn't share their scent until I cut into them. I have been assured that if you know that a bin of melons all came from the same field, or, better yet, if you can choose among a few melons on the same plant, you can expect the larger ones to be better ~ they are the ones the plant has favored. If you aren't confident but want to learn, it can be instructive to buy two melons at a time ~ choosing ones that look and feel quite, or slightly, different, and then cut and taste them side by side. If one tastes better to you, make a point of noting what it looks, feels, and smells like, and whether one end or one side is sweeter than the other. The extra melon purchase will not seem extravagant if you are learning how to choose well.

Wine: Collio Pinot Grigio, Vittorio Puiatti, 2000

FOR ABOUT 4 SERVINGS:

1-1/2 to 2 pounds ripe melon
A few pinches of anise seeds

1 teaspoon Sambuca
4 to 6 ounces thinly sliced prosciutto

Halve and seed the melon. Cut into inch-thick wedges, then carve away the rind, deeply enough to remove any rindy-tasting, hard flesh, in a continuous, smooth stroke to produce elegant crescents. Expect 3/4 to 1 pound of flesh. Place in a wide bowl.

Slightly crush the anise seeds and sprinkle over the melon. Dribble a little Sambuca over all and fold gently to distribute without bruising the melon. Leave to macerate for about 10 minutes in a cool place, or refrigerate.

Turn the melon slices over on themselves, then slide onto plates or a platter. Cut the prosciutto into wide ribbons and drape them over the melon.

PROSCIUTTO *with* WARM ROASTED FIGS
& HAZELNUT PICADA

I CAN'T EAT A WARM ROASTED FIG ANOINTED WITH NUTTY CRUMBS AND WRAPPED in a melting slice of prosciutto without remembering the sweet-salty, crispy, creamy, hot grilled peanut butter and jelly sandwiches I loved as a child. I never liked sweets much unless there was a little salt and crunch. This zesty, garlicky crumb topping, based on a Catalan culinary staple, adds both. Notwithstanding, if you don't have time to make the *picada,* roasted figs and prosciutto are delicious by themselves. {And remember roasted figs: they are good with grilled or roasted lamb or game birds. Or, if you skip the oil and roll them in sugar before roasting, they make a nice dessert.}

Wine: Steele, Santa Barbara County Pinot Blanc, 2000

FOR 4 SERVINGS:

About 8 small, ripe Black Mission figs {6 to 8 ounces total}

About 2 teaspoons extra-virgin olive oil

About 3 tablespoons Crumbly Hazelnut *"Picada"* {page 305}

4 to 6 ounces thinly sliced prosciutto

Preheat the broiler.

Cut the figs in half, roll in the olive oil to coat, and place cut side up on a small baking sheet. Broil until hot through and just beginning to caramelize on the edges, about 3 to 5 minutes. Sprinkle a few pinches of *picada* on each as you pull them from the broiler. The warmth will tame the raw garlic and heighten the other flavors in the *picada.* Lay the prosciutto on plates and carefully garnish with the hot fig halves. Serve immediately.

PROSCIUTTO & WHITE ROSE NECTARINES *with* BLANCHED ALMONDS

THE ROSE SCENT, FAINT BITTERNESS, AND LONG FLAVOR OF A RIPE WHITE NECTARINE reveal flavors in prosciutto that you can miss when you taste the ham with sweeter fruit. Choose a nectarine that yields to the touch, like a barely flexed muscle. A thin-skinned white Babcock peach, because it has a similar austere bitter-sweetness, can make a nice counterpoint to the ham as well. Smooth, lightly toasted peeled almonds are delicate enough for the subtle balance; no other preparation, or nut, will do. {During the few weeks a year we can get them, I do like to serve this dish with green almonds. Pried from their fuzzy pods and painstakingly peeled, tender unripe almonds have as delicate a flavor as I know, one that reads best against something savory, rather than sweet. See Note below.}

In any case, taste this combination slowly.

Wine: Alban Vineyards Edna Valley Viognier, 2000

FOR ABOUT 4 SERVINGS:

18 to 24 raw almonds {about 1/4 cup or 1 ounce}

1 large or 2 small White Rose nectarines {7 to 8 ounces total}

4 to 6 ounces thinly sliced prosciutto

Preheat the oven to 300°.

Bring a few cups of water to a simmer in a small saucepan. Drop in the almonds and count to ten. Fish out one nut and pinch it ~ the swollen skin ought to slide right off. {If not, blanch for a few seconds longer.} Promptly drain the remaining almonds, so they don't get waterlogged. Spread on a towel and rub dry. Pinch off all the skins, then rub dry again.

Spread the almonds on a baking sheet and place in the oven until they begin to change color ~ this may take 15 minutes or longer. They will be soft as they emerge from the oven but will crisp as they cool.

Cut the nectarines into 1/2-inch-thick wedges {if the nectarines are sliced too thick, they will dominate, and the combination will be awkward}. Arrange the slices of prosciutto and the nectarine wedges on plates. Scatter the almonds over all.

Note: If you are in an almond-growing region, or know someone with an almond tree, you may be able to get the soft green fruits. If you do, here is how to liberate the prize: Use a paring knife to gently split each fuzzy almond pod along its natural seam. Pop out the almond and peel it carefully. Occasionally some nascent almonds will be cloudy and jellylike. I eat those on the spot. The more mature ones will be ivory and pliable.

+ +
+ +

PROSCIUTTO *with* CHESTNUTS *in* SAGE OIL

FRESH CHESTNUTS ARE A BIT OF A BOTHER TO PREPARE, BUT WORTH IT FOR THIS winter antipasto. Salty-sweet prosciutto is a lovely foil for the warm chestnuts. You might also try this with smoked prosciutto, serrano ham, or raw Smithfield ham. Choose firm, shiny, heavy chestnuts. Make sure the shells are not split. If you prepare extra, they will keep for weeks refrigerated, as long as they are submerged in the scented oil. Serve them warm with roast pork or game.

Wine: Bardolino Cavalchina, 2000

FOR ABOUT 4 SERVINGS:

About 4 fresh sage leaves

About 6 tablespoons extra-virgin olive oil

12 to 16 whole fresh chestnuts {about 8 ounces}

4 to 6 ounces thinly sliced prosciutto

If the sage leaves are large, cut or tear into a few pieces. Bruise and crush the leaves with the back or flat face of your knife. This will expedite the release of their fragrant oil. Place in a 2-quart saucepan with the olive oil, and set over very low heat to steep for about 10 minutes. The oil should never get too hot to touch. Set aside.

To prepare the chestnuts: Most chestnuts have one rounder and one flatter

\ *continued*

face. Using a small knife, and holding the tip of the blade against the flatter face, slash the leathery shell as you would slide a letter opener into an envelope ~ that way you won't gouge the meat. For the occasional rotund specimen, make as shallow a slash as you can.

Place the chestnuts in a pot of just-simmering water to cover by a few inches. Large chestnuts usually take 12 to 15 minutes to cook. When ready, the flesh will be steamy but still firm. Scoop a chestnut at a time from the simmering water and hold it in a towel while you peel it: Slide the knife back into the slash and peel away the outer shell; if you are lucky, the velvety inner skin will come off as well. Working quickly, while the nut is still quite a lot hotter and more humid than the surrounding air, will improve your odds of getting both shell and skin at once. If a given chestnut cools too much to peel easily, slide it back into the simmering water. It may crumble when you return to peel it, but that will hardly destroy the dish. As you peel each chestnut, inspect carefully for hidden bits of copper-colored skin. You may need to pry the flesh apart to remove inner folds of skin. Trim any discoloration as you go. If any chestnut is over an inch in any dimension, break it in half ~ this will speed up the absorption of scented oil. As you peel them, drop the warm chestnuts {or the pieces of chestnut} into the warm sage olive oil. Stir as needed to bathe all the chestnuts.

Once you have peeled all of the chestnuts, set the pan back over the lowest heat and heat until warm to the touch. Remove from the heat and leave the chestnuts to absorb some of the oil and its perfume, about 30 minutes. Stir again.

Serve each person a spoonful of the warm chestnuts and the oil that clings to them, with a few slices of prosciutto. Save any leftover oil to stir into bean or winter squash soup, or to add to *Farrotto* {page 199} or Farro Soup {page 200}.

✢
✢ ✢

SMOKED PROSCIUTTO *with* SPICED ZANTE GRAPES *&* FENNEL

THIS IS A FESTIVE DISH TO SHOW OFF THE SIMPLE SPICED ZANTE GRAPES. Don't substitute regular prosciutto; the pickled fruit is too aggressive for the soft, sweet meat. In that case, use fresh Zante grapes. They are usually most abundant in August, although they may appear as early as July and last into September.

Wine: Boeger Vineyards El Dorado Refosco, 1999

FOR 4 SERVINGS:

6 ounces Spiced Zante Grapes {page 276}, drained {about 3/4 cup}

4 to 6 ounces thinly sliced smoked prosciutto

1 medium fennel bulb {about 8 ounces}, trimmed

2 to 3 ounces walnuts {about 1 cup}, preferably freshly shelled {optional}

Use scissors to snip the grapes into bite-sized clusters. Wrap a slice of smoked prosciutto around each cluster, fixing with a toothpick if you like, and arrange on a platter. Slice the fennel crosswise into 1/8-inch-thick sickles and offer these and the walnuts, if using, in little piles on the side.

+
+ +

SALAMI *with* RAW FAVAS, MINT, *&* MANCHEGO CHEESE

RAW FAVAS ARE A SPRING DELIGHT, OFTEN OVERLOOKED IN CELEBRATIONS OF THE first peas, asparagus, and artichokes. A friendly collision of a Tuscan idea {favas and sheep's milk cheese} and a Catalan one {favas and mint} resulted in this little

\ *continued*

dish. Basque Brebis, and aged Tuscan pecorino are good alternatives to Manchego. This antipasto is also nice made with thinly sliced, leftover rosy-pink Roasted Leg of Lamb {page 394}. In that case, strew the dressed favas and Manchego over the slices of lamb, which should be at room temperature and trimmed of all fat.

Wine: Vermentino "Vigna U Munte," Colle dei Bardellini, 2000

FOR ABOUT 4 SERVINGS:

2 pounds whole young favas

2 to 3 ounces thinly sliced pork salami

About 3 tablespoons extra-virgin olive oil

A few leaves of fresh mint

Salt and freshly cracked black pepper

About 2 ounces Manchego, Basque Brebis, or aged Tuscan pecorino

A lemon {optional}

Shell the favas, removing the fat, fleshy beans from their padded pods. Next, peel away the outer skin, which resembles nothing more than a bit of rubber glove. This is tedious, but if you trim away a sliver of this casing from the tip of the bean with your fingernail, you can usually peel away the rest in a few seconds. {Resist the temptation to blanch the favas and then pop them out of their skins~a quicker technique, good for some recipes, but one that changes their texture.} The peeled favas should be pliable and bright green~don't use any that are hard or yellowing. Split the favas into halves, as you would a shelled peanut. You should get about 1-1/2 cups "double-peeled" favas.

Cut the salami into 1/2-inch-wide ribbons.

Toss the favas with olive oil to coat. Coarsely chop the mint leaves, then add to the favas, with a little salt and lots of black pepper. Use a vegetable peeler to shave in a few curls of cheese, avoiding any rind, then fold in the salami ribbons. Taste. Fold in a trickle of lemon juice, if you like, and taste again. Transfer to plates or a platter, garnish with additional curls of cheese, and serve immediately.

Antipasto *of* Salami, Idiazabal, *&* Celery-Walnut–Dried Fig Relish *with* Grappa

A GOOD COMBINATION BUILT FROM THINGS YOU CAN KEEP IN THE LARDER. Idiazabal is the Basque town where they produce this hard sheep's milk cheese. It is very lightly smoked and retains a fruity note that marries well with figs and grappa. Manchego is a good substitute. Both cheeses keep well for weeks.

Tossed with a handful of frisée and sherry vinaigrette, the combination makes a good first-course salad. In that case, you can skip the salami or cut it into wide ribbons to fold into the salad.

Wine: Arneis, Vietti, 2000

FOR 4 SERVINGS:

12 walnut halves {about 1 ounce}, preferably freshly shelled
1 stalk celery, leaves trimmed off
4 dried white figs ~ Kadota or Smyrna {Calimyrna}
1 tablespoon pomegranate seeds {optional}

1 tablespoon extra-virgin olive oil
A splash or two of grappa
Salt and freshly cracked black pepper
4 to 6 ounces Idiazabal or Manchego
4 to 6 ounces thinly sliced pork salami
A bunch of small radishes {optional}

Preheat the oven to 300°

Go through the walnuts and discard any shriveled or very dark bits of nutmeat. If you aren't sure what the standard for too dark ought to be, taste a suspect piece and decide if you like it, then base your standard on that. Spread the walnuts on a baking sheet and warm for about 5 minutes, then rub between rough towels to remove some of the tannic, papery skin. {The fresher the walnuts, the more effective this technique will be.} Pick out the nutmeats, break into little bits, and then shake in a strainer to further cull flecks of skin.

Slice the celery crosswise into thin sickles. Trim their stems, then cut the figs into small chunks the size of the walnut bits, or halve and thinly slice. Combine roughly equal parts of celery, walnuts and figs, plus the pomegranate seeds, if using. Moisten with the olive oil just to coat, then add a few splashes of grappa, a

\ *continued*

pinch of salt, and a few grinds of black pepper. Mix well, then set aside for 5 minutes so the flavors marry.

Cut the cheese into 1/4-inch-thick wedges. Loosely fan the salami and cheese
on plates or a platter. Pile the relish in a little mound alongside. Offer crisp whole
radishes, if you like, on the side.

⁘ ⁘⁘

COPPA & WARM PARSLIED POTATO SALAD *with* ROASTED PEPPERS

THIS COMBINATION IS SO FRIENDLY AND EASY YOU MAY MAKE IT MORE OFTEN
than any other of our cured meat antipasti. No one can resist parslied potatoes. The
key to this simple potato salad is to fully season the cooking water so it seasons the
potatoes, inside and out, as they cook, and then dress them while still warm. We
use Yellow Finnish, Butterball, or Bintje potatoes; they have a much richer flavor
and a creamier texture than the shrewdly named Yukon Gold potatoes grown in our
region. But you should experiment with potatoes you find in your area and choose
the variety that tastes best to you. Regarding the parsley: Chop it just before you
need it, and not too finely. Salami would be good in place of coppa here.

Wine: Dolcetto d'Alba, Aldo Conterno, 1999

FOR ABOUT 4 SERVINGS:

Generous 1 pound peeled yellow-fleshed
potatoes cut into irregular 1-inch
chunks or a little smaller

Salt

About 1 tablespoon tightly packed,
coarsely chopped, fresh flat-leaf
parsley

About 4 to 5 tablespoons extra-virgin
olive oil

About 2 tablespoons Champagne vinegar or white wine vinegar

Freshly cracked black pepper

About 4 ounces coppa, sliced 1/16 inch
thick

1 large or 2 small red or green bell peppers {about 12 ounces total}, roasted
or charred, peeled, and cut or torn
into wide strips {see page 273}

12 oil-cured meaty black olives, such as
Nyons

Place the potatoes in a 2- to 4-quart saucepan and add cold water to cover. Salt the water very liberally, stir to dissolve, and taste~the water should taste a little too salty. {I use a generous 1-1/2 teaspoons sea salt per quart of water.} Bring to a simmer, uncovered. Cook at a bare simmer, stirring once or twice, until the potatoes are tender and the edges are starting to soften, usually about 6 minutes. Drain well.

As soon as they have stopped steaming, transfer the potatoes to a wide bowl. Using a rubber spatula, fold in the parsley and enough olive oil to coat well. The edges will break down a little, shedding potato into the oil. Cover with plastic wrap and leave for a few minutes so the parsley perfumes the oil and softens.

Fold in the vinegar and black pepper, both to taste.

Arrange the slices of coppa and the strips of roasted pepper on plates or a platter, and mound the juicy potatoes and the olives to one side.

+ +
+ +

COPPA *with* CATHERINE'S CELERY ROOT

CATHERINE BRANDEL WAS A DEAR FRIEND AND AN UNCOMMONLY GIFTED COOK who could charm a cockscomb into elegance. On her return from a cooking job in Turkey in 1998, she served me a dish of delicately preserved celery root that she had learned to make there. I could not figure out how she'd achieved the texture, color, and flavor and I asked about it. Of course, she had measured nothing, but this formula owes to her keen observations and precise explanation.

Make this whenever you have to buy a whole celery root in order to get only a chunk for a salad or a braised dish. The mild pickle keeps for about a week refrigerated and is nice as an hors d'œuvre or with grilled fish. The formula works for carrots as well, although you will want to cut back on the sugar.

Wine: Vernaccia di San Gimignano, Strozzi, 2000

\ continued

FOR 4 SERVINGS:

1/4 cup mild-tasting olive oil

3 tablespoons water

Scant 2 tablespoons sugar

1/2 teaspoon salt

1/4 teaspoon coriander seeds

1 bay leaf

1 pound peeled celery root {about 2 medium celery roots}, cut into roughly 1-inch chunks

1 to 2 tablespoons freshly squeezed lemon juice

4 to 6 ounces thinly sliced coppa

About 3/4 cup olives {4-1/2 ounces}, such as Lucques, Picholine, Ascolane, Gaeta, Niçoise, or Nyons, or a combination

Place the olive oil, water, sugar, salt, coriander seeds, and bay leaf in a 2- to 4-quart saucepan. Stir to dissolve the sugar, then stir in the celery root to coat. Set over low heat, cover, and bring to a quiet simmer. Cook, stirring once, for 5 to 6 minutes, then uncover. Cook uncovered at the same discreet simmer, stirring regularly, until the celery root is tender and the water has practically evaporated, about 10 more minutes. The celery root should not color. Remove from the heat and stir in lemon juice to taste.

You can serve the celery root warm, at room temperature, or cool. If you do wait to serve it, taste again for lemon; it will taste less assertive than when it was warm, and you may want to add more.

Arrange the coppa on plates or a platter. Spoon a juicy mound of celery root next to the meat. Offer a bowl of the olives on the side.

❖
❖ ❖

AIR-DRIED BEEF *with* BUTTER LETTUCE *&* CORIANDER VINAIGRETTE

BRESAOLA, ITALIAN AIR-DRIED BEEF, IS TRADITIONALLY CURED WITH A SPRINKLE OF crushed coriander seeds, a preserving habit that dates from Roman times at least. This easy antipasto is for purists, who will find the combination of heady, salty meat and the fragrant vinaigrette refreshing and logical. In this context, the satiny, soft leaves of butter lettuce taste and feel luxurious.

Wine: St. Innocent, Temperance Hill Vineyard, Willamette Valley Pinot Noir, 1999

FOR 4 SERVINGS:

About 6 tablespoons extra-virgin olive oil

About 1 tablespoon Champagne vinegar or white wine vinegar

Salt

Scant 1/4 teaspoon coriander seeds

A small head of butter lettuce in excellent condition, carefully washed and dried

About 5 ounces thinly sliced air-dried beef

Combine the oil, vinegar, and salt to make a mild vinaigrette. Warm the coriander seeds in a small pan over medium heat for a few seconds, then lightly crush and add them to the vinaigrette. Taste.

Pick out a combination of about a dozen large, medium, and small lettuce leaves, choosing perfect specimens {or pick nearly perfect ones and trim their minor flaws}. Toss with enough vinaigrette to liberally coat.

On cold plates or a platter, alternate slices of meat and lettuce leaves in a shingle pattern. Drizzle with a little additional dressing, stirring together more if necessary.

✢
✢ ✢

AIR-DRIED BEEF & FUYU PERSIMMONS *with* EXTRA-VIRGIN OLIVE OIL & BALSAMIC VINEGAR

THIS IS A PRETTY WINTER ANTIPASTO REQUIRING ALMOST NO WORK. The subtle, candylike sweetness of the persimmons in combination with the rich, smoky-salty lean meat is beguiling. Choose Fuyus that are a deep, saturated orange and just beginning to give to the touch, like a slightly underripe peach. The best varieties have a squat profile and are clefted, presenting a quatrefoil-shaped slice. Don't use torpedo-shaped Hachiya persimmons, which must be jelly-soft to be edible. If you see the unusual Chocolate Fuyu persimmons, snatch up a few. The gorgeous, mar-

\ *continued*

bleized flesh has faint cinnamon overtones and is worth the extra dimes. I don't usually peel Fuyu persimmons, but you should taste a small sliver of the fruit and decide if you like the skin or not.

This antipasto is a proper place to lavish the best artisan-made, aged balsamic, but, lacking that, combine good-quality commercial balsamic with the oil to make a rich vinaigrette instead. We sometimes add a few sickle-shaped slices of raw fennel to this dish. A nice variation, simpler still, constists of prosciutto or smoked prosciutto with Fuyus and almonds. Ham doesn't need the balsamic for sweetness, and is rich enough without the oil.

Wine: Buttonwood Santa Ynez Valley Sauvignon Blanc, 1999

FOR ABOUT 4 SERVINGS:

1 medium or 2 small Fuyu persimmons {about 6 to 8 ounces total}

5 to 6 ounces thinly sliced air-dried beef {bresaola}

3 to 4 tablespoons extra-virgin olive oil

2 to 3 tablespoons artisan-made balsamic vinegar

1 fennel bulb, trimmed {about 6 ounces} {optional}

Use the tip of a paring knife to carve out the stem end of the persimmons. Carve out a sliver of meat and skin and taste. If you like the texture of the skin, leave as is; if not, peel the fruit. Cut the persimmon into very thin wedges, prying out seeds if there are any, or thinly slice with a mandoline.

Spread the meat and persimmons, somewhat overlapping, on plates or a platter. Drizzle with oil, then finish with balsamic. If using the fennel, sliver crosswise into thin sickles and scatter them over. Don't feel you need to use the whole fennel bulb.

❖
❖ ❖

AIR-DRIED BEEF *with* FROMAGE BLANC *&* GREENS

My FIRST TASTE OF BRESAOLA WAS WRAPPED AROUND SOFT, DELICATE CAPRINO goat cheese on the wrong shore of Lake Como {even that, I could not really afford} in 1981. It is a well-known combination, traditional there, and it is a pleasure to transplant the idiom, using a fresh "white cheese," only lately available in

America. Friends at Cowgirl Creamery north of San Francisco make soft, delicate mixed Holstein and Jersey milk fromage blanc, which blooms next to the salty meat. You can substitute a soft, mild goat cheese or fresh ricotta.

Pair the stuffed air-dried beef with a small-leaved salad green, such as lamb's lettuce, tiny baby lettuces, or lettuce hearts, a handful of dressed chervil sprigs, or *minutina* {see About Salads, page 136}.

Wine: Apremont, Vin de Savoie, Pierre Boniface, 2000

FOR 4 SERVINGS:

About 6 tablespoons fromage blanc

12 to 16 thin slices air-dried beef {bresaola} {about 2 ounces}

3 to 4 ounces tiny salad greens, carefully washed and dried

About 2 tablespoons lemon oil {see Sources and Resources, page 518, or, to infuse your own, Lemon Oil, page 285}

Salt

Smear 1 to 2 teaspoons of cheese onto each slice of meat, fold over, and pinch closed. Toss the greens with the lemon oil to coat and a pinch of salt. Arrange the pinched meat "turnovers" around a nest of salad.

✦ ✦
✦ ✦

PORTOBELLO MUSHROOMS *with* EXTRA-VIRGIN OLIVE OIL, MINT, LEMON, *&* MOCK CRÈME FRAÎCHE

A VERY EASY AND LOVELY FIRST COURSE. Portobellos {or portabellas or portobellas, since different producers have adopted different versions of the marketing name} are a cultivated, large-capped form of *Agaricus bisporus,* the brown field mushroom that has been a supermarket staple for years. Make sure the mushrooms are firm, plump, and cold; this will make the slicing easier. Refrigerate the serving plates or platter as well. This preparation is also delicious with raw porcini mushrooms or with shavings of Parmigiano-Reggiano in lieu of the cream.

\ *continued*

Wine: Soave Classico Superiore, Pieropan, 2000

FOR ABOUT 4 SERVINGS:

6 ounces firm portobello mushroom caps {about two 5-inch caps} {save the stems for Giblet-Mushroom Sauce, page 214}

About 12 fresh mint leaves

Salt and freshly cracked black pepper

Generous 1/2 cup extra-virgin olive oil

1 lemon, halved

3 to 4 tablespoons Mock Crème Fraîche {page 286}, thinned with whipping cream if necessary to the consistency of thick paint

Using a dry pastry brush or towel, brush or wipe the mushroom caps clean. Check the gills for hidden dirt, which you can flick out with the tip of a paring knife. Don't rinse the mushrooms; this tends to damage their texture and flavor.

Using a Japanese mandoline, slice the mushrooms as thin as possible, letting them fall into a loose, layered scatter on cold serving plates or a platter. Sliver the mint and distribute over the mushrooms. Season evenly with salt and pepper, a generous drizzle of olive oil, and then a trickle of freshly squeezed lemon juice. Finish with a "scribble" of crème fraîche dripped from the tines of a fork.

❖
❖ ❖

RAW WHITE ASPARAGUS & PORCINI MUSHROOMS *with* HAZELNUTS, PARMIGIANO-REGGIANO & WHITE TRUFFLE OIL

A SIMPLE ASSEMBLY OF SUBLIME THINGS. White asparagus is in season for a few months in the spring~overlapping with the short spring porcini season. Ours comes from Fairview Gardens, an organic farm near Santa Barbara. Nourished with plenty of compost, it is tender and sweet, with a pleasant trace of bitterness. To store asparagus, white or green, trim the ends, place in an inch of water, like flowers, and refrigerate. {Use spring water if your tap water isn't great.} Choose porcini that are firm, like fresh button mushrooms, and tennis-ball–sized or smaller. Check under the caps; they should be beige and firm, not yellow-green and spongy. Buy them no more than a day before you make the dish, and store in a paper bag, refrigerated, until just before serving. If you can't get suitable porcini, you are better off substituting slices of fleshy Belgian endive. For a very luxurious version of this dish, look for Occelli's *crutin,* a delectable, aged cow-and-sheep's-milk cheese that is studded with black truffles, from the Piedmont region of Northern Italy {see Sources and Resources, page 518}. Shave it over the antipasto in lieu of the Parmigiano and truffle oil.

Wine: Aligoté de Bouzeron, A. & P. de Villaine, 2000

FOR 4 SERVINGS:

8 to 9 ounces fresh, fat white asparagus {about 8 spears}, to yield 6 to
7 ounces trimmed

About 4 ounces fresh, firm porcini
mushrooms or about 8 Belgian
endive leaves

About 24 hazelnuts {3/4 ounce, or
scant 1/4 cup}

About 1/4 cup extra-virgin olive oil

1 scant teaspoon white truffle oil

Salt

A small chunk of Parmigiano-Reggiano
{about 2 ounces}, to shave on top

Peel each asparagus spear to within a few inches of the tip, then break off the woody end. To clean the porcini, remove any loose dirt or debris with a clean towel or pastry brush. Use a sharp paring knife to scrape off or peel away any crusty dirt. Trim soft or discolored spots. Check under the cap as well. Don't worry if the stems fall off as you clean the mushrooms ~ you can slice the stems and caps separately. Place in a paper bag and refrigerate until needed. This pre-serves them and makes them much easier to slice.

Preheat the oven to 325°.

Roast the hazelnuts on a small baking sheet until their skins darken, start to split, and become papery, about 10 to 15 minutes. While they are still hot, bundle them in a towel beanbag-style and scrunch and massage them to rub off some of their skins. Don't worry if some of the skin remains. Pick out the nuts and chop them coarsely.

Combine the oils and taste ~ the truffle flavor should be subtle.

Slice the asparagus lengthwise on a mandoline, barely 1/16 inch thick {if you don't have a mandoline, slice with a sharp knife on as steep an angle as possible

\ *continued*

into elongated ovals}. Scatter most of the slices onto serving plates or a platter. Salt very lightly all over.

Use the mandoline or a razor-sharp knife to slice the porcini as thinly as possible. You will get a pretty combination of sickles, ovals, and "parasols." Or, if using endive, cut the leaves crosswise into 1/2-inch-thick sickles. Scatter over the plates, then add the rest of the sliced asparagus. Salt again, very lightly.

Use a vegetable peeler or the mandoline to shave curls of cheese over the asparagus, then scatter the hazelnuts over. Drizzle evenly with the truffle-scented oil.

⁘
⁘ ⁘

GRILLED ASPARAGUS *with* PISTACHIO AÏLLADE

AN *AILLADE* IS AN EMPHATICALLY GARLICKY THING, USUALLY A GARLIC-{*AIL* IN French} driven sauce. This one is based on a delicious pounded walnut-garlic condiment, *L'Aïllade Toulousaine,* in Elizabeth David's *French Country Cooking.* This pairing is pretty and the preparation easy.

Choose firm asparagus with elegant, smooth tips; as the tips begin to bud, the stalks become less tender and sweet. Trim a quarter inch from the ends and store upright in water, refrigerated, until using.

Don't hesitate to make extra *aïllade*; covered and refrigerated, it will keep for at least a week. It is delicious with grilled vegetables, like zucchini, leeks, or fennel, or with grilled quail or chicken. For a nice variation, try substituting hazelnuts for the pistachios. We serve hazelnut *aïllade* with Rabbit Mixed Grill {page 416}. Grilled asparagus is a versatile side dish and is also good with a drizzle of lemon-, orange-, or tangerine-scented *agrumato* oil {page 285} and mild meaty Nyons olives.

Wine: Weingut Bründlmayer, Langenloiser Steinmassel, Austrian Riesling, 2000

FOR 4 SERVINGS:

For the aïllade *{makes about 1/2 cup}:*

2 ounces raw shelled pistachios {about 1/3 cup}

1 small garlic clove

About 1/4 cup extra-virgin olive oil

1 small orange, mandarin, or tangerine, for zesting

A splash of grappa or brandy

Salt

For the asparagus:

1 to 1-1/4 pounds trimmed asparagus {allow 1-1/2 to 2 pounds untrimmed}

1 to 2 tablespoons mild-tasting olive oil

Salt

Preparing the *aïllade:*

Turn the oven to 350°.

Go through the pistachios and discard any that are shrunken or brown. {Taste a "perfect" pistachio, then taste one of the rejects. You will understand why you are taking the trouble.} Spread on a baking sheet and heat the pistachios until warm to the touch, about 2 to 3 minutes, long enough to heighten their flavor without burning their fragile oil. Coarsely chop, again watching for and culling discolored nuts.

Coarsely chop the garlic, then pound in a mortar. Scoop out with a rubber spatula and set aside.

Transfer the chopped pistachios to the mortar and pound to a dry paste, or grind finely in a processor. Blend in the pounded garlic to taste. Pound or grind in about half of the oil to bind with the nuts, then stir in the remainder.

With a few strokes of a zester, carve a teaspoonful of fragrant orange filaments. Chop, then stir them into the paste. Add the grappa or brandy and salt to taste.

The finished *aïllade* will be a dense, heavy paste. Set aside to mellow for an hour or so. As it sits, the crushed nuts will settle out of the oil, but a few stirs will reamalgamate the paste.

\ *continued*

Finishing the dish:

Prepare a grill fire and let it burn to glowing coals. Spread the coals, position the grill about 4 inches above them, and preheat it.

For standard or jumbo asparagus, 1/2 inch thick or thicker: Break off the woody ends, then peel away the toughest skin. Bring about 6 quarts water to a rapid boil. Salt lightly {about 2 teaspoons per gallon}. Blanch the asparagus for about 1 minute. They should remain crunchy and bright green. Drain. Cool in lightly salted ice water {so you don't unseason the asparagus you just seasoned}, drain, and pat dry. Oil and arrange in a single layer on the grill. Grill until hot through and emblazoned with pretty char marks, 1 to 2 minutes per side, depending on the thickness of the asparagus.

For pencil-thin or thinner asparagus: Break off the woody ends. Wash, drain, and then toss with olive oil and salt. Line up the asparagus on the hot grill, not too crowded, or the asparagus will steam instead of sizzle and char. The tips of the asparagus may frazzle and blacken slightly, but taste before you reject this on principle. I find the charred tips delicious. After about 2 minutes, use a spatula and/or tongs to turn the asparagus, several spears at a time. Cook for about 1 minute longer.

I serve a smear of the *aïllade* in the center of each warm plate and let the grilled asparagus fall like "pick-up-sticks" on top of it.

＊ ＊ ＊ ＊ ＊

BLANCHING

A SHAMELESSLY VERSATILE TERM, WHICH ONCE MEANT "TO whiten," but which is now cheerfully applied to a cluster of different culinary operations that have different goals:

1. Plunging food, very briefly, into boiling liquid, usually water, to achieve the most superficial cooking possible. The specific goal is to soften or distress the skin so it can be removed, as in the case of peaches, tomatoes, or almonds. It may be no coincidence that in English this sense of blanching as a preparation for peeling was first applied to almonds, which, once peeled, are white.

2. A more lengthy but still abortive cooking operation, where food is plunged into boiling or nearly boiling liquid, usually water, for only long enough to partially cook. The hope is for minimal flavor

loss, along with tenderizing, and/or brightening the color and/or strategic hydrating. This is all in anticipation of a secondary cooking. Hence, we might blanch leeks or fennel before adding them to a fish stew, or fat asparagus before grilling it. This type of operation is sometimes referred to as parboiling, which has come to mean "partially" boiling, a curious transformation in itself, since "par" means "thoroughly." {"Parboil," and its French and Italian equivalents, originally meant "boil thoroughly," until "par" was misunderstood to mean "part." For a while the two meanings of parboil coexisted, which must have been as confusing as "blanching" is today.} This sense of blanching also applies, sort of, to the peculiar case of french-fry cookery, where one first "blanches" {or "par-fries"} the raw potato batons in not-too-hot oil until just tender, in preparation for a second cooking in sizzling oil.

3. In the case of certain tender vegetables, such as little green beans or very skinny asparagus, rapidly boiling in lots of water until al dente, where al dente is considered quite cooked enough. No secondary cooking occurs.

4. Placing food in cold liquid {usually water, generally unsalted} and gradually bringing it to a simmer, with the goal of extracting unwanted flavor from the food so it can be discarded with the water {as in the case of blanching olives to desalt them, cardoons to draw out bitterness, or tripe to subdue its aggressive flavor.} Partial cooking is the inevitable result, and it can be arrested or prolonged, depending on the situation. {For example, in the case of blanching pig's feet, I prolong it. The first goal is to cleanse them of surface impurities, the second step is to soften the tough cartilage and meat.}

Also, certain vegetables are called "blanched" when they are cultivated in such a way that some or all parts of the plant are shielded from sunlight so they never turn green~leaving the leaves or stems pale yellow-white. This produces, for example, white asparagus, Belgian endive, and pale-hearted escarole and chicories. Hence a head of frisée is "blanched," but completely raw. It is merely "whitened."

Understanding what "blanched" means hinges on knowing what you are blanching.

＊ ＊ ＊ ＊ ＊

CHARRED EGGPLANT *with* BOTTARGA

THIS IS A SUAVE, SLIGHTLY SMOKY EGGPLANT DIP. Born of the most primitive of techniques, it is surprisingly delicate. I like to serve this with cracker bread, but thin, crispy crostini {page 122} are good as well. Comforting and delicious plain, it is unusually good garnished with grated bottarga, whether tuna or mullet {See Note, page 183}, or with thin ribbons of smoked prosciutto. Both have a pungent, feral saltiness that is perfect with the fleshly-earthy mash. This will keep for a few days covered and refrigerated.

Wine: Kavaklidere Çankaya {Turkish white wine}, 1999

FOR 4 TO 8 SERVINGS:

1 to 1-1/4 pounds globe or Japanese eggplant

1 garlic clove, peeled

2 to 3 tablespoons extra-virgin olive oil

About 2 teaspoons red wine vinegar or sherry vinegar

Salt and freshly cracked black pepper

A small chunk of bottarga {enough to grate about 1 teaspoon} or 1 ounce thinly sliced smoked prosciutto {both optional}

About 6 ounces cracker bread or 20 to 25 bite-sized crostini

Char and cook the eggplant by nesting it in barely glowing coals or placing it directly over the flame of a gas burner. Turn a few times to ensure even cooking. It should take about 15 minutes for large globe eggplant, about 8 minutes for skinnier Japanese eggplant. The once-proud specimen will have collapsed on itself, the surface coal black, the skin a thick, cakey mantle. Place in a paper bag to steam for about 5 minutes, then, when it is cool enough to handle, rub off the skin, rinsing your hands a few times as you go. Give the eggplant a very quick rinse under cold water just to rid it of some of the lingering burned specks. Don't be thorough.

Slice off the stem, then cut the eggplant in half and pry out and discard any lobes of dark, hard, mature seeds. Chop coarsely. You ought to get a generous 1-1/4 cups pulp.

Cut the garlic clove in half and rub it all over the inside of a small mixing bowl. Add the chopped eggplant, then fold in olive oil, vinegar, salt, and black pepper to taste. Don't overwork.

Mound on a serving dish and garnish with the optional grated bottarga or with smoked prosciutto cut into thin ribbons. Offer broken sheets of crispy cracker bread or crostini.

+
+ +

ARTICHOKE CAPONATA

THIS IS A STURDY VARIATION ON EGGPLANT CAPONATA. It is best when 2 to 5 days old and at room temperature. Serve it as part of an antipasto, with cured meat, hard-cooked egg, roasted peppers, or all three. I especially recommend it tossed with chunks of preserved tuna {for the method, see Pasta with Preserved Tuna and Pine Nuts, page 211}.

Choose artichokes as you would flowers. Look for perfect "blooms" with firm, unblemished "petals." The freshest artichokes, that have been handled well, feel heavy for their size and make a scrunchy sound when you squeeze them. For this recipe, you need small, tightly closed buds~if the blossom is beginning to open, you know the thistle will have begun to develop, at which point the leaves will have toughened and changed in flavor.

I don't bother rubbing the artichokes with lemon or holding them in acidulated water as I trim them~they do brown initially, but that discoloration disappears with cooking. Moreover, the lemon flavor is unwanted in this recipe, and the water just "spits" when you add the artichokes to the hot oil.

Wine: Ribolla Gialla del Friuli, Abbazzia di Rosazzo, 2000

\ *continued*

FOR ABOUT 3-1/2 CUPS:

Scant 1/4 cup tomato paste

2-1/2 tablespoons sugar

1/2 cup Champagne vinegar or white
    wine vinegar

1/2 cup mild-tasting olive oil

Salt

1-1/2 cups sliced celery {6 ounces}

1-1/2 cups sliced yellow onions {6
    ounces}

About 16 small artichokes {1-1/2 to 2
    ounces each}

1/2 cup rinsed, pitted green olives,
    such as Picholine, Lucques, or
    Ascolane, or whole Niçoise olives
    {3 ounces}

3 tablespoons capers, rinsed and
    pressed dry between towels

A handful of fresh mint leaves,
    coarsely chopped

3 tablespoons pine nuts {optional}

Stir together the tomato paste, sugar, and vinegar in a 3-quart sauté pan.

Warm about a tablespoon of the olive oil in a 12-inch skillet over medium heat. Add the celery and cook, tossing or stirring a few times, until it begins to soften and color slightly, about 4 minutes. Tip the celery into the tomato-vinegar mixture. Add another tablespoon or two of oil to the skillet and cook the onions, tossing or stirring a few times, for about 3 or 4 minutes until translucent but still firm. Some of the onions may be gold on the edges. Add to the celery, salt lightly, and stir to combine. Cover and set aside. Set the skillet aside.

Remove the dark green outer leaves of each artichoke until you reveal the softer, pale leaves at the heart. Trim the tip and stem, then, rotating the artichoke as you go, trim around the base of the leaves. You should have about 1 pound of "turned" artichokes. Halve or quarter the artichokes, depending on size.

Warm the remaining 5 or 6 tablespoons of olive oil in the skillet over medium heat. Add the artichokes and stir to coat. Cook until golden on the bottom, then stir and leave to color again, a few minutes each time. Reduce the heat, cover, and cook until the artichokes are nutty-tender, about 3 to 5 minutes. Don't worry that they are not uniform in color. Taste for salt. Fold into the celery-onion-sauce mixture. The caponata will look like a chunky, dryish vegetable chutney.

Set the sauté pan over medium heat and stir until the scant sauce bubbles hesitantly. Reduce to the lowest setting. Stir in the capers and olives, cover, and leave for about 30 minutes to finish cooking the vegetables, checking after 15 minutes to make sure the sauce isn't close to drying out. {Sprinkle with a teaspoon of water at a time if this threatens.} The vinegar will keep the vegetables from falling into a purée, but check the artichokes especially for doneness ~ they should be soft enough to crush with a wooden spoon. If they are undercooked, they will eventually blacken in the center. The caponata will now look like a *soft,* chunky, dryish vegetable chutney.

Taste the caponata, expecting it to taste out of balance~it should seem too acidic. If not, add a few drops more vinegar. Bear in mind that cooling, and time, always mute acidity. Cool to room temperature, then stir in the mint leaves, transfer to a clean storage vessel, cover, and refrigerate for at least 48 hours before serving.

Just before serving, place the pine nuts in a small pan and warm, stirring, over low heat, or heat until just warm in the oven {oven temperature matters little, so long as you watch that they don't burn}. Fold into the caponata. Taste again and notice how the flavors have mellowed, then serve.

✢
✢ ✢

FARRO & TOMATO SALAD *with* BASIL & ANCHOVIES

AMONG THE FIRST GRAINS DOMESTICATED IN THE ANCIENT NEAR EAST, AND ONE that has remained traditional in parts of Central and Southern Italy since Roman times at least, farro is lately chic. In this preparation, the farro looks like brown rice and has a delicate, nutty flavor. Mindful of this, be judicious with the vinegar. Use whole-grain farro, which is sometimes labeled as *"decorticato," "perlato,"* or *"semiper-lato"* {like "pearlized" rice}, having some of the outer brown hull removed. It cooks fairly rapidly and becomes chewy-tender. {Farro *integrale,* which has the whole outer brown hull intact, requires a few hours of soaking, takes longer to cook, and stays nutty-firm, like wild rice. You may also encounter cracked farro, which looks like steel-cut oats; it doesn't need soaking, and cooks in about 10 minutes.}

For the best flavor and texture, cook the farro specifically for this salad and then serve at room temperature. {However, leftover plain boiled farro will keep for a few days refrigerated and can be useful in other dishes. Stir it into risotto, use it for Farro Soup {page 200}, or add it to your favorite bean or vegetable soup.} This is a good summer dish, offered as part of an antipasto, with deviled eggs, radishes, and olives.

\ *continued*

Wine: Fiano d'Avellino Radici, Mastroberardino, 1999

FOR 3 TO 3-1/2 CUPS:

1 cup whole-grain farro

About 3 cups water

Salt

6 tablespoons extra-virgin olive oil

1 teaspoon red wine vinegar or sherry
   vinegar

Freshly cracked black pepper

1 cup halved ripe Sweet 100 cherry
   tomatoes {about 24 tomatoes} or
   diced ripe tomatoes

4 salt-packed anchovy fillets, rinsed
   and cut lengthwise into 3 or 4
   strips each

1/2 small cucumber {about 3 ounces},
   peeled, if you like, and sliced or
   diced

A handful of basil fresh leaves

Combine the farro with the water and salt to taste in a 2-quart saucepan and cook uncovered at a bare simmer until just tender, 10 to 15 minutes. You should get about 2 cups. Drain and spread on a sheet pan so it will cool evenly.

Whisk together the oil, vinegar, and salt and black pepper. Taste. The vinegar flavor should be barely strong enough to detect.

Combine the farro, tomatoes, anchovies, and cucumbers, if using, and toss with enough vinaigrette to coat. Tear the basil leaves, then fold into the farro. Taste again. Serve promptly, while the flavors are bright and clear and before the farro soaks up the vinegar.

❖ ❖ *Variation* CARLO'S FARRO SALAD *with* AGED TUSCAN PECORINO

An excellent variation on this dish consists of no more than the farro, tomatoes, basil, and olive oil, joined with about 1/2 cup tiny cubes of aged Tuscan pecorino in lieu of the anchovies. No vinegar at all. Carlo Cioni, during his benevolent one-week reign over the kitchen at Zuni in 1999, made that salad, for which Zuni, unjustly, still receives the compliments. Carlo is chef and owner of Da Delfina, an idyllic restaurant just outside Florence, where he furthers the cause of Tuscan food and Tuscan cooking with uncommon vigor and irresistible charm.

❖
❖ ❖

Bosc Pears *with* Fennel, Fresh Walnuts, Parmigiano-Reggiano, & Balsamic Vinegar

Sweet, fruity fresh walnuts are a luxury of the fall. At their prime, they appear constantly on our menu, especially in this, one of my favorite dishes. But even at peak season, shelled walnuts change flavor rapidly ~ look for them in their shells, or taste shelled walnuts before you buy. {And if you don't see whole walnuts in your market year-round, do not despair; consider this a reminder that they are a seasonal crop, not a pantry staple.}

Choose firm, plump, mature heads of fennel that are heavy for their size. Avoid slender, stalky "baby fennel" ~ it can be fibrous and green tasting. Choose Bosc pears with amber skins.

This is a good dish to lavish with syrupy artisanal balsamic vinegar. Otherwise, use a good-quality commercial product, but dose it more sparingly.

Serves as an antipasto, salad course, or, if you have a precious balsamic, dessert. This salad has a primitive sweetness that is as elegant as any refined sugar dessert I know. I enjoy its unmanipulated finesse at the end of a rich meal.

Wine: Wild Horse Monterey Malvasia Bianca, 2000

FOR ABOUT 4 SERVINGS:

1 medium fennel bulb, trimmed {about 8 ounces}

1 large, ripe Bosc pear {about 8 ounces}

A small chunk of Parmigiano-Reggiano {about 2 ounces}

2 ounces walnuts {about 3/4 cup}, preferably freshly shelled

About 1/2 cup extra-virgin olive oil

About 1/4 cup aged balsamic vinegar, preferably artisan-made

Just before serving, slice the fennel crosswise into thin sickles. Cut the pear in half, then carve into elegant 1/4-inch-thick wedges, avoiding the core and seeds.

Layer the fennel and pear very loosely on a platter, interspersing with slivers and curls of the cheese, cutting them with a vegetable peeler as you go. Scatter the walnuts over all. Drizzle with the olive oil and finish with the balsamic, enough that the whole thing glistens gold and chestnut.

PICCOLO FRITTO

Our "small fry" is a small assembly of fried things whose composition varies. I have dropped just about every available vegetable and not a few fruits into the fryer over the years, looking to "bronze" as many different textures and flavors as possible. What doesn't vary much here is the simple technique. It produces a light, lacy, golden fry. I offer here descriptions and frying hints for our most popular *fritto* combinations, but you can also compose your own. As you select from what is in season and delicious, look for complementary flavors, and pursue textural contrast as well. The best little mixed fries boast a variety of leafy and solid; sweet, tart, and slightly bitter; meaty, fibrous, and crunchy. Garnishes can provide interesting contrast as well.

Deep-frying food at home can be an invasive operation; while this breading technique is very easy, it does take up a lot of counter space, and then the actual frying needs to happen in batches. But don't let these concerns daunt you; once you've figured out an arrangement that works in your kitchen, the process will seem easy.

At Zuni, we fry in peanut oil. It is nearly neutral in taste and fairly stable. I also like food fried in pure olive oil, though it has a persuasive flavor and is considerably more expensive. The key to our breading is buttermilk; slightly viscous, it grabs and binds the perfect amount of flour for a light, tender, crispy *fritto.*

Here is a list of favorite *fritto* ingredients and how to prepare them, followed by general frying instructions. Having chosen to cook distinctly different things at the same temperature, one needs to tailor the thing to the temperature, so each of the items is cut with a mind to surface area, texture, and doneness. Keep this in mind if you choose to fry things not listed here. For most combinations, plan on about 1 pound of prepared vegetables for 4 servings as a first course. If you are including seafood or poultry, allow slightly more.

+ **Onions:** Peel, slice 1/16 to 3/8 inch thick, and separate into rings.
+ **Lemon or orange slices:** This is our signature fritto item. The crispy, fragrant, savory-tart chips are irresistible and beautiful. Use unwaxed fruit, or scrub in hot water to remove wax. Trim the blossom end flat, deep enough to reveal the juicy fruit. Slice, skin on, into pinwheels the thickness of shirt cardboard {about 1/32 inch}. Where it's easy to do, pick out the seeds as you go. Stop when you reach the pith at the stem end.

⁃ **Portobello mushroom caps or fresh porcini mushrooms:** Slice 1/4 to 3/8 inch thick.

⁃ **Broccoli rabe:** Leave small clusters whole; cut lengthwise in half if the stem is more than 3/8 inch thick, or if a floweret is more than 1 inch across. I prize the frazzled look and extra-crisp texture of the fried leaves and flowers.

⁃ **Radicchio:** Trim the root end clean, then cut through the core into 3/4-inch wedges.

⁃ **Fennel:** Trim, and cut across the bulb into 1/4-inch-thick slices. Separate into sickles.

⁃ **Pencil-thin asparagus:** Break off the woody ends.

⁃ **Celery hearts:** Use only the pale innermost section. Trim the root end and separate into individual, pliable stalks, up to 1/2 inch wide and 4 inches long.

⁃ **Summer squash:** Slice, in any direction, about 1/4 inch thick. Crookneck squash sliced lengthwise makes pretty arabesques.

⁃ **Squash blossoms or nasturtiums:** Check inside for bugs or flecks of dirt. Leave whole.

⁃ **Fresh sage:** Use individual perfect leaves or, where the stem is tender, small sprigs of perfect leaves.

⁃ **Capers:** Rinse or soak until not very salty, drain, and press dry between towels. {You won't be breading these.}

⁃ **Cauliflower:** Remove the leaves and trim the root end flush. Cut the head into quarters. Starting along one of the flat faces, slice 1/4 inch thick. You'll get a selection of scalloped-edged, lacy, branchy slices, a few full-width and held together by the central trunk, most broken at least in half, and lots of pea-sized, and smaller, "crumbs." Fry them all; the variety is fun.

⁃ **Prunes, with or without pits:** Plump for an hour or so in warm water to cover, drain and gently squeeze in a dry towel. Spiced Prunes or Prunes in Black Tea {page 278} are delicious deep-fried, but they should be well drained before breading. Fried prunes are great with duck confit or quail.

⁃ **Fresh figs:** Trim the stem ends, then halve or quarter depending on size.

⁃ **Fresh Zante grapes:** Cut into clusters, walnut-sized and smaller. Save the loose grapes; you can bread and fry them too, or, for contrast, scatter them raw over the crisp, hot *fritto.*

⁃ **Squid:** Clean {see page 338}, then cut the bodies into 1/4- to 3/8-inch rings

\ *continued*

and leave the tentacles whole. Rinse and drain. {1 pound whole squid will yield 10 to 11 ounces cleaned.}

⁙ **Scallops:** Leave small scallops whole; cut fat ones 1/2 to 3/4 inch thick in either direction.

⁙ **Skate:** Buy "on the wing," by which I mean a whole or partial skate wing that is still attached to the cartilage. Rinse briefly and press dry between towels. Cut between the ridges into 1-inch-wide pieces. Salt lightly all over.

⁙ **House-Cured Salt Cod** {page 328}: Soak, drain, cut into 1-ounce chunks, and press dry between towels.

⁙ **Fresh anchovies, smelt, or small sardines:** Scale, gut, and clean {see page 72}. Remove the heads if you like. Press dry between towels. Salt lightly.

⁙ **Whole sand dabs or sole:** Buy pan-ready "dressed" fish {cleaned, fins trimmed, head removed}. Rinse and press dry between towels. Leave small fish~ up to 6 ounces~whole; cut larger fish, perpendicular to the vertebrae, into 1-inch-wide segments. Salt lightly all over.

⁙ **Eggs:** Crack each egg into its own small, shallow bowl.

⁙ **Chickpeas:** Cook until quite tender, then cool in their liquid {see Dried Beans, page 263}. Drain well. {You won't be breading these.}

For breading and frying about 4 servings:

About 4 quarts peanut oil
About 2 cups buttermilk
About 4 cups all-purpose flour
About 1 cup semolina {optional, but it
 gives the crust a nutty crunch and
 makes the breading process a little
 less sticky}

Salt

Prepare the items you plan to fry.

Place the oil in stable pot, stockpot, or Dutch oven with a capacity of approximately 6 quarts. The oil should be a few inches below the rim of the pan. Clip on an accurate thermometer. Set the pan over medium-low heat to begin preheating. We fry most often at 365° to 370°; this cooks the small pieces of vegetables in the time it takes to brown the breading. We reduce the heat if we are frying fish or quail. While you bread the food, keep an eye on the thermometer and the oil, adjusting as needed to reach the proper temperature.

Place the buttermilk in a wide, shallow bowl. Mix the flour and semolina, if using, in a cake pan or deep platter. Place this right next to the bowl of milk. Set a sheet pan, tray, or platter next to the flour, to receive the breaded food. For easy handling, line this with parchment paper.

Place a few pieces of the prepared food in the buttermilk, then transfer them, dripping, to the bed of flour. "Shimmy" the breading pan so the pieces settle, coating their sides, then flip each piece with a fingertip to coat the other side. {Before you have finished, your fingers will be breaded as well.} Lift out the breaded food, tap or shake to remove excess flour, and set on the sheet pan. Be aware that this simple coating is never uniform and does not need to be. Ideally, the breading will have wrinkles and some barely coated spots; both fry nicely and, in combination, they make a *fritto* lovely and fun to eat.

Bread the remaining ingredients in the same fashion. It's fine if the pieces of breaded food touch and overlap on the sheet pan, but don't stack them outright ~ use more than one sheet pan if you need to. It is convenient, although not required, to get all the breading done before you begin frying it. Most breaded items will hold well at room temperature, or slightly cooler, for half an hour or so. {They become a little sticky, but will still fry beautifully.} If you hold the breaded food too much longer, the breading may fry to hard rather than crisp. In general, don't refrigerate the breaded food; it won't prevent stickiness, and cold food will hamper the frying process.

Line another wide bowl, or a shallow roasting pan, with a few layers of paper towels. Set on the stove, ready to receive the fried food.

Once the oil is heated to the desired temperature, add a small piece of breaded food. It should sizzle quietly, almost instantly. Now add a few more pieces of food ~ about one-third of the total. The pot shouldn't be crowded, as that would produce a soggy fry, {or worse, the oil could boil over}, but it is inevitable that some pieces of food will touch and fuse into odd couplings, which everyone will reach for first. The oil will bubble noisily as moisture vaporizes, and the temperature will fall, but the overwhelming volume of oil should recover quickly. But you are the thermostat, so monitor closely. If the oil doesn't rebound, you may need to increase the heat. If so, be very conservative; since any adjustment will only take effect gradually, it is easy to overcompensate.

\ *continued*

Leave the frying food undisturbed until a pale golden crust sets. With this volume, it generally takes about a minute or two. {Larger vats of oil~and commercial fryers~recover more quickly, and may color and cook the food in half that time.} Use tongs or a long-handled fork to very gently turn anything that won't otherwise brown on the top. Don't, however, fuss with the frying food; the fragile breading must stay integral, or the *fritto* will go limp and become greasy. Stirring and aggressive poking can easily fracture the crust. Once the food is generally golden, lift out the pieces with tongs or a mesh skimmer {you may choose to corral little things like capers, chickpeas, or cauliflower "crumbs" in a mesh strainer}, dangle them briefly over the oil to drip, and then set gently in the paper-lined bowl; try not to crack the crust. Fry and drain the remainder of the food in the same manner. Don't pile the new batches of hot *fritto* on the prior ones, lest they steam or crush one another. You ought to be able to cook the suggested pound of vegetables in about three batches.

Just before serving, season lightly all over with salt and transfer, still gingerly, to warm plates or a platter.

Note: You can usually save the oil for reuse, as long as it has not gotten too hot, you haven't cooked too much in it, and none of what you cooked was seafood. To save the oil, cool it to room temperature, letting the solids settle, then pour it off through a fine mesh strainer. Don't bother trying to salvage the sludgy oil on the bottom of the pan. Store, sealed, in a cool, dark place. It is hard to say exactly how long it will keep; smell and taste a drop before you decide to reuse it.

These are some of the *Piccolo Fritto* combinations we serve regularly:

RADICCHIO, ONIONS, & LEMON OR ORANGE SLICES

Radicchio balances the sweetness of the onions, which, in turn, play off the tart, fragrant lemon. Fry just a few wedges of radicchio, or it will dominate, volume- and flavor-wise. The outer leaves tend to pull away during the breading process, or in the fryer, and emerge looking like brittle parchment. They are delicious. Fry the citrus slices last; they cook quickly, and need to be removed from the oil slightly paler than everything else~their sugars continue to brown outside of the oil. You will have tart, crisp, lacy golden wafers, sometimes etched with inky caramel. Fry a few slices per person, at least. They are addictive. This *fritto* is delicious drizzled with artisan-made balsamic.

RADICCHIO, ONIONS, & PORTOBELLO MUSHROOMS *with* A DEEP-FRIED EGG

A variation on the preceding *fritto,* with the earthy, meaty mushrooms striking a different flavor-texture balance. The virtuoso garnish is optional, but here is how we deep-fry an egg: Lower a fryer basket or strainer at least 2 inches into the oil. {If using a strainer, the far edge probably needs to be resting on the bottom, rather than hooked on the side of the pot.} Let it preheat for at least 30 seconds, then slowly slide the egg from its bowl into the oil, positioning it so it lands in the basket or strainer. The white will begin to set as it falls through the oil; you can gently pull the egg from the mesh after it has fried for about 20 seconds. Count 1 egg per person, but plan on frying a practice egg so you can decide how done you like it, and learn how long that takes. Also good drizzled with balsamic or topped with shavings of Parmigiano-Reggiano.

PENCIL ASPARAGUS, ONIONS, & NASTURTIUMS

This spring *fritto* is about delicacy in taste, texture, and display. Slice the onions very thinly. Bread the asparagus and onions first. Thin the buttermilk with a little milk before you dip the nasturtiums, then twirl by the stem as you sprinkle them with the breading flour, rather than dredge them in it.

It is surely lily-gilding, but I sometimes offer fresh Lemon Mayonnaise {page 288} with this *fritto.*

MOZZARELLA & CORN-STUFFED SQUASH BLOSSOMS & SWEET 100 TOMATOES

Choose very fresh blossoms whose petals you can easily spread open. Tuck a few small dice of mozzarella inside, along with a spoonful of freshly scraped corn kernels {see page 148}. Gather and twist the tips of the petals together gently, then bread as usual. Fold the twisted part back and under and leave to set for at least 10 minutes. {Otherwise, the flowers may open during frying and the cheese escape.} The tiny tomatoes must be very sweet and with tender skins; underripe or tough, they will make you squint. They are the one vegetable you need to double-bread ~ otherwise, the flour will tend to slide off the shiny skins. Alternatively, you can simply halve the tomatoes and scatter them raw over the star of the plate, the fried blossoms. And if you don't have time or inclination to stuff the blossoms, fry them plain; although mild in flavor, they have an intriguing crispy, leathery texture.

SQUID, CHICK PEAS, & SWEET 100 TOMATOES

The squid may not need to be dipped in buttermilk before dredging~whenever we fry squid, we test it both ways to see which sets the nicest crust. And don't bread the chick peas at all; they fry to smooth crunchiness without. Choose sweet, thin-skinned tiny tomatoes and double-bread them. They will deliver little explosions of sauce for the squid. Garnish, if you like, with a handful of arugula or a few torn leaves of basil for counterpoint and freshness. Everyone asks for Aïoli {page 289} with this *fritto.*

SAND DAB *with* ONIONS, LEMON SLICES, & FRESH SAGE

The onion-lemon-sage combination is good with many kinds of fried fish, such as whole sardines, smelt or fresh anchovies, pieces of skate wing, or chunks of our house-cured salt cod. To fry the sage, holding it by the stem, dip each sprig or large leaf in the buttermilk, then drag through the flour. If breading a sprig, jostle it in the flour to coat each leaf. Fry to golden, about 15 seconds on each side. Fried capers are an easy alternative to the sage~don't bread them, and fry just until the little buds begin to crisp on the surface; if you are lucky they will begin to "bloom" before they set. Capers take about 30 seconds. Cook this *fritto* at 360°.

ONIONS, FENNEL, & ZANTE GRAPES

Three kinds of sweet, with distinctly different perfumes and textures. Cut the onions very thin for a lacy effect. We sometimes drizzle this *fritto* with a rich condiment called *saba* {see Sources and Resources, page 518} or with syrupy balsamic. You can substitute halved or quartered fresh figs for some or all of the grapes {and Deep-Fried Figs make a stunning dessert; see page 459}.

We sometimes strew these skinny fried onions and grapes over a wad of warm frisée salad studded with pecans. Serve this as a first or middle course, or add a piece of plainly prepared duck, squab, or quail and serve as main course.

✦ ✦ ✦ ✦ ✦

WINE & PICCOLO FRITTO

FOR RADICCHIO, LEMON, FISH, ASPARAGUS, ETC., CHOOSE A CRISP, GRASSY Sauvignon Blanc from New Zealand's cool Marlborough region Goldwater Dog Point Vineyard or Cooper's Creek, for example.

For dishes based on prunes, fennel, grapes, and mushrooms, use the softer and more melony Sauvignon Blancs from Hawkes Bay~they include Matariki and Matua Valley~and be sure they are always of the most recent vintage available.

+ + + + +

SAGE GRILLED CHEESE

Don't consign grilled cheese to lunch alone. Individual little sandwiches or diminutive wedges of sizzling grilled cheese make an irresistible, accessible hors d'œuvre. Using chewy bread, excellent cheese, and lots of fresh sage and black pepper makes the familiar icon addictive. For Zuni's twentieth anniversary, we layered the cheese with slivers of fresh black truffle, which was exquisite.

Serve with Spiced Zante Grapes {page 276}.

Wine: Hamilton's Ewell Vineyard Barossa Valley Grenache/Shiraz, 2000

FOR 4 LITTLE SANDWICHES, OR ABOUT 20 BITES:

About a dozen fresh sage leaves

2 tablespoons mild-tasting olive oil

1/2 teaspoon freshly cracked black pepper

6 ounces chewy, peasant-style bread, sliced 1/4 inch thick {8 slices from a fat French *bâtard*~a fat baguette~will do perfectly}

4 ounces Fontina or Swiss Gruyère, all rind removed and sliced 1/16 inch thick or coarsely grated

Chop the sage. You should get about 1 tablespoon. Place in your smallest saucepan, add the olive oil and cracked pepper, set over low heat, and warm to the touch. Turn off the heat and leave to infuse while you assemble the sandwiches.

\ *continued*

Blanket half of the slices of bread evenly with the cheese, taking care to bring the cheese all the way to the crust. Top each with a second slice of bread and press flat. Lay a heavy or weighted cutting board on top of the sandwiches for 10 to 20 minutes.

Use a pastry brush to spread the sage oil lightly on both faces of the sandwiches. Make sure you go all the way to the edges, and try to distribute the sage and pepper evenly over the bread.

Preheat a griddle or warm a seasoned cast-iron pan over low heat. Sprinkle with a few drops of olive oil, then rub it over the whole cooking surface with a paper towel. Add the sandwiches and cook until golden, 2 to 3 minutes per side. Keep the heat low so you don't burn the sage or pepper.

Eat quickly, while the cheese is still soft.

٭
٭ ٭

NEW YEAR'S EVE GOUGÈRES *with* ARUGULA, BACON, *&* CAROL'S PICKLED ONIONS

THIS WAS THE MOST SUCCESSFUL NEW YEAR'S EVE HORS D'ŒUVRE OF THE LAST decade, outselling foie gras, oysters, caviar, crab salad, and little truffle-laden pizzas. Many tables ordered several more after they had had one. A gougère is a savory, cheese-studded cream puff pastry; for this dish, you split and stuff the puffs like sandwiches.

Wine: Louis Roederer Brut Premier

FOR 20 TO 24 THREE-BITE–SIZED GOUGERES:
   For the batter:

1 cup water

3 tablespoons unsalted butter

1 teaspoon salt {a little more if using kosher salt}

4 ounces all-purpose flour {1 cup}

4 large eggs, cold

1/2 to 3/4 teaspoon freshly cracked black pepper

2 ounces Gruyère, cut into 1/4-inch cubes {about 1/2 cup}

To stuff the gougères:

10 to 12 slices bacon

About 1-1/2 ounces arugula, carefully
washed and dried

1 cup Carol's Pickled Onions {page
271}, drained

Preheat the oven to 400°.

In a 2- to 4-quart saucepan, bring the water, butter, and salt to a simmer over medium heat. Add the flour all at once and stir vigorously until the mixture masses and detaches itself from the sides of the pan. Reduce the heat to low and cook, beating constantly, until the batter is very stiff and almost shiny, usually a few minutes. Off the heat, add the eggs one by one, beating thoroughly with a wooden spoon to completely incorporate each egg before adding the next. The mixture will initially resist each addition; you'll find yourself cutting through and slapping together slabs of slippery, warm paste until it gradually absorbs the egg and becomes sticky again. The final mixture should be no hotter than tepid. Add the pepper to taste and stir in the Gruyère.

If you are proficient with one, transfer the batter to a pastry bag, and pipe 2- to 3-inch-long bands onto a parchment paper–lined {or nonstick} baking sheet about 2 inches apart. Otherwise, use a spoon to scoop out a heaping tablespoon of batter per gougère and a second spoon to scrape it into a peaky mound on the prepared baking sheet.

Bake until firm and a rich golden brown, about 25 minutes. Inevitably, some bits of cheese will ooze and form a delicious, crispy bib on the edges of the gougères. To check doneness, remove 1 gougère and pry open. The interior strands of dough should be tender and moist, but not mushy; if they are, close the gougère and return it to the oven to bake with the rest for another few minutes. If you are concerned they may overbrown, simply turn off the oven and leave to finish cooking in the ambient heat.

Meanwhile, cut the bacon into 1-1/2- to 2-inch segments and panfry or roast to your taste. Drain on towels.

Serve the gougères warm from the oven {or reheated}, split through the middle and overstuffed with a few pieces of bacon, several leaves of peppery arugula, and a few ringlets of the pickled onions.

⁜
⁜ ⁜

Savory Onion Tart, *with* Two Elaborations

"ROUGH PUFF" PASTRY SMEARED WITH SWEET, HONEY-COLORED STEWED ONIONS and baked hot and fast. Serve with a fistful of arugula, frisée, or watercress dressed with vinaigrette.

Wine: Claiborne & Churchill Central Coast Riesling, 2000

FOR 4 SERVINGS:

1 recipe "Rough Puff" {page 484}

For the basic onion mixture:

About 3 tablespoons mild-tasting olive oil	Salt
12 ounces thinly sliced yellow onions {about 3 cups}	A few garlic cloves {optional}
	1 bay leaf
	A sprig of fresh thyme

If the dough is frozen, thaw it in the refrigerator, then leave at room temperature long enough to roll out without cracking {see Tempering, page 120}. Roll the dough into a square about 1/2 inch thick. Cut into 4 roughly equal squares and then roll them out until barely 1/8 inch thick. The warped-squareish pieces of dough should be 7 to 8 inches across. The thickness need not be perfectly uniform~indeed, an unnoticed thick edge will bake into pillowy tenderness, and it never fails that that little tart is the first one chosen. Place each piece of dough on an 8- to 9-inch square of parchment, stack, cover, and refrigerate.

Preheat the oven to 400°.

Warm the olive oil in a 12-inch skillet. Add the onions and a few pinches of salt. Cook over medium-high heat for a few minutes, until some of the onions begin to color. Stir or toss, then cook undisturbed for another few minutes to color another layer of onions. Reduce the heat to medium-low and stir in the garlic, if using, the bay leaf, and the thyme. Continue cooking until the onions are generally golden and tender but not mushy, about 15 minutes total. If they threaten to dry out at any point, reduce the heat a little further and cover the pan to trap the remaining moisture. Taste and correct the salt. You should get about 1-1/4 cups. Cool completely. Remove the thyme and strip the leaves into the onions. Remove and discard the bay leaf.

Pull the prepared dough from the refrigerator and allow to warm just enough to fold the edges over without cracking; this will take only a few minutes in a warm kitchen.

Place the squares of dough, on their parchment, on a baking sheet. Don't worry if the papers overlap. Spread each piece of dough with 4 to 5 tablespoons of the cooled onion mixture, stopping about an inch from the edges. Fold in the sides, mitering or lapping the corners. Press lightly to secure the sides and corners.

Bake until a rich golden brown, about 20 minutes. The edges of the onions may begin to caramelize.

❖ ❖ ONION TART *with* SAFFRON, TOMATO, ANCHOVIES, & OLIVES

Prepare the dough squares and gather the ingredients for the basic onion mixture, plus:

A few saffron threads

1 small, very ripe tomato or 15 to 20 tiny, ripe Sweet 100 tomatoes {about 3 ounces}

Salt

4 salt-packed anchovy fillets, cut lengthwise into 3 or 4 strips each

A trickle of extra-virgin olive oil

4 mild black olives, such as Nyons, Niçoise, or Ligurian

Cook the onions as described in the basic recipe, adding the saffron with the bay leaf and thyme.

Slice the tomato about 1/4 inch thick, or halve the Sweet 100s, and salt very lightly. {If using a large tomato, set aside the shoulder and heel for tomato soup or sauce.} Leave to purge for a few minutes, then pat with a towel to wick a little water from the fruit. This way, the tomatoes will color a little and have more intense flavor.

Drizzle the anchovies with extra-virgin olive oil.

Smear the onions on the prepared pastry dough, crown each tart with 1 or 2 tomato slices, or dot with the tomato halves, and finish with strips of anchovy and the olives.

Bake as in the basic recipe.

⁜ ⁜ ONION TART *with* APPLES *&* BACON

Prepare the dough squares and cook the basic onion mixture. Gather:

1 small Pippin or other crisp apple
3 or 4 thin slices lean bacon {scant 3 ounces}

Cut about 12 slivers of apple, 1/16 inch thick, leaving the skin on if it tastes good to you. Cut the bacon into 1/2-inch strips, set in a small skillet, and place over low heat for a minute or so, until it has rendered a film of fat. Drain the fat and, off the heat, toss the apple slices with the bacon.

Spread the cooled onions on the prepared pastry dough and press in the warm apple and bacon. The tart will be most interesting if some of the apples poke above the surface a little and some are tucked into the onions. The bacon, on the other hand, should lay flat, or it may burn on the edges.

Bake as directed in the basic recipe.

⁜ ⁜ ⁜ ⁜ ⁜

TEMPERING

THE TERM "TEMPERING" IS AN EFFICIENT WAY TO EXPRESS AN important culinary concept: moderating the temperature of whatever you are handling. It can involve cooling or warming, either liquids or solids, and serves many purposes. In some situations, we temper to manage texture; for example, frozen desserts usually have a nicer texture when not too cold. Similarly, butter and pastry dough tend to crack if too cold, so we usually temper them before handling. And we temper tubs of cold confit in order to soften the fat just enough to remove the meat. Tempering can also improve flavor, and again, this is particularly significant for ice creams, sorbets and granitas. As really cold things warm up, you can perceive more flavors. We occasionally temper very hot things before adding them to a dish to avoid cooking the remainder, as when we cool a hot brine before pouring it over fresh meat, fruits, or vegetables, or cool hot liquids before combining them with eggs {or warm the cold eggs, tempering them by adding a little of the hot mixture.} I sometimes temper large chunks of meat before roasting them, so they cook more rapidly and evenly. But more important than memorizing specific applications, embracing the general concept~that moderating temperature extremes will frequently increase success in the kitchen and at the table~will make you a better cook. You will find yourself deciding on your own when you want to temper an ingredient or finished dish.

I should note that where chocolate is concerned, "tempering" has a different and precise meaning. It is a more complex process, involving both warming and cooling, within strict temperature ranges, that has the goal of stabilizing the chocolate, and of preventing the cocoa butter from migrating to the surface as a bloom of fine white crystals.

✦ ✦ ✦ ✦ ✦

CROSTINI

O R CROUTONS, OR CRISP CANAPES: THESE ARE THE LITTLE PIECES OF TOASTED, roasted, grilled, or fried bread, crowned or smeared with compatible toppings, that haunt our menu. A bite-sized hors d'œuvre is often the best way to fit a very rich, unusual, or expensive dish, like foie gras, or brandade, or eggs and bottarga, onto a menu~people can't resist little things on toast. Several of the other crostini toppings and combinations here are proudly based on leftovers, or larder items. When yesterday's giblet-mushroom sauce or squid stew is still delicious~often more delicious than it was yesterday~but is in short supply, it may manage to return by the spoonful, on toast, as an appetizer. It is most practical to serve those crostini when you already have a little of such a topping on hand. You will find I advise making a little extra of such things on a regular basis in these pages. Nearly all of these crostini appetizers are also comfortable next to a tangle of carefully dressed salad, to make a different sort of first course.

While the toppings may be the attention-grabbers of any crostini course, they will be squandered if the bread part is not properly prepared. For delicate crostini, the bread should be fresh, or at least fresh enough to eat "as is." Really stale bread is prone to make hard, tough, dry croûtons. Well-wrapped, carefully frozen {and carefully thawed} bread is a fine alternative to today's bake. Keep a loaf in the freezer for emergency crostini. Aside from baguettes, we use chewy, peasant-style white bread and mixed unbleached wheat and barley flour sourdough *levain* bread for crostini. Small-crumbed sandwich breads are generally too tender and often too sweet or rich for the rustic toppings I describe.

To prepare the crostini: Slice the bread about 1/4 inch thick {if the bread is particularly soft, wrapping and partially freezing it will make this easier} and, where indicated, brush with olive oil, making sure to go all the way to the edges.

Don't cook the crostini until you have to ~ it is tempting to get this done well in advance, and oven or grill logistics may force you to do so, but freshly cooked crostini are fragrant and crispy. Cooled, hours-old ones usually taste dull.

When you do cook the crostini, make sure your oven or grill is fully pre-heated ~ the goal is to achieve surface color and crispness without transforming the bread into melba toast. Bake the crostini on a baking sheet that conducts heat well. I like them to be slightly brown on the edges, with golden touches on the face. This generally takes about 5 to 7 minutes at about 425°, but timing will vary according to rack height, oven size, baking sheet, and, most of all, the bread. Check this by baking a single crostini; if it takes much longer to color, the bread risks drying out completely. Raise the heat for quicker results.

I pull the crostini from the oven with a trace of chewiness left in the bread ~ they crisp as they cool. That way, they are more flavorful and don't wick too much moisture from the topping. {They also tolerate 30 seconds of reheating if you do need to make them in advance.} If your crostini do get fully crisp in the oven, slide them off the baking sheet right away; this will keep them from getting too hard and dry. Otherwise, leave them on the baking sheet until needed.

Grilled crostini tend to be chewy-crisp and are delicious but not particularly convenient unless you are grilling something else in the meal {in which case, you should grill some bread no matter what, to enjoy with the meal, even if you don't have a crostini course}. On a hot grill, allow 30 seconds or less per side to crisp and etch lovely char marks on thinly sliced dry bread.

I have made dry crostini in a toaster by fussing with the darkness adjustment, toasting the bread once on "light" to dry it slightly, and then retoasting it on a darker setting. Making baguette croûtons in a toaster is possible if you slice the baguette lengthwise or on a very steep angle, into large slices you can safely retrieve from the appliance. Cut these down to bite-size after the fact. A toaster oven is fine for dry or oiled crostini toasting, though the cramped quarters means they tend to color quickly and stay steamy in the middle. Experiment and adjust for this as necessary.

THESE ARE SOME OF MY FAVORITE CROSTINI COMBINATIONS. Most are based on spoonfuls and slivers of other dishes in this book, with only a few, easy "from scratch" requirements. Make sure all of the toppings have concentrated flavor and are succulent and moist, but not wet or watery. If they are too dry, the bread will dominate the flavor and texture of the toppings, and the toppings will tend to fall off the bread. Very wet toppings will make the toast soggy too quickly; you can easily "tighten" these small amounts of topping, evaporating excess water as you reheat them, stirring with a spatula, in a small skillet or saucepan, preferably non-stick, over low heat.

Count on a tablespoon or two of topping per crostini, depending on the size of the toast. Where you are serving a couple of different types, don't worry if you don't have equal amounts of the toppings.

* * **CROSTINI** *with* **CHARRED SWEET 100 TOMATOES** *&* **BALSAMIC VINEGAR**

Prepare crostini with extra-virgin olive oil {see page 122}. Rub with raw garlic if you like.

Select nearly overripe red or gold Sweet 100 tomatoes, 4 or 5 per crostini, more than you think you'll need to cover the toasts. Stem, rinse, and dry well. Toss with extra-virgin olive oil to coat and salt to taste. Crowd in a shallow gratin dish and place under a preheated broiler. Cook until the skins burst, usually a few minutes, then raise the rack and leave until the surfaces begin to char. Adjust the rack or rotate the dish as needed to achieve dramatic results. Cool briefly, then drizzle with balsamic vinegar and tilt and shimmy the dish to distribute. You can prepare these tomatoes just before you need them, or up to a few hours in advance, then leave at room temperature to mellow.

Top each toast with a layer of tomatoes, pressing on them gently so they bleed juice into the bread. Drizzle any extra balsamic-oil-tomato-juice mixture from the baking dish over the crostini.

Wine: Sangiovese di Toscana, Conti Contini, 1998

CROSTINI *with* SMASHED SHELLING BEANS, GIBLET-MUSHROOM SAUCE, *&* GREENS

Prepare crostini with extra-virgin olive oil {see page 122}.

Warm a heaping spoonful of cooked Fresh Shelling Beans or Dried Beans {pages 262 and 263} per crostini. Lift the beans from the pan with a slotted spoon and mash in a mortar, adding a little of the cooking liquor, and extra-virgin olive oil to taste. Keep warm. Drain, then warm Boiled Kale {page 162}. Warm the Giblet-Mushroom Sauce {page 214} separately, then top each crostini with one of the three toppings. Finish the crostini with freshly cracked black pepper. A juicy, charred Sweet 100 tomato {see above} would also be good on each of these crostini.

Wine: Lolonis Mendocino Estate Zinfandel, 1999

CROSTINI *with* BEAN PURÉE *&* SARDINES *in* CHIMICHURRI

Prepare crostini with extra-virgin olive oil {see page 122}.

Warm, then smash well-cooked white beans or chickpeas as described immediately above, but don't add the extra-virgin olive oil. Warm sardine fillets {see page 208} in Chimichurri {page 298} for about 5 minutes in a 275° oven. Slather each crostini with the bean purée, then set a sardine fillet, or a piece of one, on top. Stir the chimichurri to recombine, then spill a little on each crostini.

Wine: Far Niente Napa Valley Chardonnay, 1999

CROSTINI *with* SALT COD BRANDADE *&* CHARD *with* LEMON OIL

Prepare crostini with extra-virgin olive oil {see page 122}.

Chop, then warm a handful of Chard with Lemon Oil {page 248}; keep warm. Mashing and stirring constantly, warm a spoonful of Brandade {page 331} per crostini in a small nonstick pan, then mound on some of the crisp bread. Spread strategically all the way to the edges. Place under a preheated broiler to brown and frazzle the tips of the fish paste, a minute or two.

Pile the warm chard on the remaining crostini.

Wine: Orvieto Classico Secco, Le Velette, 2000

CROSTINI *with* FAVA-EGG SALAD *&* SMOKED TROUT

Prepare crostini with extra-virgin olive oil {see page 122}.

Choose very young favas. Shuck, then double-peel them {see page 88}, counting a few tender, small, bright green favas per toast. Prepare 1 hard-cooked egg {see page 508} for each 3 crostini. Peel the warm eggs and mash with the favas and 1 tablespoon extra-virgin olive oil or Lemon Oil {page 285} per egg. Salt lightly. Spread on the crostini and top each with a bite-sized piece of smoked trout fillet and freshly cracked black pepper. This simple egg salad is also good with slivered raw asparagus in place of favas. Sliver just the center section of the spears ~ especially when raw, it is the sweetest part and has the best texture; save the tips to use elsewhere.

Wine: Bonny Doon Pacific Rim Riesling, 2000

CROSTINI *with* EGG SALAD, ROSEMARY-PICKLED PEPPERS, *&* SMOKED PROSCIUTTO

Prepare crostini with extra-virgin olive oil {see page 122}.

Prepare 1 hard-cooked egg {see page 508} for each 3 crostini. Peel the warm eggs and mash with 1 tablespoon extra-virgin olive oil per egg. Salt lightly. Spread on the crostini and top each with a few strips of smoked prosciutto and a few thin strips of Rosemary-Pickled Peppers {page 273}. Garnish with a few leaves of rosemary fished from the pickle brine. You can substitute regular prosciutto or serrano ham for the smoked prosciutto.

Wine: Rioja Crianza, CUNE, 1999

CROSTINI *with* GRILLED FOIE GRAS, *&* A FEW FAVORITE GARNISHES

Allow about 1-1/2 ounces foie gras for each 2 crostini. {For notes on choosing foie gras, see page 436.}

Prepare dry crostini ~ the foie gras is so rich in fat that you don't need to oil the bread. Build a small grill fire and let it burn to glowing coals. Spread the coals, position the grill about 4 inches above them, and preheat it. Set the bread

\ *continued*

over the hottest part of the fire so it quickly colors on the outside but remains tender in the middle. Then set the toast on the side of the grill, away from direct heat. Slice the foie gras very evenly, 3/8 inch thick, at an angle that will produce slices that will span a few bars of your grill ~ if the slices are too short, they may tip and fall between. Salt evenly on both sides. Set on the grill, but not directly over the hottest coals, or the inevitable dripping fat may flare up and scorch the liver. Cook until just soft and branded with chestnut-colored grill marks, about 30 seconds. Using tongs aided by an offset spatula, turn over and grill for about 25 seconds on the other side. If the grill is charring any of the liver too fast, pivot the piece of foie gras a quarter turn, but otherwise don't bother trying to get criss-cross grill marks ~ this might result in overcooking the foie gras. Slide onto the waiting toasts.

If grilling is not an option: Prepare the crostini in the oven. Cook the foie gras on a hot griddle or in your smallest skillet, preheated for about 30 seconds over medium-high heat. Don't add fat to the griddle or pan; the foie gras will produce plenty in the first sizzling seconds. Cook until golden brown and just soft, about 30 seconds per side.

Wine: Meursault Premier Cru Les Charmes, Joseph Matrot, 1999

+ *with Arugula and Hazelnuts:* Dress a few small leaves of arugula {or torn large leaves} per crostini with mild red wine vinaigrette and add a few roasted, skinned, and finely chopped hazelnuts. Arrange a few leaves flat on each warm crostini and press a slice of hot foie gras on top.

+ *with Brandied Red Currants* {page 281}: Dress a few leaves of baby lettuce with mild red wine vinaigrette spiked with syrup from the brandied currants. Lay the leaves flat on each toast and set the hot foie gras on top. Garnish each crostini with a tiny sprig of brandied currants. You can eat the tender stems.

+
+ +

Rosemary-Grilled Chicken Livers & Bacon
with Balsamic–Onion Marmalade Toasts

This is a perennial favorite appetizer, which we offer regularly during the cold winter months, and sometimes during chilly San Francisco summers as well. We occasionally substitute wedges of grilled polenta {see page 192} for the toast.

This recipe produces more onion marmalade than you need for 4 servings. I find it's difficult to cook it slowly enough to get the right texture in smaller batches, but given that it takes about an hour and a half to cook properly and keeps well, making "too much" is a fine idea. You can serve it on crostini, next to a main course of pork, squab, or quail, or with a warm frisée or dandelion salad. If you don't have time to make the marmalade, serve the warm livers drizzled with strong balsamic vinaigrette instead.

Wine: Mas de la Garrigue, Côtes du Roussillon Villages, 2000

FOR 4 SERVINGS:

4 branches of fresh rosemary, 6 to 8 inches long, to use as skewers

9 to 10 ounces chicken livers {1 generous cup, 7 to 8 livers}

Salt and freshly cracked pepper

A few tablespoons mild-tasting olive oil

4 thin slices meaty bacon {about 2 ounces}

4 large slices chewy, peasant-style bread, about 1/4 inch thick

6 to 8 tablespoons Onion Marmalade {recipe follows} or a few spoonfuls strong balsamic vinaigrette made with equal parts balsamic vinegar and extra-virgin olive oil, with salt to taste

Prepare a small grill fire and leave it to burn down to glowing coals.

Strip most of the leaves off the rosemary branches, leaving only a tassel at the tip of each; set the leaves aside. Cut the stem ends cleanly on a steep angle.

Separate the lobes of the chicken livers and trim the veins and discoloration. Season very lightly with salt, cracked pepper and a trickle of olive oil. Bruise a

\ *continued*

few of the rosemary leaves with the back of your knife to encourage them to express their flavor, then toss them with the livers.

Cut each slice of bacon into segments about 3 inches long. Assemble the brochettes, wrapping the bacon segments partially around the pieces of liver, then threading the livers on the skewers, making sure to poke through both ends of the bacon to hold it in place. The livers should be touching one another, but not pressed tightly together or the bacon will not cook properly. If you have more pieces of liver than bacon, slide the unwrapped livers on last.

Spread the coals and position the grill about 3 inches above the coals to heat.

Lightly oil the bread and grill briefly on both sides, just long enough to crisp the surface and leave faint char marks. Spread each slice with a very thin layer of the marmalade, then return to the grill to heat through. Arrange the toasts on 4 warm plates.

Meanwhile, grill the liver skewers for about 3 minutes per side. Watch closely and move the little brochettes aside if the melting bacon fat causes flare-ups.

Serve the skewers perched atop the warm toasts. {Drizzle with vinaigrette if using that in place of the marmalade.}

For the onion marmalade:
FOR ABOUT 1-1/4 CUPS:

1 pound sliced red onions {about 2 medium onions}
1 to 2 tablespoons mild-tasting olive oil
About 1/4 teaspoon salt
1 tablespoon plus 2 teaspoons honey
1 bay leaf

1 cup medium-bodied red wine, or a little less of a full-bodied variety
3 tablespoons balsamic vinegar {an inexpensive commercial type is fine here}

Place the onions in a 2-quart saucepan and toss with the olive oil and salt. Set over very low heat, cover, and cook quietly, stirring occasionally, for about 20 minutes. The onions will first "sweat" their moisture, then fall into a mauve mass about an inch deep. Uncover and continue cooking over low heat until that moisture has evaporated and they have softened.

Taste an onion ~ it should have no trace of rawness. Stir in the honey and cook for another few minutes. Add the bay leaf and red wine, bring to a low simmer, and cook until the wine is syrupy and barely puddles in the pan, about 1 hour.

{The acidity in the wine will toughen the cellulose enough to keep the onions from becoming a purée.}

Add the balsamic and cook, maintaining low heat until the liquid is syrupy again. Taste and adjust for salt, sweetness, and acidity, being aware that further cooking is going to mute the acidity of the balsamic.

Raise the heat slightly to evaporate the last of the syrupy liquid. The wine-honey concentrate can scorch rapidly, so you'll need to stir every 15 seconds or so ~ but don't be tempted to curtail this step. The onions will gradually become glossy and the color will become markedly richer as evaporation concentrates the pigments. The marmalade is ready when the mass of onions oozes no liquid and has a suave, marmalade-like consistency. This step can take from a few to 10 minutes, depending on the type of pan and the intensity of heat.

Store any extra marmalade, covered and refrigerated, for up to a few weeks.

⁺
⁺ ⁺

Beef Carpaccio, & Four Ways to Serve It

Carpaccio, a popular culinary idiom that promises a plate lined with thinly sliced meat, fish, or whatever the cook intends to glamorize, has suffered from overexposure, but this does not dim the luster of the brilliant original dish. Born at Harry's Bar in Venice, and named for the Renaissance painter, thin sheets of pounded raw beef carpaccio make a sensual, elegant first course or light main course. The meat is just resistant to the tooth and subtly flavored. Easy to overwhelm, carpaccio shows best in restrained counterpoint, with careful contrasts of flavor, texture, and temperature.

Quang Nguyen, perhaps the cleverest cook among the many I have learned from at Zuni, fine-tuned this technique for preparing the classic dish. The meat should be chilled until very cold ~ but not frozen, since that damages the flavor and the texture ~ and then sliced and pounded by hand.

\ *continued*

Use very fresh, bright red top round for carpaccio, and ask for a chunk that is all from a single muscle. At its best, it has a slight, clean tang and a firm, but not chewy, texture. All of our trials with beef fillet instead have been disappointing in comparison. Although it is easier to trim, and is conveniently shaped, tender fillet reads "mushy" in this context. What's more, served cold and raw, it can taste dull and "organy."

Count on about 3 ounces finished carpaccio per serving, but buy extra to allow for trim. Just under 1 pound should be plenty for 4 servings, and you will likely have some nice scraps left over. You can use them to make a Beef-Mushroom Sauce for pasta {based on the Giblet-Mushroom Sauce, page 214} or add them, in a small proportion, to chuck before you presalt it for the Zuni Hamburger {page 366}.

CARPACCIO *with* LEMON & OLIVE OIL

FOR 4 SERVINGS:

1 pound top round
Salt
Extra-virgin olive oil {a little to brush
    the paper, plus about 1/4 cup to
    garnish}

1 lemon, halved
A small chunk of tuna bottarga, to
    grate on top {optional}

Preparing the sheets of carpaccio:

Trim the meat of every bit of surface discoloration, fat, and sinew. Chill thoroughly to firm the muscle and make it easier to slice.

Cut 8 sheets of parchment paper 12 to 14 inches square.

Position the knife at a right angle to the grain of the muscle and slice the meat 1/4 inch thick. Cutting across the grain allows you to pound the meat evenly and produces the best texture. Excise any sinew or fat you encounter along the way.

Brush one sheet of parchment with olive oil. Lay about 3 ounces of sliced meat in the center. A serving need not be a single slice ~ you may need to compose it of a few smaller slices. If so, make sure the slices are not overlapping {1}. Place a second sheet of paper over the meat and press to smooth. Repeat with the remaining slices of meat to make 4 "packages."

Working outward from the center, pound the meat evenly with a meat pounder or a flat-faced rubber mallet {2}. Pound just hard enough to stretch the muscle without tearing the fibers. If you are too aggressive, the meat will disintegrate into uninteresting bits. Aim for a thickness of 1/16 inch. Hold the paper up to the light to check for evenness {3}. Smooth the pounded carpaccio with one light pass of a rolling pin {4}. The finished sheets of carpaccio will be two to three times bigger around than the unpounded meat.

I   2   3   4   5

Refrigerate promptly. If it suits your schedule, you can complete this phase up to 12 hours in advance, although for optimum flavor, try to serve within 6 hours.

Serving the carpaccio:

Carefully peel off one sheet of parchment from each "package," then lay its exposed meat side on a cold plate. Press to smooth, then carefully peel away the other sheet {5}.

Season lightly and evenly with salt, then finish with a long drizzle of extra-virgin olive oil and a squeeze of lemon juice. I sometimes add a dusting of finely grated bottarga as well. Bottarga is salted, dried fish roe ~ *bottarga di tonno* is made from tuna roe; *bottarga di mugine* is milder, firmer gray mullet roe {see Note, page 183}. Or try one of the following elaborations. In each case, be stingy with the garnishes, they are meant to flatter the carpaccio, not obscure it.

Wine: Domaine Drouhin Oregon Pinot Noir, 1999

CARPACCIO *with* CRISPY ARTICHOKE HEARTS *&* PARMIGIANO-REGGIANO

4 pounded sheets carpaccio {see pages 130–131}

8 small artichokes {firm and heavy for their size}

About 1/2 cup mild-tasting olive oil

Salt

A small chunk of Parmigiano-Reggiano {about 2 ounces}

2 tablespoons capers, rinsed, pressed between dry towels, and barely chopped

2 tablespoons extra-virgin olive oil

1 lemon, halved

Freshly cracked black pepper

Just before serving, "turn" the artichokes. First remove a few outer layers of leaves from each artichoke to reveal the pale, kidskin-soft inner petals. Trim off the tip and stem, then use the tip of a paring knife to trim around the circumference of the base. Thinly slice.

Warm the mild olive oil in a 12-inch skillet over medium heat. Drop an artichoke sliver in the oil, and when it begins to sizzle, add the rest. Stir to coat, then swirl the pan to spread the artichokes into an even lacy layer. They should not quite float in the oil. Stirring every 15 seconds or so, fry until just firm and pale golden on many edges, about 2 to 3 minutes. Scrape the sides of the pan whenever bits of artichoke cling to them, and adjust the heat as needed to maintain a discreet sizzle. The oil should never smoke. Drain in a strainer, then tip the artichokes onto a dry paper towel. Discard the frying oil.

Turn the carpaccio onto plates {page 131} and salt very lightly and evenly. Scatter the gilded slivers, still hot, over the meat. Use a vegetable peeler to shave thin curls of cheese over all. Scatter with the capers, then drizzle with the extra-virgin olive oil and a squeeze of lemon juice. Finish with black pepper.

Wine: Pomino Rosso, Frescobaldi, 1998

CARPACCIO *with* CELERY LEAF SALSA VERDE

4 pounded sheets carpaccio {see pages 130–131}

1/2 cup Celery Leaf Salsa Verde {page 295}

A small chunk of pecorino romano {about 1 ounce}

Turn the carpaccio onto plates {see page 131}. Salt lightly and evenly. Splatter with the salsa verde. Use a vegetable peeler to shave tiny nicks of pecorino romano over all.

For a more ambitious version, garnish each plate with a few little stalks {up to 4 inches long} of fried celery hearts, a modest handful that you can fry properly in just a few cups of peanut oil. {For guidelines, see *Piccolo Fritto*, page 108.}

Wine: Château Routas, "Rouvière," Coteaux Varois Rosé, 2000

⁕ ⁕ CARPACCIO *with* FRIED POTATOES *&* TRUFFLES

The Troisgros brothers served this carpaccio; both loved to wrap the cold meat around the warm, crispy potatoes. The truffles are an optional garnish; lacking them, add a very little truffle oil to the vinaigrette.

1 pound peeled {just over 1 pound whole} yellow-fleshed potatoes, preferably Yellow Finnish or Bintjes, cut into irregular 1-1/2-inch chunks

About 1/2 cup mild-tasting olive oil, for shallow-frying, or 4 cups peanut oil, for deep-frying

1/4 cup extra-virgin olive oil

2 teaspoons Champagne vinegar or white wine vinegar

Salt

A few drops of truffle oil if not using fresh truffles

4 pounded sheets carpaccio {see pages 130–131}

2 handfuls of arugula {about 1-1/2 ounces}, carefully washed and dried, at room temperature

1/2 to 1 ounce fresh black or white truffle {optional}

Cooking the potatoes:

Place the potatoes in a saucepan and add cold water to cover. Season moderately with salt {I use a generous teaspoon sea salt per quart}, stir, and taste. The water should taste perfectly seasoned. Bring to a simmer and cook gently until the potatoes are tender through but not soft on the outside, usually about 5 minutes. Drain and immediately spread out on towels to cool and dry.

To shallow-fry: This operation sounds more tricky than it is. Potatoes fried this way are addictive. Warm the mild olive oil in a 12-inch skillet over medium heat.

\ *continued*

Choose a small, firm piece of potato and set it in the pool of oil. When it begins to sizzle, carefully distribute the rest of the potatoes evenly around the pan. They should just fit, making a starchy mosaic. Some of the potatoes may stick initially, but don't fuss with them now ~ once freed, they are doomed to stick again, leaving a rough crust on the bottom of the pan, which will inevitably burn, instead of browning the potatoes. Adjust the heat to maintain a steady sizzle. The oil should never smoke. After about 5 minutes, the potatoes should be browning around the edges and a nice crust should have set. Swirl the pan cautiously and use tongs or a metal spatula to gently turn the potatoes. It's now okay to pry any slightly reluctant chunks cleanly from the pan. Continue to fry, turning the potatoes occasionally, for about 20 minutes, until they are mottled golden all over and crunchy. {They will shrink a lot as water evaporates from the flesh.} Drain on towels.

To deep-fry: Heat the peanut oil to about 365° in a 3-quart sauté pan. Lower the potatoes into the oil and fry until golden and crispy, usually 5 to 7 minutes. Drain on a towel.

Whichever frying method you use, keep the potatoes warm while you plate the carpaccio. {But don't pile them atop one another, or they will steam and the crust will soften.}

Finishing the carpaccio:
Combine the extra-virgin olive oil, vinegar, and salt to taste. The vinaigrette should be mild, to avoid overwhelming the truffle. If using truffle oil in lieu of truffles, add a few drops to the vinaigrette.

Turn the carpaccio onto plates {see page 131}, then brush or drizzle all over with vinaigrette. Toss the arugula with vinaigrette to coat, and add as much thinly sliced black or white truffle as you could afford. This is the one garnish you need not fear abusing in a carpaccio dish.

Scatter the salad over the meat and finish with the hot, crispy potatoes.

Wine: Baga, Beira, Luis Pato 1999

✛ ✛
✛

LEAFY SALADS

✛ ✛
✛

If you have time, confidence, and energy for no other cooking endeavor on a regular basis, focus on the salad. Simple preparation and spontaneous presentation are among its charms, and with a little careful shopping, sniffing, paring, toasting, and occasionally marinating, a bowl of leaves can become "A Dish" tailored to the season, occasion, budget {time or dollars}, and appetite. The habit of a repetitive hodgepodge of greens and familiar vegetables, often tired, generic hydrator staples, is easy to abandon. As surely as we crave variety in the main course of our meals, it is welcome in this slot.

I offer a dozen salads of leaves and a few other things, chosen and turned out to flatter one another visually, tastewise, and texturewise. As you are tempted to vary or embellish them, remember it's best to keep salad uncomplicated ~ which usually means keep the number of ingredients limited to just a few thoughtfully matched elements. A harmony of leaf, nut, cheese, and a particular vinegar can become a garbled mess when a few extra, well-meaning ingredients weigh it down. Save them.

We serve these salads most often as a first course or middle course, but some work well with the main course, next to grilled or roasted birds, fish, or meat. You will find such suggestions in the recipes. A few of the richer salads ~ Arugula with Cucumbers, Radishes, Cracker Bread, Feta, and Mint and the Caesar Salad ~ may be satisfying as a main course at lunch, or for dinner when lunch was a big meal. Many of these salads, especially those with fruits, will be as welcome after a main course as at the beginning of a meal. And I sometimes close a meal with one of the rich, savory-sweet salads in place of a traditional dessert. I keep a jar of biscotti and a tablet of chocolate in the pantry, in case anyone craves a familiar sweet afterward.

Types *of* Greens

With any of these salads, variety of flavor and texture begins with the leaves themselves. Lettuces can be sweet or pleasantly mineraly, with silky leaves or crunchy ones; chicories range from sweet to mild to bitter, and their texture from satiny {Belgian endive} to bristly {curly endive}, tendrily {frisée}, cabbagey {radicchio}, and leafy {escarole}. Stemmy dandelion has an intense, bitter, earthy flavor. We use lots of nutty, radishy arugula; crisp, refreshingly "icy-hot" watercress; and tissue-tender baby mustard leaves with their sneaky wasabi-like bite. There is the odd lot of lamb's lettuce {mâche}, which tastes to me the way crushed rose petals smell. Thoughtfully named, *minutina* resembles nothing more than tiny blades of freshly mown grass but tastes like raw spinach and is delightful to eat. It is too fragile to be widely distributed but is as easy to grow as grass. To grow your own, look for seeds for *erba stella* and harvest it young.

CHOOSING & WASHING THE LEAVES

FOR ANY OF THESE SALADS, LOOK FOR FRESHLY CUT GREENS; GROW YOUR OWN IF you can. When buying loose mixes, check the cut ends of the leaves; if they are rusty colored, chances are the greens were harvested more than a few days ago. If any of the leaves are beginning to discolor, the whole head or mix is probably old, or hasn't been kept cool enough. Inspect the greens before you wash them, culling wilted or damaged leaves or parts of leaves. Cut off the root end and check for damage inside heads of lettuce. To wash, add the inspected leaves to a large bath of cool water ~ don't run the faucet at full bore on the leaves, as that can bruise the leaves. Swish them around, then lift them out gently so grit and dirt stay behind. Repeat with fresh water baths until the water is pristine. Watch for missed flaws as you transfer the leaves to a salad spinner. Spin dry in small batches, so you don't crush the tender leaves ~ bruising will damage the flavor.

DRESSING THE SALAD

WHEN YOU ARE READY TO DRESS THE SALAD, CHECK TO MAKE SURE IT IS DRY; IF not, place the greens in the salad bowl and toss with a few pieces of dry paper towel to soak up lingering drops of water. Wet leaves will make the brightest dressing insipid. Make sure the bowl is dry too. {Occasionally I chill ~ or slightly warm ~ a salad bowl, to make sure the salad is the temperature I intend.} The bowl ought to be wide and large enough to hold twice as much salad as you are dress-ing ~ that way you can easily distribute the ingredients over the leaves and then thoroughly toss the salad without crushing any of them, or sending any over the edge. Use a ceramic, glass, or metal salad bowl, not unfinished wood, which can retain flavors. As you add the dressing, consider the character of the greens. Fleshy and strongly flavored greens generally need to be heavily dressed; tender leaves with delicate flavor, more scantily so. Likewise, the tenderest leaves want just enough gentle tossing and turning to coat each surface, while some heartier greens are best *bien fatigués* ~ "tired out" ~ with a longer, but still gentle, tossing. Your hands are the kindest tool for tossing salads ~ I love the feel of scooping up the leaves and sliding them between my fingers, coating each surface with dressing. Spoons and tongs always seem awkward and inefficient, and they tend to bruise the most tender lettuces. Where a salad has a couple of elements, the sequence in which they are dressed matters, for taste, texture, and appearance. And forget not to taste. Taste a leaf dry, and taste the dressing by itself. Dip a leaf in the dressing and taste again. Doctor the dressing if it needs it ~ with any of its ingredients, or others you have learned that you like ~ then taste again. Dress the salad, and taste again. In all the recipes that follow, amounts of leaf and dressing are only guidelines. The right amount of salad and of dressing is most easily determined by eye, taste, and feel, so follow your own instincts where they tell you to make more or less vinaigrette for your unmeasured bowl of greens. Dress all these salads just before you serve them.

Fortunately, all these advisories amount to more words than work. Each becomes second nature in no time.

* * * * *

WINE & SALADS

WINE IS NOT EASILY RECONCILED WITH VINEGAR, NO MATTER HOW discreetly it's used. When a green salad is served as a refresher after a main course, that doesn't necessarily matter. But it might when a composed salad is served as a first course ~ or even as a main course for a light lunch. A mild rice vinegar in the dressing will accommodate most white wines. Garlic ~ rubbed either on croûtons or on the inside of the bowl ~ helps bring a red wine and a conventional vinaigrette together. Yvonne Geoffray of Château Thivin used to dress her favorite lamb's lettuce salad with walnut oil brightened with a few drops of old Cognac instead of vinegar to take us from meat to cheese without a change of palate.

* * * * *

MIXED LETTUCES & GREENS *with* GARLIC CHAPONS

Shop for, or grow, a mix of young loose lettuce leaves, arugula, chervil, and frisée sprigs for this mesclun* salad. *Chapons* are a scrap of Gascony~ croûtons made from the crusty heel of yesterday's bread. They are good broken up and tossed in any salad where you like croûtons, and we float or simmer them in soups as well. Use the leftover "crumb" part of the loaf for bread salad {see Zuni Roast Chicken with Bread Salad, page 392}, for *Pappa al Pomodoro* {page 164}, or for bread crumbs.

A handful of tender, nutty, and frizzy greens is always friendly just before or after an elaborate main course but can be elegant with a simple main course as well, as an alternative to blanched, braised, or grilled green vegetables. We nest grilled or roasted birds in mesclun salad garnished with roasted Brandied Fruit {page 279} or crowd it with Roasted Figs {see page 83} next to Roasted Leg of Lamb {page 394}. It's lovely scattered over Beef Carpaccio {page 129}.

I describe here how we dress this simple salad, tossing it first with oil, then salt and vinegar. But you can stir the dressing ingredients together into a little vinaigrette in advance if you prefer.

FOR 4 SERVINGS:

For the chapons:

A crusty 4- to 5-ounce chunk of chewy, peasant-style bread

About 1 tablespoon extra-virgin olive oil

1 garlic clove, cut in half

To finish the salad:

About 1/4 cup extra-virgin olive oil

About 1 tablespoon red wine vinegar, sherry vinegar, or Champagne vinegar

4 to 5 ounces mixed young lettuces and greens, carefully washed and dried

Salt

Freshly cracked black pepper

\ *continued*

---

* Mesclun means "mixture" in Provençal dialect. I called this salad Mesclun on our menu for ten years before conceding that the exotic foreign word generated more confusion than romance. To many, it sounded hallucinogenic.

Preheat the oven to 400°.

Carve a few 1/8- to 1/4-inch-thick curved slabs of crust off the bread, you need 1 to 2 ounces. Brush them lightly all over with olive oil and sprinkle lightly with salt. Spread the crusts on a sheet pan and bake until golden brown on the edges but still pale in the middle, about 5 to 7 minutes.

When the *chapons* are just cool enough to handle, rub with the cut garlic clove, gingerly or thoroughly, depending on your fondness for garlic.

Break the crisp *chapons* into bite-sized pieces into a salad bowl. Drizzle with a little of the olive oil and vinegar and toss to distribute. Add the greens and drizzle and toss with olive oil until lightly coated. Season lightly and evenly with salt, and toss again. Taste, then sprinkle with vinegar and toss again. If the greens are sweet and delicate in flavor, it is a shame to insult them with too much vinegar; if the lettuces are minerally or if your mix is heavy on arugula or frisée, you may use the whole dose, or more. Taste again and toss with more oil, vinegar, and/or salt as you like. Offer freshly cracked black pepper at the table.

✧
✧ ✧

MIXED LETTUCES *with* MANDARINS, HAZELNUTS, & HAZELNUT VINAIGRETTE

USE SILKY YOUNG LETTUCES, BY THEMSELVES OR MIXED WITH ENDIVE OR ARUGULA. Fragrant mandarins come into season in December, and are refreshing and beautiful in salads. They will taste best in this salad if they are at room temperature or just cool, not cold. Frangelico is a hazelnut liqueur that perfumes the salad as the alcohol releases its sweet, nutty scent. For a toastier flavor, substitute a few drops of hazelnut oil. A beautiful variation on this salad consists of arugula, blood oranges, slivered fennel, and toasted almonds, tossed with sherry vinaigrette, perfumed with Amaretto, Cointreau, or Grand Marnier. Another joins endive, frisée, tangelos, and pistachios with coriander-scented vinaigrette, garnished with a drizzle of crème fraîche. The combination of satiny, scraggly, tart, nutty, crunchy, and creamy ends up being elegant.

This salad is good before or after a main course, particularly one featuring game birds or lamb.

FOR 4 SERVINGS:

About 24 hazelnuts {3/4 ounce, or a scant 1/4 cup}

2 to 3 mandarins {about 8 ounces}

1/4 cup extra-virgin olive oil

1 tablespoon Champagne vinegar or white wine vinegar

A splash of Frangelico liqueur or hazelnut oil

Salt

4 to 5 ounces mixed young lettuces, carefully washed and dried

Preheat the oven to 325°.

Roast the hazelnuts on a small baking sheet until the skins darken and begin to split, 10 to 15 minutes. While they are still hot, bundle them in a towel beanbag-style, then scrunch and massage them to rub off most of their skins. Pick the nuts from the chaff and chop them coarsely.

Slice both ends off each mandarin, cutting just deeply enough to expose the juicy flesh. Setting the fruit on end, use a paring knife to carve away the skin and pith in a series of smooth, arcing strokes from top to bottom, rotating the mandarin a little with each stroke as you work your way around the sphere. {Most of us misjudge and miss a little pith on the first go-round, but this is easy to trim once you've removed the bulky skin.} Slice the mandarins evenly into 1/4-inch-thick pinwheels. Collect the slices and juice on a plate.

Combine the oil, vinegar, Frangelico or hazelnut oil, a trickle of juice from the mandarins, and salt to taste. Dip a lettuce leaf in the dressing, taste, and correct. Spoon a little of the vinaigrette over the mandarin slices. Tilt the plate to distribute it.

Drizzle and toss the lettuces with enough vinaigrette to coat them lightly but evenly. Taste. Toss in the hazelnuts, then distribute most of the leaves among individual plates. Slide and tuck the sliced mandarins among the leaves, then scatter with the remaining leaves and the hazelnuts. Drizzle the vinaigrette from the mandarin plate over the salads.

⁜

Mixed Lettuces *with* Roasted Cherries, Hazelnuts, *&* Warm Saint-Marcellin

A HANDSOME SALAD I LIKE TO SERVE AT THE END OF A MEAL FEATURING RED MEAT, pork, or game birds. It is lovely made with tender young red lettuces whose leaves are no more than a few inches long. Mix with a little arugula or frisée if you like. Saint-Marcellin is a rich cow's milk cheese with a slightly yeasty tang and some fruity notes. I've eaten syrupy ripe Saint-Marcellin out of the cup it's sold in with a tiny plastic spoon provided by the *affineur* {cheese "refiner"}, but this salad wants a fairly firm specimen, with only a bit of downy, white mold on the surface. It should feel like firm custard, as opposed to soft pudding. A young Banon is a good alternative to Saint-Marcellin~it is the same size and has similar character. It is wrapped in chestnut leaves, which are convenient for warming purposes. Do check to make sure no gray mold hides beneath these leaves. Although it's usually inoffensive, after heating its flavor may be too strong.

FOR 4 SERVINGS:

About 24 hazelnuts {3/4 ounce, or a scant 1/4 cup}

16 ripe red cherries {about 6 ounces}, such as Bing, Van, Larian, or Burlat

About 1/4 cup extra-virgin olive oil

A few splashes of kirsch or grappa {optional}

About 1 tablespoon red wine vinegar

Salt

2 wheels Saint-Marcellin {about 3 ounces each} at room temperature

4 to 5 ounces mixed young lettuces, such as red oak leaf, red perella, and baby red romaine, carefully washed and dried

4 slices chewy, peasant-style bread

Preheat the oven to 325°.

Roast the hazelnuts on a small baking sheet until the skins darken and start to split, 10 to 15 minutes. Remove from the oven and turn the oven up to 400°.

While the nuts are still hot, bundle them in a towel beanbag-style, then scrunch and massage them to rub off most of their skins. Pick out the nuts and coarsely chop.

Rub the cherries with a few drops of olive oil, and season with a few drops of the optional alcohol and a pinch of salt.

Combine the oil, vinegar, and salt to taste. Add another few drops of kirsch or grappa, if you like, and taste again.

Place the cheeses on squares of parchment paper and place, with the cherries, on a sheet pan {the cherries might roll off a cookie sheet}. Roast until the fruit is near to bursting and the cheese is beginning to slouch, about 6 minutes. If your cheese is riper than described in the headnote, it may begin oozing fairly rapidly and you may need to remove it before it is hot throughout.

Dress the lettuces and hazelnuts very skimpily in the vinaigrette and arrange the leaves on plates, leaving the nuts behind for the moment. Garnish with the warm cherries and nest a half of the warm cheese next to each salad. {If you are using Banon, you can remove the chestnut leaves first.} Sprinkle the hazelnuts over the top of the salads. Offer toasted peasant-style bread.

✢
✢ ✢

BUTTER LETTUCE *with* ORANGES, AVOCADO, *&* SHALLOT VINAIGRETTE

A PRETTY, SATINY WINTER SALAD. The combination is good with watercress as well. Use Hass avocados that are just yielding to the touch and sweet ripe oranges, or tangerines, tangelos, mandarins, or Ruby Red grapefruit ~ or a combination of citrus. We sometimes scatter radish coins over the finished salad. I like this salad best when everything except the vinaigrette is cold. A popular variation on this salad pairs endive and frisée with grapefruit and avocado, then sweetens the vinaigrette with a little honey or Chartreuse liqueur.

Very good before, or with, cracked crab or cold shrimp.

\ *continued*

FOR 4 SERVINGS:

2 medium oranges {about 12 ounces}, chilled

1 to 2 heads green butter lettuce, trimmed of damaged or tough outer leaves {to yield 8 to 12 ounces}

About 1/2 cup extra-virgin olive oil

About 2 tablespoons Champagne vinegar or white wine vinegar

1 medium shallot {about 1/2 ounce}, finely diced

Salt

1 large or 2 small ripe avocados, chilled

Slice both ends off each orange, cutting just deeply enough to expose the juicy flesh. Setting the fruit on end, use a paring knife to carve away the skin and pith in a series of smooth, arcing strokes from top to bottom, rotating the orange a little with each stroke as you work your way around the sphere; then go back and trim any pith you may have missed. Next, working over a wide bowl, slide the blade of a paring knife close to the membranes on either side of each segment and gently pry out the fragile sections; don't worry if some of them break. Tease out any seeds you encounter as you go. Squeeze the remaining juice from the orange "carcasses" over the orange sections.

Inspect the lettuce: If the heads feel tight and solid, simply wash and dry, trim the root ends, and cut into 1-inch wedges. If the heads are light and not very hearty, carve out the root ends and wash and dry the individual leaves. In either case, look for and trim or discard bruised or damaged inner leaves.

Combine the oil, vinegar, shallot, salt to taste, and a little of the juice from the oranges. Taste. Add a splash of this vinaigrette to the oranges and swirl to distribute it.

Toss the lettuce with enough dressing to coat well, then taste. {If using wedges of lettuce, gently fan them open as you toss them to urge the dressing between the leaves.} Arrange on cold plates or a platter.

Cut the avocados in half and remove the pits. Run a rubber spatula around the edge of each avocado half next to the skin, then ease it under the meat. You should be able to pop out the halves. If they resist, cut into quarters and try again. Trim any discolorations and slice into 1/2-inch-thick wedges or slices.

Tuck the avocados randomly among the lettuce leaves. Distribute the orange sections, then strategically drizzle their vinaigrette-spiked juice, followed by some or all of the remaining vinaigrette, over the salads, targeting the avocado slices.

✢
✢ ✢

PROSCIUTTO & WHITE ROSE NECTARINES
with GREEN ALMONDS, *page 84*

AIR-DRIED BEEF *&* FUYU PERSIMMONS
with EXTRA-VIRGIN OLIVE OIL *&* BALSAMIC VINEGAR, *page 93*

RAW WHITE ASPARAGUS & PORCINI MUSHROOMS
with TRUFFLED CRUTIN, *page 96*

NEW YEAR'S EVE GOUGÈRES *with* ARUGULA, BACON,
*& * CAROL'S PICKLED ONIONS, *page 116*

MIXED LETTUCES *with* ROASTED CHERRIES,
HAZELNUTS, *& *WARM SAINT-MARCELLIN, *page 142*

ASPARAGUS & RICE SOUP *with*
PANCETTA & BLACK PEPPER, *page 166*

PASTA ALLA CARBONARA, *page 210*

ZUNI RICOTTA GNOCCHI, *page 221*

LAMB'S LETTUCE *with* RAW ASPARAGUS, PISTACHIOS, *&* PARMIGIANO-REGGIANO

USE FLESHY JUMBO ASPARAGUS FOR THIS SPRING SALAD, THE PURPLE VARIETY IF you see any in the market. Since it is served raw, it will retain its color. You may be surprised to learn that the stem of any spear of asparagus is sweeter than the tip, especially raw. So trim off the pretty tips and save them for risotto, or pasta.

By itself, this spring salad makes a good first course. It is delicious and lovely piled in a small mound on thinly sliced prosciutto.

FOR 4 SERVINGS:

2 tablespoons raw, shelled pistachios
    {about 1/2 ounce}
1/4 cup extra-virgin olive oil
1 tablespoon Champagne vinegar or
    white wine vinegar
Salt

4 spears jumbo asparagus, tips removed
    and reserved for another use
4 to 5 ounces lamb's lettuce, carefully
    washed and dried
A small chunk of Parmigiano-Reggiano
    {about 1 ounce}

Preheat the oven to 350°.

Heat the pistachios in a small pan in the oven until just warm, 2 to 3 minutes. This will heighten their flavor. They should remain bright green.

Coarsely chop the pistachios, culling any shriveled and discolored nuts.

Combine the oil, vinegar, and salt to taste.

Starting at the tip ends, slice the asparagus on a steep angle into 1/8-inch-thick ovals. As you work your way down each stalk, taste an occasional sliver, and stop slicing when the flesh becomes tough. Discard the woody ends.

Toss the lamb's lettuce, asparagus, and pistachios with enough vinaigrette to coat. Taste.

Divide among cold plates, leaving some of the pistachios in the bowl. Use a vegetable peeler to shave tiny curls of the cheese over the salads, then sprinkle the rest of the nuts on top.

Minutina Salad *with* Vegetable Confetti *&* Coriander Vinaigrette

I FELL FOR *MINUTINA* THE FIRST TIME I MISTOOK IT FOR LAWN CLIPPINGS ~ THIS AT Eastertime in a three-stall market in Impruneta, not far south of Florence. Harvested young, the leaves of *erba stella* {*Plantago coronopus*} are vaguely succulent in texture and have a pleasant, mineraly taste, a little like raw spinach. Although I have never seen *minutina* in an American market, I include it here not as a taunt or curiosity, but instead to promote the little plant, which is easy to grow and makes a fetching salad. We have clients who ask regularly if there might be a little in-house even when they don't see it on the menu. It is at least as fragile as baby lettuces and arugula ~ and with all that surface area, it needs to be dried very carefully ~ but is otherwise a friendly ingredient. Ask about it at your local produce market or farmers' market. Or, if you grow salad greens {or know someone who does} plant a little. Clip it while it is tiny. {For seed sources, see page 518.}

This salad celebrates the texture of *minutina.* Select a stout carrot for the julienne ~ it will be easier to manipulate. Choose small, firm radishes ~ really large ones often taste dank or dull, and soft, pithy ones disappoint. {The leftover truncated celery root will be handy for Catherine's Celery Root, page 91.} For richness, we sometimes garnish this salad with wedges of marinated beets. All of the ingredients should be cold. If you can't get *minutina,* and you like raw spinach salads, consider this alternative: stack a dozen tender leaves at a time, then roll like a cigar and slice into thin strings to use in place of the *minutina.*

FOR 4 SERVINGS:

4 to 5 ounces *minutina*

A few coriander seeds

About 1/4 cup extra-virgin olive oil

About 1 tablespoon Champagne vinegar or white wine vinegar

Salt

A fat 2-inch chunk of carrot, peeled {about 2 ounces}

1/2 small celery root, peeled {about 2 ounces}

1/2 fennel bulb, trimmed {about 3 ounces}

4 small radishes

Carefully wash and drain the *minutina,* then spin-dry in small batches. You may want to spin each batch with a dry paper towel, and then layer the clean leaves with fresh, dry towels. Handle very gently.

Warm the coriander seeds briefly in a small pan over medium heat to heighten their flavor. Crush lightly in a mortar.

Combine the oil, vinegar, coriander, and salt to taste. I find *minutina* tastes best when the vinaigrette is slightly high-acid and a little salty. Taste a few blades dipped in the dressing to check.

Use a mandoline to slice the carrot and celery root lengthwise as thin as possible. Stack a few slices at a time and cut them, again lengthwise, into little strings. Line up the celery root strings and cut into tiny dice. Place the carrot strings and celery root specks in a wide salad bowl.

Using the mandoline, shave the fennel into thin sickles, and the radish into coins, over the carrot and celery root. Toss with the vinaigrette to coat well. Add the *minutina,* then drizzle with more vinaigrette. Toss gently. The tender leaves will mat if overdressed or overhandled. Taste.

Fluff the salad as you serve it promptly on cold plates.

✦
✦ ✦

Arugula Salad *with* Raw Sweet Corn *&* Sweet 100 Tomatoes

While everyone seems to know that corn is at its best eaten just after it's picked, it's barely appreciated that arugula is just as fragile ~ its bright nuttiness turns stale after a day or so. Tomatoes keep a little longer, but don't refrigerate them, just store them in a cool spot. Make this salad when you can get really young corn whose tender, juicy kernels resemble pearl-like "buds." More mature ears ~ fine for boiling ~ will yield dry kernels that may taste bland or cardboardy when raw.

Good by itself, or with grilled chicken or beef. Serve at room temperature.

FOR 4 SERVINGS:

4 to 5 ounces Sweet 100 or other small, ripe cherry tomatoes {about 1 cup, 25 tomatoes}

2 very young, small ears white corn {you need about 1/2 cup kernels}

5 tablespoons extra-virgin olive oil

1 tablespoon Champagne vinegar or white wine vinegar

1 small shallot {about 1/4 ounce}, finely diced

Salt and freshly cracked black pepper

4 ounces arugula, carefully washed and dried

Stem, wash, and dry the tomatoes. Cut them in half.

To scrape the corn: Shuck the ears and remove all the silk. Trim the tip from each but don't break off the stalk; it makes a convenient handle. Holding the cob at an angle, use a sharp knife to slice off the kernels, positioning the blade flat against the ear and sliding it smoothly down the length of the ear. Aim for the base of the kernels, but try not to cut into the hard cob itself. Rotate the ear a little after each swipe, until you have harvested all of the kernels. Crumble between your fingers to separate any clusters.

Combine the oil, vinegar, shallot, and salt and pepper to taste. Make this vinaigrette low in acid, to allow the sweetness of the vegetables to define the salad.

Place the arugula in a wide salad bowl and toss with enough vinaigrette to coat well. Taste. Scatter the tomato halves and corn kernels over the leaves, add the remaining vinaigrette, and fold to distribute. Taste again and correct the oil, vinegar, or salt.

Distribute among four plates, taking care to display all the elements.

✦
✦ ✦

Arugula Salad *with* Cucumbers, Radishes, Cracker Bread, Feta, *&* Mint

This salad quietly challenges our caesar for having the most passionate advocates.

Use a small to medium-sized cucumber ~ really large ones tend to have lots of not very tasty seeds, which, having drained the best from the pulp, leave it watery and stale tasting. We use English, Japanese, or Mediterranean cucumbers, which have a melony flavor and perfume. Or look in farmers' markets for the curvy, ridged, pastel green Armenian cucumbers, which have a delicate flavor and dense, crunchy texture. In any case, taste one sliver with and another without the skin to decide whether you want to peel it. Substitute a few halved, ripe cherry tomatoes for the radishes if you like.

FOR 4 SERVINGS:

4 to 6 fresh mint leaves

About 6 tablespoons extra-virgin olive oil

About 1-1/2 tablespoons red wine vinegar

Salt

1-1/2 ounces plain cracker bread

About 4 ounces arugula, carefully washed and dried

1 small, firm cucumber {about 6 ounces} or a portion of a medium cucumber

4 small radishes, leaves and tails trimmed

2 ounces feta, drained

Freshly cracked black pepper

12 small black olives, such as Niçoise, Ligurian, or Greek Elitses

\ *continued*

Coarsely chop the mint leaves. Combine with the oil, vinegar, and salt to taste.

Break the cracker bread into bite-sized pieces into a wide salad bowl, then toss with about one-third of the vinaigrette. Add the arugula and fold to distribute the bread.

Peel the cucumber, if you choose, then use a mandoline to slice it lengthwise into very thin, rippley "serpentines." Or, if you don't have a mandoline, use a chef's knife and slice as thin as possible on a very steep angle. Slice the radishes into coins. Add the cucumbers and radishes to the salad and drizzle with the remaining vinaigrette, then fold gently but thoroughly to coat well. Crumble the feta over the salad, add a few grinds of black pepper, and fold to distribute. Taste. Don't hesitate to make and add extra vinaigrette if the salad seems dry; the cracker bread can soak up a lot of dressing. Add salt, oil, or vinegar to taste.

Distribute the salad among plates, making sure to include some of each component in each portion. Garnish with the olives.

⁜
⁜ ⁜

Shredded Radicchio *with* Anchovy Vinaigrette, Bread Crumbs, *&* Sieved Egg

A STRONG-FLAVORED SALAD WITH AN UNUSUAL TEXTURE. Good by itself or with grilled seafood ~ tuna, swordfish, or scallops in particular ~ or with roast chicken. For a different flavor balance, you can replace some of the radicchio with escarole hearts or Belgian endive, or use a bitter radicchio ~ Castelfranco or Treviso variety.

FOR 4 SERVINGS:

1-1/2 ounces fresh, soft bread crumbs {about 3/4 cup} made from slightly stale, crustless, chewy, white peasant-style bread {see page 506}

About 1/2 cup extra-virgin olive oil

About 1-1/2 tablespoons red wine vinegar

About 1-1/2 teaspoons chopped salt-packed anchovy fillets {2 to 3 fillets}

1 large shallot {about 1 ounce}, finely diced

Salt

About 2 medium heads radicchio {about 12 ounces}

2 hard-cooked eggs {see page 508}, freshly cooked and peeled

Freshly cracked black pepper

Preheat the oven to 400°.

Combine the bread crumbs with about a tablespoon of the olive oil and knead very gently to distribute it. Spread the crumbs on a sheet pan and bake until they are unevenly golden, about 6 minutes. You may need to rotate the pan or stir the crumbs with a spatula. {The crumbs will shrink to about 1/2 cup in volume.} Cool completely.

Combine the remaining oil, the vinegar, anchovies, shallot, and salt to taste.

Remove any damaged outer leaves from the radicchio, then rinse, dry, and quarter it. Remove the stem and core, then slice as if for coleslaw, about 1/8 inch thick. Place in a salad bowl and toss and fluff to separate into individual threads. Incorporate the toasted crumbs. Drizzle the vinaigrette evenly over the salad and toss well to combine. Taste and add more salt, oil, or vinegar as needed.

Press the eggs through a strainer, or grate on the finest face of a grater, letting the mimosa-like bits fall evenly over the salad. Give the salad only one or two folds to distribute the eggs, then serve. Offer cracked black pepper.

✢
✢ ✢

WATERCRESS SALAD *with* BEETS
& WALNUT-MASCARPONE CROSTINI

THIS SIMPLE WINTER SALAD STRIKES SEVERAL CHORDS: THE PEPPERY WATERCRESS IS a foil for the sweet mascarpone~as are the crunchy walnuts. Rich, meaty beets and walnuts have an earthy affinity. The black currant vinegar adds a fruity note to the iron-rich beets, and its perfume is strong enough to tame the cress. If you can't find it, use red wine vinegar and add a few drops of black currant liqueur *{crème de cassis},* a drop of raspberry vinegar, or a trickle of fruity red wine to the dressing. I always try to cook beets a day in advance; I have found that they have a rounder, sweeter, richer flavor after a night in the refrigerator. And it is nice to have them ready.

FOR 4 GENEROUS SERVINGS:

8 golf ball–sized beets {about 1 pound}

About 1-1/2 tablespoons black currant vinegar

Salt

About 6 tablespoons extra-virgin olive oil

2 ounces walnuts {about 2/3 cup}, preferably freshly shelled

A few 1/4-inch-thick slices chewy, peasant-style bread {about 2 ounces total}

1/4 cup mascarpone, at room temperature

About 4 ounces watercress, carefully washed and dried

Walnut oil, to taste {optional}

Trim, roast, peel, and retrim the beets {see page 240}. Cut into 1/2-inch wedges. Splash with a few teaspoons of the vinegar and season with salt. Coat with olive oil, folding to distribute, and taste. For the best flavor, cover and marinate overnight in the refrigerator. {The beets will keep for a week or so. If you do prepare them in advance, plan on setting them out at room temperature for a half hour or so before assembling the salad.}

Preheat the oven to 300°.

Spread the walnuts on a baking sheet and place in the oven until just warm through, about 5 minutes. Place them, still warm, between towels, and rub gently to remove some of the tannic skin. Pick out the nutmeats and shake in a strainer to cull little bits of skin.

Toast the slices of bread, then cut into 8 two-bite–sized pieces. Spread each piece thickly with the mascarpone, then stud with the walnut pieces.

Place the beets and their marinade in a bowl and toss gently with the watercress. Add more oil, vinegar, and salt to taste. If you like, add a few drops of walnut oil. Serve cool, garnished with the warm crostini.

+ + *Variation* WATERCRESS SALAD *with* BEETS & TAPENADE–GOAT CHEESE
CROSTINI

Prepare the salad as described above, adding a grating of orange zest to the beets when you dress them. Spread each crostini first with a teaspoon of Orange-Olive Tapenade {page 304}, then top with a smudge of cakey, fresh goat cheese.

+
+ +

ENDIVE & FUYU PERSIMMON SALAD *with* PECANS

A RICH, SLIPPERY, FLESHY SALAD THAT CAN SUPPLANT DESSERT. Choose Fuyus that are saturated orange in color and as firm as a slightly underripe peach, or the skin of a just ripe banana. {Don't use the torpedo-shaped Hachiya persimmons, which need to be jelly-soft before they are edible. For more on choosing Fuyus, see Air-Dried Beef with Fuyu Persimmons, Extra-Virgin Olive Oil, and Balsamic Vinegar, page 93.} This salad is also nice with a few sprigs of watercress for contrast. You'll get a very different flavor balance, still delicious and unusual.

FOR 4 SERVINGS:

About 24 pecan halves {1 ounce, or 1/3 cup}

About 1 pound endive {about 4 heads}, chilled

1 large or 2 small Fuyu persimmons {about 8 ounces total}, chilled

About 6 tablespoons extra-virgin olive oil

About 1 tablespoon Champagne vinegar or white wine vinegar

Salt

\ *continued*

Preheat the oven to 350°.

Warm the pecans on a small baking sheet for about 4 minutes, just to heighten their flavor. Let them cool, then break along the natural folds.

Remove or trim any damaged outer leaves from the endive. Rinse, dry, and then slice each one on a steep angle into long, saberlike pieces, rolling the endive a quarter-turn with each cut. Work your way down to the solid core, and discard it.

Use the tip of a paring knife to carve out the stem end of the persimmons, then remove a thin wedge and taste. If the skin is tender and you like it, leave it on; otherwise, peel with a vegetable peeler. Cut the persimmons into 1/4-inch-thick wedges.

Combine the oil, vinegar, and salt to taste. This vinaigrette should be mild.

Gently toss the endive, persimmons, and pecans in the vinaigrette to coat well. Separate any leaves of endive that remain sandwiched together. Taste.

Serve on cold plates.

✢
✢ ✢

Zuni Caesar Salad

Nothing strikes such a resonant note among Zuni kitchen alumni and current staff so much as memories of working the salad station, often referred to as "Caesar's Palace." The Caesar outsells every other salad, indeed every other dish, every day by a factor of three, and after three or four hours, the ritual of cracking, whisking, tasting, tweaking, tasting again, and so on takes its toll on the sturdiest palate.

There is nothing clever, original, or mysterious about this Caesar salad. The main "trick" we rely on is top-notch ingredients, freshly prepared. If you use a lesser cheese, or grate it too soon, you will get a different salad. If you squeeze the lemon juice ahead of time, it will have little or no fragrance. If the eggs are not particularly fresh, or you beat them into the dressing too far in advance, the dressing will not have body. Old or harsh-tasting garlic will dominate every other component and spoil the dressing. Likewise, fresh croûtons are exciting; stale ones are dull. And look for salt-packed anchovies; more delicate and nutty than oil-packed fillets, they give the Zuni dressing its distinctive flavor. {But if you can't find salt-packed fish, and must use oil-packed ones, make sure you rinse them in warm water and press between clean towels to extract as much of that oil as possible. Even fillets packed in "good" olive oil can have a vaguely rancid taste or smell straight from the can or jar.} Finally, make the effort to use very fresh romaine; after a few days in the refrigerator, or on the shelves in the produce department, its sweetness fades and it can become muddy, metallic, or bitter.

As you assemble your impeccable ingredients, bear in mind that most vary from day to day and place to place. Red wine vinegar varies in flavor and acidity, as do olive oils. Lemons vary widely in size, juiciness, fragrance, and acidity. Romaine varies in sweetness, "amount of heart," and the texture of the leaf ~ smooth or crinkly. {The latter needs a lot more dressing per leaf.} And garlic varies in pungency. All this notwithstanding, the proportions below are good guidelines, if making tens of thousands of salads means anything. Start with them, then smell and taste each component each time you make the salad, adjusting for your palate, and remember what you like and how you got there. If you know you love garlic, or anchovy, prepare extra, to make the adjusting easy.

I will be forever thankful to Paula Blotsky, who distilled our daily tweakings into these basic guidelines. Her name is on the greasy, dog-eared recipe card I wrote out fifteen years ago and still refer to.

FOR 4 TO 6 SERVINGS:
For the croûtons:

A 4- to 5-ounce chunk or slice of day-old *levain* or sourdough bread or other chewy, peasant-style bread

2 to 3 tablespoons mild-tasting olive oil
Salt

To finish the salad:

2 to 3 heads romaine lettuce {to yield about 1-1/2 pounds usable leaves}
1 tablespoon red wine vinegar
2/3 cup mild-tasting olive oil
About 1-1/2 tablespoons chopped salt-packed anchovy fillets {6 to 9 fillets}
About 2 teaspoons chopped garlic

Salt
2 large cold eggs
About 3 ounces Parmigiano-Reggiano, grated {1-1/2 cups very lightly packed}
Freshly cracked black pepper
About 1-1/2 lemons {to yield about 3 tablespoons juice}

\ *continued*

Preheat the oven to 350°.

Cut the bread into 1/2- to 3/4-inch cubes, toss with oil to coat evenly, salt lightly, toss again, and spread on a sheet pan. Roast, rotating the pan as needed, until golden all over, about 8 to 12 minutes. Taste a croûton; it should be well seasoned and slightly tender in the center. Leave to cool on the sheet pan.

Discard the leathery outer leaves of the romaine, then cut off the base of each head and wash and dry the leaves. Go through the leaves, trimming them of discolored, leathery, bruised, or wilted parts, but leave them whole. You need about 1-1/2 pounds of prepared leaves. Layer the leaves with towels if necessary to wick off every drop of water ~ wet lettuce will make an insipid salad. Refrigerate until just before dressing the salad.

Whisk together the vinegar, oil, anchovies, and garlic in a small mixing bowl. Add the eggs, a few sprinkles of the cheese, and lots of black pepper. Whisk to emulsify. Add the lemon juice, squeezing it through a strainer to catch the seeds. Whisk again, just to emulsify. Taste the dressing, first by itself and then on a leaf of lettuce, and adjust any of the seasonings to taste. If the romaine is very sweet, the dressing may already taste balanced and excellent ~ if it is mineraly, extra lemon or garlic may improve the flavor. If you like more anchovy, add it. {You should have about 1-1/2 cups of dressing.}

Place the romaine in a wide salad bowl. Add most of the dressing and fold and toss very thoroughly, taking care to separate the leaves and coat each surface with dressing, adding more as needed. Dust with most of the remaining cheese, add the croûtons, and toss again. Taste and adjust as before. In general, the tastier the romaine, the less you will need to emphasize other flavors.

Pick out first the large, then the medium-sized, and then the smallest leaves and arrange on cold plates. Add a last drizzle of dressing to the bowl to moisten the croûtons if they are at all dry and stir them around in the bowl to capture dressing on each of their faces and in their hollows. Distribute the croûtons among the salads and finish each serving with a final dusting of cheese and more pepper.

✢
✢ ✢

Soups

STRACCIATELLE *in* BROTH *with* SORREL

THIS EGG-DROP SOUP IS A LIGHT BUT RESTORATIVE DISH. It is very easy to digest, and a perfect meal when you are feeling under the weather. *Stracciatelle,* literally, are "rags," specifically the pulpy, pounded rags required for old-fashioned paper-making. The metaphor is apt; if you have ever seen pounded rag pulp, it will help you visualize the tender bits of cooked egg. I started adding sorrel to this traditional Roman formula years ago because I like its flavor with eggs and it cooks instantly with the "rags." For really fluffy "rags," use a really fresh egg and beat it just before you add it to the broth.

Wine: Bonarda Oltrepò Pavese, Castello Luzzano, 1999

FOR ABOUT 4-1/4 CUPS:

About 4 cups Chicken Stock {page 58}
Salt
1 large cold egg
1 tablespoon semolina

4 teaspoons lightly packed, finely
    grated pecorino romano or
    Parmigiano-Reggiano
Scant 2 ounces tender sorrel leaves,
    stems trimmed

Place the stock in a 2- to 4-quart saucepan and bring to a gentle simmer. Taste and correct for salt. Skim any fat.

Lightly beat the egg with the semolina and cheese just until homogenous. Cut the sorrel into skinny ribbons. Add both to the simmering broth. After 5 seconds, stir vigorously with a fork, then reduce the heat slightly. The "rags" will look like mimosa blossoms. Let cook for about 1 minute at a bare simmer. The beaten egg will clarify the broth as the "rags" firm up.

Serve instantly in warm bowls.

Onion Soup *with* Tomato & a Poached Egg

Inexpensive and easy to make. If you use duck fat, the soup will be unusually fragrant. The soup is made even better by the addition of a tablespoon of that salty gelée you can collect from the bottom of the pot after you make duck confit. If you go the olive oil route, a few ounces of soaked, flaked House-Cured Salt Cod or Brandade are delicious simmered into this soup, with or without the egg.

Wine: Moulin-à-Vent, Vielles Vignes, Domaine Bernard Diochon, 2000

FOR 4 SERVINGS:

1/4 cup duck fat {see Sources and Resources, page 518} or extra-virgin olive oil

1 pound sliced yellow onions {2 medium onions, about 4 cups}

Salt

2 garlic cloves, slivered

A sprig of fresh thyme

4 cups Chicken Stock {page 58}, warmed

1 tablespoon salty confit gelée {see page 433} {optional}

1 very ripe tomato {about 6 ounces}, peeled and coarsely chopped

A 2-ounce slice or chunk of chewy, peasant-style bread

4 ounces {2/3 cup} soaked House-Cured Salt Cod {page 328}, torn into thumbnail-sized bits, or scant 1/4 cup Brandade {page 331} {optional}

4 eggs

Freshly cracked black pepper

Preheat the oven to 400°.

Warm 3 tablespoons of the duck fat or olive oil in a 3-quart sauté pan over low to medium heat. Add the sliced onions, a few pinches of salt, the garlic, and thyme. Cook, stirring regularly until the onions are translucent and have collapsed onto themselves, about 15 minutes; don't let them color. Taste a sliver of onion; it should be sweet and tender, but not mushy.

Add the warm stock and the gelée if using. Bring to a simmer and stir in the chopped tomato. Return to a gentle simmer and cook for another 5 minutes or so. Taste for salt. Fish out the thyme, and let it cool slightly, then run it between

\ *continued*

your thumb and forefinger to strip any remaining leaves into the soup. Discard the stem.

Meanwhile, tear or cut the bread into 4 pieces and brush with the remaining 1 tablespoon duck fat or olive oil. Spread on a baking sheet and toast until unevenly golden, about 6 minutes.

If using salt cod or Brandade, stir into the soup.

Crack each egg into a saucer or small, shallow bowl. Tipping each dish just above the surface of the simmering broth, slide in the eggs, aiming to keep them separate. The freshest eggs will set to neat orbs, older eggs will spin delicate threads into the simmering broth ~ which the rustic character of the soup will forgive. Cook the eggs to the desired doneness ~ usually 3 to 4 minutes. You may wish to baste the eggs with the broth, or cover the pot to set the top of the yolks.

Set a warm croûton in each of four warm bowls. Spoon an egg, along with a tangle of onions and a bit of tomato, into each bowl and fill with the broth. Offer freshly cracked black pepper.

✢
✢ ✢

BEEF BROTH *with* MARROW CROÛTONS *&* A TRUFFLED EGG

WE SERVE A DOZEN DIFFERENT "EGGS POACHED IN *BRODO*" SOUPS. This is the most elegant and one of my favorite truffle dishes, even though it presents no truffles to the eye. The warm yolks have instead an intoxicating truffle perfume that I swoon over every time we make it. The eggs absorb the truffle scent through their porous shells. For the prettiest poached eggs, use very fresh ones. Older eggs spin a web of filaments, which would spoil the look of this pristine soup. {You can also make this soup with "un-truffled" eggs.}

This soup will serve as a fine first course for a formal meal, but would not be out of place before a rustic *Pot-au-Feu* {page 385}, where you make it with the broth from that boiled dinner.

Wine: La Calonica, Rosso di Montepulciano, 1999

FOR 4 SERVINGS:

About 2 ounces beef marrow {1/4 cup} or a combination of marrow and unsalted butter at room temperature*

8 thin slices plain baguette

Salt and freshly cracked black pepper

2 cups Beef Stock {page 63}

A little water or Chicken Stock {page 58}, as needed

4 eggs, refrigerated for a few days in a closed container with a fresh black or white truffle

A few fresh chives

Preheat the oven to 425°.

Chop, then mash the marrow, or marrow with butter. Season with 4 pinches of salt and a few grinds of black pepper. Spread on the sliced baguette. Arrange the bread on a baking sheet and toast until golden, 6 to 8 minutes. Keep in a warm spot while you finish the soup.

Bring the stock to a simmer in a small saucepan. Skim and, if it is not limpid, strain it through a clean, lint-free linen or cotton cloth. {Wet the cloth first with water and squeeze it out so it doesn't soak up your soup.} Taste for salt, and, if it seems too rich or beefy, dilute it with water, or chicken stock if you have it.

Transfer the broth to 12-inch skillet or 3-quart sauté pan and bring to a simmer over low heat. Crack each of the eggs into a deep saucer or small, shallow bowl. Tipping each dish just above the surface, slide the eggs into the barely simmering broth; stagger the additions by about 10 seconds to give each egg a chance to set slightly, so they are less likely to stick together. Large eggs will fit in the pan without overlapping; extra-large or jumbo eggs may collide. To maintain a simmer, you may have to raise the heat to compensate for the arrival of the eggs. Spoon broth over the exposed yolks, or gently tilt and swirl the pan to bathe them. Cook to desired doneness, typically 3 to 4 minutes.

Lift each egg from the broth with a large, flat spoon and slide into warm bowls. Fill the bowls with the broth. Garnish with the warm marrow croûtons and freshly snipped chives.

❖
❖ ❖

*You can poke the marrow from the shank bones before you roast them to make beef stock, or pry the marrow from about 2 pounds split beef femur bones; rinse and store in cold water, refrigerated, for up to 1 week.

BOILED KALE, FOUR WAYS

THESE DISHES ARE AS DELICIOUS AS THE TITLE SOUNDS DULL. They are simple to make, inexpensive, and restorative, and the basic boiled kale keeps well for days. Hard to classify~only certain renditions appear overtly soup-like~these primitive concoctions can appear at breakfast, lunch, or dinner or as a midnight snack or midafternoon energy booster.

I use *cavolo nero* {black cabbage}, a slender, bumpy-leaved kale, which is also marketed as *lascinato* kale, dino kale, and Tuscan kale, but curly kale will do fine, as will collard greens.

Wine: Saucelito Canyon Zinfandel, 1999

FOR ABOUT 4 CUPS:

Generous 8 ounces kale

1-1/2 cups diced yellow onions {6 ounces}

5 tablespoons extra-virgin olive oil

A pinch of dried red pepper flakes or a small dried chili {optional}

2 garlic cloves, slivered {optional}

3 to 4 cups water

Trim the kale of any discolored or damaged leaves, wash in several baths of cold water, and drain. Stack and roll up a few leaves at a time, then slice 1/8 inch thick.

Place the onions and oil in a 4-quart saucepan and set over low to medium heat. Cook, stirring once or twice, until the onions are translucent but still firm, about 3 minutes. Add the optional chili and garlic and the kale, and stir as it wilts into a heavy mass, about 5 minutes. Add water to cover by 1/2 inch and bring to a simmer. Salt to taste. Cover and simmer until the kale is tender but not mushy, about 30 minutes; add water if necessary to keep the kale just submerged. Taste for salt.

◦ ◦ BOILED KALE *on* TOAST

Grill or toast thick slices of crusty, chewy, peasant-style bread until golden or even slightly charred. Rub both sides with raw garlic while still hot. Float the toasts on the surface of the simmering kale, just long enough to soak up some "pot liquor," then transfer to wide soup plates. Generously garnish each slice of steamy bread with a few sloppy forkfuls of boiled kale, then finish with a drizzle of extra-virgin olive oil, shavings of aged Tuscan pecorino {or grated pecorino romano}, and freshly cracked black pepper. If you have a slice of leftover prosciutto or smoked prosciutto, cut it into ribbons and drop them on the warm kale. Serve with a knife, fork, and spoon.

✦ ✦ BOILED KALE *with* EGGS, FRIED OR POACHED

Prepare soggy toast as described above, garnish with the kale, and top each with an egg fried in extra-virgin olive oil. Warm a teaspoon of red wine vinegar in the skillet you used for the eggs and pour over the eggs.

Or, transfer the boiled kale to a wide sauté pan and bring to a simmer. Crack 1 egg per person into the pot, taking care to space them an inch or so apart. Drizzle the eggs with extra-virgin olive oil, cover, and cook at a bare simmer until done to your liking. Spoon each ragged egg, with plenty of extra kale and broth, into a bowl and serve with toast, rubbed with garlic if you like.

✦ ✦ KALE PAPPA *&* KALE FARINATA

Prepare the kale as directed, but increase the water by about 1 cup, enough to cover the kale by about 1-1/2 inches.

For Pappa: Return the kale to a hard boil, then stir in about 4 ounces slightly stale, chewy, peasant-style bread, torn into bite-sized wads. Add a splash of extra-virgin olive oil, cover tightly, and turn off the heat. Leave to rest for 10 minutes, then stir and serve with freshly cracked black pepper and grated pecorino romano or Parmigiano-Reggiano.

For Farinata: Cool the kale, then stir in 1 generous tablespoon semolina flour per cup. Return to the heat and stir as it comes to a simmer, then cook gently for about 15 minutes. The earthy soup will become *velouté*.

✦
✦ ✦

Pappa *al* Pomodoro

Tomato "pap" is a friendly staple of Tuscan cookery. It is a good, easy dish to make when you have too many ripe tomatoes, a half a loaf of yesterday's bread, and not much else. Its homey, porridgey texture always seduces, and the robust tomato flavor, not complicated here by long cooking or the addition of stock, is elemental. *La pappa* is traditionally served by itself, like a soup, but I also enjoy it as a side dish with roasted or grilled birds or with grilled lamb chops.

Wine: Saintsbury Pinot Noir "Garnet," 2000

FOR ABOUT 4 CUPS:

About 2 pounds very ripe tomatoes
About 1/2 cup extra-virgin olive oil
1 cup diced yellow onions {4 ounces}
Salt
About 3 garlic cloves, coarsely
    chopped
A leafy branch of fresh basil
Sugar {optional}
About 1/4 pound day-old, chewy,
    peasant-style bread, most of the
    crust removed
Freshly cracked black pepper

Core the tomatoes and trim of blemishes or underripe shoulders. Blanch, or blister over an open flame, and peel about half of them {see page 515}; leave the skins on the remainder. {Aside from giving the *pappa* more flavor, the skins give this version its distinctive texture.} Coarsely chop the tomatoes into 1/4-inch bits, taking care to capture all the juices. Collect the tomatoes and juice in a bowl.

Warm about 1/4 cup of the olive oil in a 4-quart saucepan or 3-quart sauté pan over low heat. Add the onions and a pinch of salt. Stirring a few times, cook over medium-low heat for 5 to 10 minutes while the onions soften and "sweat" in their juices; they will become translucent and sweeter. Once they are tender, stir in the garlic. Cook for a few minutes longer, then add the tomatoes~juice, seeds, and all~and another healthy splash of oil. Raise the heat and bring to a simmer.

Pick the leaves from the basil and set them aside, then push the stem into the sauce. Cook only long enough for the bits of tomato to collapse and release their skins, another 5 to 10 minutes. Watch the color of the sauce, and stop the cooking just as it takes on the characteristic orangey hue of cooked tomatoes. Taste for salt and for sweetness. If you find the sauce too acidic, add a pinch of sugar, but reserve final judgement until after you add the bread. You should have about 4 cups of sauce.

Remove the basil stem. Tear the basil leaves and add to the sauce. Tear the bread into fistfuls. Bring the sauce to a boil, add the bread, and stir just until it is saturated and submerged. Cover the pan with a tightly fitting lid, remove from the heat, and place in a very warm spot, or place over barely simmering water. Leave the bread to swell and soften for 15 minutes or so.

When you are ready to serve the *pappa,* give it a vigorous stir to break up the chunks of softened bread, taste again, and adjust for salt and sweetness. Stir in a few more spoonfuls olive oil to enrich the *pappa* and enhance its perfume. But don't overstir the *pappa* once you've added the bread, lest you sacrifice its delightful lightness and pleasantly lumpy, irregular texture.

Offer cracked black pepper and extra-virgin olive oil with the *pappa.*

✤ ✤ ✤ ✤ ✤

SWEATING

As a culinary operation, "sweating" means to make a food release and then cook in its own moisture.* This typically produces a mild, dilute flavor and a soft texture {as contrasted with browning, which deepens flavors, introduces new flavors, and firms texture}. Sweating is most efficiently accomplished by crowding the food in a straight-sided pan, which restricts evaporation {using a deeper pot or covering it will restrict it further}, and cooking over low heat. That way the cell walls slowly collapse and expel moisture, which falls back on them, preventing the sugars from caramelizing and fats or proteins from coloring. The liquid becomes part of the cooking medium {a little oil, butter, or other fat usually being the remainder}. Sweating is a generally a quiet operation; if the food is whispering, or worse, hissing, the moisture is probably evaporating too rapidly. If sweating is your goal, adding salt to the food before cooking, or early in the cooking, is a good idea, as it draws out water {although, if you drain or wipe

---

* Where vegetables and fruits are concerned, and that is most often what we sweat, the French have a useful phrase, *eau de végétation*~ "plant water" ~ for this moisture.

that water off, you will enhance browning instead}. Frequent stirring can also encourage sweating; it quietly distresses the weakening cells, encouraging their collapse. Finally, when you plan to sweat something, don't preheat the pan or the fat.

✢ ✢ ✢ ✢ ✢

ASPARAGUS *&* RICE SOUP *with* PANCETTA *&* BLACK PEPPER

THIS SIMPLE SOUP IS CROWDED WITH FLAVORS AND TEXTURES. The ingredients are dosed to strike a high-pitched balance between the sweet onion and asparagus and the pungent pancetta and pepper. The mild, tender rice mediates. You can use jumbo, medium, or skinny asparagus spears, as long as they are perky and sweet. Choose spears with neat, tight tips and bright firm stalks. I use Carnaroli or Arborio rice for this soup, because I usually have it in-house for risotto, but you can use any type of white rice you like, and gauge the cooking time accordingly.

Wine: Penfolds Eden Valley Reserve Riesling, 2000

FOR ABOUT 4 CUPS:

6 tablespoons extra-virgin olive oil
2 cups diced yellow onions {8 ounces}
Salt
1/4 cup white rice
About 3-1/2 cups Chicken Stock {page 58}

1/2 cup water
About 8 ounces asparagus, woody ends trimmed
3 to 4 ounces pancetta, finely minced {1/2 to 2/3 cup}
Freshly cracked black pepper

Warm about 1/4 cup of the oil in a 4-quart saucepan over medium-low heat. Add the onions and a pinch of salt and cook slowly, stirring regularly. Don't let the onions color; they should "sweat" their moisture and then become tender and translucent in about 10 minutes. Add the rice, chicken stock, and water and bring to a simmer. Cover tightly and cook until the rice is nutty-tender, probably 15 to 20 minutes, depending on the rice you choose. The broth will be cloudy and should taste sweet from the onions. Turn off the heat.

While the rice is cooking, sliver the asparagus, slicing it on an angle about 1/8 inch thick. Don't worry if the slivers vary a little in thickness; the irregularity will guarantee uneven cooking and a pleasantly varied texture. You should get about 2 cups.

Warm the remaining 2 tablespoons oil in a 12-inch skillet over medium heat. Add the pancetta and asparagus slivers and stir once to coat, then spread them out and leave to sizzle until those at the edges of the pan begin to color. Toss or stir once, then leave to color again. Repeat a few times until the mass has softened and shrunk by about one-third.

Scrape the pancetta and asparagus into the broth and bring to a boil. Add lots of pepper. Boil for about 1 minute. This soup is best when served promptly, while all the flavors are still bold and the texture varied.

✧
✧ ✧

LENTIL-SWEET RED PEPPER SOUP *with* CUMIN *&* BLACK PEPPER

AN EASY, HEARTY SOUP THAT CAN BE READY IN HALF AN HOUR. We use the small, plump, shrewdly marketed black lentil dubbed "Beluga" for this soup, as well as dark green French lentils. You can also use flat olive green lentils, or try other pulses, like split peas ~ green, orange, or gold. Just be prepared to adjust the amount of stock or water and the cooking time. I have served this soup three different ways: straight from the pot, irregularly mashed in a mortar, and fully puréed in a blender or processor ~ each method produces a different texture and character, and I like all three.

You can garnish the soup with a few scraps of browned braised bacon, or enrich it with a spoonful of the strong juices that braising bacon generates {see Pasta with Braised Bacon and Roasted Tomato Sauce, page 205}.

Wine: Gigondas, Château du Trignon, 1999

\ *continued*

FOR ABOUT 4 CUPS:

3 to 4 tablespoons extra-virgin olive oil

1/3 to 1/2 cup diced sweet red pepper {bells, gypsies, Corno di Toro, or sweet Italian}

1/2 teaspoon whole black peppercorns

1/4 teaspoon cumin seeds

1/4 cup finely diced carrot {1 ounce}

1/4 cup finely diced celery {1 ounce}

1/4 cup finely diced yellow onion {1 ounce}

1 to 2 garlic cloves, smashed and chopped

1 bay leaf

A sprig of fresh flat-leaf parsley, chopped {both stem and leaves}

1 cup lentils, preferably black or dark green French, picked over

4 to 4-1/2 cups Chicken Stock {page 58} or water, or a combination

Warm a tablespoon of the olive oil in a 4-quart saucepan over medium heat. Add the diced pepper and cook, stirring regularly, until it begins to color slightly, about 5 minutes.

Crush the peppercorns and cumin seeds in a mortar. Add both to the peppers and cook for another minute. Add the remaining 2 to 3 tablespoons oil, carrot, celery, onion, garlic, bay leaf, parsley, and lentils and about 3 cups of the stock or water. Bring to a simmer. Stir, and taste the liquid for salt. Reduce the heat and cook uncovered, barely simmering, until the lentils are tender and have absorbed most of the liquid, about 15 minutes. Turn off the heat, cover, and leave 5 minutes for the lentils to soften.

If you are going to purée or partially crush the lentils, do so now ~ it is most efficient to do this while the mixture is thick and dense, before you add the last of the liquid. Once you add more liquid, the lentils will find it easier to dodge the blender blades, or your pestle.

Add more liquid, in 1/2-cup doses, to bring the soup to the desired texture. Simmer, taste again, and serve.

❖
❖ ❖

La Garbure Landaise

ACCORDING TO PEPETTE, MY LODESTAR FOR ALL THINGS INVOLVING DUCK FAT, *la garbure* should include the whole *garbe*, or "everything you can grab" from the garden, in this case a modest garden in Southwest France.

Duck fat makes this an unusual and fragrant winter vegetable soup. Choose a not-so-pretty piece of confit to flavor the soup~a duck leg that got overcooked, or torn, or the flavorful but not-so-diner-friendly neck or winglet pieces. *Garbure* is traditionally made with water and flavored with *jambon cru*~the French version of prosciutto~a bone, rind, or a gnarly scrap of sinewy meat. {Ask for these where you buy prosciutto; most stores will be happy to sell you what doesn't make pretty slices at a pretty friendly price.} I also like to flavor this soup with salty duck gelatin harvested from the bottom of the confit pot, whenever we have it. You can also use chicken stock.

Wine: Château Bonnet, Bordeaux Rouge, 1999

FOR ABOUT 4 CUPS:

About 8 ounces duck confit~a small leg or a few necks or winglets {to make your own, see Duck Confit, page 429, or see Sources and Resources, page 518}

1-1/2 tablespoons duck fat {scraped from the confit}

1/4 cup carrot, peeled and sliced into half-moons {about 1 ounce}

1/4 cup sliced celery {about 1 ounce}

1/4 cup diced yellow onion {about 1 ounce}

1/2 cup sliced leeks~a mix of green and white parts {about 1-1/2 ounces}

2 large, dark green outer leaves Savoy cabbage, cut into bite-sized strips

A sprig of fresh thyme

3 garlic cloves, coarsely chopped

3/4 cup diced and peeled winter squash, such as butternut, Kabocha, or pumpkin

About 3 ounces prosciutto scraps or rind, or a larger chunk of prosciutto bone with some bits of meat attached

2-1/4 cups water plus 2 tablespoons salty confit gelatin {page 433} or 2-1/4 cups Chicken Stock {page 58}

Salt

A few fresh flat-leaf parsley leaves, coarsely chopped

1 to 1-1/4 cups cooked white beans finished with duck fat, and their cooking liquid {see Dried Beans, page 263}

\ *continued*

Set the confit in a warm spot to drain of excess fat.

Warm the 1-1/2 tablespoons duck fat in a 4-quart saucepan over medium-low heat. Add the carrot, celery, onion, leeks, cabbage, and thyme. Cook uncovered, stirring regularly, until the cabbage has turned bright green and all of the vegetables have softened slightly, about 10 minutes. Add the garlic, squash, prosciutto scrap or bone, and the water and gelatin or chicken stock. Bring to a simmer and salt lightly.

Use your fingers to "squeegee" the remaining surface fat from the confit, then add the confit to the soup. Cover and simmer for about 15 minutes.

Stir in the parsley and white beans and simmer for another 15 minutes. Pull the confit from the pan. Remove and discard the skin, slide out the bones, and then break up the pieces of meat as you drop them back in the soup. Bring back to a simmer, taste for salt, and serve. *Garbure* holds and reheats well, though the beans will thicken it somewhat, which I like.

❖
❖ ❖

CORN-SHRIMP BISQUE

Bisque does not have to be daunting, particularly if your first efforts concern shrimp, as described here. Hard-shelled crab, lobster, and crayfish bisque can be noisy, splattery, multistep operations, which are possible to botch if you are unfamiliar with the process.* The method here is easy, but do allow about 20 minutes to strain and press the purée.

We also use this formula to make soft-shelled crab bisque, an extravagance, but a good way to make the best of the not-so-soft-shelled "crunchies" that are often shipped to our coast.

---

* As I was, when I almost served a pot of thoroughly puréed lobster bisque at Chez Panisse about three months into my tenure there. Several tubs of lobster shells from dinner the night before had been iced and saved for me to transform into bisque for lunch. I did what just about every nervous young cook does one almost-fatal time: I hesitated, but didn't ask for help, or say that I had never made a bisque before. My bisque was more like clay slip than soup, so thick it was with finely pulverized shell. But Chez Panisse had angels watching over it {and my fumbling}. The head waitress took a sip just before we opened, and with well-contained panic, suggested it not be served.

We sometimes garnish this bisque with squash blossoms, grilled or sautéed and then chopped.

Wine: Raymond Napa Valley Reserve Chardonnay, 1999

FOR ABOUT 4 CUPS:

5 to 6 tablespoons unsalted butter

About 3/4 cup thinly sliced carrots {3 ounces}

About 1/2 cup thinly sliced celery {2 ounces}

About 3/4 cup thinly sliced yellow onions {3 ounces}

1 bay leaf

A small dried chili

2 garlic cloves, slivered {optional}

1 to 1-1/4 pounds shrimp in their shells or 4 plump soft-shelled crabs

1/2 cup thinly sliced fennel {2 ounces}

2-1/2 to 3 cups Shellfish Fumet {see below} or a combination of Shellfish Fumet or Shellfish Essence {also below} and Chicken Stock {page 58}

Salt

About 3 cups freshly scraped corn kernel tips and their milky juice {6 to 12 young ears, depending on size and yield} {see page 254}

Melt about 2 tablespoons of the butter in a 4-quart saucepan over medium heat. Add the carrot, celery, onions, bay leaf, chili, and garlic, if using. Stir until all of the vegetables are coated, then reduce the heat to medium-low and cook until tender, about 5 minutes.

Meanwhile, coarsely chop the shrimp or crabs in their shells. Add them, along with a second 2 tablespoons butter, to the vegetables, raise the heat to medium, and stir occasionally as the shellfish sweats and steams for about 5 minutes.

Add the fennel. Add fumet or fumet and stock to just the depth of the shellfish and vegetables. Bring to a simmer, taste for salt, and cook uncovered at a bare simmer until the liquid tastes strongly of shellfish, 15 to 20 minutes.

Stir in enough corn that the liquid is quite crowded ~ the vegetables should still be barely covered; you should have at least a few tablespoons of corn left over.

Cover and simmer until the corn is quite tender, 5 to 10 minutes. Remove from the heat.

\ *continued*

Fish out and discard the bay leaf {and chili pod, unless you want your bisque quite spicy}, then purée incompletely, using a blender or processor. Stop every few seconds to avoid homogenizing the mix. The result should be thick and creamy, but densely flecked with coarse shell bits.

The most efficient way to strain the mixture is to pass it first through a coarse strainer or food mill, pressing hard to force all the liquid and vegetable purée through, then pass it through a finer sieve to catch the smaller flecks of shell. Taste and correct the salt. If the resulting bisque is too thick, add a little fumet or stock. If it is a little thin, you can thicken it with the remaining corn: Cook the corn with a tablespoon or so of butter in a small saucepan over low heat, covered until tender. Add a little of the bisque, purée thoroughly, strain, and add this to the thin batch. Or, if your bisque already has a nice texture, simply add the cooked kernels whole.

Stir in some or all of the remaining butter, to your taste, as you heat the soup for serving. Don't let the bisque boil.

◆ ◆ SHELLFISH FUMET & SHELLFISH ESSENCE

Extracting lovely flavor from throwaway shells is as gratifying as it is easy. Use shells from crab, shrimp, crayfish, or lobster. A meal of cracked crab or boiled lobster is an excellent source, as you will have heaps of shells, some with caches of meat inside. If you have only a modest amount of shell, double-wrap them in plastic, place in a storage container and freeze for up to a few weeks, until you have enough to warrant brewing a pot of fumet.

Make as you would fish fumet {page 68}, but adjust for the following: unlike fish bones, crustacean shells yield their flavor reluctantly. Shellfish fumet takes longer to peak in flavor than fish broth, up to an hour. Accordingly, there is no need to boil off the alcohol in the wine in advance, and the vegetables should be more thickly sliced. Taste regularly as the brew evolves from bland and vaguely metallic to thinly sweet to saturated with shellfish flavor. Strain and cool completely. Freeze what you don't plan to use the same day. Unlike fish fumet, you can reduce it by 90 percent or so to make a pungent, syrupy shellfish essence that is a culinary treasure. Use this by the teaspoon to flavor bisque, risotto, or butter sauces. Reduce as you would reduce stock to glaze {see Reduction: Turning Stock into Sauce, page 56}.

◆
◆ ◆

✢ ✢
✢

Eggs

✢ ✢
✢

.

A NOTE ON CHOOSING EGGS: WHEREVER THEY APPEAR IN YOUR MEAL, SPARE NO pennies to get the freshest, tastiest eggs you can. I want yolks the color of saffron that sit plump and high on the clear, thick, jellylike whites. If the white is thin overall and watery at the edge, the egg may be too feeble to turn into a fluffy omelette or frittata. Eggshell color is about hen variety and is no guarantee of great flavor, but the best eggs we get are from well-tended and well-fed hens that produce brown or blue eggs. Try all the different colors and "brands" of eggs you can find, then choose the one that delivers flavor and freshness. Even the most expensive egg makes a very economical meal.

For the best flavor and performance, keep eggs cold and use them promptly.

⁜

MADELEINE'S OMELETTE *with* MUSTARD CROÛTONS *&* BEAUFORT CHEESE

TATA {AUNTIE} MADELEINE'S NAME APPEARS OCCASIONALLY ON THE MENU AT Zuni, though few know the reverence with which I regard her cooking. But such understatement suits her and her home cooking perfectly. *Tata* Madeleine, Jean and Pierre Troisgros's sister, quietly complemented her brothers' culinary teachings with a primer in basic Burgundian and Lyonnaise cooking. Jean usually feigned hurt feelings when he heard I was heading up to Madeleine's house for a dinner of scrambled eggs, but he'd have gone as well if he hadn't been on duty at the family restaurant, deemed by many the best in France in 1973.

At Madeleine's house, dinner omelettes were much loved, and dinner, in that case, was *an* omelette for the family. Madeleine cooked the omelette in a shallow twelve-inch "*tay-fahl*" {T-fal} skillet. The time-honored alternative, an assiduously cared for steel omelette pan, is also a great choice, but hard to find these days. You can, of course, make smaller omelettes in smaller pans. In any case, it's worth knowing how to produce a fluffy omelette for four or five people. Twelve eggs can be maneuvered successfully in a slick pan and become a lovely thing turned out onto a handsome platter, presented as proudly as a holiday turkey. Start the meal with a cured meat appetizer or with smoked fish, and follow with a salad of bitter greens, studded with nuts and slivers of sweet apple or pear and fennel. Madeleine would admonish you not to change plates after the omelette.

«Enlève-moi pas ça! C'est le meilleur avec la salade!» {"Don't take that away. It's the best with the salad!"} referring to the delicious mixture of leftover egg, vinaigrette, and greens. Try that.

Beaufort is a sweet and nutty hard cheese from the Haute-Savoie in the French Alps that rivals Swiss Gruyère in character. It is best in the early winter months and worth looking for. Swiss Gruyère, Fontina, or a not-too-strong white Cheddar are all fine alternatives; just don't use more cheese than specified or it will weigh down the eggs and quickly become the dominant flavor of the dish. In my mind, omelettes should be about the eggs, not the filling.

This scramble-then-roll technique is not really difficult, but if you've never made an omelette this way, consider making a 2- or 3-egg omelette, without the croûtons or cheese, to learn the motions. As with many simple culinary techniques, it will take longer to read the description than to execute. {If you do choose to make a smaller omelette, simply use a proportionately smaller pan, fewer eggs, and less filling.}

Wine: Chambave Rosso, Valle d'Aosta, "La Crotta di Vigneron," 2000

FOR 4 SERVINGS:

For the croûtons:

2-1/2 ounces slightly stale, chewy, peasant-style bread, most of the crust removed

2 tablespoons unsalted butter

1 tablespoon Dijon mustard

1-1/2 tablespoons dry white wine or dry white vermouth

1 teaspoon brown and/or yellow mustard seeds, lightly crushed in a mortar

Freshly cracked black pepper

Salt

For the omelette:

12 large eggs

Salt

Scant 3 tablespoons unsalted butter, cut into a few slices

Scant 2 ounces Beaufort or Swiss Gruyère, coarsely grated {about 3/4 cup loosely packed}

Making the croûtons:

Preheat the oven to 400°. Take the eggs out of the refrigerator.

\ *continued*

Tear the bread into small, fluffy wads, 3/4 inch and smaller. Tear a few of the wads into crumbs. You should get 2 to 2-1/2 cups.

Melt the butter in a small saucepan, then remove from the heat and whisk in the mustard, wine, seeds, and lots of pepper. The mixture should be the texture of a thick vinaigrette. Add the bread wads and toss well to coat. Rub the bits of bread against the sides of the pan to grab all the "dressing," then massage them gently, to make sure the "dressing" reaches the inside of the wads. Taste for salt.

Spread the bits of bread out on a sheet pan and roast for 5 to 10 minutes, until unevenly golden on the outside but still slightly chewy in the middle. The smaller crumbs will be crisp through, and the contrast is delightful in the omelette. Keep the croûtons in a warm spot.

Cooking the omelette:

Set your chosen omelette pan over very low heat. Don't skip this step ~ gently heating the pan for a few minutes means that both the bottom and sides will be hot enough to sizzle the arriving eggs. This is especially important when making a large omelette, which otherwise challenges burner power. I've found that large, heavy nonstick pans may take up to 5 minutes over very low heat to heat thoroughly and uniformly.

Crack the eggs into a deep bowl and add a pinch of salt per egg. Beat them enough to combine the yolks and whites, but leave the eggs bouncy and ropy. Don't look for homogeneity. Overbeating ~ or beating the eggs in advance ~ weakens or tears the protein strands and results in a thin, homogenous slurry that won't trap and hold the air necessary to make your omelette light. I use a dinner fork and count about 50 strokes. {If using fewer eggs, count proportionately fewer strokes.} Get out a wooden or heatproof rubber spatula.

Check the temperature of the pan by adding a trickle of water and tilting the pan: the water should bubble as vigorously on the sloped sides as on the bottom. If the water bounces and sputters, the pan is too hot; let it cool until water only boils on contact.

Turn the heat to medium-high. Add the slices of butter and swirl the pan to coat the sides with butter. When most of the butter is sizzling but is not yet coloring, dribble a tiny bit of egg into the pan. When the egg begins to puff, add the remaining eggs. The eggs should "cluck" pleasantly as they bubble on the bottom of the pan. Within a few seconds, a ring of puffy cooked egg will form around the edges. {If not, raise the heat.} Once it does, wait for about 10 seconds, then use the spatula to cut through and scramble the thick layer of puffy, cooked eggs for a few seconds. {If you notice that any of the egg folds are chestnut brown, reduce the heat slightly.} Scrape the sides, then leave briefly to set a new puffy layer of egg, which you should then scramble nearly as wantonly as you did the first batch. Continue this process until about half of the egg has set, then scatter the surface with the warm croûtons. Use the spatula to mass the cooked egg against the back {or front, it makes no difference} slope of the pan, then tip the pan forward {or backward} to allow the raw egg to flow off the cooked folds down to the hot surface of the pan. Don't worry if some of the croûtons slide out with the eggs, they'll brown on the surface and be delicious. Push the newly cooked folds of egg into the mass. Continue tipping and enlarging the mass of cooked egg until nearly two-thirds of the eggs are set, then sprinkle the cheese in the center of the cooked egg folds. Tip the pan forward and slide or push the cooked mass to the far edge of the pan. Then tip the pan more aggressively, give it a little yank, and use your spatula to nudge the far edge of the mass to roll over on itself. It will feel like a sluggish sauté gesture {which I explain more fully on page 340}. Repeat to form a cocoon-like shape. Don't worry when the omelette cracks or breaks, the surface will reset with the next roll, and the wrinkles and folds will be lovely. Some of the croûtons usually peek from the cracks. I push any escapees back into the folds so the next rolling gesture traps them back in the omelette. Repeat this tipping, nudging, and rolling gesture until all of the eggs are enfolded, then continue rolling until the "cocoon" is cooked to your taste. If you aren't comfortable guessing doneness, use a fork to pry open one of the folds and check inside. If the omelette is already nice and golden on the outside but is not yet cooked to your taste, simply reduce the heat and keep rolling the omelette every few seconds until it is as firm as you like. Tip onto a warm platter.

⁕ ⁕ ⁕ ⁕ ⁕

A NOTE ON WHY TO COOK OMELETTES HOT AND FAST: A FLUFFY omelette always begins with fresh eggs, but it ultimately depends on your cleverly trapping air in them. You start by rapidly vaporizing the water that is in every egg; this requires fairly high heat. That vapor stretches and unravels the raw egg proteins, which you then need to keep very hot until they set in that state. This means that where there was steam, there will be little air pockets in the cooked egg~this makes an omelette fluffy. Reducing the heat too much or too soon lets the steam out before the proteins set and can deflate a promising omelette {this is also the basis of the "don't-open-the-oven-on-a-rising-soufflé" rule~although soufflés may actually be less vulnerable than omelettes in this regard}. The obvious risk of high heat is burning the eggs or butter; avoiding this depends on practice and attention, until you become familiar with how your pan conducts heat and find just the right setting on your burner for the results you like. But a lightly browned omelette is not burned, and my ideal omelette is mottled golden in patches~the slightly browned butter smells and tastes delicious.

* * * * *

Note: If you are in the slightest way intimidated by these issues of heat and rolling and tipping over, I suggest the kind and worthy alternative of softly scrambling as many good, fresh eggs and adding the mustardy croûtons just as the eggs begin to set. This is a different dish, but not a compromise.

Variation MADELEINE'S POTATO & BACON OMELETTE

We alternate the above omelette at the restaurant with Madeleine's potato and bacon omelette, which is scrunched and folded around a few ounces of peeled and roughly cubed yellow-fleshed potatoes, well cooked in very salty water, drained on a towel, and then irregularly browned with a few batons of streaky bacon per person. Madeleine browns them directly in the omelette pan. Add a little less butter, due to the bacon fat, and the beaten eggs, and proceed as described above. If your pan is not in perfect condition, this omelette may stick, but a strategic scrape with a wooden spatula will usually make it cooperate.

+
+ +

FRIED EGGS *in* BREAD CRUMBS

I LIKE THESE CRUNCHY EGGS FOR DINNER WITH A SALAD OF BITTER GREENS. At Zuni, they appear on the Sunday lunch menu accompanied by house-made sausage or bacon and grilled vegetables or roasted mushrooms. This is a very easy dish and fun to eat when you are alone, so I provide proportions for one person. For more people, make it in a larger pan, in batches of four to six eggs.

Wine: Cline Cellars Mourvèdre, Ancient Vines, Contra Costa, 1999

FOR 1 SERVING:

3 tablespoons packed, fresh, soft bread crumbs made from slightly stale, crustless, chewy, white peasant-style bread {see page 506}

Salt

About 2 tablespoons extra-virgin olive oil

A few fresh thyme or marjoram leaves or coarsely chopped fresh rosemary {optional}

2 eggs

About 1 teaspoon red wine vinegar, balsamic vinegar, or sherry vinegar

Sprinkle the crumbs with salt, then drizzle with enough of the oil to just oversaturate them.

Place the crumbs in a 6- to 8-inch French steel omelette pan or nonstick skillet and set over medium heat. {If you like your fried eggs over easy, reserve some of the oiled raw crumbs, to sprinkle on the top of the eggs just before you flip them over.} Let the crumbs warm through, then swirl the pan as they begin drying out ~ which will make a quiet staticky sound. Stir once or twice.

The moment you see the crumbs begin to color, quickly add the remaining oil, and the herbs if using, then crack the eggs directly onto the crumbs. Cook the eggs as you like.

Slide onto a warm plate, then add the vinegar to the hot pan. Swirl the pan once, then pour the drops of sizzling vinegar over the eggs.

Note: If you are preparing the eggs for more than a few people, it is a little easier to toast the seasoned, oiled crumbs in advance in a 425° oven instead of in the skillet. In that case, toast them to the color of weak tea. Then scatter them in the skillet, add the remaining olive oil, and proceed as described above.

❖
❖ ❖

Frittata & Elaborations

By "frittata," I mean a skinny but fluffy cake of scrambled eggs, judiciously studded or veined with perfectly cooked and seasoned vegetable or meat condiments and delicately fried to be wrinkly golden on both faces. These skinny frittatas ~ scarcely an inch at full "puff" ~ have the right amount of inside to outside to set without toughening. Use only very fresh eggs, which will remain thick and viscous after a brief beating. And choose a fragrant extra-virgin olive oil; this simple dish will showcase its fruitiness. Use a well-seasoned steel omelette pan or a nonstick pan, but beware ~ brand-new nonstick is emphatically that, and your eggs may spread unstoppably up the curved sides of the pan. This results in a thin-edged, flat frittata, more like a crêpe.

I like frittatas best when they are freshly made, with a salad, or on a pool of light tomato sauce or sandwiched between split focaccia.

Basic Method for a 5- to 6-inch frittata, fried in an 8-inch steel or nonstick skillet:

Crack 2 eggs and beat with a few drops of water and 2 pinches of salt: beat to combine the yolks and whites, but stop short of homogeneity. I count about 30 strokes, using two splayed forks as a makeshift whisk.

Heat 1-1/2 tablespoons olive oil in the chosen pan over high heat. Test the heat by spilling a drop of the egg into the oil. If it puffs instantly, the pan is hot enough to set a fluffy frittata.

Add the beaten eggs, count to 5, then stir and mass the eggs back in the center. Count to 5 again, stir again, then re-mass the egg in the center of the pan. Swirl the pan to make sure the frittata isn't sticking, then flip it and cook for 15 seconds on the other face. {This is an easy motion to learn; see Sautéing, page 340, for a simple lesson.} Slide onto a plate immediately, so it doesn't overcook.

Note: For 3 eggs, use a 9-inch pan.

✦ ✦ Onion Frittata *with* Balsamic Vinegar

This is especially good made with a sweet onion variety, such as vidalia, Walla Walla, Granex, or Maui. Sweet red onions are also an option. An artisan-made balsamic won't be squandered here, but a good-quality commercial product is fine.

This frittata makes a great sandwich on a tender bun.

Wine: Silverado Napa Valley Sangiovese, 1998

FOR 1 SERVING:

2 large eggs
Salt
A few drops of water
1-1/2 to 2 tablespoons extra-virgin olive
    oil

About 2 ounces thinly sliced yellow
    onion {1/2 cup}
1 to 2 teaspoons balsamic vinegar,
    artisan-made or a good-quality
    commercial product

Beat the eggs with the salt and water as described in the Basic Method {page 180}.

Warm the olive oil in the pan over medium heat and add the slivered onions; they should cover the bottom of the pan in a lacy layer. The oil should sizzle as the onions hit. Let the onions color slightly, then toss them once and lightly brown the other side. Cook until nutty tender, a minute or so. Add the beaten egg and continue as described in the Basic Method. The onions will tend to cluster and drag in the frittata, so each bite is different, which I like. Slide onto a plate and dribble with the balsamic vinegar.

✦ ✦ **FRITTATA** *with* **FIDEUS** *&* **TOMATO SAUCE**

This frittata has a great texture and is a delicious way to revisit leftover *fideus* pasta. You can also make it starting with uncooked cappellini; see the Note below.

Wine: Ribera del Duero, Viña Pedrosa Crianza, 1998

FOR 1 SERVING:

2 large eggs
Salt
A few drops of water
1/4 cup fully cooked *fideus* noodles
    {2 ounces} {see page 217}, at room
    temperature or see Note

1-1/2 to 2 tablespoons extra-virgin olive
    oil
2 tablespoons Tomato Coulis {page 287}
1 thin slice prosciutto or 2 thin slices
    smoked prosciutto or coppa, cut
    into wide ribbons {optional}

Beat the eggs with the salt and water and start frying the frittata as described in the Basic Method {page 180}. Add the cooked *fideus* when you stir the eggs the first time. Finish as described in the Basic Method and slide onto a warm plate.

\ *continued*

Set the pan back on the heat, add the Tomato Coulis, and swirl until it bubbles. Pour over the frittata. Garnish with the cured meat, if using, and serve instantly.

Note: If you don't have leftover *fideus*, toss 1/2 ounce cappellini, broken into 1/2-inch pieces {1/4 cup} with about 2 drops of oil and toast to the color of cornflakes in a 325° oven, about 10 minutes. Place in a small saucepan, moisten with a few tablespoons of water, and add a pinch of salt. Set over medium-low heat and simmer until the water is absorbed, then add more water by the spoonful, as necessary, until the noodles are just tender. This should take 10 minutes or less.

✢ ✢
✢ ✢

SLOW-SCRAMBLED EGGS *with* BOTTARGA, *&* VARIATIONS

THIS IS A BASIC, SHAMELESSLY RICH FORMULA FOR A FRENCH *BROUILLADE,* A "disorder" of eggs. The method is foolproof and the result is so suave that it makes a fine hors d'œuvre, spooned onto warm crostini, or a comforting, indulgent little meal paired with a salad of lightly dressed arugula, baby lettuces, chervil sprigs, or baby greens. These eggs laced with *bottarga di tonno* are a personal favorite.

Wine: Morgan Monterey Chardonnay, 2000

FOR 3 OR 4 SERVINGS, OR TO GARNISH ABOUT 20 HORS D'ŒUVRE CROSTINI:

3 to 4 tablespoons cold unsalted butter   Salt
8 large eggs   1 garlic clove, peeled
A small chunk of bottarga {see Note}
    {enough to grate 1 teaspoon or
    more, to taste}

Cut the butter into little slivers. Crack the eggs into a bowl and beat with a few slivers of butter, a few pinches of finely grated bottarga, and a pinch of salt.

Barely melt a few more slivers of the butter in a 1- to 2-quart nonstick saucepan or a 6- to 8-inch nonstick skillet, just to coat the pan, then remove the pan from the heat. Add the eggs and return to the lowest-possible heat.

Generously rub the bowl of a wooden spoon, front and back, with the garlic and use this to stir the eggs almost constantly while you incorporate the remaining butter, sliver by sliver, over 8 to 10 minutes. If the eggs begin to set in folds, the heat is too high or you aren't stirring enough. Use a Flame Tamer if you can't keep the heat low enough, or pull the pan from the heat for 10 seconds at a time to control the cooking. As they first begin to heat through, the beaten eggs will look somewhat like buttermilk ~ heavy with occasional flecks of curd. Gradually they will thicken and the curds will proliferate. The eggs will keep cooking off the heat, so pull the pan off the burner while they are still quite soft and stir for another minute. The finished *brouillade* should be slightly curdy, like creamy cottage cheese.

Serve a few neat spoonfuls per person, flanked with warm, dry toast and a small salad.

Note: Bottarga {also *botargo* and *buttàriga* in Italian and *botargue, boutargue,* and *poutargue* in French} is dried, salted fish roe. A tradition that dates to ancient Egypt, it is still a useful, if not well-known, condiment. *Bottarga di tonno* ~ tuna bottarga ~ is quite strong in flavor, more pungent than salted anchovies. *Bottarga di muggine* ~ from gray mullet {*Mugil capito*} ~ is milder. Both show best as a counterpoint to an unchallenging partner, such as shelling beans, plain risotto, skinny noodles, or eggs. I like it shaved over Charred Eggplant {page 102}. Most bottarga is sold in chunks, usually 4 ounces or more for tuna, a few ounces for mullet. Tightly wrapped and refrigerated, your chunk can keep for months. I have also used powdered dried mullet bottarga, which is milder than the moister, chunk-version {see Sources and Resources, page 518}.

⁜ ⁜ **BROUILLADE *aux* OURSINS**

Substitute fresh sea urchin roe for the bottarga. Figure on about 1 teaspoon urchin roe per person and stir the tender "tongues" of roe into the eggs just as you pull the pan from the heat. They should break down only partially.

Wine: Morgan Monterey Chardonnay, 2000

❖ ❖ TRUFFLED BROUILLADE

A delicious relief from elaborate planning, truffled eggs and toast is my favorite Christmas dinner. Begin by storing the eggs in a sealed container with a fresh black truffle, refrigerated, for a day or so. The eggs will absorb the perfume through their shells. A few hours before the meal, crack and beat the eggs slightly with the minced truffle. Cover and leave in a cool spot. Season and cook as described above, omitting the bottarga.

Wine: Carmignano, Villa di Capezzana, 1999

❖ ❖ BROUILLADE *aux* ORTIES

A final variation, just as earthy, but more affordable, calls for a gloved handful of coarsely chopped nettles to be stirred into the eggs when you first pour them in the pan. Omit the bottarga. The combination is as compelling as it is unusual.

Wine: Carmignano, Villa di Capezzana, 1999

❖
❖ ❖

EGGS BAKED *in* RESTES

*R*ESTES ARE FRENCH LEFTOVERS. This is a by-product dish that I enjoy as much as the parent concoction. It capitalizes on leftover oxtail, *brasato*, or short rib–braising liquid, studded with whatever scraps of meat you can pick from the bones and scrape from the pan. {See Oxtails Braised in Red Wine, page 377; *Brasato*, page 373; or Short Ribs Braised in Chimay Ale, page 382.}

Choose a shallow baking dish appropriate to the amount of liquid and number of eggs you are using. The reconstituted braising liquid should be about 1/2 inch deep in the baking dish before you add the egg or eggs.

Wine: Montes Alpha, Colchagua Valley, Chile, Cabernet Sauvignon Reserva, 1999

PER SERVING:

About 3/4 cup braising liquid {from braised oxtails, *brasato,* or short ribs}

1/4 to 1/2 cup scraps boned meat and vegetables from the braise, coarsely chopped or shredded

To correct the liquid {as needed}:
A splash of water, red wine, or Chimay; Chicken Stock {page 58}, or Beef Stock {page 63} {depending on the source dish}, and/or juice from canned tomato
Pinch of sugar {optional}

If you are shy on scraps, or if you just want more solid stuff {optional}:
1 tablespoon drained, chopped canned tomato or wild mushrooms, sliced, or both, plus a trickle of mild-tasting olive oil to cook them in

To finish the dish:
1 or 2 eggs
Freshly cracked black pepper
A slice of chewy, peasant-style bread

1 garlic clove, peeled
A trickle of extra-virgin olive oil

Preheat the oven to 500°.

Warm the braising liquid in a small saucepan over medium heat. Reduce the heat and stir in the scraps of meat and vegetables. Bring just to a simmer. Taste and rectify the texture and flavor as needed. The liquid should have a little body, like maple syrup; if not, reduce it slightly, taking care it doesn't become oversalty. If it is quite thick already, thin as needed; if added wine or tomato makes the sauce too acidic, add a pinch of sugar.

If adding the tomato and/or mushrooms, warm them in a little olive oil in a small skillet and stew until their juice has evaporated and they are quite tender, 5 to 10 minutes. Add to the braising liquid, bring to a simmer, and taste again.

Pour the simmering mixture into the chosen baking dish. Crack the egg or eggs into the center. Barely prick the surface of the yolk {or yolks} ~ this will keep it from setting a rubbery skin. Set on the top rack of the oven and bake as you like your eggs, allowing 5 to 7 minutes. The meaty juices should bubble and begin to set a skin at the edges.

Eat or serve from the dish, with black pepper and warm toast or grilled bread rubbed with garlic and drizzled with extra-virgin olive oil.

Eggs Cooked *in* Spicy Tripe Stew, or Veritabile Uova *in* Trippa

Even if you are one who turns the other way when you sniff tripe, this dish may change your mind. The double-blanching technique tames the scent, a bit, and the generous blend of friendly flavors like tomato, onion, and pancetta is easy to embrace. This stew is fine without the eggs and also makes a good crostini topping, with or without a grating of Parmigiano-Reggiano or aged pecorino. Tripe stew keeps well for days and benefits from cooling and reheating.

Raw or cooked, tripe is unlike anything else in the menagerie of comestibles. The honeycombed second stomach of a calf, or ox or cow, when still intact, resembles a tough, deformed bathing cap. Blanched, slivered, and patiently stewed, tripe becomes silk-satiny and looks like ruffled ribbons.

{If these "Real Eggs in Tripe" don't seduce you, you may prefer the metaphorical ones: That *Uova in Trippa* consists of plain well-seasoned Frittata {page 180}, cut into skinny strips. Pile these, Medusa-like, in a shallow gratin dish and top with spicy Tomato Coulis {page 287}. Bake in a 500° oven until hot through and bubbling at the edges. The fluffy frittata strips will look a little like frilly tripe.}

Wine: Barbaresco Montestefano, Produttori del Barbaresco, 1996

FOR 4 TO 6 SERVINGS {ABOUT 6 CUPS}:
For blanching the tripe:

1-1/4 pounds honeycomb tripe
Salt
1 bay leaf
A few small, dried chiles

1 medium yellow onion {about 8 ounces}, quartered
1 leafy stalk celery

For finishing the stew:

6 tablespoons mild-tasting olive oil

12 ounces sliced yellow onions {about 3 cups}

6 ounces sliced celery {about 1-1/2 cups}

1-1/2 cups coarsely chopped, canned tomatoes, with their juice, or about 2 cups ripe tomatoes, peeled and coarsely chopped

12 whole black peppercorns

2 bay leaves

2 or 3 small dried chiles

Salt

1/2 cup dry white wine

4 ounces thinly sliced pancetta, cut into 1-inch strips {about 2/3 cup}

A few kale leaves, torn into bite-sized pieces {optional}

3/4 to 1 cup reserved tripe cooking liquid or Chicken Stock {page 58}

6 to 8 garlic cloves, chopped

A few sprigs fresh flat-leaf parsley, coarsely chopped

4 to 6 eggs {1 per person}

2 tablespoons extra-virgin olive oil

Freshly cracked black pepper

4 to 6 slices peasant-style bread, grilled or toasted and rubbed with raw garlic {optional}

Double-blanching the tripe {up to 2 days in advance}:

Place the tripe in a 4-quart saucepan and add cold water to cover by a few inches. Add about a teaspoon of salt, set over medium heat, and bring to a boil. Drain.

Rinse the tripe thoroughly, and wash out the pan. Return the tripe to the pan and add the bay leaf, chiles, onion, celery, and cold water to cover by a few inches. Salt to taste. Bring to a boil, adjust the heat to maintain a steady simmer, skim, and cook uncovered until just tender, about 2 hours. Leave the tripe to cool in the cooking liquid. {If preparing in advance, cool completely, then refrigerate until you prepare the stew.}

Preparing the stew:

Drain the tripe, reserving up to 1 cup of the cooking liquid. Cut into manageable 1-inch wide strips, then cut them into short slivers about 1/4 inch thick. You should get about 3 cups of little strips.

Warm the olive oil in a 4-quart saucepan or stew pot over medium heat. Add

\ *continued*

the onions and celery, stir, and leave to sizzle for a few minutes. Add the tripe and cook, stirring, for another 5 minutes. Add the tomatoes, peppercorns, bay leaves, chiles, and salt. Stir as the juice from the tomatoes comes to a simmer, then add the white wine and bring to a boil. Reduce the heat, cover tightly, and cook, barely simmering, for 15 minutes.

Add the pancetta and the kale, if using. Gradually moisten the stew, with the tripe liquid if you want a strong tripe flavor, with chicken stock if you don't, stirring in about 3/4 cup of the chosen broth. Bring to a simmer, then cover and reduce the heat to maintain a quiet simmer. Simmer until the stew becomes thick and unctuous and the tripe tender, about 30 more minutes. Add more liquid if necessary to keep the solids not quite covered. Add the garlic and parsley and simmer for 10 minutes longer. Taste. If making in advance, set aside to cool, then cover and refrigerate.

Cooking the eggs in the stew:

Transfer the tripe stew to a 3-quart sauté pan; set over medium-low heat. {If you prepared the stew in advance it will be thicker than when you first cooked it.} Taste. To make it spicier, fish out one or more of the chiles and squeeze, so the fiery juice inside drips into the stew. Stir in the extra-virgin olive oil. Make a hollow in the dense stew with the back of a ladle, then crack and slide an egg into the depression. Repeat with the remaining eggs, spacing them so they only barely touch, if at all. Shimmy the pan gently, cover, and cook at a bare simmer for 4 to 6 minutes, depending on how you like your eggs cooked.

Carefully spoon an egg each and some of the tripe stew into hot, wide soup bowls. Offer freshly cracked black pepper. Good on top of a slice of freshly grilled or toasted bread rubbed with raw garlic.

STARCHY DISHES

POLENTA

I CREDIT OUR SIMPLE FIVE-DOLLAR BOWL OF WARM POLENTA WITH KEEPING ZUNI
alive through the first days after the 1989 earthquake~business was terrible all
over town, but we stayed pretty busy, selling many more bowls than usual.
Inexpensive, reliable, and comforting, a well-seasoned bowl of polenta is satisfying by itself, but, soft, grilled, roasted, or fried, it also finds its way into dozens
of dishes at the restaurant, alongside, or under, beef, pork, or game birds. In any
of its forms, it is great with sausage or bacon.

We use organic polenta ground from a variety of yellow corn called Pioneer
{see Sources and Resources, page 518}. The grits are irregular and larger than
American cornmeal, and coarser than most commercial polenta I have seen in Italy.
It has lovely flavor, great body, and wonderful texture. {If you use a fine-textured
polenta, it will need less water; consult the package for the water-to-meal ratio. It
may cook somewhat more rapidly as well.}

There is a persistent superstition that polenta needs to be stirred constantly,
but we stir it only often enough to be sure it's not sticking and scorching. Steady,
gentle heat and a heavy-bottomed pot will also help prevent that. The light, tender, creamy, slightly viscous texture I prize, and our clients love, is the result of a
high ratio of water to meal and long, slow cooking, followed by a holding period
where the polenta meal swells and softens even more. This technique means you
can make the polenta up to a few hours in advance, which can be very convenient.

Serve soft polenta by the spoonful as a side dish, or by itself in warm bowls
with freshly grated Parmigiano-Reggiano, mascarpone, or crumbled Gorgonzola
and freshly cracked black pepper over the top. Alternatively, serve with a spoonful of rich tomato or meat sauce. Cook at least 1 cup of polenta at a time~it is difficult to cook less without much of the water evaporating before it can be
absorbed. Lots of suggestions for capitalizing on leftover polenta follow the recipe.

Wine: Merlot delle Venezie, Livio Felluga, 1999

FOR ABOUT 4-1/2 CUPS, OR 4 TO 8 SERVINGS:

5 cups water	About 2 teaspoons salt, or to taste
1 cup coarsely ground polenta	Unsalted butter, to taste {optional}

Bring the water to a simmer in a 2-quart saucepan. Whisk or stir in the
polenta, then stir until the water returns to a simmer. Reduce the heat until the

polenta only bubbles and sputters occasionally ~ use a Flame Tamer if necessary ~ and cook uncovered for about 1 hour, stirring as needed, until thick but still fluid. If the polenta becomes stiff, add a trickle of water. Taste. Add salt and a generous lump of butter, if you like.

Transfer the polenta to a double boiler set over simmering water, to rest for at least 30 minutes {or up to a few hours, if it suits your schedule}. Wrap the lid tightly in plastic wrap and cover the polenta. This will keep the polenta from developing a skin. If you don't have a double boiler, you can make do by setting the polenta pan on a small, ovenproof ramekin {or any small piece of heat-resistant crockery} centered inside a wider, deeper pot, and surrounding it with just-simmering water. Cover the pan as above.

* * *Variation* POLENTA *with* FRESH CORN

Perhaps better than plain polenta. Don't be tempted to stir the corn in raw, as some sweet corn may turn the thick polenta runny. Cooking the corn disables the guilty enzyme.

FOR ABOUT 5 CUPS:

2 tablespoons unsalted butter
About 1 cup fresh corn kernels and
    their milky juice {3 to 4 small
    ears} {see page 254}

1 recipe polenta, made without butter
    and kept warm
Salt

Melt the butter in a 10-inch skillet over low heat. Add the corn, stir, and cook until hot through, about 3 minutes. Stir into the waiting soft polenta. Taste for salt. Serve immediately, or spread on a sheet pan to firm up for roasting or grilling.

+ + Variation SAGE *&* ONION POLENTA

Very delicious by itself or with pork or poultry.

FOR ABOUT 5-1/2 CUPS:

4 tablespoons unsalted butter

About 2 cups diced yellow onions {8 ounces, about 1 medium onion}

A dozen fresh sage leaves, coarsely chopped

Freshly cracked black pepper

Salt

1 recipe polenta, made without butter

While the polenta is cooking, melt the butter in a 10- or 12-inch skillet over medium-low heat. Stir in the onions, sage, and lots of freshly cracked pepper. Salt lightly and cook slowly until the onions are translucent and soft, about 8 minutes.

Stir the onions into the thick polenta. Taste.

FIRM POLENTA *&* THREE WAYS TO SERVE IT

SPREAD SOFT POLENTA ABOUT AN INCH DEEP ON A LIGHTLY OILED SHEET PAN TO cool. You can leave the surface smooth, or wait until it is partially set and then churn the surface somewhat, giving it shallow valleys and little crags, which will become especially crispy when you later grill or roast it.

Note: For any of these side dishes, allow 5 to 6 ounces polenta per person.

+ + ROASTED POLENTA

Leftover polenta {plain or either variation} becomes delicate, if such a thing is possible, when patiently roasted this way. Cut into 2- to 3-inch triangles and brush on all sides with melted unsalted butter or olive oil. Arrange, widely spaced, on a sheet pan or in a shallow gratin dish and roast for about 30 minutes at 275°. Rather than drying out, the polenta will become crunchy outside, and surprisingly succulent and almost fluffy inside. Serve with hearty stews and braises.

+ + SAGE *&* ONION POLENTA GRATIN

An obvious idea, but one that takes a little bit of care to steer clear of stodginess. The cooked onions make it particularly tender and succulent. Serve by itself, or with roasted or grilled birds, pork, or beef. It is great with pot roast, or with warm, leftover pot roast juices added to the edge of the dish as you pull it from the oven~trust the hot dish to bring the juices to a simmer.

Preheat the oven to 350°.

Cut firm Sage and Onion Polenta {page 192} into rough 3/4-inch chunks. Ragged edges are good. Choose a baking dish that will hold the chunks in about two loose layers. Brush the dish with melted unsalted butter. Arrange the chunks of polenta in the dish, making sure that some poke higher than others so they will produce a nice irregular surface and brown more than the rest. Include the broken bits and crumbles. Dab the tips with more melted butter, or top with a lacy layer of grated Fontina or Swiss Gruyère.

Bake until the high points are quite brown, 20 minutes or longer. Don't shortcut the oven time, or the chunks of polenta will be heavy. Serve immediately.

⁜ POLENTA HASH

Serve with sausage, fried eggs, grilled birds, or saucy pot roast. You will get the crunchiest results if you make this in a well-seasoned cast-iron pan or on a steel griddle, but it is easiest to manage in a nonstick skillet.

Break firm polenta into irregular 1- to 3-inch chunks. This will produce some crumbles. If using plain polenta, prepare a few spoonfuls of diced onion or of a mixture of diced carrot, celery, and onion per serving.

Heat 1/8 inch of mild-tasting olive oil in the chosen pan over low heat. Add the vegetables, if using, and stir to coat. Pile on the chunks and crumbles of polenta, to cover the bottom of the pan in a loose, craggy, 1-inch thick layer. Press gently to encourage surface contact. {Don't add salt~the polenta is fully seasoned.} Turn the heat up until the oil begins to pop discreetly. Cook uncovered and undisturbed until the polenta sets a firm golden crust, about 10 minutes. Reduce the heat as needed so the vegetables don't burn.

Turn the polenta over, a spatula-full at a time, making sure you break a few pieces as you go, creating new faces to brown. Leave to set a crust, another 8 to 10 minutes, then turn the polenta again. Don't rush the hash; turning it when the crust is too thin will result in polenta mush. Continue turning and crisping until you have a nice balance of small and large bits and of slightly under- and slightly overcooked vegetable bits. Serve immediately, or hold in the pan, uncovered, in a 250° oven for up to 20 minutes.

⁜

ABOUT RISOTTO

Risotto makers are much esteemed in kitchens and dining rooms, as though risotto were somehow more demanding than a fine plate of pasta. In fact, producing a satiny-creamy risotto, the grains still al dente, is not such a tricky operation and is only unforgiving when it comes to mediocre raw ingredients.

For traditional risotto, we use Italian Carnaroli or Arborio rice. Look for a brand that boasts its harvest date; rice from the most recent harvest will have better flavor than the prior year's crop. And make sure the single variety is listed on the package. A cheerful box labeled "rice for risotto" may contain a profitable mix of rices that won't cook evenly. {You can make risotto with other types of rice, such as the Italian Vialone Nano, Baldo, and Sant'Andrea or, for that matter, Spanish and starchy Asian rices. I've made delicious risotto-y dishes with all at home. Perhaps the grains are smaller and have a different flavor from Carnaroli or Arborio, but the cooking method is certainly friendly to them.} Store rice in a cool, dark spot, and, if you choose a brand sold in cloth bags, be aware it may absorb surrounding odors. Rice packaged in unlined cardboard may taste faintly of that.

Regarding stock: Most of the unfixable, bland risotto I have tasted in my kitchen owes to mediocre stock. No high-concept, earnest technique, added salt, extra cheese, glamour vegetables, or final splash of great wine will mask it. Delicious stock, on the other hand, can carry a risotto by itself, and will harmonize with carefully dosed embellishments. Taste your stock critically ~ if it doesn't taste bright enough to sip "as is," it will likely compromise the risotto. If your stock is lackluster, consider serving pasta instead. {Or ponder water. I have made tastier risotto using water than I can conjure with bland stock. The water effort is at least bursting with a clean rice flavor, preferable to the muddy, noncommittal result you get with dull stock.}

Concerning technique, I use a heavy, deep saucepan ~ 2-quart for up to 1-1/2 cups rice, 4-quart for 2 to 3-1/2 cups rice, and so on. I find that a saucepan has advantages over wide sauté pan or skillet. A deep layer of rice has less surface area than a shallow layer, which makes it much easier to control evaporation and favors even absorption of liquid. {This decreased evaporation, by the way, means you may use less liquid than when you use a shallow pan.} As you cook the risotto, aim for something close to a gentle simmer, but don't worry if the rate of simmer varies. I avoid high heat, if only to prevent scorching and splattering. Gentle, regular stirring encourages even absorption of liquid and keeps things from sticking.

In my experience, risotto is forgiving when it comes to the temperature of the stock, wine, or other liquid you add to it. Although for years I added only simmering stock to the rice, I never found that this rigor guaranteed creaminess, or any other measure of risotto success. Then, after I casually made a fine risotto using room-temperature stock, I started experimenting with cold, warm, and hot stock and found I could make a creamy risotto with any one. Whatever its temperature when you add it, the stock will reach nearly 200° as it is absorbed by the rice. At home, I most often use cold or cool stock~which conserves burner space and means one less pot to clean. This convenient heresy alarms even longtime cooks at Zuni, but it has not failed me. A simmering stock will speed things up, and allows you to nearly standardize cooking time, but, all other things being equal, you can get fine results with less-than-simmering stock. {But don't take this to mean you can leave stock for hours at room temperature. "Just-warm" stock should be that way only because it simmered recently.} You'll tend to use less stock if it is cold than if it is simmering away on the back burner.

In the initial phases of a risotto, adding the stock or other liquid requires no great rigor; you can add larger or smaller increments than I suggest. Likewise, exactly how "absorbed" each early dose is is not critical to the final result, so long as you don't let the rice dry out completely. It is only the final doses that require thoughtful judgment, to make sure you don't add more stock than an al dente grain needs. At that point, treat each addition as though it will be the final one, waiting for the liquid to be absorbed and turn viscous before adding more. Add little doses of the liquid until the grains are nutty-tender. The rice should still be uniform and smooth on the outside~not rough on the surface from oversaturation. Bite into a grain~and look for a speck of white at the core. Err on the side of undercooking; the rice will continue to absorb liquid and soften after you turn off the heat. Once the rice is al dente, a final splash of liquid, brought to a simmer, will give the dish a saucy *all'onda* {wavelike} quality. With regards to timing, expect most batches of risotto to take under 20 minutes to absorb hot stock; allow a little more time if you use colder stock. I allow about 30 minutes overall for most risottos.

A cup of rice will yield about 2-1/2 cups of plain al dente risotto, a little more if you like it *all'onda*, and then more as you stir in other things~I advocate restraint here. Too much "stuff" will distract from and disintegrate the carefully nurtured texture of risotto, and you risk overwhelming the lovely flavor of the rice as well.

Citrus Risotto

This fragrant risotto surprises and delights everyone who makes, or eats, it. In our menu meeting before going upstairs to prepare for dinner service, cooks often look at me as if I've slipped a little when I explain what goes into it. It doesn't sound as if it will fall into balance, but it does. Use sweet, ripe, pink or red grapefruit. If you can get ripe limes~which have yellow rinds~they will be more fragrant and sweeter than the bright green, unripe supermarket standard.

We sometimes serve this risotto as a bed for sweet spot prawns or fat white shrimp, both of which we sauté in their shells.

Wine: Pinot Grigio, Alto Adige, J. Hofstätter, 2000

FOR 4 TO 6 SERVINGS:

1 to 2 medium grapefruit, to yield 3/4 cup sections {about 16 small sections} plus juice

1 lime, to yield a scant 1/4 cup sections {about 8 sections}

2 tablespoons unsalted butter

1/2 cup finely diced yellow onion {2 ounces}

Salt

2 cups Carnaroli or Arborio rice

3-1/2 to 5 cups Chicken Stock {page 58}

1/4 cup mascarpone

Slice both ends off the grapefruit and lime, cutting just deeply enough to expose the juicy flesh. Setting the citrus on end, use a paring knife to carve away the skin and pith in a series of smooth, curved strokes from top to bottom, rotating the citrus a little with each stroke. If you don't get all the pith on the first go-round, go back and trim any you missed. Next, cradling the citrus in one hand, slide the blade of the knife close to the membranes on either side of each segment and gently pry out the sections; work over a bowl so you capture the juice. Tease out any seeds you encounter as you go, and don't worry if some of the sections break. Squeeze the remaining juice from the grapefruit "carcasses" into the bowl.

Warm the butter in a 4-quart saucepan over medium-low heat. Add the onions and a few pinches of salt. Cook, stirring regularly, until the onions are tender and translucent, about 6 minutes. Add the rice and stir until the grains are warm and coated with fat. Add about 2 cups of the stock, adjusting the heat to maintain a gentle simmer, then stir as needed until it has been mostly absorbed. Add another cup of stock and do likewise. The risotto should look like a shiny porridge of pearls. Taste: the rice will still be hard and a little raw tasting. Correct the satiny liquid for salt. Add another 1/2 cup or so of stock and stir as needed until just absorbed. Taste again, checking flavor and doneness.

Break the citrus sections into irregular pieces as you add them, and the grapefruit juice, to the risotto. Continue to cook as described above. Taste again. If the rice is still quite firm, add more stock about a tablespoon at a time and cook until it is al dente. If your grapefruit was very juicy, you may use little of the remaining stock. Turn off the heat and, with a little vigor, stir in the mascarpone. The citrus will be reduced to pretty flecks in the creamy rice. Serve promptly.

⁘

RISOTTO *with* WILD RICE, SQUASH,
& WILD MUSHROOMS

I LIKE TO STIR A LITTLE COOKED WILD RICE INTO RISOTTO TO INTRODUCE TEXTURAL contrast and nutty flavor. Here the austere wild rice balances the sweet, soft squash and earthy mushrooms. This is a good autumn combination; in the springtime, try a similar combination of wild rice with favas or asparagus tips and morel mushrooms. You can also try stirring in cooked whole-grain farro {see page 199} in place of the wild rice.

For any version of the dish, I cook the mushrooms separately and then add them to the risotto when it is about half-cooked. This heightens the flavor of the mushrooms and keeps them from having a boiled texture. Likewise, I add the squash late enough that it will reach peak flavor and be just tender at the same moment the rice is al dente.

Wine: Toar, Rosso del Veronese, Masi, 1997

\ *continued*

FOR 4 TO 6 SERVINGS:

About 1/4 cup wild rice

3/4 cup water

Salt

4 tablespoons unsalted butter

About 6 ounces cleaned, sliced wild mushrooms, such as porcini, chanterelles, or hedgehogs {see page 516}

About 1 cup peeled butternut, Kabocha, or Red Kuri squash cut into 3/8-inch dice {about 4 ounces}

1/2 cup finely diced yellow onions {2 ounces}

2 cups Carnaroli or Arborio rice

4 to 5 cups Chicken Stock {page 58}.

About 1/4 cup freshly grated Parmigiano-Reggiano

Place the wild rice and water in a 2-quart or smaller saucepan. Bring to a simmer over low heat and stir in salt to taste. Adjust the heat to achieve a nearly imperceptible simmer and cover tightly. Cook until tender, about 45 minutes, checking occasionally to make sure the water hasn't begun to boil hard. The rice will not cook perfectly evenly; the majority should be splitting along the length of the grain, and as many as one-third of them may spread wide open and curl before the whole lot is tender. Drain in a strainer and capture the excess cooking water. You should have about 3/4 cup cooked rice and a few tablespoons of flavorful cooking water.

Melt 2 tablespoons of the butter in a 10- or 12-inch skillet over medium-low heat. Add the mushrooms, salt lightly, and cook, stirring or tossing a few times, until they color slightly, 3 to 6 minutes, depending on how wet the mushrooms are. You should just begin to smell their nutty aroma. Add the squash cubes, salt lightly, and stir or sauté just to warm through, about 3 more minutes. Remove from the heat, cover, and set aside.

Warm the remaining 2 tablespoons butter in a 4-quart saucepan over medium-low heat. Add the onions and a few pinches of salt. Cook, stirring regularly, until the onions are tender and translucent, about 6 minutes. Add the risotto rice and stir until the grains are warm and coated with fat. Add the wild rice cooking water and about 2 cups of the stock. Adjust the heat to bring it to and maintain a gentle simmer, then stir as needed until it has been mostly absorbed. Add another cup of stock and do likewise. The risotto should look like a shiny porridge of pearls. Taste: the rice will be hard and a little raw tasting. Correct the satiny liquid for salt.

Stir the mushrooms, squash, and wild rice into the risotto, then add another cup or so of stock and stir as needed until just absorbed. Taste again, checking the flavor and doneness. Add additional stock a few spoonfuls at a time until the rice is al dente; the squash ought to be nutty-tender as well.

Stir in the Parmigiano-Reggiano, off the heat.

⁘ ⁘

FARROTTO *with* DRIED PORCINI

FARRO, OR EMMER WHEAT {*TRITICUM DICOCCUM*}, GROUND INTO MEAL AND cooked into a porridge, was the life-sustaining *puls* {the original polenta} that fueled the legionnaires. This "*farrotto*," made like a risotto but with whole kernels of farro, would be the wealthy modern descendant, still elemental and nourishing, but lavishly concocted with meat stock, mushrooms, and fine oil. It is substantial winter fare. Use whole farro {which may be labeled variously as "*decorticato*," "*perlato*," or "*semiperlato*"}; cracked farro cooks much more rapidly and will lack the requisite nutty-chewy consistency that gives this dish character.

Wine: Falerno del Massico Rosso, Villa Matilde, 1999

FOR ABOUT 4 CUPS, OR 4 TO 6 SERVINGS:

1/4 cup extra-virgin olive oil, plus a little for drizzling

1/4 cup diced yellow onion {1 ounce}

3 garlic cloves, coarsely chopped

3 fresh sage leaves, coarsely chopped

Salt

About 1/4 ounce dried porcini {about 1/2 cup loosely packed}, rinsed and coarsely chopped, or about 2 ounces fresh porcini or chanterelles, cleaned and diced {see page 516}

1-1/3 cups whole-grain farro

4 to 5 cups Chicken Stock {page 58} or Beef Stock {page 63}

Freshly cracked black pepper

Warm about half of the olive oil in a 2- to 4-quart saucepan over medium heat. Add the onion, garlic, sage, and a few pinches of salt, then add the fresh

\ *continued*

mushrooms, if using. Cook, stirring regularly, until the onion is translucent, about 4 minutes. Reduce the heat to medium-low.

Add the farro and the rest of the olive oil and stir to coat the farro. Add about one-third of the stock and, if using them, the dried mushrooms and cook at a gentle simmer, stirring regularly, until the stock has been absorbed. Repeat with another third of the stock, then add the last third more gradually, checking for tenderness as each addition is absorbed; taste and adjust the salt as you go. Depending on your pan and your burner, it should take between 20 and 30 minutes for the farro to become nutty-tender. You may not need all of the stock.

Farrotto is forgiving, timing-wise; covered and held in a warm spot, it will hold for up to a half hour without the texture of the grain suffering, although you will need to add a splash of hot stock to restore the consistency. Serve very hot, drizzled with extra-virgin olive oil. Offer black pepper.

✦ ✦ TURNING FARROTTO *into* FARRO SOUP:

Leftover *farrotto* is a good base for soup. We add cooked shelling beans, greens, and my favorite leftover, stale bread. Here is a flexible recipe for how you might do that; adjust the amounts to your supplies and your taste.

FOR 3-1/2 TO 5 CUPS:

A handful of greens {kale, mature mustard, collard, turnip greens, or Savoy cabbage}, cut into bite-sized pieces

1 bay leaf

1 to 2 cups Chicken Stock {page 58} or water

About 2 cups leftover *farrotto*

1/2 to 1 cup cooked white beans, flageolets, or lentils {see page 263}, with their cooking liquid.

About 2 ounces slightly stale, chewy, peasant-style bread, torn into bite-sized wads

Extra-virgin olive oil, to taste

Freshly cracked black pepper

Place the greens and bay leaf in a saucepan and add stock or water to cover by an inch. Cover and simmer gently until the greens are tender, about 10 minutes.

Stir in the *farrotto* and the beans {with their liquid} and bring to a simmer. Add more stock or water if the result is pasty. Don't worry if it seems a little thin. Taste for salt. Simmer gently, uncovered, for about 15 minutes, until the farro is very tender and the flavors have melded. Stir in the bread and return to a simmer. Add more stock or water as needed to make a soft porridge. Cover tightly and turn off the heat. Leave to swell for about 10 minutes, then stir, taste, and serve. Offer extra-virgin olive oil and freshly cracked black pepper.

+ + + + +

GENERAL NOTES *on* PASTA COOKERY

+ Consider the package instructions concerning cooking times as guidelines only, and check the pasta regularly. With some experience and attention, you will be able to judge doneness by the color of the noodle and its "droop factor" as you dangle it from tongs, but biting into the pasta is a reliable test for all experience levels. "Al dente" means the pasta should just resist your tooth~it should have a faint trace of white at the core when you bite through and inspect the cut face of the noodle.

+ Drain cooked pasta immediately and shake hard in a colander or strainer. Don't rinse; the surface starch helps bind the sauce to the pasta.

+ Make sure the sauce or topping is piping hot when you combine it with the steaming pasta. Beware of adding pasta to a sizzling-hot pan~it will stick wherever sauce does not insulate it instantly.

+ Serve on warm plates or bowls. Most pasta preparations lose their savor as they cool.

+ + + + +

PASTA *with* CORN, PANCETTA, BUTTER, *&* SAGE

ONCE THE FIRST LOCAL SWEET CORN ARRIVES IN JUNE, WE MAKE THIS PASTA, IN one form or another, a few times a week. My favorite version is whichever one we are making on a given day. The formula is delicious with or without the Parmigiano-Reggiano, with a little cream added at the end, with prosciutto in lieu

\ *continued*

of the pancetta, or without meat at all. An unmeasured scatter of sweet peas in addition to the corn is another pretty and delicious variation.

Buy fresh-picked corn, and when choosing ears, root around for the young ones with small kernels~you'll get less corn per cob, but what you sacrifice in yield is inconsequential, given the difference in quality. Fat, full kernels tend to be tougher, dry, and starchy. Juicy, young kernels need less butter to make a succulent pasta dish. Otherwise, you can't skimp on butter without stripping the dish of succulence. {If less butter is your goal, reducing portion size makes more sense}. I have tried this dish with various olive oils and found the flavor disappointing.

Wine: Ruchè di Castagnola Monferrato, Na Vota, Cantine Sant'Agata, 2000

FOR 4 OR 5 SERVINGS:

2 to 3 ounces pancetta, minced {1/3 to 1/2 cup}

Up to 1/2 pound {2 sticks} unsalted butter

A trickle of water

6 fresh sage leaves, coarsely chopped

Freshly cracked black pepper

1 pound fettuccine, tagliarini, or other slender egg pasta

Salt

2-1/2 cups freshly scraped corn kernels and their milky juice {5 to 10 small, young ears, depending on yield; see page 254}

A small chunk of Parmigiano-Reggiano

Cook the pancetta in a few tablespoons of the butter in a 12-inch skillet over medium-low heat. Stir and scrape to make sure it cooks evenly. When the pancetta has browned slightly on the edges and is starting to sizzle, turn off the heat, add a few drops of water to cool the pan, and stir, then add another few tablespoons of butter, the sage, and a few grinds of black pepper. Swirl the pan, then leave the aromatics to infuse the melting butter.

Drop the pasta into 6 quarts of rapidly boiling water seasoned with a scant 2 tablespoons salt {a little more if using kosher salt}. Stir, and cook until the pasta is al dente.

Meanwhile, turn the heat under the skillet to medium, and add another 6 to 8 tablespoons butter, sliced. Swirl the pan. When the butter is nearly melted, add the corn, stir, and cook until heated through. Taste for salt. If the corn seems dry, add a trickle of pasta water and some or all of the remaining butter, to taste. Reduce the heat to low.

When the pasta is cooked, drain well, then toss with the corn, taste again for salt, and serve. Offer freshly grated Parmigiano-Reggiano.

❖
❖ ❖

Pasta *with* Spicy Broccoli *&* Cauliflower

A DISH CELEBRATING MOST OF MY FAVORITE SEASONINGS AND CONDIMENTS: CAPERS, garlic, chili flakes, olives, anchovies, bread crumbs. You can use all broccoli or all cauliflower if you like. You can try minced fennel bulb in lieu of seeds for a sweeter, more subtle note, or dash both and use freshly chopped mint instead. Substitute pecorino romano if you don't feel like bread crumbs, trade black olives for green ones, or skip the olives and add more capers or anchovies. But don't sacrifice the 8 to 10 minutes of care it takes to cook the vegetables to the delicately frazzled crispness that gives the dish its great texture and variety. The sautéed vegetables are great by themselves, or as a side dish with grilled or roasted poultry or meat.

This formula works with all sorts of chewy pastas ~ penne, spaghetti, orecchiette, or shells.

Wine: Somontano Chardonnay, Enata, 1999

\ *continued*

FOR 4 TO 5 SERVINGS:

About 1 cup fresh, soft bread crumbs {about 2 ounces} made from crustless, slightly stale, chewy, white peasant-style bread {see page 506} {optional}

About 3/4 cup mild-tasting olive oil

About 12 ounces broccoli, trimmed, with a few inches of stem intact

About 12 ounces cauliflower, leaves removed and stem end trimmed flush

Salt

1 generous tablespoon capers, rinsed, pressed dry between towels, and slightly chopped

1 pound penne, spaghetti, orecchiette, fusilli, or medium shells

1 tablespoon chopped salt-packed anchovy fillets {4 to 6 fillets} {optional}

6 small garlic cloves, coarsely chopped

About 1/2 teaspoon fennel seeds, lightly pounded in a mortar

4 to 8 pinches dried chili flakes

1 tablespoon tightly packed, coarsely chopped, fresh flat-leaf parsley

4 to 5 tablespoons coarsely chopped pitted black olives, such as Niçoise, Gaeta, or Nyons {rinsed first to rid them of excess brine}

If using bread crumbs, preheat the oven to 425°.

Toss the bread crumbs with 2 teaspoons of the oil, spread on a baking sheet, and bake for about 5 minutes, until golden. Keep the crumbs on the stove top until needed.

Slice the broccoli and cauliflower about 1/8 inch thick, and generally lengthwise. Most of the slices will break apart as you produce them, yielding a pile of smooth stem pieces, tiny green broccoli buds, loose cauliflower crumbs, and a few delicate slabs with stem and flower both. Don't worry if the slices are of uneven thickness; that will make for more textural variety.

Warm about 1/4 cup of the oil in a 12-inch skillet over medium heat. Add most of the sliced broccoli and cauliflower, conveniently leaving the smallest bits behind on the cutting board for the moment. {They'll burn if you add them too soon.} The oil should sizzle quietly. Swirl the pan, and leave the vegetables to cook until you see the edge bits browning, about 3 minutes. Salt very lightly and toss or stir and fold gently. Add a few more spoonfuls of oil and scrape the remaining bits of broccoli and cauliflower into the pan. Add the capers and swirl gently. Continue cooking over medium heat until the edges begin to brown, another few minutes, then give the pan another stir or toss. Don't stir too soon or too often, or you will get a homogenous, steamy pile of vegetables instead of a crispy, chewy one. Most of the capers and vegetable crumbs will shrink into crispy confetti-like bits.

Meanwhile, drop the pasta into 6 quarts of rapidly boiling water seasoned with a scant 2 tablespoons salt {a little more if using kosher salt}. Stir, and cook al dente. Set a wide bowl or platter on the stovetop {or in the still-warm oven if you made crumbs} to heat.

Once the mass of broccoli and cauliflower has shrunken by about one-third and is largely tender, reduce the heat, add another few spoonfuls of oil, and scatter the chopped anchovy, garlic, fennel, and chili over all. Give the vegetables a stir or toss to distribute. Cook for another few minutes, then add the parsley and olives. Taste ~ every flavor should be clamoring for dominance. Adjust as needed.

Toss with the well-drained pasta and garnish with the warm, toasted bread crumbs, if desired.

✢
✢ ✢

PASTA *with* BRAISED BACON &
ROASTED TOMATO SAUCE

OUR VERSION OF THE MUCH-LOVED DISH FROM ABRUZZO, *PASTA ALL'AMATRICIANA*. Since the traditional signature ingredient, *guanciale* {tender pig-cheek bacon}, is not available to us, we blanch and slow-cook a piece of slab bacon, which renders much of the fat and mellows strong cures. Consider braising a larger chunk of bacon than you think you will need; you can use the extra for other recipes {Lentil-Sweet Red Pepper Soup, page 167; Lentils Braised in Red Wine, page 267; or Salmon Cooked with Bacon and Red Wine Flageolets, page 324} or wherever you ordinarily use bacon. I like the tender leftover bits and scraps fried in the same pan with eggs, with a trickle of the bacon braising juices spooned over the top. You can prepare this multipurpose bacon up to a week in advance, which is a

\ *continued*

boon. But for those times when braised bacon is not an option, make this dish with little strips of thickly sliced bacon. {Brown them while the pasta boils, then drain off most of the fat, stir in the peppery tomato sauce, and simmer together for a minute or two.}

We always make this sauce with canned tomatoes ~ roasting them concentrates their flavor and gives them a fleshy texture. If you make extra sauce, you can use it for Pasta with Sardines and Tomato Sauce {page 208}.

Pasta all'amatriciana is traditionally made with bucatini {also called perci-atelle}, but penne, penne rigate, and spaghetti are good alternatives. Offer freshly grated pecorino romano or pecorino sardo to garnish; the salty, feral flavor is a good match for this aggressive sauce. Parmigiano-Reggiano would taste out of place here.

Wine: Rioja Reserva Viña Ardanza, La Rioja Alta, 1995

FOR 4 TO 5 SERVINGS:
For the braised bacon {makes 1/2 to 3/4 pound}:

3/4 to 1 pound slab bacon, in one piece, skin removed

1 small carrot, peeled and coarsely chopped

1 stalk celery, coarsely chopped

1 small yellow onion, thickly sliced

1 bay leaf, crumbled

About 1/2 cup dry white wine

About 1/2 cup dry white vermouth

About 1/2 cup Chicken Stock {page 58} or water

For the roasted tomato sauce {makes about 2-1/2 cups}:

2-1/2 cups drained canned whole tomatoes, juice reserved

About 1/2 cup extra-virgin olive oil

8 ounces sliced yellow onion {about 1 medium onion}

6 garlic cloves, coarsely chopped

1 teaspoon freshly cracked black pepper, plus more for serving

1 bay leaf

Salt

Sugar, if needed

1 pound bucatini, penne, penne rigate, or spaghetti

Freshly grated pecorino romano or pecorino sardo, to taste

Preparing the braised bacon:
Preheat the oven to 300°.

Place the bacon in a wide pot and add cold water to cover by a few inches. Set over medium heat, bring to a simmer, and cook until the bacon softens a little, 5 to 10 minutes. Drain and rinse. {This process will draw out some of the sweet-salty brine and more important, rehydrate the bacon, to produce a tender, succulent result.}

Place the bacon fat side up in a shallow flameproof baking dish just large enough to hold it and the vegetables in a single layer {A 1-quart gratin dish should work; cut the bacon into 2 pieces if necessary}. Add the carrot, celery, onion, and bay leaf and moisten with equal parts of the wine, vermouth, and stock, adding enough to come to a depth of 1/2 inch. Place over medium heat and bring to a simmer. Cover with parchment paper and then with foil, dull side out, transfer to the oven, and bake until melting tender, about 2-1/2 hours.

Uncover the baking dish, raise the-heat to broil, and leave just long enough the color the surface, 3 to 5 minutes. By now the bacon will have rendered about 30 percent of its weight, most of it in fat. Leave to cool completely in the baking dish, then skim or scrape off and discard the rendered fat. Strain and save the braising liquid to flavor beans, soups, or braised greens. {I usually discard the braising vegetables as too strong and too cooked to be of interest.}

If not using the bacon right away, cool completely, then replace in a clean baking dish, add the strained liquid, cover, and refrigerate.

Preparing the tomato sauce:
Preheat the oven to 500°.

Halve the tomatoes and place cut side down in a shallow roasting pan or gratin dish that holds them in one crowded layer. They shouldn't be stacked, or they will steam and stew rather than dry out and color. Add any juice they released when you cut them in half, plus enough of the reserved juice to come to a depth of 1/4 inch. Drizzle with a tablespoon or two of the olive oil.

Roast until the tomatoes char slightly and are bubbling around the edges, about 15 minutes. Use a dough cutter to very coarsely chop in the roasting dish.

Shortly before the tomatoes are done, in a 12-inch skillet, cook the onions in about 3 tablespoons of the olive oil over medium-high heat until they begin to color at the edges, about 3 minutes. Reduce the heat and stir in the garlic, pepper, and bay leaf.

\ *continued*

When the onions are just beginning to soften through, stir in the warm toma-toes and another few tablespoons of olive oil. Salt lightly to taste, and add a pinch or two of sugar if you find the tomatoes too tart. Add a spoonful of the reserved tomato juice if needed to keep the tomatoes saucy. Simmer briefly, just long enough to combine the elements, but without sacrificing their textures and indi-viduality. Set aside.

Cooking and saucing the pasta:

Cut the braised bacon into strips about 1/4 inch thick and 1 inch long.

Drop the pasta into 6 quarts rapidly boiling water seasoned with a scant 2 tablespoons salt {a little more if using kosher salt}. Stir, and cook until al dente.

Meanwhile, brown the bacon strips in a 12-inch skillet or 3-quart sauté pan over medium heat, stirring as needed, until both sides are slightly colored, a few minutes at most. If the bacon seems dry, add a trickle of olive oil. Stir in the tomato sauce. Simmer together for a minute or so.

Drain the pasta well and fold into the tomato sauce. Offer the pecorino and additional black pepper.

⁜

PASTA *with* SARDINES *&* TOMATO SAUCE

T HIS DELICIOUS, TRADITIONAL PASTA IS FOR VERA AND JIM CALCAGNO. I'd forgot-ten how good it was until my business partner, Vince, their son, reminded me how his parents loved *pasta con le sarde* and asked if we could put it on the menu to honor their visit from Ohio. What it really celebrates is their roots in southern-most Italy. This recipe has become a Zuni mainstay and is one of my favorites, but it might have languished in the crowded bin of also-rans if the Calcagno clan hadn't made it the Zuni family pasta.

The pasta here has only a light dressing of tomato sauce, so you can taste the delicate sardines. Serve with bucatini, sometimes called perciatelle, which are long, skinny tube noodles. Penne and spaghetti are good alternatives.

It is worth preparing extra sardines to fillet and preserve in warm Chimichurri {page 298}, or simply bathe them in extra-virgin olive oil with bay leaf, chili flakes, slivered garlic, a splash of vinegar, and salt. Let them cool, then cover and store refrigerated to use later on crostini {see page 124}. So long as they are well salted and thoroughly cooked, they will keep, and improve, for a week or even longer.

Wine: Regaleali, Conte Tasca d'Almerita, 2000

FOR 4 TO 5 SERVINGS:

4 to 6 fresh sardines {2 to 3 ounces each}

Salt

About 2 tablespoons mild-tasting olive oil

1 pound bucatini, penne, or spaghetti

About 2 tablespoons extra-virgin olive oil

A few fennel seeds, lightly crushed {optional}

A pinch of dried chili flakes

About 1-1/2 cups Roasted Tomato Sauce {page 205}

A sprig fresh flat-leaf parsley, or a fennel frond, or both, coarsely chopped

Preheat the broiler.

Clean the sardines: Cut off the heads, which should pull out most of the viscera. Slide a finger into the belly cavity and pry it open. Gently rinse out the bellies and rub off the scales under cold, running water. Pat dry inside and out. Salt evenly all over and drizzle and roll in the mild-tasting olive oil. Place on a small baking sheet and roast under the hot broiler until firm and cooked through, about 2 minutes per side. Adjust the height of the broiler rack so the fish doesn't char. Cool completely.

By hand, ease the sardine fillets off the bones. Once you have filleted all of the fish, go back and recheck for bones, looking especially for remnants of the fins.

Drop the pasta into 6 quarts rapidly boiling water seasoned with a scant 2 tablespoons salt {a little more if using kosher salt}. Stir, and cook until al dente.

Meanwhile, warm the extra-virgin olive oil in a 12-inch skillet or 3-quart sauté pan over low heat. Add the fennel seeds, if using, and the chili flakes. Add the sardine fillets and swirl the pan as you warm them through. Add the tomato sauce, parsley, and/or fennel frond. Continue to swirl the pan over low heat to

\ *continued*

combine the flavors, without completely breaking down the delicate fish fillets. Taste for salt. Once the sauce comes to a simmer, turn off the heat and leave on the burner until the pasta is ready.

Drain the pasta well, slide into the pan of warm sauce, and fold to distribute, then serve.

❖
❖ ❖

PASTA *alla* CARBONARA

THIS ROGUE VERSION OF CARBONARA IS BASED ON ONE I HAD IN ROME. It is not very saucy, and the ricotta makes it pleasantly curdy. The bacon should be crispy-tender and aromatic; don't be tempted to cook it in advance ~ you will sacrifice much of its aroma to convenience, and it will tend to harden. And don't substitute Parmigiano-Reggiano for the aged pecorino.

Serve with a chewy, dried semolina pasta shape that does not grab too much sauce: spaghetti, spaghettini, penne, or bucatini.

Wine: Bodega Norton, Mendoza, Argentina, Malbec Reserve, 1999

FOR 4 TO 5 SERVINGS:

5 ounces bacon {4 or 5 thick slices}, cut into 1/4- to 1/2-inch segments

5 tablespoons extra-virgin olive oil

4 large or 5 small eggs, at room temperature

1/2 cup fresh ricotta cheese, at room temperature

1 pound spaghetti, penne, or bucatini

Salt

About 3/4 cup shucked sweet English peas or mature sugar snap peas or double-peeled favas {see page 88}

About 2 ounces pecorino romano or pecorino sardo, grated {1 cup lightly packed}

Freshly cracked black pepper

Warm the bacon in the olive oil in a 12-inch skillet or 3-quart sauté pan {see Note below} over low heat. It should gradually render a little fat, which will mix with the oil.

Meanwhile, lightly beat the eggs with the ricotta.

Drop the pasta into 6 quarts rapidly boiling water seasoned with a scant 2 tablespoons salt {a little more if using kosher salt}. Stir, and cook until al dente.

When the pasta is about 1 minute from being al dente, add the peas or favas to the water, and raise the heat under the bacon. Cook the bacon until it is just crispy on the edges but still tender in the middle. Turn off the heat, slide the pan from the heat, and swirl it a few times to cool it slightly.

Drain the pasta, shake off the excess water, and slide the pasta and peas or favas into the pan of bacon; you'll hear a discreet sizzle. Place back on the burner {the one you used to cook the bacon, which should still be quite warm}. Immediately pour the beaten eggs all over the steaming pasta, add most of the pecorino and lots of cracked black pepper, and fold to combine. Work quickly so the heat of the noodles, bacon, and bacon fat slightly cooks the eggs. The eggs and ricotta will coat the pasta and form tiny, soft, golden curds.

Serve in warm bowls and offer the remaining pecorino and black pepper.

Note: If you prefer the egg cooked further, return the pan to low heat, but use a nonstick pan, or else much of the egg, and some of the pasta, will stick to the pan.

❖ ❖ ❖

PASTA *with* PRESERVED TUNA *&* PINE NUTS

THIS TUNA CONSERVATION TECHNIQUE IS A BY-PRODUCT OF THE "SUNDAY NIGHT Fish Problem," and my culinary apprenticeship in confit country. Zuni is closed on Monday, and writing off leftover yellowfin tuna would be a fiscal nightmare. But salting and then slowly cooking it to tenderness in fragrant fat, as you would duck confit, transforms tuna completely and yields a delicious, versatile larder staple. Bluefin or Bigeye tuna are even better preserved this way; they are softer than yellowfin to begin with, and stay tender with long cooking. I like their strong flavor here. This preserved tuna appears frequently as an antipasto at Zuni, tossed with

\ *continued*

white beans and fennel or crumbled into Artichoke Caponata {page 103} or traditional eggplant caponata. As little as a thimbleful of preserved tuna pounded into a few spoonfuls of Orange-Olive Tapenade {page 304} makes a good crostini topping.

But this popular pasta dish is where we use most of our preserved tuna. Use a small tube shape: penne, ziti, or ditali. And, if you aren't burdened, or blessed, with fresh tuna, leftover or otherwise, you can stir together this pasta with canned tuna~I include instructions for that as well.

Wine: Signorello Seta, Napa Valley, 1999

FOR 4 TO 5 SERVINGS:
For the preserved tuna {makes about 10 to 14 ounces, plus the preserving oil}:

3/4 to 1 pound tuna, trimmed
Salt
1 tablespoon thin strips lemon zest
   removed with a zester
2 bay leaves
Scant 1 teaspoon dried chili flakes

Scant 1 teaspoon freshly cracked black
   peppercorns
2 garlic cloves, slivered
1/4 teaspoon fennel seeds
3/4 to 1 cup extra-virgin olive oil

For the pasta:

1/4 cup pine nuts {1-1/4 ounces}
About 10 ounces preserved tuna with
   its preserving oil {from above} or
   excellent-quality oil-packed
   canned tuna, drained
2 tablespoons capers, rinsed, pressed
   dry between towels, and chopped,
   or 2 tablespoons coarsely chopped,

pitted green olives, such as
   Picholine
1 tablespoon rinsed, drained, and
   chopped Preserved Lemon or
   Limequat {page 275} {optional}
1 pound penne, ziti, or ditali

Seasoning the tuna {for the best flavor, do this step 2 to 3 hours in advance}:

Cut the tuna into walnut-sized chunks and sprinkle evenly all over with salt {we use a scant 3/4 teaspoon sea salt per pound}. This will help tenderize the tuna as it seasons it throughout. Cover and refrigerate.

Cooking the tuna:

Pat the tuna dry. Crowd the chunks of tuna in a 2-quart saucepan, distributing the zest, bay leaves, chili flakes, black pepper, garlic, and fennel between the pieces. It should be a snug fit~this minimizes oil consumption. Add olive oil to barely cover the tuna. Set over the lowest-possible heat and bring to a hesitant simmer. Don't let the oil boil. Cook uncovered, stirring and prodding a few times to coax flavor from the aromatics and to favor even doneness, for about 30 minutes. The tuna will initially turn quite hard but will gradually soften a little. Leave the tuna to cool in the oil, stirring once or twice. Store in the oil, refrigerated, until needed ~ but if using the same day, don't bother refrigerating the tuna; this would harden it needlessly.

Preparing the sauce:

Warm the pine nuts in a 12-inch skillet or 3-quart sauté pan over low heat. Use a slotted spoon to lift the preserved tuna from the oil, then crumble it into thumbnail-sized bits as you add it to the pan. Using a fork or wooden spoon, smash a few of the tuna bits: These will disperse into the oil and encourage it, and the seasonings, to cling to the pasta. Stir in the capers or olives. Use a fork to scoop up as much of the delicious "sludge" of zest, chili, pepper, garlic, and fennel seeds from the preserving oil as you want ~ if you use it all, the pasta will be quite spicy ~ and add to the pan. Then add about 6 tablespoons of the oil itself. If there is any tuna "broth" at the bottom of the preserving pan or container {it will be beige and slightly gelatinous}, drain off the remaining oil, taste the liquid, and, if you like it, add a spoonful to the sauce as well. Add the preserved lemon or limequat, if using. Raise the heat to medium-low, stir, and warm through. When the tuna and oil are hot, turn off the heat, but leave the pan on the warm burner while you cook the pasta.

Cooking and saucing the pasta:

Drop the pasta into 6 quarts rapidly boiling water seasoned with a scant 2 tablespoons salt {a little more if using kosher salt}. Stir, and cook until al dente.

Drain the pasta well and spill into the warm tuna mixture. Toss to distribute the oil, tuna, and seasonings. Add more preserving oil, if you have it, to taste.

⁕ ⁕ *If using canned tuna:* Warm 1/2 cup extra-virgin olive oil with half the amounts of lemon zest, bay leaves, chili flakes, black pepper, garlic, and fennel seeds. Leave to infuse for about 15 minutes over the lowest-possible heat. Stir in the canned tuna, pine nuts, capers or olives, and preserved lemon or limequat, if using, and warm through, then turn off the heat.

⁜
⁜ ⁜

PASTA *with* GIBLET-MUSHROOM SAUCE

We make a dozen different meat sauces following this basic formula at Zuni ~ using bits of beef {skirt, *onglet,* cheek}, fresh pork, sausage, duck, squab, or rabbit, but this version is my favorite. It has a deep, solid flavor and texture owing to the unique character of giblet meat ~ it is worth the watchful cooking it requires. I use only the gizzards and hearts here, ask for them where they carry duck and other game birds. You may have to order them, and you may have to settle for frozen ones, but this preparation will forgive that fact.

Substituting more tender cuts of meat is easy. Mince and cook them as described, but expect that they may cook more quickly and contribute more moisture to the sauce. You may not need to cover the sauce for so much of the cooking time. You can also make the sauce with a combination of giblets and game bird meat. In that case, start with the chewy giblets and add the tender cuts about 15 minutes later.

I don't recommend making less than a full recipe; smaller quantities tend to cook too fast to develop flavor, and it is difficult to keep the heat low enough to avoid scorching the sauce. Furthermore, it keeps well and a little leftover sauce is a nice thing to have on hand. Spooned onto warm crostini, it makes an easy and welcome appetizer {page 124}.

We serve this sauce with trenne ~ a big, chewy, triangular penne-like noodle ~ but substitute penne, mostaccioli, or rigatoni if you like. This sauce is also great with garganelli or wide egg noodles.

Wine: Priorato, Barranc dels Closos, Mas Igneus, 1999

FOR 4 TO 5 SERVINGS, WITH SAUCE TO SPARE:

For the sauce {makes about 3 cups}:

8 ounces duck, goose, chicken, or
squab gizzards and hearts

About 1/2 cup extra-virgin olive oil

1-1/2 cups chopped portobello mushrooms {caps and/or stems} {4
ounces} or fresh porcini,
chanterelles, black trumpets, or
morels or scant 1/2 ounce dried
porcini, rinsed, minced, and moistened with 2 tablespoons water

3/4 cup finely diced carrots {3 ounces}

3/4 cup finely diced celery {3 ounces}

3/4 cup finely diced yellow onions {3
ounces}

1 ounce pancetta, minced {about 3
tablespoons packed} {optional}

Salt

2 garlic cloves, chopped

1-1/2 cups chopped canned tomatoes,
drained of about half their juice

1 bay leaf

1 dried chili or a few pinches of dried
chili flakes

1/2 cup hearty red wine, such as
Cabernet Sauvignon, Zinfandel, or
Syrah

A few leaves fresh flat-leaf parsley,
coarsely chopped

Sugar {optional}

1 teaspoon tomato paste {optional}

To finish the pasta:

1 pound trenne {see Sources and
Resources, page 518}, penne,
mostaccioli, rigatoni, garganelli, or
wide egg pasta

A small chunk of Parmigiano-Reggiano
{about 2 ounces}

Preparing the sauce:

Rinse the gizzards and hearts, then press dry between towels. Use a paring
knife to removing the silverskin from the gizzards. Chop them finely. Chop the
hearts.

Warm about 1/4 cup of the olive oil in a 4-quart saucepan over medium heat.
Add the gizzards and hearts and cook, stirring almost constantly, until they begin
to turn a little golden on the edges, about 5 minutes. Don't worry if they stick a
little and the bottom of the pan colors slightly ~ but don't let it scorch. Stir in the
mushrooms, carrots, celery, onions and the pancetta, if using. Add a few pinches

\ *continued*

of salt and enough additional oil to coat the vegetables. Once the mixture begins to sizzle, reduce the heat to low, cover, and stew for about 15 minutes, stirring occasionally. The vegetables will throw off some moisture as they soften; this will dissolve any delicious browned juices that may have formed on the bottom of the pan when you browned the giblets.

Uncover and taste a bit of gizzard. It will be quite hard; remember this texture, so you can recognize when they begin to become tender.

Stir in the garlic, tomatoes, bay leaf, chili, and red wine. Bring to a bare simmer, cover, and cook until the bits of giblet are just tender, another 45 minutes or so. Monitor the pan closely, stirring as needed and adjusting the heat to maintain the weak simmer. {Double and triple batches of this sauce are less likely to come to a boil and will not need such close attention.} Taste for salt; if you used pancetta, it may not need much. Scrape across the bottom of the pan with a flat-edged spatula ~ the sauce will quickly release a pool of thin but tasty juices.

Stir in the parsley and another splash of olive oil. Simmer quietly, uncovered, to marry and concentrate the flavors and to reduce those brothy juices; allow 15 minutes or so, stirring and scraping the pan regularly, and stopping when the thickened juices only ooze from the mass {but don't let the sauce dry out and sizzle}. Taste. The sauce should be shiny, rich, thick, and sweet, with just enough acidity from the wine and tomato to keep it from being cloying. If it tastes too tart or lean, try adding a trickle more of olive oil. Sometimes, if the carrots or onions weren't particularly sweet or the wine was quite acid, I add a pinch of sugar, and once in a while, I add a dab of tomato paste if the sauce wants more body and a little instant character. {If you are not confident in your instincts, you can test any of these adjustments in a spoonful of the sauce before you decide to alter the whole batch.}

Leave to cool completely. {The sauce can be refrigerated for up to a week}. The juice will turn a little syrupy, the vegetables almost suave, and the giblets velvety. The flavors will blend and become richer and sweeter.

Cooking and saucing the pasta:

Drop the pasta into 6 quarts rapidly boiling water seasoned with a scant 2 tablespoons salt {a little more if using kosher salt}. Stir, and cook until al dente.

Reheat about 2 cups of the sauce in a 3-quart sauté pan or 12-inch skillet over low heat, stirring as needed. If it seems dry, add a spoonful of the boiling pasta water.

Drain the pasta well, and toss and fold with the hot sauce. The sauce should glisten on the pasta; if not, it is too lean ~ add a splash of extra-virgin olive oil. Serve in warm bowls and offer the cheese to grate on top.

+
+ +

ZUNI FIDEUS *with* WILD MUSHROOMS *&* PEAS

*F*IDEUS IS A BRAISED NOODLE DISH FROM CATALONIA, WHERE THE NOODLES ARE short threads. We use cappellini pasta broken into 1/2-inch lengths. You can also use slightly fatter fedelini or vermicelli, broken into the same lengths. Pastina shapes such as riso, orzo, and acini di pepe are also tasty cooked this way, although any of these alternatives may require more liquid and more time to cook through.

If you are comfortable with risotto making, *fideus* making will feel familiar. How much stock you use will vary according to the pasta in question, the heat, and the pan you use. You can make this dish entirely on the stovetop, or, for more textural contrast, finish it in a hot oven. Either way, as with risotto, a plate of *fideus* is only as good as the stock it is made with. In Catalonia, *fideus* is often served with a dollop of *allioli* ~ a yolk-less, mayonnaise-like garlic-oil emulsion, which is a trick to produce. Yolky Aïoli {page 289} is a very rich substitute. Another excellent option is to crack an egg per person into the bed of simmering *fideus,* gingerly prick the yolks so they won't form a skin, then slide the pan in the oven to finish cooking.

Don't be daunted by the fact that this recipe has a few subcomponents; preparing the onion base and toasting the noodles can be done well in advance, and both are easy to do. Likewise, you can make the chicken stock a few days in advance if you like. Once you have these three things ready, the assembly of the dish is no more ambitious than for risotto.

If you have leftover cooked *fideus*, they make a great Frittata {page 181}. And the raw toasted noodles are a good alternative to plain pastina for the friendliest

\ *continued*

of soups, *pastina in brodo*, especially if you use beef broth or the broth from a *Pot-au-Feu* {page 385}.

Wine: Penedès Torres Gran Viña Sol, 1999

FOR 4 SERVINGS:

For the aromatic onion base:

3 cups finely diced yellow onions {12 ounces}

6 tablespoons extra-virgin olive oil

Salt

1/4 cup chopped drained canned tomato or 1/2 cup chopped, peeled, ripe tomato

A few garlic cloves, coarsely chopped

2 small dried chiles, broken in half

A pinch of saffron threads

For the toasted noodles:

10 ounces cappellini, broken into 1/2-inch pieces

2 teaspoons mild-tasting olive oil

For finishing the dish:

1/4 cup extra-virgin olive oil

4 to 6 ounces chanterelle, porcini, or morel mushrooms, cleaned {see page 516} and sliced about 1/4 inch thick

Salt

4 garlic cloves, finely chopped

6 cups Chicken Stock {page 58}

1 cup shucked sweet English peas or shucked sugar snap peas {8 to 12 ounces whole pods}

A handful of fresh flat-leaf parsley, coarsely chopped

Preparing the aromatic onion base:

Place the onions and olive oil in a 2-quart saucepan, set over medium-high heat, and stir to combine. Let the onions on the bottom color, then stir again and reduce the heat to medium-low. Continue to cook, stirring regularly, until the onions have fallen to about half their original mass and are generally golden, about 15 minutes. Salt to taste.

Reduce the heat to low, stir in the tomato, garlic, chili, and saffron, and cook, stirring occasionally, for another hour or so on the lowest heat: When the mixture is ready, it will be suave and jam-like, with no trace of acidity. If it starts to dry out, or look oily around the edges, add a few drops of water or stock to reemulsify the mixture. You should get about 1 cup. {The onion jam will keep well for a week or so, covered and refrigerated.}

Toasting the noodles:

Preheat the oven to 325°.

Toss the noodles in the olive oil just to coat, then spread evenly in a single layer on a baking sheet. {I use a 14-inch square baking sheet and brown the noodles in two batches.} Toast until the color of cornflakes, about 10 minutes; stir the noodles or rotate the pan if they are not browning evenly. Set aside.

If you plan to finish the *fideus* in the oven, raise the heat to 475°.

Finishing the dish:

Warm about half of the olive oil in a 3-quart sauté pan over medium heat. Add the mushrooms, salt them, and cook, stirring occasionally, until they are tender but only slightly golden on the edges, 3 to 8 minutes, depending on variety and moisture content. Stir in the garlic. Taste a mushroom. It should be delicious already; if at all bland add a little more salt or garlic, or cook little longer to concentrate the flavor.

Add the onion base, toasted noodles, and about 1-1/2 cups of the stock. Bring to a simmer, and stir as the noodles absorb this first dose of stock, about 2 minutes. Add the peas and another 1-1/2 cups stock and bring to a simmer. Stir until the stock is absorbed, another 3 minutes or so, then add another 1-1/2 cups stock. Continue to cook, just simmering, until this dose is absorbed, another few minutes. Check a noodle for doneness; it should be chewy. Add the parsley, the final 1-1/2 cups stock, and the remaining olive oil. Taste for salt.

Stir and cook the *fideus* over slightly higher heat until the stock is fully absorbed and the noodles are tender through or, *to finish the dish in the oven*, slide the juicy noodles into a shallow flameproof 3-quart baking dish, bring to a simmer, and place the pan in the top half of the oven. Bake uncovered until the stock is completely absorbed, about 10 minutes. Though purists may scoff, I like the variety and contrast of the al dente surface noodles, which are especially caramelized and crisp at the edges of the pan, with the remainder underneath, cooked to tender, slippery succulence.

⁜

MARTHA'S SPÄTZLE

Spätzle are tiny, wiggly, chewy dumplings, usually overshadowed in the starch department by pasta, potatoes, polenta, and rice. {And, in my kitchen, by day-old bread} But each time we make this recipe I learned from my longstanding sous-chef Martha Buser, I eat a plateful, and then take home more for a late dinner. Squished through little holes, the sticky batter turns into a crowd of beaky "little sparrows" {which is what *spätzle* means in Swabian dialect} that bob to the surface of a pot of simmering water. They are nice freshly boiled and tossed with melted butter, or with the rich juices from a pot roast or other braise. Spätzle brown well, especially in a nonstick pan. Leftover spätzle sometimes replace pastina in our *brodo*. Spätzle are not fragile or sticky, and they can be cooked well in advance, as long as you spread them out to cool. Don't worry if some clump together; you can easily break them up by hand once they have cooled.

The technique is easy to get the knack of, but if you have never made spätzle before, or seen anyone make them, I recommend you make a practice batch. The ingredients are staples and inexpensive. Really fresh eggs will make the tastiest, fluffiest spätzle. There are several types of spätzle-makers available; I use an inexpensive model that looks like a grater with a sliding box attached. Although it's more awkward, you can also press spätzle through a colander with large holes.

FOR ABOUT 2-1/2 CUPS:

5 ounces cake flour {not self-rising} {scant 1-1/2 cups~spoon-and-level; don't pack, don't tap}

2 large eggs

5 tablespoons lukewarm water

Salt

1 tablespoon unsalted butter or mild-tasting olive oil

Shake the flour through a strainer into a bowl to break up any clumps. Crack the eggs into a separate bowl; beat lightly with a fork. Pour the eggs over the flour and stir with the fork just until the eggs are absorbed, about 10 strokes. Don't worry that most of the flour is still dry and loose. Stir in 4 tablespoons of the water, to make a heavy, lumpy batter. Trickle in the remaining tablespoon of water, stopping once the batter is soft and no longer holds a peak as you mix it. Lift the fork clad with some of the batter; it should hang for a second before dropping. As it rests, the batter will smooth out and begin to look like warm taffy.

Fill a wide sauté pan with water and bring to a boil. Salt liberally {I use about 1 teaspoon sea salt per quart of water}. Add the butter or oil.

Spoon about half of the batter into the spätzle-maker {or a colander with 1/4-inch-wide holes}, and set it over the boiling water, resting it on the edge of the pan. Press on the spätzle {or use a stiff rubber spatula or bowl scraper to smear the batter against the bottom and sides of the colander}, forcing it through the holes. The little sparrows will initially sink, but they will swell and float within 30 seconds as they fill with steam. Stop adding batter once the surface of the water becomes crowded.

Let the spätzle cook for about 1 minute after they float. Lift them out with a skimmer or strainer, shake gently to drain, and tip them onto a sheet pan to cool. {Or slide into a pan of warm braising juices.} Repeat with the rest of the batter. You may be able to manage more batter at a time once you get the knack of it, but only attack as much as you can press through in 15 seconds or less, and never add more batter than the surface of the water can safely harbor. Obviously, some of the spätzle cook a little longer than others, but the resilient little things don't go soft or soggy that quickly.

⁘ ⁘

ZUNI RICOTTA GNOCCHI

THIS RECIPE, BASED ON ELIZABETH DAVID'S *GNOCCHI DI RICOTTA* IN HER BOOK *Italian Food*, has become one of our most-often-requested house formulas. Requiring fresh, curdy ricotta, it yields succulent, tender dumplings that always beguile. But since fresh ricotta varies in texture, flavor, and moisture content, depending on the season, what the animals are eating, who is making it, and how long they drain it, we often need to tinker with recipe, adding more Parmigiano-Reggiano for flavor, or butter for richness. If the cheese is particularly wet, we add a little more egg, or we hang it overnight in cheesecloth, refrigerated

\ *continued*

{or we do both}. Very wet ricotta can weep 1/2 cup liquid per pound. Don't substitute machine-packed supermarket ricotta here; flavor issues notwithstanding, mechanical packing churns and homogenizes the curds and water~ you'll have trouble getting enough water back out. Tender fresh sheep's milk ricotta, if you can get it, makes delicious gnocchi and is worth the extra expense.

Having offered ricotta gnocchi four or five evenings per week for more than a decade, we have a large repertory of accompaniments for, and variations on, this dish. We sometimes add freshly grated nutmeg, chopped lemon zest, or chopped sage stewed in butter to the batter before forming the gnocchi. Or we form thumbnail-sized gnocchi and poach them in chicken broth for a delicate soup course. One of the nicest variations is to fold flecks of barely cooked spinach into the batter. These Spinach and Ricotta Gnocchi recall the Florentine mainstay, variously called *ravioli verdi* {"green ravioli"}, *ignudi* {"naked" ravioli}, or *malfatti* {"poorly fashioned," which they needn't be}, and are sublime.

Although these gnocchi are delicious and delicate enough to serve with just a cloak of melted butter, I list my favorite seasonal accompaniments at the end of the recipe to provoke you to think of serving ricotta gnocchi often, and year-round.

Wine: Chehalem Willamette Valley Pinot Gris, 2000

FOR 40 TO 48 GNOCCHI, TO SERVE 4 TO 6:

To prepare the gnocchi:

1 pound fresh ricotta {2 cups}

2 large cold eggs, lightly beaten

1 tablespoon unsalted butter

2 or 3 fresh sage leaves, chopped, or a few pinches of freshly grated nutmeg, or a few pinches of chopped lemon zest {all optional}

1/2 ounce Parmigiano-Reggiano, grated {about 1/4 cup very lightly packed}

About 1/4 teaspoon salt {a little more if using kosher salt}

All-purpose flour, for forming the gnocchi

To sauce the gnocchi:

8 tablespoons butter, sliced

2 teaspoons water

Testing the cheese {the day before you make the gnocchi}:

Check the cheese for wetness. If you are lucky enough to have an individual basket-drained ricotta~ you'll see the basket imprint or dimples on the cheese~ it may be sitting in a little whey; in this case, slide it out of the container and wick away the surface moisture with a dry towel. With any ricotta, place about 2 teaspoons of the cheese on a dry paper towel and wait for about 1 minute. There will always be a little wet spot under and around the cheese, but if the cheese has thrown a wide ring of moisture, it is too wet to use as is. Place it in a strainer, or double-wrap in cheesecloth, and suspend over a deeper receptacle to drain for 8 to 24 hours, refrigerated. Cheesecloth is more efficient, as it also wicks moisture from the cheese while gravity does its job of draining. You can also speed up the draining operation by cinching the cheesecloth tight and squeezing some of the moisture from the ball of cheese.

Making the batter:

Beat the ricotta vigorously, then smash a little cheese against the side of the bowl with a soft rubber spatula. If you can still make out firm curds, press the cheese through a strainer to break them up. Stir in the eggs. Melt the 1 tablespoon of butter~with the chopped sage, if using~and add to the batter. Add the nutmeg or lemon zest, if using. Add the Parmigiano and salt and beat the whole mixture very well. This is what will make the gnocchi light. You should have a soft, fluffy batter.

Forming and testing a sample gnocchi:

Make a bed of flour about 1/2 inch deep in a shallow baking dish or on a sheet pan.

Scrape the sides of the bowl, mass the batter, and smooth its surface. Use a spoon held at an angle to shallow-scoop out 2 to 3 teaspoons of batter {1, 2}. Use your fingertip to push the almond-shaped scoop of batter cleanly from the bowl

✢ ✢ ✢ ✢ ✢

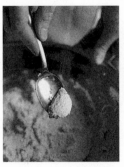

1   2   3   4

✢ ✢ ✢ ✢ ✢

\ *continued*

of the spoon onto the bed of flour {3}. Shimmy the pan gently to coat its sides, then flip the gnocchi with your fingertip to coat the top. Lift from the flour and cradle and rock it in your palm {4}. Don't squeeze it. You should have a dusty oval pod. As long as the general shape is uniform and rotund, don't worry that the gnocchi has a few wrinkles, dimples, or bumps.

To check the batter, poach this first gnocchi in a small pot of simmering well-salted water. It will initially sink but will then swell, roll, and bob to the surface. Maintaining the quiet simmer, cook until the gnocchi is just firm, usually 3 to 5 minutes from the time it floats, depending on the cheese and the size of the gnocchi. Don't boil hard, or the gnocchi may explode. If, even at a gentle simmer, the gnocchi spreads or starts to decompose, the cheese was probably too wet. This can usually be corrected by beating a teaspoon or so of egg white into the remaining batter. If the batter was very fluffy, but the sample seems heavy, beat in about 1 teaspoon beaten egg. In either case, poach another sample to make sure the fix is successful.

Taste the sample for salt, and adjust the batter if needed.

Forming the remaining gnocchi:
Use the same spoon-and-finger technique to form the rest of the gnocchi. I usually form them in groups of 4 to 6, placing them all at the same angle, and a few inches apart, in the bed of flour, then shimmy the pan to coat all of them at once; don't leave them sitting too long in the flour, or they will absorb too much. Keep scraping the bowl and smoothing the surface of the batter to permit smooth scoops. As with the sample, roll each gnocchi in your hand. Arrange them on a sheet pan lined with a flour-dusted sheet of parchment paper or wax paper. Be sure that the individual gnocchi are not touching one another.

✦ ✦ ✦ ✦ ✦

✦ ✦ ✦ ✦ ✦

You can poach the gnocchi right away, but if you refrigerate them uncovered for about an hour, they will firm up, making them easier to cook and handle. {They will keep for up to 8 hours that way}.

Cooking the gnocchi:

Place the 8 tablespoons of butter and the 2 teaspoons of water in a 12-inch skillet; set aside.

Bring 2 to 3 quarts water to a simmer in a wide pan ~ 10 or more inches in diameter, so the gnocchi won't crush each other too much as they push to the surface. A sauté pan, flared brasier, or saucier pan will work, as long as it is at least 2 inches deep. Salt the water liberally ~ about 1 teaspoon per quart. Add the gnocchi one by one, adjusting the heat to maintain the simmer. Dip your fingertips in water if you find they are sticking to the gnocchi, but don't fret if the gnocchi stick a little to the paper. Do avoid holding the tray of gnocchi in the steam. Cook the gnocchi as you did the sample, until just firm, 3 to 5 minutes from the time they float.

Meanwhile, as soon as the gnocchi float to the surface, place the pan of butter and water over medium heat. Swirl the pan as the butter melts and begins to seethe. As soon as the butter is completely melted and has turned into an opaque pale yellow sauce, turn off the heat. Swirl the pan a few more times.

Lift the gnocchi out with a slotted spoon or skimmer, slide into the ready skillet, and roll in the warm butter sauce. Serve instantly in warm bowls.

Note: *Freezing ricotta gnocchi:* Since you may not want to cook all your gnocchi at once, and they don't keep long raw, it is useful to know how you can freeze and cook them later. The results may not be quite as delicate and flavorful as fresh dumplings, and will be more wrinkly, but they are still delicious. Be aware that uncareful that freezing and cooking, however, will fail utterly.

Place the raw gnocchi, still widely spaced on their floured tray {or transfer to a smaller floured tray if appropriate}, in the freezer. Don't cover, or they may sweat before they solidify. Once they are frozen hard, slide the gnocchi, tray and all, into a plastic bag, tie the end and keep frozen until needed.

Cooking frozen ricotta gnocchi: Remove gnocchi from the freezer, slide off the plastic bag, and separate any gnocchi that have rolled together during storage. Thaw completely in a cool spot or in the refrigerator. Frozen, or partially frozen, they will not cook properly. Cook as directed for fresh gnocchi.

\ *continued*

Serving Suggestions:

The mild flavor of the ricotta marries well with many other flavors and ingredients, especially sweet, subtle, or nutty ones. Whatever the companion, it should be tender and delicate ~ like the gnocchi themselves.

Try serving the dumplings with a few leaves of sage, arugula, or spinach wilted in butter, or roll in melted butter with just-cooked baby carrots and fresh chervil. Or pair with tender flageolets finished with extra-virgin olive oil and black pepper. Or fold in matchsticks of just-cooked zucchini; it's subtle flavor becomes clearer next to these gnocchi. In the spring, we offer them with barely cooked peas, tiny favas, or finely slivered asparagus, or all three. During summer, we match them with fresh white corn kernels cooked in butter with basil, or scatter them with chopped nasturtium blossoms. When tender-skinned Sungold Sweet 100 tomatoes are at their sweetest, we halve them, warm them in extra-virgin olive oil with basil, and toss them over the gnocchi. In the fall, fresh wild mushrooms slivered, stewed, and finished with white truffle oil are delicious with the gnocchi, and in the winter, whenever we have black truffles in house, we shave some generously over the dish.

Variation SPINACH & RICOTTA GNOCCHI

Prepare the batter as above. Warm an additional tablespoon of butter in a 10-inch skillet over low heat. Add a few handfuls of spinach leaves ~ about 2 ounces. Salt lightly and, stirring and folding constantly, cook until the spinach is completely wilted but still vibrant green, 1 to 2 minutes. Slide onto a clean towel, cover with another towel, and press to extract the moisture. {The spinach will bleed green into the towel.} Peel off the spinach and chop into bits the size of fresh thyme leaves. Don't chop fine, and don't purée, or you will sacrifice the nice texture and burst of flavor it promises. Beat the spinach flecks into the prepared batter, then form and cook the gnocchi as described above.

Three Onion Panades: Chard, Sorrel, & Tomato

A *PANADE,* LITERALLY, A "BIG BREAD THING," IS A FLUFFY, GRATINÉED CASSEROLE of stale bread and stewed onions, moistened with broth or water {made with water, it might be tagged *acquacotta,* an Italian relation}. Enriched with cheese and layered with greens or tomatoes, this primitive peasant gratin becomes an affordable luxury dish. We serve a generous scoop of *panade* by itself in lieu of soup, pasta, or risotto, or a smaller spoonful next to grilled or roasted birds or meat. In either case, scoop strategically when you serve, so everyone gets some of the craggy top. Whichever *panade* strategy you choose, don't worry if it looks as if you will have too much. What isn't consumed in second helpings has a future still: it is delicious panfried {see page 230}.

You can assemble and start baking the *panade* itself hours in advance, and you can certainly prepare the chicken stock, onions, and bread even earlier. {If you do, make sure to refrigerate the bread after you moisten it.} When possible, use sweet onions ~ Granex, Vidalia, Maui, or Walla Walla ~ whichever is available in your region. As suggested above, you can make the *panade* with part or all lightly salted water; the result will be lighter. In that case, brown the onions a little longer and consider adding extra garlic to boost the flavor.

Wine: Côtes du Ventoux, Val Muzols, Delas Frères, 2000

Chard & Onion Panade *with* Fontina

Use Fontina Val d'Aosta for this recipe, not an imitation. Swiss Gruyère is also a good choice.

\ *continued*

FOR ABOUT 5 SERVINGS AS A MAIN COURSE, 6 TO 8 AS A SIDE DISH:

1-1/2 pounds thinly sliced yellow onions, a sweet variety if possible {about 6 cups}

1/2 cup mild-tasting olive oil

6 garlic cloves, slivered

Salt

1 pound green Swiss chard, thick ribs removed {which you can reserve to deep-fry~see Chard with Lemon Oil, page 248} and cut into 1-inch-wide ribbons

A little water, as needed

10 ounces day-old chewy peasant-style bread, cut into rough 1-inch cubes {8 to 10 cups}

Up to 4 cups Chicken Stock {page 58}

About 6 ounces Fontina or Swiss Gruyère, coarsely grated {about 2 cups very loosely packed}

Preparing the onions, chard, and bread:

Place the onions in a deep 4-quart saucepan and drizzle and toss with olive oil to coat, about 1/4 cup. Set over medium-high heat and, shimmying the pan occasionally, cook until the bottom layer of onions is slightly golden on the edges, about 3 minutes. Stir and repeat. Once the second layer of onions has colored, reduce the heat to low and stir in the garlic and a few pinches of salt. Stew, stirring occasionally, until the onions are pale amber colored and tender but not mushy, another 20 minutes or so. If at any point the onions look as if they may dry out, cover them to trap some of the moisture in the pan. Taste for salt. You should get about 2-1/4 cups cooked onions.

Preheat the oven to 325° {or as low as 250°, if it suits your schedule to stretch the cooking time from about 1 hour 45 minutes to 2 hours 45 minutes; in general, the longer and slower the bake, the more unctuous and mellow the results}.

Wilt the prepared chard in batches: Place a few handfuls of leaves in a 3-quart sauté pan or 10- to 12-inch skillet with a drizzle of oil, a sprinkling of water {if you've just washed the chard, it may have enough water still clinging to the leaves}, and a few pinches of salt. Set the pan over medium heat until the water begins to steam, then reduce the heat and stir and fold the leaves until they are just wilted, 3 to 4 minutes. The leaves should be uniformly bright green, the white veins quite pliable {the veins will blacken later if they are not heated through}. Taste. The chard may be slightly metallic tasting at this point, but make sure it's salted to your taste. Set aside.

Toss and massage the cubed bread with a few tablespoons of olive oil, a generous 1/4 cup of the stock, and a few pinches of salt, to taste.

Building the *panade:*

Choose a flameproof 2-quart soufflé dish or enameled cast-iron Dutch oven. Assemble the *panade* in layers, starting with a generous smear of onions, followed by a loose mosaic of bread cubes, a second layer of onions, a wrinkled blanket of chard, and a handful of the cheese. Repeat, starting with bread, then onions, and so on, continuing until the dish is brimming. Aim for 2 to 3 layers of each component, then make sure the top layer displays a little of everything. Don't try to make the layers flat or even; irregularity makes the final product more interesting and lovely. And don't worry if you need to pack the layers a bit. Drizzle with any remaining olive oil.

Bring the remaining 3-3/4 cups chicken stock to a simmer and taste for salt. Add it slowly, in doses, around the edge of the dish. For a very juicy, soft *panade*, best served on its own, like a soup or risotto, add stock nearly to the rim; for a firm but still succulent *panade*, nice as a side dish, fill to about 1 inch below the rim. Once you've added the stock, wait a minute for it to be absorbed, then add more if necessary to return to the desired depth. The *panade* may rise a little as the bread swells.

Baking the *panade:*

Set the *panade* over low heat and bring to a simmer; look for bubbles around the edges. {Heating it here saves at least 30 minutes of oven time; it also means every *panade* you bake starts at the same temperature, so you can better predict total cooking times.}

Cover the top of the *panade* with parchment paper, then very loosely wrap the top and sides with foil, dull side out. Place a separate sheet of foil directly under the *panade* or on the rack below it, to catch the inevitable drips. Bake until the *panade* is piping hot and bubbly. It will rise a little, lifting the foil with it. The top should be pale golden in the center and slightly darker on the edges. This usually takes about 1-1/2 hours, but varies according to the shape and material of your baking dish, and your oven. {You can hold the baked *panade* for another hour or so; just reduce the temperature to 275° until 20 minutes before serving.}

Browning and serving the *panade:*

Uncover the *panade*, raise the temperature to 375°, and leave until golden brown on top, 10 to 20 minutes. {If you aren't quite ready when your *panade* is,

\ *continued*

re-tent the surface with parchment and foil and reduce the heat to 275°. You can hold it another half hour this way without it overbrowning or drying out.} Slide a knife down the side of the dish and check the consistency of the *panade*. Beneath the crust, it should be very satiny and it should ooze liquid as you press against it with the blade of the knife. If it seems dry, add a few tablespoons simmering chicken stock and bake for 10 minutes longer.

Present the *panade* full-blown, then allow it to settle for a minute before serving directly from the baking dish.

⁂ Sorrel & Onion Panade

Prepare as above, but layer with raw sorrel {2 big handfuls, about 3 ounces} instead of cooked chard. Don't bother de-ribbing the sorrel; just trim the stem tips and any damaged areas. The tissuey leaves will melt into silky-tart veins.

⁂ Summer Onion Panade *with* Tomatoes

This version calls for 1/2 pound tomatoes in lieu of the chard, extra-virgin olive oil, basil, and a little Parmigiano-Reggiano instead of the Fontina. You may use a little less stock, since the tomatoes provide more moisture than chard. I suggest slicing the bread so you can layer the tomato slices more neatly, which is especially pretty if you use more than one color of tomato.

⁂ Turning Leftover Panade *into* Panfried Panade:

If you are blessed with too much *panade*, the refrigerated leftovers can be turned into an excellent, comforting supper:

Warm about 1 tablespoon extra-virgin olive oil in an 8-inch nonstick skillet over medium heat. Slide in a scoop or wedge of cold *panade* and press gently to make an amorphous 1/2-inch-thick patty. Fry gently to make a golden crust, about 3 minutes, then use a wide spatula to turn over and fry the other side, also until golden. Don't worry if it wrinkles, crumbles, or cracks as you turn it; just smash it back together. Serve piping hot with a salad of bitter greens, a poached egg, and sausage or bacon~or with nothing but freshly cracked black pepper and a glass of red wine.

⁂

VEGETABLES, SAVORY FRUIT DISHES, PICKLES & PRESERVES

Cooking with fresh, seasonal vegetables, whether the first crowd-pleasing asparagus or the first underheralded onions of the year, is an irresistible delight. The annual rediscovery of perfumes, flavors, and textures makes this branch of the repertory endlessly seductive. The daily ponder over what we shall eat seems not a bother but an opportunity when gorgeous, knobby winter squashes chase the last tomatoes from the market stalls, or when, for a few months, fresh shelling beans unseat the staple, taken-for-granted dry ones ~ which we then rediscover and reappreciate as we turn back to them in the late fall.

What follows is a collection of some of my favorite vegetable dishes. A few we make nearly year-round ~ those with spinach, chard, potatoes, dried beans ~ but the majority are dishes that explode with particular charm in peak season. Most are simple, versatile dishes that may require careful shopping but call for minimal planning or labor ~ although a few do involve some affectionate ritual. Also included here are some pickled vegetables and a few preserved fruits, all of which we use constantly, to bridge the harvests, and to add spark and heart to many dishes. I adore them. Suggestions for when to bring out these larder treasures are among the most frequent of cross-references in this book.

To supplement this collection, here is an index of other vegetable preparations that appear elsewhere in the book, as part of another dish, or playing a different role in the meal.

Grilled Asparagus {Grilled Asparagus with Pistachio *Aillade*}, page 98
Roasted Figs {Prosciutto with Warm Roasted Figs and Hazelnut *Picada*}, page 83
Artichoke Caponata, page 103
Chestnuts in Sage Oil {Prosciutto with Chestnuts in Sage Oil}, page 85
Pappa al Pomodoro, page 164
Wilted Spinach {Shrimp in Romesco with Wilted Spinach}, page 334
Spicy Broccoli and Cauliflower {Pasta with Spicy Broccoli and Cauliflower},
     page 203
Warm Parslied Potatoes {Coppa with Warm Parslied Potato Salad and Roasted
     Peppers}, page 90
Preserved Celery Root {Coppa with Catherine's Celery Root}, page 91
Fried Potatoes {Carpaccio with Fried Potatoes and Truffles}, page 133

Wine & Vegetables

Any vegetable garnish or side dish should be considered when choosing wine for a main course. With buttermilk mashed potatoes, for instance, roast chicken would be a good foil for a rich Alexander Valley Chardonnay. But the same chicken with any kind of bitter greens would show a lively young red from Touraine ~ a Chinon or a Bourgueil ~ or a California Cabernet Franc to far greater advantage. Grilled and lightly charred vegetables served hot or cold as a separate course can be good with either a light, fruity red or an aromatic white ~ especially a young German Riesling. Its acidity will keep the palate alert while the touch of residual sugar, though barely perceptible, will enhance the natural sweetness of young vegetables and bring out their flavor. The cream or béchamel sauce of a vegetable served *au gratin* as a course on its own can make a wine seem thin. So choose a fleshy Chardonnay or a substantial Riesling. If red is preferred, and there's enough cheese in the sauce or crust to support it, choose a Syrah from a warm region like Paso Robles.

✦ ✦ ✦ ✦ ✦

Buttermilk Mashed Potatoes

I am almost afraid to run these mashed potatoes at Zuni, because whatever I pair them with will outsell all other main courses four to one, roast chicken included. The cook who has buttermilk mashed potatoes on his main course looks upon his fortune with vague dread ~ he will be "slammed" all night. We always prepare an extra ten pounds' worth for side orders. I offer the recipe to the home cook with no apologies for how popular it will be with diners.

These mashed potatoes are rich in flavor but light, and slightly tangy. Sweet gold-fleshed potatoes, such as Yellow Finnish, Bintje, or German Butterballs are

\ *continued*

delicious mashed~and may not need as much dairy enrichment as white-fleshed russets. We sometimes add a handful of torn sorrel leaves and a few scrapings of nutmeg to these mashed potatoes. Or we infuse the melted butter with chopped sage before stirring it into the warm potatoes.

FOR ABOUT 3 CUPS {4 SERVINGS}:

1-1/4 pounds peeled potatoes {scant 1-1/2 pounds whole}, preferably Yellow Finnish, Bintje, or German Butterballs {but russets are fine as well}, cut into rough 1-1/2-inch chunks

Salt

2 to 3 tablespoons milk, half-and-half, or heavy cream, heated until hot

2 to 3 tablespoons buttermilk, at room temperature

About 3 tablespoons unsalted butter, just melted and still warm

Place the potato chunks in a 2- to 4-quart saucepan and add cold water to cover by an inch or so. Stir in salt until you can just taste it clearly {I use a scant teaspoon sea salt per quart of water}. Bring the potatoes to a boil, uncovered, and cook until very tender, 8 to 15 minutes, depending on the variety.

Drain and rice or mash while the potatoes are piping hot, then beat in the hot milk, half-and-half, or cream, and then the buttermilk. Finish with the butter. {Warming the enrichments is a restaurant necessity, so they won't cool the large batch of mashed potatoes, which would be a lot of trouble to get really hot again without scorching. Since it works just as well at home, I suggest it. But don't heat the buttermilk~it will separate.} Whip vigorously, taste for salt, and serve immediately, or keep warm, covered, in a double boiler, for up to 30 minutes.

Note: Generally, I don't encourage making extra *anything* with potatoes. Leftover cooked potatoes usually don't improve in flavor, tending instead to pick up a mineraly or musty taste in the refrigerator. However, the buttermilk in this recipe seems to stall their demise, and I find these mashed potatoes to be delicious baked atop leftover beef stew, à la shepherd's pie, or thinned with rich chicken stock to make a simple soup.

ROSEMARY-ROASTED POTATOES

THE SECOND MOST EFFECTIVE WAY TO SELL A MAIN COURSE AT ZUNI, AFTER
Buttermilk Mashed Potatoes {page 233}. As always, I recommend a rich,
yellow-fleshed potato, such as Finnish, Bintje, or German Butterballs, but you can
use Yukon Golds or even russets for this recipe. We usually prepare this recipe
with olive oil, but in the winter we sometimes substitute duck fat, when serving
the potatoes with poultry, or rendered beef fat, to accompany beef.

FOR 3 TO 4 SERVINGS:

About 1-1/2 pounds peeled yellow-
    fleshed potatoes {scant 1-3/4
    pounds whole}, cut into irregular
    1- to 1-1/2-inch chunks

Salt
A leafy sprig of fresh rosemary
About 1/4 cup extra-virgin olive oil

Preheat the oven to 400°.

Place the potatoes in a 4-quart saucepan and add cold water to cover by a few
inches. Salt liberally, stir to dissolve, and taste~ it should be well seasoned {we use a
scant 1-1/2 teaspoons sea salt per quart water}. Bring to a simmer over high heat and
stir again, then reduce the heat just to hold the simmer. Cook until the potatoes are
soft on the edges and tender inside, 6 to 12 minutes, depending on the variety of
potato and exact size of chunks. Drain well. Taste. The potatoes should be perfectly
seasoned and delicious already. Place in a bowl while still warm.

Strip a palmful of leaves from the sprig of rosemary, then smash and bruise
them with the back of a knife blade to release their perfume. Add them to the
bowl of warm potatoes and drizzle with the olive oil to coat liberally. The slightly
overcooked potatoes will both soak up and shed into the fat. Some of the edges or
smaller pieces may even crumble, which will produce crunchy bits and pieces
everyone will reach for.

Transfer the potatoes, clad in their potato-laden oil, to a wide shallow roasting
pan. {If roasting potatoes for a crowd, use more than one pan, rather than pile the
potatoes.} Roast until golden, rotating the pan as needed so they color evenly, 20

\ *continued*

to 25 minutes. Because they were so moist, the potatoes may stick to the roasting pan in spots~use a metal spatula to loosen them.

Once golden, the potatoes hold well, or even improve from holding in a 275° oven. To best preserve their crunchy mantle, don't stack or pile them; leave them on their roasting pan.

✦ ✦ ✦ ✦ ✦

BRUISING

"BRUISING" IS A GOOD WAY TO DESCRIBE WHAT WE DO WHEN WE crush something enough to burst some cells, but without pulverizing it or necessarily bursting its skin. The usual goal is to encourage the release of a maximum of aromatic elements without spreading tiny bits of debris throughout a mixture {which is why we twist a lemon zest, rather than chop it, before we drop it into a martini}. On other occasions, you may first bruise, then chop a leaf, seed, branch, or clove, in order to maximize both flavor extraction and distribution of solids. Sage, rosemary, garlic, and fennel seeds are among the things I frequently bruise before adding them to a dish. I use whatever is handiest~the back or side of my chef's knife, a pestle and mortar, a meat pounder, or a rubber mallet.

✦ ✦ ✦ ✦ ✦

ROASTED FINGERLING POTATOES

FINGERLING POTATOES ARE ELONGATED, DIMPLED TUBERS WITH SILKY SKINS AND dense, fine flesh. Some types tend to grow a few stubby "thumbs." This charismatic feature makes them harder to pack, so they may never find widespread commercial appreciation, but they seem to have favored status at farmers' markets. Russian Banana, Austrian, German, French, Ruby Crescent, Rosefir, Ozette, and other fingerling-type potatoes vie for my potato dollars, and it is hard to resist any new variety I encounter~but French Fingerlings are a consistent favorite. Fingerlings seem best suited to a moist cooking method~dry-roasting can leave them parched. Moreover, I think their flavor responds well to some teasing~hence this simple formula that bathes the cut tubers with wine, which combines with their starches to make a subtle, silky glaze.

FOR 4 SERVINGS:

1-1/2 pounds fingerling potatoes
Salt
About 3 tablespoons dry white wine

About 3 tablespoons extra-virgin olive
  oil or melted unsalted butter
A branch of fresh thyme {optional}

Preheat the oven to 350°.

Scrub the potatoes, pick any dirt from the eyes, and trim any green parts. Cut lengthwise in half, to expose as much of the inside of the potato as possible. Toss with a teaspoon or so of salt, the wine, and oil or melted butter. If using, strip the thyme leaves from the branch and toss with the potatoes.

Crowd the potatoes in a shallow roasting pan in a single layer, cover tightly, and bake until very tender, 20 to 30 minutes, depending on variety and size. Serve promptly.

Note: You can reheat these potatoes on a grill; just set them cut-side-down over a medium fire. They will set a golden crust with nice grill marks in just a few minutes.

+
+ +

SALT-ROASTIES

THIS IS A SIMPLE METHOD THAT MAGNIFIES FLAVOR. Salt-roasted potatoes are moist and, except for the frosted skins, not at all salty. "Salt-roasties" are rich and delicious plain, with the usual baked potato condiments, or with a spoonful of Rich Balsamic Mayonnaise {page 289} or mascarpone. Choose regularly shaped yellow-fleshed potatoes~Finnish, Bintje, German Butterballs~about 2 inches in

\ *continued*

diameter. Look for potatoes that are free of sprouts and green spots ~ since they are to be buried in salt, you don't want to have to trim away the protective skin.

You can reuse the rock salt several times.

FOR 4 SERVINGS:

1-1/2 pounds creamer potatoes, such as Yellow Finnish, Bintje, or German Butterballs, about 2 inches in diameter

Rock salt to cover {about 10 cups}

Preheat the oven to 400°.

Scrub and dry the potatoes. Spread a 1/2-inch-thick layer of salt in a 2- to 3-inch-deep baking dish. Arrange the potatoes on the salt, spaced at least 1/2 inch from one another. Add rock salt to barely cover the potatoes. It's convenient to leave a spot of each potato showing so you can locate and retrieve them easily.

Bake until tender, usually about 40 minutes, although I recommend you check the doneness after 30 minutes. To do this, press on an exposed potato "dot." {Much of the roasting time is spent heating the salt.}

Wait for 5 minutes before you try to excavate the potatoes, then scoop deeply underneath each one to unearth it. They will be humid as they emerge, and will turn dusty white as they dry. Brush off any whole grains of salt that stick to the potatoes.

You can keep the potatoes warm piled on the salt for a while, but they are never as delicious as when freshly dug from the salt.

+
+ +

HASHED SWEET POTATOES

A TRICKY DISH TO DO IN VOLUME, AND HENCE, I RARELY MAKE IT AT THE restaurant, but it is easy for the home cook. An obvious friend to bacon and eggs, these lacy cakes are also good with almost any roasted meat or bird. The sweet-salty flavor and crispy texture are irresistible and appeal to those not usually fond of sweet potatoes. These hash browns are also very pretty made with a combination of starchy yellow sweet potatoes and a little bit of orange yam. {Don't use all yams; by themselves, they would form a wet, dense mass, not a lacy cake. They don't have enough starch to stick together and form a crust. They do, on the other hand, try to stick to the pan.}

FOR 4 INDIVIDUAL "CAKES," TO SERVE 4:

Just over 1 pound yellow sweet potatoes or a combination of mostly sweet potatoes and a little bit of yam

4 tablespoons unsalted butter

Salt

Peel, then grate the potatoes on the widest face of your grater or in a processor.

Melt 1-1/2 teaspoons of the butter in an 8- to 9-inch nonstick skillet over medium heat. Add about one-quarter of the grated potatoes, to cover the bottom of the pan in a 1/2-inch-deep tangle~ you should barely be able to see the bottom of the pan. They should sizzle on contact. Season evenly with salt. Swirl the pan to urge the potatoes into a mass without compacting them, and cook for 5 minutes or so, then check gingerly at the edge of the tangle to see if the bottom has set a golden crust. Once it has, swirl the pan again to make sure the cake is not sticking, then flip the mass of potatoes like a pancake, or lift and turn it over with a spatula, in halves if necessary. Don't be tempted to "neaten-up" or compress the potatoes; their charm lies in the irregular, lacy, crispy texture~ and overhandling them makes them steam and will produce a dense, uninteresting patty. Add another 1-1/2 teaspoons of the butter to the edge of the pan, tilt in all directions to ensure it coats the whole surface, then leave it to brown the other face. This should take about 4 minutes. Serve immediately, or keep on a parchment paper–lined sheet pan in a warm oven while you make the remaining cakes. Don't overlap the finished cakes.

\ *continued*

Note: You can certainly make a larger cake in a larger pan, although it will be trickier to flip. If you have a griddle, you can free-form the cakes and then turn them with a spatula.

⁝

MARINATED ROASTED BEETS & TRUFFLED BEETS

MERCILESS COMMERCIAL CANNING PRACTICES HAVE MADE BEETS AN UNLOVED vegetable in many homes, but home-cooked, nutty-tender beets are a different matter. For the best flavor and texture, choose small beets, 1-1/2 to 2-1/2 inches in diameter. I always try to roast and marinate the beets a day in advance; they seem to taste sweeter and richer after a night in the refrigerator.

Satiny roasted beets are delicious with just a little salt, oil and vinegar, to be enjoyed by themselves, in salads, as part of an antipasto, or with grilled or roasted birds or beef. But they are stunning paired with black truffles; they absorb the truffle flavor as their own. Biting into a nutty slice of truffled beet is like biting into a thick slice of warm truffle. Truffled beets are especially good with air-dried beef, or roasted squab or duck.

FOR 4 TO 6 SERVINGS AS A SIDE DISH OR IN A SALAD:

12 golf ball–sized beets, stems and leaves removed {about 1-1/2 pounds total}
Salt

1 to 2 tablespoons red wine vinegar or black currant vinegar
About 1/4 cup extra-virgin olive oil

Preheat the oven to 375°.

Scrub the beets, trim the stem ends flat, and cut off the tails. Place in a wide baking dish, about as deep as the beets are tall, and add 1/4 inch of water. Cover tightly and bake until they feel barely tender through, about 25 minutes {figure more or less time for larger or smaller beets}; don't overcook. To test for doneness, use a cake tester, bamboo skewer, or the tip of your skinniest paring knife and stab to the center of a beet. Remove from the oven and leave covered for 5 minutes to finish cooking.

Uncover the beets, rub off the skins, and trim the ends again. Cut into slices or wedges and taste; they should be nutty-tender with a subtle, mineraly sweetness. Place in a bowl, season lightly with salt and about a tablespoon of vinegar, and fold to distribute. Fold in olive oil to coat well. Taste again. The seasonings should flatter, not overwhelm, the subtle beet flavor you first tasted.

Stir and taste again just before serving. The beet flavor tends to become stronger as the beets cool, and they seem sweeter. If not serving the same day, cover and store refrigerated. The beets will keep for up to a week.

✧ ✧ TRUFFLED BEETS

Roast and peel as described above, then slice 1/8 inch thick. Sprinkle with salt and only a teaspoon of vinegar, in deference to the truffle to come. Drizzle liberally with olive oil and fold gently. It should seem like a lot of olive oil, but you will be glad for this once it is truffle-scented. Taste for salt.

Thirty minutes to 4 hours before serving:
Preheat the oven to 275°, then turn it off.

Thinly slice up to 1 ounce black truffle, then layer it with the beets and their marinade in a small baking dish. Cover tightly and place in the oven to warm through, 15 minutes or so. Keep, still covered, in a warm spot, or in the oven if it is available, until serving.

To serve, spoon some of the fragrant oil over each plate of beets and truffles.

✧
✧ ✧

GRILLED EGGPLANT

A QUICK, SIMPLE DISH TO SERVE HOT, WARM, OR COLD, WITH GRILLED OR ROASTED meat or fish or in combination with other grilled vegetables. Offer Salsa Verde {page 292}, Green Olive-Lemon Relish {page 301} or Roasted Pepper Relish {page 302} on the side. This easy dish is a great way to show off sweet, tender eggplant,

\ *continued*

however, identifying that sweet eggplant is tricky. I do know what *not* to buy: withered or overripe specimens, where you can feel "hollows" when you press the sides. Incomplete coloration can mean underripe, and eggplant that feels really light for its size may be underripe as well. But unequivocal "buy" guidelines are scarce. I have tried to sort out reliable rules, studying color, shape, size, and condition of the blossom end, but nothing consistent has emerged. And I can't smell a good eggplant from a mediocre one.

What matters quite a lot are climate, soil, farming practices, and stage in the harvest cycle; unfortunately, these are hard to ascertain at the market. In general, full-grown specimens from early in the season will be sweeter than the last ones plucked from the plant at the end of the season; making seeds triggers unpleasant flavor and texture changes in the fruit. But since eggplant is grown and ships well from many regions, and year-round, factoring in harvest cycle can be impossible. Buying locally grown eggplant, especially at the farmers' market, is one good way to crack that nut.

The above notwithstanding, knowing the characteristics of specific varieties is very useful. For example, long, slender Chinese eggplant is predictably mild, thin-skinned, and delicate, the flesh very tender and velvety~great for grilling. Slender, curved Japanese eggplant {which, like its Chinese cousin, has an inky purple calyx} and rotund Italian varieties {whose calyx is green} run the range from very tender to a little coarse in texture, and from sweet to somewhat bitter, with the Japanese usually a safer bet. As long as they are not too mature and seedy, both are nice grilled. Unfortunately, the gorgeous streaky purple and white varieties, the pure white ones {some of which, appropriately, you might mistake for duck eggs}, and the lovely slender, pale Green Goddess eggplant are all frequently bitter. All miniature specimens I have tasted have been tough-skinned, seedy, and bitter, making them difficult to use in traditional Mediterranean preparations.

That said, I confess I choose eggplant by tasting it raw, and have done so regularly for years. This method, while it may seem impractical or unappetizing, is foolproof. First, because you get to see the flesh~the nicest eggplant has flesh that is dense, vaguely humid, and tender. It is glowing creamy white with a green tint~and it won't discolor rapidly. It may have a few barely formed seeds, or no seeds yet at all. But the most compelling information comes from the tasting itself~when a nibble of the raw tender flesh is sweet, not unlike a soft, bland apple, and it often is, I buy a case or more.

About 1 pound eggplant   Salt
4 to 6 tablespoons mild-tasting olive oil

Prepare a hot fire in a grill.

Just before grilling, slice the eggplant 3/8 to 1/2 inch thick, brush lightly on both sides with oil and sprinkle lightly and evenly with salt. I don't salt eggplant in advance, whether to tenderize it, or to purge it of bitterness. I like the fleshy texture of freshly seasoned grilled eggplant, and as for drawing out the bitterness, I have never found this ritual very effective. It does draw out liquid, but where the eggplant was truly bitter, I've never found the treated vegetable to be much mellowed as a result.

Spread out the glowing orange coals and set the grill rack a few inches above to preheat. Just as the orange begins to fade, arrange the eggplant in a single layer on the grill. It should sizzle discreetly~if the grill and fire are not hot enough, the eggplant tends to bake and dry out rather than set a crispy-smoky crust. Cook for about 1 minute, then turn over and grill the other side. Bold black grill marks promise a pleasant charry flavor and give the fleshy slabs a great surface texture. Cook for another minute or so, until the eggplant is tender, moving it away from the hottest spots if the elegant black char marks threaten to grow into fully blackened faces. Serve right away, or arrange on a wide platter to cool. To preserve their texture, avoid stacking or overhandling the slices.

÷
÷ ÷

GRILLED ZUCCHINI OR SUMMER SQUASH

SIMPLE, INEXPENSIVE, AND VERSATILE. Grilled zucchini tastes best straight off the grill; it can become dull and soggy after cooling.

Choose freshly picked firm medium-sized squash; baby ones usually lack flavor, and large ones will be busy nourishing seeds. If possible, taste the squash

\ continued

raw. Zucchini doesn't have to be bland; it should be sweet, and some varieties are reliably sweeter than others. I look for pale-green "old-fashioned" varieties, such as Lebanese, French, White, or Grise {gray}, and the tennis ball–sized Rond de Nice squash. I am glad the charismatic *tromboncino* {"little trombone"} is usually sweet; it is fun to buy, cut, grill, and serve. And costato zucchini, with little ridges from end to end, is reliably tasty. On the other hand, I find that showy banana-yellow zucchini and "starburst" squash usually disappoint flavorwise. But yellow crookneck squash can be quite sweet and is delicious grilled. So are pale green patty pan squashes.

FOR ABOUT 4 SERVINGS:

4 to 5 medium zucchini {about 1 pound}

Salt
4 to 6 tablespoons mild-tasting olive oil

Build a small grill fire and let it burn down to glowing coals.

Slice the zucchini lengthwise or on a steep angle into 1/2-inch-thick slices. Salt lightly and evenly and set aside for 5 to 10 minutes to soften. {This encourages the squash to cook more evenly and rapidly, retaining its delicate sweetness.}

Spread out the coals, position the grill rack about 3 inches above them and preheat. Brush the squash on both sides with olive oil. Arrange in a single layer on the grill. Grill for a few minutes per side, until nutty-tender. Move farther from or closer to the fire if any slices of squash threaten to char or are not coloring at all.

✢ ✢
✢ ✢

GRILLED ARTICHOKES

GRILLED RAW, IMMATURE ARTICHOKE "BUDS" HAVE A SUBTLE NUTTY FLAVOR AND present a lovely mantle of crispy, bronzed outer petals, surrounding layers of silky inner leaves. You need a very hot fire to virtually fry the outside and to cook the inner leaves before they dry out. Less-aggressive heat will merely wilt the artichokes; they will discolor and have a disappointing flavor. Grill the artichokes at the last minute. They turn leathery with time.

Choose tightly closed small artichokes, about 2 inches in diameter. They should feel heavy for their size and feel resilient when you squeeze them.

Serve as a side dish with grilled fish or meat garnished with lemon and olive oil, freshly made mayonnaise {see Aïoli, page 289, or Rich Balsamic Mayonnaise, page 289}, or with an anchovy-based sauce, such as Chopped Lemon Bagna Cauda {page 308}. Or serve them with white beans, shavings of Parmigiano-Reggiano, and a splash of extra-virgin olive oil.

FOR 4 SERVINGS:

16 young artichokes {about 1-1/2 to 2 pounds}	4 to 6 tablespoons mild-tasting olive oil Salt

Prepare a hot fire in a grill.

Remove the dark green outer leaves from each artichoke to reveal the pale green heart. Trim off the thorny tips and stem, then "turn" the artichoke, trimming around the base. Cut the artichokes in half from stem to tip and toss with olive oil and salt. Make sure the artichokes are well coated, rubbing the cut faces in the oil to encourage them to accept the seasoning. Thread the artichokes on slender wooden or metal skewers, arranging them so the cut faces will lie flat on the grill.

Spread out the coals and set the grill rack 3 to 4 inches above them to preheat. Just as the orange coals begin to fade, place the skewers cut face down on the hot grill. You should hear a very faint sizzle, and within a few minutes, they should have golden grill marks. Turn them over to grill the rounded side. Grill until the outer leaves are golden and crispy, another minute or so. Squeeze one of the artichokes; it should be soft. If not, grill for another minute or so, a few inches distant from the hottest part of the fire. Slide the artichokes off the skewers and serve immediately.

❖
❖ ❖

GRILLED RADICCHIO

Radicchio is my favorite vegetable for grilling. The sizzling combination of charred and bittersweet and papery-dry layered with fleshy-moist is one I never tire of. For a stunning display, grill a combination of familiar red Chioggia radicchio, some of the speckly ruby and green Castelfranco variety, and Medusa-like heads of Treviso, along with wedges of frisée, and/or Belgian endive. Serve grilled radicchio with balsamic vinaigrette as a first course, or as a side dish with grilled birds, fish, beef, or lamb. It is also good at room temperature or cold, again with balsamic vinaigrette, or with Rich Balsamic Mayonnaise {page 289} or Toasted Bread Crumb Salsa {page 297}. Once the radicchio is cooked, take care not to crowd or stack it, or its extraordinary texture will turn heavy and sodden.

FOR 4 SERVINGS:

3/4 to 1 pound radicchio {about 1 large head}	Salt
	4 to 6 tablespoons mild-tasting olive oil

Build a fire in a grill. Spread out coals while they are red hot. Position the grill rack a few inches above them to preheat.

Meanwhile, remove damaged or wilted outer leaves from the radicchio, then shave any discoloration from the root end of the radicchio, leaving the core intact so that all the healthy leaves stay attached. Cut into 1-1/2-inch wedges. Toss and drizzle with salt and olive oil to coat. If your radicchio is especially dense, oil and season it at least 10 minutes before you grill it. This will soften it so the heat can penetrate quickly and evenly.

Set the radicchio cut face down on the hot grill. Turn when the first side is mottled with bronze and sparsely flecked with black, usually 3 to 5 minutes, and cook another 3 or 4 minutes on the second side. The leaves will tend to fan out as the radicchio cooks. The wedges will become pliable~but don't fuss with them, or you will compact the steaming inner leaves and crumble the fragile outer ones. Left alone, the outer leaves will grill to a nice slightly charred delicacy, with a sweet, pipe tobacco-y aroma and taste. The protected inner leaves will be steamy warm and tender. The flavor dances from smoky-bacon to grapefruit-bitter.

Note: *If charcoal grilling is not an option:* Cook the radicchio under a pre-heated broiler. Space the wedges an inch or so from one another, and raise or lower the broiler rack during the process if, instead of charring, the radicchio begins to merely fade and wither or if it threatens to catch fire.

* *

GRILLED BROCCOLI RABE

TOSSING BROCCOLI RABE WITH A LITTLE WATER, ALONG WITH THE OLIVE OIL, before grilling, means it will steam as it sizzles. This helps the tough branches cook through before they dry out.

Grilled broccoli rabe is easy to prepare and good next to grilled fish, poultry, or meat, or as part of a platter of grilled vegetables. It is tasty at room temperature.

FOR ABOUT 4 SERVINGS:

About 12 ounces broccoli rabe, trimmed

3 to 4 tablespoons mild-tasting olive oil

About 1 tablespoon water

Salt

Build a small fire in the grill and let it burn down to glowing coals.

Split any stalks of broccoli rabe that are more than 1/2 inch thick. Toss the rabe as you would a salad with the olive oil, water, and salt. Leave to soften for 5 to 10 minutes at room temperature.

Meanwhile, spread out the coals and position the grill rack about 3 inches above them to preheat.

Arrange the broccoli on the hot grill and cook for about 1-1/2 minutes per side, allowing the leaves and flowerets to char slightly as the water steams the thicker stems to tenderness. Serve immediately, or slide the broccoli rabe to a cool spot on the grill or onto a warm platter to keep until needed. Don't stack, or you will compromise its pleasant papery-fleshy texture.

* *

CHARD *with* LEMON OIL

A SIMPLE, FRAGRANT SIDE DISH, ESPECIALLY GOOD WITH FISH AND CHICKEN.
Choose very fresh green chard, just mature enough to issue a comforting scrunch when you squeeze the leaves. Very young chard is too limp, grassy, and thin tasting for this dish. Bigger leaves have a mellow, earthy flavor and a satisfying fleshy texture, which is perfect here.

FOR 4 SERVINGS:

About 2 pounds green Swiss chard, damaged leaves trimmed

Salt

3 to 4 tablespoons Lemon Oil {page 285, or see Sources and Resources, page 518}

Wash the chard leaves in several baths of cold water, then use a paring knife to strip the leafy green parts from the white stems. Set the stems aside for another use {see below}.

Prepare a basin of ice water large enough to hold the cooked chard leaves.

Drop the chard into 4 quarts or more of boiling, lightly salted water {I use 2 teaspoons sea salt per gallon}. Taste a bit of leaf as soon as the water returns to a boil ~ it will be tough and slightly minerally or metallic. Continue to taste every 15 seconds or so until the chard is al dente, with no trace of metallic rawness, usually within 1 minute of boiling. The leaves should be soft but not limp; they should hold their shape and be a rich, dark green.

Lift from the water and drop the leaves into the ice water to stop the cooking. Drain and layer between towels to dry. Remove any white veins that turn gray as they cool.

Place the chard in a 3-quart sauté pan or 12-inch skillet. Drizzle with the lemon oil and set over medium-low heat. Stir and fold until the chard is warm and coated with lemon oil. It will wilt a little, but it should remain al dente. Salt to taste. Serve hot, warm, or cold.

❖ ❖ TURNING CHARD STEMS *into* CHARD FRIES

If the stems are in very good condition, try this: Trim the ends and any discolored or damaged sections. Coat each stem first with beaten egg, and then with all-purpose flour; re-dip in the beaten egg, and finish by dredging in fine fresh bread crumbs {page 506}. Refrigerate for about 30 minutes to set the crust, then deep-fry at 365°, or shallow-fry in 1 inch peanut oil until golden. Drain on towels and serve with freshly grated Parmigiano-Reggiano. See *Piccolo Fritto* {page 108} for detailed information on deep-frying.

+
+ +

WILTED ESCAROLE

Fleshy outer escarole leaves ~ too tough for salad ~ make a delicious "what-is-this?" side dish. Slowly wilted, the sturdy leaves fall into gorgeous, satiny folds with a long, earthy, sweet flavor. Don't be tempted to use the pale escarole hearts ~ they usually turn brown and lack sweetness; save them for salads. Good with fish, poultry, pork, or beef.

FOR 4 SERVINGS:

8 to 12 ounces dark green outer esca-
    role leaves, limp and discolored
    spots trimmed
1/4 cup extra-virgin olive oil or 4 table-
    spoons unsalted butter

Zest of 1 lemon, removed with a zester
Up to 1/4 cup water
Salt

Wash the escarole leaves in several baths of cold water to remove every trace of grit. Tear the leaves into 3- to 4-inch lengths. Drain well, but don't spin-dry.

Place half of the oil or butter, lemon zest, water, and escarole in a 3-quart sauté pan or 12-inch skillet. Sprinkle with salt. Cover and set over medium heat. As soon as the water begins to steam, uncover, and then stir every 10 seconds or so until all of the leaves are uniformly wilted and vibrant, glistening green. If the water evaporates before the leaves are cooked, add a few more drops at a time, just enough to keep the escarole from frying. The bright flavor and texture depend on quick cooking in even, steamy heat, not boiling water.

Transfer the leaves to a warm plate. Add the remaining butter or oil, lemon

\ *continued*

zest, and escarole and water as needed to the pan and cook as described above. Serve promptly, spooning the syrupy oil or butter that remains in the pan over the leaves. If the liquid is watery, not syrupy, raise the heat and simmer briefly until it has some body, then spoon over the escarole.

⁝⁝

LONG-COOKED ROMANO BEANS

THE FIRST TIME WE SERVED THESE BEANS, MORE THAN A DECADE AGO, I WONDERED if they would be too homey for contemporary tastes. I should not have worried. They are hours from bright green and al dente, but, perfectly prepared, they have a velvety texture and long flavor that are very satisfying. You can also use mature Blue Lake or Kentucky Wonder beans, which are inexpensive and abundant all summer and well into the fall. Choose beans that are just beginning to bulge with seeds but are still tender. Don't substitute yellow wax beans or yellow romanos.

Serve with beef, pork, or birds and soft or Roasted Polenta {page 192}.

FOR 4 SERVINGS:

About 2 pounds romano beans
About 1/4 cup mild-tasting olive oil
Salt

A few pinches of chili flakes, to taste
2 to 4 garlic cloves, lightly crushed

Break or snip the stem ends off the beans. Unless they are badly shriveled, I leave the tail ends intact. Place in a 6-quart Dutch oven or crowd in a 4-quart saucepan. Drizzle and fold with olive oil to coat all the beans generously, sprinkling with salt and chili flakes as you go. I use my hands to do this. Drop the garlic cloves on top, cover, and place over very low heat. You should barely hear a faint sizzle. Stir a few times during the first 30 minutes, to make sure the beans on the bottom don't scorch, covering the pot again quickly each time so the little steam the beans produce doesn't evaporate {don't add water ~ the flavor and texture will suffer if you do}.

Once the beans begin to soften, usually after about 45 minutes, stir again. Taste for salt. Once they have started to soften, you should notice the oil pooling shallowly on the bottom of the pot. Now check on the beans every 30 minutes or so, but stir only once more, and gently, to avoid crushing the beans. Cook until the beans are utterly tender and limp and have a rich, concentrated flavor, usually about 2 hours total cooking time {smaller beans may take less time than fleshy romanos}. Waiting for this degree of doneness will require a leap of faith for anyone trained to favor al dente vegetables. The beans at the bottom of the pot may color a little during the last 30 minutes before the whole pot is ready, but they will still be delicious.

+ +
+ +

BRAISED PEAS *with* ONIONS, SAGE, *&* PANCETTA

No CONSPIRACY OF NATURE AND CLEVER FARMER HAS EVER DELIVERED A BUSHEL of evenly sized, tiny, sweet English peas that stay that way for even twenty-four hours, so we began making this dish, which calls for those inevitable "culls" {oversized, "gone-starchy," day-old peas}. This recipe flies in the face of my long-held prejudice for just-cooked spring vegetables, but the result is delicious, and preparation easy. It is a rich dish, so serve it with lean poultry or fresh pork, rather than rich duck or squab, cured pork, or red meat. Braised peas are also good with Ricotta Gnocchi {page 221}. This dish is delicious made with fava beans; choose fairly large ones and double-peel them raw {see page 88}. You can leave out the pancetta if you feel like a meatless dish.

FOR 3-1/2 TO 4 CUPS, OR 4 TO 6 SERVINGS:

2 cups finely diced yellow onions {8 ounces}

4 tablespoons unsalted butter

4 cups large and/or starchy green peas

A sprig of fresh sage

2 to 3 ounces pancetta, finely minced {1/3 to 1/2 cup, packed}

Warm the butter in a 2-quart saucepan over medium-low heat. Add the onions with a little salt, stir, and cook slowly until they begin to soften. Add the peas, sage, and pancetta, and salt again conservatively. Stir to coat everything, cover

\ *continued*

tightly, and cook over low heat for 30 minutes to 1 hour, depending on the size of the peas. You should hear a very quiet sputtering. Don't try to rush the peas ~ you will spoil their velvety texture or, worse, scorch them. Stir occasionally, but don't leave the pan uncovered for more than a moment ~ the only moisture in the dish is that in the vegetables themselves, and you don't want it to escape as steam. Don't add water; it would change the flavor and texture.

The peas are ready when they are uniformly drab green and velvety tender but still intact. Don't cook them so long that they begin to shed their skins en masse; once they do, they quickly fall into purée and become heavy and pasty. The juice should be rich and velvety. If at all thin, simmer gently, uncovered, folding once or twice with a rubber spatula, until it thickens. Taste and serve.

⁘ ⁘

SUGAR SNAP BOATS

THE SUGAR SNAP PEA IS A BRILLIANT HYBRID THAT HAS SEVERAL ADVANTAGES OVER old-fashioned English peas. Primarily, you have a good chance of finding sweet ones and getting them to the table that way. And, as with snow peas, you can eat the whole pod, but it is fleshier and crunchier than the parent stock, and sweeter as well. As long as they are firm and bright green, and the pods neither distressed nor bulging, you can largely count on perfect yield, great flavor, and minimal labor.

I like to cook sugar snaps cut into little "boats" ~ they cook evenly and rapidly, scoop up what they are cooked in, and stay on your fork. They present a pretty clutter of saber-shapes, dots, and half-dots. They are tasty and charming tossed with Ricotta Gnocchi {page 221}.

Always cook sugar snaps just before you plan to eat them. Their improbable sweetness shows best fresh from the fire; it can turn mineraly tasting if you try to keep them warm or reheat them.

FOR 4 SERVINGS:

12 ounces sugar snap peas
1 to 2 tablespoons unsalted butter or
    extra-virgin olive oil, or as needed
Water

A fresh basil leaf, a few fresh tarragon
    leaves, or a sprig of fresh chervil,
    chopped {optional}
Salt

String both edges of the snap peas~the inside curve will yield a real filament, the outside one may be less bothersome, but check for it anyway. Cut lengthwise in half, not along the seam, but across the rounded face: one piece will be a half-almond shape, and the peas and half-peas inside will easily fall out. The other piece will look like a canoe with the bottom shaved off; its half-peas will stay attached to the pod.

Place the peas in a shallow pan that holds them in a single layer. Add the butter or oil and water to come to a depth of 1/4 inch. Turn the heat to high, cover, and bring to a boil. Check every 15 or 20 seconds and add a little more water, but not enough to come to more than 1/8 inch deep now, whenever the pan gets close to dry. After a minute or so, taste a pea pod. They are best when they have just lost their grassy raw taste but still have crunch~depending on the peas, your burner, and the pan, plan on 2 to 4 minutes. Don't overcook.

Uncover, add the optional basil, chervil, or tarragon, and boil off nearly all of the water. Add an extra nut of butter or splash of oil if you like. Salt to taste.

❖
❖ ❖

CREAMED CORN

SIMPLE AND VERY RICH. A spoonful with a few grilled or sautéed shrimp makes a nice appetizer. Pick out the youngest ears of corn in the bin, those with small, juicy kernels. They are fairly tender to start with and need little more than heating through.

This recipe includes a basic technique for shaving fresh corn kernels from the

\ *continued*

cob. Your goal is to harvest the rounded tips of the kernels, leaving most of the tough kernel casing behind, while still capturing all the sweet juice.

You can substitute crème fraîche for the mascarpone; the result will be silkier and a little less sweet. {See "real" crème fraîche, page 286.}

FOR 4 SERVINGS AS A SIDE DISH, 6 TO 8 AS PART OF AN APPETIZER:

3 cups scraped corn kernels and their milky juice {see method below} {6 to 12 ears young corn, depending on size and condition}

Scant 3 tablespoons unsalted butter

Salt

A little water, as needed

Up to 1/2 cup mascarpone, at room temperature

Freshly cracked black pepper

Scraping the corn: Shuck the corn and remove all the silk. Trim the tip of each cob, but don't break off the stalk ~ it makes a convenient handle. Holding the cob at an angle, position the knife blade flat against each ear and slide it smoothly down the length of the ear ~ don't cut too close to the cob. Rotate the ear a little after each swipe, until you have harvested all of the tips of the kernels. Now, scrape the whole cob, this time with the dull side of the knife, to force out the milky juice at the base of each kernel. Since the corn tends to fly and the juice splatter as you scrape, you may want to contain this inconvenience by setting up the operation in a wide bowl, tub, or shallow roasting pan. Holding the dull side nearly flat against the stripped cob will direct most of the juice into the vessel instead of onto your kitchen walls.

Melt the butter in a 12-inch skillet over medium-low heat, add the corn and a pinch of salt, and stir with a spatula as you slowly heat the corn through. If the corn is at all dry, flick in a little water with your fingertips and stir as it steams. Taste a kernel of corn ~ if it isn't very tender, add water by the spoonful and stir as the corn cooks to tenderness. Once the corn is tender, stir in mascarpone, a few spoonfuls at a time, to taste. Serve just as it tries to bubble at the edge of the pan. Top with pepper.

✧
✧ ✧

BRAISED FENNEL

WE ONCE MADE THIS EASY RECIPE FOR A BENEFIT FOR 400 PEOPLE, WHICH translated into gently browning 1,200 wedges of fennel in two hours' time on the only two burners we weren't using for lunch service that day. It was, in kitchen parlance, "a nightmare," but the fennel was so good that the trauma was soon forgotten and we still make it regularly. This is very easy to make for 8, 12, or more people.

Choose plump fennel bulbs that feel heavy for their size. I don't use the lovely bright green baby fennel that is popular these days. It tends to be fibrous, tough, and more "green" tasting than sweet. And I avoid bulbs, large or small, that are loosely layered and "scrunchy" rather than firm. Good with birds, lamb, and especially pork.

FOR 4 SERVINGS:

3 fennel bulbs, trimmed {about 8 to 10 ounces each}

2 to 3 tablespoons mild-tasting olive oil

Abou 1/2 cup dry white vermouth or dry white wine

About 1/2 cup Chicken Stock {page 58}

Salt

Pinch of sugar, if needed

A splash of pastis, such as Pernod or Ricard, if needed

Preheat the oven to 375°.

Cut the fennel into 1- to 1-1/2-inch wedges.

Warm a film of olive oil in a 10- or 12-inch skillet over medium-low heat. Make a crowded mosaic of fennel wedges in the pan and cook until delicately golden on the bottom, about 5 minutes, then turn and gild the other side. Salt lightly. Remove the cooked wedges, add more oil as needed, and repeat until you have browned all of the fennel.

Arrange the wedges in a flameproof baking dish that holds them in a single very crowded layer. Add vermouth and chicken stock in equal proportions to come to a depth of 1/2 inch. Bring the dish to a simmer, then transfer to the oven and bake until the fennel is tender, 20 to 30 minutes. Taste the pan juices~if they are thin tasting or too acidic, tilt the dish to one side until the juices puddle and stir in the optional sugar and/or pastis to balance the flavor. Set the baking dish over low heat until the juice bubbles. Serve promptly.

Note: This dish is good reheated. Cover very loosely and heat in a 350° oven.

BAKED ARTICHOKES *with* ONIONS, LEMONS, BLACK OLIVES, *&* MINT

I LOVE THIS DISH FOR ITS EARTHY, SATISFYING TEXTURES AND FLAVORS THAT MELD so well. It is based on the gorgeous, satiny baked artichokes that crowd the windows of Roman groceries in the spring. It is also delicious made with crisp green olives and fresh rosemary leaves.

For general notes on choosing artichokes, see Artichoke Caponata {page 103}. For this dish you will appreciate big blooms with meaty "bottoms." Thick stems are a good indication of that. I suggest sweet yellow onions here; if you can't find them, use regular yellow onions, and plan on adding a little water if they don't throw off enough juice.

FOR 4 OR 8 SERVINGS:

2 pounds thinly sliced sweet yellow onions {about 8 cups}, such as Granex, Vidalia, Walla Walla, or Maui

3/4 to 1 cup mild-tasting olive oil

Salt

4 garlic cloves, slivered

1/3 cup Niçoise or Gaeta olives {about 2 ounces}, rinsed

A dozen fresh mint leaves, very coarsely chopped

1/2 lemon {cut lengthwise}

About 6 tablespoons dry white wine

4 bright green, tightly closed artichokes, 3-1/2 inches in diameter

A little water, as needed

Preheat the oven to 375°.

Toss the onions with about 1/2 cup of the olive oil and about 1-1/2 teaspoons salt {if using kosher salt, use a little more}. Add the garlic, olives, and mint.

Trim off one pithy end of the lemon, then slice it as thin as possible into half-moons, stopping when you hit pith at the other end. Remove seeds as you encounter them. Toss the lemon slices with the onion mixture, add the white wine, and set aside to let the onions soften and "weep" their moisture while you trim the artichokes.

Trim the bottom of the stem of each artichoke and carefully peel the stalk. Remove badly damaged or dry outer leaves. Trim the thorns with scissors or slice them off with a sharp paring knife. Cut the artichoke in half, then use a stainless steel spoon to carve under and remove the thistley choke, leaving the meaty bottom intact. Rinse in cold water; don't drain well ~ a little water between the leaves helps ensure that the artichokes cook thoroughly and evenly.

Sprinkle the artichokes with salt, squeezing and folding them so some salt falls between the leaves. Drizzle and rub with olive oil to coat thoroughly, then squeeze the halves so you can trickle and rub some oil between the leaves.

Spread the juicy onion mixture about 1-1/2 inches deep in a large, flameproof baking dish {I use a 10- by-14-inch lasagna pan}. The liquid should be about 1/2 inch deep; if not, add a little water. {This puddle will generate steam to keep the artichokes moist as they cook.} Nestle the artichokes cut side down in the bed of onions. They will be crowded.

Heat gently over a low flame until the puddle is bubbling, then cover tightly ~ first with parchment paper, then foil, dull side out ~ and bake until you can easily pull out a second-tier leaf and the pulp at its base is tender. This usually takes about 1-1/2 hours; the exact size of the artichokes, as well as the baking dish and oven performance, will affect the cooking time. Be aware that the outermost layer of leaves will emerge a little leathery, which I like.

Once a test leaf is tender, raise the oven temperature to 400°, uncover, and bake for about 15 minutes longer to concentrate the flavors and lightly brown the tips of the vegetables. Serve hot, warm, or cold, as is, or with homemade mayonnaise flavored with lemon, garlic, or a few chopped anchovy fillets {see Lemon Mayonnaise, page 288}.

Cover any leftovers tightly and refrigerate; they will be silkier and sweeter the next day. Bring to room temperature before serving, or heat slowly, loosely covered, in a 300° oven.

Tomato Summer Pudding

Modeled on the traditional English dessert of juicy berries encased in tender white bread, this dish is fine way to show off really ripe tomatoes and day-old bread. Carefully layered like a dish of baked lasagne, it is uncharacteristically orderly for Zuni. Unlike the homey chopped tomato and bread salads of Tuscany, this is a tidier *panzanella,* contrived to display colorful heirloom tomatoes. Different regions, farms, or backyards will favor certain varieties, but my favorites for this dish are Brandywine, Marvel-Stripe, and Granny's Gold. I intersperse these sweet types with a few citrusy Lemon Boys, sweet, piney Evergreens, and tart-rich Purple Cherokees or Black Krims. Whatever their names, choose tender tomatoes with silky, thin skins. Avoid refrigerating tomatoes~even very ripe ones. Being a semitropical fruit, tomatoes are ill equipped for the cold; it damages the cells, leaving them less fragrant. Warming them up doesn't seem to revive the scent. And the refrigerator always seems to make tender tomatoes turn mushy.

Choose herbs and other ingredients with a view to the rest of your meal and then add them sparingly; they should flatter the tomatoes, not compete with them. Garnish with red Sweet 100s, orange Sungolds, or sprigs of tiny currant tomatoes.

Make the pudding an hour or more in advance to allow the flavors to mingle and the bread to fully soften. Serve as a first course, or as a supper dish on a hot summer night, with a plate of cured meats or cold roasted chicken.

Wine: Würzburger Stein Silvaner Spätlese Trocken, Weingut Juliusspital, 1999

FOR ABOUT 6 SERVINGS:

About 8 ounces day-old, chewy, peasant-style bread, sliced about 1/4 inch thick

A few garlic cloves, peeled

Scant 1 cup extra-virgin olive oil

3 tablespoons red wine vinegar or sherry vinegar

Salt and freshly cracked black pepper

About 2-1/2 pounds very ripe tomatoes, preferably several flavors and colors of heirlooms

About 1/4 cup fresh basil, parsley, or cilantro leaves, very coarsely chopped

1 medium shallot {about 1/2 ounce}, finely diced, or a scant 1/4 cup thinly sliced red onion

1/2 small cucumber {about 3 ounces}, peeled and diced

1 cup Sweet 100, Sungold, or currant tomatoes, to garnish

Preheat the broiler. Crisp and brown the bread lightly on one side only. Rub the crispy side of the bread with the raw garlic; set the garlic aside. Brush the soft side with water. Stack the bread and place in a plastic bag to steam and soften as it cools.

Combine the oil, vinegar, and salt and pepper to taste to make a mild vinaigrette.

Core the tomatoes. Cut in half from stem to blossom end, then slice crosswise into half-moons about 1/4 inch thick. Capture all the juice and add it to the vinaigrette. Pick out the bottoms and shoulders of the tomatoes. Coarsely chop them, salt lightly, and scrape into a strainer. Set this over the vinaigrette, smash and press the tomato bits with a spoon, and leave to drain.

Build the pudding in a soufflé dish, wide bowl, gratin dish, or other comparable vessel with a capacity of about 1-1/2 quarts; it should be at least 3 inches deep. Rub the dish with the raw garlic. Cutting the bread into appropriate shapes, carpet the bottom of the dish~leave only small gaps, but don't overlap the slices. Next, make a solid shingled double layer of tomatoes. Scatter with a little of the shallot or red onion and cucumber and the herb. Whisk, then drizzle a few tablespoons of vinaigrette over all. Add another layer of bread, then press with the back of a spoon or fork to encourage the tomatoes to release their juice. Repeat the sequence two or three more times, finishing with a layer of tomatoes. You may not use all of the ingredients, and you should have a few spoonfuls of extra vinaigrette as well. Save both for garnishing. Poke the pudding randomly with a skewer or a meat fork.

Cover with parchment paper or plastic, then choose a flat-bottomed dish that will fit just inside the pudding dish. Place on top and press down firmly. Add a weight~some kitchen item that will fit on the plate and weighs a couple of pounds {I use my heaviest mortar}. Set aside at room temperature.

After an hour or so, remove the weight and plate and check to see if the pudding is juicy enough by sliding a knife down the side of dish; angle the knife to pry the pudding away from the dish. The pudding should ooze. Taste the juice. If the pudding seems dry, drizzle a little more vinaigrette over the top, adjusting its balance first if you thought the ooze was either too acidic or too oily. Press the pudding again until ready to serve.

\ *continued*

To serve, slide a knife around the edge of the pudding, then place a platter upside down on top of the the dish and carefully turn them over together. Holding both the platter and dish tightly, rap the platter firmly on the counter to release the pudding. Ease the dish off the pudding. Present whole, then cut into wedges. Garnish with the little tomatoes, and remaining sliced tomatoes, cucumber, and/or herbs. Spoon extra vinaigrette onto each serving to taste.

⁜

ROASTED APPLESAUCE & SAVORY APPLE CHARLOTTE

ROASTED APPLES PRODUCE A CHUNKY, FLAVORFUL APPLESAUCE. We serve it hot or warm with poultry or pork. Baked in bread-lined custard cups, roasted apple charlottes make an elegant side dish.

Use crisp eating apples for this recipe, rather than soft, fine-textured baking varieties. We use Sierra Beauties, Braeburns, Pippins, or even Golden Delicious and Galas.

FOR ABOUT 3 CUPS:

3-1/2 to 4 pounds apples
Pinch of salt
Up to 2 teaspoons sugar, as needed

About 2 tablespoons unsalted butter
A splash of cider vinegar, as needed

Preheat the oven to 375°.

Peel, core, and quarter the apples. Toss with a little salt and, unless they are very sweet, a bit of sugar to taste. If they are tart enough to make you squint, add the full measure of sugar. Spread in a shallow baking dish that crowds the apples in a single layer. Drape with slivers of the butter, cover tightly, and bake until the apples start to soften, 15 to 30 minutes, depending on your apples.

Uncover, raise the heat to 500°, and return the pan to the oven. Leave the apples to dry out and color slightly, about 10 minutes.

When the tips of the apples have become golden and the fruit is tender, scrape them into a bowl and stir into a chunky "mash." Season with salt and sugar to taste, then consider a splash of apple cider vinegar to brighten the flavor. {Try a drop on a spoonful to see if you like it.}

Savory Apple Charlotte

Make these charlottes in straight-sided 6-ounce ramekins or custard cups.

For 4 servings:

A chunk of day-old, chewy, peasant-style bread {4 ounces or more~ you won't use more than 2 ounces, but you need plenty to work with in order to get the right shapes}

About 2 to 3 tablespoons unsalted butter, melted

About 1-1/3 cups Roasted Applesauce

Preheat the oven to 350°.

Slice the bread 1/8 inch thick. {Partially freeze it if necessary to get even slices.} Avoiding the crust, cut 8 circles sized to fit the bottom of your custard cups, then cut 4 long rectangles to line the sides. The side piece should rise about 1/8 inch above the rims. {Cut paper templates first to make this easy.} A snug fit and even edges will make your charlottes prettiest. {Save scraps and rejects for bread crumbs.}

Brush the bread evenly, on one side only, with the melted butter. Line the custard cups with the bread, pressing the buttered faces against the dishes. Set the 4 extra circles aside. Fill each cup with roasted applesauce. Set the remaining bread circles, buttered side up, on top, held in place by the surrounding bread. Press down lightly.

Bake until golden brown on top, about 30 minutes. To serve, slide a knife around the edge of each charlotte, then turn out onto warm plates. If the bottom circles stick to the dish; retrieve them by sliding a salad fork under the edges. The charlottes should be golden all over, with tasty caramelized spots where the applesauce bled through the coarse-textured bread.

+
+ +

FRESH SHELLING BEANS

Fresh shelling beans are more trouble to find than they are to cook. During their too-short season, they are a cheerful, tasty change from the staple dried beans we cook the rest of the year. Mottled cranberry beans seem to be the most popular fresh shelling beans, but fresh white beans and fresh flageolets are my favorites. I've found fresh chickpeas too few times; they yield a pretty, bright green "pea" and they are delicious.

Buying shelling beans is much like buying fresh peas; you pay a premium for the inedible pod, and yields can be a surprise. For the best flavor and yield, poke around the bin and pick out medium-sized, fleshy pods that are swollen with beans and heavy for their size. Keep the beans in their protective humid pods and refrigerated until you are ready to cook them ~ they discolor readily once they are shucked.

We use fresh shelling beans in soups and pastas, and simmer them with tomato and herbs {See *Fagioli all'Uccelletto*, page 265}. But they show particularly well in simple presentations. Freshly cooked and tossed with excellent olive oil, salt, pepper, and slivers of raw sweet red onion, they make a good side vegetable. Or, for a simple hors d'œuvre, garnish that same mixture with shavings of pungent tuna bottarga {see page 183}, or flank it with a few thin slices of cured meat. At room temperature, shelling beans make a lovely salad with a few leaves of arugula, a little chopped shallot, mild red wine vinaigrette, shavings of aged pecorino or Manchego cheese, and freshly cracked black pepper.

FOR ABOUT 2 CUPS:

1 to 1-1/2 pounds shelling beans in
    their pods {about 2 cups shucked}
1 carrot, peeled, split lengthwise, and
    cut into a few chunks
1 small yellow onion, quartered

1 bay leaf
Water, to cover
Salt
About 2 tablespoons extra-virgin olive
    oil

Shuck the beans and rinse in cold water. Discard any discolored or shriveled beans.

Place the carrot, onion, and bay leaf in a 2-quart saucepan and add cold water to cover. Cover and simmer over low heat until the vegetables have softened and flavored the water, 25 minutes or so.

Add the beans and enough water to barely cover them. {A few varieties of beans ~ cranberry beans and black-eyed peas in particular ~ may turn the cooking water an unappetizing gray, you can avoid this by parboiling them separately before you add them to the vegetable brew.} Bring to a simmer, then tilt the pot and skim any foam that floats to the surface.

Simmer gently uncovered until the beans are tender, 5 to 20 minutes, depending on the variety and maturity. Stir a few times to ensure even cooking, and add water as needed to keep everything just covered. To test for doneness, spoon a few beans and their liquid into a shallow dish and set to cool for a minute in the freezer. Eat a cooled bean. If there is no raw taste or feel, it is ready. If you are unsure, cut a second bean in half. You can usually read doneness in the cut face: it should be moist and tender through, with no pale, chalky core. Remove the pan from the heat and stir in salt to taste. Since it will take a while for the beans to absorb the salt, taste the liquid, not the beans, for salt. Stir in the olive oil and leave the beans to cool completely in the cooking liquid.

Cover and refrigerate, still in their liquid, until needed. They should hold well for up to 4 days.

✢
✢ ✢

DRIED BEANS

THIS IS A GOOD BASIC METHOD FOR COOKING MOST TYPES OF DRIED BEANS ~ IT forces you to get the doneness and salt right. You can double, triple, or quadruple the quantity of beans, as long as you use a larger pot, watch the liquid level, and stir regularly. Exact cooking times and yields vary with the size and dryness of the beans. Different batches of the same type of bean from different sources, or in different years, may cook differently. Soaking will always reduce cooking time and, in my experience, sometimes helps to keep the skins from splitting during cooking, but it is not obligatory, and with really freshly dried beans, can cause problems. My cooks and I struggled for weeks with one batch of cannellini beans

\ *continued*

that shed their skins completely and cooked to mushy before they'd lost their starchiness; finally, when we skipped the soaking step, they came out perfectly. Consequently, we now only soak batches of beans we've had success soaking before, and we never soak lentils or tiny "rice" beans. They are so small they cook in less than 30 minutes anyway. Since most types of cooked beans become creamier after a day or so in the refrigerator, and often the flavor improves, I usually try to cook them in advance. Cooking beans tightly covered does tend to give them a suave texture, but it doesn't improve the flavor the way the passage of time can.

Most of the other ingredients in the recipe are negotiable; you can use more, less, or different aromatic vegetables, including garlic or leeks, for example. You can add herbs, like fresh thyme or sage; spices, such as chili pods or peppercorns; or a scrap of prosciutto or bacon rind if you want. For more character, use a little stock in place of some of the water. The natural and added salts in stock will slow down the cooking and toughen the beans slightly, but the resulting depth of flavor makes it worth it. When cooking beans for confit-based dishes, finish with a spoonful of duck fat in lieu of olive oil.

Buy dried beans where they sell a lot of them. All other things being equal, this year's harvest will taste better and have a nicer texture than last year's. And pass over those attractive packets of mixed beans; they promise a confusion of under- and over-cooked.

FOR 2 TO 3 CUPS:

1 cup dried beans
Water to cover by an inch or so
1 small carrot, peeled, split lengthwise, and cut into a few chunks
1 small yellow onion, peeled and trimmed, leaving the root end intact, and halved

1 bay leaf
Salt
1 tablespoon extra-virgin olive oil {or duck fat, if using with, or in, confit dishes}

Rinse the beans and place in a 2-quart saucepan. Add cold water to cover by about an inch and bring to a simmer. Skim any foam. Stir, then add the carrot, onion, and bay leaf. Maintaining a very gentle simmer, cook the beans uncovered until tender but not mushy, anywhere from 30 minutes to 2 hours, depending on the variety of the bean and how dry it was. Stir occasionally early on, especially if you are cooking larger quantities, so those on the bottom are not crushed, and add water as necessary so that the beans remain just covered. To test for doneness,

PICCOLO FRITTO:
SAND DAB *with* ONIONS, LEMON SLICES,
& FRESH SAGE, *page 114*

SORREL & ONION PANADE, *page 230*

CHOPPED LEMON BAGNA CAUDA *with* ROASTED
TOMATO *&* ROASTED ONION CROSTINI, *page 308*

ZUCCHINI PICKLES, *page 269,*
& RED ONION PICKLES, *page 270*

FRESH CRANBERRY BEANS *with* RED ONIONS
& BOTTARGA DI TONNO, *page 262*

BAKED ARTICHOKES *with* ONIONS, LEMONS,
BLACK OLIVES, *& MINT, page 256*

SHRIMP COOKED IN ROMESCO *with*
WILTED SPINACH, *page 334*

ZUNI ROAST CHICKEN *with*
BREAD SALAD, *page 342*

place a few beans and a little cooking liquid in a cup and set in the freezer for a minute to cool a bit. {If you drain and taste one straight from the pan, piping hot, you won't get an accurate read on tenderness}. Taste one. If it is tender through and shows no trace of raw starchiness, pull the pan from the heat and add salt to taste, gently stirring to make sure it will be evenly absorbed. Taste the bean liquid for salt, not the beans, which will take a while to absorb it. Stir in the olive oil {or duck fat}.

If you serve the beans immediately they will be nutty and their cooking liquid watery and clear, making them ideal for salads, brothy soups, or pasta dishes. Otherwise, let the beans cool in their liquid, then store, still in their liquid, covered and refrigerated for up to 4 or 5 days. They will tend to be silkier and, depending on the variety, may have a sweeter, rounder flavor by the next day. The cooking liquid will gradually thicken and become cloudy.

If you choose to soak the beans: Up to about 8 hours in advance, rinse, then soak the beans in double their volume of cold water. If soaking more than a few cups of beans, swish them around after a half an hour to loosen the pile, so the beans on the bottom of the pile don't get crushed as they soften. When ready to cook, drain and rinse the beans. Notice how much they have swollen, and squeeze one: if they are already quite soft, expect them to cook rapidly, in half the normal time for that type of bean. Place in the pan, add water to just cover, and cook as described above.

⁘

FAGIOLI ALL'UCCELLETTO

"*FAGIOLI ALL'UCCELLETTO*" SOUNDS MORE CHEERFUL THAN "BEANS WITH HERBS and tomato," and I stopped pondering years ago whether cooking beans this way really makes beans {*fagioli*} taste like a little bird {*uccelletto*}, or whether I'd ever had little birds cooked like this in Italy. This version of the Tuscan staple presents

\ *continued*

a light dish of creamy beans in a silky liquid flecked with bits of tomato, rather than the usual beans saturated with tomato sauce. Look forward to occasional whole peppercorns, which soften as they simmer with the beans; I think they are exciting to bite into ~ but you can substitute cracked pepper if that sounds disturbing to you. Wild mushrooms, fresh or dried, are a good addition to the bean stew. We use fresh shelling beans or dried beans at Zuni ~ mottled cranberry beans, any sort of white bean, flageolets, or pea beans. Black-eyed peas, purple crowders, and limas are all nice cooked this way as well. The texture of the dish is best if you start with beans cooked a day in advance. And the flavor is best if you let the finished dish cool completely, then carefully reheat it just before serving.

These beans are good with little and big birds, and with beef, pork, or lamb. I like them with meaty monkfish and with salt cod too. Or make them the center of a meatless meal, paired with grilled eggplant, summer squash or porcini mushrooms. Any leftover beans are a good start on tomorrow's, or the next day's, soup.

Wine: Chianti Classico, Geografico, 1999

FOR ABOUT 3-1/2 CUPS, OR ABOUT 4 SERVINGS:

A small scrap of prosciutto ~ skin or sinewy shank meat {optional}

1/2 cup diced ripe red or gold tomato {about 4 ounces}, or chopped drained canned tomatoes

Salt

1/2 cup diced red or yellow onions {2 ounces}

About 1/4 teaspoon whole black peppercorns

1/4 cup extra-virgin olive oil

A leafy sprig of fresh sage

A leafy branch of fresh thyme

A small sprig of fresh rosemary

A sprig of fresh flat-leaf parsley or a few parsley stems {optional}

A few garlic cloves, coarsely chopped

1 to 1-1/2 ounces cleaned wild mushrooms, preferably porcini or chanterelles {see page 516}, chopped, or 1/4 ounce dried wild mushrooms, rinsed in cold water, then chopped {optional}

2-1/2 cups cooked beans with their cooking liquid {see page 262 or 263}, preferably cooked a day or two in advance

Place the prosciutto scrap, if using, in a small pot, add a few cups of water, cover, and leave to simmer while you begin the sauce. {Alternatively, simmer it with the beans when you first cook them.}

Season the diced fresh tomato, if using, with a pinch of salt and leave to drain in a strainer.

Warm about half of the olive oil in a 3-quart sauté pan or a 4-quart saucepan over medium-low heat. Add the onions, stir, and cook until just translucent, about 5 minutes. Add the peppercorns. Crush the herbs with the back of your knife so that they will release their flavor, then tie in a bundle and add to the onions. Stir in the garlic and the wild mushrooms, if using. Raise the heat slightly, stir, and cook until the onions at the edges of the pan are just threatening to color.

Reduce the heat to low and add the rest of the olive oil and the beans, with most of their cooking liquid. Add the tomatoes and the softened prosciutto scrap, if using. The beans should be just covered; add a little more bean liquid if they aren't. Bring to a bare simmer and cook for about 15 minutes, stirring occasionally. The herbs will go quite limp but the tomato should not break down. Taste.

Remove from the heat and cool to room temperature, uncovered. Cover and refrigerate the beans if you need to hold them for more than an hour. Either way, the tomatoey sauce will have more body if you let the beans cool thoroughly. If the beans seem at all shy on sauce, or if the sauce seems pasty, add more bean cooking liquid or a splash of water.

About 10 minutes before serving, reheat the beans, stirring gently once or twice over low heat. Don't boil, or the sauce may become grainy or pasty. Retrieve the bundle of herbs and squeeze out any sauce it tries to take with it. Most of the leaves will have fallen off; if not, let the bouquet cool and use your fingers to strip them off into the sauce.

Provide the remaining extra-virgin olive oil to garnish.

+ +
+ +

LENTILS BRAISED *in* RED WINE

HERE IS SIMPLE DISH FULL OF CHARACTER. If it suits your taste, and the rest of the meal, you can elaborate on the basic recipe by adding bacon rind or prosciutto scraps, or a branch of thyme or a bay leaf, all at the beginning. The stingy-with-

\ *continued*

liquid method, which will remind you of risotto-making, keeps the flavors concentrated. We use tiny, plump black lentils or dark green French lentils, both of which are about the size of a peppercorn. If you use flat olive green lentils, they may cook more rapidly and require less liquid. In either case, using chicken stock will slow the cooking a little, but will give the dish a more complex flavor.

We serve red wine lentils with game birds, sausage, and red meat. They are also tasty with grilled salmon and meaty fish like monkfish and eel. And they are delicious with fried eggs and bacon, or spooned onto crostini {page 122} and topped with a strip of anchovy and julienned roasted peppers.

If you prepare them in advance, cool, and then reheat them, they will have a mellower flavor and creamier texture than a freshly cooked batch.

FOR ABOUT 4 CUPS, OR 4 TO 6 SERVINGS:

1/4 cup mild-tasting olive oil

1/2 cup finely diced carrots {about 2 ounces}

1/2 cup finely diced celery {about 2 ounces}

3/4 cup finely diced yellow onions {about 3 ounces}

Salt

1 bay leaf

1-1/4 cups lentils {about 8 ounces}, preferably tiny French lentils or

the black lentils sometimes sold as "Beluga" lentils

1 or 2 sprigs fresh thyme {optional}

1 cup medium-bodied red wine, such as Sangiovese or Pinot Noir

2 to 2-1/2 cups water, Chicken Stock {page 58}, or a combination

2 to 3 tablespoons extra-virgin olive oil

Warm the olive oil in a 3-quart sauté pan or 4-quart saucepan over medium-low heat. Add the carrots, celery, onions, and a few pinches of salt. Stir for about 5 minutes as the vegetables release their moisture and begin to hiss, then add the lentils, bay leaf, optional thyme, the wine, and about a cup of the water and/or stock. Raise the heat slightly to achieve a gentle simmer, then cook uncovered, stirring as needed, as you would risotto, and adding more water or stock as the last of each batch is just about absorbed, until the lentils are nutty-tender and just bathed in their cooking liquid. You may not use all of the liquid. Allow about 30 minutes. Taste. If using water or unsalted stock, the lentils will need salt; if using lightly salted chicken stock, they may need none.

Add the extra-virgin olive oil to taste and simmer for a minute longer to bind it with the cooking liquid.

ZUCCHINI PICKLES

This is one of the day-glo pickles we have served next to every hamburger at Zuni, and with the Union Hotel hamburger before that. The basic recipe can be found in older editions of *Joy of Cooking,* but I learned this version from Mark Miller, whose technique produces intense, saturated flavor and nutty texture. Both qualities owe to careful purging and cold brining.

Use firm, medium-sized dark green zucchini, or pickle a combination of these and pearly pastel green patty pan squash. Avoid big, seedy zucchini; they can be pulpy and have a starchy flavor. And don't bother with "fingerling" baby zucchini; though hardly more tender than more mature squash, they rarely have fine flavor, and aren't worth the premium in price.

FOR ABOUT 2 PINTS:

1 pound zucchini or patty pan squash
1 small yellow onion

2 tablespoons salt {a little more if using kosher salt}

For the brine:

2 cups cider vinegar
1 cup sugar
1-1/2 teaspoons dry mustard

1-1/2 teaspoons crushed yellow and/or brown mustard seeds
Scant 1 teaspoon ground turmeric

Wash and trim the zucchini, then slice 1/16 inch thick on a mandoline. Slice the onion very thin as well. Place together in a large but shallow bowl, add the salt, and toss to distribute. Add a few ice cubes and cold water to cover, then stir to dissolve the salt.

After about 1 hour, taste and feel a piece of zucchini~it should be faintly salty and softened. Drain, making sure to remove any remaining ice cubes. Dry very thoroughly between towels, or spin, a few handfuls at a time, in a salad spinner. {Excess water will thin the flavor and spoil the pickle.} Rinse and dry the bowl.

Combine the vinegar, sugar, dry mustard, mustard seeds, and turmeric in a saucepan and simmer for 3 minutes. Set aside until just warm to the touch. If the brine is too hot, it will cook the vegetables and make the pickles soft instead of crisp.

\ *continued*

Replace the zucchini in the bowl and add the cooled brine. Stir to distribute the spices.

Transfer the pickle to jars, preferably ones that have "shoulders" to hold the zucchini and onions beneath the surface of the brine. Cover and refrigerate for at least a day before serving to allow the flavors to mellow and permeate the zucchini, turning them a brilliant chartreuse color. These keep indefinitely refrigerated.

⁙

RED ONION PICKLES

These are delicious and beautiful. Customers regularly request them, by the quart, to go. We serve them with our hamburger, but they are also good with sausages, smoked trout, or pâté.

Use firm round or flat red onions~mild torpedo onions are too tender and the layers of flesh are too thin to make a crunchy pickle. Make sure to cook the brine in a stainless steel pot and use stainless steel or wooden tools to stir and remove the onions~aluminum would turn the onions an unappetizing bluish mauve. Age these pickles for at least a day before serving. They keep indefinitely refrigerated.

FOR ABOUT 2 PINTS:
1 pound firm red onions {about
    2 medium onions}

For the brine:

3 cups distilled white vinegar

1-1/2 cups sugar

A cinnamon stick, broken into a few
    pieces

A few whole cloves

A few allspice berries

A small dried chili

A star anise pod {optional, but it will
    impart a very distinctive licoricey
    flavor}

2 bay leaves

A few whole black peppercorns

Combine the vinegar, sugar, cinnamon, cloves, allspice, chili, star anise, if using, the bay leaves, and peppercorns in a 4-quart saucepan. Bring to a boil, reduce the heat, cover, and simmer for about 3 minutes. Turn off the heat and let stand to allow the spices to infuse the brine.

Peel the onions, trim the ends, and slice 3/8 inch thick. Separate the slices into rings, discarding any green sprouts and thin, leathery outer rings.

Uncover the brine and bring to a boil over high heat. Immediately add about one-third of the onion rings and stir them under. They will turn hot pink almost instantly. As soon as the brine begins to simmer around the edges, about 20 seconds, stir them under again and slide the pot off the heat. Immediately remove the onions with a slotted spoon, skimmer, or tongs and spread on a platter or jelly-roll pan to cool completely. The onions will still be firm. Repeat with the remaining onions, in two batches.

Once the onions have cooled {you can refrigerate them to speed things up}, repeat the entire process, again in three batches, two more times, always adding the onions to boiling brine, pulling them promptly as the brine begins to simmer again, and cooling them completely after each bath. After the third round of blanching, thoroughly chill the brine, then add the pickled onions. This slightly tedious process saturates onions with fragrant brine without really cooking them~they should still be crunchy. It also guarantees that the volatile purple color sets to a charismatic fuschia pink. {Simply simmering the onions in the brine makes a soft, dull pickle~we've tried.}

Place in jars, preferably ones with "shoulders" to hold the onions under the surface of the brine, cover, and store refrigerated.

✦
✦ ✦

CAROL'S PICKLED ONIONS

CAROL BEVER, A VETERAN ZUNI CHEF WHO COOKS WITH LIGHTHEARTED PASSION, came up with this diminutive pickle. Crunchy and complex, but not too sweet, they are good as a foil for grilled birds or fried fish; as a condiment with *Pot-au-Feu* {page 385}; or as a surprise tucked into a sandwich of grilled skirt steak and smashed white beans with arugula. Or add a few rings to your next BLT. We

\ *continued*

serve them with New Year's Eve Gougères {page 116}, and with Crostini with White Beans and Sardines {page 124}.

This easy pickle tastes best made a day or more in advance. It is versatile and inexpensive, and it keeps indefinitely refrigerated and becomes more complex and dramatic, so it makes sense to make more than you need for a given meal. Small onions, no more than 2-1/2 inches in diameter, make a prettier pickle.

FOR ABOUT 1-1/2 PINTS:
12 ounces firm yellow onions, preferably
   no more than 2-1/2 inches in diameter

For the brine:

1-1/4 cups Champagne vinegar or white wine vinegar	2 bay leaves
	1 small dried chili
1-1/4 cups water	A few whole black peppercorns
2 generous tablespoons sugar	Salt

Peel and slice the onions into rings about 1/8 inch thick, discarding the end cuts; a mandoline will make this job very easy. The slices will tend to fall into rings on their own, but you may need to separate the tight centers. Discard any green sprouts or pithy or discolored rings.

Combine the vinegar, water, sugar, bay leaves, chili pod, peppercorns and a few pinches of salt in a small saucepan. If you like things spicy, break the chili pod in half before you add it. Bring to a simmer over medium-low heat, then turn the heat up to medium and add the onion rings. Gently stir the crowded onions as they return to a simmer. Simmer for a little less than 1 minute.

Pour the hot onions and brine into a wide bowl or directly into jars. The skinny rings will turn glassy as they cool. Cover and store refrigerated.

❖
❖ ❖

Rosemary-Pickled Gypsy Peppers

A gypsy pepper is a thin-skinned sweet pepper hybrid. I choose ripe red or orange gypsy peppers for salads and for grilling, but this is a good recipe for the pale chartreuse gypsies that always seem more abundant, and less expensive, but are not so flavorful on their own. If your gypsy peppers are red-ripe, you may want to reduce the amount of sugar here.

Serve with hamburgers, with sausages and fried potatoes, or as part of an antipasto along with salami or coppa, olives, and deviled eggs. We also serve them with Manchego, the hard sheep's milk cheese from Spain, serrano ham, and toasted almonds. Fleshy slabs of the pickled peppers are great on Egg Salad Crostini, topped with ribbons of smoked prosciutto {page 125}.

This pickle tastes best after a few days in the refrigerator ~ the peppers lose their grassy taste and the brine mellows. It keeps indefinitely refrigerated.

FOR ABOUT 4 PINTS:

3 pounds gypsy peppers {6 to 8 peppers}   Salt
About 2 teaspoons mild-tasting olive
    oil

For the brine:

3 cups Champagne vinegar or white   1-1/2 cups sugar
    wine vinegar   A handful of fresh rosemary leaves

Combine the vinegar, sugar, and rosemary leaves in a small saucepan. Simmer covered for about 3 minutes. Set aside.

Preheat the broiler and position the oven rack about 8 inches from the element {or prepare a hot grill}.

Wash and dry the peppers and cut lengthwise in half. Cut away the seed clusters and trim any soft spots. Drizzle with the olive oil and salt. Toss and rub gently to coat all the surfaces.

Arrange on a baking sheet and broil just long enough to slightly soften the

\ *continued*

flesh and slightly blister and color the skins, about 10 minutes {or grill for 3 to 4 minutes per side}. Pack the warm peppers into jars and add the still-warm brine.

Cool, then cover and store refrigerated.

✢
✢ ✢

PICKLED GLASSWORT

This unpromising-sounding and -looking marsh succulent may be slightly overrepresented on Zuni's menu, owing to my sentimental attachment to what Jean Troisgros referred to as *"les algues."* Everyone in his extended family seemed to love pickled glasswort, and a jar was always brought out anytime you might be expecting cornichons {French gherkins}. The Troisgros brothers garnished their famous *Poulet au Vinaigre* {Chicken with Vinegar} with pickled glasswort.

Glasswort *is* actually an algae. It is a naturally briny *salicorn* that the English used to call "chicken claws" {which the fleshy, leafless stems resemble, sort of}. It is always a hard sell, hopeful marketing names like "sea beans" notwithstanding. Discovering that it owes its common name to a high alkali content, making it useful in the manufacture of glass, hardly enhances the romance. "Marsh samphire" is another name that provokes no understanding, or appreciation. The French have called it *pousse-pied* ~ "sprout-foot" ~ not a revealing concept to me or a pretty phrase in English, so this name is not very helpful in America.

On our coast, the glasswort harvest starts in early May, in the coastal marshes of southern Oregon. I look for tender small sprigs, bright green, with little or no budding at the tips. When it is abundant, we serve glasswort fresh, sautéed in butter and deglazed with vinegar as a garnish for the local sand dabs, rex sole, or skate wing {See Sand Dabs with Shallots, "Sea Beans," and Sherry Vinegar, page 317}. This is a delicacy. And then we pickle a few gallons to use the rest of the year as a condiment with *Pot-au-Feu,* or chopped into salsa verde, stirred into brown butter sauces, or with potato salad ~ in short, anywhere we might use capers.

To pickle glasswort, you need only good white wine vinegar and patience. Go through the glasswort sprig by sprig, checking for woody stems. Only the nibs and stems that are so young that they are truly "succulent" will be tasty. Discard mature branches that have a tough fiber running through them, after harvesting any tender branchlets. Discard also any desiccated or discolored sprigs. Rinse the glasswort, then pack in jars {with "shoulders," to keep the glasswort submerged} and add vinegar to cover. I sometimes tuck 1 small, peeled garlic clove into each pint jar. Cover and age the pickles for 2 weeks in a cool, dark place, then refrigerate for long-term keeping.

A note on finding glasswort: If you don't live near a salt marsh where it grows, ask about glasswort at produce markets that offer a good selection of wild mushrooms from the Pacific Northwest. Since it is abundant in the same region, glasswort is often shipped by the same brokers who handle wild mushrooms.

❖
❖ ❖

PRESERVED LEMONS OR LIMEQUATS

A GOOD CONDIMENT TO HAVE ON HAND. Its distinctive flavor is unmistakable and makes everything it touches seem exotic and special. Chopped preserved lemon is good in relishes, sauces {see Preserved Lemon-Caper Butter, page 309}, stews, and pastas. Use fully ripe unwaxed lemons. Limequats are lemon-yellow, look like kumquats, and are in season at the same time. Although not traditionally prepared this way, preserved limequats are delicious. They can be used in as little as one week, retain their firm texture, and present pretty coins when sliced. Rinsed, slivered, and generously moistened with extra-virgin olive oil, preserved limequats are delicious smeared on grilled fish or chicken while still hot from the grill. Our experiments with other types of citrus have been little more than entertaining, with results ranging from odd to awful.

FOR ABOUT 2 PINTS:
About 1-1/2 pounds lemons or limequats

\ *continued*

For the brine:

2 to 3 quarts, plus 2 cups water
About 3 tablespoons salt
1 cinnamon stick

A few whole black peppercorns
A few coriander seeds
1 bay leaf

A few tablespoons mild-tasting olive oil

Add the lemons or limequats to 2 to 3 quarts boiling water and simmer for about 4 minutes for lemons, 2 minutes for limequats, to soften the skin. Drain and rinse in cold water. Pack into jars that have "shoulders" to keep the fruit submerged. You can cut some of the lemons into wedges, or slash them deeply, to make for an easier fit.

Combine the 2 cups water, the salt, cinnamon stick, peppercorns, coriander, and bay leaf in a small saucepan and bring to a boil. Cool slightly.

Pour over the prepared citrus to cover it completely. Coat the surface with olive oil, and screw on the lids.

Age lemons for about 4 weeks, limequats for 1 week, in a cool, dark spot. To preserve the texture of the limequats, refrigerate after that 1 week.

Note: Always use clean tongs or a fork, not your fingers, to remove the citrus from the jar. Taste a sliver. Rinse briefly under cool water if they seem intolerably salty. Refrigerate after opening.

⁺
⁺ ⁺

Spiced Zante Grapes

We serve these "as is" or briefly roasted, with pork, game birds, or sausage, or as a garnish for pâté or cured meats. The individual berries are nice tossed into frisée salad with walnuts and crumbles of Gorgonzola, Roquefort, or Stilton cheese. Scatter a few over a warm Savory Onion Tart with Apples and Bacon {page 120}. Or add to a pan of sizzling sautéed chicken livers and onions about 1 minute before serving.

If you can't find Zante grapes, use small, very ripe Red Flame grapes, fleshy wine grapes, or very small, amber-ripe Thompson seedless grapes.

FOR 2 PINTS:

1 pound Zante grapes or other very ripe,
    small grapes

For the brine:

3/4 cup sugar

1 cup Champagne vinegar or white
    wine vinegar

1 cup dry white wine

A few allspice berries

1 bay leaf

Wash and dry the grapes, then cut into small clusters. Cut away any cracked, bruised or moldy grapes, but leave naturally "raisined" fruit in place ~ it will take the brine well. Place in wide jars with "shoulders" to keep the fruit from floating above the surface of the brine.

Combine the sugar, vinegar, wine, allspice and bay leaf in a small saucepan. Bring to a simmer, stirring, then cover and adjust the heat to a bare simmer for about 1 minute. Taste. The brine should be tart but should not make you squint; add sugar or vinegar, as needed, to correct. Leave until barely warm to the touch.

Pour the cooled brine over the grapes. {If the brine is too warm, it will cook and soften the fruit, spoiling this elegant pickle.} Seal and store refrigerated for at least 1 week before using. Keeps indefinitely.

÷
÷ ÷

PRUNES PRESERVED THREE WAYS

Make any of these recipes at least a day, but ideally a few days, before you want to serve them; the prunes will mellow in flavor and develop a suave texture. And they will keep and improve for months. Store in the refrigerator ~ processing these for room-temperature storage cooks the tender prunes and ruins their texture. For the same reason, the syrup mustn't be too hot when you combine it with the prunes, or it will cook the fruit.

Pitted prunes will soften more rapidly than whole prunes and emerge more

\ *continued*

uniform in flavor and texture. They ultimately absorb more syrup. But I prefer the meatier result you get with whole unpitted prunes, and I like to chew on the pits.

✦✦ SPICED PRUNES

Serve as a condiment with pâté, cured meat, roasted duck or squab, confit, braised goose, or roasted brined turkey {page 403}.

FOR ABOUT 2 PINTS:

1 cup Champagne vinegar or white wine vinegar
1 cup water
1 cup sugar
1 cinnamon stick, splintered

4 allspice berries
8 whole black peppercorns
1 bay leaf
1 pound prunes ~ about 2-1/2 cups with pits, closer to 3 cups if pitted

Combine everything except the prunes in a small saucepan and simmer for 3 minutes. Cool the brine until it is not quite too hot to touch, about 130°, if using unpitted prunes. For pitted prunes, it should be just warm to the touch, about 100°.

Place the prunes in a jar or jars and add the brine to cover completely, distributing the spices evenly. Cool completely, then cover tightly and refrigerate for at least 24 hours, or up to several months. Shake the jar{s} occasionally to redistribute the seasonings.

✦✦ PRUNES *in* BLACK TEA

These barely sweetened prunes are delicious for breakfast, or with roasted duck, quail, or squab. We usually use English breakfast tea, but I once made these with jasmine tea when I had nothing else in the house; the result was delicate and floral.

FOR ABOUT 1-1/2 PINTS:

2 cups water
1 tablespoon plus 1 teaspoon loose tea leaves
About 2 tablespoons sugar
1 pound prunes ~ about 2-1/2 cups with pits, closer to 3 cups if pitted

3 strips orange or lemon zest, about 1 inch long and 1/2 inch wide ~ removed with a vegetable peeler

Bring the water to a simmer, pour over the tea, and infuse for about 8 minutes. Strain. Stir in sugar to taste. Cool until not quite too hot to touch, about

130°, if using unpitted prunes. For pitted prunes it should be only warm to the touch, about 100°.

Place the prunes in a jar or jars, a narrow bowl, distributing the zest evenly. Don't pack. Pour the tea over the prunes to just cover. Cover, or, if storing in a bowl, weight the prunes with a small plate to keep them submerged. Cool completely, shaking or stirring under once or twice, then store refrigerated.

‡ ‡ PRUNES & CRANBERRIES *in* TEA

Prepare Prunes in Black Tea, making an extra 1/2 cup of tea syrup. Spoon the extra syrup into a small saucepan, add sugar until it is candy sweet, and bring to a boil. Add about 1/4 cup fresh cranberries. Swirl the pan over the heat until the skins split, then pull from the heat and leave the cranberries to cool and absorb the syrup.

Drain the cranberries, discard the pink syrup, and fold the berries into the softening prunes. Cool, cover, and refrigerate. Makes a generous 1-1/2 pints.

‡
‡ ‡

BRANDIED FRUIT

DURING MY FIRST YEAR AT ZUNI, I PUT UP MASSIVE STOCKS OF THESE BRANDIED fruits. Recalling the image of my mentor Pepette's tiny, timbered dining room in rural Southwest France, its walls ornamented with rows of the translucent amber-, ruby-, and plum-colored jars, I imagined the whole of urban Zuni thus transformed. This proved to be colossally expensive, given my choice of brandy, and not terribly practical, given the size and layout of the restaurant. The resulting oversupply provoked a lot of invention, and we found that the fruits were a stunning addition to savory dishes as well as sweet ones. Each time I show a cook how to souse cherries, raspberries, figs, red currants, grapes, prunes, Italian plums, or greengages, I still fight the urge to make more than we will use. {Fortunately, this year's batch of brandied fruit will still be good next year, as long as you keep it refrigerated.}

\ *continued*

Basic Method:

Choose sound, just-ripe fruit with no blemishes or soft spots. Time will magnify every flaw, so inspect each piece of fruit carefully. Rinse the fruit and leave
to drain on a clean towel. Gently pack in sterilized jars with shoulders that will
keep the fruit submerged in the brandy.

Dissolve the sugar in the spirits with a small measure of water. The ideal
amount of sugar will vary according to the sweetness of the spirit and the type
and ripeness of fruit in question. Remember to take into account the flavor of
skins ~ the flesh of a grape or a plum may be supersweet, but some have tart, tannic skins, which require lots of sugar to tame. In that case, you may want to use
more than the recommended dose of sugar.

Pour the sweetened liquor over the fruit to cover. Seal the jars and tap gently
to release air bubbles. I record the amount of sugar and spirits {or at least a ratio}
on the jar when I label it with the date and type of fruit.

Store the jars in a cool, dark place for a few weeks to allow the fruit to
exchange flavor with the liquor, then refrigerate. {You can also place them
directly in the refrigerator, but this will slow the flavor-mellowing process.} If
serving the brandied fruit raw, open the jar a few hours before using and poke
gently once or twice to encourage some of the alcohol to evaporate, or pour the
desired amount of fruit into a wide bowl.

Here are guidelines for making and serving some of the most versatile fruits.

◆ ◆ **BRANDIED CHERRIES**

Crisp red Bing or Van cherries are the best choice for brandying. Firm Queen Ann
and Rainier are also good, but they aren't the best choice for really long keeping,
since the brandy eventually overwhelms their delicate flavor ~ plan to use them
within a month.

FOR ABOUT I PINT:

About 8 ounces cherries   6 to 7 tablespoons sugar
Scant 1 cup good-quality inexpensive   About 2 tablespoons water
    brandy

Wash and dry the cherries. Leave the stems on, but clip the very ends. Pack
according to the Basic Method {above}.

Serving suggestions:

‡ Serve with pâté and wedges of raw fennel.

‡ Roast briefly and serve with quail or squab, along with a salad of bitter greens and toasted hazelnuts.

‡ Sauté and add to braised duck, or serve with sautéed duck breast, cooking the cherries briefly in the pan juices before pouring them over the sliced breast.

‡ Serve in a pretty bowl with biscotti and chunks of dark chocolate on the side.

‡ Pit and sauté briefly in butter with a splash of the syrup, and serve with ice cream and crêpes.

‡ Preserve in bourbon instead of brandy and use about 2/3 cup sugar, then substitute for maraschino cherries in a Manhattan cocktail.

‡ ‡ BRANDIED RED CURRANTS

Sprigs of raw red currants are beautiful but frustrating. The fruit is not very tasty in this, its most beautiful form. Brandying them allows you to showcase the lovely fruit *en branche,* knowing that it tastes as lovely as it looks.

FOR ABOUT I PINT:

About 8 ounces red currants on branches
Scant I cup good-quality inexpensive
   brandy

7 to 8 tablespoons sugar
About 2 tablespoons water

Rinse the currants, drain, and leave to dry. Snip off damaged fruit. Prepare according to the Basic Method {page 280}, taking care to handle very gently. These are ready to use in a week.

Serving suggestions:

‡ Serve with pâté or *rillettes* {see Rabbit *Rillettes,* page 442}.

‡ Serve with Rabbit Sausage {page 426} or as part of a Rabbit Mixed Grill {page 416}.

‡ Serve as a condiment with lamb chops or Roasted Leg of Lamb {page 394}.

‡ Pick off the branches and mix with fresh berries in a traditional English summer pudding.

‡ Serve with bread pudding, rice pudding, or Panna Cotta {page 500}.

Here are two more fruit conserves I keep on hand to serve with cheese. {For suggested pairings, see pages 449 to 454.}

+ + DRUNKEN RAISINS

Place raisins in a narrow container and add enough brandy, grappa, or Port to barely cover, then top off with a little water. Cover, shake, and set in a warm spot. Taste in about an hour and sweeten with sugar or honey to taste. Cover, shake again, and leave at room temperature for a few days, then refrigerate.

You can serve these raisins as soon as a day after making them, but they only improve as they become swollen with syrup. In any case, leave uncovered for an hour or so before using. Once refrigerated, they keep for ages, eventually becoming very suave and mellow.

+ + DRIED FIGS *in* RED WINE

This condiment is easy to put together and keeps for months. Make it at least a few days before you plan to serve it, to allow time for the figs to swell and the flavors to mellow. Dried figs vary in dryness; the ones I use are chewy-moist ~ like the paste in a Fig Newton. They are fairly tender to begin with and absorb most of the scant wine syrup after a few days. If your figs are really dry, rinse them quickly under water before combining with the wine.

FOR ABOUT 1 PINT:

1-1/2 cups red wine {you can use a light, medium, or full-bodied red here}
2 bay leaves
A wide, 1-inch-long strip of orange zest, removed with a vegetable peeler

8 ounces dried Black Mission figs {about 20 large or 36 small figs}
About 1 teaspoon honey

Place the wine in a small saucepan with the bay leaves and simmer to reduce to a scant 1/2 cup. While the wine is reducing, cut the figs in half and place in a 2- to 4-cup storage vessel with a tightly fitting lid. Drop the orange zest in with the figs.

Add the honey to the warm reduced wine, stir, and pour over the figs. It won't seem like enough liquid. Cover and shake. Leave to swell for a few days, shaking or stirring a few times to redistribute the scant wine syrup, then refrigerate. Serve at room temperature.

Sauces & Relishes

Vinaigrette

Vinaigrettes are the simplest of sauces, easy to make and to adjust for whatever they are destined to dress. Though vinegars vary in intensity and acidity, a ratio of about 4 parts oil to 1 part vinegar will usually produce a pleasant balance. At 2 or 3 parts oil to 1 part vinegar, the acidity and perfume of the vinegar will be assertive, desirable for rich dishes or for food that has already been rubbed with oil or another fat. At the other extreme, about 6 parts oil to 1 part vinegar may be perfect for dressing starchy vegetables or grains, or in dishes with delicately flavored vegetables such as green beans, asparagus, mushrooms, or truffles. In these cases, the vinegar flavor should be elusive and the presence of a little acid only teases and excites the palate to better taste the other flavors. Likewise, the very best olive oils want the stingiest trickle of vinegar when you are using them for vinaigrettes.

Most of our vinaigrettes are made with Champagne vinegar or red wine vinegar. We occasionally make cider or sherry vinaigrettes where the dishes respond to those flavors, and we sometimes use a small of measure of black currant vinegar to add rich fruitiness to vinaigrette. When making balsamic vinaigrette, we choose a rich, tasty balsamic, with a few years of age perhaps, not a precious artisan-made product.

We use a not-too-spicy Tuscan or Umbrian olive oil for most vinaigrettes, sometimes spiked very judiciously with nut oil or citrus-scented *olio agrumato* {see Homemade Lemon-Infused Olive Oil, page 285}.

Salt is the only constant seasoning in our vinaigrettes. If a dish wants pepper, we usually add it to the dish, not to the vinaigrette. A few recipes ask you to add shallot, spices, mustard, honey, liqueur or brandy or meat glaze to the vinaigrette. I suggest amounts, but you should decide on the final dose by tasting. When tasting any vinaigrette, you cannot do better than to taste it on a leaf of salad, or a piece of whatever it is going to dress. The flavor dynamics will be very different than on a spoon, or your fingertip.

With the exception of some herbed concoctions, vinaigrette rarely improves with age. So, make what you need just before you need it. Be prepared to make more of the vinaigrette, or add extra oil, vinegar, or salt, once you actually dress the dish.

FOR 5 TABLESPOONS, GENERALLY ENOUGH FOR 3 TO 4 SERVINGS OF SALAD GREENS:

1 tablespoon vinegar   Salt

1/4 cup extra-virgin olive oil

Combine the ingredients and stir briskly into an emulsion. Taste and correct. Stir well again just before using.

✢
✢ ✢

HOMEMADE LEMON-INFUSED OLIVE OIL

Necessity is the genius behind much culinary tradition, and lemon oil is a rarely acknowledged case in point. In the Abruzzo region of Southern Italy, it is traditional to press lemons~rich in citric and ascorbic acids~with the season's first batch of olives. This process serves to clean the olive press, but it can also produce a hauntingly fragrant oil. This treasure was quietly bottled and guarded for family use, until in recent years it became commercially available as *Olio Agrumato* {"citrus-ed" oil}. For artisan-made Italian lemon, orange, or mandarin olive oil, see Sources and Resources, page 518.

Even if you don't press your own olives, you can make a creditable substitute by crowding 1 cup extra-virgin olive oil with the zest of 1 or 2 lemons. Use unwaxed, organic lemons and only the yellow part of the rind, carving wide zests with a vegetable peeler. Set the oil to infuse over the lowest heat for about 10 minutes. Don't allow it to simmer. Remove from the heat and leave for 30 minutes, or longer. Strain out the zest before using. This lemon-scented oil is not as pungent or saturated with flavor as the traditional product but, lacking that, choose this simple alternative rather than squeeze harsh lemon juice over a dish. The fragrance of homemade *olio agrumato* is fleeting, so make only as much as you are likely to use right away.

✢
✢ ✢

Mock Crème Fraîche

THIS POPULAR METHOD OF CULTURING HEAVY CREAM CAME INTO GRAND VOGUE in the 1970s as an earnest surrogate for the real thing from France, which was unavailable in America. I've never thought of it as a substitute, however. It doesn't taste or behave like its namesake. Mock crème fraîche is downright tart in comparison to the genuine product, which is nutty-sweet, with a hint of acidity. Owing to the realities of most American cream, mock crème fraîche is typically lower in milkfat and lacks the nutty-sweetness altogether. It also doesn't really tolerate cooking. Hence, it's less than ideal for slathering on desserts or enriching sauces. But all those "flaws" make a little of this thickened cream an ideal last-second garnish for salads or soups. A lacy drizzle of something thick and tangy can just as easily balance a very rich dish as animate and enrich a lean one.

To make Mock Crème Fraîche: Stir about 2 tablespoons buttermilk into 1 cup heavy cream. Heat until warm to the touch ~ about 85°. Cover loosely and leave to culture in a warm place. Mock crème fraîche usually takes at least 8 hours to thicken, but this varies with quantity, the ambient temperature, and the condition of the buttermilk you are using {see below}. Monitor the process and refrigerate it when you like the taste and texture. The cream will continue to thicken, albeit much more slowly, in the refrigerator. If it becomes too thick for drizzling purposes, you can thin it with more plain heavy cream.

Regarding "real" crème fraîche: Traditional, farmhouse crème fraîche "happens" when raw cream, naturally swarming with the proper lactic cultures, thickens and matures on its own. Pasteurization prevents such culturing. Commercially produced crème fraîche, whether in France or elsewhere, is the result of inoculating pasteurized cream with strategically chosen pure, live lactic cultures. When you inoculate pasteurized heavy cream with supermarket buttermilk at home, you are not doing the same thing. You could, perhaps, find the proper cultures in natural farmhouse buttermilk, but commercial buttermilk is a cultured product itself, the result of adding a mix of desirable bacteria to low-fat or nonfat milk. The exact composition of this mix varies from buttermilk to buttermilk, and from region to region. It may well include the "right" cultures for crème fraîche, plus others, but the fermenting process, which turns the milk into cultured buttermilk, alters the ratios of those organisms. Many may die off completely. All of this affects flavor. This situation, coupled with the milkfat deficiency and flavor differences in the cream itself, begins to explain why you can't produce real crème fraîche this way.

Fortunately, it is no longer difficult to find authentic nutty-sweet crème fraîche made in America. We buy ours from Cowgirl Creamery, in nearby Tomales Bay; Vermont Butter and Cheese makes an excellent one as well. Where you are serving crème fraîche by the dollop, adding it to Creamed Corn {page 253}, or stirring it into a simmering sauce, you should use one of those products, not mock crème fraîche.

⁘
⁘ ⁘

TOMATO COULIS

A LIGHT, FLUID, BARELY COOKED TOMATO SAUCE, GOOD WITH FRIED FOOD, A Frittata {page 180}, or grilled or broiled swordfish, sea bass, or sardines. It will be only as good as the tomatoes you use; pithy, underripe fruit will not make a great coulis. Make this simple sauce with fragrant high-season fruit. You can infuse the coulis with a branch of basil or thyme if you like, or perfume it with a lightly crushed clove or two of garlic or a pinch of dried chili flakes. If you peel the tomatoes first, the sauce will be more delicate, and sweeter; if you leave the skins on, it will be more robust. It is a good way to use up the awkward but tender heels, shoulders, and leftovers you generate when you serve sliced tomatoes on sandwiches or salads.

FOR ABOUT 1 CUP:

About 12 ounces ripe tomatoes
Salt
A sprig of fresh thyme or basil
    {optional}
1 or 2 garlic cloves, lightly crushed
    {optional}

A pinch or two of dried chili flakes
    {optional}
About 2 tablespoons extra-virgin olive
    oil
Sugar, if needed

If you choose to peel the tomatoes, plunge them into a pot of rapidly boiling water for a few seconds, then remove and cool them in ice water, or blister each one in direct flame, just long enough to split and shrink the skin all over. In either case, the skins should then slide off easily.

\ *continued*

Core the tomatoes, then trim any hard shoulders or carve out woody cracks. Cut into a few thick slices or chunks, salt very lightly, and toss with the optional thyme or basil, garlic, or chili flakes. Place in a strainer set over a bowl to purge for about 20 minutes. {Draining a little water from the raw tomatoes reduces the time needed to concentrate the flavor over heat. The result is brighter tomato flavor.}

Warm the olive oil in a small skillet over low heat. Add the tomato, and any aromatics, and crush with the back of a fork. Raise the heat slightly and cook until the tomatoes have "melted" and are just taking on the characteristic orange cast that comes from cooking, about 1 minute. Swirl and stir the pan to encourage maximum evaporation. Mass the tomatoes on one side of the pan and tilt it. They should barely ooze. Scrape into a strainer or food mill and press through. Cool slightly and taste. The coulis will likely not need salt, but may appreciate a pinch of sugar.

Serve at any temperature. If serving warm or hot, reheat just before serving.

⁘

LEMON MAYONNAISE

FOR 1/2 TO 3/4 CUP, BOTH GENEROUS:

1 egg yolk
A few pinches of salt

1/2 to 3/4 cup mild-tasting olive oil
1/2 lemon

Whisk the yolk with a pinch of salt. Whisk in a trickle of oil, then another, gradually increasing the flow to a stream, whisking constantly to maintain an emulsion. The sauce will begin to turn opaque and tacky. Keep adding oil until the mayonnaise is a little firmer than you like, then add a long squeeze of lemon juice. Drop another pinch of salt on the lemon juice, then whisk again. Taste, and whisk in more lemon, salt, or oil to taste.

⁘ *Variation* ANCHOVY MAYONNAISE

Prepare as described for Lemon Mayonnaise, adding 3 or 4 finely chopped salt-packed anchovy fillets after you have added about 1/4 cup of the oil. Flavor with lemon juice to taste. This mayonnaise may need no more than the initial pinch of salt.

⁂ ⁂ Variation RICH BALSAMIC MAYONNAISE

This toffee-colored mayonnaise is good with Salt-Roasties {page 237}, boiled or Grilled Artichokes {page 244}, Grilled Radicchio {page 246}, grilled chicken or lamb. Make a batch for your next bacon, lettuce, and tomato sandwich.

FOR SCANT I CUP:

I egg yolk

A few pinches of salt

About 3/4 cup mild-tasting olive oil

1/4 teaspoon Dijon mustard

I or 2 salt-packed anchovy fillets, finely chopped {optional}

About 2 tablespoons balsamic vinegar, a good quality commercial product is fine here

Whisk the yolk with a pinch of salt. Starting with a bare trickle, gradually whisk in about 1/3 cup of the olive oil as described for lemon mayonnaise, above. Stir in the mustard, anchovy if using, and about I tablespoon balsamic vinegar. Whisk in the remaining oil, then finish by adding more balsamic to taste.

⁂

AÏOLI

I LIKE GARLIC MAYONNAISE BEST MADE WITH JUST GARLIC, EGG YOLK, OIL, AND salt ~ with no acid of any sort. So long as the 4 ingredients are excellent in quality, the flavor will be bold, but balanced. At home, I make small batches of Aïoli in a 2-cup wooden mortar; for larger batches, I use the same pestle, but do the binding in a wide, unfinished wooden bowl.

FOR A GENEROUS I/2 CUP:

I large or 2 small garlic cloves, peeled

A few pinches of salt

I egg yolk

About 1/2 cup mild-tasting olive oil

\ *continued*

Cut the garlic into a few pieces and then pound them in a mortar. Add the salt. It should act as an abrasive and help you smash the last solid bits of garlic. Add the yolk and stir with the pestle to amalgamate. Still using the pestle, work in the oil, a cautious trickle or a few drops at first, gradually increasing the flow as the yolk becomes tacky and opaque. As the yolk reaches saturation, the mixture will make a satisfying clucking sound.

If you add a few drops of water to the Aïoli, it will whiten and soften, allowing you to add more oil, which you may choose to do if you find the garlic remains too aggressive with only 1/2 cup oil. {1/2 teaspoon water will bind an additional 1/2 cup oil.} I find this is the best way to stroke an Aïoli into balance, preferable to introducing lemon or other new flavors.

✦ ✦ ✦ ✦ ✦

THE TRICKIEST MAYONNAISE TO MAKE IS A ONE-EGG-YOLK ONE. All of us have failed at least once, usually for adding too large a dose of oil early on. The foolproof rescue technique I learned was to start with a new yolk in a new bowl, gradually sneaking in the damaged goods. The price is making twice as much mayonnaise as you wanted to. But you can sometimes avoid this:

Anytime you accidentally spill in too much oil, don't panic. Resist the urge to whisk wildly. Instead, tilt the bowl strategically, so the excess oil flows into a puddle, off to the side, away from the yolky part. Now whisk only the yolky part, which can mean whisking it partway up the side of the bowl, steering clear of the oil puddle. Once you can see the yolk emulsion is stable {stop whisking, check that it is still thick and opaque}, begin to very gradually draw in the problem oil, working from the edge of the puddle. As this effort succeeds you can gradually level the bowl again. Whether saving a mayonnaise or not, I find it easiest to control how much oil gets to the yolk when I make mayonnaise in a wide, flat-bottomed bowl in which I can trickle oil on the edge of the emulsion and know it will stay there until I am ready to drag it in with the whisk.

✦ ✦ ✦ ✦ ✦

FOUR-MINUTE EGG GRIBICHE

OUR RICH HALF-COOKED VERSION OF *SAUCE GRIBICHE,* WHICH IS USUALLY A vinaigrette bound with chopped hard-cooked egg, shallots, capers, and herbs. This one is inspired by the mustardy gribiche the Troisgros brothers drizzled over beef carpaccio and crowned with a pile of crispy hot fried potatoes, as an alternative to the familiar raw-egg steak tartar. This herby, shalloty mayonnaise is good with grilled fish or poultry, on sandwiches, or with fried shrimp, scallops, clams, mussels, or soft-shelled crab, as well as boiled shrimp or cracked crab. It will turn ordinary boiled potatoes into excellent potato salad.

FOR ABOUT 1-3/4 CUPS:

1 large egg
Salt
2 teaspoons Dijon mustard
1-1/4 to 1-1/2 cups mild-tasting olive oil
1 tablespoon finely diced shallot
{about 1 medium shallot}
1 tablespoon tightly packed chopped
fresh herbs {a combination of

parsley, chervil, and chives, plus a
little tarragon or dill}
1 tablespoon capers, rinsed, pressed
dry between towels, and slightly
chopped
About 2 teaspoons sherry vinegar or
red wine vinegar

Place the egg in a small pot of barely simmering water and bring to a boil, then reduce the heat and simmer for about 4 minutes. Drain and leave to cool in a bowl of ice water.

When the egg is sure to be cool, crack it and scrape into a small bowl. Stir in a pinch or two of salt and the mustard. Mash together, then begin whisking in the oil, a trickle or a few drops at first, then gradually increasing the flow to a thin stream. Stop adding oil when the mayonnaise is satiny and has lots of body, like hot fudge sauce. Stir in the shallots, herbs, and capers. Add vinegar and salt to taste.

Salsa Verde

Salsas, especially green ones, are great democratizers in the kitchen. Anyone can make an excellent one, they go with humble as well as fancy dishes, they are crowd pleasers, and they need not be expensive. They are not, of course, forgiving of mediocre ingredients, so make the effort to gather perky, fragrant herbs. Chop them only just before you assemble the salsa~and don't do that too far in advance. Time will dull the bright taste and texture.

Guidelines regarding the herbs and preparing them:

⁜ Choose herbs as you would flowers~go for pretty and fragrant, avoid wilted and bruised. Pick off the leaves, culling any yellowed ones that may have snuck into your pristine bouquet. When using parsley, chervil, and cilantro, I include some of the slender, tender terminal stem~it usually tastes sweet and adds another texture to the salsa. Try this.

⁜ Wash and dry the herbs carefully. A little grit will spoil a salsa, and water will make it dull. I spin the leaves in a salad spinner with a dry paper towel to absorb hidden water.

⁜ Chop the herbs with a very sharp knife. A dull knife smashes as much as it chops, extracting the green juice from the herbs. This juice oxidizes rapidly and can give the salsa a tired flavor. {Or it stays on the cutting board. You want it to stay in the leaves.}

⁜ Don't chop the herbs too fine. Most cooks enjoy the smell as they chop herbs, but I spoil that pleasure if they are being too thorough, reminding them that all that scent is gone now, not to be captured in any salsa, or other dish. The finer you chop, the fewer remaining intact cells full of scent you save for your guests. Chop the herbs into little flakes just small enough to produce a pleasant texture.

⁜ Likewise, don't chop the herbs too evenly. Leave some flakes slightly larger than others; they will give the salsa a pretty look, but more important, the bigger flakes explode with flavor when you bite through them. If combining different herbs in one salsa, try leaving one type fairly coarse~it won't shed as much flavor into the oil, but it will make up for it later. This makes a salsa multilayered, and fun to eat.

⁜ Don't chop the herbs in advance, or add leftover chopped herbs to a salsa. Once you've chopped the herbs, trap their fragrance in the oil as soon as possible.

Regarding the rest of the ingredients:

Most of our green salsas are bound with olive oil and usually include capers, or something briny, like chopped glasswort; someone from the onion family; citrus zest; and cracked pepper or crushed chili.

It doesn't usually make sense to use your most precious extra-virgin oil here, as the collision of aromatics may overwhelm it, but do use delicious oil~it will be noticed. As you decide how much oil to add to a salsa, take into consideration the dish it is going with~is it dry or wet, lean, or succulent? Grilled fish with lean white beans will tolerate a well-lubricated salsa, but a rib-eye steak needs very little extra fat, just enough oil to bind the herbs. Likewise, boiled green beans or grilled zucchini are good with a rich salsa, but grilled eggplant wants little extra oil.

Use the same kind of reasoning to decide whether to add body-building ingredients to salsas~chopped hard-cooked egg, mustard, avocado, nuts, and finely diced ripe tomato {or other ripe fruits} all make a salsa fleshier or at least thicker, but each in a different way. Consider the flavors and richness of the dish before you choose to enrich a salsa this way. Mustard will give spark and muscle to a salsa destined for a wintry *Pot-au-Feu* {page 385} or a robust steak, while chopped egg or avocado will flatter quiet salmon, bass, or chicken dishes, and so on. That said, don't clutter the salsa with too many supplemental flavors.

\ *continued*

SALSA VERDE *with* PARSLEY *&* ONE OTHER PUNGENT HERB

This is a basic formula you may never make the same way twice.

FOR 1 TO 1-1/4 CUPS:

1/2 cup tightly packed chopped fresh
flat-leaf parsley {nearly 1 cup
loosely packed}

2 to 3 tablespoons tightly packed
chopped other herb, such as fresh
tarragon, chervil, chives, cilantro,
mint, watercress, spicy broadleaf
cress, garden cress, nasturtium
blossoms, small nasturtium leaves,
or basil~green or purple, and
consider lemon- or cinnamon-
scented basil as well

1 tablespoon capers, rinsed, pressed
dry between towels, and coarsely
chopped, or 1 tablespoon chopped
glasswort, fresh or pickled {see
page 274}

About 2 teaspoons finely chopped
lemon zest {from 2 small lemons},
or a combination of lemon and
orange zest

1 tablespoon finely diced shallot or red
onion or thinly slivered scallion

Salt

Freshly cracked black pepper or dried
chili flakes, crushed

1/2 to 3/4 cup extra-virgin olive oil {a
part of this could be lemon
oil~see Sources and Resources,
page 518, or, to infuse your own,
Lemon Oil, page 285}

Optional ingredients to add body, tooth, and character to the salsa:

1 to 1-1/2 teaspoons Dijon mustard

1/2 hard-cooked egg {see page 508},
chopped, or 1/4 just-ripe medium
avocado, neatly diced

1 tablespoon chopped walnuts or pine
nuts

1 teaspoon rinsed, chopped Preserved
Lemon or Limequat {page 275}

1 teaspoon chopped salt-packed
anchovies {about 2 fillets}

Combine the parsley, other herb, capers, zest, shallot or red onion or scallion,
a few pinches of salt, pepper or chili flakes to taste, and barely 1/2 of the olive oil.
Stir and taste. Add more oil and salt to taste; since salt will not dissolve instantly
in the olive oil, allow each sprinkle time to dissolve before you decide the salsa
needs more. Stir in any optional ingredients and transfer to a tall storage vessel, so
very little of the salsa is exposed to the air. Don't refrigerate, but set in a cool
spot until needed. Do refrigerate leftovers.

❖ ❖ CELERY LEAF SALSA VERDE

Every kitchen I have worked in has a discreet stash of unloved pale, leafy celery hearts. So pretty, but their flavor is not popular raw. They are unwelcome in stocks and uninteresting in sautéed dishes. I do like the tiniest ones deep-fried {see *Piccolo Fritto,* page 108}, but confronted with a constant glut, we devised this salsa, which transforms their brash flavor into an exciting, peppery condiment. It is good with grilled chicken breast, roast pork, or grilled or broiled fish and smeared on Carpaccio {page 132}.

FOR ABOUT 1 CUP:

2 tablespoons tightly packed chopped fresh flat-leaf parsley

1/4 cup tightly packed chopped celery leaves

2 tablespoons finely diced tender, pale yellow inner celery stalks

2 tablespoons capers, rinsed, pressed dry between towels, and coarsely chopped

1 lemon {to yield about 1 teaspoon chopped zest plus juice to taste}

1 teaspoon finely diced jalapeño, preferably red

1 tablespoon finely diced red onion

1 teaspoon chopped salt-packed anchovies {about 2 fillets} {optional}

About 1/2 cup extra-virgin olive oil

Salt and freshly cracked black pepper to taste

Combine all the ingredients, adjusting any to your taste. Allow the salt time to dissolve before adding more. Don't refrigerate, but set in a cool spot until ready to use. Stir occasionally to encourage the flavors to mingle. Refrigerate leftovers.

❖
❖ ❖

Melting Marrow Gremolata

A PASTE THAT BECOMES SALSA-LIKE WHEN YOU SMEAR IT ON A HOT STEAK.

Gremolata is an aromatic condiment that depends on osso buco for its fame, but it can be used on other dishes as well. Contemporary versions are usually a loose mix of chopped herbs, garlic, and zest that is sprinkled raw on a finished dish. Not so, traditional Milanese *gremolada:* Habit was to stir a bit into a bubbling osso buco a few minutes before serving. This sensible technique mellows the raw condiment and infuses the whole dish with flavor. This marrow-enriched version lies somewhere in between. Allow about 1 tablespoon per serving.

A note on buying beef marrow: The best marrow bones are femurs; expect 1 pound of bones to yield about 1 ounce {2 tablespoons} marrow. Have the bones split lengthwise, then pry out the buttery lumps of marrow. Keep in water, refrigerated, until needed.

FOR 1/4 CUP:

2 tablespoons tightly packed chopped fresh flat-leaf parsley

1 small garlic clove, finely chopped

1 teaspoon chopped lemon zest {from 1 small lemon}

1 teaspoon freshly cracked black pepper

Salt

1 tablespoon cold beef marrow {1/2 ounce}

Combine the parsley, garlic, zest, pepper, and a few pinches of salt. Chop the marrow and place in a small bowl. Sprinkle with the aromatics and toss to amalgamate, without warming the marrow. Cover and store refrigerated until needed.

To serve, spread or sprinkle the mixture over a steak a few minutes before you remove it from the grill or pan. As the marrow warms and melts, the flavor of the trapped aromatics will bloom and spread over the surface of the steak.

⋆
⋆ ⋆

TOASTED BREAD CRUMB SALSA

THIS RECIPE IS BASED ON ONE SOUS-CHEF KELSIE KERR SPIED IN AN OLD ITALIAN cooking magazine and brought into work. Restaurant cooks are not so different from home cooks in that respect, but among her many genial culinary instincts, Kelsie knew a really good idea, or recipe, when she saw one, and envisioned how this one could be delicious with many different foods. I believe this salsa was originally described as an excellent condiment for *bollito misto,* which it is. But it is also great with simple grilled food, such as tuna, skirt steak, game birds, radicchio, or leeks. It is delicious with warm roast beef or tossed with cold roasted chicken or warm green beans.

You can fine-tune this recipe for the specific meat, fish, or vegetables you are serving, or in response to the other courses in the meal. If you are serving the salsa with mild white sea bass, you might cut back on the thyme; a little bit gives a nice note of earthiness and complexity, but the whole amount could overwhelm the delicate fish. By contrast, the pungent herb complements rich red meat so well that you might want to add extra if serving with beef or lamb.

FOR ABOUT 1-1/4 CUPS:

2 ounces fresh, soft bread crumbs {about 1 cup} made from slightly stale, crustless, chewy, white peasant-style bread {see page 506}

1 tablespoon mild-tasting olive oil

1 to 2 teaspoons chopped salt-packed anchovy fillets {2 to 4 fillets}

1 teaspoon fresh thyme leaves, barely chopped

1 tablespoon capers, rinsed, pressed dry between towels, and barely chopped

1 tablespoon finely diced shallot {about 1 medium shallot}

1 cup extra-virgin olive oil

About 3 tablespoons Champagne vinegar or white wine vinegar

Salt and freshly cracked black pepper

Preheat the oven to 275°.

Very gently knead the bread crumbs together with the 1 tablespoon olive oil and spread in a thin even layer on a baking sheet. Bake until the crumbs are the color of strong tea, about 30 minutes. Don't try to rush this step; if the crumbs are too pale, or not dry enough, the salsa will go soggy in minutes. You should get a scant 2/3 cup very hard crumbs. Cool completely.

\ *continued*

Stir together the anchovies, thyme, capers, shallot, extra-virgin olive oil, vinegar, and salt and pepper to taste. Combine this base with the crisp bread crumbs about 10 minutes before serving, then taste, and add more of any of the ingredients if you like. The salsa should be brightly flavored and juicy. Stir and taste again just before serving.

❖
❖ ❖

Connie & Maryanna's Chimichurri

Chimichurri is an herbed chili-vinegar mixture used everywhere in Argentina, whether for basting grilled meat {often mixed with salty water, not unlike a Sicilian *salmoriglio,* which follows}, or as a tabletop condiment. No two chimichurris seem to be alike, but oregano and a dried red chili called *ají molido* are constants. This lavish interpretation of chimichurri marries and mellows the flavors with lots of extra-virgin olive oil; we use it as both a salsa and a marinade. We learned it from a team of wonderful cooks from Argentina who spent a week in our kitchen in 1998, and their names come up every time we make it. It has a pungent, autumnal flavor, a nice change from delicate, summery green sauces. Resist the urge to chop all the herbs ~ the whole leaves quietly perfume the oil, and then explode with flavor when you bite into them. This sauce-marinade keeps well for weeks refrigerated, improves with time, and is versatile, so make more than you think you need.

We also use chimichurri to preserve sardines, which we grill first, then bathe in the warm marinade. They make a great hors d'œuvre ~ whole or filleted and perched on a white bean crostini {page 124}. Likewise, you can marinate Grilled Quail {page 359} in chimichurri, then reheat them and serve with grilled bread, roasted potatoes, or white beans. Try frying eggs in it. Or drizzle chimichurri, in the traditional manner, on grilled meat just before pulling it from the fire.

FOR ABOUT 1-1/4 CUPS:

1 jalapeño {about 1/2 ounce}, prefer-
    ably red
2 teaspoons tightly packed fresh
    oregano leaves
2 teaspoons tightly packed fresh thyme
    leaves
1 teaspoon tightly packed fresh rose-
    mary leaves
About 1 cup extra-virgin olive oil

1 tablespoon sweet paprika {or crushed
    ají molido}
1 tablespoon tightly packed coarsely
    chopped fresh flat-leaf parsley
1 to 2 teaspoons finely chopped garlic
2 bay leaves, crumbled
2 tablespoons red wine vinegar
About 1/2 teaspoon salt
Freshly cracked black pepper, to taste

Char the jalapeño, either directly in the open flame of a gas burner or charcoal fire or close under the heat of a hot broiler. Use tongs to turn the pepper a few times until it is generally freckled with black and smells good, about 1 minute. When the pepper has cooled slightly, halve, seed, and mince it. Don't rub off the tasty black blisters ~ include them in the chimichurri.

Place the oregano, thyme, and rosemary in a mortar and pound lightly.

Warm the oil in a small saucepan until it is hot to the touch. Pull from the heat and stir in the bruised herbs, plus all the remaining ingredients, including the jalapeño. {If making the chimichurri more than a few hours in advance, wait to add the parsley until you are about to use it.} Taste. Leave to infuse for at least 1 hour at room temperature before serving.

·⬩·
⬩·⬩

SALMORIGANO, OR SALMORIGLIO

A PUNGENT SICILIAN SAUCE THAT IS SORT OF A SALSA, SORT OF A MARINADE. {Its name betrays its origins as a *salamoia,* or brine.} This delicious slurry is good for soaking raw things, basting cooking things, or moistening cooked ones. Use it with chicken, beef, pork, fish, or grilled or roasted vegetables ~ onions, summer squash,

\ *continued*

tomatoes, eggplant, or peppers. It is delicious on grilled bread, whether you drizzle it on before or after grilling. I like eggs fried in it and ricotta baked in it.

Although salmorigano is traditionally made with fresh oregano, I like the long, persuasive flavor of dried oregano and violate the standard with this version. At home, I stir together the sauce base and age it at room temperature for at least a few days, but it always tastes best when I forget about it for a month or longer. Add the lemon juice and hot water no more than a minute before using the sauce.

FOR ABOUT 3/4 CUP:
For the base:

4 small garlic cloves, peeled

About 1/4 teaspoon salt

1 tablespoon dried oregano

About 1/2 cup extra-virgin olive oil

1/4 teaspoon freshly cracked black pepper or dried chili flakes

To finish the sauce:

About 2 tablespoons simmering water

1 lemon, halved

Thickly slice the garlic, then place in a mortar and pound it to a rough paste. Add a pinch of salt and pound until smooth, then add the oregano, oil, and black pepper or dried chili, pounding lightly as you stir them in with the pestle. Cover and store at room temperature.

Just before using, add the simmering water, squeeze in the lemon juice, whisk, and taste. The sauce should not be tart ~ the lemon should contribute perfume more than acidity, and the water should tame all sourness, to better reveal the fruit of the lemon and scent of the other aromatics. Spoon the warm salsa over cooked meat, fish, or vegetables.

Or, if using as a marinade, rub the raw meat, poultry, or fish with the salmorigano to encourage it to impregnate the flesh with its flavor. Leave to marinate for up to an hour. Roast or grill over medium heat. The water may make the meat stick to the grill or pan, so allow time for that water to evaporate before you try to turn whatever you are cooking.

GREEN OLIVE–LEMON RELISH

A BRIGHT-TASTING RELISH FOR FISH, CHICKEN, OR PORK, ALSO DELICIOUS WITH grilled summer vegetables. Use unwaxed very ripe lemons. Fragrant Meyer lemons are particularly good here, or you can add a spoonful of chopped preserved lemon or limequats to give the relish an exotic flavor. Lucques olives, fleshy, nutty, and fruity, are great for this recipe. Fat Ascolane or Ceregnola olives are also suitable. Crunchy Picholines are a fine choice too, but I recommend you rinse them, then place in cold water and bring to a simmer to cook for 2 minutes before pitting them. This blanching will soften them a bit, and purge them of the brine that obscures their fruity flavor.

FOR 1 TO 1-1/4 CUPS:

12 raw almonds {about 1/2 ounce}
1 cup green olives, such as Lucques, Ascolane, Ceregnola, or Picholine
About 1/4 small unwaxed lemon
2 tablespoons capers, rinsed, pressed dry between towels, and barely chopped

1 to 2 tablespoons freshly squeezed lemon juice
1/4 to 1/2 cup extra-virgin olive oil
1 tablespoon chopped rinsed Preserved Lemon or Limequat {page 275} {optional}

Preheat the oven to 300°.

Drop the almonds into a small pot of boiling water and leave for about 10 seconds. Drain, slide off the skins, and rub dry. Toast on a small baking sheet until slightly colored, about 15 minutes. Chop coarsely.

Rinse the olives, roll dry between towels, and then pound lightly with a mallet, meat pounder, or heavy saucepan. Pick out and discard the pits. Coarsely chop, so the bits of olive are pine nut–sized on average. Strive for irregularity, so some of the bites will be fleshier than others. You should get about 1/2 cup.

Very thinly slice the lemon, stopping when you get to the pithy end. Watch for and discard seeds. Chop the slices into coarse confetti. You should get about 2 tablespoons.

\ *continued*

Combine all of the ingredients, adding oil according to the intended use. For a crumbly relish, nice with grilled eggplant, braised pork, or simple chicken or rabbit dishes, use the lesser amount of oil. The full dose of oil will produce a perfumed salsa, perfect stirred into white beans or spooned over grilled or broiled bass, scallops, or salmon.

✢
✢ ✢

ROASTED PEPPER RELISH

THIS IS A LUSCIOUS, MEATY RELISH THAT BLENDS SWEET, TART, AND NUTTY flavors. We pair it with full-flavored meats, poultry, or fish. Serve a spoonful with lamb, quail, swordfish, tuna, or sea bass. It's great in a roast beef or lamb sandwich. Or serve it on crostini with fresh mozzarella and an arugula salad.

I suggest two different ways to roast peppers here; both depend on distressing and shrinking the skin so that it pulls easily from the flesh. How aggressively you destroy the skin determines how much you cook the peppers in the process, how much peppery syrup precipitates, and the flavor of the peeled flesh. Oven roasting, even at high heat, is slow enough to soften and cook the peppers pretty thoroughly. The finished product will be mild, sweet, and slippery. Stovetop charring or char-grilling peppers burns the skin off more rapidly, often before the flesh of the pepper is thoroughly cooked. This method typically yields less syrup, a firmer texture {sometimes pleasantly leathery}, and a richer, slightly smoky flavor.

Choose between the techniques according to your taste, and convenience.

FOR ABOUT 1-1/3 CUPS:

1-1/2 tablespoons dried currants

2 teaspoons sherry vinegar

1/2 teaspoon warm water

12 ounces bell peppers {1 large or 2 small}

3 tablespoons pine nuts

1 tablespoon freshly chopped basil or arugula

2 small garlic cloves, pounded to a paste

3 tablespoons extra-virgin olive oil

1 to 2 tablespoons sweet sherry or sweet Marsala

Salt

Combine the dried currants, vinegar, and warm water, kneading the currants lightly.

Roasting and peeling the peppers:

Note: Handle the roasting peppers gently ~ the collapsing cells release moisture, which you want to keep inside the peppers until you peel them. If you puncture the tender flesh, the sweet juice will spill into the roasting pan and dry out, or trickle into the fire.

To use the oven method, preheat the oven to 450°. Set the peppers in a baking dish or shallow roasting pan and place on the top rack of the oven. Turn as the tops brown and blister, and roast until they have nearly collapsed, 20 to 35 minutes, depending on size.

To char the skins with live fire, place the peppers directly on hot gray coals, in the flame of a gas burner, or on a grill grate about an inch from glowing coals or live fire. Monitor closely and turn the peppers as soon as any side has turned black, repositioning strategically until the whole is fairly evenly charred. Allow 10 to 20 minutes, depending on pepper size and heat source.

Transfer the roasted peppers to a bowl and cover tightly with plastic wrap. Once the peppers are cool enough to handle, slide or rub off the skins ~ not worrying if some spots don't want to release {do this over a second bowl, so you can capture the delicious juice}. Charred skins tend to come off in chunks and bits; dip your fingertips in water occasionally as you remove them. Don't rinse the peppers.

Still working over the bowl, pull out the stems, hopefully with most of the seeds attached, and discard. Separate each pepper into slabs. Combine the juice from both bowls and strain out skin and seeds.

Lay the pepper slabs on a cutting board, brush away any remaining seeds, and scrape or peel off any remaining large patches of skin with a paring knife. Again, don't rinse the peppers, as you would only be washing away the flavorful syrup. A few stubborn flecks of charred skin will taste nice.

\ *continued*

Assembling the relish:

Cut the peppers into small dice and combine with their juice. You should get about 1 cup.

While the peppers are roasting, set the pine nuts in the oven, if using, or in a small skillet over low heat to warm through, a few minutes at most. Coarsely chop.

Add the currants, pine nuts, basil or arugula, garlic, oil, and sherry or Marsala. Salt to taste.

٭ ٭
٭ ٭

ORANGE-OLIVE TAPENADE

AN OLIVE PASTE NAMED FOR A MINORITY INGREDIENT: CAPERS {*TAPENO* OR *tapeino* in Provençal}. Use olives you love the taste of, and rinse them, or even purge them for half an hour, in warm water before you pit and chop them. That way, you will taste olive, not just brine. We most often use Niçoise or Nyons olives; briny black Gaeta or Kalamata olives lack their rich, nutty flavor and can make a one-dimensional tapenade. When mandarins are in season, we substitute them for oranges in this recipe.

Tapenade is very happy on crostini; those toasts make a versatile garnish, whether surrounded by a collection of grilled vegetables or on a platter with radishes, sliced fennel, and wedges of baked ricotta cheese. We sometimes pound a spoonful of preserved tuna into a batch of tapenade; crostini topped with this richer version make a good stand-alone hors d'œuvre. You can also stir tapenade into a vinaigrette to spoon over grilled sweet peppers or meaty bass, or tuna, or sprinkle a little inside a boned leg of lamb before you tie it up to roast {see page 394}. Tapenade-Grilled Cheese is delicious, especially when the cheese is Fontina, fresh Asiago, or Manchego. {Spread a little of the black paste inside one piece of bread.}

1 cup black olives, such as Niçoise or
    Nyons

1 small garlic clove, peeled

1 tablespoon capers, rinsed and pressed
    dry between towels

2 salt-packed anchovy fillets
    {optional}

A walnut-sized lump of Preserved
    Tuna {page 212} {optional}

1 orange

1 teaspoon pastis, such as Pernod or
    Ricard, or ouzo

1 teaspoon to 1 tablespoon extra-virgin
    olive oil

Drain and rinse the olives. Roll dry between clean towels, then pound lightly with a mallet, meat pounder, or heavy saucepan. Pick out and discard the pits. You should get about 1/2 cup.

Slice the garlic, then pound in a mortar. By hand or in a processor, chop and combine the olives, capers, garlic, and optional anchovy until you have a crumbly paste. Transfer to a bowl.

If using tuna, pound it in a mortar and then knead into the olive paste. Grate and work in about 1/2 teaspoon orange zest. Add the pastis or ouzo and oil to taste. Squeeze a few drops of orange juice into the tapenade just before serving. Keeps well for a week or so refrigerated.

✢
✢ ✢

CRUMBLY HAZELNUT PICADA

To CALL THIS CRUMB TOPPING A *PICADA* IS CAVALIER. A *picada* is typically a pounded paste of nuts, crisp bread crumbs, and aromatics, bound with oil. It is used in Catalan cooking to both thicken and add sparkle to stews and sauces. This recipe is chopped, not pounded, it lacks the extra oil, and we don't generally use it to thicken anything. But it is an affectionate appropriation of the Catalan formula.

This recipe will produce more crumbly *picada* than you may use right away, but it is a versatile condiment you will be happy to have on hand. Spread it on

\ *continued*

meaty grilled fish or rib-eye steak a minute or two before you pull it from the heat. I like it tossed into the warm frisée salad we serve with roasted birds or with duck confit. Try it sprinkled on pasta, especially egg noodles, instead of traditional seasoned bread crumbs. It adds a complex crispy, salty note to unctuous roasted figs, which are then delicious with roasted leg of lamb {page 394} or with prosciutto {page 83}.

Store extra *picada* sealed in a small jar, refrigerated, for up to a week.

FOR ABOUT 1/2 CUP:

A cup or so mild-tasting olive oil, for frying

1 ounce chewy, peasant-style bread, sliced about 1/2 inch thick

About 16 hazelnuts {1/2 ounce, or 2 tablespoons}

1/4 teaspoon orange or mandarin zest

1 very small garlic clove or 1/2 medium clove

4 small fresh mint leaves

Salt, if needed

Pour olive oil to a depth of 1/2 inch into an 8-inch skillet or 2-quart saucepan and set over medium-low heat. Test the temperature with the edge of bread: when it barely sizzles on contact, reduce the heat slightly and add the bread. {You may need to cut it into pieces so it fits into the pan in a single layer}. Check the underside at 1 minute; it should just be beginning to color. Fry until it is the color of cornflakes, 2 to 3 minutes per side; poke the center~it should be firm. Take care that the olive oil never smokes. Drain and cool the bread on a paper towel.

Break the bread into coarse chunks, discarding any doughy unfried parts. Spread the bread chunks between two clean brown paper bags, then use a rolling pin to crush into crumbs. The bag will absorb quite a bit of the oil. Alternatively, you can grind the bread in a processor, which will not absorb any oil, and produce a richer *picada*. Either way you should get a generous 1/4 cup of crumbs.

Meanwhile, preheat the oven to 325°.

Roast the hazelnuts on a small baking sheet until their skins start to split and become papery, about 10 to 15 minutes. While still hot, bundle them in a towel beanbag-style, and scrunch and massage them to rub off some of their skins. Don't worry if some of the skin sticks. Pick the nuts from the chaff and finely chop them. You should get about 2 tablespoons.

Finely chop the orange or mandarin zest together with the garlic and mint, then combine with the bread crumbs and nuts. If your bread is bland, you may need to add a pinch of salt.

✢
✢ ✢

SAGE PESTO

AN EXUBERANT CYNTHIA SHEA HATCHED THIS IDEA ON HER SECOND OR THIRD DAY of writing the daily lunch menu. I worried that a bowl of pounded raw sage might smell more like camphor than lunch, but her enthusiasm was persuasive and the pesto was a success. For a nicely perfumed sage pesto, we pick out tender, velvety leaves and then warm them in oil over low heat. Cynthia's pesto has become a mainstay in the autumn and winter as a garnish for soups. Stir it into white bean purée, potato soup, or minestrone. A spoonful tossed with penne or spaghetti is shockingly good. But you can also fold in a few charred tomatoes, a spoonful of tomato sauce, or sautéed zucchini for a more elaborate pasta dish. Try the pesto smeared on broiled tomatoes, roasted onions, or grilled mushrooms, or stir it into polenta. Or spread a tiny bit on a steak or pork chop as you pull it from the heat.

FOR I SCANT CUP:

1/4 ounce fresh sage leaves {3 table-
    spoons packed}
1/2 cup mild-tasting olive oil
1 garlic clove, peeled
Salt
1/2 cup walnuts, preferably freshly
    shelled, or pine nuts, coarsely
    chopped {about 2 ounces}

1 ounce Parmigiano-Reggiano, grated
    {about 1/2 cup very lightly
    packed}
Freshly cracked black pepper

Coarsely chop the sage. Place it in your smallest pan and moisten with a few spoonfuls of the olive oil. Stir and smash over low heat until it is quite hot to the touch. Turn off the heat and leave for about 1 minute. Remove from the heat.

Slice the garlic, then pound in a mortar. Once you have a rough paste, add a pinch of salt, then continue pounding until the garlic is nearly smooth. Add the warm sage and sage-y oil, and continue to pound until the leaves are pulverized.

\ *continued*

Add the nuts and pound the whole to a paste. Stir in the remaining oil, the cheese, and salt and pepper to taste. {Don't try to make this pesto in a processor, you won't be able to properly grind the sage, and it wouldn't be terribly efficient in this small quantity anyway.}

Covered and refrigerated, the pesto will keep for a week or so.

⁘
⁘ ⁘

CHOPPED LEMON BAGNA CAUDA

TRADITIONALLY SERVED IN THE PIEDMONT REGION OF NORTHERN ITALY AS A "hot bath" {dip} for raw vegetables, this sauce is very good spooned over grilled fish, which is how we usually serve it at Zuni. The bits of chopped lemon make this version of bagna cauda more pungent and chunky than most. The optional walnuts give it an unusual texture and richness. Pair it with grilled tuna, swordfish, sea bass, salmon, or shrimp, and serve roasted potatoes or white beans and grilled fennel, peppers, zucchini, or leeks on the side. It is also good drizzled on grilled bread crowned with warm thinly sliced tomatoes, roasted onions, or Boiled Kale {page 162}.

FOR ABOUT 1 CUP:

1/4 small lemon, plus optional lemon juice, to taste
2 garlic cloves, chopped
3/4 cup extra-virgin olive oil
3 tablespoons chopped salt-packed anchovy fillets {12 to 16 fillets}

About 6 walnuts {1/2 ounce}, preferably freshly shelled {optional}
Freshly cracked black pepper

If using walnuts, turn the oven to 300°.

Cut the lemon into thin slices, removing seeds as you go. Chop the slices into coarse confetti. You should get about 2 tablespoons.

In your smallest saucepan, combine the lemon confetti with the garlic and moisten with about half of the olive oil. Set over low heat until the oil is hot to

the touch, then remove from the heat and let cool. {This will soften the lemon.}
Add the anchovies and the rest of the oil, and stir and reheat until warm to the
touch. Set aside.

Spread the walnuts, if using, on a baking sheet, and place in the oven to warm
through, about 5 minutes. Rub between rough towels to remove some of the tannic,
papery skin. Pick out the nutmeats and then shake in a strainer to further cull little
bits of skin. Pound the walnuts to a crumbly paste. You should get 1 to 2 tablespoons.

Add the nuts to the warm sauce. Stir in plenty of freshly cracked black pepper. Taste. Add more lemon juice if you like. Rewarm and stir just before serving.

⁺
⁺ ⁺

PRESERVED LEMON–CAPER BUTTER

THE ONE BUTTER SAUCE I HAVE NOT ABANDONED FOR SALSA OR VINAIGRETTE.
Unapologetically rich, but pungent and chunky with bits of fragrant citrus. Serve
it with salmon, Pacific swordfish, bass, spearfish, or albacore. Garnish with potatoes roasted in their skins and wedges of slightly bitter grilled escarole or endive
or blanched leeks. Or offer with artichokes or asparagus as a first course.

FOR ABOUT I CUP:

2 tablespoons dry white wine
A few drops of water
1/2 pound unsalted butter {2 sticks},
    sliced and chilled
1 tablespoon capers, rinsed, pressed
    dry between towels, and barely
    chopped

1 tablespoon rinsed, chopped Preserved
    Lemon or Limequat {page 275},
    seeds removed
Champagne vinegar, white wine vine-
    gar, or freshly squeezed lemon
    juice, as needed

Choose a heavy saucepan 6 to 8 inches in diameter. I use a 2-quart saucepan:
for a larger quantity of sauce, you can use a wider pan, but for this small quantity,

\ *continued*

a relatively small surface area is desirable. In a wide pan, changes in the necessarily shallow pool of liquid would happen very quickly, before you noticed, much less had time to cool the pan to slow or stop them. This leads to caramelized wine, or separated butter sauce.

Place the wine in the saucepan and reduce by half over medium heat. {If you are concerned that you won't know when it reaches that point, first measure 1 tablespoon of wine into the pan and tilt it, and try to remember what that amount looks like in that pan. Then add the second tablespoon of wine.} The reduced wine should be deep yellow, not amber. Taste it: it should be pungent, but not acrid. {If it is, pour it out, rinse the pan and start again.} As soon as the wine is reduced, pull the pan from the heat and immediately add a few drops of water and a few slices of the cold butter. Swirl, reduce the heat slightly, and return the pan to the burner. Whisk, continuing to swirl the pan on the burner, until the first pats of butter are nearly melted. Add another few, and continue whisking to encourage emulsion. The emerging sauce will gain body as you add more butter. Don't allow it to boil; if it starts to, quickly pull the pan from the burner, add a drop, or a few drops, of water at the edge, and swirl the pan to restabilize the emulsion.

Once all of the butter is added, stir in the capers and preserved lemon. Taste. The sauce will taste underseasoned at first, but it will get saltier as the condiments infuse it. Add a few drops of white wine, vinegar, or lemon juice if you would like the sauce more tart.

You can keep the warm sauce covered in a warm spot, but not over direct heat~a double boiler is a fine idea, but it is imminently possible to break the sauce by resting it over, or in, hot water. We hold butter-based sauces in a double boiler, but instead of using water we stuff the bottom chamber with crumpled newspaper. This arrangement insulates the fragile sauce both from direct heat and from drafts.

+
+ +
+ +

PORCINI PEARÀ SAUCE

I NO LONGER THINK TWICE BEFORE TYPING "WARM BREAD CRUMB–MARROW SAUCE" on our menu, although for years I obscured the facts behind its beautiful Italian name: *pearà*. When we first served this unusual and delicious sauce from the Veneto in the late eighties, it seemed a singularly hard sell. But what sounded unappetizing to many a decade ago has become one of our mainstay cold-weather sauces, either in the original formula, or as a variation. *Pearà* is a shortened form of *peperata*~"peppered"; keep that in mind when you make this very rich sauce. Short on pepper, the sauce can be insipid. Traditionally served in Verona with bollito misto, *pearà* is a primitive but rich foil for that dish of lean boiled meats and vegetables. It is also delicious with roasted or grilled meat, poultry, or meaty mushrooms, and with crispy grilled radicchio, pencil asparagus, or artichokes.

Most traditional versions of *pearà* contain some freshly grated Parmigiano-Reggiano, added minutes before serving, which makes the sauce even richer. If you substitute bits of foie gras or foie gras fat for the marrow, and chicken stock for the beef broth, the sauce becomes a nice companion for quail, chicken, or guinea hen. We sometimes add scraps of black truffle, or a few drops of truffle oil to the humble *pearà,* and the results are delicious. Try that variation with grilled asparagus.

A note on buying and preparing beef marrow: the best marrow bones are femurs; expect 1 pound of bones to yield about 1 ounce {2 tablespoons} marrow. Have the bones split lengthwise, then pry out the buttery lumps of marrow. Keep in water, refrigerated, until needed. Soaking draws out the blood and will make the sauce cleaner tasting and prettier.

FOR ABOUT 1 CUP:

1 ounce beef marrow {2 tablespoons}
1 tablespoon unsalted butter
About 1/2 ounce cleaned fresh porcini, chopped, or a slice of dried porcini, rinsed in warm water and chopped
Freshly cracked black pepper
1-1/2 ounces fresh soft bread crumbs {about 3/4 cup} made from slightly stale, crustless, chewy, white peasant-style bread {see page 506}
10 to 12 tablespoons clear broth, from *Pot-au-Feu* {page 385} or Beef Stock {page 63} {dilute the beef stock with water as necessary until it is no richer than a light broth}
Salt

\ *continued*

Optional:

1/4 ounce Parmigiano-Reggiano, grated {about 2 tablespoons, very lightly packed}

Up to 1 tablespoon chopped black truffle or a few drops of truffle oil

Coarsely chop the marrow. Place in a 1- to 2-quart saucepan with the butter and chopped porcini. Cook over medium-low heat, stirring constantly, until the butter and marrow melt but do not color, about 3 minutes. Raise the heat slightly, add a generous amount of pepper and the bread crumbs, and stir to incorporate. The soft crumbs will become well saturated with fat and the mixture will be fragrant. Stirring gently, add about 10 tablespoons of the broth. The sauce should be the texture of soft oatmeal, and the crumbs should look like fat curds. Reduce the heat to the lowest setting and let the sauce seethe and swell for about 3 minutes. Gradually add more broth if the sauce is stiff or stodgy. The bread you use will determine how much stock you need. Don't overstir, overcook, or overmoisten this simple sauce, or you risk producing a smooth, uninteresting porridge. Taste for salt and pepper.

Serve immediately, or keep covered in a double boiler over just simmering water until needed. The fat will tend to separate from the sauce as it sits, but the sauce will reamalgamate with a few stirs. If it doesn't, add a few drops of broth or water and stir again.

❖ ❖ *Variation* FOIE GRAS PEARÀ SAUCE

Substitute 2 tablespoons {1 ounce} foie gras scraps or foie gras fat {see Foie Gras *en Terrine,* page 439} for the marrow and Chicken Stock {page 58}, or Duck, Guinea Hen or Squab Stock {page 67} for the broth.

SEAFOOD

Choosing Seafood

Beyond the usual concerns with freshness and proper handling, it is especially important when buying seafood to know where the product is coming from and how it was harvested or raised. The tenuous state of many world fisheries owes to years of unsustainable, indiscriminate fishing practices, aggravated by problems associated with certain types of aquaculture. But determining what you should and shouldn't buy can be difficult; new problems are emerging constantly, and existing ones are evolving rapidly, as populations recover, or as their decline accelerates. In addition to that volatility, specific issues and remedies vary from species to species and from region to region for the same type of seafood~the status of Atlantic versus Pacific swordfish and tunas being good examples of that.

Although there will be no quick or permanent solution to the crisis in our oceans, consumers' preferences and purchases will make a difference. Supporting well-managed fisheries and fisherman who fish sustainably is imperative. For example, you can begin by purchasing only hook-and-line-caught cod instead of accepting trawler fish, or by turning down farmed shrimp or salmon; both will send a signal to your fish market that constant availability and the lowest price are not your highest priorities. Paying a little extra for sustainable seafood rewards the stores and fishermen who are making the extra effort to preserve the ocean's resources. You will find guidelines for certain items in individual recipes, and in Sources and Resources, page 520, I recommend a publication that can help you understand the issues and sort out what is sustainable for a given type of seafood.

⁂

Boiled Dungeness Crab

Dungeness crab {*cancer magister*} is a relative of the rock crab, named for the spot on Washington's Olympic Peninsula where they were first commercially harvested. Today, commercial crabbing operations extend from Northern California to Alaska. Fresh, perfectly cooked Dungeness crab is fluffy, succulent, and sweet with a briny nuance. When it is in season {mid-November through early May}, we serve cracked crab every day that we can get frisky, live ones. Dungeness crab is so pure and good that way that I largely forget that it is also delicious grilled or smokily roasted in the brick oven. A platter of cracked crab can make a great main course, although I usually prefer to start with it ~ the ritual of cracking and extracting meat may hamper conversation, but, like oysters on the half-shell, it is such a complete and rich delicacy that I feel it deserves a clean palate and ready appetite. The elaborations I like the best are simple composed salads; freshly cooked, cracked and picked from the shell, crabmeat is delicious in a salad of endive, grapefruit, and avocado {page 143}. This is a low-margin, or no-margin, labor of love in a restaurant, but a seductive one that home cooks can enjoy without that concern. You can glean about 8 ounces of hard-earned meat from a 2-pound Dungeness crab.

It is simple to prepare a great cracked crab, although it is also easy to produce a dull one. The critical work is in choosing the crab, the pot, and the burner. Select feisty crabs that were caught that day, or the night before. Don't buy a crab that is already dead, or barely alive ~ it will have released autolytic enzymes that damage flavor and texture. Expect it to taste dull to awful; its texture will be limp and stringy. In the best case, where live crabs are displayed in a tank full of sea-water, ask when they were pulled from the ocean. Choose a crab that is heavy for its size and has a really hard shell. Dark, saturated shell color is a good sign as well. That crab will be more full of meat than one that, just a few weeks from molting, is still spending energy building its shell rather than tasty muscle. For this reason, the first hard-shelled crabs of the commercial season often yield less meat, and can be less tasty. {And this is also why the best eating soft-shells are *just*-molted ones ~ they haven't redirected their energies to shell production yet.}

Keep the live crab cool and moist ~ wrapping in wet newspaper is one method, but the paper tends to cling to the crab and tears easily when the crab thrashes. A more convenient way to store an angry crab is to place it in a brown paper grocery bag, fold it shut, and run the bag under cold water. Slide this inside a second bag and refrigerate until just before cooking. Cook the crab the same day you buy it, ideally within a few hours.

For a 2- to 2-1/2-pound crab, choose a 10- to 12-quart pot, preferably not a lot wider than your most powerful burner. Bring at least 6 quarts of water to a boil. Salt liberally ~ my fish broker suggests the boil should rival seawater for saltiness {that is, if you can't get seawater, which he actually prefers}; I add only 2 table-

\ *continued*

spoons salt per gallon, a lot, but not as salty as seawater. I don't add herbs, spices, or aromatic vegetables to the water; there is no perfume I'd add to improve upon the purity and subtle sweetness of unadulterated Dungeness crab. Likewise, wine, vinegar, or lemon can toughen the meat if you add them to the boil. And, far from adding finesse, their pungent flavors readily dominate delicate crabmeat.

Rinse the crab with cold water just before you cook it. Place in the boiling water and cover the pot to encourage the water to return to a full boil as rapidly as possible. This is to rapidly disable those autolytic enzymes mentioned above throughout the crab. {Once the water has boiled again, you can remove the lid, if only to prevent boiling over and the mess that makes.} Cook for about 6 minutes per pound, timed from the returned-to-a-boil moment. To check for doneness, twist a leg from the body and look at the feather of flesh it pulls with it; it should be opaque, glowing white, and firm. If it is translucent and grayish white, like skim milk, cook for another minute or so. Don't undercook. Use tongs to lift the crab from the pot, supporting the steamy catch with a slotted spoon or strainer. Rinse under cold running water. If you can't clean the crab right away, shock it in ice water to stop the cooking, then drain and keep cold until you can clean it, which should be within the half hour.

To clean the crab, remove the top shell to reveal the body cavity full of soft purple, gold, and white fat and tissue. Remove the ten feathery gills that flank either side of the body cavity. Rinse the crab quickly but thoroughly under cold water. Turn it over and lift the tip of the triangular piece of armor that lays flat against the breast. Fold it backward, and pluck it from the carapace. {You can save this piece and the top shell to make shellfish fumet.}

Turn the crab over and cut it in half down the middle. Cut each half into 5 pieces, corresponding to the legs, cutting straight down through the center of each of the smooth sections of translucent shell that protect the body meat. This will expose all that meat, making it perfectly accessible to the clumsiest fingers with no special tools. To crack the sturdier of the legs, gently fracture each section with the backside of a heavy knife or with a clean hammer. Whack the shell with restraint, so you don't shatter it and smash the meat. You can, of course, use a nut- or crab-cracker, or serve uncracked crab with enough crackers for your likely impatient diners. You can usually break into the smaller legs by hand, and use the thornlike claw tips as a tool to retrieve bits of meat from inside the skinny ones.

For the best flavor, serve immediately. If not serving within half an hour, wrap loosely and refrigerate. Time and refrigeration will gradually stiffen and dry out the meat and mute the delicate flavor, so aim to cook no more than a few hours before serving.

Rinse, drain, and triple-wrap shells, and, if they occur, scraps of meat, and freeze for Shellfish Fumet {page 172} or bisque {page 170}.

Wine: Saint-Véran, Domaine Corsin, 2000

⁂

Sand Dabs *with* Shallots, Sea Beans, *&* Sherry Vinegar

A RICHLY FLAVORED PANFRY THAT HAS A PUNGENT, DELICIOUS AROMA. "Sea beans" are glasswort, a crunchy, briny marsh succulent. We use fresh sea beans in the late spring when they are briefly in season, and pickled ones the rest of the year {see Pickled Glasswort, page 274}. You can substitute capers or caperberries. In lieu of sand dabs, a mild, succulent flatfish that is a San Francisco delicacy, you can use small, whole, pan-ready sole or flounder. By "pan-ready," I mean gutted, scaled, head and tail removed, and fins trimmed. Filleted fish is an option as well, but adjust the cooking time accordingly, and be prepared for it to curl as it cooks. Skate wing is another good choice~the skate in black butter of French tradition is the obvious inspiration for this dish.

A large nonstick skillet is the best choice here. If you don't have one, clarify half of the butter {see Note below} before you brown the fish in it {or any time you plan to pan-brown a wet protein or starch in butter}. To keep wet fish from sticking to a non-nonstick pan, you need to use higher heat, and the solids in whole butter would burn at that temperature. Clarifying also removes the water, which makes food stick, from the butter.

If you are new to panfrying fragile things, you should opt for the larger fish~it will be easier to manage 4 sizzling, slippery objects than 8.

Serve with new potatoes, boiled or steamed in their skins.

Wine: Kaseler Nies'chen Riesling, Kesselstatt, 1999

\ *continued*

FOR 4 SERVINGS:

8 small or 4 large pan-ready sand dabs, about 3 or 7 ounces, respectively, and 1/2 inch thick, or 4 pan-ready flatfish, such as sole or flounder, about 7 to 8 ounces each, or about 1-1/2 pounds sole or flounder fillets

About 1 cup all-purpose flour

3 ounces slivered shallots {scant 3/4 cup or about 3 large shallots}

2/3 cup fresh glasswort or 1/3 cup drained Pickled Glasswort or 1/3 cup rinsed caperberries or 1/4 cup rinsed capers

8 tablespoons {1 stick} unsalted butter {or 4 tablespoons clarified plus 4 tablespoons whole unsalted butter, if using a non-nonstick pan}

2 tablespoons sherry vinegar

Briefly rinse the fish and pat dry. Lightly salt them all over. {You can do this step up to a few hours in advance; if you do, cover the fish loosely and refrigerate.}

Ten minutes to an hour before cooking the fish, pat dry again and dredge in flour. Tap to remove the excess flour, arrange, barely touching one another, on a platter or sheet pan, and refrigerate. This will help set the crust for easier handling and less flour will shed into, and taint, the pan sauce.

Heat about half of the butter in a 12-inch skillet over medium heat. When it has melted and separated, but before it begins to color, give the fish a last flour-shedding tap and gently lay them in the pan; they should sizzle on contact. Don't try to move the fish until they have set a crust. Cook until golden on both sides and cooked through, about 3 minutes per side, adjusting the time if your fish are thicker or thinner than 1/2 inch. Monitor closely, and reduce the heat if the butter is threatening to color beyond golden, or raise it if the fish are not coloring at all. Turn the fish gently, trying not to crack the golden crust; I lift and turn them with a metal spatula, nudging with a wooden spoon so they land where I want them to. When the fish are cooked, remove the pan from the heat and transfer to warm plates or a platter. Protect from drafts while you concoct the simple pan sauce.

Pour off the butter if it is darker than hazelnut colored. Return the pan to medium-low heat and add the remaining butter, the shallots, and glasswort, caperberries, or capers. Cook, stirring constantly, until the shallots have just lost their raw edge. Raise the heat slightly and add the vinegar. Taste as it comes to a boil, but it shouldn't need salt ~ the briny wort or capers will likely provide enough. Spoon over the fish and serve piping hot, while the heady aroma of brown butter and evaporating vinegar is still concentrated.

Note: To clarify butter, melt the butter in your smallest, narrowest saucepan, or a butter warmer, over low heat. Monitor it as it comes to a controlled, quiet simmer, then let it bubble for a minute. Pull from the heat and leave to settle and separate, which should take 10 minutes or less. Skim the surface, then gently tilt the pan and pour the clear yellow butter off the water and solids at the bottom of the pan.

⁘
⁘ ⁘

WHOLE SEA BREAM ROASTED *on* ONIONS *with* TOMATOES, PARSLEY, *&* MINT

A SIMPLE METHOD TO FLATTER SMALL WHOLE FISH. Where open roasting can dry out larger fish, a higher proportion of skin and bone keeps small fish succulent. Count one of these fish per two diners; for larger groups, cook two or more fish in separate pans or placed a few inches apart in one large pan. You can substitute whole striped bass, black sea bass, tautog {blackfish}, snapper, or pompano, or, on the Pacific Coast, the best of the rockfish, Bolina rock cod. Choose shiny, firm fish that smell faintly of the ocean. Ask the fishmonger to clean and scale the fish, or allow about ten minutes to clean it yourself.

Use the sweetest onions you can for this dish ~ tender, sweet red ones or Vidalia, Walla Walla, Granex, Imperial Valley, or Maui. If you can't get a sweet onion variety, you may need to stew the salted onions briefly to soften them before you roast the fish. If you like fennel, try sprinkling a few crushed seeds on the fish or stuffing a branch into its belly before you roast it. Then use the chopped feathery fronds in lieu of the mint with the onions. Or use a half cup of Salmorigano {page 299} to marinate the onions and baste the fish.

Wine: Mercurey Blanc, Clos Rochette, Faiveley, 1999

\ *continued*

FOR 2 SERVINGS:

8 ounces sliced red or yellow onions {2 cups, about 1 medium onion}

Salt

About 1/2 cup extra-virgin olive oil

A handful of fresh flat-leaf parsley leaves, coarsely chopped

A dozen fresh mint leaves, coarsely chopped

1 sea bream or black sea bass, about 1-3/4 pounds, or about 1-1/2 pounds cleaned and scaled

1 small, ripe, juicy tomato {about 4 to 5 ounces}

About 1 tablespoon red wine vinegar or sherry vinegar

Seasoning the onions and fish {several hours in advance}:

Combine the onions with a few pinches of salt, enough olive oil to coat, and most of the parsley and mint. Knead and toss until the onions begin to soften. Set aside at room temperature to continue softening.

If necessary, clean and scale the fish. Rinse the fish under cold running water, opening the belly and throat to wash out blood or remaining viscera. Pat dry, inside and out.

Make two parallel slashes in the thickest section of each side of the fish, about halfway down to the bone. {This will expose more surface area to the seasoning and will also ensure the fat sections cook as rapidly as the skinnier parts.} Sprinkle the fish all over with salt, making sure some salt falls in the slashes. Open the belly and sprinkle a little salt inside. Cover loosely and refrigerate until needed.

Cooking the fish:

Preheat the oven to 500°.

Check the onions: they should be quite soft and moist. Taste one. If it is still firm or harsh tasting, cook the onions in a small saucepan over low heat, covered, until softened, 5 minutes or so. Spread the onions 1/2 inch deep in a shallow oval or rectangular 1-quart gratin dish or ovenproof 10-inch skillet. Whether raw or cooked, add a few tablespoons of water if they are dry.

Core, halve, and slice the tomato a scant 1/4 inch thick. Tuck about half of the slices into the bed of onions. {If the shoulder and heel pieces are tender, include them here; if they are tough, set aside for tomato sauce.}

Rub the fish thoroughly all over with a few spoonfuls of the olive oil and nestle it in the onions. If the fish hangs far over the edge of your dish, trim the tail, or consider removing the head. Arrange the remaining tomato slices on the fish, more or less echoing the curve of the gills. Press them into place, so they adhere to the fish, and to make them release juice. Season lightly with salt and drizzle with a little more olive oil. Place in the center of the oven and roast until just cooked through. A 2-1/2- to 3-inch-thick 1-1/2-pound fish should take about 17 to 20 minutes. The edges of the tomatoes and tips of the onions should brown~if they aren't coloring within 14 minutes, raise the heat to broil and watch closely so that they don't char. Cooking time will vary according to the fish, your oven, the size and shape of the dish, and the material it is made of. {You will get lovely results with glazed terra-cotta~it absorbs and transfers heat gently, but it may take longer than porcelain, Pyrex, or an ovenproof skillet. In any case, if you use the same roasting vessel even a few times, you will learn how evenly and rapidly it conducts heat, and you may eventually opt for a different oven temperature. Here, as elsewhere, this sort of attention and experience allows you to thoughtfully subvert the strictures of a recipe.}

While the fish is cooking, stir together about 1/4 cup olive oil with the vinegar and the rest of the parsley and mint. Salt to taste.

Bring the fish, in the baking dish, to the table. To serve, first remove the dorsal and ventral fins and any attendant little bones they try to drag with them {I pull the fins out by hand}. Slide a knife in at an angle under the "collar" of the fish, freeing the neck end of the fillet. Carve a line down the center of the top fillet from head to tail. Slide the knife blade flat against the vertebrae and lift the top fillet out in two sections, serving one tomato-topped section to each diner. Since the section around the belly is no more than a slip of flesh lined with long, scythe-shaped bones, don't bother trying to lift that part of the fillet. Gently lift the exposed central bone by the tail, and use the tip of your knife to gradually free the other fillet, so it falls back into the bed of onions. Discard the central bone. Serve the second fillet, then drizzle the onions with a little of the vinaigrette and shimmy the pan gently so it disperses. Spoon some of the juicy onions onto each plate, checking for fugitive bones as you go. Offer the remaining vinaigrette on the side.

+ + + + +

To Clean a Whole Fish

Remove the scales by scraping the fish from tail to head with the dull side of a knife held at an angle. First the scales will "pop up"; with a few more strokes, they will fall off. Continue dragging the knife over the whole surface of the fish until the skin is soft and smooth. Rinse the fish briefly under cold water, then use the tip of a boning knife to open the belly, cutting from the peppercorn-sized vent at one end toward the "chin" of the fish and making a shallow cut, away from yourself, and with the blade facing out. Pull out the entrails and rinse the belly cavity. Lift the hard collar-flap {the *operculum*} to reveal the gills. Cut through the bone where the belly meets the chin of the fish. Trace the comb-like gills to where they attach to the spine and cut them free. Flip the fish over and repeat on the other side. Remove the gills, which will drag a little viscera with them. If you or your guests are skittish about the head, lift the collar-flap again and make a clean cut through the spine to remove the head.

✦ ✦ ✦ ✦ ✦

SEA BASS *with* LEEKS, POTATOES, *&* THYME

SORT OF A BASS *BONNE FEMME,* THE FISH BEING COOKED IN A CHUNKY STEW OF leeks and potatoes that recalls that traditional French soup. We use plump white sea bass fillets, but black bass and turbot are good alternatives. The fillets need to be between 1 and 1-1/2 inches thick in order to cook properly, which means avoiding tail pieces.

The first time you make this dish, plan to watch it closely while it is in the very hot oven {all of about 10 minutes}. My pan placement instructions and cooking times are necessarily only guidelines~you may need to adjust one or both to the characteristics of your oven, pan, or fish.

Wine: Chassagne-Montrachet, E. Sauzet, 1999

4 pieces sea bass fillet, about 6 ounces
    each and 1 to 1-1/2 inches thick
Salt
About 3/4 pound peeled
    yellow-fleshed potatoes, prefer-
    ably yellow Finnish, Bintje, or
    German Butterballs, cut into irreg-
    ular bite-sized chunks
1-1/2 cups diced or thinly sliced leeks
    {including a little bit of the green
    part}

A few sprigs of fresh thyme
About 1-1/4 cups Chicken Stock {page
    58}
A splash or so of dry white vermouth
6 tablespoons unsalted butter, sliced
    and chilled
A trickle of Champagne vinegar or
    white wine vinegar, if needed

Seasoning the fish {For the best flavor, do this a few hours in advance}:
    Season the fish lightly and evenly with salt. Cover loosely and refrigerate.

Cooking the fish:
    Preheat the broiler. Position the rack so it is about 6 inches from the element.

    Place the potatoes in a saucepan, add cold water to cover, and set over medium
heat. Season liberally with salt {we use a scant 1-1/2 teaspoons sea salt per quart},
stir, and taste. The water should taste as seasoned as you would like the potatoes
to be. Cook the potatoes at a gentle simmer until quite tender and soft on the
edges, about 5 minutes. {Some of the soft potatoes will later diffuse in the sauce,
giving the dish its homey character.}

    Drain the potatoes well and place them, still steaming, in a 12- or 14-inch
ovenproof skillet. Add the leeks, thyme, about 1 cup of the chicken stock, and a
splash of vermouth. Set over medium heat and swirl as the broth comes to a simmer. Add about 4 tablespoons of the butter, and swirl until it melts. Taste for salt.
Reduce the heat to low and add the fish. Swirl and tilt the pan to baste the surface
of the fish with the buttery broth. The liquid level should rise as the bass releases
moisture into the broth. If it doesn't, add a little more chicken stock.

    Make sure no bits of leek are stuck to the sides of the pan, or marooned on
top of the fish, and place the pan under the broiler. Cook until the surface of the
fish and potatoes is lightly gratinéed, about 5 to 6 minutes. The liquid should be

\ *continued*

bubbling vigorously. Reduce the oven temperature to 500°. Cook until the fish is medium-rare, another 1 to 5 minutes.

While the fish is cooking, set a small, shallow platter and four plates to warm in the oven for a minute or so, then remove.

Transfer the fish pan to the stovetop. Using a spatula and tongs, lift the fish, tilt to drain slightly, then place on the warm platter, protected from drafts {don't stack the pieces of fish}. The fish will finish cooking as it rests.

Swirl the pan gently over medium heat to encourage the potatoes to thicken the sauce as it simmers. Taste. Add the remaining butter and adjust the salt. Tilt the platter of fish over the pan and carefully drain any liquid into the simmering sauce. Continue simmering to reduce the sauce as needed, until it has a little body, then taste again. If it seems flat, add a splash of vermouth or a few drops of vinegar. {Don't reach for lemon; its perfume can easily dominate all others and it is out of character for this dish.} Transfer the fish to the warmed plates and spoon the sauce and potatoes over all.

Note: At Zuni, this dish and the two fish dishes that follow brown and reduce beautifully in our brick oven; the burner-then-hot-broiler technique mimics those blistering conditions.

❖
❖ ❖

SALMON COOKED *with* FLAGEOLETS, BACON, *&* RED WINE

AN EARTHY SALMON DISH, BEST MADE WITH FAT, LATE-SUMMER SALMON WHICH will stand up to the challenge of the other long, rich flavors. We use Pacific salmon~Sacramento River Basin Kings or wild Alaskan~for this, or any salmon dish. All commercial salmon labeled "Atlantic" is farmed; I find its flavor disappointing to dreadful, and the environmental effects of salmon farming can be devastating to surrounding waters and wild fish. Choose fat pieces of fish; thin tail pieces will cook too rapidly. As long as you don't overcook the salmon, or over-reduce the sauce, the result will be satiny and succulent. If you have a scrap of bacon left from a recent Pasta with Braised Bacon and Roasted Tomato Sauce {page

205}, it will be delicious in this dish. You can substitute lentils for the flageolets.

Be prepared to adjust the oven temperature or distance from the broiler as necessary when you make this dish.

Wine: Iron Horse Alexander Valley Sangiovese, 1998

FOR 4 SERVINGS:

4 pieces salmon fillet, preferably King, about 6 ounces each and 1 to 1-1/2 inches thick

Salt

1-1/3 cups medium-bodied red wine, such as Sangiovese, Pinot Noir, or a light Merlot

3/4 cup Chicken Stock {page 58}

3 ounces thickly sliced bacon or braised bacon {see page 205}, cut into 1/4-inch strips

About 6 tablespoons unsalted butter, sliced and chilled

1/2 cup finely diced carrots {2 ounces}

1/2 cup finely diced celery {2 ounces}

1/2 cup finely diced yellow onions {2 ounces}

2 cups cooked flageolets {see page 263}, drained, cooking liquid reserved

A few sprigs of fresh thyme

1 bay leaf

Seasoning the salmon {For the best flavor, do this several hours in advance}: Season the salmon evenly with salt. Cover loosely and refrigerate.

Cooking the salmon:

Preheat the broiler. Position the rack about 6 inches from the element.

Place the wine in a small saucepan and reduce to about 1/3 cup. Add the chicken stock and return to a simmer. Turn off the heat.

Place the bacon in a 12- or 14-inch ovenproof skillet and lightly brown it in its own fat over medium heat. Reduce the heat slightly and pour off all but a film of the fat. Add about 2 tablespoons of the butter, the carrots, celery, onions, and 1 sprig of the thyme. Cook, stirring, until the vegetables are tender, about 6 minutes.

Add the flageolets, about 1 cup of the red wine–stock mixture, the bay leaf, another sprig of thyme, and about 3 tablespoons of the butter. Raise the heat to medium and swirl as the liquid comes to a simmer. Reduce the heat to low, add the salmon, and swirl and tilt the pan to baste the top of the fish. Make sure no

\ *continued*

beans, bacon, or bits of vegetables are perched on top of the fish, where they could burn. The pieces of fish should not be touching one another.

Place the pan under the broiler. Cook for about 6 or 7 minutes; the salmon should be quite rare and the whole surface of the dish should be sizzling and beginning to color. Watch closely; if the fish or beans threaten to char at any point, reduce the oven temperature to 500°.

While the fish is cooking, set four plates in the oven to heat for a minute or so, then remove.

Transfer the pan to the stovetop. Using a spatula and tongs, transfer the salmon onto the warm plates, where it should reach medium-rare as you finish the sauce. Protect from drafts.

Set the pan over medium heat and bring to a simmer. Taste. If the liquid looks or tastes thin, simmer briefly to reduce and allow the starch from the beans to bind the sauce. If it seems winy, add a splash of the reserved bean cooking liquid. If you want more sauce, add the last splash of red wine–stock mixture and some bean liquid. Correct the salt. Reduce the heat and swirl in some or all of the remaining butter, to your taste.

Spoon the saucy beans over the waiting fish.

＋
＋ ＋

MONKFISH BRAISED *with* WHITE BEANS, FENNEL, *&* TOMATO

THIS DISH REAPPEARS IN A NUMBER OF FORMS AT ZUNI, SOMETIMES WITH THICKLY sliced boiled potatoes instead of beans, or with house-salted cod in lieu of monk-fish, or with big chunks of blanched leeks in place of the fennel. In summer, we shove a bouquet of basil stems into the tomato sauce, or stir whole leaves into the simmering sauce just before baking it. In any variation, the recipe is forgiving with regard to exact amounts, so long as each of the elements is delicious to begin with. And succulent, meaty monkfish is fairly forgiving with regard to cooking time.

If you plan to make the fumet, ask for monkfish bones when you buy the fillets. {The fumet will take less than an hour to make.} You can cook the beans a day or two in advance.

Wine: Fleurie, Domaine Berrod, 2000

FOR 4 GENEROUS SERVINGS:

4 chunks monkfish fillet, about 6 ounces each, skin and translucent membrane removed

Salt

1/2 cup mild-tasting olive oil

1 medium fennel bulb, trimmed and cut into 1/2-inch-thick wedges {about 8 ounces}

3/4 cup diced yellow onions {3 ounces}

1/2 cup dry white wine

6 ounces very ripe tomatoes, peeled, cored {1 large or 2 small}, cut into wedges, and lightly salted, or 3/4

cup drained canned tomatoes, quartered

A few garlic cloves, coarsely chopped

1 small dried chili or a pinch of dried chili flakes

A pinch of saffron threads

A splash of pastis, such as Pernod or Ricard, or ouzo {optional}

About 1 cup Monkfish Fumet {page 68} or Chicken Stock {page 58}

About 1-1/2 cups cooked white beans {see page 263}, drained, cooking liquid reserved

About 1/2 cup Aïoli {page 299}

Seasoning the fish {for the best flavor, do this 4 to 12 hours in advance}:

Briefly rinse and then dry the monkfish fillets. Salt them lightly and evenly. Cover loosely and refrigerate.

Warm about 2 tablespoons of the olive oil in a 12-inch skillet over medium heat. Add the fennel and cook until slightly golden, about 3 minutes per side. Reduce the heat, add the onions, another tablespoon or two of oil, and a few pinches of salt, and cook gently for about 10 minutes, stirring and turning the pieces of fennel as needed. The salt, low flame, and stirring should coax the onions to "sweat" their water without browning.

Add the white wine and raise the heat to boil it briefly, then add the tomatoes, garlic, chili, saffron, and the pastis or ouzo, if using. Bring to a quiet simmer and cook for about 5 minutes. Add the fumet or chicken stock {or a combination

\ *continued*

of fumet or stock and reserved bean liquid} and another tablespoon of the olive oil. Add the beans and simmer briefly, then correct for salt and set aside.

Cooking the fish:

Preheat the broiler. Position the rack so it is about 6 inches from the element.

Pat the fish fillets dry. Warm about 1 tablespoon of the oil in a 10-inch skillet, nonstick if you have one, over medium heat. Arrange the pieces of monkfish in the oil; they should sizzle on contact. Don't crowd the fish, or it will steam, but make sure that you don't have too much empty pan space either ~ the oil will rapidly overheat in these spots. As long as the oil is hot enough and the fish is dry on the surface, it should not stick, even in a *non*-nonstick pan, but in any case, don't fuss with it. Let the fish develop a pale golden crust before you try to turn it; this should take about 3 minutes. Then cook until golden on the second side.

When you finish searing the monkfish, nestle it in the pan of sauce. Set over medium-low heat and swirl as you bring to a simmer. Cook gently for about 6 minutes, until medium-rare.

Transfer to the broiler to finish cooking and brown the tips of the fish, fennel, and tomatoes, about 5 minutes. Look for the juices to begin caramelizing around the rim, but reduce the oven temperature if it looks as if the dish might burn. I sometimes assemble, finish, and serve the dish in a 2-inch deep, 4-quart ceramic baking dish or similar-sized copper roasting pan. I like to bring the whole dish, still bubbling, to the table. Offer the Aïoli on the side.

❖
❖ ❖

HOUSE-CURED SALT COD

ZUNI HAS ALWAYS HAD A SALT COD–LOVING CLIENTELE, AND MORE SO SINCE WE started salting fresh cod ourselves in 1993. Commercial salt cod wasn't bad or unavailable, but in the spirit of "stop, think, there must be a harder way," I figured starting from scratch might be more gratifying. It was, and it produces very succulent versions of traditional Mediterranean dishes ~ where pungent salt cod is most frequently served as a first course, and either pounded, fried, or otherwise affectionately manipulated. But home-cured cod is delicate enough to feature intact and in main-course portions. It is delicious broiled or poached, with Salsa Verde {page 292} or Preserved Lemon–Caper Butter {page 309}, or simmered in romesco {page 334} or briefly stewed with fennel, saffron, and white wine {page 333}.

This home-cured cod has none of the sinewy, oversalted sections you can count on with the commercial product, and it doesn't have the musty smell or flavor that some boast, even after they are cooked. Salted raw cod is, however, pungent, and will announce its presence to everything else in the refrigerator. It is, frankly, "stinky" to anyone who doesn't love it. We use dayboat hook-and-line-caught Atlantic cod, *Gadus morhua*. Its Pacific cousin, *Gadus macrocephalus,* is too soft to be a viable substitute. The confusingly named lingcod, rock cods, and black cod are not appropriate.

Salting the cod:

Buy skinned cod fillet, rinse it quickly under cold water, and press it gently between towels to wick out excess water. Pay attention to how soft the fish feels; this will be a reference point when you soak and rinse the fish. Weigh the fish, and season it with 1-1/2 tablespoons {3/4 ounce} salt per pound. Use an even hand over all at first, then go back and reseason the center section just a little more than the edges and tail end. If the center section is thicker than 1-1/2 inches, cut a 1/2-inch-deep slash in the thickest section to increase the surface area and ensure that the salt will reach and cure the whole mass rapidly and evenly.

Place the frosty-looking fillet flat on a stainless steel rack or shallow perforated pan and set this inside a larger, deeper pan to catch the drips. If that pan has a lid, use it; otherwise, loosely drape the assembly with plastic to protect from contamination, and contain odor, somewhat. The lid or plastic should not touch the fish.

Refrigerate and cure for up to 7 days. The fillet will get firmer as it dries out. You can desalt and cook the cod after as little as 24 hours, but it won't start to acquire its distinctive character until it has cured for about 72 hours. In the interest of minimizing odor, you will probably want to rinse and dry the "drip pan" daily until the fillet stops dripping. The cod usually weeps a tablespoon or so of liquid per pound, most of it in the first 24 hours. If you are keeping the cod

\ *continued*

salted for longer than 5 days, you should lift out the fillet, rinse and dry the rack, and lightly resalt the cod, especially the underside if it feels humid. Flip the fillet over before you return it to the refrigerator.

Soaking the cod:

To desalt the cod, cut off the desired portion {if you are not using it all}, rinse it under cold water, and then soak it in fresh cold water, about 2 quarts per pound of fish. Refrigerate. Remember how firm the salted fillet felt before you rinsed it ~ once it is perfectly desalted, it will feel a little firmer than it did to start.

Desalting times will vary according to the dimensions of the piece of cod, the exact size of the water bath, the water temperature {the colder the water, the slower the process}, and how long the cod was salted. Pay attention to each of these things as you desalt the cod, so you can duplicate or modify them the next time you soak a batch.

If the cod was salted for only 24 hours, allow 4 to 8 hours to desalt it. For longer cures, allow 24 hours, stirring it in the soaking water once or twice. To determine whether the cod is purged enough, feel the fillet ~ it should feel softer and heavier than when you started to soak it ~ nearly as soft as the unsalted raw fish did. If you are becoming courageous, pinch off a bit of cod and taste it {see below}; spit it out if you wish ~ but not before you decide whether or not it is nicely seasoned. This will probably be a new experience, but don't underestimate your ability to taste and judge correctly. Remember that the edge will be the least salty part of the slab you are desalting. Once the cod is desalted, pat dry and refrigerate until cooking, up to 6 hours.

Don't try to rush the desalting process by washing the salt out under running water ~ you will wash out more than just salt. Cod rinsed this way will be deficient in the connective stuff and juices that make cooked salt cod dishes succulent.

∗ ∗ ESQUIEXADA

If you try the raw cod and like the taste, consider making the delicacy *esquiexada:* torn bits of just-soaked cod, pressed dry, then moistened with extra-virgin olive oil and tossed with slivered raw onions and sweet peppers, maybe a few olives, vinegar, and, yes, salt to taste. Our house-cured cod produces an excellent version of this genial Catalan dish.

Wine: Dry Creek Vineyard Clarksburg Dry Chenin Blanc, 2000

SALT COD CARPACCIO

We serve never-soaked raw salt cod, sliced thin like smoked salmon, garnished with radish coins, slivered avocado, spicy garden cress {or chopped nasturtiums or arugula}, and drizzled with shallot vinaigrette. For this dish, use cod that has been salted for only 2 or 3 days.

Wine: Nautilus, Marlborough, New Zealand, Sauvignon Blanc, 2001

+
+ +

HOUSE SALT COD BRANDADE

I CAN'T RESIST INCLUDING THIS TRADITIONAL DISH OF SALT COD BEATEN WITH OLIVE oil, cream, and pounded garlic. Some brandade recipes call for boiled potato or bread crumbs ~ either to stretch a small amount of cod or tame the flavor ~ but I have abandoned both since we started using delicate, freshly salted cod. I recommend making brandade in the traditional way, pounded by hand with a pestle in a mortar. I use an inexpensive wooden salad bowl that I never use for salad, only as a mortar for brandade. If you are making a larger batch, it will be tempting to beat it with a paddle in an electric mixer, but you won't get the same fluffy result that comes from smashing every flake of cod down to fibers.

Serve this delicacy warm on croûtons, to enjoy by themselves, with a salad, or with fried or poached eggs, or in broth. Or press 1/8-inch-thick slices of tomato onto thin slices of baguette, brush with oil, and bake until they are leathery crisp, then mound these with warm brandade. Or form cold brandade into 1-inch balls, roll them in beaten egg and fresh bread crumbs, and deep-fry them. These are good with Tomato Coulis {page 287} or with a frisée or arugula salad.

Wine: Mâcon-Lugny Les Charmes, 2000

\ *continued*

FOR ABOUT 1 CUP:

2 to 3 garlic cloves, peeled
Salt
About 1 cup whole milk
About 1 cup water
1 pound House-Cured Salt Cod {page 328}{18 ounces fresh skinned cod fillet}, cut into 2 or 3 pieces, soaked for 4 to 24 hours, and drained
About 3 tablespoons heavy cream
About 3 tablespoons extra-virgin olive oil

Cut the garlic into a few pieces, then put in a mortar and pound to a rough paste. Add a pinch or two of salt and pound until smooth. Scrape into a small bowl and set aside.

Place the milk and water in a 2-quart saucepan and bring to a simmer. Add the salt cod. The fish should be just submerged; if not, add a little more hot water. Adjust the heat to maintain a gentle simmer. Simmer until the cod is just cooked through, about 5 minutes for a 1-inch-thick fillet. Don't let the liquid boil, and don't overcook the fish ~ both will damage the proteins that give the brandade body. You will sacrifice flavor too. Lift the cod from the poaching liquid {set it aside for now} and set to drain on a dry towel.

Heat the cream and oil separately until both are warm to the touch. Set aside.

As soon as the fish stops steaming, begin flaking it to make sure it is not *under-cooked* ~ if any flakes are translucent, return them to the simmering watery milk for a few seconds, and drain as before. You should get about 3/4 pound cooked cod.

Place the warm cod in a mortar or wooden bowl and pound and beat until nearly all of it is reduced to a fibrous pulp. The more thoroughly you smash the cod, the more cream and oil it will accept. Since house salted cod is tender compared to commercial product, you can leave some bits of cod intact for bursts of flavor, but most of the fish must be broken down to individual fibers to achieve the fluffy texture prized in brandade.

Still using the pestle, gradually work in the cream, oil, and garlic to taste, making a rich emulsion with the pounded fish. Taste for salt. If not serving immediately, hold in a double boiler, or rewarm in a small, nonstick pan, or on croûtons under the broiler.

✦
✦ ✦

HOUSE SALT COD CHOWDER *with* FENNEL, SAFFRON, ONIONS, *&* CRACKER BREAD

Rᴇᴍɪɴɪsᴄᴇɴᴛ ᴏꜰ ᴛʜᴏsᴇ ᴛʀᴀᴅɪᴛɪᴏɴᴀʟ ᴄʜᴏᴡᴅᴇʀs ᴡʜᴇʀᴇ ᴅʀʏ ᴄʀᴀᴄᴋᴇʀs ᴛʜɪᴄᴋᴇɴᴇᴅ and gave bulk to a broth meager in fish or fresh vegetables. This is fun to assemble, it is cooked almost as soon as it simmers, and it has a wonderful texture. I flavor this chowder with sprigs of wild fennel gone to seed that grows around the Bay Area; you can substitute a few crushed fennel seeds plus some of the feathery fronds from the fennel bulb.

Wine: Crozes-Hermitage Blanc, La Mule, Paul Jaboulet Aîné, 2000

FOR 4 SERVINGS:

1-1/4 pounds House-Cured Salt Cod {page 328}{1-1/2 pounds skinned fresh cod fillet}, soaked {see page 330} and drained

1 large or 2 medium fennel bulbs, trimmed {about 12 ounces total}, a few sprigs of feathery frond reserved and chopped if using fennel seeds

A pinch of saffron threads

About 1/2 cup extra-virgin olive oil

8 ounces sliced yellow onions {2 cups, about 1 medium onion}

Salt

A few garlic cloves, slivered

1/2 cup diced or sliced leeks {including a little of the green part}

A few sprigs of wild fennel flower that has gone to seed or a few fennel seeds, crushed

About 2 ounces plain cracker bread

1/4 cup dry white wine

3/4 to 1 cup Chicken Stock {page 58}, warmed, or lightly salted warm water

1/4 cup Aïoli {page 299} {optional}

Slice the salt cod on an angle into 1-1/2-inch-thick slabs.

Cut the fennel bulb into wedges about 3/4 inch thick. Bring about 3 quarts unsalted water to a simmer, add the fennel, and cook until al dente. Drain, cool in ice water, drain again promptly, and spread on a towel.

Place the saffron in a 3-quart sauté pan or 12-inch skillet over medium-low heat. When the bottom of the pot is just too hot to touch, add about 1/3 cup of

\ *continued*

the olive oil and swirl the pan. The saffron will "bloom" in the oil. Add the sliced onions and a few pinches of salt and stir. Cook covered, stirring occasionally, until the onion is translucent and just soft, about 15 minutes. Add the leeks, garlic, and a little more olive oil to coat and cook another few minutes uncovered. Turn off the heat.

Nestle the cod and fennel wedges evenly in the bed of onions. Tuck in the cracker bread, distributing it evenly as well. Scatter the wild fennel or fennel seeds plus chopped fennel frond over all, then moisten with the wine and enough warm chicken stock or salted warm water, to not quite cover the fish and vegetables. Bring slowly to a simmer, swirling the pan occasionally to encourage mingling of flavors. Taste for salt. Simmer for about 2 minutes. Turn off the heat, cover, and leave for about 1 minute, to let the fish finish cooking and the cracker bread swell.

Spoon out the tender cod, then distribute the vegetables, velvety bread, and juices. Offer the optional Aïoli on the side.

✧
✧ ✧

SHRIMP COOKED *in* ROMESCO *with* WILTED SPINACH

In tarragona, on the catalonian coast, where romesco is traditional, the word refers to the sauce base, the chili pepper used to make it, and the finished dish it defines, and when there's enough of it, it seems to become a *romescada*.

The romesco sauce base is a bit labor-intensive, but it is versatile, keeps well, and improves as the flavors mingle, so we always make a large amount and use it with different seafood over the course of a week. This shrimp dish is the easiest of our romesco dishes, but it is nearly as easy to steam open and then simmer mussels or clams in romesco. Or you can cook medallions of halibut, monkfish, or House-Cured Salt Cod {page 328} in the sauce. Or make a delicious event of combining a few kinds of fish and shellfish. Regarding ingredients: I encourage you to avoid farmed shrimp. Buy American-caught wild shrimp at specialty fish markets~all of which, by law, ought to be "turtle-safe" {meaning the traps exclude sea turtles}. {A similar system that permits shrimpers to avoid destroying massive numbers of juvenile fish has also been mandated by federal law, although its use is not yet well enforced.} Asking for and paying a little more for these sustainably harvested shrimp is a good way to encourage responsible shrimping.

I like to cook the shrimp in their shells, but you can also prepare this dish with peeled and deveined shrimp. {If you are doing the peeling, you may want to turn the shells into a little fumet to flavor the sauce. Allow about an hour to do this.}

As for the sauce, ancho chilis are a good substitute for the romesco pepper, which so far remains elusive on my coast. We use a high-acid, oaky Spanish red wine vinegar from l'Estornel, which imparts a distinct character to the sauce. We also use Spanish paprika, although Hungarian products will do as well~in either case, make sure it is pungent and fresh. Buy all ground spices in quantities that you will exhaust promptly.

Wine: St. Amant Amador Roussanne, 1999

FOR 4 SERVINGS:

For the romesco base {makes 1 generous cup}:

1/2 ounce raw almonds {about 2 tablespoons, or 12 nuts}

1 ounce hazelnuts {1/4 cup, or about 32 nuts}

1/2 cup coarsely chopped drained canned tomatoes or peeled ripe tomatoes

About 1/4 cup extra-virgin olive oil

1 ancho chili

About 1 cup mild-tasting olive oil

1-1/2 ounces chewy, white, peasant-style bread {about 1 thick slice}

2 to 3 garlic cloves, peeled

1 teaspoon l'Estornel brand red wine vinegar {see Sources and Resources, page 518} or other red wine vinegar fortified with a few drops of sherry vinegar

1 teaspoon hot paprika

1/2 teaspoon mild paprika

Salt

\ *continued*

To finish the dish:

1 cup Chicken Stock {page 58},
    Shellfish Fumet {page 172}, water,
    or a combination
3 tablespoons dry white wine
1/2 cup diced yellow onions {2 ounces}
About 1/4 cup extra-virgin olive oil

Salt
About 1-1/4 pounds shrimp in their
    shells or just over 1 pound peeled
    shrimp
3/4 pound spinach, carefully washed
    and dried

Making the romesco base {up to a week in advance}:

Preheat the oven to 325°.

Drop the almonds into a small pot of boiling water and leave for about 10 seconds. Drain, slide off the skins, and rub dry. Set aside.

Roast the hazelnuts on a small baking sheet until the skins darken and start to split, 10 to 15 minutes. While they are still hot, bundle them in a towel beanbag-style, then scrunch and massage them to rub off most of their skins. Pick out the nuts and set aside.

Turn the oven to broil. Spread the tomatoes 1/2 inch thick in a small, shallow baking dish. Trickle with a little of the olive oil and place under the broiler about 4 inches from the element. Cook until the tomatoes char slightly and bubble, a few minutes. Remove from the broiler.

Reduce the oven temperature to 425°.

Meanwhile, pour a few cups of boiling water over the chili and leave to swell for a few minutes. Drain, then stem and seed the pepper.

Pour mild-tasting olive oil to a depth of 1/2 inch into an 8- or 10-inch skillet and set over medium-low heat. Test the temperature with the edge of the slice of bread; when it barely sizzles on contact, reduce the heat slightly and add the bread. {You may need to cut the bread into pieces so it fits into the pan in a single layer.} Check the underside at 1 minute; it should just be beginning to color. Fry until it is the color of cornflakes 2 to 3 minutes per side. Drain and cool on a paper towel.

Thickly slice the garlic, then pound to a paste in a mortar. Scrape into a processor and add the chili, fried bread, almonds, and hazelnuts. Grind to a fine, moist paste, scraping the sides frequently. Scrape in the tomato and process to a paste. Add the vinegar, paprika, the remaining extra-virgin oil and salt to taste. Taste; it should be bursting with flavor, although not overly spicy. The flavor of the paprika will come out over time.

Spread the paste in a thick layer in a small shallow baking dish and bake until the surface has turned dark orange with occasional flecks of brown, about 8 minutes.

Finishing the dish:

Bring the stock, fumet, or water and the white wine to a simmer in a small saucepan. Turn off the heat and stir in the romesco base. Taste for salt. Cover and set aside for about 30 minutes. As this brew cools, the crumbs will begin to swell and soften, which will give the sauce a nice texture.

Place the diced onions in a 3-quart sauté pan with about 2 tablespoons of the olive oil and a few pinches of salt. Cook over medium heat until translucent and tender, about 5 minutes. Add the romesco and warm through. Add the shrimp and turn the heat to medium. Cook gently, turning each one over once in the thickening sauce, until the shrimp are just firm and opaque. This should take no longer than 4 minutes, but depends on the size of the shrimp.

Meanwhile, warm another 2 tablespoons olive oil in a 12-inch skillet over medium heat. Add the spinach and sprinkle with salt. Gently turn and fold leaves until they are uniformly wilted and bright green. Taste for salt and add another trickle of oil if the spinach seems lean.

Divide the spinach among warm plates. Arrange the shrimp on top of the spinach. Taste the sauce, and correct the salt. The romesco should be fluid but thick~reduce briefly or add a splash of water if it seems either watery or pasty. Spoon the sauce over all.

+
+ +

SPICY SQUID STEW *with* RED WINE
& ROASTED PEPPERS

HERE IS A DISH TO CHALLENGE THE DOGMA THAT THE BEST COOKING LETS ingredients and flavors sing clearly in the finished dish {or only nudges them into harmony}. In this recipe, you radically change the character, flavor, look, and texture of every ingredient~and the murky, complicated result is delicious. We make many variations on this recipe, adding diced fennel or leeks to the vegetable mix, or finishing the stew with a spoonful of cooked lentils, charred cherry tomatoes, or coarsely chopped blanched chard leaves.

Squid stew makes a great first or main course, followed by a roasted bird or grilled lamb chops with salad on the side. A few spoonfuls of leftover stew make a great crostini topping.

Wine: Quivira Dry Creek Cuvée, 1999

FOR 4 TO 6 SERVINGS:

2-1/4 pounds whole squid

About 6 tablespoons mild-tasting olive oil

Salt

1 cup plus 2 tablespoons red wine

3/4 cup chopped drained canned tomatoes or 1-1/2 cups chopped peeled ripe tomatoes

3/4 cup diced carrots {3 ounces}

3/4 cup diced celery {3 ounces}

3/4 cup diced yellow onions {3 ounces}

1 or 2 small dried chiles

3 garlic cloves, coarsely chopped, plus 1 clove, peeled, to rub the toasts

2-1/2 teaspoons tomato paste

A branch of fresh basil

A few wide strips of orange zest {removed with a vegetable peeler}

2/3 cup peeled roasted red or green bell pepper {about 8 ounces raw pepper, 1 medium}, cut into large dice, with its juice {see page 303}

4 to 6 thick slices of chewy, peasant-style bread

Begin to clean the squid by pulling out the tentacles as you grasp the body with the other hand. Look in the soft matter attached to the tentacles for the silver ink sac~it looks like a drop of mercury. Carefully transfer it to a small cup. Trim away the soft matter, cutting between the eyes and the "neck" of the tentacles. Squeeze the neck; a hard pea-sized "beak" should pop it out. Discard it. Set the tentacles aside. To clean the bodies, starting at the closed tip of each, use your finger or the dull edge of a knife to gradually press and flatten the body, forcing out the insides. {Imagine you are flattening a toothpaste tube.} Cut the bodies into 1/3-inch rings. Rinse and drain the bodies and tentacles. You should have about 1-1/2 pounds cleaned squid.

Warm a tablespoon or two of olive oil in a 10-inch skillet over medium heat. Test with a piece of squid; when the oil sizzles on contact, add about half of the squid and cook briskly for about 45 seconds, stirring or tossing to cook evenly. Season lightly with salt, then tip the barely cooked meat into a 4-quart saucepan. Add another tablespoon or two of oil to the skillet and cook the rest of the squid.

Pour the red wine into the skillet to deglaze the squid juices, and stir and scrape as the liquid reduces by one-third. Add the tomatoes. If using canned tomatoes, simply heat through; if using fresh tomatoes, simmer to reduce by about half. Pour the mixture over the squid. It should be about half submerged in liquid.

Add the remaining 2 to 4 tablespoons olive oil, the carrots, celery, onions, chilis, chopped garlic, and tomato paste. Pick the leaves off the branch of basil and set them aside. Drop the stems into the stew. Twist and drop the strips of orange zest into the pan. Place the ink sacs in a fine strainer, hold over the stew, and bathe with a few spoonfuls of the red wine and juices, pressing to extract the ink. Stir it into the darkening stew. Cover and simmer gently for about 20 minutes. The squid and vegetables will now be nearly submerged in liquid. The squid will be shrunken and may be disturbingly hard.

Taste for salt and add the roasted peppers and their juice. Simmer uncovered until the squid becomes just tender. How long this takes varies enormously, depending on the squid, the pan, and the burner; allow 10 to 30 minutes. Check again for salt, and spiciness~if the stew is too mild for your taste, fish out the chili pods, crush them with a little of the liquid in a small dish, and add a little, or all, of this super-spicy dose to the pot. Otherwise, remove the chilis and the basil stems and cool the stew completely. Cooling and then reheating the stew makes the squid more tender.

To serve, reheat gently, adding the reserved basil leaves as the stew comes to a simmer. Taste. The finished stew should be rich and slightly thick. Offer toasted or grilled bread rubbed with the garlic.

＊ ＊ ＊ ＊ ＊

Sautéing

To saute means, literally, to make something jump. In the kitchen, this is usually hot food in a pan, although the technique is useful for tossing food in a wide bowl as well. When we sauté, we set the food into motion, thrusting the pan {or bowl} forward and then, with a short, firm tug, pulling the pan back, using the edge of the vessel to change the direction or merely break the momentum of its contents. Depending on the tilt of the pan, and the force of the tug, sautéing can allow the cook to gently and efficiently flip or fold masses of ingredients onto themselves without using a utensil {which is less efficient and, to some degree, distresses the food}. It is a fun skill to master. Learning can be messy, with hot food and fat jumping to the floor or stovetop, but you can practice with a few handfuls of dried beans in a cold pan. They slide easily, and you can make them jump, or roll over, with a fairly slow push-then-pull motion that is easy to get the knack of. Add more beans, and you will get a feel for how to adjust your motion as the weight and volume increases. It will be easier to control the larger quantity of beans. I prefer to sauté in a skillet rather than what is classically called a sauté pan; the straight-sided sauté pan thwarts the "jump" so soon that it is hard to get much food flipped over. A curved pan encourages movement.

＊ ＊ ＊ ＊ ＊

POULTRY

ZUNI ROAST CHICKEN *with* BREAD SALAD

The zuni roast chicken depends on three things, beginning with the small size of the bird. Don't substitute a jumbo roaster~it will be too lean and won't tolerate high heat, which is the second requirement of the method. Small chickens, 2-3/4 to 3-1/2 pounds, flourish at high heat, roasting quickly and evenly, and, with lots of skin per ounce of meat, they are virtually designed to stay succulent. Your store may not promote this size for roasting, but let them know you'd like it. I used to ask for a whole fryer, but since many people don't want to cut up their own chickens for frying {or anything else}, those smaller birds rarely make it to the display case intact; most are sacrificed to the "parts" market. But it is no secret that a whole fryer makes a great roaster~it's the size of bird favored for popular spit-roasted chickens to-go. It ought to return to retail cases.

The third requirement is salting the bird at least 24 hours in advance. This improves flavor, keeps it moist, and makes it tender. {For more on this idea, see The Practice of Salting Early, page 35.} We don't bother trussing the chicken~ I want as much skin as possible to blister and color. And we don't rub the chicken with extra fat, trusting its own skin to provide enough. Our brick oven does add a lovely smoky flavor, but it is its tender succulence that really distinguishes this chicken, and this you can achieve at home. I have shared our method with many home cooks, who report the results are startling and delicious when they prepare a chicken this way in their gas or electric ovens. And over the years, I've cooked at least a hundred of these preseasoned chickens in a 1940s O'Keefe and Merritt oven at home, roasting variously in a cast-iron frying pan, a tin pie pan, a copper Tarte Tatin pan, and a 10-inch All-Clad skillet, with no anxiety, or apologies, and with fine results. {For a general discussion of roasting, see page 391.}

But if the chicken is about method, the bread salad is more about recipe. Sort of a scrappy extramural stuffing, it is a warm mix of crispy, tender, and chewy chunks of bread, a little slivered garlic and scallion, a scatter of currants and pine nuts, and a handful of greens, all moistened with vinaigrette and chicken drippings. Tasting as you make it is obligatory, and fun. I recommend you allow a little extra bread and vinaigrette the first time you make the recipe so you can taste with impunity. For the best texture, use chewy peasant-style bread with lots of big and little holes in the crumb. Such loaves are usually about 1 or 2 pounds, so plan on a half or a quarter loaf, respectively, per chicken. I don't use sourdough or *levain*-type bread for this recipe, finding the sour flavor too strong and rich for this dish. And make sure to use day-old bread; fresh bread can make a soggy, doughy salad.

Although everyone seems to love bread salad, it is optional here. The roast chicken is so versatile and appealing you'll want to serve it often, and with your own favorite side dishes.

Wine: Handley Anderson Valley Pinot Noir, 1999

FOR 2 TO 4 SERVINGS:

For the chicken:

One small chicken, 2-3/4 to 3-1/2-pounds

4 tender sprigs fresh thyme, marjoram, rosemary, or sage, about 1/2 inch long

Salt

About 1/4 teaspoon freshly cracked black pepper

A little water

For the salad:

Generous 8 ounces slightly stale open-crumbed, chewy, peasant-style bread {not sourdough}

6 to 8 tablespoons mild-tasting olive oil

1-1/2 tablespoons Champagne vinegar or white wine vinegar

Salt and freshly cracked black pepper

1 tablespoon dried currants

1 teaspoon red wine vinegar, or as needed

1 tablespoon warm water

2 tablespoons pine nuts

2 to 3 garlic cloves, slivered

1/4 cup slivered scallions {about 4 scallions}, including a little of the green part

2 tablespoons lightly salted Chicken Stock {page 58} or lightly salted water

A few handfuls of arugula, frisée, or red mustard greens, carefully washed and dried

Seasoning the chicken {1 to 3 days before serving; for 3-1/4- to 3-1/2-pound chickens, at least 2 days}:

Remove and discard the lump of fat inside the chicken. Rinse the chicken and pat very dry inside and out. Be thorough ~ a wet chicken will spend too much time steaming before it begins to turn golden brown.

Approaching from the edge of the cavity, slide a finger under the skin of each of the breasts, making 2 little pockets. Now use the tip of your finger to gently

\ *continued*

loosen a pocket of skin on the outside of the thickest section of each thigh. Using your finger, shove an herb sprig into each of the 4 pockets.

Season the chicken liberally all over with salt and the pepper {we use 3/4 teaspoon sea salt per pound of chicken}. Season the thick sections a little more heavily than the skinny ankles and wings. Sprinkle a little of the salt just inside the cavity, on the backbone, but don't otherwise worry about seasoning the inside. Twist and tuck the wing tips behind the shoulders. Cover loosely and refrigerate.

Starting the bread salad {up to several hours in advance}:
Preheat the broiler.

Cut the bread into a couple of large chunks. Carve off all of the bottom crust and most of the top and side crust {reserve the top and side crusts to use as croûtons in salads or soups}. Brush the bread all over with olive oil. Broil very briefly, to crisp and lightly color the surface. Turn the bread chunks over and crisp the other side. Trim off any badly charred tips, then tear the chunks into a combination of irregular 2- to 3-inch wads, bite-sized bits, and fat crumbs. You should get about 4 cups.

Combine about 1/4 cup of the olive oil with the Champagne or white wine vinegar and salt and pepper to taste. Toss about 1/4 cup of this tart vinaigrette with the torn bread in a wide salad bowl; the bread will be unevenly dressed. Taste one of the more saturated pieces. If it is bland, add a little salt and pepper and toss again.

Place the currants in a small bowl and moisten with the red wine vinegar and warm water. Set aside.

Roasting the chicken and assembling the salad:
Preheat the oven to 475°. {Depending on the size, efficiency, and accuracy of your oven, and the size of your bird, you may need to adjust the heat to as high as 500° or as low as 450° during the course of roasting the chicken to get it to brown properly. If that proves to be the case, begin at that temperature the next time you roast a chicken. If you have a convection function on your oven, use it for the first 30 minutes; it will enhance browning, and may reduce overall cooking time by 5 to 10 minutes.}

Choose a shallow flameproof roasting pan or dish barely larger than the chicken, or use a 10-inch skillet with an all-metal handle. Preheat the pan over medium heat. Wipe the chicken dry and set it breast side up in the pan. It should sizzle.

Place in the center of the oven and listen and watch for it to start sizzling and browning within 20 minutes. If it doesn't, raise the temperature progressively until it does. The skin should blister, but if the chicken begins to char, or the fat is smoking, reduce the temperature by 25 degrees. After about 30 minutes, turn the bird over {drying the bird and preheating the pan should keep the skin from sticking}. Roast for another 10 to 20 minutes, depending on size, then flip back over to recrisp the breast skin, another 5 to 10 minutes. Total oven time will be 45 minutes to an hour.

While the chicken is roasting, place the pine nuts in a small baking dish and set in the hot oven for a minute or two, just to warm through. Add them to the bowl of bread.

Place a spoonful of the olive oil in a small skillet, add the garlic and scallions, and cook over medium-low heat, stirring constantly, until softened. Don't let them color. Scrape into the bread and fold to combine. Drain the plumped currants and fold in. Dribble the chicken stock or lightly salted water over the salad and fold again. Taste a few pieces of bread ~ a fairly saturated one and a dryish one. If it is bland, add salt, pepper, and/or a few drops of vinegar, then toss well. Since the basic character of bread salad depends on the bread you use, these adjustments can be essential.

Pile the bread salad in a 1-quart baking dish and tent with foil; set the salad bowl aside. Place the salad in the oven after you flip the chicken the final time.

Finishing and serving the chicken and bread salad:
Remove the chicken from the oven and turn off the heat. Leave the bread salad to continue warming for another 5 minutes or so.

Lift the chicken from the roasting pan and set on a plate. Carefully pour the clear fat from the roasting pan, leaving the lean drippings behind. Add about a tablespoon of water to the hot pan and swirl it.

Slash the stretched skin between the thighs and breasts of the chicken, then tilt the bird and plate over the roasting pan to drain the juice into the drippings.

\ *continued*

Set the chicken in a warm spot {which may be your stovetop}, and leave to rest while you finish the bread salad. The meat will become more tender and uniformly succulent as it cools.

Set a platter in the oven to warm for a minute or two.

Tilt the roasting pan and skim the last of the fat. Place over medium-low heat, add any juice that has collected under the chicken, and bring to a simmer. Stir and scrape to soften any hard golden drippings. Taste – the juices will be extremely flavorful.

Tip the bread salad into the salad bowl. {It will be steamy-hot, a mixture of soft, moist wads, crispy-on-the-outside-but-moist-in-the-middle wads, and a few downright crispy ones.} Drizzle and toss with a spoonful of the pan juices. Add the greens, a drizzle of vinaigrette, and fold well. Taste again.

Cut the chicken into pieces, spread the bread salad on the warm platter, and nestle the chicken in the salad.

Capitalizing on leftovers: Strain and save the drippings you don't use, they are delicious tossed with spätzle or egg noodles, or stirred into beans or risotto. You also can use them, plus leftover scraps of roast chicken, for the chicken salad which follows.

✣
✣ ✣

ROAST CHICKEN SALAD *with* PEPPERS, PINE NUTS, OLIVES, *&* BITTER GREENS

SINCE RUNNING OUT OF ROAST CHICKEN IS NOT AN OPTION AT ZUNI, WE DO SOMEtimes find ourselves with way too many birds in house and so have explored the options of chicken sandwiches and chicken salads extensively. This is my favorite of the repertory. It is a warm, bright, crunchy alternative to mayonnaise-based chicken salad, an attractive tangle to make for one or two when you have a little leftover roast chicken, or for four to six if you roast a bird expressly. Treat the amounts in this recipe as guidelines; you can alter them to accommodate your supplies and preferences. More important is that each element be tasty on its own and that everything be warm, including the bowl where you combine everything just before serving.

If you are using leftover chicken, wait to pull it off the bones until you are set to make the dish. Once it is "picked," it will start to dry out and absorb other flavors, especially in the refrigerator.

Note: A 2-3/4-pound roast chicken will yield about 1 pound meat, a 3-1/4-pound bird about 1-1/4 pounds.

Wine: Chinon, Charles Joguet Jeunes Vignes, 1999

FOR 4 SERVINGS:

About 8 ounces roast chicken meat {see Zuni Roast Chicken, page 342}, at room temperature or warmer

About 2 tablespoons gelatinous drippings from the roast chicken

A crusty chunk ~ 4 to 8 ounces ~ of chewy, peasant-style bread {or the curved crusts you generated if you made the bread salad}

About 1/2 cup extra-virgin olive oil

1 garlic clove, peeled

2 tablespoons pine nuts

1 small red, yellow, or green bell pepper {about 6 ounces}, cored, seeded, and thinly sliced, at room temperature

3 handfuls ~ about 3 ounces ~ hearty greens, such as arugula, dandelion, chicory, or watercress, at room temperature

12 pitted, oil-cured olives, such as Nyons, or 24 pitted brined black olives, such as Niçoise, Ligurian, or Greek Elitses {about 1/3 cup}

About 1-1/2 tablespoons red wine vinegar

Salt and freshly cracked black pepper

Preheat the oven to 400°.

Tear the roast chicken into bite-sized pieces or smaller and remove any bits of fat and sinew, and skin if you wish, so that each bit is impeccable. Place in a small bowl.

Warm the drippings in a small saucepan. Tilt the pan and skim and discard any fat. Moisten the chicken with the drippings, adding enough to coat all the surfaces well. {This will make the chicken succulent and more flavorful, and prevent it from absorbing the vinegar.} Set in a warm spot.

Carve enough of the crust from the chunk of bread to make an awkward handful of irregular curved croûtons {save the chunk of bread for bread crumbs,

\ *continued*

or to tear into bread wads for Madeleine's Omelette, page 174}. Brush the crusts with olive oil to coat, spread on a sheet pan, and toast until golden on the edges, about 6 minutes. Cool slightly, then rub the hot crusts with the garlic ~ be as thorough as you as you are fond of garlic.

Set the pine nuts and olives in a small dish and place in the turned-off oven to warm for a few minutes, then remove.

Whisk together the remaining oil, the vinegar, salt, and pepper to taste, to make about 1/2 cup vinaigrette.

Set the salad bowl and four plates in the oven for a minute or two to warm through.

Place the peppers and greens in the warm bowl and toss with vinaigrette to coat liberally. Add the warm chicken, pine nuts, and olives and toss well, coating every surface. Break the croûtons into bite-sized pieces directly over the bowl so the garlicky crumbs fall into the salad. Drizzle a little more of the vinaigrette over the crusts and toss the whole salad again. Taste and add more vinaigrette {or vinegar, or oil, and salt or pepper}. Serve promptly on the warm plates.

+
+ +

CHICKEN BOUILLABAISSE

THIS IS AN EASY, CROWD-PLEASING DISH I OWE TO MADELEINE SERRAILLE, SISTER of the famous frères Troisgros. It is one of the distracting dishes her brother Jean would sniff and sample when he happened by her house on his way back to the restaurant to cook salmon in sorrel sauce and steak *à la moelle.* Madeleine claimed it was from Ali-Bab's *Gastronomie Pratique,* an idiosyncratic eleven-pound treasury of French cooking that she insisted I buy and study the summer before I went to college.

Aïoli gives this dish richness along with a jolt of garlic; a lighter alternative is to rub the hot toasted bread with raw garlic.

Wine: Pellegrini Alexander Valley Carignane, Old Vines, 1999

FOR 4 SERVINGS:

4 chicken legs {about 8 ounces each} or one 3-pound chicken, back removed and quartered

8 ounces sliced yellow onion {2 cups, about 1 medium onion}

1/4 cup extra-virgin olive oil

Salt

1 bay leaf

A sprig of fresh thyme

1 small dried chili

1/4 cup dry white wine

1/4 cup coarsely chopped drained canned tomatoes or 1/3 cup chopped, peeled, ripe tomatoes

Pinch of saffron threads

2 garlic cloves, coarsely chopped

2 cups Chicken Stock {page 58}

4 small slices chewy peasant-style bread, about 1/2 inch thick

About 1/2 cup Aïoli {page 289} {optional} or 1 garlic clove, peeled

Seasoning the chicken {for the best flavor and succulence, do this step 12 to 24 hours in advance}:

Trim the excess fat, then season the chicken evenly all over with salt {we use 3/4 teaspoon sea salt per pound of chicken}. Cover loosely and refrigerate.

Combine the onions with the oil and a few pinches of salt in a 4-quart saucepan and place over medium heat. Cook, stirring frequently so they do not color, until the onions are nutty-tender and translucent and have fallen to half their former mass, about 5 minutes.

Add the bay leaf, thyme, and chili, breaking the pod in half if you want the bouillabaisse to be a little spicier. Add the white wine and boil for 1 minute. Add the tomatoes, saffron, garlic, and chicken stock and bring to a simmer.

Add the 4 or 2 chicken legs and bring back to a simmer. Skim any foam. Adjust the heat to maintain a quiet simmer and cook uncovered for about 1 hour, stirring once or twice. If using a cut-up chicken, add the breasts after about 30 minutes of cooking time. The chicken should be quite tender, but not falling off the bone.

Meanwhile, grill or toast the bread. Spread each warm slice with about 1 tablespoon of Aïoli, if using, and place in a warm bowl.

Lightly skim the surface of the bouillabaisse, then raise the heat and boil vigorously for 1 minute. Place a piece of chicken on each toast and moisten with the golden, oniony broth. Offer the remaining aïoli as a garnish.

CHICKEN BRAISED *with* FIGS, HONEY, *&* VINEGAR

LEARNING TO IDENTIFY GOOD FIGS IS AN ANNUAL RITUAL AT ZUNI. As each year's fig crop appears, I always ask the new cooks if they have eaten many before. Often, particularly from those new to California, the answer is, "Not really," and I envy them the pleasure of what lies ahead.

"Look at them. Feel them. Plump can be good, but not unless they are really heavy for their size and they need to be tender."

A tentative squeeze.

"Taste it. How is it? And that cracked one. It's kind of light, but check anyway. How about that one, it looks flawless, and it's heavy, but it is kind of hard. Taste it."

After a wary nibble, "It's not that great."

"Now look at that one. Shrunken and wrinkled is actually good, as long as it is heavy. 'Pristine' isn't usually a good sign. If you look for pretty, you may miss the best ones. Just keep tasting until you can tell. And then try to remember how 'that look' and 'that feel' taste."

This last applies to all produce, all meat, all fish, all cooking.

We use a lot of figs at Zuni, in every course. This dish is Greek in inspiration, and it is a crowd pleaser. We use fleshy Kadota figs, syrupy and with a blush of pink in the center when ripe, though you can use Smyrnas {re-christened "Calmyrna" or "Calimyrna" when grown in California}, Excel, Adriatic, or plump-ripe Black Mission figs as well. Use wildflower or chestnut honey. The flavor of lavender honey is too persuasive.

We sometimes serve this dish with a salad of raw fennel ribbons and frisée or arugula, with wedges of fried pizza dough to sop up the sauce. Grilled bread is a fine and practical alternative.

Wine: Boutari Nemea, 1999

FOR 4 SERVINGS:

4 chicken legs {8 to 9 ounces each}
Salt
About 2 tablespoons mild-tasting olive
    oil
1 medium yellow onion {about 8
    ounces}, root end trimmed flat,
    peeled, and cut into 8 wedges
About 1/2 cup dry white wine
About 2 tablespoons dry white
    vermouth

About 1/2 cup Chicken Stock {page 58}
1 bay leaf
A sprig of fresh thyme
A few black peppercorns, barely
    cracked in a mortar
About 2 tablespoons cider vinegar
About 1 tablespoon honey
8 to 10 ripe fresh figs ~ Kadota,
    Smyrna, Excel, Adriatic, or Black
    Mission

Seasoning the chicken {for the best flavor and succulence, do this step 12 to 24 hours in advance}:

Trim the excess fat, then season the chicken evenly all over with salt {we use a scant 3/4 teaspoon sea salt per pound of chicken}. Cover loosely and refrigerate.

Cooking the chicken:

Preheat the oven to 375°.

Pat the chicken legs dry; this will make them less likely to stick. Heat a scant 2 tablespoons olive oil in a 12-inch skillet over medium-low heat, then add the chicken legs, skin side down. The oil should sizzle, not pop explosively, when you add chicken. Adjusting the heat as necessary, cook until the skin is evenly golden, about 8 minutes. Turn the legs over and color only slightly on the other side, about 4 minutes. Pour off the fat.

If your skillet is ovenproof, arrange the onion wedges in the spaces between the chicken legs; otherwise, transfer the chicken to a shallow flameproof braising dish that will easily hold the chicken and onions in a single layer, and add the onions. Add the wine, the vermouth, and enough stock to come to a depth of about 1/2 inch. Bring to a simmer and add the bay leaf, thyme, and cracked black peppercorns.

Place, uncovered, in the oven, and cook until the meat is tender but not quite falling off the bone, about 40 minutes. The exposed skin will have turned golden and crispy; the liquid ought to have reduced by about half. Remove from the oven and set on a slight tilt so the fat will collect at one side of the pan.

\ *continued*

Combine the vinegar and honey and warm slightly. Taste. The vinegar should dominate, but without making you squint. Trim the stems and cut the figs in half.

Skim as much fat as possible from the braising liquid, then set the pan over medium heat. Bring to a boil and swirl as you reduce the liquid to a syrupy consistency. Distribute the figs evenly around the pan, add about 2 tablespoons of the vinegar-honey syrup, and swirl the pan to diffuse the bubbling, amber syrup without smashing the tender fruit. The sauce will be glossy. Taste~it should be rich and vibrantly sour-sweet. Add more, or all of the syrup, to taste. The vinegar adds a bright but unstable note of acidity, which will fade with boiling, so simmer for only a minute or less.

Serve each chicken leg with 2 wedges of sweet, soft onion and 4 or 5 fig halves, bathed in a few spoonfuls of the sauce.

✢
✣ ✣

DUCK BRAISED *with* RED WINE *&* PRUNES

A RICH OLD FRENCH DISH. If you use the orange zest or the clove, it will have a dramatic impact on the flavor and character of the dish, making it sneakily festive. I like it both ways.

Muscovy, or *Barbarie* {Barbary}, duck has firm, almost beefy, dark red flesh that supports long cooking and generous old-fashioned flavors. Very good with roasted polenta {page 192}.

Wine: Cahors, Château du Cayrou, 1996

FOR 4 SERVINGS:

4 Muscovy duck legs {10 to 12 ounces each}{see Sources and Resources, page 518}

Salt

4 cups medium-bodied or hearty red wine, such as Sangiovese, Merlot, Syrah, or Cabernet Sauvignon

2 cups Duck Stock or other bird stock {page 67} or Chicken Stock {page 58}

2 medium yellow onions {about 8 ounces each}, root end trimmed flat, peeled, and cut into 1-1/2-inch wedges

2 ounces garlic cloves {about 1/2 cup}, unpeeled

1 bay leaf

2 wide strips of orange zest about 1-1/2 inches long, removed with a vegetable peeler, and/or 1 whole clove {optional}

12 prunes, preferably with pits

Trimming and seasoning the duck legs {for the best flavor and succulence, do this step 1 to 3 days in advance}:

Trim lumps of fat, ragged edges or meatless flaps of skin {it's worth saving and rendering these [see page 432]; even a few scraps can be enough to flavor a soup}. Rinse the duck legs, lay between dry towels, and press to absorb surface moisture. Season evenly all over with salt {we use a scant 3/4 teaspoon sea salt per pound of duck}. Cover loosely and refrigerate.

Cooking the duck:

Preheat the oven to 300°.

Reduce the red wine and the stock separately to about 1 cup each. The stock should have body and will be slightly salty. Set aside.

Press the duck between towels to wick off excess moisture. Place a dry 10- or 12-inch skillet over medium heat. When the pan is hot enough that the duck hisses on contact, add the legs, skin side down, and leave to set a golden crust, about 10 minutes. The duck will begin to render fat within a few minutes; reduce the heat if the fat starts to smoke. Turn the legs over and brown for just a few minutes on the flesh side, then arrange skin side up in an ovenproof 3-quart sauté pan. Pour off the rendered fat from the skillet; if any appetizing golden bits

\ *continued*

remain in the skillet, add the reduced red wine to the pan and simmer briefly, stirring, to dissolve them. Set aside.

Nestle the onion wedges in between the duck legs. Add the garlic, bay leaf, and optional orange zest and/or clove. Add enough of the reduced wine and stock, in about equal doses, to come to a depth of 1/2 inch; save any extra wine and stock for extending the sauce. Swirl the pan as you bring to a simmer over medium heat, then cover tightly, place in the oven, and cook for about 1 hour.

Turn the duck legs over and add the unpitted prunes, making sure they are submerged in the braising liquid; work quickly, so you don't lose too much heat. {If you are using pitted prunes, add them after 30 minutes more.} Cover the pan tightly and return to the oven.

After another hour {or about 40 minutes if the duck legs are on the small end of the range listed}, turn the legs over, turn the heat up to 375°, and return the pan to the oven uncovered. When the legs feel just tender and are slightly browned, usually within another 20 minutes, remove the pan from the oven. Turn off the oven and place a serving platter to warm in the oven for a minute or two. Leave the duck legs to rest for about 5 minutes, then carefully lift from the sauce to the warm serving platter.

Skim the abundant fat from the surface of the braising liquid, and taste the liquid. If it seems thin in flavor or texture, set the pan over medium heat and, skimming attentively, reduce to the texture of warm maple syrup. If the sauce tastes too rich, dilute it with a trickle of water. If you seem shy on sauce and you have extra wine and reduced stock, add a little of each, then simmer to bring the sauce to a slightly syrupy consistency.

Serve each duck leg with 3 prunes and a few silky onion wedges and slippery garlic cloves. There should be a few tablespoons of sauce for each leg.

✦
✦ ✦

ROASTED GUINEA HEN *with* BAY LEAVES, MADEIRA, *&* DATES

GUINEA HEN IS A FLAVORFUL BUT UNDERAPPRECIATED GAME BIRD. Roasted whole, as it often is, it tends to cook unevenly and can be tough, which discourages further experiments with this premium product. But if you handle the breasts and legs separately, and roast them hot and fast, you can get great results. It becomes an elegant, lean alternative to chicken and duck. This recipe was inspired by the stunning guinea hen with Vin Santo that my Tuscan colleague and friend Carlo Cioni made at Zuni when he graced our kitchen in 1999. He taught us to perfume the bird with a fistful of buoyant aromatics and to sauce it stingily. Salting the meat in advance enhances succulence, and I especially recommend it for guinea hen dishes.

You can serve 4 with one guinea hen, or consider buying two birds and using the four legs and wings for this dish, and the breasts for Guinea Hen Breast Saltimbocca, which follows.

This is a winter dish, and the aromatics make it festive and friendly to big red wines. Allspice berries can replace the cloves if you prefer that flavor. Substitute dry Marsala or Vin Santo for the Madeira, if either is more convenient. You can also make this dish with whole quail {count 2 per person}, although instead of browning them first, simply rub them with a little of the Madeira before you set them to roast. Finish them under the broiler if they haven't turned golden. They will take only about 10 minutes. {See Roasted or Grilled Quail, page 359.}

Serve with wild rice; soft, grilled, or roasted polenta {page 190}; or, for a lighter meal, with a wad of watercress, with or without a splash of sherry vinaigrette.

Wine. Qupé Central Coast Syrah, 1999

\ *continued*

One 3-1/4- to 3-1/2-pound guinea hen (see Sources and Resources, page 518)

Salt

About 3/4 cup Guinea Hen Stock (page 67) or Chicken Stock (page 58)

1 tablespoon mild-tasting olive oil

6 bay leaves

2 whole cloves or allspice berries

2 matchstick-sized pieces cinnamon stick

1/2 cup Madeira

A wide strip of orange zest, about 1-1/2 inches long, removed with a vegetable peeler

8 small dates, pitted and halved

Cutting up and seasoning the guinea hen {for the best flavor, do this step 12 to 24 hours in advance}:

Make a long incision in the skin between each leg and the breast meat, then tug the leg away from the carcass. Fold it all the way back to pop the ball joint, then fold even farther and use the tip of your knife to carve out the lentil-shaped muscle known as the "pope's nose." Then tug at the leg as you cut through the remaining muscle and skin.

To extricate the meaty wings, tug the wing straight out and make a circular cut around the shoulder joint. Twist the wing, straining that joint, to reveal the stubborn connective tissue. Sever with the tip of your knife. Continue to twist and fold the wing back, cutting through remaining muscle, sinew, and skin.

To remove the breast meat, first make a deep clean cut with the knife flat against each side of the sternum. Next, tugging the breast away from the collarbone, use the tip of your knife to make a shallow cut along each arc of collarbone {the wishbone}. Pulling the breast away from the sternum, make a series of little cuts flat against the sternum and under the wishbone to progressively free the breast as you go. Repeat with the other breast.

Season the 6 pieces of guinea hen evenly all over with salt {we use a scant 3/4 teaspoon sea salt per pound of meat}. Fold the wing tips back behind the shoulders to secure them in twisted triangles. Cover loosely and refrigerate.

If desired, make the carcass and scraps into Guinea Hen Stock. Reduce about 3/4 cup of it, or of the chicken stock, to about 1/3 to 1/2 cup.

Roasting the guinea hen and making the sauce:

Preheat the oven to 500°.

Pat the pieces of guinea hen dry. Warm the olive oil in an ovenproof 12-inch skillet over medium heat. When the oil is hot enough to sizzle boldly on contact, arrange the pieces of meat skin side down in a single layer. Reduce the heat only if the oil threatens to smoke. Leave to set a golden crust, about 5 minutes; turn off the heat. Turn over the legs and wing pieces. Remove the breasts and set aside. Pour off all but a film of fat, then tuck the bay leaves, cloves or allspice berries, and cinnamon under the legs. Set the pan in the lower half of your oven and roast for about 15 minutes. Add the breast pieces, skin side up, and roast until just cooked through, another 8 to 10 minutes.

Remove the pan from the oven and pour off the few drops of fat. Add the Madeira and orange zest and set over medium heat. Swirl the pan and use a wooden spoon to scrape the sides and rub the pan with the orange zest. When the Madeira has boiled hard for about 5 seconds, add the reduced stock and the dates and continue swirling the pan and stirring the sauce. Taste every few seconds, and pull from the heat when the sauce has a little body and concentrated flavor. Bear in mind that the big pan will continue cooking and reducing the little sauce until it is served, so be prepared to work quickly. If the sauce does get too strong or thick, add a few drops of water to correct.

Distribute the meat among the plates and spoon the sauce over. {Don't pour directly from the pan ~ the hot lip of the pan will boil the sauce along the way, further reducing it and producing splatters that will land on the plates.}

‧
‧ ‧

GUINEA HEN BREAST SALTIMBOCCA

BASED ON THE WELL-KNOWN VEAL DISH THAT PROMISES TO JUMP INTO YOUR MOUTH. Guinea hen has enough character to welcome salty-sweet prosciutto and pungent sage in this variation on the Roman classic. We substitute extra-virgin olive oil for the usual butter; it adds spiciness to a chord of rich flavors.

Serve with wilted spinach or asparagus. and roasted potatoes.

Wine: Savigny-les-Beaune Premier Cru Les Vergelesses, Simon Bize, 1999

\ *continued*

FOR 4 SERVINGS:

4 boneless guinea hen breasts {see
    page 356} {about 5 ounces each}
Salt
About 1-1/4 cups Guinea Hen Stock
    {page 67} or Chicken Stock {page
    58}

4 thin slices prosciutto with a ribbon
    of fat around the edges
12 small fresh sage leaves
3 to 4 tablespoons extra-virgin olive oil
1 lemon
Freshly cracked black pepper

Trimming and seasoning the breasts {for the best flavor and succulence, do this
step a few hours in advance}:

Peel the skin from the guinea hen breasts and discard it. Turn the breasts with
the skinned side down. Trim any ragged edges and gently pound the thickest section of the meat. If it resists, you may need to make a few shallow parallel incisions, with the grain, at the thickest spot and then try again. The goal is to
produce a 1/2- to 3/4-inch-thick cutlet. Salt the breasts very lightly on the skinned
side and more liberally on the other side. Cover loosely and refrigerate.

Reduce the guinea hen stock or chicken stock to about 3/4 cup.

Position a slice of prosciutto neatly on the lightly salted side of each breast,
then decorate with 3 sage leaves. Pin each leaf, through the prosciutto, to the
breast with a toothpick: hold the toothpick flat against the breast and poke it on a
shallow angle into the meat; if you stab all the way through, you'll have a curvy
saltimbocca that won't sit flat in the pan and won't cook evenly.

Warm about 2 tablespoons of the oil in a 12-inch skillet over medium heat.
Lay the saltimbocca prosciutto side down in the oil. You should hear a friendly
sizzle~if it starts to crackle, reduce the heat. Cook for about 1 minute, then turn

✦ ✦ ✦ ✦ ✦

✦ ✦ ✦ ✦ ✦

over. The ham should be mottled with bronze. Brown the other side for 1 minute, then reduce the heat and cook through, another 2 to 3 minutes per side.

Remove the pan from the heat and place the saltimboccas on warm plates. Pour off a little of the oil from the pan. Slide out the toothpicks and steal 1 sage leaf from each saltimbocca. Add the stolen leaves to the skillet. Use a zester to carve about a teaspoon of thin strips of lemon zest directly into the pan. Add a long squeeze of lemon juice. Set over low heat and add the reduced stock. Stir and scrape to encourage any caramelized juices to dissolve in the sauce. Simmer just until the sauce has a little body. Taste. Finish with a long trickle of extra-virgin olive oil.

Spoon the sauce over the breasts. Offer black pepper.

✣
✣ ✣

Roasted or Grilled Quail, & Marinated Grilled Quail

QUAIL IS A VERSATILE BIRD WHOSE LEAN FLESH AND SMALL SIZE MEAN IT BOTH cooks quickly and welcomes pretty salsas or the richest side dishes, such as Braised Peas {page 251} or Creamed Corn {page 253}. I like it with a dollop of Porcini *Pearà* Sauce {page 311} or *Pappa al Pomodoro* {page 164}. We always salt the little birds in advance, which makes them a little more succulent; if you add herbs, the salt will drag those flavors into the bird as well.

Quail is finger food ~ once you get past the plump breast meat, utensils become obstacles between you and the tasty bits of meat. I don't bother with "boneless" quail; it is only mostly that, and unless you prop it up with stuffing, it makes a floppy roast. That poses less of a problem when you butterfly them for grilling, but I still cling to the delicious ritual of picking at the bony birds. Grilled quail marinated for a few hours, or days, in Salmorigano or Chimichurri makes a great hors d'œuvre.

Wine: St. Francis Sonoma Valley Merlot Reserve, 1997

\ *continued*

PER SERVING:

2 whole quail {about 6 ounces each} or 2 dressed quail {about 4 ounces each}

Salt

Freshly cracked black pepper {optional}

A sprig or two of fresh rosemary, sage, thyme, or marjoram {optional}

2 teaspoons mild-tasting olive oil or unsalted butter, softened

A trickle of brandy {optional}

Seasoning the quail {for the best flavor and succulence, do this step 12 to 24 hours in advance}:

If using whole quail, first cut off the feet at the knee joint and the head at the base of the neck. {You can double-wrap and freeze these meager trimmings for a future bird stock.} Season the quail lightly all over with salt, and pepper, if using. If using herbs, strip the leaves from the sprigs, then lightly pound and bruise them in a mortar to release their flavor. Sprinkle over the quail and massage lightly. Cover loosely and refrigerate.

Cooking the quail:

Turn on the broiler and position the rack so the quail will be about 3 to 4 inches from the element.

Wipe the quail dry. Pick off any bits of herb {so they don't burn}, then use your fingers to rub with oil or butter. To enhance browning, rub with the optional brandy.

Place the quail breast side up on a shallow-rimmed heavy baking sheet. The quail need to be a few inches apart so they will brown evenly; since they won't throw off much juice, there is no concern with its burning in the wide pan. A wide ceramic gratin dish is also a workable choice, though you should preheat it thoroughly.

Slide the pan under the broiler. Turn the quail over after the breasts have browned, 5 to 6 minutes. Leave for a few minutes to brown the back, then turn back over for a minute or two before removing from the oven. The breasts should be firm, like a ripe peach; the inside should be opaque and beige with a tinge of pink. The few minutes it will take you to serve the quail and for diners to assess how to attack them will give the meat a chance to rest.

◦ ◦ **To Butterfly & Grill Quail:**

Dress the quail and season as described above, but, before seasoning, remove {and discard} the backbone, then spread each quail open and use your fingers to crack the sternum where it meets the collarbone. Give each butterflied bird a restrained whack with a meat pounder to flatten it further.

Prepare a fire and let it burn to glowing coals. Spread out the coals; position the grill about 4 inches above them and preheat it.

Wipe the quail dry, brush lightly with the oil or butter {which you can set in a dish on the grill to melt first}, and place skin side down on the grill. Grill for 4 to 6 minutes per side. {Alternatively, you can use the same specifications to pan-fry quail over medium heat. In this situation, I like to use cast iron.}

To Marinate Grilled Butterflied Quail:

These are good with beans, roasted potatoes, polenta, or grilled bread rubbed with garlic. Crowd the warm quail, more or less flat, in a gratin dish. Warm up enough Salmoriglio {page 299} or Chimichurri {page 298} to bathe the quail liberally. Stir, then pour the sauce over the warm birds. Turn the quail over in the sauce after 30 minutes. Serve at room temperature, or rewarm briefly in a 300° oven. If you don't intend to serve the quail within an hour or two, cover tightly and refrigerate.

To rewarm refrigerated marinated quail, preheat the oven to 275°. Cover the quail loosely and heat until warm through, about 25 minutes.

✧
✧ ✧

QUAIL & SAUSAGE BRAISED *with* GRAPES

A FALL DISH, TRADITIONALLY MADE WITH WINE GRAPES ~ AND WITHOUT QUAIL ~ in Umbria. This is a tame interpretation of that dish, *salsiccia all'uva* {sausage with grapes}, which is intensely flavored and crunchy with grape seeds. For our version, we use mostly seedless grapes, Black Emerald or Red Flame, in combination with a few seedy ones ~ wine grapes when we can get them. Choose varieties that are not too sweet, or the result will be cloying. Small grapes with lots of skin in proportion to flesh cook down quickly and produce the best flavor and texture. I don't recommend cooking this dish in advance; the grape sauce quickly loses its bright flavor and the quail and sausages risk drying out. And it's so quick and easy, there is no need to.

\ *continued*

Serve with polenta ~ soft, grilled, or roasted {page 190} ~ or grilled bread, and a salad of bitter greens mixed with thinly sliced raw fennel.

Wine: Rosso di Montalcino, La Gerla, 1998

FOR 4 SERVINGS:

4 whole quail {about 6 ounces each} or 4 dressed quail {about 4 ounces each}

Salt

About 6 tablespoons extra-virgin olive oil

A few pinches of fennel seeds, barely crushed

About 2 pounds stemmed, small, red or black grapes {5 to 6 cups}, at least two-thirds of which are seedless varieties

Balsamic or red wine vinegar, as needed

4 fresh sausages {3 to 4 ounces each}, preferably fennel sausage {to make your own, see Pork Sausage, page 424}

Seasoning the quail {for the best flavor, do this step 12 to 24 hours in advance}:

If using whole quail, first cut off the feet at the knee joint and the head at the base of the neck. {You can double-wrap and freeze these meager trimmings for a future bird stock.} Season the quail evenly all over with salt, cover loosely, and refrigerate.

Cooking the quail:

Warm about 1/4 cup of the olive oil with the fennel seeds in a 3-quart sauté pan over medium heat. Add the grapes. Stir regularly as the grapes sizzle and release their fruity aroma, until the skins begin to split and the grapes yield their juice. Cook uncovered, stirring occasionally until the grape sauce has a little body, 20 to 30 minutes. You should have about 2 cups. Taste. If the grapes are quite sweet, add a pinch of salt and/or a dribble of vinegar.

Warm about 2 tablespoons olive oil in a 12-inch skillet over medium heat. Wipe the quail and sausages dry, then place in the pan. They should sizzle on contact. Brown the quail and sausages evenly, 3 to 4 minutes on each side. Reduce the heat, tilt the pan, trapping the quail and sausages behind tongs or a strainer, and pour off the excess fat. Add the grapes. They will seethe regally as they bubble up around the quail and sausages ~ a moment to look forward to when making this dish. Cover and cook over medium-low heat until firm, like a ripe peach, another 12 minutes or so, turning the quail and sausages a few times to ensure even cooking. Uncover and simmer to reduce the sauce to a rich, jammy consistency. Taste and correct with salt or vinegar.

Serve immediately.

✛
✛ ✛

ROASTED SQUAB

T HE "RED MEAT" BIRD, SQUAB {YOUNG PIGEON} IS A QUICK, CONVENIENT single-portion roast. It requires nothing more than a little salt and about fifteen minutes in a very hot oven. Roasted whole and hot, the skin sets to a delicious, caramel crispiness. We don't bother to truss squab~I prefer to leave as much skin as possible exposed, to render its fat and crisp it. I like to eat squab rosy; it can taste livery if cooked beyond medium-rare. {For a general discussion of roasting, see page 391.}

Many of the vegetable dishes in this book are good with squab: Hashed Sweet Potatoes {page 239}, *Fagioli all'Uccelletto* {page 265}, and Rosemary-Roasted Potatoes {page 235} are some of my favorites. I also like squab with Brandied Fruit {page 279}, warm Spiced Prunes {page 278}, or with roasted fresh fruit~figs, cherries, sprigs of Zante grapes, or ripe apricot halves {whose cut face we dredge in sugar before roasting}. When we serve squab with fruit, we nest it in a room-temperature salad of frisée, arugula, or watercress, with a few ribbons of raw fennel tossed in. Squab is gorgeous next to a Savory Apple Charlotte {page 260}.

Wine: Château Langoa-Barton, Saint-Julien, 1996

PER SERVING:

1 squab {about 1 pound whole, or 3/4 pound dressed}
Salt

A few tablespoons Squab Stock {page 67}, a scant 1/2 cup "squab tea" {see below}, or a generous splash of Chicken Stock {page 58}, dry white wine, or balsamic vinegar

Seasoning the squab {for the best flavor and succulence, do this step 12 to 24 hours in advance}:

If using whole squab, cut off the feet, head and neck, and the last two wing joints. {Use these parts to make Squab Stock, or simply roast until golden at 475°,

\ *continued*

then place in a small saucepan, add water to cover, and simmer for about 30 minutes to make a quick half-cup or so of "squab tea".} Rinse and dry the squab inside and out. Sprinkle evenly all over with salt. Cover loosely and refrigerate.

Cooking the squab:

Preheat the oven to 500°.

Wipe the squab dry and set it in a shallow baking pan. A flameproof gratin dish is a workable choice, though you should preheat it thoroughly. If cooking more than one squab, make sure they are several inches apart, so they brown evenly.

Place the pan of squab in the center of the oven. In most ovens, it should begin browning within 7 minutes ~ if it hasn't, turn on your broiler for a few minutes to coax it to color, then turn the heat back to 500°. Roast for about 12 minutes for rosy meat, a few minutes longer for medium. In either case, let the squab rest in the roasting pan for about 5 minutes after removing it from the oven.

A minute or two before serving, remove the birds, and do one of the following to stretch the usually meager drippings in the roasting pan:

⁃ Add the squab stock or "squab tea" to the roasting pan and simmer until it has a little body.

⁃ Add the chicken stock, dry white wine, or balsamic vinegar and stir and scrape to tease the few drops of drippings into a spoonful or so.

To serve, cut each squab in half and remove the backbone. Arrange on plates and dribble with sauce. We don't usually carve the bird ~ figuring a pretty display would require leaving juice, fragrance, and some delicious nibbles of skin in the kitchen in quest of refinement. Fingers are the best tools for full enjoyment of squab.

⁃ ⁃ **GRILLED SQUAB**

Before seasoning, remove and discard the backbone, then flatten ~ butterfly ~ the bird, making sure to completely crack the sternum so it will not revert to its original shape on the grill.

Prepare a fire and let it burn down to glowing coals. Place the grill grate about 4 inches over the coals. Don't oil the squab; simply place it skin side down on the grill. Grill for about 5 minutes, moving the birds if dripping fat starts to flare up. Grill the other side another 5 minutes or so, then return to the skin side to cook another 2 minutes for a rosy result. The breast should feel firm but not hard. Let the squab rest for about 5 minutes before serving.

⁃
⁃ ⁃

BEEF, LAMB, PORK, & RABBIT

THE ZUNI HAMBURGER

THREE-STAR CHEF JEAN TROISGROS COULD NOT HAVE KNOWN WHAT HE WAS seeding when, in 1973, in the most revered kitchen in France, he grandly announced he was planning a special dish for the Sunday family meal in the bar of Les Frères Troisgros. He prepared fourteen generous *«ahm-bour-gaires poêlés»* and explained his selection with an incredulous, *«Et pourquoi pas?» Cuisiné* with care, his hamburger was worthy of his signature *filet au poivre* or benchmark *entrecôte à la moelle.* The Troisgros brothers' rogue attitudes about what is okay to cook in a "serious restaurant" still color my every culinary decision.

The Zuni hamburger is made with fresh chuck and sea salt. Look for firm, bright red meat with hard, bright white fat. Pale, flaccid, wet meat produces a listless result. It cooks up dryer than its fresh counterpart, and tastes old within hours of grinding. For this reason, we avoid meat that has been vacuum-packed {"Cryovac'd"}. Although the process does prolong shelf life, it doesn't enhance flavor or texture. The vacuum process weakens the cell walls, which is why the meat weeps progressively more and more water and blood into its package. The meat smells unpleasant when you unwrap it, and although rinsing helps, the odd scent doesn't always go entirely away. For largely the same reasons, we avoid meat that has been frozen.

Where fat is concerned, don't trim it all off. We aim for 18 percent fat overall ~ which sounds hard to judge, but if you think of it as barely one-fifth of your prepared product, it's possible to get close enough by eye. You can moderate this, at the cost of some flavor and juiciness. {Bear in mind that commercial ground chuck is 20 to 25 percent fat; 18 percent is within the margins for ground sirloin.}

But what finally makes the Zuni hamburger particularly succulent and delicious is seasoning the meat with salt a day before grinding it. Aside from guaranteeing that it is evenly and properly seasoned, this brief curing makes the meat retain moisture better and enhances the texture. We use 1 tablespoon sea salt per 5 pounds of meat. You can use more or less salt, to your taste. It is important to keep the meat cold during all phases of handling.

The Zuni hamburger arrives on a rosemary-flecked focaccia bun with a few leaves of oak-leaf lettuce, a smear of Aïoli {page 299}, and our Zucchini and Red Onion Pickles {pages 269 and 270}.

Wine: Joseph Phelps California Le Mistral, 1998

FOR 4 SERVINGS:

1-1/2 pounds boneless beef chuck, trimmed of discoloration but with some fat intact

1 scant teaspoon salt {a little more if using kosher salt}

Seasoning the meat {18 to 24 hours in advance}:

Cut the meat into 1-inch strips or chunks and toss with the salt. Cover loosely and refrigerate.

Assemble your meat grinder with a 3/16-inch blade and sharp knife. Refrigerate to chill thoroughly. A warm grinder can warm the meat, melt the fat, and produce more of a "smash" than a clean, crumbly grind. The result will have inferior flavor and texture and then degenerate rapidly. {For more on grinding meat, see A Lesson in Sausage Making, page 420.}

Grind the meat two times, paying special attention on the first pass to make sure that the meat is emerging cleanly and evenly. If it is not, turn off the grinder immediately. Remove and clean the blade and knife: an errant sinew wrapped around a cutting edge is usually responsible for a mushy grind. Reinstall and finish grinding the meat.

As an alternative to grinding the meat, you can finely chop it, by hand or by the fistful in a food processor with a very sharp blade. The patties will be a little more fragile and the texture of the cooked meat more crumbly, but neither of these is necessarily a defect. The flavor and succulence will not suffer.

Form 6-ounce patties by hand, first forming balls, then flattening them to 3/4-inch thickness. Press the patties a bit thinner in the middle; the meat shrinks as it cooks and the patties will emerge an even thickness only if they start out skinny in the middle. If the edges crack, smash them back together. In all events, work quickly and don't overhandle or warm the meat.

Cook the hamburgers immediately, or refrigerate loosely covered until needed. The hamburgers will taste best if cooked within 12 hours.

To grill the hamburgers: At Zuni, we grill hamburgers over mesquite charcoal. The grill sits about 3 inches from the just-graying coals. We flip the patties three times to ensure even cooking and to make sure they don't char. A cold 6-ounce

\ *continued*

patty will take about 9 minutes to cook to a rosy medium-rare, but allow another 2 to 3 minutes away from the direct heat for this thick hamburger to rest, as you would a roast. Short of that, it will be a bit overdone on the edges and perhaps too rare in the center.

To cook the hamburgers on the stovetop: Choose a pan not much larger than will accommodate the patties, and make it cast-iron if you have one the right size. This will encourage a nice crust. Preheat the pan until the meat sizzles on contact. Start over medium heat, and flip the patties after about 3 minutes. They should have set a tender golden-brown crust. Cook another 3 minutes to make a crust on the other side. Reduce the heat to cook through without toughening the crust, flipping each patty twice more to guarantee even doneness. For rosy medium-rare, allow about 10 minutes total cooking time, plus 2 to 3 minutes' resting time away from direct heat.

To broil the hamburgers: Make sure to fully preheat the broiler and broiler pan. Also, make sure the patties are widely spaced, so they don't steam one another. Failing either of these, the patties will not look very appetizing and the surface will taste insipid. Start by browning both sides of the patties close to the heat, about 3 minutes per side. Then lower the broiler rack a few inches and finish cooking, flipping each patty twice more. For a rosy medium-rare, allow about 9 minutes' total cooking time, then turn off the broiler, leave the door slightly ajar, and let the hamburgers rest for a few minutes before serving.

⁂

SKIRT STEAK & HANGER STEAK

BOTH THESE CUTS ARE HARDWORKING ABDOMINAL MUSCLES AND ARE VERY flavorful. Ask for the "outside" skirt ~ it will be plumper than the "inside" cut. The "hanging tender" steak is a single convoluted muscle, among the select cuts that butchers everywhere used to try to keep for themselves. It has a rich flavor that more than makes up for its awkward shape. The French call it *onglet* and accord it an honored role in the traditional repertoire; specifically, sizzled in butter and finished with lots of minced shallot, coarsely chopped parsley, a stingy splash of white wine, and then more unsalted butter.

Both cuts are flavorful unadorned but also stand up to sauces like Porcini *Pearà* {page 311}, Chimichurri {page 298}, Salmorigano {page 299}, Salsa Verde {page 292}, or Toasted Bread Crumb Salsa {page 297}, in which case we serve them with grilled vegetables. Or serve with a rich Onion *Panade* {page 227}, Buttermilk Mashed Potatoes {page 233}, Hashed Sweet Potatoes {page 239}, Braised Fennel {page 255}, Long-Cooked Romano Beans {page 250}, Lentils in Red Wine {page 267}, or *Fagioli all'Ucelletto* {page 265}.

Hanger steak and skirt steak both make great sandwiches. My favorite marries them with salsa and white bean purée. Either cut makes delicious pasta sauce {see Pasta with Giblet-Mushroom Sauce, page 214}.

Wine: Chimney Rock Stags Leap District Reserve Cabernet Sauvignon, 1998

PER SERVING:

5 to 6 ounces skirt steak or hanger
    steak
Salt

Mild-tasting olive oil, to coat, or as
    needed

Trimming and seasoning the meat {for the best flavor, do this step in advance, about 4 hours for skinny skirt steak, up to a day ahead for stumpy hanger steak}:

Trim any fat or discoloration from the meat, then press lightly between dry towels to wick away surface moisture. Season evenly all over with salt {we use a scant 3/4 teaspoon sea salt per pound}. Cover loosely and refrigerate.

Just before cooking, press the meat dry between towels and rub with olive oil. Sear over high heat ~ on a preheated grill, or in a hot skillet with a few additional drops of oil. Sear each side of the meat until splotched with a little color, a minute or so per side, then move to slightly lower heat, or reduce the burner heat, to cook to the desired doneness. Skinny skirt steak will take only minutes more at most; a thick hanger steak may take 8 more minutes to cook to medium-rare. But these times are hugely affected by the cooking medium, size of cut, how cold it is when you begin cooking it, how thoroughly you sear it, and so on. Hanger steak benefits from resting for a few minutes before slicing.

Slice straight across the grain, rather than on a uniform indiscriminate steep angle ~ this popular habit produces wide, elegant-looking slices, but they can be

\ *continued*

pretty chewy, regardless of how well the meat is cooked. Cutting strategically across the grain minimizes the chewiness problem. Also in view of chewiness, I like to slice both skirt and hanger steak no more than 3/8 inch thick. Cutting skirt steak across the grain is easy, since the fibers run in regular, parallel formation across the full width of the muscle. Try to forgive the skinny slices and enjoy the improved texture. The grain of a hanger steak is not so ruly; and most cooks puzzle over the cooked thing, flipping it a few times, before making a calculated, counter-intuitive stab. It may help to study the direction of the fibers before you cook the meat, when they are much easier to make out. The grain does alter course within the cut; be prepared to change the angle of your knife accordingly. Cutting the hanger steak this way, you will get a collection of oval and oblong slices.

✢ ✢ *Variation* SKIRT STEAK OR HANGER STEAK *&* WHITE BEAN SANDWICH

Toss thin slices of warm meat with Chimichurri, {page 298}, Salsa Verde {page 292}, or Salmorigano {page 299}. Warm a spoonful of white beans {page 263} with a splash of their cooking liquid and taste for salt. Smash and spread on a slice of warm grilled or toasted chewy country bread or focaccia. Pile the meat on the beans, add a few leaves of arugula or sprigs of watercress, and top with a second piece of bread.

✢
✢ ✢

MASTERING THE BRAISE

Few of us think of glowing coals when we set out to make a braised dish, though the name traces to *la braise,* the steady coal fire that was heaped on and under a closed cooking vessel ~ the *braisière* ~ filled with meat and aromatics. A modern braise, largely defined by content and technique, not by the cooking vessel, is composed of gently browned meat, typically crowded by vegetables and moistened with stock and wine, then covered tightly and cooked slowly in the oven. It lacks the romance and risk of the original technique but relies on the same principal of trapping the meat and its juices in a moist, fragrant chamber surrounded by steady, low heat. Stovetop braising can approximate this condition if the vessel is heavy enough to really surround the food with uniform and steady heat.

In contemporary kitchens, or at least in ours, braising has succeeded sauce making as the most appealing of culinary endeavors. And with good reason. Braising integrates protein cooking and sauce making in one dish, and the result is usually the heart of any meal. "Building" a tasty braise requires good judgement in the choice of ingredients and how they are prepared, portioned, and assembled. Producing a successful braise depends on appreciating a clutch of variables and how they will interact through long cooking. The succulence of a braised meat depends on slow, steady cooking with internal temperatures high enough to gradually melt sinews {which begins at about 150°} and weaken tough muscle fibers without drying them out. If the meat gets too hot for too long, too much moisture evaporates and the proteins become so denatured that they can't hold on to the melted sinew {collagen} that gives the meat succulence. That melted collagen will give body to the braising liquid, but the muscle itself will collapse and become stringy.

Hence, successful braising requires low to moderate heat and time. And still, as fragile as all that may sound, and as elaborate as any of these braising recipes may appear, the technique is, in fact, easy. The particulars don't require absolute precision and, happily, no great dexterity is needed to produce a fine braise. And the slow, gentle cooking process permits great latitude with regard to timing.

Some guidelines and "braising habits" you'll encounter in most of our braised meat recipes:

⁃ The meats are salted in advance, usually 1 to 3 days before braising. We usually use 1 scant tablespoon of sea salt for 4 pounds of meat. I find this improves flavor and enhances succulence and is worth the little planning it requires. If your schedule is tight, reducing the lead time will diminish the effect, but is better than skipping this preliminary step.

⁃ Good, rich flavor depends on carefully browning the meat. Brown meat gently over medium heat, or a good 5 inches from a broiler element. This will preserve the flavor of the fat and allow the whole surface of the meat to brown before any fraction of it gets a chance to burn. The tiniest spot of overbrown or scorch will affect the flavor of the braising liquid. Trim any such defect. When pan-browning, use only a film of fat. If there is too much fat in the pan, the meat will shallow-fry, and the gorgeous, crunchy surfaces that might taste delicious now will seem like so much boiled cardboard after braising. {To appreciate this point, imagine taking a bite of freshly cooked, crispy brown bacon, and then consider how that same slice would feel in your mouth after simmering for two hours in stock.}

And bear in mind that browning *is* for flavor, not sealing in juices. The persistent saw that "searing seals in the juices" is only a blessing if it causes cooks to continue to brown carefully ~ it has long been understood that no amount of well-meaning browning will hold in moisture. Close attention to a lovingly seared steak reveals that plenty of moisture escapes no matter what, but if you resist trusting your eyes when it comes to abandoning such a successful myth, an explanation of the dynamic is in Harold McGee's *On Food and Cooking* {Scribner, 1984}. It is worth noting that searing does, however, keep slowly cooking meat from oozing unappetizing globs of protein, as, for example, happens when you place hamburgers under a not-very-hot broiler. {For more on browning, see page 382.}

❖ Concerning the "surrounding" vegetables: We very rarely brown them, not only because the braising process is long enough to thoroughly cook the brawniest of roots, but also because aggressively browning generally dims their individual flavors in favor of subtly cloying caramel. And I prefer to avoid introducing more cooked fat into the long-cooked braise. I think the resulting sauces are clearer in flavor and more digestible. All of this is relevant even if you don't plan to serve the braising vegetables.

❖ The braising liquid consists of stock, wine, or beer, and sometimes tomato. The depth of the liquid ranges from one-quarter to one-third of the height of the meat, depending on how much liquid we expect the meat and vegetables to release as they cook. It is critical that the liquid be seasoned and rich in flavor and body, to avoid leaching too much flavor, succulence, and salt from the meat. {Where the stock is not terribly gelatinous, a pig's foot is a good, inexpensive off-the-shelf fortifier. It is mild in flavor, but rich in the collagen that gives the sauce body. After a brief parboiling, the pig's foot will be primed to shed that protein into the braising liquid.} This formula produces satiny, syrupy, clear tasting sauces that hold and reheat well. I prefer them to the slightly starchy texture and duller taste of sauces whose body owes to flour.

Reheating a Braised Dish:

These meaty braises generally taste best and have a silkier texture if they are allowed to cool, at least partially, and are then reheated. Cool them with the pot at a slight tilt, which makes it easier to remove the fat.

We always strain off, taste and "rectify" the braising liquid before we reheat the braise, whether by reducing it or adding salt, sugar, wine, stock, water, tomato, and/or vinegar. If you aren't confident making such an adjustment, I recommend you tinker with only a spoonful of the braising liquid and then taste the effect before you gamble on the whole affair. Once you are happy with the sauce, recombine it with the meat.

We reheat the meat and any vegetables we've salvaged, together with the braising liquid, slowly and still crowded, either in the original braising vessel or in one suited to the amount we are reheating. To evenly reheat a fully cooled braise, set the pan over low heat and bring to a simmer, then cover and place in a 300° oven until the meat is piping hot. If you are reheating a small amount, you can do so successfully on the stovetop, as long as you gently swirl the pan and turn the pieces of meat over occasionally. The braise shouldn't boil hard when you reheat it.

✦
✦ ✦

BRASATO

THE NOTION OF COOKING IN A COVERED PAN HEAPED WITH COALS {LA BRAISE} gave us the name of this dish and cooking method, although in English we focused on the vessel, not the fire, and came up with "Pot Roast." This *brasato* was inspired by the Piedmontese version, which is a pot-roasted chunk of beef loyally bathed with the red wine of that Northern Italian region. {When they do the same thing around Florence, they call it *stracotto,* meaning "overcooked," but "extra-cooked" sounds more encouraging} When we make *brasato,* we reduce the wine first and then add rich beef or chicken stock to the braising liquid. If using chicken stock, we fortify the liquid with a piece of pig's foot, which many supermarkets carry fresh or frozen {or can order for you}, as do many Latin or Asian markets. I always buy more than I need, cut it into chunks, and wrap and freeze them individually. They keep well for months and are a boon to have on hand for enriching this and other dishes.

Shoulder chuck is excellent for pot roasting ~ choose firm, bright red meat with bright white fat, and ask for a piece where different muscles meet: this means there will be plenty of gelatinous connective tissue to render the pot roast succulent. Lean, uniform single-muscle cuts, like eye-of-the-round and bottom round roasts, advertise "pretty," but do not have better flavor and will readily dry out; I don't recommend them. The ritual of artificially enriching lean cuts by

\ *continued*

larding them with alien fat is a curious one ~ it doesn't contribute what you need, collagen, and the channels of introduced fat always taste and feel like, well, channels of fat {unless you roll the strips of fat in salt and other seasonings first, which can make them worthwhile}. But fat does improve flavor; so I simply choose a cut that has some of its own fat and I don't trim it too scrupulously. We try to tie the roast in such a way that a little of that compatible fat is inside the roast. Fat and gelatin notwithstanding, salting the chunk of meat a few days in advance will make any pot roast more flavorful and succulent.

Red-wine pot roast calls for hearty vegetable and starch dishes. Polenta is its constant companion in the Piedmont, but root vegetables ~ roasted, braised, or mashed ~ are welcome too. And Long-Cooked Romano Beans {page 250}, Braised Fennel {page 255}, Martha's Spätzle {page 220}, watercress salad, roasted winter squash, and Lentils Braised in Red Wine {page 267} have all accompanied pot roast at Zuni. By adding an egg or two, you can turn leftover bits of meat and braising liquid into a hearty meal for one, or a few. {See Eggs Baked in *Restes,* page 184.}

Wine: Barolo "Bussia Soprano," Aldo Conterno, 1996

FOR 6 GENEROUS SERVINGS:

One 4-pound beef shoulder chuck roast, trimmed of any discoloration, but with some fat intact

Salt

One 750-milliliter bottle hearty red wine, such as Nebbiolo, Cabernet Sauvignon, Zinfandel, or Syrah

About 4 cups Beef Stock {page 63}, or 2 cups Chicken Stock {page 58} plus 12 ounces pig's foot, cut into pieces

About 1 tablespoon mild-tasting olive oil

1 large carrot {about 4 ounces}, peeled and cut into 2-inch chunks

1 small celery root, top trimmed {about 8 ounces}, peeled, and cut into 2-inch chunks

1 medium yellow onion {about 8 ounces}, cut into 2-inch wedges

A handful of garlic cloves, unpeeled

1 or 2 bay leaves

12 black peppercorns, barely cracked

A pinch of sugar, if needed

About 1 teaspoon balsamic vinegar {optional}

Seasoning the meat {for the best flavor and succulence, do this step about 3 days in advance, or as close to 3 days ahead as you can}:

Salt the meat evenly all over, making a point of sprinkling it into any of the natural seams between the muscles {we use 1 scant tablespoon sea salt for 4 pounds meat}.

Tying up the meat:

Tie the meat tightly into a stout log about 6 to 7 inches in diameter, knotting about four individual loops around the circumference and one loop around the length of the meat {see Hints for Tying Up Meat, page 406}. Given the sought-after irregularity of the cut, you may need to push the muscles into slightly unnatural alignment to produce a regular shape.

Preparing the braising liquid {about 20 minutes, and you can do this well in advance}:

Simmer the red wine to reduce to just over 1/2 cup. It will be very dark.

If using beef stock: Place in a small saucepan and simmer, skimming as needed, to reduce the stock to about 2 cups. It should have a little body.

If using chicken stock plus the pig's foot: Place the pig's foot in a small saucepan and add cold water to cover. Bring to a boil, reduce the heat, skim, and then simmer until the foot begins to feel slippery, about 20 minutes. Drain, and set aside.

Browning the meat {allow 15 minutes}:

Lightly brown the meat, either under a preheated broiler or on the stovetop; you are browning for flavor ~ if the fat or meat scorches you defeat that purpose.

To broil: Preheat the broiler. Rub the roast with the olive oil, set in a small roasting pan and place about 5 inches below the element. Roll a quarter-turn as each side takes on a little color. Trim any bits that overbrown.

To pan-brown: Choose a skillet not much larger around than the largest side of the roast. Add the olive oil and warm over medium heat. Set the roast in the pan and leave it to color, then roll and pivot it as necessary to brown the sides and ends.

Assembling the braise {about 5 minutes}:

Preheat the oven to 325°.

Choose a heavy flameproof braising vessel that can accommodate the roast surrounded by a 2- to 3-inch wide moat of vegetables. A deep Dutch oven, flared brasier, or wide saucier-type pan is ideal, although I generally use my 3-quart suaté pan. Set the browned meat in the center of the pan, flanked by the pig's

\ *continued*

foot, if using, then scatter the bay leaves and cracked pepper in the "moat." Surround with the vegetables. The vegetables should be crowded; your pan size will determine whether you can fit them all. Add the reduced red wine, then add enough stock to come to about 1 inch. You may not use all the stock ~ save what you don't use for extending or correcting the sauce.

Bring the braise to a simmer {this will save about 30 minutes of oven time}. I usually then take the temperature at the center of the piece of meat and make a mental note of it. These two habits help manage and predict cooking time; using the same pan and the same oven every time helps as well. This allows you to focus on the more elusive variables that affect the timing and flavor of the pot roast and its sauce, or of any braised dish: the characteristics of the particular piece of meat, vegetables, and moistening agents.

Braising the meat {3-1/2 to 4 hours}:
Cover the pot tightly and place in the oven. After about 2 hours, uncover and turn the meat over. It will be very firm, like a flexed muscle. Work quickly, so neither the roast nor the oven loses too much heat. Cover and cook for another hour or so, then turn the meat again.

Continue cooking until fork-tender, usually another 30 minutes to 1 hour. {If you like, uncover the roast for the last 30 minutes to glaze the surface slightly.} Properly cooked, the pot roast will yield, but not collapse, with a gentle poke. Remember, a piece of cooked meat never feels harder than when it is piping hot; the roast will soften further as it cools. A tender pot roast will have surrendered about 30 percent of itself to the sauce.

If you need your pot roast to mind itself while you are gone, you can skip the turning over steps; and you can slow the cooking down by an hour, or even a few, by cooking it at 275°. The most succulent pot roast I have ever made spent nearly 6 hours in the oven, the last 4 at 250°. This flexibility makes the dish appealing, as you can tailor it to your schedule; the window of succulent tenderness is not narrow, and an extra 30 minutes at low temperatures will not ruin the result.

Finishing the sauce and serving the pot roast {about 15 minutes}:
Transfer the pot roast to a new pan and set in a warm, protected spot.

If you used the pig's foot, place it in a strainer, hold it over the braising pan, and rinse with a few splashes of warm water. This will wash the sticky braising juice into the pan below. Another option is to bone and chop the meat and skin and add some or all of it to the sauce.

Fish out the braising vegetables, set in a medium-mesh strainer perched over a bowl, and press with a spatula or wooden spoon until you have about 1 cup of homey mixed-root vegetable purée. I like the garlic in particular, so I make sure it all goes through.

Tilt the braising pan and skim the fat. Skim and add any juice the meat may have oozed as it rested. Taste. The sauce ought to be rich and have a little body. Stir in enough of the vegetable purée to give the sauce a little more bulk and sweetness. Taste again. If you find the flavor too acidic, consider adding a splash more stock or a pinch of sugar. Or trickle in the balsamic, which will add both sweetness and acidity and a waft of perfume to the sauce. {If you are unsure of what to add, and how much, adjust only a spoonful of the liquid to make sure you are on the right track. Then rectify the lot.}

Carve the pot roast into thick slices, removing strings you go: for the best texture, slice across the grain. You may have to change the angle of the knife a few times to do this. Sometimes we pry the whole roast apart into major muscles that want to be carved on different angles. Serve a few spoonfuls of hot sauce with each portion of pot roast.

✥
✥ ✥

OXTAILS BRAISED *in* RED WINE

W E HAVE BRAISED NEARLY 7,500 OXTAILS SINCE THEY BECAME A ONCE-A-WEEK item at Zuni in 1989. But the ugly-duckling cut of over a decade ago is very much in demand now, and since no one can arrange for more than one 2-1/2-pound tail per beast, we can't always get as many as we need. This became a happy problem when we began supplementing them with beef cheeks, which are even richer in

\ *continued*

flavor, or short ribs, which are easy to find and, it seems, loved by everyone. Cheeks and short ribs both cook more rapidly than tails, so we remove them from the braise an hour or so early.

As with any braised dish, I am just as interested in the character of the sauce as the meat itself, so we use rich beef stock to ensure that it is flavorful and has body, without wicking all the succulence from the meat. If you don't have time to make a full-blown beef stock, you can use chicken stock plus a pig's foot ~ the foot is an inexpensive package of mostly skin, tendon, and cartilage that slowly melts, giving the braising juice wonderful body. {Many supermarkets carry them, or can get them; Latin and Asian markets are also a good place to find them. Buy split feet, and more than you need. Wrap in small chunks and freeze for future projects}. Whichever approach you take, do know that this dish does take time, although not so much your time as *its* time. Don't try to rush it. On the other hand, preparing it in advance and reheating it is an excellent idea; the flavors and textures do nothing but improve.

Serve the oxtails over Polenta {page 190}, with Buttermilk Mashed Potatoes {page 233} or Martha's Spätzle {page 220}. Or arrange the oxtails in a casserole on a slice of stale bread you have first soaked in a mixture of red wine and olive oil, add the braising liquid, and reheat slowly. Garnish with a wad of watercress.

And I hope you have some leftover braised oxtails to serve in one of the following ways: with eggs, poached or baked in the meat-flecked braising liquid {see Eggs Baked in *Restes,* page 184}; tossed with egg noodles or chewy pasta tubes; over risotto; or boned and recombined with their braising liquid, topped with mashed potatoes, and baked into a wealthy shepherd's pie.

Wine: Jacob's Creek South Australia Shiraz Reserve, 1998

4 generous pounds oxtails {or a combination of mostly oxtails and the balance in beef cheeks or short ribs}

Salt

4 cups Beef Stock {page 63}, or 2 cups Chicken Stock {page 58} plus 1 pound pig's foot, cut into a few pieces

1 to 2 tablespoons mild-tasting olive oil

1-3/4 cups hearty red wine, such as Cabernet Sauvignon, Zinfandel, or Syrah, or as needed

A splash of brandy

1 or 2 bay leaves

1 small head garlic {about 2 ounces}, root end trimmed and cut crosswise in half

A branch of fresh flat-leaf parsley, fresh thyme, or both

A few black peppercorns, barely cracked

1 large carrot {about 4 ounces}, peeled and cut into 2-inch chunks

A few stalks celery, leaves trimmed {about 4 ounces} and cut into 2-inch lengths

1 medium yellow onion {about 8 ounces}, cut into thick wedges

About 1 cup coarsely chopped, drained canned tomatoes

Trimming and seasoning the meat {for the best flavor and succulence, do this step 2 to 3 days in advance, or as early as you can manage}:

Trim the oxtails of excess fat, but don't remove the shiny silverskin. If you have bought a whole oxtail, cut between the vertebrae to make about 9 chunks. The skinny tip of the tail has almost no meat, but include it in the braise anyway, it will add gelatin and flavor. If using beef cheeks, trim any tough-looking silverskin, then cut each cheek into 2 pieces. If using short ribs, trim most of the fat, but leave the silverskin and bones in place. Season all the meat liberally all over with salt {we use 1 scant tablespoon sea salt for 4 pounds of meat}. Cover loosely and refrigerate.

Preparing the braising liquid and browning the meat {about 1/2 hour}:

If using beef stock: Place in a small saucepan and simmer gently to reduce to about 2 cups. Skim as needed. It should be syrupy, not gluey.

If using chicken stock plus a pig's foot: Place the pig's foot in a small saucepan, cover with cold water, and bring to a boil. Reduce the heat, skim, and simmer until the foot starts to feel slippery, about 20 minutes. Drain.

\ *continued*

Preheat the oven to 300°.

Choose a heavy flameproof braising vessel that will hold the pieces of meat in a single layer with the vegetables piled and crowded in between. I use a 10- by 14-inch roasting pan that is 2-1/2 inches deep.

Wipe the pieces of meat dry. Warm a film of olive oil in a 12-inch skillet over medium heat. Add enough pieces of meat to loosely crowd the pan. Let brown lightly, usually 3 to 4 minutes, then turn to color the other sides. {This can be tedious, since these cuts of meat have multiple awkward faces, but conscientious, gentle coloring overall will repay you with a well-flavored braise.} If the oil smokes at any point, transfer the meat to a dry towel, discard the oil, and clean the skillet; wipe the burned oil from the meat and start again. Transfer the browned meat to the braising pan, and brown the remainder in one or two batches. Once you have browned all of the meat, pour off the fat and wipe the skillet clean.

Set the skillet over medium heat and add the 1-3/4 cups red wine and brandy. Stir and scrape as it sizzles. Then simmer until the wine has reduced by about half. Add the reduced stock and bring to a simmer. Turn off the heat.

Assembling the braise {5 minutes}:
Arrange the meat, including the pieces of pig's foot, if using, evenly in the braising pan. Distribute the bay leaves, garlic, parsley and/or thyme, and black pepper around it, followed by the carrot, celery, onion, and tomatoes, filling the crannies between the chunks of meat. Add enough of the hot wine-stock mixture to come to about one-third the depth of the meat. You may not need all of the liquid; save it for finishing the sauce {or freeze it for your next red wine–beef braise}. Set the braising pan over low heat and bring to a simmer. Heating the pan and liquid will save about 20 minutes of oven time, and routinely doing so means that every braise you make, oxtail or otherwise, starts at the same temperature; controlling this variable can help you to better predict cooking times.

Tent the surface of the braise with parchment paper, then cover the pan with a tightly fitting lid or with foil, dull side out.

Braising the meat {3-1/2 to 4 hours}:
Place the pan in the oven and cook until the oxtail meat has just begun to pull from the bone, usually 3-1/2 to 4 hours. Check the doneness at 2-1/2 hours. The meat and vegetables will have released lots of moisture ~ the meat may be nearly

submerged. {If you have included other cuts than oxtails, they may be tender already. If so, transfer them to a shallow bowl and set aside, loosely covered.}

After checking the doneness, leave the lid slightly ajar, or the foil loose, when you return the pan to the oven. This will allow the now-abundant braising liquid to begin reducing. Check meat again at 20- to 30-minute intervals until it is tender, but not collapsing. It will continue to soften as it cools.

Cooling and skimming the braise {about 20 minutes}:

Once the oxtails are tender, remove the braise from the oven and prop the pan at a slight angle so the fat will collect at one side. Turn each piece of meat over to remoisten the dryer face. If the braising juice is already quite syrupy, add a trickle of water. Tent with the parchment.

When the braise has cooled slightly, spoon off the fat. Transfer the pieces of meat to a separate pan, with the cheeks or shortribs, if applicable. {Cover and refrigerate if you are not planning on serving the dish within an hour or so.}

Correcting the sauce {about 15 minutes}:

If you used the pig's foot, remove it and use your fingers to bone it. Discard the bones. Chop the meat and skin. Set aside.

Taste the vegetables. If you like the flavor and texture, you can serve them as is. If their flavor is nice but their texture insipid, press them through a food mill or strainer and stir some or all of that purée into the finished braising liquid. {I usually salvage at least the garlic and press it through a strainer to recuperate the mellow paste~ or simply break it up and scatter the paste-filled cloves into the braise.} If the vegetables are utterly spent, collect them in a strainer and place over a bowl to capture whatever liquid they release. Rinse them with a trickle of warm water, stirring the vegetables as you add it, to dilute and retrieve the sticky braising liquid clinging to them, then discard the vegetables.

Skim the braising liquid again. Add the optional chopped pig's foot and the liquid from the vegetables, bring to simmer over low heat, and skim again. Taste, then spoon a little of the liquid onto a plate. If it tastes weak and looks watery, simmer to reduce further, do the "plate test" again, and taste. If the liquid is less than rich and delicious, consider further reduction, or add wine, stock, or extra

\ *continued*

wine-stock mixture to a spoonful of the liquid to see if it makes it taste better, then adjust the lot accordingly {which may mean not at all}.

Reheating the braise:

Combine the meat and liquid in the original braising vessel or in a wide sauté pan. Bring to a simmer, then cover and continue to simmer until the meat is piping hot, 10 to 15 minutes. {To reheat oxtails you braised yesterday, or the day before, you should bring to a simmer as described, place in a 350° oven, and heat until the meat is piping hot, usually 30 to 45 minutes.} Serve.

✦ ✦ ✦ ✦ ✦

ABOUT BROWNING

WHEN YOU BROWN FOOD, YOU ARE COLORING THE SURFACE BY using heat to rapidly evaporate its moisture. Once the water is gone, the natural sugars can caramelize and/or the carbohydrates, proteins, or fats can turn gold, chestnut, or brown {or, eventually, black}. "To golden" might be a more appropriate instruction, since that is most often what is sought, but that word hasn't risen to verb status in English. {However, in French, the term *dorer,* and in Italian, *dorare* [both meaning "to gild," or "to make golden in appearance"], are used liberally in the kitchen.} Browning always firms the surface of the food, and successful browning introduces delicious new flavors, which one counts on to give character to braises and stews.

The simplest, least active form of browning is "top-browning," where a dish is placed under a hot broiler for quick results, or in a somewhat cooler oven for slower coloring. Pan-browning is a more active operation and requires a little finesse from the cook. It is best done in a slope-sided pan so the moisture has a wide avenue of escape. You should preheat the fat, so it issues some sort of sizzle as the food hits it~just how noisy depends on the food in question. If the surface of the food is quite moist, pat it dry before you add it to the fat; this will quiet it down, and help prevent sticking. Don't crowd the food~if the pieces of food are too close together, they will trap moisture and steam rather than brown. {But don't space the food too far apart, or you risk burning the fat.} The food will stick to most cooking surfaces until its surface moisture has evaporated and a crust, however minimal, has formed, so be patient. If a chunk of meat, {or poultry, or fish} wants to stick, don't fuss with it. Stirring or prying tends to create new problems~it makes the food release more moisture, and if you rip it from the pan, you will simply expose a new moist surface of meat, which will in turn want to stick to the pan. Any bits of meat you leave stuck to the pan will readily burn, and you won't be able to brown anything on top of them. If time doesn't encourage a piece of meat to release, use a metal spatula to scrape it cleanly from the pan.

Always monitor browning operations closely and adjust the heat as needed to prevent burning or to encourage that brown, or golden, crust to form.

+ + + + +

Short Ribs Braised *in* Chimay Ale

A SIMPLE BRAISE INSPIRED BY THE STALWART BELGIAN DISH *CARBONNADE flamande.* Chimay is the smooth Belgian ale we use for this dish at Zuni; it has a delicate sweetness, a touch of clove flavor, and only the faintest note of bitterness. Similar Belgian-type ales are made by Ommegang in New York and Unibroue in Canada. A mellow porter is another alternative, as is stout, as long as it is not too bitter.

Choose meaty slabs of short ribs, 3 or 4 ribs each, and have them sawn across the bones into floppy bands. Thickly slice the onions, so they don't dissolve into the sauce.

These are good with browned spätzle {page 220} or mashed potatoes. Husband all leftover juice and bits of meat and onion to reheat with eggs {see Eggs Baked in *Restes*, page 184}.

You can also make this recipe using large Muscovy duck legs or goose legs.

Wine: Santa Barbara Winery Santa Ynez Valley Syrah, 1998

\ *continued*

FOR 4 SERVINGS:

About 2-1/2 pounds short ribs, cut across the bone into 2-inch-wide bands {have the butcher do this}

Salt

1 to 2 tablespoons mild-tasting olive oil

1-1/2 pounds yellow onions {about 3 medium}, sliced 1/4 inch thick

2 bay leaves

A few whole white peppercorns

A few slices dried wild mushrooms, rinsed in warm water and coarsely chopped {optional}

Up to 1 cup Beef Stock {page 63} or Chicken Stock {page 58}

Up to 1 cup Chimay ale or similar Belgian-style ale or a mellow porter or stout

About 1/4 cup Dijon mustard

Trimming and seasoning the short ribs {for the best flavor and succulence, do this step 1 to 2 days in advance, or at least a few hours ahead}:

Trim most of the fat from the short ribs, but leave the silverskin and tough sheathing around the bones intact. This will help keep the meat succulent and will give body and character to the braise. Salt evenly all over {we use a scant 3/4 teaspoon sea salt per pound of meat}. Cover loosely and refrigerate.

Cooking the short ribs:

Warm the oil in a 3-quart sauté pan over medium heat. Wipe the pieces of meat dry. Brown the short ribs evenly and gently on the three meaty sides, about 4 minutes per side. Pour off excess fat.

Rearrange the meat bone side down in the pan. Add the onions, bay, peppercorns, the optional mushrooms, and equal parts stock and ale, porter, or stout to come to a depth of about 3/4 inch. Bring to a simmer, cover and cook over low heat, until fork-tender, about 2 to 2-1/4 hours. {You can cook the braise in a pre-heated 300° oven if you prefer.} Check two or three times to make sure that that the liquid is barely simmering, and turn each piece of meat each time you check. When the meat is done, uncover, prop the pan at a slight angle, and leave to rest for about 5 minutes.

Turn on the broiler.

Skim the fat that has collected at the lower side of the pan. Taste the juice and simmer as needed to concentrate the flavor. Salt as needed. Make sure each piece of meat is bone side down, then brush or smear the tops with the mustard. Set

QUAIL & SAUSAGE BRAISED *with* GRAPES, *page 361,*
with GRILLED POLENTA, *page 190*

HANGER STEAK, *page 368,*
with PORCINI PEARÀ SAUCE, *page 311*

PRE-SALTED MEAT FOR SHORT RIBS
BRAISED IN CHIMAY ALE, *page 383*

MOCK PORCHETTA, *page 408*

FOUR CHEESE COURSE PAIRINGS
{*clockwise from upper left*}: TOMME DE SAVOIE *with* WALNUTS,
STILTON *with* BRANDIED MUSCAT RAISINS, PUTNEY TOMME
with FENNEL, *&* SALLY JACKSON'S SHEEP'S MILK CHEESE *with*
DRIED BLACK MISSION FIGS IN RED WINE, *page 445*

ESPRESSO GRANITA *with* WHIPPED CREAM, *page 474*

ORANGE-CURRANT SCONES *with*
CAFÉ AU LAIT, *page 479*

PEACH CROSTATA, *page 498*

the pan under the broiler, about 5 inches from the element, to brown the mustard and glaze the surface of the onion stew, about 5 minutes.

Serve the short ribs very hot, mustard plaster up, with a spoonful of the syrupy sauce and onions.

❖
❖ ❖

POT-AU-FEU

*P*OT-AU-FEU IS AN IMPORTANT MEMBER OF THE LARGE FAMILY OF TRADITIONAL dishes that consist of flavorful but inexpensive cuts of meat or poultry cooked in their own broth with the humblest of vegetables. Such dishes are advertised, unpromisingly, as "boiled dinner" in English, although "simmered dinner" sounds more appetizing, and more accurately describes the primitive but gentle cooking method that coaxes the bony, sinewy cuts of meat and earthy roots to melting tenderness. *Pot-au-Feu* is a comforting meal ~ or even two, when you consider the delicious broth and leftovers it usually generates. Both sumptuous and elemental, it makes a fine family dinner or a delectable, unpretentious dish to serve family-style to friends. Unfortunately, lackluster renditions of this type of dish are not uncommon, persuading many to avoid "simmered dinners." On the other hand, a successful one is a triumph of pure and balanced flavor. It is a restorative dish that I am always happy to turn to as an alternative to the more usual braises, roasts, and *grillades.*

Making these simmered dinners regularly over the years, I've grown fiercely loyal to a few principles and techniques. These simple steps will help ensure your simmered dinner will be limpid and bright tasting.

❖ Start by choosing a deep, narrow pot that will crowd the meat and vegetables. A pot that is too wide obliges you to add too much liquid, which will result in bland broth, and plenty of it. A narrow pot will limit evaporation and oxidation, both of which, for the sake of bright flavor, you want to avoid.

❖ Concerning the meat, I presalt both the beef and chicken for these dishes,

\ *continued*

which helps keep them juicy and flavorful. I also blanch and rinse the beef before assembling our *pot-au-feu*. This rids the meat of surface impurities that may add off-flavors to the broth. This technique is foolproof, easy, and more efficient than the alternative of compulsive early skimming. After plenty of experimenting, I always begin this "blanching" in warm water. This seems to precipitate unwanted substances to the water's surface, without extracting the "good" flavors from the meat.

 ⊹ When it comes to assembling the actual dish, I use a combination of stock and water to moisten it. This indulgence violates the tradition of all water, but it means that a little more flavor can stay in the meat.

 ⊹ Finally, gently simmer, don't boil, the *pot-au-feu*, and, farmhouse origins notwithstanding, don't cook it indefinitely. Boiling will make the broth both murky and murky tasting. Boiling and overcooking make the meats unnecessarily stringy and will turn the vegetables into bland, moisture-logged, formless lumps.

A basic *pot-au-feu,* which comes from the French farmhouse tradition of a "pot on the fire" {where it lived, simmering indefinitely, to be replenished as often as a meal was drawn from it}, may be no more than one cut of beef plus carrots, onions, and leeks, served with a few kernels of rock salt, mustard, and cornichons {pickled gherkins}. This modest combination can be shockingly good, the taste and texture of each element still bright and clear, and the broth fragrant and saturated with flavor. More ambitious versions include multiple cuts of meat or are embellished with chicken and other root vegetables ~ such as parsnips, turnips, or celery root. Carol's Pickled Onions {page 271}, Pickled Glasswort {page 274}, and Spiced Zante Grapes {page 276} are fun alternatives to the ubiquitous French gherkins.

I am married to short ribs ~ the thick *plates de côtes* of French butchery ~ for this dish. They have a bright flavor and a great loose-grained texture. Beef shank is often recommended, but the meat is quite dense and can give a dark, bloody flavor to the broth. Cooking only one cut of meat makes this recipe easy to time. You can adjust the amount, and relative amounts, of vegetables if you like, leaving out what you don't like or emphasizing what you do. Included in this recipe is a recipe for my favorite garnish, mustard vinaigrette, which you can stir together at the last minute.

In France, the broth from the *pot-au-feu* is often served as a first course, by itself, or with croûtons and sometimes grated cheese. But even if you honor this tradition, you should still have plenty of broth leftover to serve with an egg poached in it {page 160} or with pastina cooked in it. It is also good with toasted *fideus* pastina {page 217} cooked in it, or with Martha's Spätzle {page 220} swimming in it.

Leftover beef is a prize that will allow to you make *Miroton* {page 389}.

Wine: Gevrey-Chambertin, Vielles Vignes, Dominique Laurent, 1997

FOR 4 TO 6 SERVINGS, WITH EXTRA BROTH:

4 pounds short ribs, cut across the bone into 3-inch-wide slabs {have the butcher do this}

Salt

Water

About 3 quarts Chicken Stock {page 58} or Beef Stock {page 63}, or a combination

2 small yellow onions {about 12 ounces}, root ends trimmed flat, peeled, and halved

1 or 2 bay leaves

2 whole cloves

A few black peppercorns, barely cracked

A small branch of fresh thyme {optional}

2 large carrots {about 8 ounces}, peeled, ends trimmed

2 medium leeks {about 8 ounces}, root ends trimmed flat, green parts trimmed ~ leaving a few inches of green intact ~ and quartered lengthwise and thoroughly rinsed

1 medium celery root, top trimmed {12 ounces}, peeled, and quartered

2 medium white turnips {scant 8 ounces}, peeled and quartered

1 medium rutabaga {scant 8 ounces} peeled and quartered

For the mustard vinaigrette:

FOR 1/2 CUP:

Just over 1 tablespoon broth from the *pot-au-feu*

2 teaspoons Dijon mustard {the seedy kind is particularly good here}

1-1/2 tablespoons red wine vinegar

6 tablespoons mild-tasting olive oil

1 teaspoon walnut oil {optional}

Salt and freshly cracked black pepper

Optional garnishes:

Spiced Zante Grapes {page 276}, Pickled Glasswort {page 274}, Carol's Pickled Onions {page 271}, or French cornichons

Fleur du sel or coarse sea salt {see Choosing Among Salts, page 38}

Trimming and seasoning the meat {for the best flavor and succulence, do this step 1 to 2 days in advance}:

Trim most of the fat from the short ribs, but leave the silverskin and tough sheathing around the bones intact. This will help keep the meat succulent and

\ *continued*

will give character to the broth. Salt evenly all over {we use 1 scant tablespoon sea salt per 4 pounds meat}. Cover loosely and refrigerate.

Blanching the meat {15 to 20 minutes}:

Pour a few quarts of cold water~enough to cover the short ribs~into a deep 6- to 10-quart stockpot. Set over high heat. When the water is warm to the touch, add the short ribs, a teaspoon or so of salt {so you don't desalt the meat in the water}, and bring to a simmer. Simmer for 2 minutes. The water will be dingy and crowned with unappetizing foam. Drain, rinse the meat in cold water, and wash out the pot.

Assembling and simmering the *pot-au-feu* {about 2-1/2 hours}:

Replace the short ribs in the clean pot and add enough stock to leave the meat poking about an inch above the surface. Add cold water to cover by a few inches. Bring to a simmer and skim any last bits of foam that pop up. Taste for salt. Add the onions, bay leaves, cloves, peppercorns, and the thyme, if using, and stir under. Cook uncovered at a gentle but very steady simmer, skimming occasionally, for about 1 hour.

Skim, then add the carrots, leeks, celery root, turnips, and rutabagas. Add more stock or water as needed, so everything is just covered. Stir once. Bring to a simmer then taste for salt. Simmer until the meat is yielding but not soft, about another hour. The vegetables should be tender but not mushy. Skim.

Making the vinaigrette and serving the *pot-au-feu* {10 minutes}:

Chill the tablespoon of broth, then skim any fat. Whisk together the mustard and vinegar in a small bowl, then slowly whisk in the oil, or oils. Whisk in a trickle of the cooled *pot-au-feu* liquid to stabilize this emulsion. Add salt and pepper to taste. Set aside.

{If serving a first course of broth, ladle off the desired amount, skim and pour through a fine-mesh strainer into another pot. Return to a simmer, taste for salt, and then serve in warm bowls.}

Lift the meat from the pot and slide off the bones. Thickly slice across the grain. Pile on a warm, deep platter or in individual deep plates. Garnish with the vegetables, whole, chunked, or wedged. Skim the rich broth and serve a splash of it with each plate. Offer the vinaigrette, along with something pickled and/or *fleur du sel* or coarse sea salt, if desired.

✦
✦ ✦

Beef & Onion Gratin *with* Tomatoes, or le Miroton

An elaboration of the comforting stand-by of *cuisine bourgeoise, miroton* is to the French home cook what roast beef hash or shepherd's pie is to an American cook: an unpretentious way to transform tasty leftovers into a totally different dish. Made with beef and broth from a *pot-au-feu,* it is the delicious reason I routinely simmer more meat that I need when I make that dish. {You could also use fork-tender braised beef brisket or chuck, as long as you then moisten the gratin with light beef stock rather than syrupy rich braising liquid.} Since you are likely to make this dish with whatever amount of meat you have, I provide basic moderate-appetite per person measures. The amounts are easy to multiply for larger gratins. A shallow 1-quart gratin dish is about the right size for 4 servings.

This variation begs for others, and my favorites include using sliced black truffles in lieu of the tomatoes or, more modestly, layers of blanched swiss chard. In the latter case, use melted butter spiked with a dab of mustard, instead of olive oil for the bread crumb topping.

This is a two-helping sort of dish, so follow it with, or begin with, a simple green salad.

Wine: Eberle Paso Robles Barbera, 1999

PER SERVING:

About 5 ounces leftover beef from *Pot-au-Feu* {page 385}, boned and trimmed of cartilage and fat

About 1 tablespoon mild-tasting olive oil

8 ounces sliced yellow onions {2 cups}

Salt

1 teaspoon all-purpose flour

1/2 cup strained broth from the *pot-au-feu,* or as needed

Freshly cracked black pepper

1 small ripe tomato {about 4 ounces}

A splash of water as needed

\ *continued*

For the topping {per portion}:

1/2 ounce soft, fresh bread crumbs {about 1/4 cup} made from slightly stale, chewy, white peasant-style bread {see page 506}

About 1 teaspoon extra-virgin olive oil
A splash of dry white wine

Slice the meat, across the grain 1/4 inch thick.

Choose a skillet that will hold the onions in a 1/2- to 1-inch-deep layer. Warm a film of olive oil in the skillet over medium heat, add the onions, and stir or toss once or twice. Leave to color slightly. Salt lightly and stir or toss again, then reduce the heat to low, cover, and cook until the onions have fallen into a soft, silky, wet pile, about 15 minutes. {If preparing the gratin for 6 or more, you may need to brown the onions in batches, then consolidate them in a saucepan to cook through.}

Sprinkle the onions with the flour, stir, and simmer until the juices have thickened. Stir in the broth, to produce a syrupy stew. Cook for a few minutes over low heat. Salt and pepper to taste.

While the onions are cooking, preheat the oven to 425°.

Sliver off the ends of the tomatoes, core, and slice 1/4 inch thick. If they seem quite wet, place between paper towels to purge for a minute or so~this will concentrate their flavor, and ensure they do not dilute the flavor of the gratin.

Combine the bread crumbs, olive oil, and white wine and knead very gently to distribute.

Construct the *miroton* in a shallow gratin dish. Begin with a smear of the onion stew, then pave with barely overlapping slices of meat. Spread with a second, thicker layer of onions, and then a layer of tomatoes. Repeat the sequence, finishing with a Spartan layer of tomatoes. Tamp lightly and gently shimmy the pan to encourage the layers to settle into one another. The assembled gratin should be quite moist~if not, add a splash of broth, or a few drops of water. The liquid will thicken and reduce during baking; you want enough to guarantee a saucy gratin.

Top with a lacy layer of the bread crumbs. Depending on the shape of your dish, you may not need them all. Using too much topping will result in a pasty gratin, shy of the promised sauce.

Bake the *miroton* until it bubbles at the edges and the crumbs are golden brown. This may take anywhere from 15 to 30 minutes.

Serve family-style from the dish.

✢
✢ ✢

SUCCESSFUL ROASTING

By a "successful" roast, I mean an evenly cooked piece of meat that is the doneness you hoped for and is as juicy as possible. Clever carving will show off that success with the tenderest possible slices of meat. Whatever your doneness preference, an understanding of how roasting works, and a few disciplined habits, can help you roast successfully.

As a technique, roasting is uncomplicated, and this suggests that the cook's role is passive: a "chunk" of something is cooked by surrounding it with dry heat. The heat first dries the outside and colors it, more or less, depending on the conditions on the surface. As the heat penetrates the muscle, the affected proteins contract and "cook," and the meat changes color internally and begins to dry out from the edges in. The roast shrinks and becomes firmer. How much heat reaches the center, and how rapidly and evenly it does so, begins to determine how the meat will ultimately be cooked. But the process continues outside the oven.

As you set the roast on the cooler stovetop, or "in a warm, protected spot," heat begins to escape from the meat, most dramatically from the hottest part, the surface. As the hotter regions cool, the proteins relax somewhat and the meat becomes softer. Unless the roast is quite well done, some of the moisture left in the center of the roast travels back toward the cooling surface, where it is reabsorbed by thirsty proteins. These changes are responsible for making the roast more tender and succulent. While this is going on, however, the internal temperature of the roast continues to rise, sometimes 20 degrees or more. How much it rises is a function of at least four things: first, how hot the oven was, which determines how hot those outer regions are; second, how big the roast is~a large roast has not much surface proportionate to its volume, and so it cools more slowly than a small roast; third, where the roast is resting~how hot or cool the spot is, and whether it is drafty or protected; and fourth, how long you permit it to rest. This resting period is a critical part of roasting ~ correcting for some of the damage and irregularity wrought by the oven.

Understanding how a roast absorbs and then bleeds heat demystifies roasting. And it suggests a few active measures the cook can take to manage the process. Controlling a few variables and tracking temperature changes will help you to roast successfully, consistently. And with a little experience, you can learn to dispense with most, if not all, of the temperature taking.

Begin by considering the conditions imposed by your oven. First, check its accuracy with a reliable oven thermometer ~ check it in a few different spots. Knowing your oven can be just as important for a long roast as it is for a quickly baked muffin. Next, realize that if the oven is small, the roast will be close to the walls and it will color fairly quickly. If your oven is shallow, with a wide door, it will lose a lot of heat every time you open it ~ an electric oven may take as long as 20 minutes to recover. If you are using a convection oven, expect the roast to brown quickly and cook more rapidly than in an oven without that extra force. And remember that any time a roast must share the space with another dish, it may affect results, if only because each dish deflects some heat from the other.

Although recipes routinely provide oven temperatures, consider them as guidelines; adjust for your oven, and for your piece of meat. If the meat is much larger or smaller than specified, you may need to reduce or increase the heat by 25 to 50 degrees. In general, the larger the piece of meat, the lower the temperature. I don't bother starting at a high heat to brown a large roast ~ the long cooking time will eventually color the meat, and you can best control the doneness and assure even cooking if you stick with a steady temperature. Basting a roast can make the surface tasty and can help to color it, but only if the basting juices are laden with enough solids to brown well {and if you don't leave the oven open too long as you do so}. However, moistening the surface this way won't affect the juiciness of the roast itself.

Just before cooking, I usually take the temperature of the raw roast. Where a large roast is concerned, rather than cook it straight out of the refrigerator, I leave it at room temperature for a few hours before roasting. I aim to set the prepared meat in the oven when it is 50° to 60° in the center. This reduces oven time and, more important, favors even cooking.

Next, I choose a shallow roasting dish that is just large enough to hold the piece of meat. This permits the heat to circulate evenly and freely around the roast. Deep roasting pans mean the lower regions steam, and if the pan is too large the juices will tend to dry out and burn. Shape and size are more important here than material. Other than Pyrex and disposable foil roasting pans, both of which can scorch easily, most metal roasting pans or earthenware dishes conduct heat evenly enough to be suitable for controlled roasting.

If the roast is uniform in shape, it will tend to cook most evenly. Where it is uneven, plan on shielding the skinny parts or narrow ends with foil {shiny side out to reflect the heat} once they have colored, and/or situating the roast so those parts are in the coolest part of the oven or near the door. That way, those parts will cook more slowly than the rest. You can also choose to leave them exposed, and produce a roast with a variety of donenesses to satisfy different tastes. This is another kind of successful roast.

Wipe the roast dry. This will encourage good browning, and it is particularly important for small roast that might otherwise be nearly cooked before the surface dries out enough to color. For the tiniest, leanest roasts ~ like quail ~ you may need to rub the surface with fat or brandy after you rub it dry. Set in the pan and notice how firm or soft the meat feels. Place in the preheated oven. Shortly after you reach the halfway point of the expected oven time, take the temperature at the center of the thickest part of the roast. {And make sure you know where on the shaft of your thermometer the sensor is; most sensors are partway up the shaft, but I prefer a model where it is conveniently located in the tip.} Next, check the temperature closer to the surface and note how rapidly, or not, it climbs. If the roast has a narrow end, check the temperature there; it may be ready to be protected. Feel and check the temperature again in short order to see how the process is accelerating. And add 5 to 20 degrees to the temperatures you discover at the center, in function of the variables listed above ~ size is predominant ~ to account for the post-oven cooking that will happen as the roast rests. Use the thermometer to "watch" the meat cook. And as you check the temperature, notice also how firm the roast is and how much it has shrunk ~ both are indications of doneness, but, by themselves, they are less reliable or revealing than temperature. However, once you have roasted a certain cut of meat "by thermometer" a few times, you can begin to associate a degree of doneness with an amount of shrinkage or firmness in a piece of meat. These associations are primary tools for an experienced cook, but, happily, a novice cook can recognize them just as readily. Always take the final temperature reading at the center of the thickest part of the roast.

Once you remove the roast from the oven, let it rest ~ and finish cooking ~ in a warm, protected spot. {Tenting it very loosely with foil is an easy way to deflect most drafts. Don't wrap the roast, though, or it will steam, spoiling any crispy crust} Now, admonish yourself, and everyone else in the room, that the roast is not done. At that point, it will be hot, tough, and dryish on the outside and, in most cases, only slightly less tough and too rare on the inside. Depending on size, it will need up to 30 minutes to finish cooking and relax, and to allow the juices to redistribute. Take the temperature once or twice more {since a little juice will run out each time you poke it, you may want to leave the thermometer in place}. If you should overcook a roast in the oven, the best solution is to select a relatively cool or drafty spot for it to rest in. Don't try to compensate by cutting into the meat before it has rested. Cutting interrupts the regular redistribution of heat and juices, and, while it will stop the cooking, it will stop it at a moment when the meat is still unevenly cooked and in the least succulent state.

Finally, your approach to carving will, literally, determine whether the tasty, succulent, evenly cooked slices of meat will be chewy or not. Look at the surface of the roast and read the direction and pattern of the muscle fibers. Disregard the overall shape of the cut of meat, and don't put a premium on impressive wide, regularly shaped slices. Instead, cut at a right angle to the direction of the grain and don't worry about the size or shape of the slices. Unless the roast is very well done, the muscle fibers will still be quite intact, and if you carve with the grain, you will have to chew through those fibers. The roast will seem tougher than it ought to. Carving across the grain means your knife takes care of as many fibers as possible. You may need to adjust the angle of the knife a few times, whenever the direction of the muscle fibers changes.

By the same logic, *do* worry about the thickness of the slices. Except for beef fillet or similar pampered muscles, slice fairly thinly.

Beyond these general considerations on how roasting works, I am an advocate of presalting most meats for roasting at least 24 hours in advance. This technique produces a particular succulence and consistency in results. {See The Practice of Salting Early, page 35.}

✢ ✢ ✢

ROAST LEG *of* LAMB

THESE ARE THE ROASTING GUIDELINES I LEARNED FROM KATHI RILEY AND HAVE followed religiously since 1980, when we roasted leg of lamb every night together at the Union Hotel in Benicia, California. Over the course of cooking hundreds of legs of lamb, we tried plenty of alternative methods~higher heat, lower heat, variable heat, initial searing, roasting "bone-in," and firing the meat cold~but none produced as fine or consistently rosy pink a result as this one. Even now, whenever I see a leg of lamb at the restaurant that is not evenly cooked, or looks dry, it invariably turns out it wasn't brought to room temperature before cooking, or that someone tried to rush it. Roasting the meat "off the bone" worries some purists, but the moist, flavorful results answer that. And, more important, when carving a boneless leg, it is easy to respect the grain of the meat, making each slice as tender as possible. Mentioning that I fully season the lamb a few days in advance still provokes skepticism, reminiscent of dire assurances I heard twenty years ago that this would draw out all the juices. In our experience, it only improves the flavor and produces a tender and succulent roast. {For more thoughts on roasting, see Successful Roasting, page 391.}

I give instructions here for boned whole legs of lamb ~ that is, with the shank and sirloin ends attached. Ask for the leg of lamb to be "corkscrewed" ~ that way, the bones are first loosened and then twisted out without severing many muscles.

Depending on butchering and marketing practices in your store or your region, you may be offered "short legs" or half-legs, where the loin or shank has been trimmed off. In this case, you may find starting weights are less than I specify, and some trussing and carving concerns become irrelevant, but the temperatures and basic principles of preseasoning, roasting slowly and evenly, and resting thoughtfully are still valid. If you want to make a reduced lamb sauce to serve with the lamb, ask the butcher to cut the bones from your leg of lamb into a few pieces so they will fit into your pot. {You'll need to buy some extra shank or neck, shoulder, or breast meat to supplement.} Plan to make the stock the same day you season and tie up the lamb.

✦ ✦ ✦ ✦ ✦

To Corkscrew a Leg of Lamb

If you want to corkscrew a whole leg of lamb yourself, you need to first separate the shank meat along a natural seam, then gradually whittle it away from the bone with a boning knife. Leave it attached where it joins with the next muscle group. Then, without making any further incisions from the outside, work the tip of the knife up inside the leg, as close to the bone as possible, making a series of little cuts that gradually free the leg muscles. The freed muscles will be like a loose cuff around the bone. When you reach the knee joint, flip the leg around and begin to free the loin end. Use the tip of the knife to make a series of little cuts around the awkward piece of pelvic bone that may be in place. This is a consummate feel-as-you-go operation, and you will find yourself flipping and turning the leg in order to approach all the angles of the bone you are trying to liberate. Once it is removed, begin to excavate the femur with a series of little cuts close to the bone, just as you did from the other direction. Flip the leg as needed. Once you reach the knee joint again, you'll need to stretch the opening and begin to gingerly free the kneecap, severing shiny connective tissue. Do the same from the shank side. Once you've cut most of the connections, grasp the femur in one hand, hold the meat in the other, and twist like a corkscrew. This motion should tear through the rest of the connections. {If not, return to the probing and severing until you can.} I have seen professional butchers corkscrew a leg of lamb in 45 seconds, with what seemed like only a dozen strategic incisions; my personal best is about 15 minutes, and it never looks nearly as nice as their effort.

✦ ✦ ✦ ✦ ✦

Wine: Château Sociando-Mallet, Haut-Médoc, 1995

FOR 8 TO 10 SERVINGS:

One 6- to 7-pound corkscrewed whole leg of lamb {shank and sirloin end attached}; if making the optional stock, have the bones {about 2 pounds} cut into chunks

Salt

For the sauce:

1/2 to 2 cups Lamb Stock {page 65}, about 1/2 cup Chicken Stock {page 58}, or a few tablespoons water

1 tablespoon dry vermouth

Preparing the leg of lamb, and making the optional lamb stock {ideally 2 to 3 days, but at least 1 day, in advance. If you can't get to all of this in advance, do at least try to get the meat seasoned ~ the trimming and tying can wait}:

Shave away all but a thin layer of fat from the smooth, rounded muscle of the haunch side of the leg of lamb. Flip over and trim any ragged bits of meat that resulted from boning the leg. {Add them to the bone pile if making the stock.} Season all over with salt, including the inside, where the bone was, salting the thick middle section more heavily than the skinny shank and loin ends {we use a scant 3/4 teaspoon sea salt per pound of meat}.

Tie the leg tightly into a log, tying it about every 1-1/2 inches with a separate piece of string {see Hints for Tying Up Meat, page 406}. Make the first "truss" about an inch from the center, toward the shank end, and then work your way toward the loin end. Return and make one or two more "trusses" on toward the shank end. The result will resemble a crooked log, fattest in the middle, a little skinnier at the loin end, and "floppy" at the shank end. Cover loosely and refrigerate.

Prepare and strain the lamb stock. You can reduce it all immediately to make a glossy sauce with a little body, or simply use some of the stock to deglaze the roasting pan later on and save the remaining stock for another use.

Remove the leg of lamb from the refrigerator about 4 hours before you plan to roast it.

Roasting the lamb and letting it rest:
Preheat the oven to 325°.

For reference, take the temperature of the leg of lamb at the center of the thickest section. It should be about 50°. Place on a shallow roasting pan or heavy rimmed sheet pan that is not much larger than the meat. Place in the center of the oven and roast undisturbed for just under an hour, then take the temperature, again at the center of the thickest part of the leg. Expect about 100° ~ however, the size of the leg, your oven, and the starting temperature may skew that somewhat. Then, quickly check the temperature at the center of the loin end of the leg ~ it will be 10 to 15 degrees hotter. Unless you want this portion to be well done, loosely wrap this skinny section with aluminum foil, shiny side out, for the duration of the cooking. Wrap the floppy shank end as well.

Check the temperature at the center of the roast again after another 10 to 15 minutes. I cook whole leg of lamb to 118° ~ this produces rosy pink meat that is still juicy. Typically, this takes 1 hour and 20 minutes total time. If you like your lamb more red than pink, remove it at 113°; if you don't want to see any pink, remove it at 124° ~ it will still be juicy.

\ *continued*

When the lamb has reached the desired temperature, remove the roast from the oven, tent loosely with foil, and leave for about 20 minutes in a warm, protected spot. As it "rests," the center will keep cooking even as it cools on the outside. For rosy lamb, I look for the internal temperature to peak at 140° after resting for 15 to 20 minutes.

Making a sauce with the pan drippings:

Lift the meat from the roasting pan and tilt to pour off the fat. Don't pour off the tasty juices. Add 1/2 cup or so of stock or water, and a trickle of vermouth. Set over low heat and stir and scrape to dissolve golden drippings. Pour into a small saucepan and skim again. Reduce over high heat for a few minutes to concentrate the flavor if necessary. {If you have prepared reduced lamb stock, you can use this to deglaze the roasting pan as just described, or simply serve it as is, pristine and satiny.}

Carving the lamb:

Remove the first string from the loin end. Thinly slice the lamb at a right angle to the grain of the muscle. This is convenient at the loin end, as you will be slicing at a right angle to the "log" itself. Snip the strings only as you near them. When you have sliced a 1/2 inch or so into the bend at the fattest part of the leg, stop and look at the grain of the muscle on the cut face. In order to continue at a right angle to it, you'll need to change the angle of your knife by about 45 degrees. This will feel counterintuitive, and the first slices from this angle will be small, but after carving a few slices, it will make sense. Continue carving at this angle until you reach the dense gelatinous meat of the shank, then readjust the carving angle to stay perpendicular to the grain. Slice only as much meat as will be eaten right away.

Note: Refrigerate leftover leg of lamb to serve thinly sliced as a first course with fresh raw favas {see page 88} and shaved aged Tuscan pecorino or in a sandwich with a slice of Grilled Eggplant {page 241} and a spoonful of Roasted Pepper Relish {page 302}; serve with arugula salad. In either case, bring the meat to room temperature first and slice it as thin as you can, trimming off every bit of fat as you go.

✦ ✦ **ROASTING SPRING LAMB LEGS**

If you have a much smaller leg of spring lamb, about 3 to 4 pounds corkscrewed, then make the following adjustments:

⚬ The tender meat usually does not need to be seasoned in advance, but it won't suffer if you want to get the seasoning and tying up done a day early.

⚬ Remove the meat from the refrigerator only about 2 hours before roasting.

⚬ Roast at 400°.

⚬ For a just-pink roast, cook to 124° at the thickest part of the leg. A small leg will cool more efficiently than a large one~hence the higher target temperature in the oven.

⚬ Check a few times, but expect the smaller roast to take only about 45 minutes. Allow about 15 minutes for resting.

Here are a few of my favorite ways of flavoring leg of lamb before roasting it.

⚬ ⚬ LEG *of* LAMB *with* ROSEMARY *&* GARLIC

Trim and season the leg of lamb as in the basic recipe. Strip a branch of rosemary of its leaves; pound them lightly. Peel and smash a few small cloves of garlic. Tuck the rosemary and garlic inside the leg, poking the aromatics deep into the natural separations between the muscles~don't make unnecessary incisions in the muscle, whether from the inside or outside. Tie up and roast as described above.

Roast as indicated and serve with Rosemary-Roasted Potatoes {page 235} or *Fagioli all'Uccelletto* {page 265}.

⚬ ⚬ LEG *of* LAMB *with* MUSTARD

Season and tie up the leg of lamb as in the basic recipe. Smear the outside with a thin layer of Dijon mustard just before roasting it; allow about 1/2 cup mustard. Don't worry if a little mustard gets on the roasting pan, it will give a good flavor to the pan drippings.

Roast as indicated, and serve with Buttermilk Mashed Potatoes {page 233}.

⚬ ⚬ LEG *of* LAMB *with* LAVENDER

This is best with small legs of lamb, whose flavor is mild. Season and tie up the leg of lamb as described in the basic recipe. Rub with a bit of olive oil. Crush a spoonful of lavender buds and rub them all over the leg of lamb. Don't poke

\ *continued*

them inside the roast ~ their flavor will be too strong and their texture unwelcome. Refrigerate overnight, then roast as above.

Serve with a salad of baby lettuces, arugula, and thin ribbons of raw fennel and roasted figs {page 83}. Offer grilled bread or sprinkle the figs and salad with Hazelnut *Picada* {page 305}, or with plain bread crumbs toasted in olive oil.

✢
✢ ✢

HOUSE-CURED PORK CHOP & TENDERLOIN *with* GUIDELINES *for* OTHER CUTS *of* PORK, CHICKEN, TURKEY, & DUCK

THIS IS OUR EVERYDAY WET CURE FOR FRESH PORK. It reliably transforms the lean loin chop into a succulent cut of meat. You can experiment with other flavorings, like garlic or herbs, but the ratio of salt to sugar to water is just right for a thick chop, or for a pork tenderloin. For larger cuts of pork like shoulder, leg, or a whole loin, we use a more dilute formula that I include as well. The variations for chicken breasts or duck are less sweet. A diluted version of the chicken brine can be used for a whole turkey, or turkey breast.

To make sure the brine "takes," it should be at room temperature, or only slightly cooler, when you immerse the meat in it. Cold slows down movement ~ hence, curing action ~ substantially.

Don't reuse this simple, inexpensive brine.

Wine: Côtes du Rhône, Belleruche, M. Chapoutier, 1999

THE BASIC BRINE

FOR 4 PORK CHOPS, 10 TO 11 OUNCES EACH AND 1-1/4 INCHES THICK, OR 2 TRIMMED PORK TENDERLOINS, ABOUT 1 POUND EACH:

A few crumbled bay leaves, dried chiles, and crushed juniper berries {optional}

5 cups room-temperature water

6 tablespoons sugar

3 tablespoons salt {a little more if using kosher salt}

If using the aromatics, place them in a small pot with about 1 cup of the water. Bring to a simmer, stirring and crushing with a wooden spoon, to encourage them to release their flavors. Remove from the heat and leave to infuse for about 10 minutes. Combine the remainder of the water, the aromatic mixture, if using, the sugar, and salt in a deep bowl or 3-quart plastic storage container. Rinse the meat and pat dry. Place in the brine and use a plate to keep the meat submerged. Cover and refrigerate for 2 to 4 days.

Cooking and serving brined pork chops:

A couple of hours before cooking, remove the chops from the brine. They will feel firmer than before you cured them. Rub and massage the meat as you rinse it thoroughly under cold running water. Press dry between towels. Refrigerate until about 15 minutes before cooking.

Brush the chops with olive oil and grill over medium coals, or cook in a heavy skillet with a film of olive oil over medium heat. Move the chops or adjust the heat if the sugar threatens to burn, and turn at least three times as they cook. Cold chops should take about 18 minutes to cook. They will hold well for another 10 minutes in a warm, protected spot.

Serve with Roasted Applesauce {page 260}, sage or sorrel-mashed potatoes {see Buttermilk Mashed Potatoes, page 233}, Hashed Sweet Potatoes {page 239} and Spiced Prunes {page 278}, or Boiled Kale {page 162} and Roasted Polenta {page 192}. Reduced Rich Pork Stock {page 61} makes a lavish sauce.

Cooking brined pork tenderloins:

Rinse as for pork chops and pat very dry. Rub with olive oil and grill, or sear in a skillet and then roast at 425°, for about 25 minutes. Let rest 5 to 10 minutes before carving into thick slices.

❖ ❖ BRINE *for* LARGER CUTS *of* PORK:

Increase the water in the Basic Brine to 7-1/4 cups. Follow the basic procedure, making enough brine to cover the meat. Larger cuts need to cure more slowly, about 5 to 7 days, in this milder brine. Remove the meat from the brine and rinse

\ *continued*

it 1 full day in advance; this allows the cure to diffuse evenly. Failing this, the outer part of the pork may be noticeably saltier than the center.

Note: To make "Shoulder Ham": If you add a scant 1/2 teaspoon curing salt {see Sources and Resources, page 518} to this brine, you can use it to make a small "ham" out of a fresh pork shoulder. Stab the meat all over with a wooden or metal skewer, to encourage the brine to penetrate, then leave to cure for about 1 week refrigerated. Twenty-four hours before cooking, rinse and dry the meat thoroughly and refrigerate. Truss tightly {see page 406} and then simmer in lightly salted water until about 130° in the center, then drain, dry, and roast at 375° until golden brown, about 30 minutes.

✦ ✦ BRINE *for* CHICKEN BREASTS {5 *to* 8 OUNCES EACH}:

Increase the water in the Basic Brine to 6 cups, and reduce the sugar to 3 tablespoons. Follow the basic procedure, making enough brine to cover the breasts. Brine for 2 to 3 days. An hour or so before cooking, rinse and dry as for pork chops. Brush with olive oil and grill or pan-fry over gentle heat, to avoid burning the sugar.

✦ ✦ BRINE *for* TURKEY:

This recipe marries the two formulas for chicken and pork. The only difficulty here may be finding a vessel big enough to hold the bird, and making space for it in the refrigerator. A roasted brined turkey throws off a lot of sweet-salty juice that doesn't lend itself to gravy making, but the startling succulence of the meat makes up for it.

Increase the water to 7-1/4 cups, and reduce the sugar to 3 tablespoons. Follow the basic procedure, making enough brine to completely submerge your bird. I usually roast small turkeys ~ 15-pound Toms. Cure for 5 to 6 days, rinse, dry, and refrigerate for 1 more day, so the brine can diffuse evenly. Then, before roasting, rinse again, inside and out, and prop upright to drain for at least 1/2 hour. Dry very well inside and out with paper towels. I roast my turkey at 350°, starting breast side up, turning once to brown the back, until it registers about 150° in the thickest part of the breast meat. Let it rest for at least 20 minutes before carving.

Increase the water in the Basic Brine to 6 cups, reduce the sugar to 3 tablespoons, and increase the salt to 6 tablespoons. Follow the basic procedure, making enough brine to submerge the breasts or legs. Cure breasts 2 to 3 days, legs 3 to 4. A few hours before cooking, rinse and dry as for pork chops. Grill or panfry breasts as described above for chicken breasts. For legs, sear lightly in olive oil, then roast at 375° for 20 to 35 minutes, depending on size.

Standing Rib Roast *of* Pork

This impressive roast is a perennial hit at Zuni and a family favorite for Christmas Eve dinner. The loin is succulent and perfumed, and the crispy meat-clad bones are irresistible. We use the same butchering and roasting specifications year-round but vary the aromatics according to the season or weather, and the rest of the menu. This version, sprinkled and rubbed with barely crushed fennel and coriander seeds and garlic, is inspired by an *Arista Perugina* {a boneless roast pork loin, Perugia-style} in Elizabeth David's *Italian Food.* We serve it in the fall with roasted grapes or figs and a salad of bitter greens, or with Braised Fennel {page 255} and Fresh Shelling Beans {page 263}. In the winter, we smear the roast with a paste of Dijon mustard, crushed mustard seeds, and cracked black pepper. That version begs for Buttermilk Mashed Potatoes {page 233} and greens or carrots. The same cut of meat seasoned with rosemary, lemon, garlic, and black pepper becomes a Florentine-style *Arista,* which wants roasted potatoes. A fourth variation, made with a bright blend of orange zest, chili flakes, and garlic, with or without a few fennel seeds, is good with wilted spinach and Polenta {page 190}.

Order the rib roast with the featherbone and chine bone in place. Ask the butcher to make a cut through the chine between each rib, as for a crown roast ~ or make this series of cuts yourself, as described below. Buy and season the rib roast

\ *continued*

at least 3 days before you plan to cook it. This allows time for the salt and flavor from the aromatics to permeate the whole piece of meat, essential for deep flavor and great succulence. At the restaurant, we carve off and serve one roasted "chop" per person. This makes a handsome presentation, and very generous portions, at 11 to 14 ounces. To get the smallest such chops, ask for the center-cut section of the loin; this will be the leanest section as well. An alternative is to bone the loin after roasting, and slice and serve based on appetite ~ and hope people don't fight over the bones. If preparing a larger, or, more accurately, longer rib roast, prepare proportionately more of the seasonings.

You can also use this method to prepare a rib roast of veal. {For a general discussion of roasting, see Successful Roasting, page 391.}

Wine: Beaune Premier Cru Les Grèves, Tollot-Beaut, 1997

FOR 4 TO 6 SERVINGS:

One 4-pound standing rib roast of pork {about 4 ribs} {if desired, have the butcher crack the chine}
Salt

4 garlic cloves, peeled
2 teaspoons fennel seeds
2 teaspoons coriander seeds

To sauce the roast:

About 1/2 cup Rich Pork Stock {page 61}, Chicken Stock {page 58}, or water plus a splash of dry white

wine, or about 1/2 cup reduced Pork Stock {see page 56}

Seasoning and tying up the roast, 3 to 4 days in advance {if you didn't have the butcher do this}:

Place the roast, bone side up, on a cutting board and locate the rubbery seams between the vertebrae. Crack through each one by first easing the blade of a heavy cleaver or the hefty bolster of a heavy chef's knife into each joint and then tapping firmly with a rubber mallet {or a hammer wrapped in a towel}. It may take a few taps to go all the way through the seam and joint, but take care not to cut deeply into the meat itself. The blade of your knife ought to sink no more than 1-1/2 inches into the seam {1}.

Flip the roast over and trim away all but a 1/4-inch-thick layer of fat. Begin boning the loin, starting with the thin layer of meat and fat near the cut end of the rib bones {2}. Resting the tip of your knife flat against the curved rack of bones, make a series of smooth cuts between the loin and bones until you reach the "elbow" of each rib bone {3}. Leave the loin attached to other angle of the "elbow," so you can open and close the roast like a book {4}.

✦ ✦ ✦ ✦ ✦

✦ ✦ ✦ ✦ ✦   I   2   3   4

Season the whole roast including the rack of bones liberally inside and out with salt {we use about 1 tablespoon sea salt for 3 pounds of roast}; target the thickest sections most heavily, and the two end faces of the loin most lightly. Roughly chop the garlic, then crush in a mortar. Smear on the inside face of the loin. Slightly crush the fennel and coriander seeds. Scatter about two-thirds of them on the inside of the loin and the facing bones, then close the loin back up and sprinkle the remainder evenly over all of the other surfaces.

Truss the roast, looping and knotting a string between every two ribs {5} {see Hints for Tying Up Meat, page 406}. Cover loosely and refrigerate.

Remove the pork from the refrigerator about 3 hours before roasting.

✦ ✦ ✦ ✦ ✦

✦ ✦ ✦ ✦ ✦   5

\ *continued*

Roasting the pork and letting it rest:

Preheat the oven to 400°.

I usually take the temperature of the roast just before cooking it, looking for 50° at the center of the thickest section. Stand the roast in a shallow roasting pan or on a heavy rimmed baking sheet not much larger than the meat. Place in the center of the oven. For a juicy roast that is cooked through, but with a faintly rosy cast, roast to 135°. {If the eye of your roast is smaller than 4 inches across, cook it to about 140°; it will stop cooking more abruptly when you remove it from the oven.} Start taking its temperature at about 45 minutes, and allow between 1 and 1-1/2 hours for a 4-pound roast. Turn the roast or adjust rack height if it is browning very unevenly.

Set the roast on a platter, tent loosely with foil, and leave to rest in a warm, protected spot for about 20 minutes, then take the temperature again. Like any roast, it will continue to cook as it rests, but the rack of bones retains heat particularly well, so the temperature should climb to about 160°. The meat will be cooked through but still moist.

Preparing the sauce:

Pour any fat from the roasting pan, then moisten it with the pork stock, the chicken stock, or the water and wine, to capture any fallen aromatics and deglaze the baked-on meat drippings. Pour into a small saucepan and simmer until the sauce has good flavor. Add any juice from the pork platter. Alternatively, for a more lavish sauce, simply heat up reduced pork stock.

Serving the roast:

The rib roast is easy to serve; just carve between the rib bones, then break into chops. Snip the trussing strings as you go. Alternatively, you can remove all of the strings, bone the loin completely, and slice into medallions. Then break the rack into crusty ribs to eat with your fingers.

✴ ✴ ✴ ✴ ✴

HINTS *for* TYING UP MEAT

When I tie up meat for roasting or braising, instead of using one continuous string, I make a series of independent loops and knots so that when I snip one, the remainder stay in place and snug. This makes it much easier to carve properly. It is important that each trussing string is pulled very tight. To do this, first loop the string around the meat in the intended location. Using one "tail" of the string, make a simple knot around the other "tail" of the string {1}. Pull that knot snug, but not so tight that you can't slide it along the "tail" of the string {2}. Slide the knot down that string until it butts against the meat {3}, and tighten the simple knot a little more {4}, then, holding onto the first "tail" with one hand, use the other hand to pull the second "tail" back away from the knot {5}. This ratcheting action will tighten the loop. Now tie the "tails" together to secure the snug fit {6}. I use 16-ply all-cotton string to tie up meat. Skinnier string can cut through the meat as you tighten the loops.

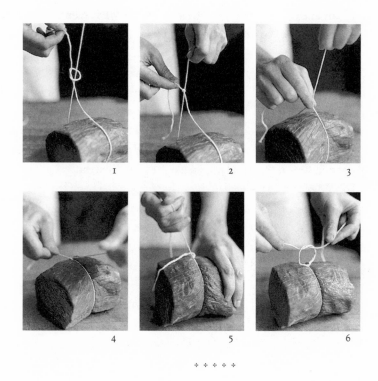

1   2   3

4   5   6

* * * * *

MOCK PORCHETTA

A VERY MODEST, VERY MANAGEABLE INTERPRETATION OF THE TUSCAN "BIG PIG" that few Americans, or Italians, could ever manage at home. {It is a formidable production even at the restaurant.} That gargantuan dish is a whole roast pig, typically stuffed with fistfuls of stemmy herbs, capers, casually chopped garlic, and sometimes fennel or pickled gherkins, all challenged by bold doses of salt and pepper. This diminutive *porchetta* is made with a small piece of pork shoulder, an inexpensive, underappreciated cut. Its mosaic of muscles provides plenty of places to stuff the seasonings, and it has enough internal fat and connective matter to self-baste and stay juicy as it slow-roasts. Buy, season, stuff, and tie-up your would-be *porchetta* 2 or 3 days before you plan to roast it, to give the flavors a chance to permeate the meat. Crowd this little roast with whatever root vegetables you like, choosing a larger or smaller roasting pan, depending on how many vegetables you want.

Make sure you have leftover *porchetta* so you can have a sandwich of the warm meat, spread with a spoonful of fresh ricotta cheese, on a crusty bun moistened with the pan juices. Leftover bits of *porchetta* are also good torn into bite-sized bits and shreds, moistened with olive oil and drippings, and roasted for a few minutes in a 400° oven. Toss with frisée or bitter greens, add a few pecans, and serve with Balsamic Onion Marmalade {page 128} on crostini.

If your pork shoulder is a little larger than the 3 pounds specified, you should increase the stuffing amounts accordingly. If it is close to 4 pounds, or larger, I recommend you turn it into two roasts; to maintain the cooking times, and so you get plenty of the caramelized, chewy outside with every slice.

Minus all the Tuscan herbs and seasonings, this is a good basic pork roast method. Try it seasoned with nothing more than salt kneaded with a few crushed juniper berries. That version is excellent with sauerkraut.

Wine: Weingut Robert Weil Rheingau Riesling Kabinett, 1999

One 2-1/2- to 3-pound boneless pork
  shoulder butt roast

Salt

1 tablespoon capers, rinsed, pressed
  dry between towels, and barely
  chopped

1 teaspoon chopped lemon zest

3 garlic cloves, coarsely chopped

About 12 fresh sage leaves, crushed,
  then coarsely chopped {about 1-1/2
  teaspoons, packed}

A leafy sprig or two of fresh rosemary, leaves stripped and crushed
  {about 2 teaspoons, packed}

2 teaspoons fennel seeds, barely
  crushed

1-1/2 teaspoons freshly cracked black
  pepper

1 to 2 pounds prepared vegetables of
  your choice: chunks of peeled carrot; onions cut into wedges; quartered fennel bulbs; chunks of
  peeled celery root, turnips, rutabagas, or parsnips; unpeeled garlic
  cloves; and/or chunks of potato

A little mild-tasting olive oil

About 2/3 cup Rich Pork Stock {page
  61}, Chicken Stock {page 58}, or
  water

A few tablespoons of dry vermouth

Trimming, seasoning, and tying up the pork {1 to 3 days in advance}:

Trim any discoloration and all but a 1/4-inch thick layer of superficial fat from
the pork. Study the natural seams between the muscles on each side of the meat.
Choose one that runs the length of and close to the center of any face. Use the tip
of a knife to gingerly separate the muscles along that seam, gradually exposing
more seams, which you should then separate as well. The goal is to create lots of
internal surfaces to cake with seasonings. If your initial foray doesn't expose many
internal seams, you can take a second stab at a different face, so long as you don't
cut the pork in two. Salt the splayed piece of pork evenly all over {I use 1/2 teaspoon sea salt per pound of meat}.

Combine the capers, lemon zest, garlic, sage, rosemary, with most of the fennel seeds and black pepper. {You should get about 1/2 cup, loosely packed.} Spread
and pack this mixture all over the excavated insides of the pork butt, making sure
the seasoning falls deep into the crannies where you've separated the muscles.
Re-form the pork butt into its natural shape and tie tightly into a uniform shape,
tying 4 or 5 strings around the circumference and another around the length of
the roast {see Hints for Tying Up Meat, page 406}. Rub the remaining fennel and

\ *continued*

pepper on the outside of the roast. Collect and refrigerate any loose herbs and seasonings. Cover the pork loosely and refrigerate.

Roasting the *porchetta* {2-1/4 to 2-1/2 hours}:
Preheat the oven to 350°.

Toss the vegetables in a minimum of olive oil, barely coating the surfaces. Add a few pinches of salt and toss again.

Heat a 12- or 14-inch ovenproof skillet, depending on how many vegetables you are roasting, over medium heat. Place the pork roast in the pan; it should sizzle. Surround with the vegetables. Place in the oven. The roast should begin to color at 45 minutes; if not, turn the heat up to 375° until it does, then turn the heat back down. At 1 hour, turn the roast over and roll the vegetables in the rendered fat. Work quickly, so you don't lose too much oven heat and the roast doesn't cool off. Turn the roast again at 2 hours and add about 1/3 cup of the stock or water. Add any excess herbs and seasonings to the pan juices at this point and swirl the pan so they sink into the liquid. Roast for another 15 to 30 minutes, to about 185°. The pork should be fragrant and glistening golden caramel.

Transfer the meat to a platter, tent loosely with foil, and leave in a warm, protected spot while you make the pan sauce. Place the vegetables on a separate warm plate.

Preparing the pan sauce and serving the roast:
Tilt the skillet and spoon off the fat. Add the vermouth and the remaining 1/3 cup stock or water and set over low heat. Scrape and stir to dissolve the caramelized drippings on the bottom and sides of the pan. Skim the fat as the liquid comes to a simmer. Add any juice that may have trickled from the resting roast.

Slice the pork, removing the strings as you go, and serve garnished with the vegetables and a spoonful of the rich pan sauce.

Cutting Up a Rabbit, & What to Do *with* the Parts

I HAVE NEVER UNDERSTOOD THE CLASSIC METHOD FOR CUTTING UP RABBIT, WHICH consists of cutting off the fore- and hind-quarters and then whacking through the central section ~ ribs, loins, flanks, and all ~ to produce three or four flappy chunks that look like bats. These pieces are impossible to cook properly, since they are composed of two very different types of muscle, neither of which, by the way, cooks at the same rate as the front- and hindquarters, which are also quite dissimilar. Yet recipes often call for all of these parts to be cooked together in the same dish, by the same method and frequently at the same time.

Here is an unorthodox method for butchering rabbit that produces four different cuts of meat {two pieces of each}, plus the innards, and a carcass for stock. We try to cook each part of the rabbit in a fashion that suits it.

Lay the rabbit on its back. If the arc of the rib cage is still intact, cut down the center, between the tips of the opposing ribs. Spread the rib cage open and remove the kidneys and liver. Set aside.

Turn the rabbit on its side and fold the hind leg away from the body, to reveal where it is connected. Use a boning knife to cut away just the leg, not the whole hindquarter, feeling with the tip of the knife and cutting the muscle where it attaches to the pelvic bone. Then fold the leg farther back, pop the ball joint, and cut through the remaining meat and cartilage. Flip the rabbit over and do the same with the other leg. The end of the vertebrae should now be exposed, poking out like a stub tail.

Pull a front leg forward until you feel it resist. Slide your knife underneath the shoulder blade, flat against the carcass, and cut through the sheath of connective muscle, then fold the leg away from the body to reveal the joint. Cut through the joint. Do the same to remove the other foreleg.

Open the belly flaps and splay the carcass, so the ribs are resting on the work surface. Set the tip of a boning knife about 1/8 inch to one side of the spine, and make a shallow cut the full length of the rabbit. Use your fingertips to pry the loin meat back on that side to reveal the vertebrae, which will look sort of like a zipper. If the loin is still tightly tethered to the vertebrae, make another long cut,

\ *continued*

this time a little farther from the spine, and pry again. Now, with a series of little cuts and tugs, gradually free the loin from the carcass, finally peeling it from the tough outer layer of silverskin that encases it. Cut across the loin at the base of the shoulder to release it there. You will have a "floppy log" about 6 inches long and tapered at one end. Remove the other loin.

Remove the semicircular flank muscles, cutting along the "dotted line" formed by the tips of the ribs. We call these the "belly flaps."

You will have: 2 plump hind legs {top of photo}, 2 smooth, tapered loins {center of photo}, 2 belly flaps {center right and left of photo}, 2 bony forelegs {near bottom of photo}, the liver and a pair of kidneys {bottom of photo}, and 1 carcass {not shown}.

✢ ✢ ✢ ✢ ✢

✢ ✢ ✢ ✢ ✢

We handle each of these pieces of rabbit differently:

✢ Cure the hardworking front and hind legs with rock salt and milk as described on page 413. We braise, grill, or roast these cuts as a main course. The plump hind legs can be big enough to serve by themselves, which frees you to turn the bony front legs into excellent *rillettes* {page 442}.

✢ Season the loins liberally with salt and with crushed fresh thyme, sage, or rosemary leaves, if you like. Refrigerate overnight. Grill or sauté, then slice into little medallions; or cut into chunks, skewer, and grill {see Rabbit Mixed Grill, page 416}. Or use for Rabbit Sausage {page 426}.

✢ Season the tough belly flaps liberally with salt and freshly cracked black pepper. Refrigerate overnight. This is the ugly-duckling cut, but this curing method and a very hot grill produce a delicacy we call rabbit "bacon," which is delicious on salads, or as part of a Rabbit Mixed Grill. You can also use belly flaps in the sausage or *rillettes* mix.

❖ Trim the liver and separate it into lobes. Coat it and the kidneys with a little olive oil to protect them from the air, and refrigerate. Both are mild in flavor and are good grilled or sautéed. Season just before you cook them.

❖ Make a stock with the carcass {see page 67}.

❖ ❖

ALL-PURPOSE RABBIT CURE

THIS METHOD MAKES RABBIT LEGS RELIABLY TENDER AND SUCCULENT.

Measure 1 ounce {5 teaspoons} rock salt per pound of rabbit pieces and toss well to distribute. Stack the pieces 2-deep in a wide dish, cover loosely, and leave at room temperature for 1 hour.

Rinse each piece of meat quickly under cold water. Make sure you remove all kernels of salt. Drain and place, again two deep, in a clean dish. Add cold milk to cover by about 1/2 inch {about 3/4 cup milk per pound}. Swish the rabbit around in the milk. Cover loosely, and leave at room temperature for 1-1/4 hours to desalt. Stir the rabbit pieces once or twice during that time to encourage them to desalt evenly.

Drain the rabbit and discard the milk. You can rinse off the slightly salty film of milk if you want, depending on the dish the rabbit is destined for and whether a little bit of dairy protein on the surface might taint the sauce. {For Rabbit with Marsala and Prune-Plums [page 414], do rinse off the milk. For delicious Fried Rabbit, just lift the pieces from the milk, dredge in flour, and refrigerate for a few hours for the crust to set, then pan- or deep-fry. You can cure rabbit up to a few days in advance of cooking it; in that case, do rinse the milk off.

A delicious elaboration on this all-purpose cure adds 1 teaspoon coarsely cracked black peppercorns and a few pounded and bruised branches of fresh

\ *continued*

thyme for each pound of rabbit. Toss them with the rabbit right before you add the rock salt. Their flavors will migrate into the flesh with the salt, perfuming it assertively. As in the most primitive marinade, salt triggers the transfer of flavor. In the absence of salt, any rub or shower of herbs or spices is destined to have a superficial effect at best. Juxtaposing aromatics and proteins can, via friction, deposit some flavor components on the surface of the food {where they can burn or be rubbed off}, but salt lets them permeate the food.

This thyme-pepper cure also produces astonishingly tasty fried chicken. It is the cure Kathi Riley and I worked out for the Union Hotel Panfried Chicken in the early 1980s. It was nearly too well received ~ meaning we couldn't fry it fast enough. The germ of the idea {the rock salt part} came from a gifted 80-plus-year-old Texas chuckwagon chef named Milum, who had told Kathi he'd learned to cook from the wind in the trees. Unable to get a white chef's toque shipped to his mobile kitchen, he fashioned his own out of a stiff medium-sized brown grocery bag. He insisted that when he got too old to walk, he would have his wheelchair outfitted with a cutting board.

+
+ +

RABBIT *with* MARSALA *&* PRUNE-PLUMS

WITH AN AFFECTIONATE NOD TO THE TRADITIONAL FRENCH DISH *LAPIN AUX pruneaux* {rabbit with prunes}, we make this succulent and fruity variation in the fall with ruddy French prune-plums {sometimes called "sugar prunes"}; purple Italian {Stanley} prune-plums will work just as well. Both are firm oval plums with amber flesh. Their flavor is subtle compared to the rounder tart-sweet varieties native to Asia {such as Santa Rosa, Elephant Heart, Laroda}. Their dense meat holds up to braising, and their skin is not too acidic, which makes them ideal for savory dishes. The result is a mellow, balanced fruitiness. Duck legs are also good with this compôte-sauce. You can brown and braise them in similar fashion; just make sure you skim all the fat before you add the fruit.

Make this dish with rabbit that you have cut up and cured as described on pages 411–414. For slightly smaller portions, leave out the forelegs ~ use them for Rabbit *Rillettes* {page 442}. Serve with soft or roasted polenta {page 190}.

Wine: Oxford Landing South Australia Grenache, Limited Release, 1998

FOR 4 SERVINGS:

About 2 cups Rabbit Stock {page 67}
  or Chicken Stock {page 58}
4 cured rabbit hind legs {about 6 to 7
  ounces each} and 4 cured forelegs
  {about 3 to 3-1/2 ounces each}
2 to 3 tablespoons mild-tasting olive
  oil

1 large yellow onion {about 12
  ounces}, root end trimmed flat,
  peeled, and cut into 8 wedges
1 bay leaf, crumbled
3/4 cup sweet Marsala
1 pound prune-plums {about 14
  medium}

Reduce the stock over medium heat until it has some body ~ to test this, spoon a little stock on a plate and set it in the refrigerator to chill. Tilt the plate ~ it should be slightly viscous.

Wipe the rabbit legs dry. Warm about 2 tablespoons olive oil in a 12-inch skillet or 3-quart sauté pan over medium heat. Add a layer of rabbit pieces and cook until golden brown on both sides, about 4 minutes per side. {You may need to do this in two batches.} Pour off the excess oil.

Crowd the browned meat back into the pan, if necessary, and poke the onion wedges in between. Add the bay leaf.

Add enough of the reduced stock to come to a depth of about 1/2 inch. {If you don't use it all, you can add it when you finish the dish, or save it to sauce rabbit sausages.} Add 1/4 cup of the Marsala. Bring to a simmer, cover tightly, and cook at a bare simmer for about 20 minutes. Alternatively, you can instead place the covered pan in a preheated 350° oven and cook for about 40 minutes.} About halfway through the cooking, turn the pieces of rabbit over and give the pan a swirl.

While the rabbit is cooking, halve the plums along the natural crease in their skin and remove the pits. I like to add the pits to the simmering rabbit, to add flavor, then retrieve them before serving.

After 20 minutes or so {or about 40 minutes in the oven}, the rabbit should be cooked through and tender, but far from falling off the bone.

The onions should look like translucent fantails, and the pieces of meat will have shrunken somewhat ~ which is convenient, as it will make room for the plums. If the braising liquid looks or tastes thin, pour or ladle it off very care-

\ *continued*

fully, reduce it in a small saucepan, and then pour it back over the rabbit. {You can set the dish aside for an hour or so at this point.}

Distribute the halved plums around the pan, add the remaining 1/2 cup Marsala, and simmer gently, uncovered, for 10 to 15 minutes, swirling the pan regularly. Try not to crush the pretty onions. The amber plum flesh will brighten to yellow gold and the skins will turn the sauce a deep mauve red, or plummy purple. The skins will curl at the edges, but they generally don't slide off of this type of plum. Stop simmering when the plums are uniformly soft, like freshly made preserves, and the sauce is just syrupy.

Serve the rabbit pieces {one foreleg and one hind leg per serving}, each carefully garnished with silky onion fans and a few plums, all bathed in the glossy sauce.

⁺
⁺ ⁺

RABBIT MIXED GRILL

When WE DEBUTED THIS DIMINUTIVE MIXED GRILL IN THE CALIFORNIA PAVILION at a wine exposition in Bordeaux, the host French chef and his brigade arched eyebrows and whispered. This was no way to handle a rabbit. But the dish was very tasty and it is now entrenched in the Zuni repertory.

This dish was originally contrived to use the pile of odd but delectable "little parts" of the rabbit you generate when you braise a lot of legs. {See Cutting Up a Rabbit, and What to Do with the Parts, page 411, for how to prepare the cuts listed here.} The "off-cuts" from 2 small rabbits will provide enough pickings for a Mixed Grill for 4. But you can buy extra rabbit to generate additional off-cuts, and to provide meat for sausage or *rillettes.* At Zuni, the composition of the dish varies constantly, according to what parts, in what quantities, we have, and what compatible greens and fruits are available. We sometimes arrange the mixed grill on a smear of hazelnut *aïllade* {see page 98}.

Serve as a first course, either on individual plates, or family-style on a platter, with toothpicks. In more generous portions, this makes a fun main course.

Wine: Château Robin, Côtes de Castillon, 1998

FOR 4 SERVINGS AS AN APPETIZER:

About 1/2 cup hazelnuts, walnuts
   {preferably freshly shelled}, or
   pecan halves
About 1 tablespoon red wine vinegar,
   sherry vinegar, or cider vinegar
About 1/4 cup extra-virgin olive oil
Salt
A few drops of hazelnut or walnut oil
   {optional}
2 to 3 tablespoons mild-tasting olive
   oil
About 1-1/4 pounds prepared rabbit
   parts and confections ~ *choose from:*
   ⁛ Rabbit belly flaps {about 2
      ounces each}, salted and pep-
      pered a few hours in advance if
      possible
   ⁛ Rabbit loins {about 3 ounces
      each}, salted a few hours in
      advance if possible
   ⁛ Kidneys and liver {about 2
      ounces per rabbit}

   ⁛ Rabbit Sausages {page 426}
      {about 2 ounces each}
   ⁛ Rabbit *Rillettes* {page 442},
      about 1 ounce per serving, at
      room temperature, plus
      bite-sized crostini made from
      baguette or other chewy,
      peasant-style bread
Freshly cracked black pepper
About 4 ounces fresh or drained
   brandied red currants or grapes
   {page 279}, fresh Black Mission figs,
   halved, or fresh red or white cherries, or 2 tablespoons pitted chopped
   Spiced Prunes {page 278} ~ to spread
   on the *rillette* crostini
A few handfuls of arugula, frisée,
   watercress, or mixed young lettuces and greens, carefully washed
   and dried, at room temperature

Preheat the oven to 350°.

Toast the hazelnuts, if using, on a small baking sheet until the skins darken and begin to split, 10 to 15 minutes. Bundle them, still hot, in a towel, beanbag-style, and scrunch and massage them to rub off most of their skins. Alternatively, warm the walnuts for about 5 minutes, then rub off the skins, or warm the pecans until fragrant. Chop the nuts very coarse.

Prepare a hot fire in a grill.

Spread the coals and place the grill grate a few inches above the coals to pre-heat. Preheat the broiler. Set a salad bowl in a warm spot.

\ *continued*

Combine the vinegar, extra-virgin olive oil, and salt to taste. Add a very few drops hazelnut oil or walnut oil, if you like.

Grill the rabbit parts, simultaneously if possible, according to the following guidelines:

Belly flaps: Lightly oil, then grill over very hot coals until golden in spots and crispy on the edges but not brittle, about 2 minutes per side.

Loins: Lightly oil, then grill over medium heat, turning as needed, until firm, about 5 minutes; the loins should feel like a just-cooked chicken breast.

Sausage: Grill, starting over medium heat and finishing on a hotter spot, until just firm, about 5 minutes.

Kidneys and liver: Oil and season with salt and pepper. Skewer if necessary, to keep them from falling through the bars, and grill over high heat until just cooked through, a minute or two per side.

Rillettes *crostini:* Lightly oil the bread and grill until just crisp on both sides, then spread thickly with *rillettes* {if using, spread with a little prune paste first}. Set over gray coals to warm through.

If using grapes, currants, figs, or cherries, coat lightly with oil, salt lightly, and broil briefly, until the skin sizzles and begins to blister.

Place the greens in the salad bowl and toss with vinaigrette to coat. Arrange most of the leaves on plates or a platter, reserving some to garnish.

Slice the loin into thin medallions. Cut the belly across the grain ~ spanning the arc of the semicircle ~ into very thin strips. {If you cut the other direction the strips will be tough.}

If you have as many sausages as diners, leave them whole; otherwise, cut into bite-sized chunks. Do likewise with the innards.

Distribute the loin, sausage, and innards randomly over the salad, taking care not to pile them. Add a few more strategic leaves of salad, tuck in the fruits and the *rillettes* crostini, if using, and garnish with the chopped nuts and slivers of belly.

✛ ✛

Sausage & Charcuterie

✛ ✛

I WILL NOT FORGET THE DAY IN 1983 WHEN BILLY WEST, THE FOUNDER OF ZUNI Café, came to my apartment in Berkeley to introduce himself, and {he confessed years later} figure out what to do with the then-tiny restaurant. He thought I might want to work there, but he was also thinking about selling the place.

There were strings of freshly cased salami spanning my front hallway, and the floor was covered with newspapers strategically taped in place beneath the occasionally dripping garlands. The whole apartment smelled like potpourri, thanks to an open bin of lavender where, once it had dried out, I had buried an earlier batch of sausage, thinking it would give a nice perfume to the tangy meat. I was busily unemployed, doing "research" for a restaurant I hoped to open. That restaurant never happened, but Billy liked the salami quite a lot and said the whole scene convinced him we would get along. We only made lavender salami a few times at Zuni, but sausage and charcuterie are an important part of our repertory, and the episode suggests one can certainly attack such exotics at home. I include here a basic sausage-making method and two treasured sausage recipes, culled from years of dabbling. They are resolutely oldfangled, but I've never grown tired of them. {Given the need to control humidity and temperature, tricky for both home and restaurant cooks, I've left out the lavender salami recipe, but I do recommend you try burying a good quality store-bought salami in dried lavender. Leave for a few days, then brush off the lavender, slice thin, and enjoy with a glass of Beaujolais and some olives.} Beyond sausage, you will find a lesson in confit-making; a classic foie gras terrine; an unusual *rillettes* formula, and a recipe for *Graisserons,* an obscure relation of confit that looks like pâté.

A LESSON *in* SAUSAGE MAKING

SAUSAGE MAKING OUGHT NOT TO INTIMIDATE THE HOME COOK: GRINDING AND seasoning is easy ~ only the stuffing part requires a special technique, but even that is not hard to master. And you can certainly serve many sausages in patties. As for specialized equipment, a meat-grinding and sausage-stuffing package for an electric mixer can be had for about $50. The grinder attachment should come with a feeding pan to hold the meat, a stomper to push the meat into the tube, two perforated plates ~ for medium and coarse grinding {by "medium" I mean a grind the texture of hamburger} ~ and an X-shaped four-bladed knife. I recommend ordering a second knife~which I explain on page 422. To care for the blades, keep them scrupulously clean, dry, and lightly oiled when not in use, stored where they will not get nicked. That way they will continue to produce the clean, crumbly grind you need for top-notch sausage. The sausage-stuffing attachment will usually consist of no more than the funnel-like "horn" you mount on the front of the grinder. {You can invest in a separate sausage stuffer~a cylinder with built-in plunger~but this is not essential; I've made sausage at restaurants for more than twenty years without ever using one.}

Once you have the equipment, getting the meat into the casings requires no great dexterity, only a little patience. The casings themselves may not be a supermarket item, but they have lately become available by mail-order, and in home cook–appropriate quantities {see Sources and Resources, page 518}. I've also found that many specialty food stores that prepare fresh sausages on site are happy to sell small quantities of casings over the counter. Even so, consider buying more casings than you need right away; stored in brine and refrigerated, they keep indefinitely.

BASIC SAUSAGE-MAKING TECHNIQUE

Seasoning the meat:

Cut the meat into cubes that will easily fit into the opening of the grinder. Trim off thick sinews or silverskin. Season with 1 scant teaspoon sea salt per pound of meat {allow a little more if using kosher salt}. We generally incorporate most of the other seasonings and ingredients at this point so they permeate the meat with the salt, as well as to ensure they are well distributed. {Working seasonings evenly into ground meat is problematic, and that kneading process changes the texture.} Refrigerate the meat for 8 to 24 hours. This slight cure improves the texture, and helps keep it juicy even when cooked well-done.

Preparing the grinder:

You will get the cleanest grind and brightest tasting sausage if the grinder, plate, and knife and the meat are well chilled when you begin. As meat warms up, it softens and the fat starts to melt, both of which cause it to slip and slide in the mechanism~the meat gets kneaded and mashed rather than passing through neatly. This taints the texture of the sausage. It will also spoil more rapidly than meat that has been kept very cold.

Whenever you assemble the grinder, always place the same face of the perfo-

\ *continued*

rated plate against the four-edged knife. {Incise a mark into the nongrinding face of the plate to keep track.} On its initial uses, the cutting edge of the knife shapes itself to the plate; alternating the face unnecessarily wears and dulls this edge. For this reason, we buy and store plates and knives in sets, and never trade parts.

Grinding and tasting the sausage:

As you grind the meat, watch that it is emerging evenly and that the grind is speckled red {or pink} and white. Occasionally a piece of sinew will catch on the plate or knife and clog the grinder. If the grind is uneven, or "smeared pink," this is the likely cause. Turn off the machine immediately, unscrew the face of the grinder, slide out the plate and knife, and remove any trapped meat and sinew. Reassemble the grinder and resume grinding.

Once all of the meat is ground, form a small patty and cook it in a small skillet over medium-low heat to check the salt and other seasonings. If it needs more seasoning, spread the meat out in a wide baking dish or on a platter and reseason it evenly, so most of the distributing is done without handling the meat. Use your hands or a spatula to cut and fold in the seasonings to finish the job. Cook another sample. Once you are happy with the flavor, return the ground meat to the refrigerator. Clean and refrigerate the grinder in preparation for stuffing. Or you can form sausage patties by hand right away.

Preparing the casings and stuffing the sausage:

While the meat is chilling, prepare the casings, whether skinny, tender lamb casings or fatter, stronger hog casings. All should be sold in saltwater brine that will allow you to preserve your supply for months. Each type of casing can vary

✦ ✦ ✦ ✦ ✦

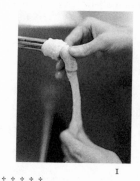  

✦ ✦ ✦ ✦ ✦　　　　　I　　　　　　　　　　2　　　　　　　　　　3

in width, and holes and tears can happen, so it is impossible to know exactly how long a piece you will need, but a generous 1/2 ounce of casing per pound of sausage meat should be adequate. This will amount to about 6 feet of lamb casing or 2 feet of hog casing. As you become adept at stuffing, you may use less. Rinse the casing in cold water, then thread the end over the spout of the faucet and run a gentle stream of cold water through it {1}. The casing should feel and smell clean. It is inconvenient to run out of prepared casing in the middle of a stuffing operation, so I encourage you to err on the side of cleaning too much~you can re-brine any casings you don't use.

Reinstall the cold grinder, substituting the stuffing horn for the knife and plate. Slide the casing over the tip of the horn. Feed the meat into the mouth of the grinder and turn it on to the lowest speed. When the first bit of meat appears at the tip of the horn, turn off the grinder, pull the casing forward, and knot it {2,3}; that way, you will avoid trapping air in the casing. Now, holding the casing in place at the tip of the stuffing horn, turn the machine on to the lowest speed, and gradually release the casing as the meat fills and tugs at it {4}; turn the machine off any time the extruding end gets ahead of you. Always stop the grinder a few seconds before you reach the end of a casing. Once you have cased all of the meat, slide the remaining casing off the horn, and pinch and twist off the links. For 4-ounce sausages in hog casings, or 2 ounce sausages in lamb casings, pinch off about 6-inch links and squeeze the meat from both ends of each one to produce a plumper 5-inch link. Give each sausage about four complete twists, and alternate directions from one sausage to the next. This will produce a twisted thread of casing about 1/2-inch-long between each link {5}. One can also, with a patient helper to feed the meat into the grinder, and a little practice, use

✦ ✦ ✦ ✦ ✦

4   5

✦ ✦ ✦ ✦ ✦

\ *continued*

both hands to release the casing and cradle and twist off the sausages as you stuff them. This is fun once you get the hang of it. Lay the sausages in a wide dish, cover loosely, and refrigerate.

Storing and cooking the sausage:

It is best to age most sausages 4 to 8 hours in the refrigerator before cooking them. That way, the meat will adhere to the inside of the casing and be less likely to burst out the ends. Before cooking, snip the sausages apart at the center of the "twisted thread" that links them. The 1/4 inch of twisted casing should keep the ends from popping open when you cook the links.

Leave the sausages at room temperature for about 15 minutes before cooking them, to reduce pressure on fragile casings; to further reduce the risk of explosion, start the sausages over medium heat, and only raise the temperature to brown them after some of the moisture has evaporated or seeped out of the sausage. Initial high heat may blister and tear the casings. I don't advocate pricking the raw sausages; too much moisture escapes with this method. Don't blanch or poach the links before grilling or panfrying them. Precooking may ensure that no bursting occurs, but it also leaches out flavor and succulence from the sausage.

Allow about 12 minutes to cook a fat sausage stuffed in hog casing. Brown each side for 3 or 4 minutes over medium heat or glowing coals, then finish cooking over lower heat. Skinny sausages stuffed in lamb's casing should take 4 to 6 minutes.

✢
✢ ✢

PORK SAUSAGE

THIS IS THE FORMULA I HAVE RELIED ON FOR DECADES TO PRODUCE ROBUST, succulent sausage. The balance of fat to lean {1 to 2}, the ratio of salt to meat {1 teaspoon to 1 pound, and strategic preseasoning are the key elements here ~ even without the fennel seed or sage, this recipe makes a tasty sausage. Choose pork that is firm and rosy pink, streaked with creamy white fat. Pork shoulder is usually well trimmed for the consumer, but if you can get a chunk with fat intact, you can cut back on the amount of pork belly and use proportionately more shoulder.

Serve this sausage, cased or in plump patties, with grilled or braised vegetables, with *Fagioli all'Uccelletto* {page 265}, or with eggs. We use it in pasta dishes with braised bitter greens or with English peas. You can also use it to make a hearty pasta sauce that keeps well for several days; follow the method for Giblet-Mushroom Sauce {page 214}. It is also good crumbled, browned, and cooked into risotto with favas or mustard greens. The fennel seed–dried currant version is perfect for Quail and Sausage Braised with Grapes {page 361}.

Wine: Pinot Blanc d'Alsace, Zind-Humbrecht, 1999

FOR ABOUT 2 POUNDS {ABOUT EIGHT 4-OUNCE LINKS IN HOG CASINGS, OR SIXTEEN 2-OUNCE LINKS IN LAMB CASINGS}:

1 pound boneless pork shoulder butt, cut into 1-inch cubes

8 ounces pork belly, cut into 1-inch cubes

1-1/2 ounces pancetta or a mixture of pancetta and fatty prosciutto scraps, coarsely chopped

Scant 1-1/2 teaspoons salt {a little more if using kosher salt}

Scant 1 teaspoon dried chili flakes

1 tablespoon fennel seeds, lightly crushed, or a few fresh sage leaves, lightly pounded, then chopped

5 to 10 garlic cloves, peeled {1 to 2 ounces}

3/4 cup diced yellow onions {3 ounces}

2 tablespoons dried currants {about 1/2 ounce}, soaked in a spoonful of brandy {optional}

Generous 4 feet hog casing or 12 feet lamb casing, cleaned {to buy, see Sources and Resources, page 518; to clean, see page 422}

Seasoning the meat {8 to 24 hours in advance}:

Combine the pork shoulder and belly with the pancetta or pancetta and prosciutto. Sprinkle evenly all over with the salt, chili, and fennel or sage, then toss well to distribute. Cover loosely and refrigerate.

Assemble your grinder attachment, with a knife and the medium plate {3/16- to 1/4-inch holes}, and chill.

Just before grinding, coarsely chop the garlic and scatter it and the diced onion over the meat. Fold to distribute. Attach the grinder attachment to your mixer or grinding machine, and grind the meat. {For guidelines, see pages 421–422.}

\ *continued*

Scatter the currants, if using, over the meat, then fold in. Form a small patty and cook gently in a small pan with a few drops of olive oil over medium-low heat. Taste for salt and other seasonings, adjust as needed, and cook another small sample. The raw onion may taste strong at this point, but it will mellow as the sausage ages.

Form the meat into patties, or chill well and then stuff into hog or lamb casing. {For stuffing guidelines, see page 422}. Cover loosely and refrigerate for at least 8 hours. Remove cased sausages from the refrigerator about 15 minutes before cooking.

As long as you have kept the ingredients cold, uncooked loose sausage should keep for a few days in the refrigerator; cased sausage for a few days longer.

⁜

Rabbit Sausage

This elegant sausage is my favorite; tender and delicate, it shows off the subtle flavor of rabbit better than any other dish we make. I first made it for a special Easter menu at the Union Hotel in Benicia. In that intimate kitchen, I always made it myself, measuring nothing, concocting entirely by "feel" and feeling vaguely proprietary about it. The reality of the bigger and busier Zuni Café made it difficult to always do *anything* myself, so I reluctantly allowed "feel" to be transformed into ounces. But not entirely.

The variable quantities and options here reflect the range of delicious textures and flavors that is possible. Cream makes the sausage rich, bread crumbs add tenderness, and egg will make it fluffy *and* rich, but all three compete with the flavor of the rabbit. Taste and decide what you like as you make the sausage. A good rule of thumb is that if the mixture tastes good and has a good texture, stop messing with it. Simple, clear tastes that emerge with no teasing are a lucky treat; don't risk stifling them beneath virtuoso layers of complexity. Availability will affect your decisions as well, as should the rest of the menu. For example, if you have cream or egg elsewhere in the meal, you may want to leave it out here.

We usually serve rabbit sausages with a salad as a first course, or as part of a Rabbit Mixed Grill {page 416}. They are delicious with mashed potatoes or favas, roasted butternut squash purée, or warm green beans and white truffle oil. Try them on top of a risotto flecked with wild rice and fresh sage. This sausage shows best next to things tender, suave, and elegant. It will falter next to rustic dishes with strong flavors and coarse textures. And don't pair it with tomato.

Yield varies with the quantity of the optional ingredients you use.

Wine: Mitchelton Victoria, Australia, Marsanne, 1999

FOR 1-1/4 TO 2 POUNDS {TEN TO SIXTEEN 2-OUNCE LINKS}:

1 tablespoon unsalted butter

1/2 cup finely diced yellow onions or shallots {2 ounces}

1 teaspoon salt {allow a little more if using kosher salt} plus a few pinches

A few fresh sage leaves, chopped {optional}

14 ounces rabbit~loin, belly flap, or hind leg {see Cutting Up a Rabbit, and What to Do with the Parts, page 411}; a 2-1/2-pound rabbit will yield about 18 ounces of these cuts~use any excess, plus the forelegs, for Rabbit *Rillettes,* {page 442}

2 ounces pancetta, minced {about 1/3 cup}

Freshly grated nutmeg

Freshly ground black or white pepper {optional}

Up to 1 cup cold heavy cream

Up to 1 ounce soft, fresh bread crumbs {about 1/2 cup} made from slightly stale, crustless, chewy, white peasant-style bread {see page 506}

1 or 2 small eggs, chilled {optional}

Up to 1/2 ounce fresh black truffle {optional}

About 9 feet lamb casings, rinsed {to buy, see Sources and Resources, page 518; to clean, see page 422}

A few teaspoons mild-tasting olive oil or unsalted butter

Preparing and seasoning the meat {8 to 24 hours in advance}:

Warm the butter in a small skillet over low heat. Add the onions or shallots, a few pinches of salt, and the sage, if using. Cook, stirring a few times, until the onions or shallots are translucent and very soft, 6 to 7 minutes. Scrape onto a plate and chill thoroughly.

Cut the rabbit into bite-sized pieces. {If using hind legs, they are quite easy to bone by simply carving the plump meat away with a paring knife. Trim the thickest

\ *continued*

sinews and cut through the smaller ones that might otherwise catch in the grinder blade. Cut any belly flaps across the grain into strips. Toss together the rabbit meat and pancetta, and sprinkle evenly with 1 teaspoon salt, the nutmeg, and pepper, if using. Fold in the chilled onions. Cover loosely and refrigerate.

Assemble your grinder attachment, with a knife and the medium plate {3/16- to 1/4-inch holes} and chill.

Attach the grinder attachment to your mixer or grinding machine and grind the cold meat mixture. {For guidelines, see pages 421–422.} Form a tiny patty and cook in a small skillet in just a film of olive oil over low heat. Taste. One in a dozen times the meat will already taste delicious and have a great sausagey texture; you can stuff such a mixture right away if you like. More often, the rabbit is a bit hard at this point, and needs help.

Mix half the cream with half of the bread crumbs, and leave for a few minutes to allow the crumbs to swell and soften.

Add the bread crumb mixture to the ground rabbit and beat with a wooden spoon. Cook another small sample and taste. The sausage will be softer, richer tasting, and less crumbly. You can stuff the sausage now, or add a little more cream, or make and add more cream-crumb mixture if you want to enhance those qualities.

To make the sausage slightly bouncy-tender, incorporate 1 egg, beaten first with a pinch of salt. Cook and taste another sample, and add a second beaten egg, or part of one, if you want to emphasize that quality.

Mince the black truffle, if using, and fold into the sausage mixture. Cover and chill well.

Stuff the mixture into the prepared lamb's casings; for 2-ounce sausages, twist every 6 inches or so. {For stuffing guidelines, see page 422.} Refrigerate for at least 3 hours before cooking.

If you have kept all of the ingredients cold, the uncooked cased sausage will keep in the refrigerator for about 4 days.

Remove the sausage from the refrigerator about 15 minutes before cooking. Rabbit sausage is fragile, owing to the high moisture content and the tender lamb casings. As the moisture vaporizes, the pressure can easily burst the skins, so take care to start the sausages over gentle heat, whether in a pan or on the grill, then increase the heat gradually. If grilling, first rub the sausages with a little mild-tasting olive oil; if cooking in a pan, start in a little olive oil or melted unsalted butter. Cook until just firm, turning to brown both sides, about 5 minutes.

+
+ +

DUCK CONFIT

CONFIT IS A TYPE OF PRESERVED MEAT, USUALLY DUCK, GOOSE, OR PORK. It is native to Southwestern France, where the farmhouse tradition lives on in homes and restaurants alike. To prepare confit, the fresh meat is first salted, then rinsed, dried, and simmered in duck, goose, or pork fat until tender. Well-made, it is neither salty nor fatty. Carefully stored, well-made confit will keep for months. Compared to simple drying, salt and sugar brining, or smoking, this method of preservation conserves the basic character of the meat very well. It also preserves succulence. Confit is served panfried until crispy, or simmered or baked in well-known concoctions like cassoulet, or less well-known ones, such as *Garbure* {page 169} Cold confit is good sliced as an hors d'œuvre or shredded into winter salads, garnished with brandied or pickled fruit.

The best duck for confit is the moulard {*mulard* in French, literally, a "mule" duck}, the sterile offspring of a Muscovy and Pekin cross. It is the duck of choice in southwestern France, since, not incidentally, it is efficient for producing excellent foie gras. Muscovy duck does well confited, although it can be tougher and stronger in flavor than the moulard. You can also confit white Pekin duck {the Long Island Duckling variety}, although it is so tender and mild that you'll need to abbreviate the curing and cooking times. The result won't have the hearty character of moulard or Muscovy confit, but can be delicious.

I have produced large amounts of duck confit over time, and a number of unusable failures have forced me to figure out how to get the salt right. I spent years ~ the better part of one in the Southwest of France ~ earnestly, hopefully, warily rolling duck legs in salt, trying to gauge how much needed to cling to the flesh, contemplating how hard to tap the frosted limb to remove excess.

\ *continued*

Everybody there seemed to produce perfect confit by feel and I was anxious to acquire that touch.

En route to that knowledge, I made some very good but also many very salty, confits. For this, I overcompensated, tending to overrinse or undersalt the duck legs. Ergo, I produced some very bland confit. I tried different types of salt~kosher, coarse sea salt, rock salt, *fleur du sel.* I then asked my mentor in Les Landes, in Southwest France, Pepette Arbulo, to send her preferred *flocons de sel* {salt flakes}. To complicate things further, I overcooked some batches and undercooked others. Bedeviled by my duck confit problems, I explored confiting quail and rabbit and chicken, and, of course, encountered the same inconsistency. I couldn't get a feel for what was right, because, like most non-Landaise cooks, I wasn't making confit often enough to remember exactly what I had done the last time and exactly what it felt like. So, I started taking notes. And then experience started to become a reliable teacher after all. The unromantic truth is that a ratio of 2 teaspoons {1/3 ounce} of sea salt per pound of meat, for 18 to 24 hours, will largely preserve you from the disaster of oversalt and the dullness of undersalt. {If using kosher salt, measure a little more than 2 teaspoons~still 1/3 ounce per pound}. Then pay attention to how evenly you distribute the salt, how well you rinse it off, and how long you cook the duck, which should be over a gentle, always-steady flame. It is easy to keep track of all this and get a feel for confit if you prepare the same amount of meat, and use the same pot, a few times in a row.

The method that follows is tailored to duck legs, which make a handsome main course, but you can also use these guidelines to confit other parts of the duck. Boneless breast makes a lean but excellent confit, which is especially good cold, thickly sliced, as an hors d'œuvre. I often confit necks or the first joint of the wing {or the *aileron,* which I call the "winglet"}. Both are inexpensive flavorful ways to flavor soup or cassoulet. I offer a few separate guidelines for *Gésiers Confits* {preserved gizzards}. You can also use this formula to confit comparable cuts of goose or chunks of pork. Where pork is concerned, the shoulder butt makes the best confit.

Wine: Côtes du Frontonnais, Château Bellevue La Forêt, 1998

Salting and rinsing the duck legs:

Rinse the legs and pat them dry. The flesh will feel fairly soft. Trim ragged edges {set aside the trim to render for fat or to make *Graisserons,* page 440}. Weigh the meat, then measure 2 teaspoons {1/3 ounce} sea salt per pound of meat. Working on a sheet pan or a sheet of parchment paper, salt the legs all over, targeting the thickest sections with a heavier dose than the skinny edges and ankles. Then roll the legs on the salty pan or paper to grab the salt that fell from or missed the target. Arrange the legs in a wide glass, glazed earthenware, stainless steel, or hard plastic bowl or storage vessel, placing the first layer skin side down. Don't stack the legs more than three deep, or the bottom layer will be submerged in pink brine by the next morning, and those pieces will be too salty. Refrigerate for 18 to 24 hours.

Rinse the legs one at a time under a stream of cold running water. Don't soak. Pay attention to the texture of the meat as you rinse it. The flesh will be a little darker, and feel a little firmer than before. But if any spots feel particularly hard ~ sometimes the edges will be almost clay-like ~ knead those areas lightly as you target them with rinse water, to urge excess salt out. Spread the rinsed legs on a clean, dry towel. If you are anxious about the saltiness, do a simple test. Trim off a nugget of meat, place in a small saucepan with just enough warm duck fat to submerge it, and cook at a near simmer for about 5 minutes. Taste. Ignore the texture ~ it will be very tough ~ and consider the salt. The meat should taste well seasoned, like fresh sausage. If it is too salty for your taste, briefly rinse each leg again. You will notice this softens the meat further. Once you are content with the saltiness, pat each leg dry.

Place the legs in a wide, sterilized bowl or tub, cover, and leave for an hour or so at room temperature. The shock of being aggressively salted and briefly rinsed means the salinity will be uneven within each piece of meat. As it rests, the salt will diffuse more evenly. You can leave the legs overnight refrigerated if it better suits your schedule.

The fat:

A ratio of 2 cups fat to 1 pound meat should be generous enough to submerge most cuts of duck in most pots. It is most practical to purchase rendered duck fat, in which case you need merely warm it up {see Sources and Resources, page 518}. You can render your own, but be aware that the duck you are confiting will not yield enough fat to submerge it. The phrase "duck cooked in its fat" always makes me smile, because that duck almost certainly cooked in another duck's fat as well. To get sufficient fat, you will need to either purchase extra duck {which you won't be confiting} or ask your poultry butcher to save lumps of fat and big slabs

\ *continued*

of fatty skin for you to render. Neck skin is a very good candidate for rendering. These odd bits can be frozen, which may make your request seem more reasonable. A pound of scraps and skin will yield about 3/4 pound or 1-1/2 cups of fat.

To render duck fat: Thaw the clods of fat and skin if necessary, then rinse. Place in a heavy saucepan, add about 1/2 inch of cold water, and set over low heat. Stir once or twice in the first 10 minutes, then leave to melt. Once the solids are no more than a handful of shrunken, misshapen bits and the fat is clear and golden, strain. It will take at least 30 minutes to reach this point, but exact timing depends on the pan, amount and type of scraps, and heat. If any of the shrunken bits are meaty, save them for *Graisserons* {page 440}. The remaining bits of rendered skin can be coarsely chopped, lightly salted, and browned in a pan to make cracklings, which I like to add to frisée salad.

Cooking the confit:

Choose a heavy pot that will crowd the duck legs, without stacking them more than two or three pieces deep. A crowded fit reduces the amount of fat needed to submerge the meat, but if it is piled too high, the meat can cook unevenly. Stirring and rearranging prevents this but is difficult to do without tearing the skins and losing track of which leg was where. I can confit up to 3-1/2 pounds of meat {4 large duck legs} in a 4-quart saucepan with just over 5 cups of fat. When making a large batch of confit, I use a *saucier*-type pan and never stack more than two-deep.

When you are ready to start cooking the confit, heat what should be just enough fat until it is warm to the touch. Add the duck legs, and then add more fat if they are not submerged. Bring the fat to a near simmer and skim any foam. Adjust the heat to maintain the fat at a steady near simmer. In my experience, uneven heat means the meat releases lots of its tasty juice, producing a less succulent confit. I try to hold the fat at 200° to 205°.

Judging doneness:

The duck will initially firm up and then gradually soften as it cooks in the fat. How long this takes is a function of the type of duck, size of the cut, and the quantity. Meats vary widely; even two batches of the same type of meat from the same source at different times of year can behave differently. In general, allow between 1-1/2 and 2 hours for 12-ounce duck legs, or comparable chunks of goose or pork, checking every 10 minutes after the first hour. Allow an hour for small, bony, sinewy winglets. Prod the meat in the pot; if it yields at all, remove a piece, carve off a sliver, cool it to the touch, and taste. {Very hot meat will always feel tough; it needs to cools slightly before you can accurately judge tenderness.} Perfectly cooked confit should be tender but still resilient. If it is allowed to cook to "fork-tender" it will be dry. Once the meat is tender, turn off the heat and leave for about 10 minutes for any juices to settle at the bottom.

Storing confit:

Skim the surface of the fat. Carefully remove the pieces of meat, without tearing the skins or stirring the fat, and place in sterilized glass, porcelain, glazed earthenware, hard plastic, or stainless steel vessels. Skim the fat again and then ladle it through a fine strainer over the cooked meat. Take care as you reach the bottom of the pot not to collect any of the delicious, salty, gelatinous broth that resides there. {Strain and save it for other recipes, such as *Graisserons,* page 440; Onion Soup with Tomato and a Poached Egg, page 159; or *La Garbure Landaise,* page 169.} Make sure the pieces of meat are completely submerged in fat, then cool completely, cover with a lid or plastic, and store refrigerated until needed. {Actually, properly salted, cooked, and sealed confit doesn't really need to be refrigerated, although it should be kept cool. In Les Landes, I saw lots of confit in un–air conditioned barns or cellars, and even out all day in working kitchens. It seems prudent, though, and it is convenient, to store it in the refrigerator.} It will improve during the first month and then can keep well for months longer. Label the vessel with exactly what is in it and the date. The clear yellow fat turns opaque white when it solidifies, and you could never guess what it hides.

"Tempering" the confit {see Tempering, page 120}:

Always pull the dish of confit from the refrigerator an hour or so before you need it, to begin to warm and soften the fat. You can speed the process by setting the pan in a warm spot near the oven, but don't set the whole thing in a hot oven, you'll just melt the edges. Once the fat is malleable, reach in and ease out the pieces you need. Slide them through your fingers to remove the squishy mantle of excess fat. As long as your hands were clean and you see no beige or brown liquid at the bottom, you can usually return the vessel with unused confit to the refrigerator. Just make sure no meat is exposed, and do use the remaining confit within a week or so. Otherwise, you should rewarm the remaining confit and fat,

\ *continued*

place the meat in a clean smaller vessel, and strain the fat back over it to reseal. In either case, note on the label what you did.

To pan-brown confit:

I recommend the pieces of confit be at room temperature or close to it when you brown them. Place a cast-iron or other heavy skillet over medium heat. When it is hot enough to sizzle the confit quietly on contact, arrange the pieces in a single crowded layer skin side down in the pan. The duck will shed some fat. Adjust the heat as needed to maintain that quiet sizzle. It should take about 9 minutes to set a pretty golden crust. You can check progress once or twice, but don't fuss with the confit, or you may compromise that crust. {If your confit was much colder than room temperature, trap some heat in the pan by partially covering it with a lid~don't cover it completely, or the confit may steam. I also suggest you work over lower heat and take a little longer to color the skin.} Once the skin is crispy and golden, turn the duck over and cook for only 4 or 5 minutes on the other side. Don't overcook this side, or the skinless flesh will develop a tough, jerky-like crust.

If you need to brown more than one batch of confit, spread the browned pieces in a roasting pan and hold in a 275° oven while you brown the rest.

Prepared this way, duck confit welcomes many different vegetables and garnishes. Beans, mashed root vegetables, roasted winter squash, hashed sweet potatoes, deep-fried or spiced prunes, roasted applesauce, polenta, lentils in red wine, grilled radicchio, roasted cherries or figs, and frisée, watercress, and arugula salad are all on my short list. I don't pair confit with creamy or cheesy dishes.

❖ ❖ GÉSIERS CONFITS

«Gésiers confits» sounds pretty in French and they are one of my favorite confits. "Preserved gizzards" are a hard sell in English, but absolutely worth trying. The toughest muscle I can think of, the hard-working gizzard is also the most flavorful. In southwestern France, I first enjoyed preserved gizzards as a cold hors d'œuvre, sliced the thickness of poker chips and speared with toothpicks. They are delicious in warm chicory salads with walnuts and apples. Warm confited gizzards and Warm Truffled Beets {page 241} are extraordinary together. Count an ounce or two of gizzards per person for salads or as part of an hors d'œuvre.

To confit duck, goose, or little chicken gizzards, trim off the silverskin {1,2}, rinse, and dry, then toss with 3/4 teaspoon {1/8 ounce} sea salt for every pound of innards {count about 2 dozen duck gizzards per pound}. Gizzards often come with an errant heart or two in the mix; they make a tender and delicious confit, so salt them as well. They require no trimming; just rinse and press dry.

+ + + + +

1   2

+ + + + +

1.   *Use the tip of a paring knife to free the edge of the silverskin.*

2.   *Flip the gizzard over, and, holding the freed edge of the silverskin, slide the knife flat against the work surface to remove the rest of the silverskin. Repeat to remove the silverskin on the other side.*

Cover loosely and refrigerate. Allow 6 to 8 hours for the salt to penetrate duck or goose gizzards, a few hours less for smaller gizzards or the tender hearts.

Rinse the gizzards {and hearts} thoroughly, dry, and cook very slowly in enough fat to cover by a few inches ~ figure on about 2 cups fat for 1 pound gizzards. Don't skimp on fat, or you'll have trouble keeping it from boiling. Skim foam as it accumulates. Goose and duck gizzards will take 45 minutes to 1-1/2 hours. With hearts and smaller chicken gizzards, start checking for doneness at 30 minutes. To test for doneness, spear a gizzard with the tip of a paring knife; it should enter easily. Carve off a sliver and taste. The meat should be dense and firm, but not crunchy. I compare the texture of a perfectly cooked gizzard to cold, hard Gruyère cheese. Once the gizzards are tender, turn off the heat, leave to cool for about 5 minutes, skim, and then lift the confited gizzards from the fat to a

\ *continued*

small container. Ladle the fat through a fine strainer onto the confit. They should be completely submerged. Refrigerate. Any juice at the bottom of the pot will be strong and is difficult to use, but save it if you will be making Giblet-Mushroom Sauce {page 214} or *Graisserons* {page 440} anytime soon. Discard any leftover fat.

In a pinch, when I have no duck fat on hand, I confit gizzards in mild-tasting olive oil. This is heretical, but gizzards have enough flavor and character to withstand the challenge of mild olive oil. It is a convenient alternative, of particular interest if you plan to serve the gizzards thinly sliced in a salad or in an hors d'œuvre that is prepared with olive oil.

✦
✦ ✦

FOIE GRAS *en* TERRINE

THIS IS THE SIMPLEST OF THE CLASSIC FOIE GRAS PREPARATIONS, WHOLE LOBES, gently baked in their own fat, to be served cool or cold in satiny slices. This particular method produces a rosy foie gras, which tastes exactly and only of that. My purist roots preclude adding truffles, pepper, sweet wine, or any seasoning other than salt, but you can use this technique for recipes that include those things.

Regarding your choice of foie gras: There is much discussion over whether duck or goose produces the superior foie gras; however, the issue is largely moot in America, since, as of this writing, there is no domestic goose foie gras available. Both birds have their partisans in France, but the people I worked with in Les Landes in Southwest France preferred duck for its finesse. {Notwithstanding, a combination of economics and biology determines availability. Geese need more days of forced feeding, and more food per day, to develop a fat liver than ducks do, so goose foie gras is more expensive to produce. And, since, unlike ducks, geese can't be cajoled into laying eggs year-round, you can only produce goose foie gras during part of the year~the late fall, just in time for the holidays~which helps explain how foie gras became a holiday specialty in France. I have also heard that fattened geese don't support hot summers as well as fattened ducks, which makes geese a risky undertaking in the hot Southwest of France.} Our local foie gras producer did raise geese for foie gras when they started out, and the results were good, but lacking a steady market for the meat, it wasn't a viable endeavor.

What fresh foie gras is produced in America is from either the moulard or the Muscovy duck. The moulard, or *mulard* {a sterile "mule-duck" cross between the Muscovy and the Pekin duck}, is *the* foie gras duck in France, and even though its father may be Muscovy, it is not customary there to raise that bird for its liver. Again, economics play a role; Muscovy chicks are more expensive than moulards, and require more days of forced feeding. My mentor, Pepette Arbulo, was perplexed when I first told her she'd be cooking Muscovy foie gras when she flew from France to be guest chef at Zuni, but she approved once she tasted the product. {For both kinds of duck foie gras, see Sources and Resources, page 518.}

Whatever its pedigree, the best foie gras is fleshy pink and uniformly firm. Commercial foie gras is vacuum-packed, and it begins to sweat a little blood mixed with water within three days. Although this is not an intrinsic defect, I avoid livers that have exuded a lot of brownish liquid. A small bruise or two seems to be inevitable, but check to see that there are not too many. A foie gras whose plastic pack has lost its vacuum may be fine as long as it still has good, bright color and you are planning on cooking it within a day or two. Alas, foie gras is not labeled with packing dates, but if it is kept consistently quite cold, the vacuum-pack keeps well for 3 weeks.

Preparing the foie gras for baking:

Rinse the liver in cold water and pat it dry. Gently pry the two lobes apart. If the liver starts to crack, let it warm up a few degrees, until you can ease the lobes apart. Using the tip of a boning or paring knife, gingerly trace and liberate the blood vessels that connect the lobes. Carve out the vessels as deeply into the liver as they are blood-filled. Occasionally you will discover a green vessel or green specks on the liver: this is bile and should be completely removed.

Preheat the oven to 275°.

Weigh the foie gras and season all over with 1 scant teaspoon sea salt per pound {allow a little more if using kosher salt}, concentrating the distribution on the thickest parts, where it must penetrate most deeply. Reassemble the lobes in their natural configuration. Press any loose chunks of foie gras into the natural hollows of the lobes.

\ *continued*

Baking and cooling the foie gras:

Choose a terrine or small, deep baking dish that at least vaguely echoes the shape of the foie gras and is barely large enough to contain it. Pepette baked her foie gras *en bocaux*, upright, in straight-sided canning jars, which, if not glamorous, work perfectly and have the advantage of an airtight lid for storage. Press the foie gras into the chosen baking dish. Remember how high the foie gras sits in the dish. Take the temperature at the center of the liver. This will help you predict how long it will take to cook. I usually start with the liver between 55° and 60°. If it is colder than that, it tends to cook less evenly. Cut a piece of parchment paper to rest on the surface of the liver, then cover with a lid or foil, shiny side out. If using foil, don't wrap it around the bottom of the dish; you need to be able to lift it easily during cooking.

Place the dish in the center of a larger pan, ideally about an inch taller than the level of the foie gras and wider and longer than the baking dish by at least 4 inches. Set in the center of the oven and add very hot tap water, up to 135°, to come to the depth of the foie gras, or nearly so. {This water bath will regulate the cooking temperature.}

After about 15 minutes, the liver will begin to slump in its fat. Begin checking the temperature at the thickest spot in the mass of liver. When it registers 98°, remove the terrine from the water bath, remove the foil and droopy parchment, and leave to cool. If any part of the liver projects dramatically above the rest, push on the warm, soft lobe to lower its profile. The melted fat will be much hotter than the liver, and it will, coupled with the retained heat in the vessel itself, finish cooking the liver. Continue to monitor the temperature, however, and if it rises to 105° in the thickest spot, place the dish in an ice water bath until it is cool to the touch. The rate of cooking and cooling will depend almost entirely on the material your "terrine" is made of ~ earthenware, porcelain, enameled cast-iron, and ovenproof glass absorb and bleed heat at different rates. {Try to use the same baking dish each time you bake a foie gras so you become familiar with how it affects cooking time ~ although by the time you are, you may discover the liver cooks more quickly because you won't be opening the oven so often to check it.}

By the time the liver has cooled, it will have rendered 15 to 25 percent of its mass as bright yellow fat and settled into it. This sounds dramatic in view of the cost of foie gras, but that fat is a culinary treasure as well {see page 439}.

Storing and serving:

Place a clean piece of parchment on the surface, then wrap the dish with foil. Don't use plastic, or the terrine may sweat. Refrigerate. The foie gras will have better flavor after a few days. An uncut terrine will keep for up to 2 weeks, although in that case, you should wrap plastic around the foil once the terrine is quite cold.

To most easily slice the foie gras, use a slender knife, and warm the blade in a tall glass of hot water and wipe dry before each slice. Count on an ounce or two of foie gras *en terrine* per person as an hors d'œuvre.

This fine terrine tolerates all the classic embellishments, but at Zuni we most often present it with freshly grilled, thinly sliced, peasant-style bread, lightly toasted hazelnuts, and Brandied Cherries or Red Currants {page 279}, or Spiced Zante Grapes {page 276}. We always add a few leaves of arugula, Belgian endive, or young lettuces dressed with mild vinaigrette.

Capitalizing on the Scraps:

Conserve every crumble of foie gras and every dab of the bright yellow fat. You can use both to flavor a *Pearà* Sauce {page 311} to serve with quail, squab, or duck, or to offer with grilled asparagus. Even a little bit of foie gras fat will make a simple pan of fried potatoes excellent. Pepette's mother, who was a venerable figure in the culinary community and nearly belligerent in her traditionalism, enjoyed the golden fat spread on warm toast more than the liver itself. In Roanne, a decade before, I watched great-aunt *Tata* {Jean-Baptiste Troisgros's sister} fashion the same warm *tartine* of slightly charred country bread and foie gras fat. Both *Tata* and Georgette lived well into their nineties.

✤
✤ ✤

GRAISSERONS

DESPITE THEIR INAUSPICIOUS BAPTISM AS "LARGE FAT THINGS," *GRAISSERONS* ARE in fact not terribly fatty. They are a fortuitous, and widely unknown, by-product of making a lot of confit. Traditionally, the scrappy bits of meat that fall to the bottom of the cauldron of fat are greedily gathered by the cook, drained, and then pressed into a jar or small terrine. Then the flavorful *gelée,* which also accumulates at the bottom of the pot, is skimmed of fat and poured warm over the precious scraps. Once cold, these scarce *graisserons* become a cherished stash, saved for a lucky few to enjoy as an hors d'œuvre, sliced like pâté, with pickles and toasts.

Not content to have a scant supply for a lucky few, we use a method contrived by my friend and teacher Pepette, who generated *graisserons* by the potful in her restaurant in rural Southwest France. It involves salting a selection of meats, mincing some and grinding others, and then confiting them. We add a pig's foot for gelatin. The recipe itself is flexible; as long as you follow the basic ratios for salting, and procedures for rinsing and cooking, you can alter the mix of meats. You can use goose instead of duck, or replace some of the dark Muscovy or moulard meat with pale Pekin duck, or incorporate some squab or even a little chicken. You can also alter the quantity of pork or giblets, or mince the pork instead of grinding it, or grind the duck instead of mincing it. {Or mince them both if you don't have a grinder.} If you have a little bit of tasty but ragged-looking leftover confit, shred it and add to the pot of simmering "fat things." I am certain that before this writing I had never assembled exactly the same combination twice, but I do know that the best *graisserons* are mostly dark meat, contain a combination of poultry and pork, and boast some textural variation.

Graisserons keep for months refrigerated. It is practical to pack them in 1-cup batches, to pull out as an hors d'œuvre for 4, or to give as gifts. Serve cold with warm toasts and pickled fruit, such as Spiced Zante Grapes {page 276}, Pickled Onions {page 271} or Glasswort {page 274}, or Marinated Roasted Beets {page 240}.

Wine: Morgon Javernières, Domaine Louis-Claude Desvignes, 2000

1 pound lean boneless pork shoulder butt, cut into 2-inch chunks

1 pound Muscovy or moulard duck breasts, skin on, cut into 3-inch chunks

About 10 ounces Muscovy or moulard duck leg {about 1 small leg}

4 ounces poultry hearts or trimmed gizzards {see *Gésiers Confits,* page 434}

Salt

8 ounces pig's foot

2 bay leaves

About 1/2 cup Chicken Stock {page 58}

About 1-1/2 cups duck fat {12 ounces} {to buy, see Sources and Resources, page 518; to render your own, see page 432}

Salting the meats {for best flavor, salt 12 to 24 hours in advance}:

Toss each type of meat separately and evenly with 2 teaspoons sea salt per pound {if using kosher salt, allow a little more}. Cover loosely and refrigerate overnight.

Rinse all of the meats well and pat dry. Grind the pork through a grinder fitted with a knife and the medium plate {3/16- to 1/4-inch holes}. Mince the duck breast, skin and all. Split the duck leg at the knee joint.

Place the pig's foot and duck leg and thigh in a 4-quart saucepan. Add the duck breast, pork, bay leaves, and chicken stock. Add about 1 cup of the duck fat and set over low heat to warm through, then add enough duck fat to not quite cover the meat. Once the duck skin renders, the meats should be fully submerged.

Cover and cook at a bare simmer, stirring occasionally, until the meats are very tender, about 2 hours. Remove and bone the duck leg {or, if it has already boned itself, fish out and discard the bones}. Lift the pig's foot from the pot and cool slightly, then remove and discard the bones and cartilage. Mince the meat, and skin if you like, and stir this, and the chunks of boned duck, back into the pan of *graisserons.*

Leave the *graisserons* to settle for about 10 minutes, then skim the surface and strain them from the fat. Pile them in a deep bowl. Let the fat and juices settle and separate in the pan, or transfer to a fat separator, then slowly pour off the fat

\ *continued*

and set aside. There should be about 2 cups of juices remaining ~ they will be strong, salty, and very gelatinous. If they are too salty, dilute very gingerly with water, up to a few teaspoons. {And plan to rinse the meat a little more thoroughly next time.}

Use a pestle or wooden spoon to lightly knead and amalgamate the drained *graisserons.* Add the strained juices.

Pack the *graisserons* in small straight-sided canning jars, small terrines, or custard cups. Press down so that the bits of meat are submerged in the liquid. Cool completely, then spoon a little of the duck fat over the surface to seal. Store in the refrigerator.

To serve, scrape the fat from the surface, and slice as you would pâté. If you pack the *graisserons* in jars, you can easily unmold a "loaf" by holding the sealed jar under warm water, then running a knife around the edge and sliding out the *graisserons.*

✦
✦ ✦

RABBIT RILLETTES

Most often made with pork or duck, *rillettes* are an earthy concoction of gently cooked meat teased into a meltingly tender, succulent, well-seasoned spread whose texture resembles a smashed forkful of perfectly yielding pot roast. Where traditional *rillettes* are concerned, the succulence owes to a fair bit of pork fat.

For years I made my rabbit *rillettes* in that time-honored way, marrying the lean, mild rabbit with plenty of fatty pork belly, before defecting to this unorthodox, hybrid method. Inspired by an underappreciated dish of preserved pork chunks curiously named *grillons,* this version calls for cooking the rabbit with wine and aromatics. In a further departure from canon, these *rillettes* derive their succulence not from the sacrosanct pork fat, but from pig's feet and extra-virgin olive oil. The result is lighter and more flavorful. You can use any cut of the rabbit for this recipe, but this is an excellent way to make the most of the bony forelegs.

These *rillettes* have the best flavor at room temperature or warmed. Serve with warm toasts as an hors d'œuvre, or spread on the toasts and tuck them into a salad garnished with nuts and Brandied Fruit {page 279}. These same toasts make a nice garnish for braised rabbit, and they appear in our Rabbit Mixed Grill {page

416}. Or try one of my favorite canapés, which consists of a warm baguette croû-ton smeared with a coarse paste made from Spiced Prunes {page 278} and topped with warm *rillettes*. *Rillettes* are also good stuffed into the yolk-less hollow of a hard-cooked egg and served with a slaw of finely slivered celery root, carrots, fennel, and radicchio, tossed in mustard vinaigrette.

Wine: Taltarni, Victoria, Australia, Sauvignon Blanc, 2000

FOR ABOUT I-I/2 CUPS:

I pound rabbit parts, preferably 4 forelegs and 4 belly flaps {see Cutting Up a Rabbit, and What to Do with the Parts, page 411}

I teaspoon salt {a little more if using kosher salt}

I bay leaf, crumbled

About 6 black peppercorns, crushed

A small piece of pig's foot {about 4 ounces}

I small carrot, peeled and cut into large chunks

I small stalk celery, cut into I-inch chunks

I/2 medium yellow onion, cut into wedges

4 garlic cloves, crushed

Up to 6 tablespoons extra-virgin olive oil

I/4 cup dry vermouth

Up to 3/4 cup Chicken Stock {page 58}

A nutmeg, or a piece, for grating

Freshly cracked black pepper {optional}

Seasoning the rabbit {for the best flavor, do this step 8 to 24 hours in advance}:
    Season the rabbit evenly all over with the salt, bay leaf, and black pepper. Cover loosely and refrigerate.

    Preheat the oven to 300°.

    Place the pig's foot in a saucepan of plenty of lightly salted water and bring to a boil. Skim, reduce the heat, and simmer for about 30 minutes. Drain. {This pre-cooking tames the porky flavor and assures that the tough sinew will already be at the point of yielding succulence when you start cooking the rabbit.}

    Crowd the rabbit parts and aromatics, pig's foot, carrot, celery, onion, and garlic in a shallow flameproof I-quart baking dish that accepts everything in a single, crowded layer. Chop the pig's foot into a few pieces if it pokes above the pieces of

\ *continued*

rabbit. Add the vermouth, 1/4 cup of the olive oil, and enough stock to not quite half-bathe the rabbit.

Place the dish over low heat and bring to a simmer. Cover tightly and bake until the meat is just falling off the bones, 1-1/2 to 2 hours. Check at 1 hour and turn the rabbit pieces over if they are browning.

Let cool only slightly, then remove the rabbit from the dish; set the dish aside. As soon as it is cool enough to handle, bone the rabbit. You should get about 1/2 pound of meat. Work quickly to tear and shred the meat with intrepid fingers or, if you are skittish or tradition-minded, two forks. Grate a little nutmeg over it. Pound the boned meat lightly in a mortar, in about 1/2-cup batches. As long as the meat is still quite warm, it will quickly and easily fall into a tender, fluffy mass; once the meat cools completely, it will resist separating into the fine filaments that give *rillettes* their charm. {I do like to leave a *few* thicker strands of meat in the *rillettes* for contrast. I also bone the pig's foot, chop the meat and skin finely, salt to taste, and smash it into the *rillettes* with a pestle. This is optional, but gives the *rillettes* added succulence.}

Strain the cooking liquid; skim and add the oil to the *rillettes*. Taste the remaining liquid. If it looks or tastes thin, simmer it until it has some body and tastes concentrated. A few drops at a time, add just enough of this potion, usually no more than a teaspoon or two total {see Note below}, to the meat mixture until it begins to mass. Taste. Add more salt, pepper, and/or nutmeg if you like. If you want more richness, work in a little more extra-virgin olive oil.

Serve immediately, or refrigerate until ready to use. If you make more than you will consume in one sitting, divide it among small jars or ramekins, packing it lightly, and coat the surface with a film of extra-virgin olive oil. The *rillettes* will keep a week or so this way. For longer keeping, pour a 1/8-inch-thick layer of clari-fied butter or melted pork or duck fat over the surface. Scrape or lift off and dis-card that fat before serving.

Note: Save any extra cooking liquid; you can add it to braised rabbit dishes, or spoon it over Rabbit Sausages {page 426}. It is also good tossed with egg noodles, enriched with a nugget of unsalted butter, or stirred into risotto ~ whether plain or studded with mushrooms, asparagus, peas or favas. I sometimes add it to a pot of white beans just before I reheat them.

A SIMPLE CHEESE COURSE

THE CHEESE COURSE AT ZUNI IS A MODEST ONE ~ I PAIR A SINGLE CHEESE WITH A fruit, nut, or condiment that complements it taste-wise, fragrance-wise, and texture-wise. It's meant to be a balanced, pretty, and satisfying little plate of flavors and textures that can easily close a meal, or gracefully leave room for dessert. We offer five different cheeses each day, changing the selection to take advantage of whatever precariously wonderful cheeses become available to us. This strategy is in contrast to the grand *plateau de fromage* ~ an extravagant tradition whose magnificence can distract from the charms of individual cheeses. The seductions of variety and quantity are fun, but I find I can only really appreciate one or two cheeses after a meal, and then I usually carve off additional slivers of one or the other to get to know it better. This no doubt traces to the example of my French aunt Madeleine, who reliably sniffed out the prime cheese on any *plateau* and contented herself to a helping, or two, of that cheese alone.

Finding the affinity between a particular cheese and a specific variety of apple, pear, or cherry, or a type of nut, or dried fruit ~ plain or macerated in wine syrup or spirits ~ is a delight. And raw fennel ~ nutty-crunchy and quietly sweet ~ is surprisingly friendly to many different types of cheese. The affinity can be based in contrast or similarity, or a combination of both, and a successful pairing enhances the perfume, taste, and texture of both partners. In general, I find that low-acid fruit is friendliest to cheese ~ only the most pungent blue cheeses stand up to a hard tart {underripe} Granny Smith apple, and even those cheeses show better next to a mellow variety, like a Pippin. Or a honeyed Bosc pear. I don't serve boldly fragrant, juicy, or sugary fruits ~ peaches, nectarines, or melon ~ with cheese, they tend to dominate or clash. Likewise, highly perfumed berries rarely flatter any but the freshest, sweetest cow's or sheep's milk cheeses, like ricotta, *fromage blanc,* or farmer's cheese. On the other hand, moist, honey-sweet fruits ~ like figs or dates ~ can be perfect. Nuts are especially interesting; their subtle flavors blossom next to certain cheeses, hard ones in particular ~ and vice versa. This is fun to discover. {As is deciding whether they should be raw, toasted, or barely warmed, with or without their skins.} In any pairing, temperature matters; in most cases, the cheese and accompaniment are both at room temperature. Fruit, or fennel, should be impeccable and sliced seconds before serving; or leave your guests to cut to their own tastes. Nuts should be warmed or toasted within an hour of serving them. {For notes on buying and handling nuts, see page 510.}

I propose here dozens of pairings, all culled from our menu archives. I've arranged the cheeses primarily by milk type, and for the most part, I begin with harder cheeses and finish with softer ones. The cheeses are generally in groups, where some similarity of character suggests it and triggers how I choose a complement. The precise flavor, texture, and aroma of any cheese, fruit, or nut is of course subject to many variables, so not every pairing will always be successful. But the patterns and guidelines should make it easy to consider the choices yourself. Imported cheese is well represented in the mix, although domestic artisan-made cheeses are more abundant, varied, and delicious than could be imagined when I began offering this cheese course in 1987, and they steal one or more spots on my short menu these days. In particular, imported fresh cheeses and imported high milk-fat cheeses can be very salty, to satisfy FDA, and now, EU, scrutiny; their domestic counterparts are often more lightly seasoned.

Many of the combinations I propose can be incorporated into salads or combined with cured meats for antipasti.

CHOOSING & STORING CHEESE

WHEN CHOOSING A CHEESE, LOOK FOR SIGNS THAT IT HAS BEEN HANDLED WELL. The look of "perfect condition" is different for different cheeses, but there are some reliable commonsense guidelines. The cheese should not look overhandled {read: "beat up"}, oily, or dried out on the edges. Mold on the rind, however, is often a friendly sign, to be scraped off or enjoyed, depending on the cheese and the diner. As you taste and buy different cheeses, and return to the ones you like, you will learn what each type looks, smells, and feels like when you like it best. It is wisest to buy cheese that is ready to eat ~ it is difficult to ripen or age a cheese at home, unless you buy whole wheels and have a room that maintains a steady temperature between 50° and 60° {54° is ideal} and is neither too dry nor too humid ~ 80 percent, or just over. {More likely, you will need to store cheese in the refrigerator. In that case, the cheese should be carefully wrapped to prevent dehydration, preferably in waxed or parchment paper; plastic wrap tends to make cheese sweat and damages the aroma. Store in the "crisper" if you have one.} I have successfully, if unscientifically, coaxed small nearly ripe cheeses, such as Camembert or Pérail, to ripeness at home, but the vagaries of temperature and humidity pose constant threats. In any case, a perfect ripe cheese of that sort is usually a fragile and volatile thing whose peak flavor lasts only a few hours once the cheese is brought to room temperature. Plan on eating all of it at one sitting.

* * * * *

Wine & Cheese

As a trainee in the London wine trade, I was taught to buy on bread and sell on cheese. A mild cheese makes a young red wine seem softer and rounder. But there are cheeses that can make a mature wine seem thin or distort its flavor. That's why at formal dinners in Bordeaux the oldest and most delicate of the red wines, always arriving on the table last with the cheese, is rarely seen at its best. Goat cheese, in particular, whether soft or hard, is usually best with youthfully vigorous red wines~Chinon, for example, stout Beaujolais *crus* like Morgon and Moulin-à-Vent, young California Zinfandels or Merlots~and brisk, fruity, dry whites, like Sancerre, produced from Sauvignon Blanc. For creamy cow's milk cheeses, especially Brie and Camembert, an elegant red wine with some fruit and a little bite~a light California Cabernet Sauvignon of quality, for example, or a young Burgundy from Volnay or Savigny-les-Beaune~would be a good match. Creamy cheeses with a pungent crust~Pont l'Evêque, Livarot, Epoisses, Maroilles, and so on~need solid red wines with generous bouquet: the more substantial Burgundies of the Côte de Nuits, Pinot Noirs from Russian River Valley, or muscular wines from Roussillon and the northern Rhône. They sometimes go well with mellow and sweet white wines too, especially the kind for which blue cheeses have a known affinity: Coteaux du Layon from the Loire, or Sauternes and its neighboring wines from Loupiac and Sainte-Croix-du-Mont, as well as Monbazillac and the sweeter versions of Jurançon. Firm, creamy cheeses~Reblochon, Tomme, Saint-Nectaire~are good with Beaujolais and soft white wines like Mâcon Blanc and Saint-Véran. But really fine white Burgundies and California's most elegant Chardonnays, as well as mature red Bordeaux, show best against the hard cheeses of eastern France and Switzerland~Comté, Beaufort, and Emmenthal~and mild farmhouse English Cheddar. Parmigiano-Reggiano, hardly surprisingly, is best with the big, flavory Italian reds~Barolo, Barbaresco, and the Brunellos of Montalcino and Montepulciano. But whether at home or in a restaurant, when cheese is intended simply to accompany the last of the wine, the bottle already on the table should guide the choice.

+ + + + +

COW'S MILK CHEESES

Parmigiano-Reggiano {*Emilia-Romagna, Italy*}. Serve a combination of thick shards, thin shavings, and crumbles with ripe dates~Medjool, Black Precioso, Zahidi, Bahri, Dayri, or Deglet Noor {see Sources and Resouces, page 518}. Nibbling all three "shapes" of the cheese gently forces you to savor its complex texture and flavor.

Pierre Dorée {*Burgundy, France*} is a richly flavored, golden, grana-like *crottin* made with the milk of the Montbéliard cow. Use a vegetable peeler to shave into satiny "petals" and serve with toasted almonds, fennel, or very wrinkly ripe Black Mission figs or soft, dried Black Mission figs. *Also:* Cowgirl Creamery's **Los Reyes** {*Marin County, California*}, inspired by Pierre Dorée, and made with organic Holstein milk.

Tête de Moine, Gruyère, and **L'Etivaz** {*Switzerland*}, **Beaufort** {*Savoy, France*}, and **Roth Käse USA Gruyère** {*Wisconsin*}, all hard cow's milk cheeses, are good with freshly shelled, warmed and skinned walnuts, firm, sweet ripe apples like Pippins, Russetted Goldens, or Ashmead's Kernel, or ripe Bing or Van red cherries. Tête de Moine should be thinly shaved, and is particularly good with lightly toasted hazelnuts.

Truffled Crutin {*Piedmont, Italy*} is a richly perfumed, hard, humid mixed cow's and sheep's milk cheese, studded with black truffle. Good with warm hazelnuts or ribbons of fennel.

Morbier {*Franche-Comté, France*} is a mild, semi-hard cow's milk cheese. Nice with slivered fennel or warmed and skinned fresh walnuts. Aged wheels, with a fuller, nuttier flavor, are good with Zante grapes or with chewy dried apples.

Tomme de Savoie {*Savoy, France*} is the firm cow's milk cheese made throughout the High Alps. Individual cheeses often boast the locality of production. They generally have a thick gray rind, a pleasantly musty scent, and are generally mild in flavor. Age, size, and provenance determine precise flavor and texture, but I prefer well-aged tommes with rich yellow-gold interior paste and a mellow nutty flavor. Most are good with meaty, ripe Bing or Van cherries, raw, fresh walnuts, small ripe red wine grapes, or ripe, fine-textured Arkansas Black apples. Younger wheels with a stronger lactic flavor are good with quince poached in light sugar syrup or quince paste {membrillo, see Sources and Resources, page 518}.

Putney Tomme {Vermont} is an aged cow's milk cheese with an earthy, vaguely Cheddary flavor. Made with Jersey milk, it has a rich, golden hue and an extraordinary packed-crumbly texture. Lovely with fennel or hard sweet apples.

Montgomery's Cheddar {England} and **Matos' Saint George** {Sonoma, California} are complex, not-too-sharp cow's milk Cheddars. The sweetness of raw fennel is a good foil for that hint of sharpness, as are Pippin apples or nutty-tender, sweet pecans, barely warmed. *Also:* **Cantal** {Auvergne, France}.

Appleby's Double Gloucester {England} is a hard cow's milk cheese with a mellow nuttiness, sometimes a touch of sharpness. Good with just-warmed pecans or a sweet apple, such as Fuji, Mutsu, or very ripe Golden Delicious.

Mimolette {Flanders, France} is a bright orange, hard cow's milk cheese with a floral note; I sometimes detect orange blossom. Look for Mimolette that has been aged for a year or longer. We serve it with just-warmed pecans or prunes, or both, or with French sugar plums.

Vella Aged Dry Jack, Special Reserve {Sonoma, California} is a hard cow's milk cheese. Rich, nutty, saturated flavor and texture. Good with toasted almonds, lightly toasted pecans, prunes, or dried white figs.

Pont l'Evêque {Normandy}, **Munster** {Alsace}, **Munster-Gérômé** {Lorraine}, **Livarot** {Normandy}, and **Maroilles** {Picardy} are pungent French cow's milk cheeses, which we serve with sliced fennel, not-too-crisp-apples, or meaty ripe cherries. Sweet ripe grapes, such as really ripe Riesling, Gewürztraminer, or Zante, are good as well. Nuts are usually too delicate for these strong cheeses.

Reblochon {Savoy, France} is a mild, supple, cow's milk cheese with a delicate, nutty finish. Nice with fennel or raw pistachios. Just warm, this cheese is good with shaved black truffle.

L'Edel de Cléron and **Vacherin** {Franche-Comté, France} are rich cow's milk cheeses that become almost syrupy when ripe. Wrapped in spruce bark, which can give the cheese a faintly resiny note. Sometimes taste musty or mushroomy. Good with raw hazelnuts or the first small, soft, ripe red Burlat or Larian cherries of the spring. Or little fennel wedges.

Artavaggio and **Toma della Valcuvia** {*Lombardy, Italy*} are unctuous, creamy, soft-ripening, bloomy cow's milk cheeses. Sometimes mushroomy or truffley. Best with fennel wedges, or sometimes with tender, not-too-tart, red cherries.

Robiola di Mondovi {*Piedmont, Italy*} is a pungent, creamy-sticky, soft-ripening cow's milk cheese. Sometimes has a pleasant trace bitterness; sometimes earthy, mushroomy, or truffley. We serve it with fennel, warm pistachios, or shaved black truffle. *Also:* **Tuma dla Paja** {*Piedmont, Italy*}, a mild sheep and cow's milk cheese, and **Pérail** {*Rouergue, France*}, a tender sheep's milk cheese.

Banon {*Provence, France*} is a tangy, lactic cow's or goat's milk cheese wrapped in a chestnut leaf; **Saint-Marcellin** {*Rhône-Alpes, France*} is a similarly tangy, lactic cow's milk cheese. Both have a pleasant, fruity, grape-pit finish. The flavors and textures of both evolve dramatically as they age, but both are good with raisins in grappa or brandy, served with a little of the syrup clinging to them {see Drunken Raisins, page 282}.

Coulommiers, Brie, and **Fougérus** {*Ile-de-France, France*} are soft-ripening cow's milk cheeses, lactic and salty sweet, the latter flavored and decorated with a fern {*fougère*} frond. Both present a combination of cakey and creamy textures. Offer fennel or, if the particular cheese is not too salty, pistachios.

Chaource {*Champagne-Ardennes and Burgundy, France*} is a suave, rich, creamy cow's milk cheese with a pleasant, bloomy rind. I prefer Chaource young~just oozey and strong tasting beneath the rind, but still cakey and fresh, lactic-tasting inside. Good with red or white cherries and slivered fennel.

L'Ami du Chambertin and **Epoisses** {*Burgundy, France*} are rich cow's milk cheeses, sticky and pungent when ripe. Often salty. Both are bathed with marc de Bourgogne, a potent grappa-like brandy. Good with honeyed, ripe Bosc pears, brandied raisins {see Drunken Raisins, page 282}, or red or white cherries. *Also:* **Langres** {*Burgundy, Champagne, and Ardennes, France*}.

Sheep's Milk Cheeses

Manchego {*La Mancha, Spain*} is a hard sheep's milk cheese, firm, full-flavored, and nutty, with a characteristic pleasant sheepy taste I can only describe as barnyardy. Manchego is traditionally served with quince paste {*membrillo,* see Sources and Resources, page 518}, but it is also good with dried figs or really ripe, wrinkly Black Mission figs, or toasted almonds, blanched or not.

Petit Basque and **Abbaye de Belloc** {*Pyrénées, France*} are hard, aged sheep's milk cheeses with a balanced, mellow flavor ~ fruity or nutty, or both, sometimes faintly lactic. They have a lingering, delicate aftertaste. Both are good with tender Burlat cherries, lightly toasted and blanched almonds, or raw almonds and fennel.

Vermont Shepherd Cheese {*Vermont*} is a hard sheep's milk cheese with mellow, nutty, herbaceous flavors. Good with almonds, fennel, and dried apples ~ fresh apples can be so strong they shroud some of the subtle, elegant flavor notes.

Brin d'Amour and **Fleur du Maquis** {*Corsica, France*} are slightly tangy sheep's milk cheeses, firm to oozing ripe, crusted with aromatic ~ rosemary, savory, juniper. They are good with fresh figs or dried figs in red wine {see page 282} and slivered fennel. *Also:* **Sally Jackson's Sheep's Milk Cheese Wrapped in Chestnut Leaves** {*Washington*}.

Fromage Blanc, Farmer's Cheese, and **Fresh Ricotta** are fluffy, fresh cheeses. We serve sheep's and cow's milk varieties cool, with small, tender, ripe strawberries, wild strawberries, tender blueberries, perfumed red or golden raspberries, loganberries, or tayberries. Tangier goat's milk versions often overwhelm delicate berries and are best with figs or the ever-friendly fennel, thinly slivered.

Goat Cheeses

Among the many delicious fresh goat cheeses ~ domestic, French, and Italian ~ on the market, flavor varies widely, as does tanginess. Textures range from fluffy to cakey to dense and pasty. Aged goat cheeses range from just-firm, with slightly oozey rinds, to hard *crottins* {"little turds"}. Their character varies according to age, whether or not the surface is dusted with ash, and somewhat reliably, region of production. I love the flavor of Loire goat cheeses, particularly the rich, lactic **Crottin de Chavignol** and **Selles-sur-Cher. Cypress Grove Humboldt Fog**

{*Humboldt County, California*} and pyramid-shaped **Hy-Ku Baba** {*Napa County, California*} are two ash-covered California goat cheeses we use frequently. **Chevrier** from Vermont Butter and Cheese is a lovely goat cheese with a tender white rind. The paste is creamy on the edges and cakey in the center, and it has a mellow, round flavor with notes of field mushroom. Nearly all of these fresh and aged goat cheeses taste good with ripe figs or fennel. I like freshest, fluffiest ones with freshly cracked black pepper.

Several aged goat cheeses merit separate attention:

Garrotxa {*Catalonia, Spain*} is a semi-hard goat's milk cheese with a suedey-gray natural rind. Good with fresh Black Mission figs, it is also excellent with Dried Figs in Red Wine {page 282}. *Also:* **Sally Jackson's Goat Milk Cheese Wrapped in Grape Leaves** {*Washington*} and **Juniper Grove Tumalo Tomme** {*Oregon*}.

Queso Majorero {*Canary Islands, Spain*} is a hard goat's milk cheese that is particularly good with fresh Kadota figs, sometimes brushed with a few drops of Galliano liqueur. Also good with Adriatic figs or blanched toasted almonds.

A FEW BLUE CHEESES

Mountain Gorgonzola {*Lombardy, Italy*} is a firm, nutty, occasionally crumbly, cow's milk cheese, much milder than the creamy, pasty *Dolcelatte* {"sweet-milk"} types, which don't taste sweet at all to me. Serve with a puddle of wildflower or chestnut honey, or honey with a mixture of walnuts, pistachios, and pine nuts folded in. Also good with ripe Bosc, Seckel, or Winter Nelìs Pears, or dried pears.

Stilton {*England*} The mild, firm, nutty cow's milk cheese is good with Pippin apples, dried apples soaked in Madeira, raisins soaked in brandy or port {see Drunken Raisins, page 282}, walnuts, black walnuts, or warm pecans. *Also:* **Fourme d'Ambert**, **Fourme de Montbrison**, and **Bleu de Laqueuille** {*Auvergne, France*}.

Roquefort {*Rouergue, France*}, the tangy, salty, sheep's milk cheese. Good with toasted walnuts and intensely ripe pears ~ Bartletts, Comice, Anjou.

Picon and **Queso Cabrales** {*Cantabria and Asturias, Spain*}, made with mixed cow's, sheep's and goat's milk, are very strong, very blue cheeses. They are good with Bartlett or Bosc pears, for different reasons: Bartletts have a fragrant fresh, almost tangy, flavor that survives and balances the forward, intense flavor of the cheese; Boscs have a deep, rich character that tempers and lasts through the long flavor of the cheese. Very ripe Muscat grapes show well too.

Montbriac and **Rochebaron** *{Auvergne, France}* are mild, creamy-sticky, slightly blue cow's milk cheeses. We serve them with slivered fennel, Zante grapes, or warmed pistachios. Slightly musty or mushroomy specimens will be good with hazelnuts.

✦ ✦
✦

DESSERTS & PASTRY

✦ ✦
✦

Dessert has the interesting duty of teasing out the last gasps of your appetite. For me, the best dessert is simple and bright, and often overtly sensual. A few elements, rigorously in season~in this hemisphere~can charm even a jaded eye and provoke new appetite. Most of the sweets here are familiar and traditional~fruit tarts, shortcake and pots de crème. My enthusiasm for sorbet and granita, the easiest of seasonal desserts, is unbridled. A few dishes, like fried figs, or stuffed dates, are frivolities that are exquisitely fun to eat. In deference to the fruits, nuts, dairy products, or chocolate that define the dish, most of these desserts are not very sweet. I try to keep the sugar from numbing the palate by using a tiny measure of salt in almost every concoction, and often a dribble of fragrant vinegar~cider, sherry, black currant, Champagne, or balsamic~for acidity. These techniques routinely trick me into enjoying dessert at the close of a meal, even if I am no longer hungry.

✦ ✦ ✦ ✦ ✦

WINE & DESSERT

A dessert wine that is delicious on its own can be overwhelmed by creamy or chocolate desserts. Fresh fruit is kind to a sweet wine, and so are biscotti and tuiles~provided they are not overly sugared. The best accompaniment for a glass of Château d'Yquem, I swear, is a plain English whole-meal biscuit, something like a slightly sweet, crumbly Graham cracker. With a moment's thought, it's easy to see why I've matched these particular wines with some of Zuni's most popular desserts.

✦ ✦ ✦ ✦ ✦

ORANGES *with* ROSEMARY HONEY

This is an easy, inexpensive, and aromatic dessert that can seduce even the die-hard non–dessert eater. It is welcome after a rich winter meal. Choose firm, heavy seedless oranges, or a combination of oranges and blood oranges. I use wildflower honey and infuse it with Tuscan blue rosemary.

Wine: Quady Essensia, California Orange Muscat, 2000

FOR ABOUT 4 SERVINGS:

1/4 cup honey

4 teaspoons water

A small sprig of fresh rosemary

4 to 6 oranges

Place the honey and water in your smallest saucepan. Pick off a dozen or so rosemary leaves and pound them lightly with a pestle or the back of your chef's knife blade, then add them to the pan. Set over low heat. Stir and warm gently, without boiling. Remove from the heat and leave to infuse for about 15 minutes.

Slice both ends off each orange, cutting just deeply enough to expose the juicy flesh. Set the fruit on end and use a paring knife to carve away the skin and pith in a series of smooth arc-like strokes from top to bottom, rotating the orange a little with each stroke. {Most of us misjudge and miss a little pith on the first go-round, but this iseasy to trim once you've removed the bulky skin.} Slice the oranges evenly into thin pinwheels~removing any seeds as you go~just under 1/4 inch thick, and lay them slightly overlapping on a platter or plates.

Just before serving, drizzle the tepid honey over the fruit.

÷
÷ ÷

MANDARINS & DATES STUFFED *with* MASCARPONE, POMEGRANATES, & PISTACHIOS

THIS RAVISHING DESSERT IS A STUDY IN CONTRASTS ~ SWEET AND ACID, JUICY AND dry, sticky and creamy, crunchy and soft, floral and nutty.

Look for tender, sticky-ripe fresh dates. I love their exotic names ~ Halawi, Khadrawi, Dayri, Barhi, Zahidi, Deglet Noor ~ and discovering their nuances of honey, butterscotch, molasses, and caramel is fun. All of these varieties can be delicious, although the fat Medjool, "the elusive, wonderful, unattainable thing," as defined by one guide in southern Morocco, is most available and is very reli-

\ *continued*

able. {I asked him to pronounce and try to translate the names of every date we saw in every market. But nearly all the names changed from oasis to oasis, which made any goal of cataloguing them delightfully hopeless.} My favorite date in California is the Black Precioso, which has a molasses note. Whatever the variety, "natural" dates will have the best flavor and texture; hydrated ones have been showered and steamed for hours, which makes them plump and pretty, at the expense of taste.

Clementines or Satsuma mandarins are a good choice here, but any variety of mandarin {which embraces everything we call a tangerine as well} is fine, as long as it is flavorful and fragrant. As with most citrus, look for saturated skin color. Loose-skinned varieties always worry me ~ decades of scrutinizing produce makes me think "plump and heavy" is best ~ but these self-peeling mandarins are often rich and delicious. Flavorful oranges and blood oranges are options as well. Seedless varieties will be the easiest to prepare.

If you come across a blushing yellow-white pomegranate, try it; the pulpy seeds are perfumed and look like little opals. Look for firm pomegranates whose skin has begun to shrink and become leathery, but avoid cracked and dried out fruit. Pomegranates should be heavy for their size.

Wine: Antigua California Muscat de Frontignan, Merryvale Vineyards

FOR 4 SERVINGS:

About 30 shelled raw pistachios {2 tablespoons or 1/2 ounce}

1 pomegranate

About 8 small "natural" dates or 4 large ones {about 4 ounces total}

About 8 teaspoons mascarpone

8 mandarins or 4 medium oranges or blood oranges, or a combination of all three

A few splashes of orange flower water {available at Middle Eastern or Indian markets and some liquor stores}

Turn the oven to 350°.

Discard any pistachios that are shrunken or brown. Warm the pistachios in the oven for a few minutes, just long enough to heighten their flavor, but without letting them brown. Coarsely chop, again watching for and culling discolored nuts.

Cut about halfway through the pomegranate, then pry the halves apart.

Harvest a handful of the seeds and remove every bit of tannic pith from them. Save the remainder of the pomegranate for Celery-Walnut-Dried Fig Relish {page 89} or toss the seeds into simple green salads.

Slash each date and remove the pits. If the dates are large, cut them in half. Use two small spoons to neatly stuff each cavity with about a teaspoon of the mascarpone. Lightly press a few pomegranate seeds and bits of pistachio into the mascarpone.

Slice both ends off the citrus, cutting just deeply enough to expose the juicy flesh. Set on end and use a paring knife to carve away the skin and pith in a series of smooth, arc-like strokes from top to bottom, rotating the fruit a little with each stroke. Go back and trim any pith you missed on the first try. Slice into thin pinwheels.

Arrange the citrus slices randomly on plates or a platter. Sprinkle with a few drops of orange flower water, and tilt the plate to distribute. Add the stuffed dates and scatter with a few more pomegranate seeds and the remaining pistachios. The array will be prettiest if not too crowded. Serve immediately.

✣
✣ ✣

FRIED FIGS *with* WHIPPED CREAM, RASPBERRIES, *&* HONEY

THIS IS MY FAVORITE DESSERT. Choose tender, ripe figs and sweet, fragrant raspberries.

For detailed instructions on deep-frying, see *Piccolo Fritto* {page 108}.

Wine: Isabel Marlborough, New Zealand, Noble Sauvage, 2000

\ *continued*

FOR 4 SERVINGS:

About 4 cups peanut oil, for
    deep-frying
1/2 cup cold heavy cream
8 to 12 ripe Black Mission, Adriatic, or
    Kadota figs, or a combination of
    varieties {about 12 ounces}

About 1 cup buttermilk
About 1 cup all-purpose flour, for
    dredging
1 cup raspberries
2 to 3 tablespoons lavender honey

Place the oil in a heavy 2-quart saucepan over medium-low heat and heat to
365°.

While the oil is heating, whip the cream to soft peaks; refrigerate it.
Refrigerate four dessert plates as well.

Trim the stem ends and cut the figs in half. Dip each piece in the buttermilk,
then roll in the flour to coat. When the oil is ready, lower about half of the figs
into the oil and deep-fry to golden brown, a minute or two. Remove to drain on
paper towels. Fry and drain the second batch of figs.

Place a mound of cold whipped cream on each of the cold plates. Set the figs
on top. Garnish with the red berries and drizzle with the honey. Serve instantly,
while the figs are still hot and crispy and the cream still cold and thick.

❖
❖ ❖

FRUIT GRANITA & SORBET

FRUIT GRANITA {CHOPPED ICE} AND SORBET ARE PERHAPS THE SIMPLEST, MOST
refreshing, and most versatile of prepared desserts. A few unadorned spoonfuls of
either are welcome after a rich meal, or on a very hot day, and both accept trap-
pings of cookies or pastries to become the center of an elaborate final course. And
a pair or trio of different granitas or sorbets is both elegant and charming enough
to end any sort of meal.

I've grouped granita and sorbet into a joint lesson here, taking advantage of
the fact that the simple tasting skills and testing techniques involved apply to
both. Addressing them together also accommodates the fact that in many cases
you ought to taste your fruit before you decide which you are going to make. The

recipes and variations are grouped by fruit and are short and easy, with far more words devoted to finding delicious fruit~which is as much of a coup as transforming it into a primitive chopped ice or suave sorbet. Selecting fruit begins with the imperative to seek what is in season, and grown locally if possible; but choosing the right specimens is largely an issue of using your senses. Some types of fruit are more scrutable than others, but most give at least good hints of their quality.

DECIDING WHICH TO MAKE: START *with* THE FRUIT

Granita is the simpler of the two confections; the process consists of little more than letting a block of big ice crystals happen, and then teasing it back apart. Sorbet is the result of managing the crystal-forming process, doing everything you can to prevent big ones {see About Sorbet, page 463}. Since sugar helps reduce crystal size, fruit for sorbet should be fragrant and ripe, but with enough acidity to tolerate that necessary sugar. When you have really sweet, ripe fruit, granita can be a better choice than sorbet.

GENERAL SEASONING GUIDELINES

All of the recipes ask you to season, or *not* season, to taste, and always to adjust "your taste" for the fact that cold dulls our perception of flavor in general, and of sweetness in particular. {Think of the difference in sweetness between a warm Coke and a very cold one} I repeatedly suggest you make the mixture too sweet for your taste, and sorbet needs to be even sweeter than granita. In many cases, I suggest you try a few grains of salt or drops of a selected vinegar to derail sugar's dulling effect on the palate. {Unless I am making lemon granita or sorbet, I don't look to lemon juice for acidity~its perfume seems to dominate all others.} Sometimes water will "open up" the flavor and reveal the perfume of a fruit; sometimes it will mellow a puckery tart juice or purée. As always with seasoning, test adjustments on only a spoonful of the mix, so you don't impose a misjudgment on the whole batch. If you are uncertain as to whether the sample's seasoning is optimal, then season it further and further, until it is clearly flawed. You

\ *continued*

will have exposed your palate to the range of flavor change and can then season the whole batch confidently.

It will be easiest to dissolve the sugar when the juice or purée is at room temperature.

BASIC GRANITA METHOD

Seasoning and tasting the fruit juice or purée:

Prepare the juice or purée, and taste. Begin by freezing a small puddle of juice or purée. If the chip of fruit ice is crisp, full flavored, and pleasantly sweet, do nothing to it. Freeze the juice or purée as is. If the sample is not perfect, or you don't trust yourself to know if it is, begin tinkering with it. Try the suggested seasonings; you may reject some, and you may go back and forth with others~adding, for example, a little more sugar after you add vinegar. You can freeze more chips as you go, to check how the changes read ice-cold. The final mixture should be only slightly sweet to your taste.

Freezing the seasoned juice or purée:

Pour the mixture into a wide glass or stainless steel receptacle {I use my 3-quart stainless sauté pan}; it should form a pool about an inch deep. Cover and place in the freezer.

Choose a plastic, glass, or stainless steel storage container with a tightly fitting lid just large enough to hold the chopped granita {1 cup of the unfrozen mixture will make slightly more than 1 cup frozen.} Make sure it is completely dry, snap on the lid, and place in the freezer.

Chopping the granita:

I know of no mechanical chopping system that will produce a granita with the elegant texture of a hand-chopped one. We chop with a pair of stainless steel pastry scrapers. They are easy to maneuver, and the relatively dull edges tease the crystals apart without slicing them up. {You can make do with one scraper; it will just take longer.} A knife blade produces a finer, denser texture.

Once the juice or purée has set a very thick crust but has not quite frozen through, usually 1 to 2 hours, give it a preliminary round of chopping: Place the pan on a cool surface in a cool room. Use the scraper to cut through and lift the layer of coarse-crystal ice, amalgamating it with the unfrozen core. A few cuts and folds are usually sufficient. Cover the pan and return to the freezer. Check hourly, and when the whole is firm to the touch but still yields easily to a stab with the scraper, it is ready for the final chopping.

Set the pan on a cool surface and methodically chop the crystalline blocks into a regular flaky, granular mass. This can be tedious, but is easy~ as long as you have not let the liquid freeze too solid. If it is rock hard, it will take more brawn to cut through the chunks, and you may overwork some bits as you try to split the harder pebbles. At the opposite extreme, in rare instances where the mixture is fairly sweet, or where the purée was thick, the liquid may never fully freeze hard, and it will chop to a rich, grainy-slushy texture. Such "defective" granitas can be exquisite.

Transfer to the chilled container, snap on the lid, and place in the freezer.

Serving the granita:

Place serving dishes in the freezer to chill. {I like to eat granita out of a pretty wineglass.} At the same time, check the granita. When granita is on the sweet side, the fruit syrup sometimes drains from the ice crystals, like a snow cone {or a *shar-bah;* see About Sorbet, below}. To redistribute it, turn the container upside down. In other cases, where the juice or purée was thin, and you didn't add much sugar, the granita may be dryish; if so, set the container out at room temperature for 5 to 10 minutes before serving. This will improve the texture, and the flavor as well.

Use a fork to fluff the crystals, then slide the granita by the forkful into the chilled dishes or glasses.

✢ ✢ ✢ ✢ ✢

ABOUT SORBET

THE SUAVE TEXTURE OF GREAT SORBET OWES TO VERY FINE crystals~ the size of which you can manage with several tools. Friction does its part as the motion of the dasher in an ice cream machine keeps the crystals from growing large. Adding sugar also interrupts the formation of crystals and lowers the freezing temperature. Heating that sugar with a little bit of the purée or juice is even more effective. The acid from the fruit breaks up~ *inverts*~ the sugar and makes it more efficient at "interrupting." This syrup acts like a magiric antifreeze whose only flaw is that it introduces a cooked fruit flavor into the mix. {So I try to use as little as possible}. You can also manage the mixture by adding spirits, from "flavorless" vodka to grappa to perfumed brandies. This won't make a sorbet creamy and chewy, the way sugar does, but it enhances the effect of whatever sugar is there by further lowering the freezing point of the mixture.

For flavor and richness, we occasionally add milk or cream to a sorbet mixture, which, according to federal regulations, we can then call "sherbet," although a distinction on that basis is historically, or at least linguistically, unfounded. We honor it though, because it has gained currency and the presence of milkfat is worth announcing~which is the point of the regulation.

Sherbet, sorbet, and *sorbetto* are the almost contemporaneous English, French, and Italian stabs at the Arab word we transcribe as *sharbah,* which comes from *shariba,* "to drink." A *sharbah* was a drink of sweetened fruit juice or flower-infused syrup poured over ice or snow. Icy confections with these and other abandoned names had long been a fabulous luxury in parts of France and Italy, but then became a commercial rage by the late 1700s. These treats evolved to sometimes include milk or cream, but the presence of dairy products is unrelated to the emergence of the English pronunciation and spelling.

✦ ✦ ✦ ✦ ✦

BASIC SORBET METHOD

Seasoning and tasting the fruit juice or purée:

Prepare the juice or purée, and taste. Season the mixture, tasting as you doctor with the suggested sugar, water, fruit syrup, salt, vinegar, and so on. The mixture should be oversweet but still have bright fruit flavor~too sweet to drink as a beverage, but not cloying.

Freeze a puddle of the mixture. It should be pliable and perfectly sweet. If it is brittle and icy, add a little more sugar to the whole batch as necessary, and rebalance with a few drops of vinegar if appropriate, until a frozen sample is pliable. Cover and place the mixture in the refrigerator to chill. {You can also chill it in the freezer; just don't let it freeze}.

Freezing the sorbet:

Choose a plastic, glass, or stainless steel container with a tightly fitting lid just large enough to hold the churned sorbet {1 cup of unfrozen mixture will yield just over 1 cup sorbet}. Make sure it is dry, snap on the lid, and place in the freezer.

Churn the sorbet according to the instructions for your ice cream machine. Scrape into the chilled storage container. To avoid a blanket of frost on the sorbet, snap on the cover immediately, before moisture precipitates on the surface.

If the sorbet is already fairly firm, you may be able to serve it nearly immediately, or within an hour. In most cases, though, allow a few hours for it to firm up.

Serving the sorbet:

Check the firmness of the sorbet at least half an hour before serving. If too hard to scoop, set out at room temperature or in the refrigerator to soften. This will improve the flavor as well. I usually chill the serving dishes.

RECIPES

HERE ARE RECIPES FOR MAKING GRANITA AND SORBET WITH FIVE DIFFERENT fruits, plus shopping and seasoning guidelines for another three. All of the recipes suggest quantities for sugar and the other seasonings based on ripe fruit. Since yield can vary quite a lot from one batch of fruit to the next, I have based the recipes on 1 cup of prepared juice or purée. This should make it easy to apply the proportions to whatever amount you have. {Most ice cream freezers need at least a few cups of mix to perform well.}

STRAWBERRIES

Choosing the fruit: Great-tasting strawberries generally have rich, saturated color. However, not all deep-red berries will be great; sometimes the color is skin

\ *continued*

deep and the fruit has little flavor. It may be hard, fibrous, or hollow. Hence, don't buy on color alone. Fragrance is a better guideline. If the berries are trapped behind plastic wrap, turn the basket over and smell from underneath. If the berries at your market are cold, you'll have to work a little harder to read the scent, but you should still perceive one. If you detect no perfume at all, consider another fruit.

In strawberry choosing, especially for sorbet or granita, don't focus on size or regularity. First-harvest spring berries tend to be large {and expensive, given the premium accorded to things jumbo and "first" in the supermarket}, but these trophy berries may not have the concentrated flavor of smaller summer or early fall berries, when water is scarce or withheld. While not all varieties tolerate late-season stress, some older varieties do, and I look forward to that intensely flavored small fruit.

But with any variety of strawberry, growing conditions, harvesting decisions, and shipping conditions can dramatically enhance or undermine its genetic baggage. Strawberries are fast-growing and absorb soil amendments rapidly, whether in the water that literally becomes the strawberry, or through their very permeable skins. To guarantee the highest possible yield, it is common practice to fumigate entire fields. For a few dimes or quarters more, you spare the land and those that work it, or near it, the insult of a chilling dose of sterilizing chemicals. For all of these reasons, I encourage you to look for, and ask for, organically farmed strawberries.

You can often improve the texture and sweetness of strawberries by leaving them at room temperature for up to 12 hours. For granita, use the sweetest berries you can find; for sorbet, choose fruit with a little acidity.

Preparing the purée: *Count 1/2 pound berries {a very full pint basket should weigh 1 pound} for about 1 cup strained purée.* Rinse the berries in cool water ~ don't soak. Drain and roll them around between towels to rid them of excess water. Hull, and trim any bruises and hard tips. If making granita, trim hard or pale shoulders. If you are making sorbet, a little underripe shoulder may serve to balance the necessary sugar. Purée in a blender or process, and press through a fine-mesh strainer, and taste.

* * **STRAWBERRY GRANITA**

This will be a little thick and slushy, but refreshing. Since the purée is initially whipped full of air, let it sit for a few hours at room temperature before freezing.

You can speed this up by warming the purée slightly, or pouring it into a warm bowl. Once the air escapes, the liquid will be able to form nicer crystals.

FOR 1 GENEROUS CUP:

1 cup strained strawberry purée

Up to 1 tablespoon sugar

A pinch of salt, if needed

Freeze a spoonful of the purée and taste. If needed, gradually sweeten the remaining purée. Test the effect of a few grains of salt, and adjust accordingly, then freeze and chop as described in the Basic Granita Method {page 462}.

⁘ **STRAWBERRY SORBET** *&* **STRAWBERRY BALSAMIC SORBET**

Both of these are easy and reliably suave. The thick purée virtually guarantees a nice texture. Although the balsamic is optional, it adds a complexity I find irresistible.

FOR 1 GENEROUS CUP:

1 cup strained strawberry purée

1 to 3 tablespoons sugar

A pinch of salt, if needed

About 1/2 to 3/4 teaspoon balsamic vinegar plus about 1/2 teaspoon sugar {optional}

Taste the purée, then gradually add sugar until it is quite sweet. See if salt heightens the flavor, and adjust accordingly. If considering balsamic, add a drop to a spoonful of the mixture and taste. If you like it, cautiously season the whole batch. The flavor change should be subtle. Rather than tasting the balsamic outright, you should just taste the strawberry better. Correct the sugar to taste. Freeze a sample, taste, and adjust if needed. Chill, then freeze according to the instructions for your ice cream machine.

BLACKBERRIES *&* RASPBERRIES

Choosing the fruit: The bramble genus, *Rubus,* provides a happy confusion of delicious options: Blackberries, raspberries, and the crossbreeds ~ boysen, olallie, sylvan, and marion {the black ones} and tay, burgundy, and logan {the red ones} ~ all make gorgeous, thick sorbet, and the most intensely flavored berries,

\ *continued*

with strategic thinning, make an unusually rich granita. Although the berries vary wildly in sweetness, their flavors typically stand up to sugar and cold quite well and then explode as the crystals melt in your mouth. Choose very tender, perfumed fruit, although a few slightly less ripe berries won't harm a sorbet.

Preparing the purée: *Count 2 to 3 cups {3/4 pound} berries for 1 scant cup strained purée.* Go through the berries one by one, looking for any speck of mold that would taint the flavor of the whole batch. Process briefly and press through a strainer, or pass the whole berries through a food mill whose holes are smaller than the seeds. Taste.

❖ ❖ BERRY GRANITA

This regal granita will have smallish crystals and will melt to a potent slush in short order, but that doesn't bother me. Spoon into frozen glasses to prolong the pleasant meltdown.

FOR ABOUT 1-1/4 CUPS:

1 cup strained berry purée	Up to 3 tablespoons sugar
2 to 4 tablespoons water, sparkling wine, or fruity dry white wine, such as dry Muscat	A pinch of salt, if needed

Add water or wine to thin the purée to the texture of cold half-and-half. Freeze a sample and taste. Sweeten the remainder accordingly ~ which may mean not at all. Add salt if it improves the flavor. Freeze and chop according to the Basic Granita Method {page 462}.

❖ ❖ BERRY SORBET

Reliably stunning. Consider buying a few different types of berries ~ to blend, or to make a few different sorbets. Careful seasoning can reveal their nuances: black currant–flavored vinegar can add spark to a blackberry sorbet; a dribble of Cognac or Armagnac may enhance a raspberry one.

FOR 1 GENEROUS CUP:

1 cup strained berry purée

2 to 5 tablespoons sugar

A pinch of salt, if needed

For the blackberry family: a few drops
of black-currant vinegar {optional}

For raspberries: about 1/4 teaspoon
Cognac or Armagnac {optional}

Taste the purée and gradually add sugar until quite sweet. See if salt heightens the flavor, and season accordingly. Add optional vinegar or brandy to taste, then correct sugar or salt as needed. Freeze a sample, taste, and correct as needed. Chill, then churn according to the instructions for your ice cream maker.

PLUMS

Choosing the fruit: Not many plum varieties are reliably delicious for eating raw; often you have to tolerate tart skin and sour flesh around the pit in order to enjoy the sweet meat in between: Fortunately, puréeing and sweetening usually improves on nature's arrangement. Among well-known varieties, the Santa Rosa, with its surprising note of banana flavor, is my favorite, for eating and for cooking. Its relatives ~ Casselman, Duarte, and Fortune ~ can be good as well. Ruddy Satsumas, Mariposas, and Elephant Hearts, yellow Shiros, and green Kelseys and Greengages can make nice sorbet. Handsome, round "black" plums ~ Friar and Galaxy ~ have lots of meat, small pits, and not a lot of flavor for eating raw, but even they can be coaxed into fine sorbet, provided they are ripe. In all cases, choose plump ripe plums that yield slightly when you squeeze them.

Preparing the purée: *Count 9 to 10 ounces ripe plums for 1 cup strained purée.* Cut the flesh off the pits, working over a bowl so that you capture the juice. Purée or process, strain, and taste. Save some of the bits of skin you trap in the strainer. These flecks can add a potent note of acidity and flavor; so you may want to stir a spoonful back into the purée. This will make a beautifully flecked sorbet.

⊹ ⊹ PLUM SORBET

The one sorbet that is routinely better than the fruit you make it from. The purée accepts generous scoops of sugar, virtually guaranteeing a lovely creamy-chewy texture. With or without freckles of skin, this sorbet is intensely flavorful. If you have the opportunity, serve a few different types of plum sorbet together, showing off a few shades of pink, yellow, green, or burgundy and the complex, unexpected flavors of several varieties.

FOR 1 TO 1-1/4 CUPS:

1 cup strained plum purée, with about 1 tablespoon reserved chopped skins

3 to 8 tablespoons sugar

A pinch of salt, if needed

Up to 1 tablespoon water, if needed

Up to 2 teaspoons grappa {optional}

Taste the purée. Gradually add sugar until quite sweet. See if a few grains of salt improve the flavor, then season the whole batch accordingly. If the purée is puckery or too intense, try adding a splash of water. In the event that it lacks dimension, a teaspoon or two of grappa can be ravishing. Try stirring a bit of the tart skin back into the sweetened purée~then add a bit more sugar to compensate. Freeze a sample, taste, and correct as needed. Chill, then freeze according to the directions for your ice cream machine. If you have added the skins, they may collect on the dasher; scrape off and fold them back into the sorbet.

⊹ ⊹ *Variation* NECTARINE SORBET

Choose perfumed, "dead ripe" fruit. {It should yield to the touch.} I prefer gold varieties for sorbet; the subtle succession of bitter, sweet, floral notes of a ripe white nectarine can fall out of balance when you purée and freeze it.

Prepare as indicated for Plum Sorbet, above, including the part about the skins, but omit the optional grappa. Expect to use the minimum amount of sugar, and thin with dry white wine or water as needed.

LEMONS

Choosing the fruit: With an unassailable market niche as a universal source of all-purpose "sour" for every cooking operation imaginable, commercial lemons are often picked underripe~high in acid, and shy on varietal fragrance and flavor. I always look for the ripest lemons in the bin, or on the tree; they deliver a lovely complex of flavors, and require less sugar. Both major commercial varieties ~ Lisbon and Eureka ~ and the rare backyard Ponderosa are best when saturated yellow overall, plump, and heavy for their size. Meyer lemons, a charismatic hybrid that is almost certainly part orange, are naturally sweeter than most true lemons and can be fragrant and flavorful even before they reach their fully ripe, saturated yellow-orange hue. Pale, banana yellow Meyers can be delicious.

Preparing the juice: *Count about 5 medium lemons {about 1-1/4 pounds} for 1 cup juice.* Halve and juice the lemons. Pick out seeds and large bits of pith, but don't strain. To capture the most fragrance, season and freeze promptly. If making sorbet, use a zester to remove about 1/2 teaspoon zests before you juice the lemons.

❖ ❖ **LEMON GRANITA**

Pretend you are making lemonade. At Zuni, we pour a trickle of limoncello liqueur over this granita when we serve it.

FOR 2-1/4 TO 2-1/2 CUPS:

1 cup lemon juice	A pinch of salt, if needed
1 to 1-1/4 cups water	Limoncello {1 teaspoon per serving},
Up to 1/2 cup sugar	to garnish {optional}

Combine the lemon juice, water, and sugar to taste. See if a pinch of salt heightens the flavor. Freeze a sample and taste. Correct the rest as needed, then freeze and chop according to the Basic Granita Method {page 462}

❖ ❖ **LEMON SORBET**

Chewy and intensely flavorful.

FOR ABOUT 2-1/2 CUPS:

1 cup lemon juice {1 or 2 of the juiced lemon halves reserved for zest}	About 1 cup water
	About 6 tablespoons sugar

\ *continued*

For the sugar syrup:

3 tablespoons sugar

3 tablespoons water

1/2 teaspoon lemon zest, chopped

Combine the lemon juice, water, and sugar to produce a batch of lemonade that makes you squint slightly.

Making the sugar syrup: In your smallest saucepan, combine the sugar and water. Chop and add the lemon zest. Simmer until the syrup is the texture of warm honey and the zest has candied. Cool completely.

Gradually stir syrup into your tart lemonade, stopping as it becomes quite sweet to your taste. Add a little more water if the mixture still makes you squint. Freeze a spoonful, taste, and adjust the rest as needed. Chill, then churn according to the instructions for your ice cream machine.

❖ ❖ *Variation* ORANGE SORBET

Allow about 3 tablespoons sugar per cup of juice. Dissolve the sugar in a little bit of the juice to make a syrup, simmer for 10 seconds, then proceed as for Lemon Sorbet. See whether salt improves the flavor; correct acidity with sherry vinegar.

HONEYDEW MELON

Choosing the fruit: "No, you don't want that one, but that one will be good."
"Oh?"

"I grew 'em. You want the ones that look like that. See all the netting on the skin? That's good. That's what you want. That's sugar. Let's cut one and try it."

My anonymous advisor was confident. He had just delivered the pallet of honeydews to Monterey Market in Berkeley. And in one sliver, one July morning, choosing honeydew melon was unexpectedly demystified. I gave up smelling and pressing the stem end, and have followed the friendly command for over a decade, and have never been disappointed.

Preparing the purée: *Count 1 to 2 pounds melon for 1-1/3 cups purée {1 cup strained purée}, with larger melons providing better yield than small ones.* Halve and seed the fruit, then scoop out only the tender portion of the flesh. Don't press for yield; the hard pale flesh near the rind is thin and vegetal tasting and will spoil the flavor of the rest. Purée or process, press through a fine-mesh strainer, and discard the pulp. Taste.

◦ ◦ **HONEYDEW MELON GRANITA**

This pale granita blooms with flavor in your mouth. Sweeten cautiously; sugar can shroud the honeyed natural sweetness and mask the perfumes of the fruit. {I find that adding lemon or lime juice obscures, rather than flatters, the perfume and flavor. Likewise, I haven't found a vinegar that doesn't try to outbid the melon flavor.} I like to serve this granita studded with other ripe, yellow-, green-, or orange-fleshed melon, diced into coffee bean–sized bits. To do so, incorporate the melon confetti, a few at a time, as you spoon the granita into glasses. Don't add the bits of melon any sooner; you risk freezing the raw fruit, sacrificing all but its visual charm. Serve in chilled, not frozen, glasses.

FOR ABOUT 1 CUP:

1-1/3 cups strained honeydew melon purée

A pinch or two of salt, as needed

About 1 tablespoon sugar

About 1/4 cup diced ripe melon, several colors and types if possible {optional}

Taste the juice plain, then a little of it with a pinch of salt, then add a pinch of sugar and taste again. Then taste some with sugar only. Decide which you like best, and season accordingly. {It helps to freeze a sample if you are unsure.} Freeze and chop as described in the Basic Granita Method {page 462}.

◦ ◦ *Variation* **WATERMELON GRANITA**

Watermelon granita is easy and satisfying; it can be better than the best watermelon. Choose a melon that is heavy for its size. Watermelons usually have a pale patch on their "resting" side: select one where that flush is more yellow than white; this promises maturity, which is when sugar happens. Most sweet watermelons vibrate like a drum when you tap them. You may need to thump, buy, and taste a few watermelons before you get a feel for this, but once you do, the sensation is easily recognized. If not foolproof, this time-honored technique returns better results than chance.

Prepare as for Honeydew Melon Granita, noting that a *1-1/4-pound piece of ripe watermelon should yield 10 to 12 ounces of flesh, or about 1 cup strained purée.*

✦
✦ ✦

ESPRESSO GRANITA *with* WHIPPED CREAM

THIS GRANITA IS THE SWEETEST THING WE MAKE AT ZUNI, AND YET IT IS SURPRISINGLY refreshing. This effect requires fiercely rich espresso. Weaker espresso will make an insipid, pale, sugary granita not worth the effort. Our espresso is made with equal parts dark-roasted Costa Rican, Papua New Guinean, and Colombian beans. Our machine doses 1/4 cup water per espresso; we use 1/4 ounce ground espresso beans {1-1/2 tablespoons, very tightly packed} per dose. Don't use instant espresso, or any sort of brewed coffee.

FOR 5 TO 6 SERVINGS:

1 cup sugar, or to taste   3 tablespoons water
2 cups espresso, room temperature

For the whipped cream:

About 1/2 cup cold heavy cream   About 2 teaspoons sugar

Dissolve all but 2 tablespoons of the sugar in the espresso and taste. It should taste too sweet; if not, gradually add some or all of the remaining sugar, until it does. Add the water. Pour into a stainless steel pan or glass dish in which forms a pool about an inch deep. Freeze until solid. Due to the high concentration of sugar, this may take up to 8 hours.

Choose a glass, plastic, or stainless storage vessel, about 3 cups capacity, with a tightly fitting lid. Make sure it is dry, snap on the lid, and place in the freezer.

Place the pan of frozen espresso on a cool surface and chop according to the method on page 462 {see Chopping the Granita}.

Ten to 15 minutes before serving, turn the container upside down in the freezer. {The espresso syrup sometimes drains from the ice crystals, like syrup in a snow cone; turning it upside down will redistribute the syrup.} Place 5- to 6-ounce serving bowls or glasses in the freezer to chill. I like to use clear, narrow, fluted stemware to show off the layers and crystals.

Combine the cream and sugar and whip very stiffly.

To serve, layer the granita and whipped cream like a parfait in the chilled glasses. There should be nearly as much whipped cream as granita. The surface of the cream will freeze where it is in contact with the granita, and the succession of voluptuous chewy and slushy textures is delightful.

⁘

SHORTCAKE *with* SUMMER FRUIT

THIS SHORTCAKE RECIPE IS NO MORE THAN A GREAT CREAM BISCUIT RECIPE PLUS sugar. It produces an addictive salty-sweet, crispy-tender biscuit, which almost does not need the fruit. We serve strawberry shortcake throughout the spring, then anoint the biscuits with this cocktail of soft summer fruits when they all come into season together. Choose fragrant, tender berries and stone fruits; a single hard or acidic mouthful will spoil the whole effect. The fruit is moistened with heavily sweetened white wine; you can use almost any light-bodied dry white wine, such as Trebbiano, but a floral dry Muscat makes a particularly lovely syrup.

Cut and macerate the fruit an hour or two before you plan to serve it.

Wine: Moelleux, Chappellet Napa Valley Late Harvest Chenin Blanc, 1999

FOR 6 SERVINGS:

For the "fruit cocktail":

3/4 to 1 cup light dry white wine, chilled

6 tablespoons sugar, or as needed

4 small or 2 large perfectly ripe peaches or nectarines {about 1 pound total}, or a combination of both

About 3 cups mixed ripe berries, such as strawberries, blackberries, olallieberries, loganberries, boysenberries, raspberries, and/or tayberries {1-1/2 pounds total}

for 6 biscuits:

2 cups all-purpose flour {9 ounces}, plus a little more for rolling out

2-1/2 tablespoons sugar

1 tablespoon baking powder

3/4 teaspoon salt {a little more if using kosher salt}

4 tablespoons salted butter, cut into 1/4-inch-thick slabs and chilled

1 cup plus up to 1 tablespoon cold heavy cream

Water {to brush the tops}

For the whipped cream:

1 to 1-1/4 cups cold heavy cream

Sugar to taste

\ *continued*

Preparing the fruit:

Stir together 3/4 cup of the wine and the sugar in a wide bowl; it should taste quite sweet {add more sugar if needed}.

Whatever fruits you choose, place them in the sweetened wine as you go, layering in the following sequence.

Peaches: Lower 1 or 2 peaches at a time into a few quarts of simmering water; remove after 10 to 15 seconds, as soon as the skin has loosened from the flesh. Slide into a bowl of ice water and swirl to cool evenly without bruising. Leave just long enough to cool the surface, then lift out and peel off the skins. Trim any bruises and hard shoulders. Working over the bowl of wine, so you capture any drips of peach juice, cut the flesh off the pits in 1/4-inch-thick wedges. Let the slices fall into the wine as you go; swirl to submerge the fruit.

Nectarines: Working over the bowl of wine, cut the flesh neatly off the pits in 1/4-inch-thick slices; trim bruises and carve around hard shoulders as you go. Let the nectarine wedges fall into the wine, and swirl to submerge.

Strawberries: Rinse, drain, and roll on a dry towel to wick excess water. Hull, then trim bruises and hard shoulders or tips. Halve small strawberries; thickly slice large berries. Add to the bowl of wine.

Other berries: Inspect one by one, discarding any that are hard or have even a speck of mold. Leave whole, and add to the bowl of wine.

Swirl and tilt the bowl to moisten everything without bruising the tender fruit. The wine should come just over one-third of the way up the fruit. If not, stir together a little more wine-sugar mixture, counting 1 tablespoon sugar per 2 tablespoons wine. Cover loosely and leave to macerate for an hour or so at room temperature, gently turning the fruit with a rubber spatula after about 30 minutes. The fruits will gradually bleed their juices, noticeably increasing the amount of liquid in the bowl. Taste this wine-fruit syrup and add a sprinkle more sugar or unsweetened wine if you find it either oversweet or not sweet enough. Swirl to distribute.

Cover loosely and leave in a cool spot, but not refrigerated, until serving.

Baking the biscuits {you can do this while the fruit is macerating}:

Preheat the oven to 375°.

Stir and toss together the flour, sugar, baking powder, and salt in a large bowl or a mixer bowl. By hand, or using the dough hook of the mixer, cut and smash the butter into the flour mixture, stopping when the butter is reduced to dusty flakes about as big as cornflakes. Some irregularity is inevitable and will give the biscuit a pleasant texture. Pour in 1 cup of the cream, distributing it over the whole of the flour. Work it in quickly {about 1 minute on low speed if using a mixer}. The dough will look mottled and may be sticky in spots. Target any really dry spots with as much of the remaining cream as necessary to bind the flour, but don't worry if the dough is a little ragged in spots. {Although different flours and creams behave differently, how much cream you need depends primarily on the size of the butter flakes}.

Lightly dust a cool work surface with a little flour. Gently flatten the mass of dough into a roughly rectangular form. Dust the top of the dough with flour and roll 1 inch thick. If it sticks on the bottom, lift the dough, scrape the sticky spot, and dust with flour. Use a sharp knife to cut the dough into 2-1/4- to 2-1/2-inch squares {a dull dough scraper will crimp the edges and restrict the rise}. For the best rise, trim the outside edges of the dough. Or leave it as is if you aren't afraid of the rustic. {When making large batches of this dough, I miter the scraps together to fashion a couple of amorphous biscuits~I prefer this to pressing, flouring, and rerolling to cut into orderly shapes, since that process makes drier, denser biscuits.} Brush the tops lightly with water.

Place on a baking sheet at least 2 inches apart, so the biscuits don't steam each other as they rise. Bake until golden brown, 20 to 25 minutes. Don't underbake, or the centers will become heavy as they cool. Cool on a rack to preserve the crispy bottoms. These are best served within an hour. {If you need to make the dough a few hours in advance of baking it, roll it and cut the biscuits, cover loosely, and refrigerate promptly.}

Serving the shortcake:
Softly whip the cream, sweetening to taste. Split the biscuits and top the bottom half of each with a generous spoonful of the fruit and its wine syrup. Add a dollop of whipped cream. Crown with the craggy top pieces.

CORNMEAL BISCOTTI

THESE BISCOTTI ARE A STAPLE AT ZUNI. Not very sweet, they are generously seasoned with anise and roasted nuts. I enjoy them for breakfast. They are best if aged for a few days before serving.

Wine: Veuve Clicquot Ponsardin Demi-Sec Champagne

FOR ABOUT 24 LARGE OR 36 TWO-BITE–SIZED BISCOTTI:

3/4 cup hazelnuts or almonds {4-1/2 ounces}

4 tablespoons cold salted butter

1/2 cup plus 2 tablespoons sugar

1 large cold egg

1-1/2 teaspoons anisette

1-1/4 cups all-purpose flour {about 5-1/2 ounces}

2 tablespoons fine cornmeal

1 teaspoon baking powder

1/2 teaspoon salt

1-1/2 teaspoons anise seeds

Preheat the oven to 325°. Line a baking sheet with parchment paper.

Roast the nuts on a small baking sheet until they are fragrant and beginning to color on the inside, about 15 minutes. If using hazelnuts, gather them in a towel, beanbag-style, rub to remove some of the papery skin, and then pick out the nuts. Finely chop 1/4 cup of the nuts; coarsely chop the remainder.

In a medium bowl, barely cream the butter with the sugar. Beat in the egg and anisette.

In a separate bowl, combine the nuts, flour, cornmeal, baking powder, salt, and anise seeds. Add to the butter mixture and mix until homogenous.

Divide the dough in half. Roll the dough into logs about 1 inch in diameter. The dough should be cold enough to handle without difficulty, though you may need to dust the counter with a little additional flour if the logs start to stick.

Place the logs on the baking sheet, spacing them at least a few inches apart; they will swell considerably. Bake until slightly brown and firm on the surface, but yielding to light pressure, about 15 to 20 minutes. Rotate the pan if they are browning unevenly. Don't underbake, or the baking powder will not complete its job, and the cookies will be hard and dense rather than crisp and with a great coarse texture.

Transfer the cookie logs to a cutting board and slice on an angle about 1/2 to 3/4 inch thick. Place cut side down on the warm baking sheet and bake for another 5 minutes or so to brown lightly. Cool completely, then store in an airtight container.

✦ ✦ *Variation* CORNMEAL-PISTACHIO BISCOTTI

Substitute very coarsely chopped raw pistachios for the almonds and grappa for the anisette.

✦
✦ ✦

ORANGE-CURRANT SCONES

A CONSTANT ON OUR SUNDAY BRUNCH MENU ~ AND A CONSTANT REMINDER OF ten years of sleepy weekday morning breakfasts at Zuni. We served breakfast from 1987 through 1997. Everyone loved lingering over a scone, while sipping a third cup of coffee in the warm, bright morning sunlight in an almost empty bar with classical music in the background. Over the years, these scones always outsold sticky buns, fresh fruit turnovers, *pain au chocolat,* lemon coffee cake, and everything else the pastry department scrambled to bake for the one or two customers who might arrive at 7 in the morning. The Zuni scone is so well loved that we no longer bother making special pastries for Sunday brunch either.

FOR 12 SCONES:

3 cups all-purpose flour {13-1/2 ounces}
Scant 1/2 cup sugar
4 teaspoons baking powder
1/8 teaspoon salt

1/2 pound cold butter {2 sticks}
1/2 cup dried currants
1 tablespoon freshly grated orange zest
1 large egg
1/2 cup whole milk

Preheat the oven to 350°. Line two baking sheets with parchment paper.

Combine the flour, sugar, baking powder, and salt in a large bowl and mix

\ *continued*

well. Cut in the butter until it is the size of small peas. Add the currants and orange zest and toss well.

Whisk together the eggs and milk. Add to the dry ingredients and mix and fold until the dough masses and the flour is absorbed. Don't worry if the dough is a little streaky.

Divide the dough in half and shape into 2 balls. Pat each one into a 6- to 7-inch circle on a lightly floured surface. Roll about 1 inch thick and cut like a pie into 6 wedges each.

Bake until golden brown and firm to the touch, about 25 to 30 minutes. These are best served warm from the oven.

✧
✧ ✧

BASIC RICH TART DOUGH, & TWO VARIATIONS

"A STICK OF BUTTER, A CUP OF FLOUR," MY FRIEND BETH WOOD-SETRAKIAN happily assured me, made a great tart, and was an easy formula to remember. As undergraduates in the late 1970s, Beth and I bonded over things culinary, and her pastry standard casually became mine. I always base my analysis of a pastry recipe on where it stands with respect to that rich ratio. Armed with little more than Beth's proportions, I've rubbed together and rolled out lots of different types of dough over the years, three of which I detail here. Grouping them together makes it easy to see exactly how differences in water content and handling affect texture, an important lesson in pastry making.

I use salted butter for pastry dough, which may sound inelegant, and has pro-voked a polite "Really?" from many a purist, but it really does makes delicate, crisp pastry with rich flavor. But do be aware that salted butters vary in flavor and saltiness, and the term "lightly salted" is not entirely reliable. Although it suggests that the product has less salt than simply "salted" butter, in practice, it doesn't always. {It is the word "light" that is regulated, and it merely promises you are getting half the amount of whatever thing you would get in that producer's "not light" product.} Check instead the nutritional data on the label that details sodium, typically 45, 75, or 90 milligrams per tablespoon. The 90-milligram salted butter I use for pastry making is one I find way too salty for spreading on toast, or tossing with pasta or gnocchi, but it is justly seasoned for mixing with my cup of flour. I recommend you try different salted butters~and choose the one that gives you the results you like best.

As for these individual recipes, the basic, very short pastry is cookie-like. It reminds me of my favorite French butter cookie, called *Traou Mad* {from Pont Aven, in Brittany, which is, not suprisingly, the domain of salted butter in France}. But, starting with Beth's lavish proportions, you can make flakier pastry as well. By working the butter progressively less, and adding progressively more water, you can produce flakier and flakier dough. I've made this dough with every increment of water ranging from none to nearly 7 tablespoons over the years. I describe two distinct variations here~a dough "with a little flake" and a friendly "rough puff" pastry. But you could easily, even accidentally, produce a dough that is somewhere in between the two, and it will be delicious. Don't worry if you've taken the butter a little further than you intended, just add a little less water to compensate; or, if you leave more of the butter in larger chunks than described, expect to add extra water. The main concern in variations containing water is to allow time for the muscley gluten strands to relax between dough handlings.

In any version, start with cold {but not hard} butter that you can smash between your fingers like soft clay. It shouldn't crack, and it shouldn't be oily. This is especially important when flakiness is sought. And notice that my scoop-with-a-spoon-and-level-with-a-knife cup of flour weighs 4-1/2 ounces. Then, don't use too much extra flour on the counter and the dough as you form and roll it out. To limit the amount of flour you use, always scrape the counter before you dust it with flour for rolling, and if you aren't good at throwing a fine layer of flour, try dipping your fingers in a bowl of flour and then flicking them over the troublesome areas. When flouring the dough itself, brush off the excess with a dry pastry brush. Working in a cool room, on a cool board, with a cool pin and cool hands will reduce the need for flour and make any dough easier to handle. Wiping the rolling pin clean with a dry towel at the first sign of sticking will also help.

It's easy to make a double, triple, or quadruple batch of any of these doughs, then divide it into smaller balls or slabs before the final rolling out. Once you have a feel for how the doughs come together by hand, you can make the basic

\ *continued*

dough and the "with a little flake" variation successfully in a mixer, although I don't see much advantage unless you are making at least three times the recipe. I always make the "rough puff" by hand. In any case, tightly wrap and freeze any dough you aren't planning on using within a day.

I should add that each of these recipes will likely take more time to read and visualize than you will spend pressing the dough together. The flaky doughs need resting time between handlings, but the active work remains minimal.

Use this basic dough to line tart or tartlet pans. This recipe makes enough for one 9-1/2-inch pan; double it if you are making a double-crusted or lattice-topped tart.

FOR 8-1/2 OUNCES DOUGH, ENOUGH FOR ONE 9-1/2-INCH TART SHELL:

1 cup all-purpose flour {4-1/2 ounces}   8 tablespoons cold salted butter
Up to 2 teaspoons sugar {optional}   {1 stick}

1. Place the flour, mixed with the sugar, if using, on a cool work surface or in a wide bowl.

2. Cut the stick of butter lengthwise into approximately 1/4-inch-thick slices {illus. 1}. Lay in the flour and flip over to coat each slice with flour. Press each of the dusty butter slices thin, pinching it between your thumbs and fingertips. The slices will break into dimpled, cupped sheets, some poker chip–size, some larger, with the balance in 1/4- to 1/2-inch shards {illus. 2}. You won't have incorporated much of the flour.

3. Slide your fingers under the pile and lift and toss the sheets and chips of butter. Press them flat again, sandwiching a few chips together with each squeeze. Repeat ~ the chips will begin to turn into flakes. Continue until you have a combi-

✦ ✦ ✦ ✦ ✦

1   2

✦ ✦ ✦ ✦ ✦

nation of about one-third flakes~ some as large as cornflakes, some more like rolled oats~ and about two-thirds crumbs that look like moist, clumpy sawdust.

4. Work the dough with your fingertips until the whole mixture turns into crumbs and then quickly forms a mass. Shape the mass into a ball. Knead just long enough to produce a coherent, shiny dough, then reshape into a ball. If you have added sugar, the dough will be a little sticky. Place between sheets of plastic wrap, press into a 1-inch-thick disk, and then use a rolling pin to roll smooth. If the dough cracks on the edges, press back into a ball and knead a bit longer, then place between plastic and roll smooth again. Fold over the edges of the plastic to enclose, and refrigerate until just firm enough to roll out, wrap tightly and freeze if you don't plan to use within a day or so.

Guidelines for rolling out the basic dough:
  ⁑ Make sure the dough is just soft enough to roll without cracking. If not, leave at room temperature until it is pliable. {See Tempering, page 120.}
  ⁑ Thaw frozen dough in the refrigerator, then "temper" as described above.
  ⁑ Roll the dough in all directions to a round just over 1/8 inch thick to fit your tart pan {if you leave the original dough ball between the sheets of plastic wrap, you can gain the first few inches of diameter with no need for flour; then peel off the plastic to finish the process}. Or cut into smaller portions and roll out to fit your tartlet pans. This dough will tear easily as it gets thin, but you can just as easily smash and rub the fractures back together.
  ⁑ Wrap the lined tart pan or tartlet pans in plastic and freeze for at least 1 hour before using.

⁑ ⁑ *Variation* DOUGH *"with* A LITTLE FLAKE*"*

Use this dough for sweet or savory tarts or tartlets. It tolerates juicy fruits and fillings a little better than the Basic Rich Tart Dough does. This recipe makes enough for one 9-1/2-inch tart pan; double it if you are making a double-crusted or lattice-topped tart.

FOR 9 OUNCES DOUGH, ENOUGH FOR ONE 9-1/2-INCH TART SHELL:
  Complete steps 1 through 3. Trickle 1 tablespoon of ice water evenly over the

\ *continued*

flakes and crumbs. Stir and work with your fingertips and watch the "moist saw-dust" begin to look like humid Grape-Nuts. Mass the dough and knead a few times. The dough may be a little sticky in spots. Dip your fingers in flour if necessary to keep them from sticking to the wetter spots. On a lightly floured surface, gently knead into a smooth ball. The dough will have a little bounce. Place between sheets of plastic wrap, press into a 1-inch-thick disk, and use a rolling pin to smooth the surface. Fold over the edges of the plastic wrap to enclose the dough, then refrigerate for about 30 minutes before rolling out. This will allow the gluten in the flour, activated by the water, to relax. Freeze if you don't plan to use within a day or so.

Roll out as described above. Because of the gluten, this dough is less fragile than the basic dough.

⁘ ⁘   *Variation*   "ROUGH PUFF" PASTRY

This method produces a surprisingly puffy, flaky pastry. Once you get the hang of it, you can use it for classic puff paste recipes, if you don't mind a slightly uneven rise. I use it primarily for Fruit Crostata {page 494} and for Savory Onion Tarts {page 118}.

FOR 11 TO 11-1/2 OUNCES DOUGH {ENOUGH FOR 1 CROSTATA TO SERVE 8}:
Omit the sugar, and make this dough on the counter, not in a bowl. Follow Steps 1 and 2. Spread the pile of flour and butter sheets and chips into a lumpy, roughly circular bed. Trickle 5 to 6 tablespoons ice water over it, stirring with your fingers as it puddles in the dry flour. If water starts to flow away from the floury bed, and it nearly always does, shove a little of the loose flour on the leak, then use a scraper to redirect the water to the dry mass {illus. 3,4}.

⁘ ⁘ ⁘ ⁘ ⁘

                   3   4

⁘ ⁘ ⁘ ⁘ ⁘

Use a scraper to roughly consolidate the mass, scraping in from the edges. Then slide the scraper under the shaggy, sticky, lumpy mass and fold it over itself. Lots of bits of dough and loose flour will have dodged this first folding; scrape them up and tuck them in the crack. Lift the whole mass, scraping it off the counter if necessary, then press the mass flat enough to fold again. Repeat. A couple more of these casual folds ought to produce an unpromising display that looks like chips and shards of yellow wax stuck in chewing gum. Continue pressing, scraping, lifting, and folding this mass one or two more times, until all loose bits are incorporated and there are no major dry spots. The dough should not look homogenous; you should see large sheets of butter, and the surface should be mottled and dimpled {5–9}. If you have used the full 6 tablespoons of water, the dough will be baby-bottom soft.

Wrap loosely and refrigerate for 30 minutes to allow the gluten to relax. {If you chill the dough much longer than that, you may need to leave it briefly at room temperature so you can roll it out without cracking the sheets of butter.} Scrape the work surface clean.

| 5 | 6 | 7 | 8 | 9 |

Measure out about 2 tablespoons of flour. Try to use no more than this to finish the dough.

Dust the counter with a minimum of flour, then roll the dough, going toward and away from yourself, into a roughly rectangular shape about 1/2 inch thick. Turning the dough over once or twice can make this easier to do. Fold the short ends of the dough in over itself, in approximate thirds {10, 11}. Roll out as before, and repeat. Rewrap loosely and refrigerate another 20 minutes or so. Scrape the work surface clean.

\ *continued*

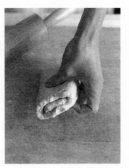

10   11

Roll and fold the dough in thirds two more times. At this point, the dough should be generally smooth, but slightly streaky, with a few discernable bits of butter~most should have been pressed too thin to see. If the dough seems coarser than that, roll and fold it one or two more times, until it is as described. Wrap and refrigerate for at least 1 hour before rolling. Or wrap tightly and freeze if you don't plan to use within a day or so.

Guidelines for rolling out the pastry:
  ⁜ Make sure the dough is just soft enough to roll without cracking the remaining streaks of butter. {See Tempering, page 120.}
  ⁜ If the dough is frozen, thaw in the refrigerator, then leave at room temperature until pliable.
  ⁜ This dough can become elastic and slightly sticky when you roll it out; if your kitchen is warm, it may be easiest to do this in two steps: Roll the dough to just over 1/4 inch thick and refrigerate for 15 minutes or so, then roll to finished size on a clean lightly floured surface.

⁜
⁜ ⁜

FRUIT TARTS

HERE ARE INSTRUCTIONS FOR 8 FRUIT TARTS, GROUPED ACCORDING TO THE character of the fruits. All are made with either the Basic Rich Tart Dough or the "with a Little Flake" variation. You can use either dough for fruits that cook without bleeding lots of thin juice, like apples, pears, figs, and blueberries; the flakier version is the best choice for wetter fruits like nectarines, peaches, plums, or boysenberries. The tarts are open-faced, lattice-topped, or double-crusted, again in function of the filling. Using the right type of crust and format for a given fruit means the dough will cook through, and you need little or no flour or other thickening agent in the filling, leaving the fruit flavor bright and clear.

Wine: Château Guirand, Premier Grand Cru Classé Sauternes, 1999

Guidelines for making these tarts:
 ⁜ Open-faced tarts allow the fruit to dry out as it bakes. The surface sugars caramelize the edges of the fruit, making them pleasantly chewy and delicious.
 ⁜ A lattice top traps some of the fruit's moisture as the tart bakes, but lets enough escape to keep the filling from being soupy.
 ⁜ A double crust generally traps the most moisture and perfume~but you can fine-tune that by making more and wider slashes in the top crust.
 ⁜ In each case, roll out the pastry at least an hour before baking it, place it in the pan, and freeze solid. Then prepare the fruit, and place in the dough-lined pan.
 ⁜ Placing filling in a frozen shell and baking it promptly in a hot oven reduces the chance of leaks or syrup-saturated, undercooked dough.
 ⁜ Avoid sweetened dough for wet fruits: sweetened dough tends to absorb moisture from the fruit and to seep or bake up gummy more readily than versions made without sugar.
 ⁜ These recipes are for 9-1/2-inch tarts baked in a 1-inch-deep false-bottom, fluted steel pan. These pans can corrode if not kept clean and dry, but don't worry that they darken with time~this will improve their performance, as they will absorb heat and brown the pastry more readily and evenly than shiny new pans. Blue-black steel pans dodge the newness problem. For larger pans, increase the amount of filling proportionately; i.e., a 10-1/2-inch pan will take nearly one-third again as much filling as a 9-1/2-inch pan.
 ⁜ If the filling of any of these tarts bubbles over the edges while baking, it may caramelize and the tart stick to the pan at that spot as it cools. To free the tart, you'll need to rewarm that section of the pan to remelt the sugar. Do that by setting the "stuck" part on the edge of a warm burner, then gently push the bottom of the pan up from underneath. You may need to cut through the caramel with the tip of a paring knife.

The recipes that follow use eight kinds of fruit, but you can apply the principles involved to other fruits. It's always best to rely on weight rather than volume when measuring awkward things like wedges, slivers, and big berries. What's more, packing them in measuring cups tends to bruise them.

Regarding sweetening: In general, dryish, low-acid fruits, like pears and many types of apples, whose skins are neither very tart nor tannic, or are removed, require little sweetening, and you can assess the amount necessary by tasting the raw fruit. Wetter fruits, like plums and most berries, need lots of sugar to thicken their juices, and even more if they have tart or tannic skins. In those cases, the necessary sugar may obscure the flavor of the raw fruit and will overwhelm most palates, so it is difficult to judge by taste alone. Flour can't be gauged by taste. You can, however, learn to adjust within a range of "lots of sugar" and "a little flour" by making at least a mental note of how sweet or juicy a batch of raw fruit was~and how it baked up with a particular amount of sugar and flour. Rely on those recollections to help you sweeten, salt, or thicken future batches of the same type fruit. They are as useful as any recipe.

Preparing the bottom crust for any of the tarts:

Remove the dough from the refrigerator and leave at room temperature just until it will roll out without cracking. Roll into an 11-inch circle just over 1/8 inch thick. Carefully lift the dough and drape it across the tart pan. Lift the edges of the dough and let the slack fall into the corners of the pan. Don't worry if it tears. Smooth the dough against the bottom, then press it against the sides. Pinch off a bit of excess dough if necessary to patch cracks or fortify thin spots, and press and smooth all repairs. Fold the remaining excess dough over the edge of the pan, then trim with a gentle pinch all the way around to make it adhere to the sides of the pan. This will help prevent the dough from slumping when you bake it. Loosely wrap, then freeze until solid before filling and baking. {You can do this step a day or two in advance. In that case, double-wrap the pan.}

Rolling out the top crust and assembling a double-crusted tart:

Remove the second ball of dough from the refrigerator and leave at room temperature just until it will roll out without cracking. Roll into a 10-inch circle, lay on a sheet pan or plate, and refrigerate. Place the filling in the frozen bottom crust, then lay the cold circle of dough on top. Press around the edges to seal. Trim and save any excess dough {see Note, page 489}. Slash the top crust with a sharp knife. If desired, brush with a wash made of 1 egg yolk stirred with a splash of water.

Rolling out and preparing a lattice top and assembling the tart:

Remove the second ball of dough from the refrigerator and leave at room temperature just until it will roll out without cracking. Roll into a 9- to 10-inch circle just under 1/4 inch thick. Cut into strips just under 1/2 inch wide. If the dough becomes very soft, chill it until it is firm enough to handle. Place the filling in the frozen bottom crust.

To make the lattice: arrange the strips of dough to form a grid pattern, using the shortest strips on the sides. Press the ends in place and trim the excess.

If you like, you can daub the slats of dough with a bit of egg yolk beaten with a splash of water to glaze it.

Note on using the leftover scraps of dough: If you make a double-crusted tart or a lattice, you will have extra dough. Pile the scraps strategically into a rough circle, smash the edges into line, and roll smooth between plastic wrap {with no added flour}. Freeze to use for individual tartlets. Or, sprinkle with sugar, roll out, and turn into a few tender cookies.

✧
✧ ✧

OPEN-FACED APPLE OR PEAR TART

Use ripe sweet eating apples with tender flesh, such as Sierra Beauty, Gala, Braeburn, or Arkansas Black for the apple tart. Golden Delicious are good as long as they are really yellow-gold ripe. Rough-skinned Golden Russets have great flavor~watch for them. Really hard, dense apples, like Pippins, will turn leathery cooked this way; use them for Crostata {page 494} instead.

Choose ripe Anjous, slightly underripe Comice, or very ripe Boscs for the pear version of this tart.

\ *continued*

TO SERVE 8:

1 recipe Basic Rich Tart Dough {page 482} or Dough "with a Little Flake" {page 483}

1 pound apples or pears

2 or 3 pinches of salt

3 to 4 tablespoons sugar

2 tablespoons honey, to glaze {optional}

Roll out the crust, press it into a 9-1/2 inch pan, wrap, and freeze until solid {see page 488}.

Preheat the oven to 375°.

Peel, halve, and core the apples or pears. Place cut side down and slice evenly into 1/8-inch slivers: Cut apples across the missing core; cut pears from stem to flower end. Collect the butt ends and incomplete slices, and taste one to check the sweetness.

Lay the ends and irregular slices flat in the center of the frozen shell. Starting at the edge of the pan, arrange the neater slices in any pattern that you like, as long as each sliver overlaps and nearly hides the one beneath. The result should be a layer of cantilevered fruit about three slices thick overall. It may be difficult to get sufficient overlap at the center of the tart, but the scraps will make up for that. Once you have carpeted the dough with apples or pears, sprinkle the fruit very lightly but evenly with salt. This will bring out the fruit flavor and, just as important, it will pull moisture to the surface to mix with the sugar and keep the surface from turning leathery. Sprinkle with sugar evenly all over. If your fruit was quite sweet, use the minimum amount of sugar; if tarter, use the full amount.

Bake until the crust is golden brown and the fruit is tender and brown on the edges, about 40 to 45 minutes. If the surface looks dry, you can brush with a simple glaze made by boiling the honey for a minute or so.

❖
❖ ❖

PRUNE-PLUM OR APRICOT TART

I GROUP THESE FRUITS TOGETHER BECAUSE EACH IS "STICKY-WET" AND BECOMES succulent inside and candy-like on the edges when baked in an open tart.

Italian {Stanley} or French prune-plums make excellent tarts. Both are firm and dryish when ripe, don't need much sugar, and bake to a chewy-meaty consistency.

TO SERVE 8:

1 recipe Basic Rich Tart Dough {page 482} or Dough "with a Little Flake" {page 483}

About 1 pound prune-plums
About 1/4 cup sugar
2 to 4 pinches of salt

Roll out the crust, press it into a 9-1/2-inch pan, wrap, and freeze until solid {see page 488}.

Preheat the oven to 375°.

Cut the fruit in half, remove the pits, and then quarter the fruit. Place in a wide bowl and very gently toss with the sugar and salt to taste. The amount of sugar may look alarming, but the salt will balance the sweetness, as will cooking, since it brings out the acidity and tannins in the skins of the fruit. Quickly place the fruit, cut side up, in neat concentric circles or randomly in the frozen shell. Crowd the fruit, but don't overlap the pieces. Scrape the sugar remaining in the bowl over the fruit.

Bake the tart until the crust is golden brown and the fruit has sunken into itself, 50 minutes or longer. The prune-plums will self-glaze, and, if you are lucky, they will emerge edged with chewy caramel.

⁘ *For* APRICOT TART

Choose small, slightly firm, fragrant apricots ~ soft ripe fruit tends to be bland and mushy. Use 1 pound apricots and about 1/3 cup sugar. Prepare as described above.

⁘
⁘

Double-Crusted Blueberry
or Blackberry Tart

You can use basic rich tart dough for blueberry tart, since blueberries won't burst until the crust is largely set, but use the flakier variation for the other fruits listed here. Blackberries and their kin~ marionberries, sylvanberries, olallieberries, loganberries, boysenberries~ need a large dose of sugar, and usually some flour to give the filling body. In that family, boysenberries tend to be wettest, and they call for the full measure of flour.

Choose flavorful, tender, but slightly tart fruit {which is, woefully often, the best you can hope for in many stores} for these fillings.

TO SERVE 8:

Double recipe Basic Rich Tart Dough {page 482} {if using blueberries; see headnote} or Dough "with a Little Flake" {page 483}
About 1 pound berries {4 cups}

For blueberries: about 1/2 cup sugar
For the blackberry family: about 2/3 cup sugar, plus up to 2 teaspoons all-purpose flour
2 to 4 pinches of salt

Roll out the bottom crust, press into a 9-1/2-inch pan, wrap, and freeze until solid {see page 488}. Roll out and chill the top crust {see page 488}.

Preheat the oven to 375°.

Go through the berries, tasting a few for sweetness, and discarding any that are dried out, very hard, or have the slightest speck of mold. Place in a wide bowl.

Combine the sugar with the salt and the flour, if appropriate. Sprinkle about half of this on the berries. Toss to coat all the surfaces. If using very fragile berries, shimmy the bowl to distribute the seasoning without damaging the berries and releasing the juices. Slide the fruit into the frozen shell, scraping the sugar from the sides of the bowl. Distribute the remaining sugar mixture evenly over the fruit.

Lay the cold top crust over the berries and press in place. {A good seal will keep the filling from bubbling over the edge and caramelizing into a stubborn, tarry glue that will bond the crust to the pan.} Cut vents in the top crust, about 5 short ones for drier berries, more, or wider ones, if the berries seemed wet.

Bake about until the crust is golden brown, usually just under 1 hour. The inky fruit syrup may bubble up through the vents. Cool completely before attempting to cut.

⁜ ⁜

LATTICE-TOPPED OR DOUBLE-CRUSTED SWEET CHERRY TART

USE RED OR WHITE SWEET CHERRIES, OR A COMBINATION OF BOTH. Choose small, tender fruit; fat, firm ones may not cook through in time.

TO SERVE 8:

Double recipe Dough "with a Little Flake" {page 483}
About 1-1/4 pounds sweet cherries
1/4 to 1/2 cup sugar
2 to 3 pinches salt
A few drops of artisan-made balsamic vinegar or a mellow, rich commercial brand {optional}

Roll out the bottom crust, press it into a 9-1/2-inch pan, wrap, and freeze until solid {see page 488}. Roll out and refrigerate the second dough ball for the lattice or top crust {see page 488}.

Preheat the oven to 375°.

Pit the cherries. You should get about 3 cups. Place in a wide bowl and season with sugar and salt to taste. A few drops of balsamic will add dimension if the cherries are really meaty and sweet. Slide into the frozen shell. Cut and form lattice, or add the top crust and slash boldly.

Bake until golden brown, about 1 hour. If the filling looks watery, reduce the heat by 25 degrees and bake until it thickens somewhat. It will continue to thicken as it cools.

⁜ ⁜

FRUIT CROSTATAS

Flaky, free-form crostatas, baked to a puffy, dark golden brown in a hot oven, are my favorite kind of tart to make and to eat. The crust, which defines the tart here ~ *crostata* means "big crust" ~ will be especially crisp and delicate, and the fruit most fragrant, during the first 45 minutes or so after you pull the crostata from the oven, so try to time it to be ready not much sooner than your diners are. Serve the crostata as is, or with ice cream, a dollop of real crème fraîche, or a drizzle of Mock Crème Fraîche {page 283}.

Wine: St. Supéry California Moscato, 2001

BASIC CROSTATA METHOD

Rolling out the dough:

Leave the "Rough Puff" Pastry out at room temperature until it becomes pliable. As you begin rolling out, anticipate the final shape you want, a rough square or rectangle. If the dough begins to stick ~ to your pin, your hands, or the work surface ~ wipe or scrape clean and flick a tiny bit of flour on the problem area. Chilling the dough again will help as well. As the dough gets thinner, it will become elastic and you can usually flip and fold it with some abandon. Roll very thin ~ just under 1/8 inch thick ~ into a roughly 15-inch square or comparable rectangle {approximately 14 by 16 inches}. Don't worry if you accidentally roll "wrinkles" into the dough, whether in the center or at the edges. These accidents will add textural variety, and look lovely when they bake. Bear in mind that the dough will retract when you lift and transfer it to the baking sheet. Don't worry if the edges of the dough are irregular. Even if they crack in spots, these flaws can make the finished crostata beautiful.

Lay the sheet of dough on a baking sheet, lined with parchment if you like. Where the dough overhangs the edge of the pan, fold it over until you are ready to assemble the crostata. Refrigerate while you prepare the fruit.

Assembling the crostata:

Arrange the fruit in the center of the dough, leaving about 2 inches of border. This border doesn't need to be consistently wide. {To make smaller crostatas, use a sharp knife to cut the dough into smaller squares or rectangles and reduce the width of the border proportionately.} After arranging the fruit, loosely fold over the edges, enveloping the outer chunks of fruit and creatively lapping or mitering the corners~don't pinch the folds; just press to secure them, and they will bake into tender, puffy shoulders.

Baking the crostata:

Bake in a preheated 425° oven until the pastry is crisp and the color of corn-flakes. This usually takes 40 minutes to 45 minutes, but depending on the baking sheet, oven, and the type, quantity, and temperature of the filling, it could take as long as an hour. Be prepared to reduce the heat to 400° if the pastry threatens to burn; some ovens and pans will color more aggressively than others. {If you always bake in the same oven and on the same pan, you should be able to choose a fixed temperature.} Don't underbake, or the pastry will have inferior flavor and will stale and toughen rapidly. If you have a convection function on your oven, consider turning it on for the last 10 minutes of the bake to aggressively brown the edges of the fruit.

÷
÷ ÷

APPLE CROSTATA *with* ZANTE GRAPES

Use a medium-firm variety of sweet apple, and select not-too-ripe specimens. I use the local favorite, Gravensteins, or Sierra Beauties, Galas, or Braeburns. Ripe Golden Delicious apples can make a fine crostata. Firm, flavorful Pippins are also good for crostatas, so long as they are very ripe.

\ *continued*

FOR ABOUT 8 SERVINGS:

1 recipe "Rough Puff" Pastry {page
    484}
About 1-3/4 pounds apples {generous 5
    cups}
A few pinches of salt

Up to 4 tablespoons sugar
About 1/4 cup stemmed Zante grapes,
    fresh or brandied {see page 279}
    {optional}

Preheat the oven to 425°.

Roll out the dough, place on the baking sheet, and refrigerate {see page 494}.

Peel and core the apples, and cut into irregular 1/2- to 3/4-inch wedges. You
need about 1-1/4 pounds. Taste.

Seasoning the apples:

Place in a bowl and toss with a few pinches of salt. Taste a tiny bit of apple. It
should taste seasoned, but not salty. Toss the apples with a few spoonfuls of sugar
and taste again. You should no longer directly perceive the salt; add more sugar if
you do, then take another nibble. {The raw sugar will quickly dull your palate if
you take healthy bites.} If it tastes too sweet, add the tiniest pinch of salt to
strike a balance. The salt heightens your perception of the apples' flavor, so it
isn't obscured by the one-dimensional taste of sugar.

The same salt will also make the apples sweat their moisture in no time, so
once you have seasoned them, quickly spread the fruit on the sheet of chilled
dough, leaving a roughly 2-inch-wide border around the edges. Don't bother
arranging the fruit in a pattern, but do make sure it its not piled more than two
deep in any spot. Leave a few small islands of bare dough and a few apple wedges
poking higher than the rest. They will caramelize rapidly and be delicious. Fold
over the edges, lapping or mitering as needed.

Bake until the pastry is crisp and well browned, about 40 to 45 minutes.
Reduce the heat by 25 degrees if the pastry threatens to burn. If using, scatter the
grapes over the craggy apples about 5 minutes before the tart is done. For the best
flavor, fragrance, and texture, serve right away, or within 45 minutes.

✢
✢ ✢

APRICOT CROSTATA *with* ALMONDS

CHOOSE BRIGHTLY COLORED, FRAGRANT APRICOTS THAT JUST YIELD WHEN YOU squeeze them.

FOR ABOUT 8 SERVINGS:

1 recipe "Rough Puff" Pastry {page 484}

About 15 raw almonds

1-1/4 pounds apricots {about 14 small or 8 large}

A few pinches of salt

6 to 7 tablespoons sugar

Preheat the oven to 425°.

Roll out the dough, place on the baking sheet, and refrigerate {page 494}.

Drop the almonds into a small pot of boiling water and leave for about 10 seconds, then drain. Pinch and slide off the skins and rub dry.

Halve the apricots and discard the pits. Cut each half into 2 wedges, or 3 if the apricots are large. Taste a sliver of apricot for reference. Spread the apricots in a wide bowl and season with salt and then sugar as described above for the Apple Crostata {page 496}. Don't overhandle; fold gently so you don't smash the tender apricots as you season them. Arrange the apricots cut side up on the sheet of dough, spaced a scant 1/4 inch apart and leaving a roughly 2-inch-wide border. Don't feel you must use all the apricots. Rub the almonds with your sugary fingers, then tuck them into or in between the apricots. They need to be below the surface, or they may burn. Fold over the edges of the dough, lapping or mitering them as needed.

Bake until the pastry is crisp and well browned, about 40 to 45 minutes. Reduce the heat by 25 degrees if the pastry threatens to burn. If your apricots were very wet, you may have to spoon off a little excess syrup. Serve immediately, or within 45 minutes at the latest.

Prepare as for Apricot Crostata, but reduce the sugar to 4 or 5 tablespoons, and then season the sweetened fruit with a trickle of Armagnac, Cognac, or grappa. The almonds are optional.

+
+ +

PEACH CROSTATA

THIS IS THE MOST DELICATELY FLAVORED AND FRAGILE OF THE CROSTATAS ~ AIM TO serve fresh from the oven. Choose just-ripe, fragrant peaches with thin skins.

FOR ABOUT 8 SERVINGS:

1 recipe "Rough Puff" Pastry {page 484}

1-1/4 pounds peaches {about 4 small or 3 medium}

A pinch or two of salt

About 3 to 4 tablespoons sugar

Preheat the oven to 425°.

Roll out the dough, place on the baking sheet, and refrigerate {see page 494}.

Wash and rub the peaches to remove as much fuzz as possible. Cut the flesh off the pits in 1/2- to 3/4-inch wedges. You need just over 1 pound {4 cups}. Place in a wide bowl and season with first salt, then sugar, as described for the Apple Crostata {page 496}. Don't overhandle; fold gently so you don't bruise the peaches as you season them. Arrange randomly on the dough, leaving a roughly 2-inch-wide border; there should be lots of thumbnail-sized bare spots between the wedges. Scrape remaining sugar from the bowl and sprinkle over the fruit. Fold over the edges, lapping or mitering them as needed.

Bake until the pastry is crisp and well browned, about 40 to 45 minutes. Reduce the heat by 25 degrees if the pastry threatens to burn. Serve immediately, or within 45 minutes at the latest.

+
+ +

CHOCOLATE POTS *de* CRÈME

JULIE COOKENBOO, WHO MADE SWEET THINGS AT ZUNI FOR OVER TEN YEARS, perfected this recipe. It is very easy to put together. Take care not to overcook; this rich custard is nicest when it is still slightly soft.

FOR 4 SERVINGS:

3 ounces bittersweet chocolate,
    coarsely chopped
3/4 cup heavy cream
3/4 cup whole milk

2 tablespoons sugar
4 egg yolks
A splash of Cointreau or Frangelico
    {optional}

Preheat the oven to 300°.

Melt the chocolate with 1/2 cup of the cream in a small pan or bowl poised over simmering water, stirring occasionally. Remove from the heat.

Warm the remaining 1/4 cup cream, the milk, and sugar in a small saucepan, stirring just to dissolve the sugar.

In a medium bowl, whisk the yolk, then slowly stir in the warm milk mixture. Pour the mixture through a strainer into the melted chocolate and stir to combine. Stir in the liqueur, if using.

Pour the mixture into four 4- to 5-ounce ramekins or custard cups and place them at least an inch apart in a baking pan. Add hot water to come to barely 1/2 inch beneath the lip of the cups. Bake until the custard is just set at the edges but still quite soft in the center, about 45 minutes. To check, lift a *pot* and tilt; the center should bulge. The eggs will continue to cook after you pull the custards from the oven and the chocolate will harden as it cools. If the custard is already firm when you first check it, then remove from the oven and set the cups in a shallow bath of salted ice water to stop the cooking. Cool, cover, and refrigerate. They will keep well for several days, although I prefer their texture when only hours from the oven.

⁛
⁛

TOASTED ALMOND PANNA COTTA *with* SABA

THIS "COOKED CREAM" IS DELICATELY FLAVORED AND VERY TENDER. *Saba* is not well known outside the region of Modena, Italy, where it is the staple syrup that spends generations becoming artisanal balsamic vinegar. It is made from Trebbiano grape must, traditionally boiled down in copper cauldrons. The *saba* we use is chestnut colored and has a honey-raisin flavor that is lovely with the suave almond cream {see Sources and Resources, page 518}.

FOR 4 SERVINGS:

1/4 cup raw almonds	Salt
3/4 cup whole milk	2 tablespoons water
1 cup heavy cream	1-1/2 teaspoons unflavored gelatin
2 tablespoons plus 1 teaspoon sugar	4 to 6 teaspoons *saba*

Preheat the oven to 325°.

Spread the almonds on a baking sheet and toast lightly, about 8 minutes. They should be fragrant and just beginning to change color on the inside. Chop immediately, and place, still warm, in a small saucepan with the milk and about half of the cream. Add the sugar and a pinch of salt, and stir as the mixture comes to a simmer. Remove from the heat and leave to infuse for about 10 minutes.

Measure the water into a small mixing bowl and sprinkle with the gelatin. Leave to soften for about 3 minutes.

Rewarm the milk-almond mixture until it is hot to the touch, then pour through a fine strainer into the gelatin and water. Stir until the gelatin is fully dissolved. Add the remaining cream. Taste. It should seem a bit sweet; chilling will correct this imbalance.

Pour into four 4- to 5-ounce ramekins or custard cups. Tent with plastic and chill for at least 6 hours. The panna cotta will have the nicest texture if served within 6 to 12 hours; the gelatin will continue to set for up to 24 hours.

To serve, place each ramekin or custard cup briefly on a warm burner, then slide a knife cleanly around the edge. Invert onto a plate, and, holding the ramekin or custard cup in place on the plate, rap the ensemble gently on the counter, then leave for a minute to give the panna cotta a chance to slide out. Top each with a drizzle of *saba* at the table.

Peaches *in* Muscat Wine

SIMPLE, BEAUTIFUL, AND DELICIOUS. Based on the impromptu dessert of peaches in Beaujolais that Jean-Baptiste Troisgros often concocted in his wineglass after turning down prepared desserts. Sweet Muscat wines vary in sweetness; choose one you like and then dose the sugar accordingly. I generally use one from Beaumes-de-Venise, but you could try a sweeter Muscat de Rivesaltes, or Vin de Glacière from Bonny Doon in California.

Choose peaches that are fragrant and just yielding to the touch, with sound, tight skin. Look for fruit that is free of large bruises and soft spots, although some tiny dimples may be a good sign ~ the best peaches are picked by hand, and even the gentlest of fingers may leave modest marks in the tender surface. Overripe or mishandled fruit discolors and loses perfume and delicate flavor notes rapidly. You can use either yellow or white peaches, or a combination; white ones have a touch of bitterness that plays well off the sweet wine. Freestone varieties will be most cooperative; to coax pretty wedges off cling-type peach pits, use a sharp knife, a gentle grip, and patience.

Serve cold, in pretty wineglasses. Perfect with Tuiles {page 502}.

Should you have any leftovers, Peach-Muscat Granita is an excellent way to revisit them. {Simply purée the fruit with the wine, strain, freeze, and chop as explained in the Basic Granita Method, pages 462–463.}

FOR 4 TO 5 SERVINGS:

1/2 bottle sweet Muscat wine {about 1-3/4 cups}	4 medium perfectly ripe peaches
Sugar, if needed	4 handfuls red or white wild strawberries, if available

Pour the wine into a bowl and taste. Sweeten, as needed, until it tastes "like dessert" to you ~ how much sugar you use will depend on your wine, and your taste for sugar. You may use none at all.

Prepare a bowl of ice water large enough to hold the peaches. Slide the peaches one or two at a time into a few quarts of simmering water. Remove as soon as you can slide a spot of skin free of the flesh. {Lift a peach with a slotted spoon and rub gently with your thumb to check}. With truly ripe peaches, this

\ *continued*

will take no more than 15 seconds~leaving them too long will cook and spoil the outer layer of fruit. Immediately slide the hot fruit into the bowl of ice water and swirl to ensure rapid, even cooling. Repeat with the remaining fruit.

Remove the skins, then carve the flesh off the pit in neat wedges about 1/2 inch thick, letting them fall into the bowl of wine. The fruit should be submerged. Swirl the bowl gently. Lay a sheet of plastic or parchment over the surface so the edges don't discolor, and place in the refrigerator to macerate for up to an hour.

About 30 minutes before serving, remove the peaches from the refrigerator and taste. Sprinkle with more sugar as needed and swirl the bowl to dissolve.

Spoon into glasses and garnish with the wild strawberries.

✢
✢ ✢

TUILES

THIS IS MY FAVORITE RECIPE, AND IT IS THE FIRST ONE IN THE DOG-EARED NOTEPAD I filled with recipes in Roanne in 1973. I owe the original formula to André Délorme, longtime pastry chef at Troisgros, but I have reduced the sugar over the years. These "tiles," so-called because they are shaped like traditional terra-cotta roof tiles, require a bit of fussing to make, and they are fragile to boot, but they are also so elegant and delicious as to merit the trouble. Although not essential, a nonstick cookie sheet will reduce the fuss-factor {see Note}. If you don't have the single-purpose pastry item called a *moule à tuiles* {a tray of curved troughs, in which to cradle the warm cookies as they cool}, you can lay the warm cookies over a rolling pin to shape them as they cool. I caution you, though, to set up your cooling operation in a no-traffic zone~I once spent hours baking more than a hundred tuiles for a charity dinner at a friend's winery, carefully draping them, like little sheets of pasta, over every broomstick and mop handle on the property. Unfortunately, every whack of a cleaver, every footstep, sent some of the fragile tiles to the floor. We christened the replacement batch "floor tiles," because we opted to leave them flat. This sensible alternative tastes the same and precludes calamity.

We serve tuiles with ice creams and sorbets, with fruit compôtes, and with sabayon and berries. They are pretty next to glasses of Peaches in Muscat Wine {page 501}.

Wine: Veuve Clicquot Ponsardin Demi-Sec Champagne

FOR ABOUT 20 COOKIES:

1 tablespoon salted butter	2 tablespoons all-purpose flour {scant
Generous 1/3 cup superfine sugar	1/2 ounce}
{2-1/2 ounces}	1/4 cup freshly separated egg whites
Generous 1/2 cup sliced almonds	{between 1 and 2}
{2-1/2 ounces}	1/8 teaspoon salt

Preheat the oven to 400°. Set a mixing bowl near or on the oven to warm through.

Melt the butter in a small pan over low heat, and monitor it as it turns a pale hazelnut color and starts to release its nutty fragrance. Promptly pour into the warm mixing bowl. Add the sugar, almonds, flour, and egg whites and stir and fold gently to combine. Don't beat. Add the salt and taste. It should taste salty-sweet. The batter will be viscous, ropey, and glossy.

Spoon about 1 teaspoonful of the batter onto a nonstick cookie sheet and use a fork to spread it into a rough 3-inch circle, barely thicker than a slice of almond. Try to scoop about half almonds, half batter for each tuile, and dip the fork into a glass of water between efforts, to keep it from "grabbing" the batter as you spread it into translucent puddles. The batter will spread a little more as it bakes, so leave an inch between each finished puddle. You can fit about 9 tuiles on a 14-inch square baking sheet. Bake until the cookies are mottled golden in the center and tea colored on the edges, about 3 to 5 minutes. Because many ovens don't bake evenly, the cookies may not either. Watch and either rotate the cookie sheet to correct for this or remove any tuiles that brown much more quickly than the rest. Pull the pan from the oven and immediately transfer the tuiles one by one to the chosen cooling spot with a thin-bladed metal spatula. If the cookies start to stick before you get them all off the pan, you need only return the pan to the oven for long enough to remelt the caramelized sugar, then peel them off the pan

\ *continued*

while they are still pliable. Wipe the baking sheet clean between batches. {To speed up production, you may want to use two pans, spreading the batter on the second one while the first set of cookies bakes.}

The caramelized sugar will readily grab humidity out of the air, which could quickly soften the cookies, and collapse their curves, so as soon as they are cool, place the tuiles, cantilevered like roof tiles, in an airtight container.

Note: If you don't have a nonstick baking sheet, then use a heavy-gauge regular sheet, brushed with clarified unsalted butter. Wipe clean and rebutter between batches.

✦ ✦
✦ ✦

Notes *on* Frequently Used Ingredients *&* Related Techniques

Bread

THE BREAD I CALL FOR MOST OFTEN IN THESE RECIPES, AND EXCLUSIVELY WHEN IT IS to be cooked into a dish, is chewy white peasant-style bread. I usually call for it to be slightly stale, because it tends to have better flavor and texture for cooking. The bread should not be dry and hard, but the crumb should be firm, not squishy-tender; day-old is right for most such loaves. {After a day, I place the loaf or partial loaf in a plastic bag, where it will keep well for another few days at room temperature or in the refrigerator, or for a few weeks in the freezer.} The original shape of the loaf isn't critical, but content is: choose one made with only white flour, yeast, water, and salt~no milk, eggs, fat, seeds, or rye, whole wheat, or other grains. Firm loaves with an open, irregular crumb-and-hole structure, and that are slightly heavy for their size, are usually chewy. They will likely have been made with fairly wet dough and have enjoyed a slow rise before being baked, both of which encourage great flavor. Such loaves have the right character for bread-based dishes, whereas a soft or dense loaf would produce a doughy texture and could taste too sweet. The bread we use at Zuni is called *pagnotta,* but I have experimented with variety of breads sold variously as *pain de campagne,* country bread, *boule de campagne,* Italian country loaf, *pugliese,* even a fat *ciabatta* that felt heavy for its size. But beware; names tend to be a function of marketing trends, making them the least useful guideline in choosing this sort of bread; rely instead on the look, the feel, and the ingredient list on the label.

For garnished crostini, I generally call for plain fresh white baguette. Seeded varieties may clash with the flavor of the toppings.

I very rarely call for any type of sourdough bread, whether the tangy, all-white-flour "San Francisco"-type or the mellower, mixed-flour *levain*-type breads. While many types are delicious for eating by themselves or with meals, I find their flavor is usually too strong and too rich to use in dishes like bread salad, *pappa al pomodoro,* or *Pearà* sauce. Where I do use sourdough, it is only for occasional crostini or salad croûtons. For example, we use *levain* bread to make super-crunchy croûtons for our Caesar Salad.

Measuring Bread I generally provide both weight and volume measurements for bread, although weight is distinctly more reliable, and that is critical for recipes where bread acts as a thickening agent, as in *romesco* or *Pearà* sauce. Knowing that your quantity of bread or bread crumbs is correct is particularly reassuring if you are not familiar with using bread this way. But once you have made such a dish successfully, you can probably gauge the bread by volume or even by eye in the future. I do occasionally specify the thickness of slices or size of chunks of bread, where the finesse of a dish depends on it, as for the croûton-wads for Madeleine's Omelette, or even the thinly sliced bread for a simple sage-grilled cheese. Nevertheless, don't feel that you need to measure every piece with a ruler.

Fresh Bread Crumbs By fresh bread crumbs I mean fluffy, soft crumbs made from chewy, peasant-style bread. You'll need to make them in the processor ~ I've never seen this type of crumb marketed. Do not substitute fine, dry, toasted bread crumbs, whether store-bought or homemade. For the best and most reliable results, use day-old bread. It is less humid and tends to make lighter, looser crumbs than fresh. Occasionally, when some types of peasant bread are very fresh, they turn into heavy, gummy nibs rather than fluffy crumbs when you process them. There is no foolproof way to stale such bread artificially ~ I've tried slicing it and leaving it in the refrigerator to dehydrate as well as slow-drying it in the oven at the lowest-possible heat. In nearly every case, I got either gummy crumbs or sawdusty ones. The best solution is to keep a little stale bread around, or identify a type of peasant bread in your market that makes light crumbs even when it is fresh.

To make fresh bread crumbs: Carve off all of the crust. {Set aside to use for croûtons, see below.} Cut or tear the tender insides of the loaf into walnut-sized wads and grind in a food processor. Don't grind too fine or evenly. Variation in the size of the crumbs makes them more fun to eat; every batch should have some fat "snowflakes" and some mustard-seed–sized crumbs. A cup of these tender crumbs will usually weigh about 2 ounces and shrink by about one-third when toasted. But the precise character of the bread you use and how fine you grind it can skew these numbers. If not using the crumbs immediately, place in a plastic bag and refrigerate for up to a few days. You can also double-bag them and freeze for a week or so.

Chapons: Croûtons Made from Crusts Anytime you make tender bread crumbs, you can salvage most of the orphaned crust for croûtons we call *chapons.* Pick through the pieces of crust, and select those from the top and sides of the loaf; the bottom crust tends to be tough. Don't worry if they are irregular in size and shape. Crusts that still have a little of the white part of the loaf will be particularly good. Brush the crusts evenly all over with mild-tasting olive oil and toast in a preheated 400° oven until just golden on the edges, then break into bite-sized pieces to float on soup or toss in a salad. In Gascony, in southwestern France, *chapons* are always rubbed with raw garlic.

CITRUS

RELIABLE GUIDELINES FOR CHOOSING CITRUS ARE ELUSIVE. No standard of scent, size, or heaviness indicates good flavor ~ although fruit that is light for its type and size tends to be dry and have poor flavor. Knowing peak season for each type helps ~ as with most fruit, citrus that is allowed to fully ripen on the tree will be the best. Saturated skin color is generally a reliable sign of ripeness, although make sure you don't confuse hue with color saturation {a deep-orange Satsuma mandarin may be paler than a deep-red-orange Page tangerine, but both may be very ripe}. And, unfortunately, skin color can be manipulated with ethylene gas.

Given these vagaries, the best way to learn to choose citrus is to buy and taste it. Try every variety of mandarin, or grapefruit, or orange you see over the course of the year. Although the particular sweetness or juiciness of a given piece of fruit depends on where it was grown, how it was farmed, and when it was harvested, you can at least develop a sense of the typical flavors of each variety and of which ones are most likely to be full flavored, acidic, delicate, bland, fragrant, and so on.

Citrus Zests Zest is the aromatic, pigmented outer rind of a citrus fruit. Use unwaxed citrus, organic whenever possible, for zesting. {Commercial citrus is bathed in wax to make the surface shiny and to keep it from dehydrating. It can contain fungicides. This practice means perfect-looking citrus is abundant in markets year-round. Although the waxing products are deemed safe for consumption, my instinct is to avoid eating them. Where you can't get unwaxed fruit, washing treated citrus in warm water and then completely rubbing off the haze that appears is a reasonable compromise.} Carve zest just when you need it and, except when it needs to be chopped, directly into the dish. This way it arrives with a maximum of its delicate perfume aboard. Zesting in advance will not save time and will squander flavor. For last-minute additions of flavor, usually uncooked, I favor the tendrils you get with a zester. For wide bands of zest or zests that are cooked into stews and compôtes, I use a vegetable peeler. In either case, make sure your tool is sharp, and don't dig deeply into the skin.

Turning and Filleting Citrus By "turned" citrus, I mean fruit that has had the skin and pith completely and neatly carved off with a knife, to produce bright, smooth, juicy spheres. These you can either slice into pretty pinwheels or "fillet," which means using a knife to remove only the tender sections, leaving all the membrane behind. I detail both of these techniques in Citrus Risotto {page 196}.

EGGS

FOR ADVICE ON CHOOSING EGGS, SEE PAGE 174.

Hard-Cooked Eggs Place cold eggs in a pot of not quite simmering water to cover by an inch or two. Bring to a gentle simmer. Timed from that simmer, cook large eggs for 9 minutes for yolks that are just pasty in the middle and set on the edges. For softer yolks, cook a minute less. For extra-large or jumbo eggs, count nearly 10 minutes. If you like your eggs more cooked, remove the pot from the heat and leave to cook for another minute or two in the hot water.

The eggs will continue cooking until they are cool, so once they are cooked as you like, promptly run them under cold water or place in a large bowl of ice water and roll gently to fracture all of the shells~this will let cooling water inside. Only then begin peeling the lot of them. Very fresh eggs will cling to the shell membrane, but the resulting imperfect surface is not a great offense. The cure, toughening the white with a bout of hard-boiling, is worse than the flaw. I always cook eggs close to when I need them; chilling them turns the flavor toward stodgy and spoils the delicate texture.

GARLIC

CHOOSE HEADS OF GARLIC THAT ARE HARD, DRY, AND HEAVY FOR THEIR SIZE. Squeeze a few different spots; while some of the outer cloves may feel perfect, others may be desiccated or rotten. Don't buy heads of garlic that are sprouting green "cowlicks." Garlic tastes best within a few months of harvest~which usually occurs in July in California. When choosing garlic, condition can be more important than variety~I love the flavor of many red-skinned varieties but will pass over them if white garlic is in better shape. Don't substitute elephant garlic; its flavor is dull and stale tasting.

Deciding How Much to Use and How to Prepare It Garlic varies wildly in flavor, as does people's taste for it. And heads and cloves vary in size. Consequently, the amounts of garlic in these recipes are negotiable; feel free to adjust to suit your taste, and your garlic. Although the character of the garlic you choose and the quantity you use is obviously important, its flavor in a finished dish is also a function of how you prepare it and when you add it. In general, fine chopping and/or long cooking mellows the flavor, as does cooking whole garlic in its skin. Coarsely chopped garlic will be more assertive, especially if it is barely cooked. Pounded raw garlic delivers the most intense and, usually, the brightest, cleanest flavor and perfume. Hence a single clove of garlic, "bruised" with the side of the knife and dropped into a vinaigrette, sauce, or broth, can perfume the whole preparation, without adding any harsh notes. I am not fond of the flavor of browned garlic; I always add garlic to dishes when the heat is low enough for it to infuse without scorching.

Peeling and Preparing Garlic Always peel and prepare garlic just before you use it. Remove as many cloves as needed from the head of garlic~or break up the whole head, if you need that much~by laying it on its sloped shoulder and pressing on the root end with the heel of your hand. This usually splits the outer layers of skin, sending the cloves skittering across the counter. If you are using the cloves in their skins, squeeze each one to make sure it is well formed. If a clove feels hollow or spongy, discard it.

To peel garlic, first fracture and loosen the skin by gently crushing each clove with the flat side of a wide knife or a cleaver. Press just hard enough to split the skin. Use the tip of a paring knife to cut off the root end, then trim away the papery skin. Discard any cloves that are shrunken or rubbery, and trim the remainder of discoloration. Split each clove lengthwise and remove any green sprouts. Then crush, sliver, chop, or pound as needed. For pounded garlic, first cut each clove into a few pieces, then place in a mortar and pound. For the smoothest result, add a pinch of salt once the garlic is pasty, then continue pounding.

The only way I know of to remove the smell of raw garlic from your hands is also a foolproof way: wash your hands well before you start the project, then wash them promptly afterward in *cold* tap water with no soap or detergent of any kind. Don't handle anything oily before you wash off the garlic.

NUTS

NUTS ARE A FRAGILE TYPE OF PRODUCE THAT OFFER WONDERFUL NUANCES OF flavor and texture. Buy nuts in small quantities, as you would any perishable product, and from stores where stocks are replenished regularly. Store in a sealed container in a cool spot and use within a few weeks. Walnuts in particular are season-sensitive; they are best when freshly harvested in the fall and rapidly decline in flavor once they are shelled. Always toast, roast, or warm nuts shortly before you plan to use them. Heating heightens their perfume and reveals subtle flavors, and it usually makes them crunchier; although they may be slightly soft when they first come out of the oven, they become crisp as they cool.

Oven temperatures are fairly negotiable when you are heating nuts, as long as you keep an eye {or nose} on their progress. In general, the oven needn't be fully preheated. A toaster oven is convenient for warming nuts.

OLIVE OIL

WE STOCK A FEW DIFFERENT COLD-PRESSED EXTRA-VIRGIN OLIVE OILS, CHOOSING among them according to their flavor and how it will show in concert with the other ingredients. In these recipes, I specify extra-virgin olive oil where I feel the dish will showcase the virtues of a full-flavored oil. This is usually where the oil is not heated at all or where the heating is gentle or brief. I specify a mild-tasting olive oil where it is likely to experience high or very prolonged heat, or where an assertively flavored extra-virgin olive oil might clash with other flavors in a dish. This oil may or may not be extra-virgin, depending on your supplies and budget. In either case, the oil is never just a "cooking medium," so make sure the oil you use tastes good straight from the bottle.

OLIVES

MY FAVORITE GREEN OLIVES, IN NO PARTICULAR ORDER, ARE CRUNCHY, BRINY Picholines; softer, mellower Lucques; fat Sicilian Ceregnola; and meaty Ascolane.

For black olives, I use small, mild Niçoise, Ligurian, Greek elitses, and Spanish arbequiñas or plumper, brinier Gaetas or Kalamatas. We also use oil-cured black Nyons olives, which are soft, nutty, and pleasantly leathery. We sometimes marinate whole olives with thyme and orange zest to serve as an antipasto, but we don't use commercially marinated olives and I don't specify them in any of these recipes. Although these medleys can be tasty, the seasonings may clash with the dish in question. Never substitute canned "Lindsay" olives.

When cooking with olives, I often recommend you rinse them, soak them in warm water, or even blanch them to leach out some of the brine. Even so, consider their residual saltiness when you add them to the dish.

Pitting Olives Rinse, drain, and roll between towels to dry. Leaving the olives sandwiched between the towels, tap them firmly with a meat pounder, mallet, or the bottom of a small heavy pot. Remove the pits from the split fruit.

ONIONS

CHOOSE ONIONS THAT ARE HARD, DRY, AND HEAVY FOR THEIR SIZE. Avoid specimens that have sprouted.

In general, prepare onions only when you need them ~ sliced and diced onion does not improve in flavor and can become acrid tasting {likewise shallots}. I make an exception when I want to soften onions before I cook them: In this case, I cut and lightly salt them in advance. This forces them to release moisture, which means they will cook to tenderness without high heat, or in less time, and without coloring.

Sometimes cutting onions will make your eyes tear; this depends primarily on the onions themselves but is exacerbated by lack of ventilation. I usually tough it out if I am only slicing an onion or two ~ or I move the cutting board to a better-ventilated spot in my kitchen. If you have to slice a lot of aggressive onions, it will help somewhat to array the halves cut face down on a clean, dry towel as you prepare for the slicing operation. The towel will wick some of the offending juice from the onions. The match-between-your-teeth trick has never provided me much relief.

Measuring Onions For accuracy, quantifying onions by prepared weight is the most reliable index. Measuring by volume works pretty well for diced onions, but it is awkward for sliced ones. Confident descriptions, like "1 large onion," are terrific for shopping lists but permit huge variation in yield. {My "large" onion may be half again larger than yours, and one's idea of large onion may vary from day to day. And the yield of one onion can vary plenty from that of another similar-looking specimen, once you trim the papery skin, root, neck, tough outer layers, or spongy cores.} Consequently, I generally list onions by prepared weight and then include whole weight or prepared volume in function of how the onions are used in the dish. All of this said, onions head the category of ingredients where you can fudge somewhat without debacle. Once you have bought, trimmed, and prepared a few onions, whether by weight or by volume, you should be able to estimate your needs by eye. Keep an extra pound or so on hand to prevent shortfalls.

Peeling Onions Use the tip of a paring knife to carve out the tassel end with a shallow circular incision ~ this will leave a conical pit. If you plan on slicing the onion, carve out the root end as well; this way the slices will not be attached to each other. Where you don't want the onion to fall apart, say for stock making, trim the root end flat. Peel away dry outer layers and trim partially dry inner layers.

Slicing Onions Use a chef's knife to cut the onion in half from end to end. Remove any newly revealed sprouts. Set face down and slice into the desired thickness, again from end to end. Hold the onion in place with your fingertips curled under and bent slightly away from the knife blade, and rest the flat face of the knife against the first knuckle above your fingertip. Use your gradually retreating knuckle to control the thickness of the slices. Watch for and remove any sprouts that reveal themselves as you slice. When you can barely hold the diminishing heel of onion, turn it widest face down on the cutting board, pivot it 180 degrees, and slice your way from the cut edge toward the rounded heel.

Dicing Onions By diced onions, I mean bits of onion that are fairly regular in size and are cleanly cut, though most won't be perfect cubes. They are the result of a series of even parallel cuts. Randomly chopping onions produces much more uneven results; some bits are so small they will shrivel before larger ones have begun to soften. In many cases, this matters little, but where even cooking does matter, it is nice to be able to produce a pretty dice. There are a number of ways to dice onions. Some suggest you leave the root end intact to help keep the onion from sliding apart. But the elegance of any technique depends on the sharpness of the knife. You can substitute force for sharpness when you are merely slicing onions, but a dull knife makes the second or third set of cuts for a dice problematic at best, regardless of whether the slices are tethered to the root or not.

The usual method of dicing onions is to start by cutting a peeled onion into halves with the root end intact. Then make a series of parallel cuts end to end, as for slicing, each of which stops just short of the root end. Next, holding the onion in place from above, make a second series of parallel cuts, this time with the blade of the knife parallel to the counter, working your way up to your vulnerable steadying hand. Again, stop short of the root end. Don't press too hard from above, or you'll pinch the blade in place. Finish the project by cradling the onion from the sides and slicing crosswise. Discard the root stub.

A better alternative is an ingenious method devised by Quang Nguyen. His technique is faster and more efficient, and it requires only two sets of cuts. Prepare onion halves, coring both ends. Use a razor-sharp slender-bladed paring knife to slice neatly crosswise through the onion. The halves should emerge neat and assembled like a pre-sliced ham. Now, gently press down on the sliced onion-ham, so the slices recline evenly away from your hand. Switch to a very sharp chef's knife for the second set of cuts. Line the knife blade up with the tips of the reclining onion slices and make a series of parallel cuts, adjusting the angle of the knife two times as you progress through the onion {see illustrations}.

✦ ✦ ✦ ✦ ✦

✦ ✦ ✦ ✦ ✦

I   2   3   4   5

 1. Slice the onion crosswise.

 2. After pressing the onion flat, start dicing with the knife angled toward 2 o'clock.

 3. About one third of the way through, switch the knife angle to 12 o'clock and continue dicing.

 4. About two thirds of the way through, switch the knife angle to about 10 o'clock and dice the remaining onion.

 5. A schematic illustration of steps 2, 3, and 4.

SALTED ANCHOVIES

WE USE COMMERCIAL SALT-PACKED ANCHOVIES EXTENSIVELY, FOR MANY DIFFERENT sauces and condiments, for pizza toppings, and for our Caesar Salad in particular. They are far more delicate than most commercial oil-packed fillets; they have a clear fish flavor but are slightly nutty. Some delicatessens sell them individually, but often you will have to buy a whole can, usually a kilogram or more, much more than you will need right away. In that case, simply remove as many fish as you need, make sure the remaining fish are covered with moist salt, wipe the exposed inside rim clean and dry, and double-bag the whole can in plastic. Refrigerate. The anchovies should keep well for months.

Filleting Salt-Packed Anchovies Rinse the fish under cool water, rubbing gently to remove the scales. Slide a fingertip into the belly of each anchovy and rinse the cavity. Pull off the dorsal and ventral fins. When you've removed all the scratchy surface parts, place the fish in a bowl of cool water and soak until it begins to feel pliable, a minute or so. Slide your finger back into the belly cavity and gently pry one fillet from the bone; if the flesh wants to rip, it's still too dry ~ return it to the soaking water for another minute. Once you've peeled off the first fillet, you can pull the central bone off the second fillet. Rinse the fillets in cool water, rubbing gently to remove any scratchy bones. Don't worry about the silky bones you can see but barely feel. Drain and lay the fillets, not touching one another, on a dry towel. Lay a second dry towel on top and press to draw out excess water. Lift and replace the towel in a different position, then press again to draw out a little more water. Pinch off a bit of fish and taste. It should be nutty and not all that salty, and toothy-tender, not mushy. If it is still too salty, soak for another minute or so; if too soft, press again between towels. Chop, pound, or sliver as directed in the recipes, or add olive oil to just cover, then cover and refrigerate. They will keep well this way for weeks. At home I usually fillet a few more fish than I actually need; having a few ready to use is an easy way to start a dinner project.

Other Preserved Anchovies Commercial oil-packed anchovy fillets are usually quite salty and sometimes taste metallic, bitter, or muddy, or all three. The oil they are packed in generally starts out or becomes dreadful tasting. However, if you are forced to use them, they can be improved. First drain off and discard the oil. Gently rinse or soak the fillets in tepid water. Press dry between towels as described above. The oil makes it difficult to leach out the salt, but this rinsing usually mellows it somewhat and minimizes the taste of the bad oil.

White anchovy fillets, especially the Spanish version sold as *boccarones,* have lately become more available in American specialty markets and can be delicious. Do not, however, confuse them with or substitute them for salted anchovies. They are "cooked" in vinegar and have a very different texture and flavor. Likewise, don't substitute Zuni House-Cured Anchovies for the commercial version.

Although anchovies vary in size, count on 2 to 3 fish {4 to 6 fillets}, whole or chopped, per tablespoon.

TOMATOES

WHILE IT IS POSSIBLE TO GET FRESH TOMATOES YEAR-ROUND, I ENCOURAGE YOU TO honor their season. The fragrance, flavors, and silkiness of sun-ripened summer and early fall fruit justify eight or nine months' abstinence; the bland, scentless crops that burden the market the rest of the year rarely deliver more than a little color and moisture. Most varieties ought to be heavy for their size, just yielding but not soft, and they should have saturated color ~ whether red, orange, yellow, oxblood, or a streaky, multicolored palette ~ and be virtually free of green blushes {barring the few varieties that ripen to a rich, saturated green}. Handle gently and store at room temperature ~ refrigeration disables the perfume while damaging the texture. If you do find yourself with a bounty of slightly overripes that you must refrigerate, plan on turning them into sauce or soup {see Tomato Coulis, page 287, and *Pappa al Pomodoro,* page 164}.

Peeling Tomatoes I don't peel fresh tomatoes all that often ~ never when serving raw, since the peeling process {heat} mutes much of their delicate perfume, and for most cooked dishes, I like to include at least some of the skin for flavor and texture. But when you do need peeled fresh tomatoes, you can choose between blanching and blistering.

For peeling just a few tomatoes, blistering is the easier and quicker of these two methods, but it can be tricky with really large, heavy fruit or extremely ripe soft fruit that can sink into the hot burner grate. {Blistering under the broiler is an option, although it tends to cook much more than just the skins.} I like the rich flavor open-flame blistering encourages and, in particular, I like the flavor of the charred skin ~ I make a point to not rub it all off. Blanching is more efficient for large quantities and where you can't risk insulting the tender flesh with brand marks or where you want to preserve the delicate flavor of the surface of the fruit from caramelizing heat. It is also the obvious choice if your stove is electric. If blanching, you can core the tomatoes before or after boiling them; if blistering, wait until you have charred the skins.

Blanching method: Lower a few tomatoes at a time into a pot of rapidly boiling water. Leave just long enough to loosen the skins, usually 15 seconds or less, then remove and cool them in ice water. Drain promptly and slide off the skins.

Blister method: Set each tomato directly in the flame of a gas burner and leave just long enough to split and shrink the skin ~ usually less than 30 seconds. If the tomatoes are less than perfectly ripe, or if you just like the charry skin, turn them to shrink the other side.

Canned Tomatoes Outside of tomato season, we use a large quantity of canned whole, peeled organic tomatoes. We chop them as needed, rather than use canned chopped tomatoes. They are packed in their own juice with salt and no other aromatics. They are obviously far more cooked than peeled fresh tomatoes, so when substituting one for the other, flavor differences are inevitable, and I sometimes specify a little extra if the peeled tomato is to be fresh.

WILD MUSHROOMS

WILD MUSHROOMS ARE UNLIKE MOST OTHER PRODUCE IN THAT YOU DON'T WANT specimens that are quite heavy for their size ~ weighty mushrooms are usually waterlogged ones. The water you are paying for will need to be evaporated, and if you are cooking the mushrooms sliced in a pan, this will give them a boiled quality. Beyond that concern, look for perky mushrooms, ones that bounce back when you prod or bend them. The best mushrooms will be free of discoloration and feel fleshy-humid, not outright moist, and never slimy. As long as the mushrooms are reasonably dry, don't worry if they are a little dirty; they will be easy to clean. {Although do factor in the weight of the dirt when you make your purchase, or harvest.} Remember that fresh mushrooms are a living fungus that is primed to decompose. Don't put them in a plastic bag ~ even at the market. Place them, uncrowded, in a brown paper bag, so they won't sweat and won't crush or soil one another. Store refrigerated, or in a very cool spot.

Cleaning Mushrooms Pick off loose dirt or debris or brush it off with a clean, dry towel or pastry brush. {An old brush whose bristles you crop short is more effective than one with long, soft bristles.} A brush works especially well to clean fluted gills. Use a sharp paring knife to scrape or carve off crusty dirt. Trim bruised, discolored, or soft spots; the fungus is past its prime there. Split trumpet-shaped mushrooms lengthwise to expose the inside of the tubular stem. If cleaning porcini, check under the cap~if the sponge is firm and creamy beige, leave it in place. If it is very soft or greenish-brown, remove and discard it. Cut porcini in half and check for worms, or wormholes; trim any colonized sections. Refrigerate mushrooms promptly after cleaning. On occasion, black chanterelles {also known as horns of plenty and trumpets of death} are dusted with fine grit that cannot be seen, much less scraped off. We rinse and swish them in tepid water, then press dry between towels. This is the only instance where washing is a good option for mushrooms. Fortunately, black chanterelles are thin and slightly leathery, so they don't absorb much water, and they tolerate the sort of cooking it requires to evaporate it without turning mushy.

SOURCES & RESOURCES

HERE ARE ONES I USE OR KNOW ABOUT ~ BUT I ENCOURAGE YOU TO FIND OR nurture your own local sources by asking for products you want at your grocery, produce, fish, or meat market. Or ask where they get related products. Then contact the producers or brokers yourself and ask if they already raise, produce, or broker the thing you are looking for ~ or just let them know you're looking for it. They can frequently guide you to a retail or mail-order source.

The Apple Farm
18501 Greenwood Road
Philo, California 95466
Telephone: 707-895-2333 or 707-895-2461
Organic dried apples and seasonal organic apples by the peck; also organic cider vinegar.

D'Artagnan
280 Wilson Avenue
Newark, New Jersey 07105
Telephone: 800-327-8246
www.dartagnan.com
Moulard, Muscovy, and Pekin ducks, duck confit, fresh foie gras, quail, squab, rabbit and duck fat.

Carlson Butcher Supplies
50 Mendell #12
San Francisco, California 94124
Telephone: 415-648-2601
Ships all types of sausage casings {hog, lamb and beef middles} in small quantities for the home cook; also carries sausage-making equipment.

The Cook's Garden
P.O. Box 535
Londonderry, Vermont 05148
Telephone: 800-457-9703
Fax: 800-457-9705
www.cooksgarden.com
See note under Johnny's Selected Seeds.

Johnny's Selected Seeds
1 Foss Hill Road
Albion, Maine 04910-9731
Telephone: 207-437-4301
Fax: 800-437-4290
www.johnnyseeds.com
The Cook's Garden and Johnny's Selected Seeds are good sources for seeds, some organic; both carry minutina *seeds.*

The Date People
P.O. Box 808
Niland, California 92257
Telephone: 760-359-3211
Fax: 760-359-3212
datefolk@brawleyonline.com
Many varieties of fresh organic dates.

Dean & Deluca
Telephone: 800-221-7714
www.deandeluca.com
Balsamic vinegar, cheeses, cured meats, olives, olive oil, spices, truffles {seasonal}, and many Manicaretti products {see below}.

Formaggio Kitchen
244 Huron Avenue
Cambridge, Massachusetts 02138
Telephone: 888-212-3224
Fax: 617-547-5680
www.formaggiokitchen.com
Will hand-select and ship a wide selection of cheeses, charcuterie, oils, vinegars, olives, quince paste {membrillo}, truffles {seasonal}, and many Manicaretti products {see below}.

Giusto's Specialty Foods
334 Littlefield Avenue
South San Francisco, California 94080
Telephone: 888-873-6566
Fax: 650-873-2826
www.giustos.com
Organic flours, some dried beans, polenta, sea salt.

Grimaud Farms
1320-A South Aurora
Stockton, California 95206
Telephone: 800-466-9955
www.grimaud.com
Muscovy duck, Sonoma foie gras {Muscovy and moulard}, duck fat, duck giblets.

Manicaretti
5332 College Avenue, Suite 200
Oakland, California 94618
Telephone: 800-799-9830
www.manicaretti.com
An importer of artisan-produced Italian foods, including balsamic vinegar, bottarga {tuna and mullet}, dried porcini, farro, honey, olive oil and agrumato oil, olives, rice, saba, vinegars, organic and conventional pasta, including trenne.

Molinari and Sons
1401 Yosemite Avenue
San Francisco, California 94124
Telephone: 415-822-5555
Fax: 415-822-5834
www.molinarisalame.com
Coppa and spicy coppa.

Niman Ranch
1025 East 12th Street
Oakland, California 94606
Telephone: 510-808-0330
www.nimanranch.com
Sausage casings, pig's feet.

The Pasta Shop
5655 College Avenue
Oakland, California 94618
Telephone: 888-952-4005
www.rockridgemarkethall.com
Will ship a wide selection of cheeses, cured meats, and fresh sausages; carries most Manicaretti products {see above} and quince paste {membrillo}.

Perfect Addition
P.O. Box 8976
Newport Beach, California 92658
Telephone: 949-640-0220
Fax: 949-640-0304
email: perfectadd@aol.com
Gelatinous beef, chicken, and fish stocks with no additives; these stocks are salt-free; be prepared to adjust when you use them in place of the lightly salted versions I make. They are available in the frozen food section of specialty and natural food markets.

Phipp's Ranch
2700 Pescadero Road
P.O. Box 349
Pescadero, California 94060
Telephone: 650-879-0787
Fax: 650-879-1622
www.phippscounty.com
Large selection of pesticide-free shelling beans, including unusual heirloom varieties.

The Chefs Collaborative
Telephone: 617-236-5200
www.chefnet.com/cc2000
See note under Environmental Defense.

Environmental Defense
Telephone: 800-684-3322
www.environmentaldefense.org
The Chefs Collaborative and Environmental Defense have collaborated to produce a user-friendly booklet that tackles the complex issues of sustainability when it comes to fish and shellfish: Seafood Solutions, A Chef's Guide to Ecologically Responsible Fish Procurement. *You can download it from their Web sites, or order it from either organization. The Collaborative is a nonprofit organization dedicated to promoting healthy, environmentally sound culinary practices.*

SELECTED BIBLIOGRAPHY

Ali-Bab. *Gastronomie Pratique, Etudes Culinaries.* Paris: Ernest Flammarion, 1928.

Andrews, Colman. *Catalan Cuisine.* New York: Atheneum, 1988.

Ayto, John. *The Diner's Dictionary.* Oxford: Oxford University Press, 1993.

Cavalcanti, Ottavio. *Il Libro d'Oro della Cucina e dei Vini di Calabria e Basilicata.* Milano: Mursia, 1979.

Correnti, Pino. *Il Libro d'Oro della Cucina e dei Vini di Sicilia.* Milano: Mursia, 1985.

David, Elizabeth. *A Book of Mediterranean Food.* New York: Horizon Press, 1952.

———. *French Country Cooking.* Baltimore: Penguin Books, 1969.

———. *Italian Food.* Harmondsworth, Middlesex, England: Penguin Books, 1977.

———. *Harvest of the Cold Months,* Edited by Jill Norman. New York: Viking, 1995.

Davidson, Alan. *North Atlantic Seafood.* New York: Perennial Library, Harper & Row, 1989.

Fàbrega, Jaume. *Traditional Catalan Cooking.* Barcelona: Edicions de la Magrana, 1997.

Fitzgibbon, Theodora. *Food of the Western World.* New York: Quadrangle Books/The New York Times Book Company, 1976.

Grigson, Jane. *Charcuterie and French Pork Cookery.* Harmondsworth, England: Penguin Books, 1978.

Lladonosa i Girò, Josep. *El Libro de los Arroces.* Barcelona: Ediciones Península, 1977.

McGee, Harold. *On Food and Cooking.* New York: Charles Scribner's Sons, 1984.

Menus Papiers des Troisgros Mémoire Gourmande d'une Famille. Médiathèque de Roanne 16 septembre–4 novembre 2000.

Oxford English Dictionary. Oxford: Oxford University Press, 1971.

Ray, Richard, and Lance Waldheim. *Citrus: How to Select, Grow, and Enjoy.* Tucson: HP Books, 1980.

Root, Waverly. *The Food of Italy.* New York: Vintage Books, 1977.

———. *The Food of France.* New York: Alfred A. Knopf, 1978.

———. *Food.* New York: Simon and Schuster, 1980.

Sawyer, Alexis. *The Pantropeon, or A History of Food and Its Preparation in Ancient Times.* London: Paddington Press Limited, 1977 (reprint of 1853 edition by Marshall Simpkon).

Tozzi, Franco. *Pennino l'Oste.* Signa, Italy: Masso delle Fate, 1996.

Wolfert, Paula. *Couscous and Other Good Food from Morocco.* New York: Harper and Row, 1973.

———. *The Cooking of Southwest France.* Garden City, New York: Dial Press/Doubleday and Company, 1983.

INDEX

truffled, 240, 241

    watercress salad, with walnut-mascarpone crostini and, 152–53

    watercress salad with tapenade-goat cheese crostini and, 153

Belon oysters, 76

berry:

    granita, 468

    sorbet, 468–69

Bever, Carol, 271

biscotti:

    cornmeal, 478–79

    cornmeal-pistachio, 479

bisque, corn-shrimp, 170–72

bitter greens, roast chicken salad with peppers, pine nuts, olives and, 346–48

blackberry(ies):

    for granita and sorbet, 467–69

    tart, double-crusted, 492–93

black olives, baked artichokes with onions, lemons, mint and, 256–57

black tea, prunes in, 278–79

blanching, 100–101

    double-, tripe, 186–87

    meats for *pot-au-feu*, 386, 388

blenders, 45

Bleu de Laqueuille, 453

blueberry tart, double-crusted, 492–93

blue cheeses, 453–54

blue point oysters, 75

boiled Dungeness crab, 314–17

boning knives, 44

Bosc pears with fennel, fresh walnuts, Parmigiano-Reggiano, and balsamic vinegar, 107

bottarga, 183

    charred eggplant with, 102–3

    slow-scrambled eggs with, 182–84

bouillabaisse, chicken, 348–49

braised:

    bacon, pasta with roasted tomato sauce and, 205–8

    chicken with figs, honey, and vinegar, 350–52

    duck with red wine, 352–54

    fennel, 255

    lentils in red wine, 267–68

    monkfish with white beans, fennel, and tomatoes, 326–28

    oxtails in red wine, 377–82

    peas with onions, sage, and pancetta, 251–52

    quail and sausage with grapes, 361–63

braising, mastering of, 370–73

brandade:

    house salt cod, 331–32

    salt cod, crostini with chard in lemon oil and, 123

Brandel, Catherine, 55, 91

brandied fruit, 279–83

    basic method for, 280

    cherries, 280–81

    red currants, 281–82

brasato, 373–77

bread, 505–7

    see also cracker bread; chapons; croûtons

bread crumb(s):

    fresh, 506

    fried eggs in, 178–79

    salsa, toasted, 297–98

    shredded radicchio with anchovy vinai-grette, sieved egg and, 150–51

bread knives, 44

bread salad, Zuni roast chicken with, 342–46

bresaola, 81

    see also air-dried beef

Brie, 451

Brin d'Amour, 452

brining, 36, 269, 401–3, 429

broccoli, spicy, pasta with cauliflower and, 203–5

broccoli rabe:

  grilled, 247

  in *piccolo fritto,* 109

broth:

  beef, with marrow croûtons and a truffled egg, 160–61

  stracciatelle in, with sorrel, 158

  see also stock

brouillade:

  aux orsins, 183

  aux orties, 184

  truffled, 184

browning, 382–83

bruising, 236

burners, 46

Buser, Martha, 220

butter, preserved lemon-caper, 309–10

butter lettuce:

  air-dried beef with coriander vinaigrette and, 92–93

  with oranges, avocado, and shallot vinaigrette, 143–44

buttermilk mashed potatoes, 233–34

Caesar salad, Zuni, 22, 24, 26, 154–56

Calcagno, Vera and Jim, 208

Calcagno, Vince, 24–26, 208

Cantal, 450

caper-preserved lemon butter, 309–10

capers, in *piccolo fritto,* 109

capocollo, 81

caponata, artichoke, 103–5

carbonara, pasta alla, 210–11

Carlo's farro salad with aged Tuscan pecorino, 106

Carol's pickled onions, 271–72

  New Year's Eve gougères with arugula, bacon and, 116–17

carpaccio, beef, and four ways to serve it, 129–34

  with celery leaf salsa verde, 132–33

  with crispy artichoke hearts and Parmigiano-Reggiano, 132

  with fried potatoes and truffles, 133–34

  with lemon and olive oil, 130–31

  salt cod, 331

carving, meat, 394

cast-iron pans, 49

Catherine's celery root with coppa, 91–92

cauliflower:

  pasta with spicy broccoli and, 203–5

  in *piccolo fritto,* 109

celery hearts, in *piccolo fritto,* 109

celery leaf salsa verde, 295

  carpaccio with, 132–33

celery root, Catherine's, with coppa, 91–92

celery-walnut-dried fig relish with grappa, antipasto of salami, Idiazabal and, 89–90

Chaource, 451

chapons, 507

  garlic, mixed lettuces and greens with, 139–40

  see also bread

chard:

  fries, 248–49

  with lemon oil, 248

  in lemon oil, crostini with salt cod brandade and, 123

  and onion panade with fontina, 227–30

charlotte, savory roasted apple, 260, 261

cheese:

  about service at Zuni, 27

  aged Tuscan pecorino, Carlo's farro salad with, 106

  Beaufort, Madeleine's omelette with mustard croûtons and, 174–78

  blue, 453–54

grilled (*continued*)

broccoli rabe, 247

cheese, sage, 115–16

eggplant, 241–43

foie gras, crostini with a few favorite garnishes and, 125–26

quail, 359–61

quail, marinated, 359, 361

radicchio, 246–47

sausages, 424, 428

skirt or hanger steak, 368

squab, 364

summer squash, 243–44

zucchini, 243–44

grills, 46–47

Gruyère, 449

guinea hen:

breast "saltimbocca," 357–59

roasted, with bay leaves, Madeira, and dates, 355–57

stock, 67–68

gypsy peppers, rosemary-pickled, 273–74

hamburger, Zuni, 366–68

hanger steak, 20, 368–70

and white bean sandwich, 370

hard-cooked eggs, 508

see also eggs

hash, polenta, 193

hashed sweet potatoes, 239–40

hazelnut(s):

mixed lettuces with mandarins, hazelnut vinaigrette and, 140–41

mixed lettuces with roasted cherries, warm Saint-Marcellin and, 142–43

picada, crumbly, 305–6

picada, prosciutto with warm roasted figs and, 83

raw white asparagus and porcini mushrooms with Parmigiano-Reggiano, white truffle oil and, 96–98

vinaigrette, mixed lettuces with mandarins, hazelnuts and, 140–41

heat sources, 46–48

herbs, fresh, guidelines for preparing and chopping, 292

honey:

chicken braised with figs, vinegar and, 350–52

fried figs with whipped cream, raspberries and, 459–60

rosemary, oranges with, 456–57

honeydew melon:

granita, 473

for granita and sorbet, 472–73

house-cured pork chop and tenderloin, 400–403

house salt cod, 328–31

brandade, 331–32

chowder with fennel, saffron, onions, and cracker bread, 333–34

in *piccolo fritto,* 110

Hy-Ku Baba, 453

Idiazabal, antipasto of salami, celery-walnut-dried fig relish with grappa and, 89–90

ingredients, choosing, 31–35

iodized salt, 39

Italian prune-plum crostata, 498

Juniper Grove Tumalo Tomme, 453

kale:

boiled, on toast, 162–63

boiled, with eggs, fried or poached, 163

farinata, 163

pappa, 163

Kennedy, Diana, 24

Kerr, Kelsie, 297

kitchen tools, 42–46

mock crème fraîche, 286–87
    portobello mushrooms with extra-virgin
        olive oil, mint, lemon and, 95–96
mock porchetta, 407–10
monkfish braised with white beans, fennel,
        and tomato, 326–28
Montbriac, 454
Montgomery's Cheddar, 450
Morbier, 449
mortar and pestle, 45–46
Moullé, Jean-Pierre, 21
Mountain Gorgonzola, 453
mozzarella and corn-stuffed squash blossoms
        and Sweet 100 tomatoes, *piccolo fritto,*
        113
Munster, 450
Munster-Gérômé, 450
Muscat wine, peaches in, 501–2
mushroom-giblet sauce:
    crostini with smashed shelling beans,
        greens and, 123
    pasta with, 214–17
mushrooms:
    cleaning and choosing, 516–17
    farrotto with dried porcini, 199–200
    in *piccolo fritto,* 108, 109
    porcini and raw white asparagus with
        hazelnuts, Parmigiano-Reggiano, and
        white truffle oil, 96–98
    porcini pearà sauce, 311–12
    portobello, radicchio, and onions with a
        deep-fried egg, *piccolo fritto,* 113
    portobello, with extra-virgin olive oil,
        mint, lemon, and mock crème fraîche,
        95–96
mushrooms, wild:
    cleaning and choosing, 516–17
    risotto with wild rice, squash and,
        197–99
    Zuni fideus with peas and, 217–19

mustard:
    croûtons, Madeleine's omelette with
        Beaufort cheese and, 174–78
    leg of lamb with, 399

nasturtiums, in *piccolo fritto,* 109
nectarine(s):
    sorbet, 470
    White Rose, and prosciutto with blanched
        almonds, 84–85
"New American Cooking," 22
New Year's Eve gougères with arugula,
        bacon, and Carol's pickled onions,
        116–17
Nguyen, Quang, 129, 513
nonstick pans, 49
nouvelle cuisine, 17, 23
nuts, 510
    see also specific nuts

olive oil:
    carpaccio with lemon and, 130–31
    extra-virgin, air-dried beef and Fuyu per-
        simmons with balsamic vinegar and,
        93–94
    extra-virgin, portobello mushrooms with
        mint, lemon, mock crème fraîche and,
        95–96
    homemade lemon-infused, 285
    lemon, chard in, crostini with salt cod
        brandade and, 123
    lemon, chard with, 248
    sage, prosciutto with chestnuts in,
        85–86
    white truffle, raw white asparagus and
        porcini mushrooms with hazelnuts,
        Parmigiano-Reggiano and, 96–98
olive(s), 510–11
    black, baked artichokes with onions,
        lemons, mint and, 256–57

pepper(s), roasted:
    coppa and warm parslied potato salad
        with, 90–91
    relish, 302–4
    spicy squid stew with red wine and,
        338–39
Pérail, 451
persimmon(s), Fuyu:
    and air-dried beef with extra-virgin olive
        oil and balsamic vinegar, 93–94
    and endive salad with pecans, 153–54
pestle and mortar, 45–46
pesto, sage, 307–8
Petit Basque, 452
picada, hazelnut, crumbly, 305–6
    prosciutto with warm roasted figs and, 83
piccolo fritto, 108–15
    about, 108–12
    mozzarella and corn-stuffed squash blos-
        soms and Sweet 100 tomatoes, 113
    onions, fennel, and Zante grapes, 114
    pencil asparagus, onions, and nasturtiums,
        113
    radicchio, onions and lemon or orange
        slices, 112
    radicchio and portobello mushrooms with
        a deep-fried egg, 113
    sand dab with onions, lemon slices, and
        fresh sage, 114
    squid, chick peas, and Sweet 100 tomatoes,
        114
    and wine, 114–15
pickles, pickling:
    glasswort, 274–75
    gypsy peppers, rosemary-, 273–74
    onions, Carol's, 271–72
    onions, Carol's, New Year's Eve gougères
        with arugula, bacon and, 116–17
    red onion, 270–71
    salting vegetables before, 37

spiced prunes, 278
spiced Zante grapes, 276–77
zucchini, 269–70
Picon, 453–54
Pierre Dorée, 449
pine nuts:
    pasta with preserved tuna and, 211–13
    roast chicken salad with peppers, olives,
        bitter greens and, 346–48
pistachio(s):
    aïllade, grilled asparagus with, 98–100
    -cornmeal biscotti, 479
    lamb's lettuce with raw asparagus,
        Parmigiano-Reggiano and, 145
    mandarins and dates with mascarpone,
        pomegranates and, 457–59
plum(s):
    choosing for granita and sorbet, 469–70
    sorbet, 470
poached egg(s):
    beef broth with marrow croûtons and a
        truffled egg, 160–61
    boiled kale with, 163
    onion soup with tomato and a, 159–60
polenta, 190–94
    basic, 190–91
    firm, three ways to serve, 192–93
    with fresh corn, 191
    gratin, sage and onion, 192–93
    hash, 193
    roasted, 192
    sage and onion, 192
pomegranates, mandarins and dates with
        mascarpone, pistachios and, 457–59
Pont l'Evêque, 450
porchetta, mock, 407–10
porcini:
    dried, farrotto with, 199–200
    fresh, in *piccolo fritto,* 109
    pearà sauce, 311–12

rabbit (*continued*)

    stock, 67–68

radicchio:

    grilled, 246–47

    onions, and lemon or orange slices, *piccolo fritto,* 112

    onions, and portobello mushrooms with a deep-fried egg, *piccolo fritto,* 113

    in *piccolo fritto,* 109

    shredded, with anchovy vinaigrette, bread crumbs, and sieved egg, 150–51

radishes, arugula salad with cucumbers, cracker bread, feta, mint and, 149–50

raisins, drunken, 282

raspberries:

    choosing for granita and sorbet, 467–69

    fried figs with whipped cream, honey and, 459–60

raw asparagus, lamb's lettuce with pistachios, Parmigiano-Reggiano and, 145

raw favas, salami with mint, Manchego cheese and, 87–88

raw sweet corn, arugula salad with Sweet 100 tomatoes, 148–49

raw white asparagus and porcini mushrooms with hazelnuts, Parmigiano-Reggiano, and white truffle oil, 96–98

Reblochon, 450

red currants, brandied, 281–82

red onion pickles, 270–71

red pepper, sweet, -lentil soup with cumin and black pepper, 167–68

reduction, 56–57

red wine:

    dried figs in, 282

    duck braised with prunes and, 352–54

    lentils braised in, 267–68

    oxtails braised in, 377–82

    salmon cooked with flageolets, bacon and, 324–26

spicy squid stew with roasted peppers and, 338–39

relish:

    dried fig-celery-walnut, with grappa, antipasto of salami, Idiazabal and, 89–90

    green olive-lemon, 301–2

    roasted pepper, 302–4

restes, eggs baked in, 184–85

rib roast of pork, standing, 403–6

ribs:

    short, braised in Chimay ale, 383–85

    short, in *pot-au-feu,* 385–88

rice:

    and asparagus soup with pancetta and black pepper, 166–67

    for risotto, 194

    wild, risotto with squash, wild mushrooms and, 197–99

rich balsamic mayonnaise, 289

rich pork stock, 61–63

ricotta gnocchi:

    spinach, 226

    Zuni, 221–26

Riley, Kathi, 394, 414

rillettes, rabbit, 442–44

risotto:

    about, 194–95

    citrus, 196–97

    with wild rice, squash, and wild mushrooms, 197–99

roast chicken:

    salad with peppers, pine nuts, olives, and bitter greens, 346–48

    Zuni, with bread salad, 25, 342–46

roasted:

    apple charlotte, savory, 260, 261

    applesauce, 260

    beets, marinated, 240–41

    cherries, mixed lettuces with hazelnuts, warm Saint-Marcellin and, 142–43

virginica oysters, 75, 77

walnut(s):
-celery-dried fig relish with grappa, antipasto of salami, Idiazabal and, 89–90
fresh, Bosc pears with fennel, Parmigiano-Reggiano, balsamic vinegar and, 107
-mascarpone crostini, watercress salad with beets and, 152–53
see also nuts
watercress salad:
with beets and tapenade-goat cheese crostini, 153
with beets and walnut-mascarpone crostini, 152–53
watermelon granita, 473
Waters, Alice, 20–21, 22
weights, 40–42
West, Billy, 24–26, 420
white asparagus, raw, and porcini mushrooms with hazelnuts, Parmigiano-Reggiano, and white truffle oil, 96–98
white bean(s):
monkfish braised with fennel, tomato and, 326–28
and skirt steak or hanger steak sandwich, 370
white truffle oil, raw white asparagus and porcini mushrooms with hazelnuts, Parmigiano-Reggiano and, 96–98
wild mushrooms, 516–17
risotto with wild rice, squash and, 197–99
Zuni fideus with peas and, 217–19
wild rice, risotto with squash, wild mushrooms and, 197–99

wine:
cheese and, 448–49
choosing, 52
cured meats and, 81
dessert and, 456
Muscat, peaches in, 501–2
piccolo fritto and, 114–15
salads and, 137–38
vegetables and, 233
see also red wine
Wood-Setrakian, Beth, 480

Zante grapes:
apple crostata with, 495–96
fresh, in *piccolo fritto,* 109
onions, fennel and, *piccolo fritto,* 114
spiced, 276–77
spiced, smoked prosciutto with fennel and, 87
zests, citrus, 507–8
zucchini:
grilled, 243–44
pickles, 269–70
Zuni:
Caesar salad, 154–56
chicken stock, 58–60
fideus with wild mushrooms and peas, 217–19
hamburger, 366–68
ricotta gnocchi, 221–26
roast chicken with bread salad, 342–46
salt-cured anchovies, 72–73
Zuni Café, 14–16, 24–28, 420

A NOTE ABOUT THE AUTHOR

Judy Rodgers is widely regarded as one of the most creative and thoughtful cooks in America today. A native of St. Louis, she developed a passion for food while a student at Stanford University and nurtured it by studying in Roanne, France, at the Troisgros Brothers' three-star restaurant. After graduating from Stanford in 1978, she continued her apprenticeship under Alice Waters at Chez Panisse. In 1980, she worked with Marion Cunningham as chef at the Union Hotel in Benicia, California, earning a place in the 1984 inaugural edition of *Who's Who in Cooking in America*. Judy joined the Zuni Café in 1987; she owns and manages the San Francisco restaurant with her partner, Vince Calcagno. In May 2000, she was honored with the James Beard Foundation's Best Chef award for California. This is her first book.